Developing Sustainable Digital Libraries:
Socio-Technical Perspectives

Tariq Ashraf
University of Delhi, India

Jaideep Sharma
Indira Gandhi National Open University, India

Puja Anand Gulati
University of Delhi, India

INFORMATION SCIENCE REFERENCE

Hershey · New York

Director of Editorial Content:	Kristin Klinger
Director of Book Publications:	Julia Mosemann
Acquisitions Editor:	Lindsay Johnson
Development Editor:	Elizabeth Arder
Typesetter:	Gregory Snader
Quality control:	Jamie Snavely
Cover Design:	Lisa Tosheff
Printed at:	Yurchak Printing Inc.

Published in the United States of America by
Information Science Reference (an imprint of IGI Global)
701 E. Chocolate Avenue
Hershey PA 17033
Tel: 717-533-8845
Fax: 717-533-8661
E-mail: cust@igi-global.com
Web site: http://www.igi-global.com/reference

          Library of Congress Cataloging-in-Publication Data

Developing sustainable digital libraries : socio-technical perspectives / Tariq Ashraf, Jaideep Sharma and Puja Anand Gulati, editors.   p. cm.
  Includes bibliographical references and index.
  Summary: "This book provides tools to complement an organization's burgeoning information treasuries, exploring new frontiers by looking at social and economic aspects of digital libraries and their sustainability"-- Provided by publisher.
  ISBN 978-1-61520-767-1   ESBN 978-1-61520-768-8 1. Digital libraries. 2. Library materials--Digitization. 3. Digital preservation. 4. Digital divide. 5. Digital libraries--India. I. Ashraf, Tariq, 1961- II. Sharma, Jaideep. III. Gulati, Puja Anand, 1978-
  ZA4080.D487 2010
  025.00285--dc22
                    2009036022

British Cataloguing in Publication Data
A Cataloguing in Publication record for this book is available from the British Library.

All work contributed to this book is new, previously-unpublished material. The views expressed in this book are those of the authors, but not necessarily of the publisher.

Table of Contents

Preface xiv

Acknowledgment xvi

Chapter 1
Digital Libraries: A Sustainable Approach 1
    Tariq Ashraf, University of Delhi, India
    Puja Anand Gulati, University of Delhi, India

Chapter 2
Digital Libraries and Scholarly Communication: A Perspective 19
    S. C. Jindal, University of Delhi, India

Chapter 3
Digitisation: Methods, Tools and Technology 40
    Jagdish Arora, INFLIBNET, Ahmedabad, India

Chapter 4
Tools and Techniques for Digital Conversion... 64
    Pravin Kumar Choudhary, DLF Limited, India

Chapter 5
Building Digital Libraries: Role of Social (Open Source) Software 90
    Kshema Prakash, Dayalbagh Educational Institute, India
    Jason A. Pannone, Harvard University, USA
    K. Santi Swarup, Dayalbagh Educational Institute, India

Chapter 6
Web 2.0 and Social Web Approaches to Digital Libraries... 108
    Arun Kumar Chakraborty, Bose Institute, India

Chapter 7
Information Preservation and Information Services in the Digital Age 133
    Manisha Saksena, Independent Scholar, USA

Chapter 8
Digital Preservation Challenges, Infrastructures and Evaluations 145
    David Giaretta, Science and Technology Facilities Council, UK

Chapter 9
Managing Change in Reference and Information Services in Digital Environment 160
    Shantanu Ganguly, TERI New Delhi, India
    Shweta Pandey, Indus World School of Business (IWSB), India

Chapter 10
Digital Library and Repositories: An Indian Initiative 184
    Bharat Kumar, Management Development Institute, India

Chapter 11
Collaborative Digital Library Development in India: A Network Analysis 206
    Anup Kumar Das, Jawaharlal Nehru University, India
    B.K. Sen, New Delhi, India
    Chaitali Dutta, Jadavpur University, India

Chapter 12
Intellectual Property Rights 223
    Jaideep Sharma, Indira Gandhi National Open University, India

Chapter 13
Facilitating Access to Indian Cultural Heritage: Copyright, Permission Rights and Ownership
Issues vis-à-vis IGNCA Collections 235
    Ramesh Gaur, Indira Gandhi National Centre for the Arts (IGNCA), India

Chapter 14
Harnessing Technology for Providing Knowledge for Development:
New Role for Libraries 252
    M. Ishwara Bhatt, Birla Institute of Technology and Science, India

Chapter 15
Digital Library and E-Governance: Moving Towards Sustainable Rural Livelihoods 265
    P. K. Upadhyaya, National Informatics Centre, India
    M. Moni, National Informatics Centre, India

Chapter 16
Bridging the Digital Divide: A Review of Critical Factors in Developing Countries 286
Leila Nemati Anaraki, Islamic Azad University, Iran
Azadeh Heidari, Islamic Azad University, Iran

Chapter 17
Digital Divide and Economic Wealth: Evidence from Asia- Pacific Countries 311
Shampa Paul, Institute of Economic Growth, New Delhi, India

Compilation of References 321

About the Contributors 346

Index 351

Detailed Table of Contents

Preface xiv

Acknowledgment xvi

Chapter 1
Digital Libraries: A Sustainable Approach 1
    Tariq Ashraf, University of Delhi, India
    Puja Anand Gulati, University of Delhi, India

The chapter discusses the concept of the digital libraries and their structures. It delves into their role in the virtual learning environment and examines the issue related to preservation and building of sustainable digital libraries. It argues that a sustainable digitization program, needs to be fully integrated into traditional collection development strategies. The assessment of what libraries have achieved so far in this direction can be discerned upon a close examination of key factors common to sustainable collection development, be it of analog, digitized, or born-digital materials. Key factors for achieving financial sustainability are described.

Chapter 2
Digital Libraries and Scholarly Communication: A Perspective 19
    S. C. Jindal, University of Delhi, India

The chapter examines various components of scholarly communication in the context of digital technologies as being applied in libraries. It highlights the role of digital environment in research and its impact. Chapter provides both a historical and contemporary perspective of digital library movement and discusses issue s like sustainability and preservation. It argues that Research libraries have begun to take on the provision, organization and preservation of digital information with the same long-term commitment they have made for print materials.

Chapter 3
Digitisation: Methods, Tools and Technology 40
    Jagdish Arora, INFLIBNET, Ahmedabad, India

This chapter provides a practical approach to digital libraries. The authors present a comprehensive picture of digitization and explains the process of digitization in a step-by-step approach. The chapter also describes different file formats and alternatives to digitization.

Chapter 4
Tools and Techniques for Digital Conversion 64
    Pravin Kumar Choudhary, DLF Limited, India

In the last two decades, significant theoretical work has been done in the area of electronic conversion of documents. There are different methods, tools and techniques to carry on digitization activities. This chapter tries to bridge the gap between theory and practice by presenting generalized tools that link digitization and electronic document management practices. This connection can be understood most readily at the organization process level where workflow, information flow, and service delivery come together, i.e. Electronic Document Management Goals. The detailed tools and techniques which need to be integrated into the system design process, and result in the identification of technology specifications and opportunities for improving performance through improved access to documents has been incorporated. Different products and technology options have also been discussed. The content discussed in this chapter can form the models for action: Practical approaches to Electronic Records Management and Preservation. It also presents practical tools that seamlessly integrate into the system design process and result in the identification of technical specifications and opportunities for improving performance through improved access to records. At the end different considerations with regard to the tools also identify critical management and policy factors which must be in place to support a full system implementation have been discussed.

Chapter 5
Building Digital Libraries: Role of Social (Open Source) Software 90
    Kshema Prakash, Dayalbagh Educational Institute, India
    Jason A. Pannone, Harvard University, USA
    K. Santi Swarup, Dayalbagh Educational Institute, India

Blogging is a relatively recent phenomenon, and its use in academic libraries is in nascent stage. The authors of this chapter use blogs as part of their outreach to patrons, though in slightly different contexts and for slightly different purposes. Blogging can be an important component of digital libraries, one that allows for timely two-way communication of news, information, bibliographic instruction, and the like. While challenges have been raised to the worth and value of academic library blogs (e.g., Gorman, 2005), the authors believe, based on the research and their experience, that blogging is a useful tool for academic librarians and digital libraries.

Chapter 6
Web 2.0 and Social Web Approaches to Digital Libraries 108
    Arun Kumar Chakraborty, Bose Institute, India

The Chapter begins with a definition of digital library approaches and features, examines ways in which open source and social software applications can serve to fill digital library roles. In order to incorporate

Web 2.0 functionality effectively, digital libraries must fundamentally recast users not just as content consumers, but as content creators. This chapter analyzes the integration of social annotations – uncontrolled user-generated content – into digital collection items. The chapter briefly summarizes the value of annotations and finds that there is conceptual room to include user-generated content in digital libraries, that they have been imagined as forums for social interaction since their inception, and that encouraging a collaborative approach to knowledge discovery and creation might make digital libraries serve as boundary objects that increase participation and engagement. The chapter concludes with a review of positive and negative outcomes from this approach and makes recommendations for further research.

Chapter 7

Information Preservation and Information Services in the Digital Age 133

Manisha Saksena, Independent Scholar, USA

In the digital world, library services need to be transformed utilizing the advancements possible due to that automation and machine-to-machine communication of information . In this chapter prime focus is laid upon the need of digitization and how to achieve it effectively and appropriately. The strategies for digitization have also been discussed at reasonable length. The issues debated are digital decay as against paper decay, accessibility interpretation in digital world, utility of e-journals, gray content boom, problems of access to excess, human dependence of information sharing and collaboration, disintermediation. In this chapter adequate care has been taken to visualize the importance of traditional conservation as well. The main emphasis is on the spirit of collaboration and skill to take initiative for digitization project. It has been repeatedly mentioned that institutional collaborations at national and international level have given more fruitful results in the area of digitization. This chapter shows the changed picture of librarianship in digital environment along with the change in user perspectives and service perspective.

Chapter 8

Digital Preservation Challenges, Infrastructures and Evaluations... 145

David Giaretta, Science and Technology Facilities Council, UK

This chapter will describe implementations of tools and infrastructure components to support repositories in their task of long term preservation of digital resources, including the capture and preservation of digital rights management and evidence of authenticity associated with digital objects. In order to justify their existence, most repositories must also support contemporaneous use of contemporary as well as "historical" resources; the authors will show how the same techniques can support both, and hence link to the fuller science data infrastructure.

Chapter 9

Managing Change in Reference and Information Services in Digital Environment 160

Shantanu Ganguly, TERI New Delhi, India
Shweta Pandey, Indus World School of Business (IWSB), India

Libraries and librarians are no longer the sole providers of reference and information services. Reference services have traditionally played a crucial role in the delivery of library services both in the public and academic spheres. However, developments in Web technologies have seen the emergence of online or digital reference services, which many initially feared sought to replace the traditional library-based personalized service. A digital library is not merely a means of access to information over the network. As long as "library" word is attached to the concept, a digital library does and should care about users and communities that are in need of information and services just like conventional libraries. "Services", therefore, should be one of the crucial aspects of digital libraries. In the recent trend, reference services have taken a central place in library and information services. Sometimes, they are also regarded as personalized services since in most cases a personal discussion takes place between a user and a reference librarian. The librarian point to the sources that are considered to be most appropriate to meet the specific information needs of the user. Since the Web and digital libraries are meant for providing direct access to information sources and services without the intervention of human intermediaries, the pertinent question that appears is whether we need reference services in digital environment, and, if so, how best to offer such services. This chapter looks at the inevitable change taking place in the platform of reference services.

Chapter 10
Digital Library and Repositories: An Indian Initiative 184
      Bharat Kumar, Management Development Institute, India

This chapter discusses digital libraries and repositories. The purpose of this research is to identify digital libraries and repositories in India available in the public domain. It highlights the state of digital libraries and repositories in India. The digital libraries and repositories were identified through a study of the literature, as well as internet searching and browsing. The resulting digital libraries and repositories were explored to study their collections. Use of open source software especially for the creation of institutional repositories is found to be common. However, major digital library initiatives such as the Digital Library of India use custom-made software.

Chapter 11
Collaborative Digital Library Development in India: A Network Analysis 206
      Anup Kumar Das, Jawaharlal Nehru University, India
      B.K. Sen, New Delhi, India
      Chaitali Dutta, Jadavpur University, India

Digital library provides an excellent opportunity to widely disseminate our documentary heritages and greatly increases access to library collections of rare documents as well as current research literature. Indian digital library initiatives aim at producing a vast amount of digitized documents pertaining to different forms of recorded human knowledge, ranging from the rare manuscripts to current research literature. Digitized documents are made accessible in online information systems either through intranet or Internet channels. However, maintaining an Internet-based online digital library system has several problems such as availability of web server for 24X7 timeframe, robust broadband connectivity, efficient retrieval engine, ownership of digitized documents, etc. This chapter tries to address and document some of the prevailing social networking issues affecting Indian digital library initiatives, particularly the collaboration patterns among participating institutions as well as funding agencies. This chapter also tries to identify social relationships amongst the networked institutions in terms of nodes and ties. Nodes are the individual actors within the networks, and ties are the relationships between the actors. This chapter shows how social networks in the collaborative digital libraries play a critical role in determining the way problems are solved, organizations are run, and the degree to which individual projects succeed in achieving their goals. Digital Library of India (DLI) is the largest digitization initiative in India spreading across states of India and involving over ninety organizations to ensure several thousands of rare books written in Indian languages as well as non-Indian languages are accessible through Internet channel. This chapter critically appraises the formation of a formal social network in the DLI project embracing local memory institutions across the states of India as well as the funding agencies. Similarly, this chapter also critically analyses and elaborates another collaborative digital library initiative in India, namely, Traditional Knowledge Digital Library (TKDL).

Chapter 12
Intellectual Property Rights 223
      Jaideep Sharma, Indira Gandhi National Open University, India

This chapter explains the concept of IPR. The authors throw light on the global problem of copyright violation and software piracy and discuss the legal measures to control these at international level as well as in India. The authors also discuss the scenario of digitization of information and the digital measures to overcome copying and ensure IPR.

Chapter 13
Facilitating Access to Indian Cultural Heritage: Copyright, Permission Rights and Ownership
Issues vis-à-vis IGNCA Collections 235
      Ramesh Gaur, Indira Gandhi National Centre for the Arts (IGNCA), India

This chapter attempts to describe factors considered as hindrance to providing access to Indian cultural heritage material. Lack of proper policy guidelines especially on copyright issues and intellectual property rights concerning both cultural heritage materials in original as well as in digital form are an obstacle. Open access initiatives worldwide are advocating access to even current information. Cultural heritage belongs to the humanity worldwide, therefore, access should be given to all. These issues, which may not be solved at individual level or institutional level, require debate, deliberations and formulation of policy framework at the highest level.

Chapter 14
Harnessing Technology for Providing Knowledge for Development:
New Role for Libraries 252
      M. Ishwara Bhatt, Birla Institute of Technology and Science, India

Rural poor people particularly in developing countries do not get the knowledge and information which they need for their day to day living. Yet, there are no mechanisms for making this knowledge available. This marginalized sector includes small farmers, fishermen, micro-entrepreneurs, small businessmen, unemployed youth etc. They need information for day to day life, such as daily weather forecast, market prices of agricultural produce, how to treat a crop disease, where to get application for the police-men's vacancies, addresses of local masonry persons, etc. Local content is what is most important. Many times, such information is available freely, but the needy person does not get it because of lack of awareness. Such information has to be collected on daily basis from the right sources such as agri-cultural departments, meteorology offices, bank branches, primary health centers or wholesale markets. The information has to be disseminated through the fastest media such as Internet, community radio, loudspeakers, community newspapers or interactive meetings. Libraries need to work closely with the various agencies, both in government and private sectors and the civil society in order to find out the knowledge requirements of the poor and research into how to package it and deliver efficiently. The chapter gives examples of successful knowledge initiatives for the poor in five countries: Bangladesh, Ethiopia, India, Nepal, and Malawi.

Chapter 15

Digital Library and E-Governance: Moving Towards Sustainable Rural Livelihoods......................265
    P. K. Upadhyaya, National Informatics Centre, India
    M. Moni, National Informatics Centre, India

Rural Connectivity is the lifeline of Indian economy. India is a land of diversity with different types of terrain, various agro-climatic conditions, different levels of socio-economic conditions, and varied levels of regional development. At the beginning of the new millennium, 260 million people in the country did not have incomes to access a consumption basket, which defines the poverty line. Sustainable livelihood is a multi-faceted concept. Rural India thus desires to take advantage of "knowledge-intensive" tech-niques for its sustainable development and sustainable consumption. Grassroots level Information access (Contents) and Grassroots level access to Information (Networking) are the two essential components for grassroots level development strategies through ICT. Community Information and Communication Centres (CICC), as a concept and model, aim to "boost efficiency and enhance market" integration through Internet/ Intranet technologies for sustainable remote/regional development at grassroots level. Libraries can play an important role and participate in community action and enhance their function as proactive catalysts of social change. Community Information & Communication Networks in India empower disadvantaged community for effective information & communication, in view of the stated pronouncement of "India to become Knowledge Society", and also facilitate "social inclusion" of mar-ginalised rural poor to access knowledge and information. There are about 56000 Public Libraries (which include 51000 at village level), 400000 School Libraries, 11000 University/College Libraries, 13000 R&D Libraries, 28 State Libraries, and 526 District Libraries in India. Only 8.4 % of the Villages have access to Public Libraries in India. Rural Public Libraries are a part of this revolution and will serve as the backbone for "literacy mission and poverty alleviation". There are empirical evidences to support that rural digital libraries will sustain Community Information & Communication Centres (e-Community Centres). Granthalaya, a Sanskrit word means 'Library'. This chapter deals with "e-Granthalaya: a digital agenda of library automation and networking" facilitating "rural digital libraries" and promoting "local contents" through UNICODE and interoperability capabilities of XML. Networked Library environ-ment play an important role in rural revitalization, as libraries have emerged as a sunrise industry due to globalization and liberalization at regional level, and decentralization trends at grassroots level.

Chapter 16
Bridging the Digital Divide: A Review of Critical Factors in Developing Countries 286
    Leila Nemati Anaraki, Islamic Azad University, Iran
    Azadeh Heidari, Islamic Azad University, Iran

Recent developments in Information and Communication Technologies (ICT), while making our life easier, created a social divide that is known as the digital divide. The global information gap is likely to widen the North – South divide and this global digital divide raises many issues for discussion that will be explored and reviewed further in this research. This chapter provides a brief overview of digital divide and the effects of some critical factors on it. Unequal investment of Information and Communication Technologies (ICTs), the potential of the Internet, the important role of education, literacy, education, e-governance, librarians, libraries and also digital libraries etc. are some discussed factors in this paper. It concludes that paying attention to all so called critical factors can bridge and decrease this global digital divide.

Chapter 17
Digital Divide and Economic Wealth: Evidence from Asia- Pacific Countries 311
    Shampa Paul, Institute of Economic Growth, New Delhi, India

This chapter aims at identifying and analyzing the factors that have resulted in a digital divide in Asia-Pacific countries. There are several factors that can be used as proxy of the digital divide. In this study, Internet density has been used as a proxy of the digital divide along with other variables such as gross domestic product, computer density, telephone density, & information and communication technology expenditure. Using data from 1995 to 2007 for 10 countries, the study finds evidence of the pivotal role played by communication infrastructure in the diffusion of ICTs, and there is also a high correlation between Internet usage and telephone density. It appears that GDP has been a major factor influencing varying degrees of the diffusion of ICTs and the consequent digital divide.

Compilation of References 321

About the Contributors 346

Index... 351

Preface

Digital information has occupied a central place in our lives today. Libraries are acquiring digital information and providing access to users. Most of the information accessed today is digital, Internet playing an important role in the process. Even analogue information is being converted to digital for ease of access and use. Digitisation that was initiated as project in different institutions is now gaining ground. Libraries are digitizing their collections to make their presence felt outside the physical environs of the library. With all the benefits of digitized information, there are certain issues that invite discussion. Preservation of digital information, the phenomena of digital divide are some of these that are being discussed in professional circles. The present book is a compilation of articles on different aspects of digital information. Contributors in the book are from different fields and diverse backgrounds. A blend of young and old, the theoreticians and practitioners have contributed to the book.

The book, Developing Sustainable Digital Libraries: Socio-Technical Perspectives is spread over 17 chapters. The first chapter "Building Sustainable Digital Libraries," by Dr. Tariq Ashraf and Ms. Puja Anand sets the background for the theme. It dwells on the concept, development, issues and achievment of digital libraries. It also discusses the role of DL in learning.

The second chapter by Dr. S.C. Jindal, "Digital Libraries and Scholarly Communication: Issues and Perspectives," examines various components of scholarly communication in the context of digital technologies as being applied in libraries. It highlights the role of digital environment in research. The Chapter provides both a historical and contemporary perspective of digital library movement and discusses issues like sustainability and preservation. The author observes that research libraries have begun to take on the provision, organization and preservation of digital information with the same long-term commitment they have made for print materials.

Chapter 3 and 4 focus on the technological aspects of digitisation. Anyone interested in knowing the details of the techniques and equipments for digitizing would find these two chapters of use. A student learning digitization as well as a librarian interested in digitizing his/her library will find useful tips in these two chapters.

Blogging as a tool to outreach users in academic libraries is the subject of chapter 5. It is an important component of digital libraries, that allows for timely two-way communication of information, bibliographic instruction, and news. It discusses the history and value of blogging. There are some case studies of blogging that demonstrate its use in libraries.

"Web 2.0 and Social Web Approaches to Digital Libraries," by Dr. Arun Kumar Chakraborty, analyzes the integration of social annotations – uncontrolled user-generated content – into digital collection items. It briefly summarizes the value of annotations and finds that there is conceptual room to include user-generated content in digital libraries that they have been imagined as forums for social interaction since their inception, and that encouraging a collaborative approach to knowledge discovery and creation might make digital libraries serve as boundary objects that increase participation and engagement. Chapter 7 by Manisha Saksena, "Information Preservation and Information Services in the Digital Age," discusses the strategies of storage and preservation. Information services in the digital age and their benefits have also been discussed.

David Giaretta dwells on the challenges of digital preservation, infrastructure needed in preservation. The chapter discusses the OAIS reference model for preservation. Also discussed are the threats and challenges to preservation. There is a description of the implementations of tools and infrastructure components to support repositories in their task of long term preservation of digital resources, including the capture and preservation of digital rights management and evidence of authenticity associated with digital objects .

In their chapter, "Digital Reference and Information Services in Digital Environment," Shantanu Ganguly and Shweta Pandey begin with an important concept, information literacy which assumes importance in the era of digital information. After presenting a review of literature on digital reference service, issues in digital reference service are discussed. E-publishing which has a bearing on digital reference services has also been discussed. Web enabled reference services and marketing digital services also find a place in the chapter.

Chapter 10 by Bharat Kumar presents a description of digital repositories in India. It provides a comparative picture of the scope and software used in different digital libraries in India. Digital Library of India and Traditional Knowledge Digital Library, two important digital libraries, have been discussed at length in the chapter. The chapter, "Collaborative Digital Library Development in India," by Dr. Anup Kumar Das and others addresses and documents some of the prevailing social networking issues affecting Indian digital library initiatives, particularly the collaboration patterns among participating institutions as well as funding agencies. It also tries to identify social relationships amongst the networked institutions in terms of nodes and ties. The chapter critically appraises the formation of a formal social network in the DLI project embracing local memory institutions across the states of India as well as the funding agencies.

There are a number of advantages of digtising information. But a serious issue that has cropped up due to it is the unethical use of information. Intellectual Property Rights (IPR) has come up as one of the most important and debated issues due to digital information. The chapter discusses all the issues in detail.

Preserving cultural heritage by digitizing information is one of the major advantage of digitization. Dr. Ramesh Gaur in his chapter, "Facilitating access to Indian Cultural Heritage: Copyright, Permission Rights and Ownership issues vis-à-vis IGNCA Collections," presents an overview of the problems involved in accessing and providing services based on digitized heritage collections.

Chapter 14-17 discuss issues related to empowerment of the masses by digitizing information. Digital divide is a serious issue affecting the society due to unequal access to information. Different issues related to digital divide as well as overcoming the same have been discussed in different contexts by authors in these chapters. Examples of libraries putting efforts to overcome digital divide have been given. Efforts by the Government in this regard by establishing information kiosks and knowledge village centres have also been discussed.

Acknowledgment

We are thankful to our respective organizations where we have been working during the editing of the publication. The authors have taken off from their valuable time and busy schedule for contributing chapters; our sincere thanks are due to them. We acknowledge our reviewers and members of advisory board for going through the manuscript and suggesting suitable changes adding value to the book. We also take this opportunity to thank M/s IGI Global for undertaking the publication in extremely professional manner.

Tariq Ashraf
University of Delhi, India

Jaideep Sharma
Indira Gandhi National Open University, India

Puja Anand Gulati
University of Delhi, India

Chapter 1
Digital Libraries:
A Sustainable Approach

Tariq Ashraf
University of Delhi, India

Puja Anand Gulati
University of Delhi, India

ABSTRACT

The chapter discusses the concept of digital libraries and their structures. It delves into their role in the virtual learning environment and examines the issue related to preservation and building of sustainable digital libraries. It argues that a sustainable digitization program, needs to be fully integrated into traditional collection development strategies. The assessment of what libraries have achieved so far in this direction can be discerned upon a close examination of key factors common to sustainable collection development, be it of analog, digitized, or born-digital materials. Key factors for achieving financial sustainability are described.

INTRODUCTION

A loosely-defined concept "Digital Libraries" consists of amorphous borders and crossroads and has attracted visionaries and entrepreneurs, lawyers, scientists, technicians, librarians and serves as an umbrella for a great many of diverse activities.

Denoted by terms having slightly different connotations, electronic library, virtual library, library without walls, it has a number of different interpretations given by different communities having a concern with it.

The closest definition matching the approaches taken by the research community is the one given by Lesk (1997) in the first textbook on the topic. It defines a digital library as an organized collection of digital information. The digital representation is made possible due to computers and the structuring and gathering has always been done by librarians.

Arms (2000) in a newer text on digital libraries, also from a research community and technology applications perspective, provides what he calls an informal definition: "a digital library is a *managed collection* of information, with associated *services*, where the information is *stored in digital formats* and *accessible* over a *network*."

DOI: 10.4018/978-1-61520-767-1.ch001

After considerable deliberation, Digital Library Federation agreed on a *working definition of digital library,* "Digital libraries are organizations that provide the *resources,* including the *specialized staff,* to *select, structure, offer intellectual access to, interpret, distribute, preserve the integrity of, and ensure the persistence* over time of *collections of digital works* so that they are readily and *economically available* for *use* by a defined *community* or set of communities."

Borgman (2000) provides a more complex definition of digital libraries, considered as a bridge between the research community definition and practical community definitions: Digital libraries are a set of electronic resources and associated technical capabilities for creating, searching, and using information they are an extension and enhancement of information storage and retrieval *systems* that manipulate digital data in any medium. The content of digital libraries includes *data,* [and] metadata. Digital libraries are constructed, collected, and organized, by (and for) a community of users and their functional capabilities support the information needs and uses of that community.

In the light of above definitions and different perspectives, the content may be said to fall into following categories: systems, networks, and technology; collection and resources in various media; representation, organization, and operability; storage and searching; functionality, access and use; institutions and services; and user communities and related applications.

The recent spurt in the growth of digital libraries has essentially come from two forces: recognition of the social and technical trends and availability of substantial funding to address the problems. Issue of the future of libraries as social, cultural and community institutions, along with related questions about the character and treatment of "intellectual property" in our society, form perhaps *the* most central of the core questions within the discipline of digital libraries.

The emergence of digital libraries with the overcoming of physical barriers in accessing information, has dramatically accelerated scholarly research. The barriers of space and time in the search for knowledge are being eliminated. "Today, students, researchers, information professionals, and the general public can directly access many of the world's rarest artifacts—from high-quality images of each page of the Gutenberg Bible to a digital likeness of the Mona Lisa—right at the desktop or other Web-enabled device, at any time and from any location. Audio recordings of historic speeches or exotic birdcalls, video clippings from televised news programs, geospatial data, and more are being delivered directly to the desks of students and researchers" (Pasquinelli, 2002).

Accordingly, we see a great deal of funding for digitisation across the higher education, cultural memory, and government and commercial sectors in systems and services like digital asset management, digital collection creation and management, and institutional repositories using largely tools of digital libraries. The approach is developmental, operational, and eminently practical, with relatively little or no research involved. As a result, thousands of digital libraries have emerged worldwide, with more becoming operational every day. The efforts are diverse and disparate depending upon approach. Many types of collections and media are included and processed in many different ways. Many are located in libraries, creating a hybrid library (combination of a traditional and digital library); others are not bound to brick and mortar libraries at all.

ORIGIN

DL, both as a concept and practice has an incredibly rich, and yet, poorly chronicled history. The concept goes back to mid- twentieth century and has not simply emerged all of a sudden from nowhere.

The technological component of digital libraries reaches back several decades, to the 1960s, consisting of on-line research and commercial information services, library automation systems, document structuring and manipulation systems, human computer interface work and a wealth of other efforts. Technologies like distributed search (for example, Z39.50) were well established by the late 1980.

Digitisation took up initially as library projects that were largely experimental activities. Library automation software packages were also introduced developed from the experimental work. These products were aimed at educational institutions that seek easy-to-install and easy-to-maintain solutions. Many groups have become involved in the expansion of digital library technologies and techniques. These include the European Union, Association for Computing Machinery (ACM), the Institute of Electrical and Electronics Engineers (IEEE), the International Federation of Library Associations and Institutions (IFLA), the American Library Association (ALA), the Coalition for Networked Information (CNI), and the Digital Library Federation (DLF).

Up till the mid-1990s, as the Internet reached the larger public consciousness, the reality of unimaginable cornucopia of knowledge and human creativity accessible worldwide through the network; began to take a concrete shape. "While such aspirations were at least deflated if not largely shattered by the onslaught of commercial and government interests, the censors, snoops and copyright maximalists, they still run not far under the surface of the public mind, as witnessed by the reactions to Google's recent announcement that it would digitize the contents of several major research libraries" Lynch (2005).

The period of experimental digital library projects has been christened the 2nd generation digital libraries. With this new knowledge in hand, Greenstein suggests that the third-generation digital library abandoned this experimentation and started integrating digital material into the library's collections through a modular systems architecture. "This modular approach is fundamentally liberating since it permits libraries to

think creatively about how to build upon services supplied by others" (Malik and Jain, 2006).

Digital library research from 1995 onwards could really get substantial support from the major research sponsoring bodies, legitimizing digital libraries as a field of research which captured the attention of scientists, scholars, librarians, educators, political figures, and the general public. Digital libraries got a push due to several trends in the society. *First,* rapid transformation of western societies into a new form referred to as information-, knowledge-, society. Managing knowledge records became an ever more important part and problem of that evolving society, especially since the phenomenon of information explosion, the exponential growth of knowledge records of all kinds, kept accelerating. *Second,* the digital and networked technology reached a certain level of perfection and spread rapidly, which provided for more involved, varied, and broader opportunities and problems at the same time. *Third,* in most, if not all fields, the nature of scholarly communication changed drastically, creating problems and fueling exploration for new approaches for supporting and sustaining it. *Fourth,* funds started pouring in for research and for practical developments and explorations on a variety of solutions to these problems.

E-LEARNING AND THE CAMPUS ENTERPRISE

The emergence of digital libraries must also be observed in the light of initiatives to unify the IT structures and to transform the learning process through innovative technology. Economic, social, and cultural pressures are forcing schools and universities to rediscover and reinvent themselves. Akin to business process re-engineering activities of the last decade that repositioned corporate sector, education organizations are now viewing themselves in a new light. New types of students and changing student expectations are driving the integration of core campus functions and deployment of student services on the Web. Fragmented, monolithic approaches are falling away as educators realize the need to link learning and administrative resources in a more effective way to become a "knowledge enterprise," the 21st century version of the traditional campus. During the past decade steep declines in the cost of commodity components, combined with the availability of high bandwidth networks, have made sophisticated IT applications for education affordable. A mix of sophisticated digital and Internet-based services and rapidly expanding global digital content have made possible a "virtual learning environment" that delivers the capability to enhance the classroom experience or conduct learning apart from a physical campus. The digital library is a core component of this virtual environment.

With the maturity of these projects, more practical digital library implementations began to take shape and the libraries began to assume a more central role. Digital library use shifted to a large and diverse campus audience, and information technology (IT) groups began to partner with the library to develop campus-wide standards for the deployment and operation of digital libraries as an integral part of the education enterprise. This development paralleled the development of heightened student requirements for access to library resources.

"These developments are extending the role of the library, and changing the relationshis between the library and other parts of the academic enterprise," according to Clifford Lynch, Director of the Coalition for Networked Resources and a noted authority on digital libraries. "I think we will see a continued evolution from thinking about digital collections to thinking about networked information services, which will integrate authoring, analysis, and distribution tools that facilitate the reuse and repurposing of digital content. In almost all cases, the collections and services must be integrated into the institutional, national, and worldwide fabric of research and teaching" (Lynch 2005).

DIGITISATION: KEY COMPONENTS AND FEATURES

A fully developed digital library environment involves the following elements:

1. Initial conversion of content from physical to digital form.
2. The extraction or creation of metadata or indexing information describing the content to facilitate searching and discovery, as well as administrative and structural metadata to assist in object viewing, management, and preservation.
3. Storage of digital content and metadata in an appropriate multimedia repository. The repository will include rights management capabilities to enforce intellectual property rights, if required. E-commerce functionality may also be present if needed to handle accounting and billing.
4. Client services for the browser, including repository querying and workflow.
5. Content delivery via file transfer or streaming media.
6. Patron access through a browser or dedicated client.
7. A private or public network

The ability to digitally sample an object carries with it numerous advantages. Among them:

Easy Manipulation

Digital objects, by their very nature, can be easily stored, recalled, and manipulated. Current photo editing software allows digital images to be resized, duplicated, and edited using techniques simply aren't possible using the established print or analog methods for image processing.

Easy Access

The most important advantage of digital objects, however, is accessibility. Digital documents can be easily posted on web sites and online resources, allowing anyone with Internet access the ability to retrieve them. The storage of images and documents in digital format, and making them accessible through digital libraries, allows numerous simultaneous users the ability to view the same documents at once, while eliminating analog duplication costs.

DIGITAL OBJECTS: SOME UNCERTAINTIES

While easy accessibility and manipulation are strong arguments for the exclusive use of digital media, a number of drawbacks and uncertainties still persist. It is these concerns which discourage the exclusive use of digital formats to permanently store and preserve images.

All concerns regarding digital storage and archiving stem from the fact that digital objects are machine-dependent technology – that is, the use of a computer is required to decode and translate a digital image into something that can be understood by a human being.

Uncertainties Over Technology and Storage Media

As technology advances, equipment currently in use becomes obsolete. This includes storage media – the material used to store data, including digital images. Countless instances have occurred where old records, stored on old, obsolete discs and tapes, have been rendered unreadable because the required equipment is no longer available. As a result, preparations need to be made when technology is upgraded to ensure that data is transferred to current storage equipment.

Obsolescence of Imaging Equipment

Analog film, cameras and related equipment are a mature technology, and have remained largely unchanged over several decades. Digital imaging technology, however, is constantly evolving and improving. As old imaging equipment becomes obsolete, newer computers and graphic design equipment will drop support for a product in favor of a more up-to-date version. As a result, it may become necessary to incur added expenses by purchasing updated cameras and scanners.

Uncertainties Over Image Standards

Digital imaging standards are also not immune to technological evolution. A stored digital image must adhere to a file format – a standard describing how to encode and decode an image - in order to be useable. As technology changes, so do file formats, and newer formats will continue to replace older, less robust standards.

To be fair, image file formats dating back to the introduction of consumer-based computer graphics in the mid-1980s continue to be supported and widely used today. Yet, while current image-viewing software continues to support major file formats that were created more than a decade ago, there is no guarantee that a shift in standards will not render these older file formats obsolete.

These drawbacks, while substantial, are not insurmountable. Effective planning for the transition of archives during a major technology shift is necessary to avoid the pitfalls of having digital images become victims of obsolescence. When considering digital archiving over analog, the implications of such planning should be considered and compared to the expense and planning required in preserving analog materials in order to determine the best solution.

RATIONALE FOR DIGITIZATION

In view of the features of digital objects libraries usually identify two reasons for digitization: to preserve analog collections; and to extend the reach of those collections. Most individual projects and full-scale programs, while perhaps giving priority to one over the other, end up serving a mix of both purposes. As librarians have learned from tackling the brittle book problem through deacidification and reformatting, it is difficult and often pointless to pick apart preservation and access. Nonetheless, because it has been generally conceded that digital conversion is not as reliable for preservation purposes as microfilm reformatting, it is worthwhile to consider what institutions are doing and saying that they are doing in terms of preservation *per se*.

Preservation

The purpose of preservation is to ensure protection of information of enduring value for access by present and future generations. Libraries in addition to providing access to resources, have always served both as the central institutional focus and concern for preservation, as one of its core functions. The use of scanning made of rare, fragile, and unique materials, from print and photographs to recorded sound and moving image are universally acclaimed as an effective tool of preventive preservation. For materials that cannot withstand frequent handling or pose security problems, digitization has proved to be a boon.

During the last decade, many major libraries have started regular preservation programs for traditional materials which include provision of resources for preservation, measures to arrest deterioration of materials, and the incorporation of preservation needs and requirements into overall planning. Scanning of literature has been done for preservation and used quite extensively. Microfilming has also been an alternative but preference today is being given to high quality scans over it.

But there is an issue of migrating the scans over to the latest technological improvements.

University of Michigan-has a policy to scan brittle books and use the scans as replacements, not surrogates. They have created a policy for the selection and treatment of these books, and they explicitly talk of digital replacements as a crucial strategy for collection management. "This policy is premised on their view that books printed on acid paper have a limited life span and that, for those with insignificant art factual value, they are not only rescuing the imperiled information, but also making it vastly more accessible by scanning in lieu of filming" (Smith, 2001).

Accessibility

Digitization is a system and service that enhances functionality, adds to convenience, leads to preservation and also aggregation of physically dispersed collections, and an expanded reach. Among all the important acts of digitization activities at major research institutions, there are essentially two models of collection development based on access: one that serves as outreach to various communities; one that is collection-driven by users. All libraries engage in these models to one degree or another.

Outreaching and Community Goals

Libraries are also undertaking digitization of their analog holdings for reasons that are important to the institution as an outreach activity not directly related to teaching and research. Libraries are social institutions and are parts of larger networks that look to them for purposes that go beyond the educational mission of the library. "As custodians of invaluable institutional intellectual and cultural assets, the outreach programme of libraries help in cultivating alumni allegiance, public relations and raising funds" (Smith, 2001).

User-Driven Selection

Explicit user-driven needs often force libraries to digitize documents rather than the general access purposes. The focus is on the user as part of a plan that carefully prioritizes relatively modest resources for digitization. In such cases libraries decide to concentrate on working with faculty and students to develop digital objects designed to enhance teaching and research. Many of the scholar-driven projects may be highly useful resource in themselves. But they would, by library standards, fail the test of comprehensiveness as a collection. Indeed, "one could say that the value added by the scholar lies precisely in its selectivity" (Smith, 2001).

DIGITAL IMAGING: TECHNOLOGICAL ISSUES

As the digital libraries become more heavily involved in projects that require the digitization of documents and images, it becomes increasingly necessary to ensure that everyone involved in such projects have a working knowledge of digital imaging technology. This is not an easy task, and requires as much hands-on experience as it does knowledge of the theories and concepts behind digital imaging.

A digital image is little more than a file which contains instructions to appropriately illuminate and color a group of pixels, in order to create what the human eye sees as an image. Each pixel can be made any of up to 16 million colors, by varying the levels of red, green and blue light that illuminate each pixel. A digital image is produced using a similar method. All computer displays divide a screen into a number of pixels, or digital image elements.

Digital Imaging General Principles

When digitizing documents, it is important to consider possibilities beyond the scope of the immediate project. The goal is to eliminate as much as possible the prospect of having to repeat steps, and re-digitize a document whenever a new need with different requirements arises.

Without such a plan in place, one may find himself re-scanning the same material as a result of poor image quality, inability to meet changing project requirements, or obsolescence of the technology being used. While such possibilities can't be eliminated, we can reduce the likelihood of such an occurrence by implementing a plan for scanning at high resolutions, in open formats.

Scanning Resolution

The image resolution determines how many pixels per inch are used to define an image. The higher the resolution, the more definition and detail can be stored in an image, permitting greater options in enlargement and manipulation.

File Types

A number of standards exist for storing digital images. Each have advantages and disadvantages in terms of image quality, storage space, and compression capability.

TIF - Best quality for master and archive files.
TIF without LZW compression - Gives maximum compatibility with PC, Mac, UNIX etc, while being a lossless compression.
JPEG - Best quality for use copies, good resolution, small file size. Works best with photographs and other continuous-tone images.
GIF - Small file but limited in color hence is not good for photographic images. Works best with images composed of lines and solid blocks of color, such as text, cartoons, or buttons.

As digital libraries scale in size and functionality, it is critical for the underlying technology platform to deliver the performance and reliability required. Patrons expect high service levels, which means that downtime and poor response time are not tolerable. Moreover, because cost is a foremost concern, scalability and efficiency with a low total cost of ownership are also key requirements. This type of digital library implementation requires a scalable enterprise-level technology solution with built-in reliability, availability, and serviceability (RAS) features.

Storage capacity also must be scalable to adapt to rapid growth in demand, and must be adapted to the mix of media types that may be stored in a digital library, such as:

- Text, which is relatively compact.
- Graphics, which can be data-intensive.
- Audio, which is highly dynamic.
- Video, which is highly dynamic and data intensive.

Storage capacity should be expandable in economical increments and should not require redesign or re-engineering of the system design as requirements grow.

An open systems architecture provides both a robust platform and the best selection of digital media management solutions and development tools. The inherent reliability and scalability of open platforms have made them the most popular choice of IT professionals for Internet computing. This computing model features an architecture that is oriented totally around Internet protocols and stresses the role of Web sites for a vast and diverse array of services that follow a utility model.

Metadata

The key to locating, using, and preserving digital content is metadata, or structured data about digital objects and collections. Many digitization efforts have been unsuccessful due to inadequate metadata. Metadata contains information that a) allows discovery of collections or objects through the use of search tools, and b) provides sufficient context for understanding what has been found. When collections become large or when searching multiple collections (such as over the Internet) the discovery of objects of interest becomes a "needle in a haystack" exercise. Without agreed-upon metadata standards and the discipline of capturing and storing appropriate descriptive metadata, all but the smallest digital collections would be useless.

Metadata for individual objects varies by the type of object, but would include such things as its title, what it is, who created it, contributors, language, when it was created, where it is located, the subject, etc. At the collection level, users should be able to determine the scope, ownership, any access restrictions, and other important characteristics that would assist in understanding the collection. The best-known and widely accepted descriptive metadata standard for libraries is MARC (Machine-Readable Catalog) used for cataloging books and other publications. MARC has served the traditional library well, but was not designed for describing images, sound files, and other new media types.

An important descriptive metadata standard for images and other multimedia objects is Dublin Core, a group of 15 items of information designed to be simple to understand and use. Dublin Core was designed to provide a very widely accepted mechanism to allow discovery, but with the option for different communities of users to adapt and customize it by adding more fields of particular importance to the community.

Digital Rights Management

Sustained and increasingly wide focus on developing platforms that link patrons both to the library's own electronic resources and to networked digital resources available both freely and owned or controlled by other organisations, management of digital rights becomes a major concern. "In constructing a digital library service environment, the library becomes responsible for configuring access to a world of information of which it owns or manages only a part," says the California Digital Library's Dan Greenstein. "Accordingly, the digital library is known less for the extent and nature of the collections it owns than for the networked information space it defines through a range of online services." In this type of cooperative resource sharing environment, mechanisms for identifying information users and their access privileges are essential. Greenstein(2000)

Quality Control in Digitization

Quality control is by far one of the most important factors in a digital library project. In digital library projects, a lack of quality in the finished digital document can impact the overall usability of the collection: poor quality equates to reduced usefulness for patrons.

In spite of this, it is not common for digital libraries projects to have an instituted, standardized process in place for error checking and quality management. As a result, such projects run the risk of making materials available that omit information, are difficult to read or understand, or are otherwise unusable due to inattention to quality. In many cases, these problems are only fixed when a patron gives feedback to site developers about these problem a process which is unreliable at best, and depends on patrons to spot the errors. Patrons may come away with the sense that a digital collection which does not pay attention to such details may not be a reliable source for research information.

DIGITAL PRESERVATION

For Preservation of digital materials on large scale and as per the storage capabilities and in standard formats that are accessible and usable, it is necessary to articulate some basic requirements. Digital preservation requirements needs to be examined both from the perspective of users of digital materials and from the view of libraries, archives, and other custodians who assume responsibility for their maintenance, preservation, and distribution as separate but integrated stakeholders.

To achieve their preservation goal and satisfy the requirements of their users, librarians need to preserve materials in formats that enable the types of analyses that users wish to perform despite resource constraints. By making explicit preservation requirements from both the users' and custodians' perspectives, libraries and archives will be better able to integrate digital preservation into overall planning and resource allocation.

The use of digital materials has immense potential but has a varied and unpredictable nature. Accordingly any generalization, even if restricted to one community of users such as humanities scholars would be hazardous and runs the risk of overlooking and understating potential user needs. Exact needs for presentation and analytical tools may have a variation among disciplines, yet some intrinsically basic requirements are likely to transcend fields and disciplines. "The ability to establish the authenticity and integrity of a source is critical to users, whether it is generated by an individual, created in the conduct of institutional business, or produced through a formal publication process" (Lynch, 2005).

System that will facilitate establishment of authenticity of an object require archives and libraries to store much more than the content of digital documents. According to Graham (1995), "attributes such as formal document structures, metadata that document the maintenance and use history of the document, time and date stamps, and a series of references among documents are essential for determining authenticity and for understanding the provenance of sources and placing them in a larger context."

Largely depending upon requirements of users, availability of sufficient funds and technical resources, digital preservation requirements may be expressed differently by libraries, and other types of repositories that are struggling to meet. Storage systems should be capable of handling digital information in a wide variety of formats, including text, data, graphics, video, and sound.

Digital storage both as an only and alternative means for storing print formats should have a long life expectancy, a high degree of disaster resistance, sufficient durability to withstand regular use, and very large storage capacities. Conversion from analog to digital formats and migration to new generations of technology should permit very large scale transfers of heterogeneous materials.

Developing and sustaining digital library is an expensive and resource-intensive process. Hence it is important to consider some basic principles underlying the design, implementation, and maintenance of any digital library. These principles apply across the spectrum covering not only projects in which analog objects are converted to digital form, but to mixed digital libraries in which the objects may be of both types.

Changing technologies can quickly outperform the ability of designers to maintain a particular digital library. We must be able to anticipate and plan for changes needed to provide lasting access to its information. Since most digital library projects are long-term efforts, they require the commitment of long-term resources .

Beginning such a project involves an implicit, if not explicit, commitment to the continuation of the work and a promise that the digital materials will continue to be available. Lacking organizational commitment, it may not make sense to even begin a project.

The Challenges of Digital Preservation

Librarians have been instrumental in developing wide ranging tools and methodologies to reduce the decay of traditional materials and to restore books and documents that have deteriorated to such an extent that their longevity and usability are threatened. Much remains to be done to preserve cultural, intellectual, and scholarly resources in traditional formats that form the foundation for humanities research and teaching.

An estimated 80 million embrittled books reside in American libraries, 10 million of which are unique; and countless journals, newspapers, photographs, and documents require preservation treatment to survive well into the next century. Headstorm (2004)

However preservation of digital objects is a problem and challenge of an altogether different kind which is quite different from preserving traditional format materials. Preservation and guaranteed maintenance of digital materials is much discussed. Whereas the preservation of printed materials harbours several specific and well-known problems, these issues differ from those encountered with digital materials, where there exist many technical issues, ultimately solvable by technical means but with few standard solutions available, as yet.

The situation is described as being "at an interesting juncture" by Smith (2003). He sets out the complexities involved, making a useful separation into the concepts of "'bit preservation' where a digital file is carefully preserved exactly as it was created without the slightest change, and 'functional preservation', where the digital file is kept useable as technology formats, media, and paradigms evolve."

Alemneh (2002) point out that the complication of preserving digital resources is that "in order to ensure long-term access to digital resources, we need to preserve all the software, hardware, and operating systems on which the software ran." But on a practical and planning level, as Smith (2003) says, as yet, "we have very little information about actual production strategies, costs, user reaction to information loss, or how much technical metadata is needed to support all of this."

Recording media for digital materials are susceptible to degeneration and losses of other kinds, and even under normal conditions they are short lived as compared to traditional format materials. Although librarians have been fighting acid-based papers, thermo-fax, nitrate film, and other fragile media against deterioration since long, the preservation challenge posed by magnetic and optical media is altogether of different kind as they can deteriorate rapidly, making the time frame for decisions and actions to prevent loss is a matter of years, not decades.

Since advances and innovation in the computer hardware, storage, and software industries continues at a fast pace, generating greater storage and processing capabilities at reduced cost, more than media deterioration is the problem of obsolescence in retrieval and playback technologies.

Devices, processes, and software for recording and storing information are being replaced with new products and systems both unexpectedly and on a regular two- to three-year cycle, driven primarily by innovation and market forces rendering records prepared in digital form in the first instance and those converted retrospectively from paper or microfilm to digital form equally vulnerable to such a fast technological obsolescence.

The absence of well established standards, procedures, and well tested methods for preserving digital information has further aggravated the problem of long term preservation. Digital library research has largely focussed on architectures and systems for information organization and retrieval, presentation and visualization, and administration of intellectual property rights (Levy and Marshall, 1995). The important role of digital libraries and archives in ensuring the future accessibility of information with enduring value has taken a back seat to enhancing access to current and actively used materials. Since digital preservation requirements have not been factored into the architecture, resource allocation, or planning for digital libraries, digital preservation remains largely adhoc and experimental and is replete with the risks associated with untested methods; and

Current Preservation Strategies

Copying, also referred to as "refreshing" or "migration" has emerged as most reliable method of digital preservation. Copying, is more complex than simply transferring a stream of bits from old to new media or from one generation of systems to the next. But complex and expensive transformations of digital objects often are necessary to preserve digital materials so that they remain authentic representations of the original versions and useful sources for analysis and research.

The most frequently and commonly used digital preservation strategy is to migrate digital information from less stable magnetic and optical media by printing page images on paper or microfilm. It may seem both ironic and contradictory that just as librarians are discovering digital conversion as a cost-effective preservation method for certain deteriorating materials, same information is printed on paper or microfilm for safe, secure long-term storage.

Yet another widely used strategy to preserve digital objects is to preserve information in digital formats which are simple in order to minimize the requirements for complex and advance retrieval software so that it can be transferred across successive generations of technology in a "software-independent" format as ASCII text files or as flat files with simple, uniform structures. "Several data archives hold large collections of numerical data that were captured on punch cards in the 1950s or 1960s, migrated to two or three different magnetic tape formats, and now reside on optical media. As new media and storage formats were introduced, the data were migrated without any significant change in their logical structure." This approach is easy to implement and is cost-effective in those cases where retaining the content is important without particular format.

As long as the preservation community lacks more robust and cost-effective migration strategies, printing to paper or film and preserving flat files will remain the methods of last resort for many institutions and for certain formats of digital information.

Most of the current methods fall far short of what is required to preserve digital materials due to which most repositories are coping by employing interim and less than dependable strategies for tackling digital preservation matters which often eliminate the structure of documents and relationships imbedded in databases along with other computation capabilities.

CHALLENGE OF SUSTAINABILITY

A larger challenge today before digital library projects is of long term sustainability of their digitisation programmes. While a great majority of research libraries have undertaken digitization projects of one type or another, only a few have reached the point where they are moving forward to developing full-scale digitization programs, rather than just a series of projects. It is a serious challenge as there have been cases where programmes launched with great effort and dedication had to be abandoned due to a variety of reasons. Tanner (2009) argues that the major unresolved issues in the transition [towards digital libraries] revolve around money, infrastructure, scalability and sustainability. According to him ICT in digital libraries is no longer showing the immediate return investment delivered in the 1980s and 1990s, such that future developments will not necessarily instantly save staff time or reduce costs. The current benefits from technology for libraries are improving resources, processes and services, not replacing the human factor.. making the issues of sustainability and scale become paramount.

In the past, the question of sustainability was addressed towards the end of projects but now it has emerged as an integral part of any project's development. It is important not only to obtain initial funds but to have regular flow of grant, technical expertise and required equipment.

Though the concept of sustainability is applicable universally but traditional libraries may not regularly have to justify their existence though most of them need to fight to maintain their budgets. Those who do not have to battle for their core funding every year have reached the position after sustained efforts.

The question arises so frequently in the digital library world because digital initiatives, as Zorich (2003) points out, tend to be introduced as special projects. In many cases, insufficient thought has been given at the outset as to how they will turn into long-term developments. And at times of economic pressure, when even the core is questioned, anything else is vulnerable. "The key to sustainability, therefore, is to reach a position where the digital library is no longer regarded as an add-on, but as part of this integral core" (Zorich, 2003).

A sustainable digitization program needs to be fully integrated into routine collection development process. The assessment of what libraries have achieved so far in this direction can be discerned upon a close examination of key factors common to sustainable collection development, be it of analog, digitized, or born-digital materials.

It can be revealed in many cases by the collection development process, involvement of faculty in decision making and ultimate usage of the collection in meeting the mission and objectives of the institution.

A carefully conceived life cycle management is another key factor in ensuring sustainability of digital collections. How is the library budget allocated for the creation of the digital scans, metadata, storage capacity, preservation tools (e.g., refreshing, migration), and user support, the sorts of things that are routinely budgeted for book acquisitions leads to an element of perpetuity to digitization process. How much of the program is supported by grant funding and how much by maintenance grant? If presently grant-supported, what plans exist to make the program self-sustaining? (Smith 2001).

According to Smith (2001), amongst numerous and widely available documents, very few libraries have formal written policies for conversion criteria. The focus of these documents is on the planning of digital projects or various elements of a larger program instead of rationalization of digitization itself.. The University of Michigan, for example, does have a written policy and it clearly aims to fit digitization into the context of traditional collection development. It states that "Core questions underlying digitization should be familiar to any research library collection specialist" (Smith, 2001).

The rationale for expending resources to essentially digitize items already in the library's possession is necessarily more complex as against purchasing born digital. A library should only choose to digitize existing items if it adds value and additional benefits outweigh the costs.

Joint Information Systems Committee, UK ("JISC," n.d.) digitisation strategy lists a number of critical success factors to ensure that money spent and the collections produced are worthwhile, that is to ensure that the public gets value for money and that resources have been invested appropriately to create content that is standards based, interoperable, user focused, innovative contextualized sustainable and legal

One of the biggest reason for non- sustainable projects has been going forward with digitization projects without knowing how to measure either cost or benefit. The problem is aggravated further due to dependence on a technology that is constantly changing, along with the associated costs rendering the budgeting models downright meaningless or misleading.

In addition to cost, the other sustaining factor is the benefit of this technology in enhancing teaching and learning along with other number of possible goals that digitization is intended to achieve. However, most academic institutions have not done much in this direction in terms of gathering meaningful data .

Financial Sustainability

Economic sustainability is a pressing concern for many digital library projects. One key to ensure constant flow of funds and achieving economic sustainability is to diffuse digitisation process into over all policies of parent organisation rather than treat it as a special project. This can be done only by having a viable product strongly backed by user community.

Alongwith ensuring provision for reasonable funds, influential patrons and promoters for the digital library are also required and librarians must be prepared to network and cultivate useful contacts. Additional funding sources can include sponsorship, in-kind support, fee charging .

According to Smith (2003), economic sustainability is a difficult and more political area than preservation, and consequently solutions are less tangible and concrete. in a useful presentation, sums the position up as "the hardest part of sustainability – how to pay for it all".

Since there are no easy and permanent solutions in the past so many digital library projects have bloomed briefly and then ended. Funders are always short and under pressure. For instance, JISC ("JISC," n.d.) a major source of funding for digital library projects in UK higher education, is project funded and has no revenue budget of its own. One view is that at this juncture, more money should be spent on sustaining services and less on initiating projects, but in most cases it is best to start from the premise that external funding obtained to establish a project will rarely be an appropriate source to provide ongoing, unlimited funding for its continuation.

Costing Digital Libraries

According to Baker and Evans (2009) there are many ways in which digital libraries increased cost and /or create different types of costs. There is a cost to digitising materials. Copyright clearance needs to be obtained in many cases. Costs are rising partly because there are more materials to choose from, partly because acquisitions costs are increasing exponentially and partly because there is a constant need for technological development and implementation.

The challenges of digitization on an industrial scale go beyond a single institution s capabilities to digitise complete run of materials- this can usually only be achieved in collaboration with others. In the short history of digitisation there has been an emphasis on short-term costs-capital equipment, recruitment and so on-and less on the long-term costs associated with the onging development of digital collections. This course leads to more concerns over sustainability.

Some of the mechanisms for pursuing sustainability in digitisation initiatives are highlighted in a jointly funded report by JISC and Ithaka, a US non-profit organisation- sustainability and Revenue Models for Online Academic Resources (Guthrie, Griffiths, and Maron, 2008).These mechanisms included a discussion of several major revenue-generating methods, including philanthropic support, subscription, advertising and other models.

Additional evidence on charging models can be found in studies undertaken by Tanner and Deegan in 2003, and by Tanner alone in 2004. *The Handbook on Cost Reductions in Digitisation* by Tanner (2006) identifies three key factors influencing cost:

- The nature of the orginal item to be digitised;
- The digitisation processes and mechanism possible;
- The information, content and delivery objectives to be achieved.

The costs associated with preparing analogue materials prior to digitisation vary significantly with the type of content, condition, rarity and curatorial intervention and policies.

Another very significant cost associated with pertains to clearing rights. These will be dependent on the age of the object, whether the rights holders are known or the works are 'orphan works', whether expertise to clear rights is in-house or needs to be outsourced and the market value of the objects. So, for example, popular music recordings will generally cost more than spoken-word materials as their market value is considered by rights owners to be greater.

The Ithaka report commissioned by the strategic Content Alliance on Sustainability and Revenue Models for Online Academic Resources (Guthrie, Griffiths, and Maron, 2008) succinctly states that 'there is no formulaic answer or single approach to achieving sustainability'. The report gives an overview of many of the issues which are pertinent to digitisation initiatives, including creating the culture and structure for success, leveraging value and some of the pros and cons of revenue-generating options which they outline as:

- Advertising;
- Content licensing.
- Contributor pays;
- Corporate support;
- Host organisation support;
- Pay-per-use;
- Philanthropic support;
- Subscription;

An emerging trend in sustaining digitisation initiatives over the long term has been the development of public-partnership, where the roles of the content creators and revenue generators to sustain the assets created are split. In the case of the latter this has included commercial publishers and not-for-profit organisations such as JSTOR.

In addition, hybrid sustainability models have emerged, where materials are served through different platforms, such as the 18th Century Official Parliamentary Publications Portal 1688-1834 at the University of Southampton, which includes nineteenth-and twentieth-century materials through the use of ProQuest as aggregator. This commercial hybrid, meeting the aspirations of open access (OA) through a University of Southampton website and delivery via a commercial publisher's aggregation of eighteenth-, nineteenth-and twentieth-century parliamentary papers, illustrates the convergence of business models. In this case, a percentage of the commercial publisher's revenues are shared among the consortia, led by the University of Southampton assisting in maintaining and developing the 'open access' eighteenth-century materials.

Increasingly, consortia of research libraries are contributing content to joint ventures where the production costs are lowered. Digitisation centres, such as those at Queen's University Belfast and the University of Southampton, undertake digitisation for 'special collections' or are outsourced through vendors for less valuable objects and then delivered through either not-for-profit agencies such as JSTOR or via commercial partners- adding e-infrastructure and track records in the delivery of collections to various markets

Some Sustaining Factors

While launching any digital initiative, it must be ensured, as a first step, that it is soundly conceived so as to make it intrinsically sustainable. Issues of scope and coverage are particularly important in the early stages. This relates to the question of when to go live with a service. Developers will, of course, be focused on the need for a newly launched service to be hitch -free, and sufficient piloting and testing of technical aspects will be necessary to ensure users are not distracted from the product's value due to dead hyperlinks, orphan pages or spurious contents.

Funding Support

The funding issue is probably the single largest barrier to digital library development; this is why most existing collections are essentially pilot projects or R&D activities. "The challenge

of mounting a large-scale digitization effort, encoding appropriate metadata to ensure ease of discovery and use, and making a commitment to long term preservation can be daunting to libraries already struggling to pay for existing activities" (Pasquinelli, 2002).

According to Val Hamilton, "it is a rare digital library project that is so high profile and so intrinsically valuable that the host institution is forced to find funds for continuation. One route towards bucking the 'withering' trend is to ensure strong branding, linking a successful product with the institution. Most projects require rallying support through conscious efforts to gain champions beyond the immediate circles and this is where strong, ideally charismatic, project leadership is important."

A further approach which can be productive is developing cross-sector links between different types of education, between university and public libraries, or with business or local enterprise organisations. It will require hard work but may provide access to different funding sources. "Collaboration will be a key feature of future digital library economics as the technologies become so great as to be unobtainable or unsustainable within a single institutional context Just as collaborative cataloguing proved the most economically sustainable way forward in the 1980s the collaborative models for tools and infrastructure will prove fiscally attractive for digital libraries" (Tanner, 2009).

Charging for access can be a soft option if applicable for similar physical information. Charges may also be acceptable for added-value services where basic services are free. The availability of so much free information in public domain creates a barrier to payment by individuals who have to be convinced of the value of the particular information being accessed.

Sponsorship and in-kind support can take many forms and creativity may be required to overcome institutional antipathy to and restrictions on advertising. Campbell (2000) gives examples of varied sources of sponsorship for Australian subject gateways ranging from endorsement through free publicity to solid financial support. In-kind contributions are often overlooked. As Zorich (2003) points out, this can lead to problems if the contribution is withdrawn and also means that organisations "cannot effectively use this support as evidence when funders seek tangible proof of outside financial commitments to a project."

Integration is the ultimate goal for many digital library project leaders. But it is hard to integrate a project once its funding has run out. It is also hard to plan for such integration from the outset but this must be the main approach. The formal business plan required by many funders should not be regarded as one more bureaucratic hurdle but the passport to a successful, sustainable digital library.

OPEN SOURCE AND OPEN ACCESS SOLUTION

Open source movement has emerged as the most obvious example of collaboration that will deliver benefits to the digital library community. "While open source offers the possibility for the whole community to benefit from license-free software tools then open access offers the chance to access and engage with current intellectual discourse without having to pay an excessive entrance fee" (Tanner, 2009).

CONCLUSION

It is clear that digital library technology is becoming a common tool for providing enhanced library services. As the focus of digital library activity has completely moved from its initial computer science experiments to mainstream library implementations, the current generation of digital library research is focusing on evolving standards, sustainability, and increased interoperability among digital collections.

Digital access is important for libraries of all kinds but, perhaps for the academic library in particular. The delivery across multiple sites or to large numbers of off-site students is already much eased by digital provision. The same is true of any kind of autonomous learning given the instant access to materials that the digital library can provide. "The move towards digital provision has the potential to put the library at the centre of its user community, though there are significant economic consequences, including in broader areas as well as ICT policies such as staffing policies, collection strategy, housing and extra-mural cooperation" (Roosendal et al., 2003). Digital library strategies are inevitably integrated with other digital developments and it is important to be clear about the economic impact and the necessary economic decision surrounding digitization and digital provision. The economic impact of ICT on the academic institution and its library cannot be discussed in an isolated way… "The cost of establishing a digital academic library should be considered as part of the integral costs of establishing an overall digital information environment for the entire academic institution" (Roosendal et al., 2003). The extent and level to which this happens will affect a number of things, including the institutions ability to take over some of the roles of the other actors in the value chain its ability to develop interoperability and cooperation with other institutions, thereby increasing economics of scale and reducing costs, and the level of autonomy between the institutional center and the departmental units, as for example in human resource management. It will be essential no spend money in line with strategies that enable sustainability fair distribution liaison with other providers, interactive resources and use by multiple users in diverse and flexible ways.

REFERENCES

Z39. *50*. (n.d.). Retrieved from www.loc.gov/z3950/agency/

Alemneh, D. (n.d.). *Metadata Quality Assessment: A Phased Approach to Ensuring Long-term Access to Digital Resources*. Retrieved from http://www.asist.org/Conferences/AM09/posters/80.pdf

Arms, W. Y. (2000). *Digital Libraries*. Cambridge, MA: The MIT Press.

Baker, D., & Evans, W. (2008). *Digital Library Economics: Digital library economics: An academic perspective*. Oxford, UK: Chandos Publishing.

Borgman, C. (2000). *From Gutenberg to the Global Information Infrastructure: Access to information in the networked world*. Cambridge, MA: MIT Press.

Campbell, D. (2000). Australian subject gateways: political and strategic issues. *Online Information Review, 24*(1), 73–77. doi:10.1108/14684520010320266

Digital Library Federation (DLF). (n.d.). Retrieved from www.clir.org/diglib/

Graham, P. S. (1995). Requirements for the Digital Research Library. *College and University Research Libraries, 56*(4), 331–339.

Greenstein, D. (2000). Digital Libraries and Their Challenges. *Library Trends, 49*(Fall), 290–303.

Greenstein, D. (2002, March 15). Digital Library Orchestrating Digital Worlds. *Library Journal.*

Guthrie, K., Griffiths, R., & Maron, N. (2008). Sustainability and revenue models for online academic resources. *Ithaka Online*. Retrieved from http://www.ithaka.org/.../sustainability-and-revenue-models-for-online-academic-resources

JISC. (n.d.). Supporting. *Education and Research*. Retrieved from http://www.jisc.ac.uk.

Lesk, M. (1997). *Practical Digital Libraries: Books, Bytes, and Bucks*. San Francisco: Morgan Kaufman.

Levy, D. M., & Marshall, C. C. (1995). Going Digital: A Look at Assumptions Underlying Digital Libraries. *Communications of the ACM, 58*(4), 77–84. doi:10.1145/205323.205346

Lynch, C. A. (2005, July/August). Where Do We Go From Here? The Next Decade for Digital Libraries. *D-Lib Magazine, 11*(7/8).

Lynch, C. A. (2007, June 19). *Networked Information Applications and Future Internet Developments*. Presented at the event "Internet Innovation: Applications and Architectures, An Industry Perspective on Internet Research," in Santa Clara, CA.

Malik, M., & Jain, A. K. (2006). Digital Library: Link to E-learning. In *ICT Conference on Digital Learning Environment*, Bangalore, 11 –13 January. Retrieved from http://72.14.235.132/search?q=cache:MYRR4Ten8dYJ:https://drtc.isibang.ac.in/bitstream/handle/1849/232/paperY_Malik.pdf%3Fsequence%3D1+This+modular+approach+is+fundamentally+liberating+since+it+permits+libraries+to+think+creatively+about&cd=1&hl=en&ct=clnk

Pasquinelli, A. (2002). Digital Library Technology Trends. Retrieved from http://www.lib.buu.ac.th/webnew/libtech/digital_library_trends.pdf

Roosendal, H., Huibers, T., Guerts, P., & van der Vet, P. (2003). Changes in the value chain of scientific information: economic consequences for academic institution. *Online Information Review, 27*(2), 120–128. doi:10.1108/14684520310471734

Smith, A. (2001). *Developing Sustainable Digital Library Collections: Strategies for Digitization*. Digital Library Federation Council on Library and Information Resources. Retrieved from http://www.clir.org/pubs/reports/pub101/contents.htm

Smith, M. (2003). D-Space: an open source dynamic digital repository. *D-Lib, 9*(1). Retrieved April 8, 2004, from http://www.dlib.org/dlib/january03/smith/01smith.html

Tanner, S. (2006). Handbook on cost reductions in digitisation. *Minerva online*. Retrieved from http://www.minervaeurope.org/.../CostReductioninDigitisation_v1_0610.pdf

Tanner, S. (2009). The economic future for digital libraries: a 2020 vision. In Baker, D., & Evans, W. (Eds.), *Digital Library Economics: An academic perspective*. Oxford, UK: Chandos Publishing.

Zorich, D. M. (2003). *A Survey of Digital Cultural Heritage Initiatives and Their Sustainability Concerns*. Council on Library and Information Resources, Washington, DC. Retrieved April 8, 2004, from http://www.clir.org/pubs/abstract/pub118abst.html

Chapter 2
Digital Libraries and Scholarly Communication:
A Perspective

S. C. Jindal
University of Delhi, India

ABSTRACT:

The chapter examines various components of scholarly communication in the context of digital technologies as being applied in libraries. It highlights the role of digital environment in research and its impact. Chapter provides both a historical and contemporary perspective of digital library movement and discusses issue s like sustainability and preservation. It argues that Research libraries have begun to take on the provision, organization and preservation of digital information with the same long-term commitment they have made for print materials

INTRODUCTION

The term "digital library" is simply the most recent in a long series of names for a concept that was written about long before the development of the first computer. The idea of a"computerized library" that would supplement, add functionality, and even replace traditional libraries was invented first by H.G. Wells and other authors, who caught the imagination of millions with speculative writing about "world brain" and similar fanciful devices.

There is general agreement that much of the early actual application of computers to information retrieval was stimulated by the prominent scientist Vannever Bush who wrote about the "memex", a mechanical device based on microfilm technology that anticipated the ideas of both hypertext and personal information retrieval systems. The first real world application of computers to libraries began in the early 1950s with IBM and punched card applications to library technical services operations, and with the development of the MARC (machine readable cataloging) standard for digitizing and communicating library catalog information. In 1965 J.C. R. Licklider coined the phrase "library of the future" to refer to his vision of a fully computer based library, and ten year later F.W. Lancaster (Lancaster, 1978) wrote of the soon-to-come pa-

DOI: 10.4018/978-1-61520-767-1.ch002

perless library. About the same time Ted Nelson invented and named hypertext and identified later in this paper in some detail, but never built to refer to the concept of a digitized library, including electronic library, virtual library, library without walls, bionic library and others.

The relatively recent use of the term digital library can be traced to the Digital Libraries Initiative funded by the National Science Foundation the Advanced Research Projects Agency

There are many definitions, fringing from the electronic catalog that describes physical items in a "brick and mortar" library to advanced multimedia environments housing all-digital collections. H. Thomas Hickerson, Cornell University's associate University Librarian for Information Technologies & Special Collections, believes it is time to erase the line between physical and digital libraries. "A major portion of library activities are technology-supported and have been for years. The internet has had an incredible impact, but libraries have a history of managing large systems and using technology to deliver bibliographic information," says Hickerson (Personal Correspondence).

Sun Microsystems (http://www.**sun**.com) defines a digital library as the electronic extension of functions users typically perform and the resources they access in a traditional library. These information resources can be translated into digital form, stored in multimedia repositories, and made available through Web-based services. The emergence of the digital library mirrors the growth of e-learning (or distance learning) as the virtual alternative to traditional school attendance.

Digital libraries began to appear on the campus in the early 1990's as research and development projects centered within computer science departments, sometimes funded by government grants. Campus librarians were often uninvolved in these early projects, which focused on digitization technology, metadata schemes, data management techniques, and digital preservation. Digital library use shifted to large and diverse campus audience, and information technology (IT) groups began to

partner with the library to develop campus-wide standards for the deployment and operation of digital libraries as an integral part of the education enterprise. This development paralleled the development of heightened student requirements for access to library resources.(Headstrom, 2004) With the advent of the Internet, individuals' expectations for access to information have increased dramatically. Patrons increasingly expect instant access to all the information resources they require, from any location, at any time, and from any device. This is the objective that the digital library is fulfilling. With digital libraries, and individual can:

- Gain access to the holdings of libraries worldwide through automated catalogs.
- Locate both physical and digitized versions of scholarly articles and books.
- Optimize searches, simultaneously search the Internet, commercial databases, and library collections.
- Save search results and conduct additional processing to narrow or qualify results.
- From search results, click through to access the digitized content or locate additional items of interest.

All of these capabilities are available from the desktop or other Web-enabled device such as a personal digital assistant or cellular telephone. Additionally, the user can customize his or her information request so that search results reflect individual needs and preferences. Sun considers personalization the next killer application, creating a more valuable and richer user experience in the digital library environment. (www.sun.com)

These components might not all be part of a discrete digital library system, but could be provided by other related or multi-purpose systems or environments. Accordingly, integration is a consistent issue cited by digital library developers. To interoperate with the existing library infrastructure, the digital library must be designed to work with existing library catalogs and incorporate industry standards, formats, and protocols.

DIGITAL LIBRARIES: DEVELOPMENT

Throughout the world, libraries, museums and archives are digitizing the important documents and images of our culture, both to preserve them for future generations and to make them more accessible to our own. As digital imaging technology has advanced, so have opportunities for preservation of irreplaceable artifacts. Today, students, researchers, information professionals, and the general public can directly access many of the world's rarest artifacts-from high-quality images of each page of the Gutenberg Bible to a digital likeness of the Mona Lisa-right at the desktop or other Web-enabled device, at any time and from any location.

- Through the 1990s, digital library projects were largely experimental activities. Digital library techniques came about through research sponsored by the U.S. National Science Foundation (NSF) and the U.K. Joint Information Committee (JISC). (www.**nsf.gov**)

In 1999 these projects began expanding internationally when NSF linked its digital library research program with similar activities being undertaken by JISC, resulting in the JISC-NSF International Digital Library Initiative (Wiseman, 1999). The objectives of this three-year program were to:

- Assemble collections of information that were not otherwise accessible or usable because of technical barriers, distance, size, system fragmentation, or other limits.

- Create new technology and the understanding to make it possible for a distributed set of users to find, deliver, and exploit such information.
- Evaluate the impact of this new technology and its international benefits.

The development of digital libraries must be considered in the overall context of initiatives to unify the IT structures of the campus and to transform the leaning process through innovative technology. Economic, social, and cultural pressures are forcing schools and universities to reinvent themselves. As in the business process re-engineering activities of the last decade that transformed corporate enterprises, education organizations are now viewing themselves in a new light.

New types of students and changing student expectations are driving the integration of core campus functions and deployment of student services on the Web. Fragmented, monolithic approaches are falling away as educators realize the need to link learning and administrative resources in a more effective way to become a "knowledge enterprises," the 21st century version of the traditional campus. During the past decade steep declines in the cost of commodity components, combined with the availability of high bandwidth networks, have made sophisticated IT applications for education affordable.

A mix of sophisticated digital and Internet-based services and rapidly expanding global digital content have made possible a "virtual learning environment" (VLE) that delivers the capability to enhance the classroom experience or conduct learning apart from a physical campus. The digital library is a core component of this VLE. "These developments are extending the role of the library, and changing the relationships between the library and other parts of the academic enterprise," according to Clifford Lynch, Director of the Coalition for Networked Resources and a noted authority on digital libraries (**drtc.isibang.ac.in/bitstream/1849/232/1/paperY_Malik.pdf, n.d.**).

DIGITAL LIBRARY COMPONENTS

By its nature, digital collection development requires extensive use of technological resources. In the early days of digital library development, when collections were typically small and experimental, a wide variety of hardware and software was utilized. Today, the leading digital library developers are putting substantial collections online. Some of these collection include millions of digital objects; collections are being planned that will require storage measured in petabytes-the equivalent of more than 50,000 desktop computers with 20-gigbyte hard drives. According to Lynch (1994) "As digital libraries scale in size and functionality, it is critical for the underlying technology platform to deliver the performance and reliability required".

Storage capacity also must be scalable to adapt to rapid growth in demand and must be adapted the mix of media types that may be stored in a digital library, such as:

- Text, which is relatively compact.
- Graphics, which can be data-intensive.
- Audio, which is highly dynamic.
- Video, which is highly dynamic and data intensive.

Storage capacity should be expandable in economical increments and should not require redesign or re-engineering of the system design as requirements grow. Open systems architecture provides both a robust platform and the best selection of digital media management solutions and developments tools. The inherent reliability and scalability of open platforms have made them the most popular choice of IT professionals for internet computing. This "computing model features an architecture that is oriented totally around internet protocols and stresses the role of Web sites for a

vast and diverse array of services that follow a utility model" (www.sun.com/software/whitepapers/wp.../wp-dhbrown99.pdf).

The use of new internet and portal computing models the explosion of off-campus, lifelong learners and the growing need to better manage heterogeneous, round-the clock IT environments has fueled the move to Sun technologies. Sun Microsystems continues to lead the way in RAS, resource management, real-world performance capability, and cost of ownership, setting a standard that other technology platform offering cannot match.

Software is evolving from local desktop and client-server software applications to Web applications. Today, it is very common for organization to move their local application to the Web and in some cases to subscribe to additional application services over the Web from external service providers. The this evolution has led to the development and proliferation of true Web services.

Several key technologies must interact to allow Web services to work in this way. Extensible Markup Language (XML) and Standard General Markup Language (SGML) are important standards influencing our ability to create broadly interoperable Web based applications. SGML is an international standard for text markup systems and is very large and complex, describing thousands of different document types in many fields of human activity. XML is a standard for describing other language, written in SGML.

XML allows the design of customized markup languages for limitless types of documents, providing a very flexible and simple way to write Web-based applications. This differs from HTML, which is a single, predefined markup language and can be considered on e application of XML. The primary standards powering.

Web services today are XML-based. These include:

- Simple Object Access Protocol (SOAP).
- Universal Description, Discovery and Integration (UDDI).

- Web Services Description Language (WSDL).
- Electronic Business XML (ebXML).

These standards are emerging as the basis for the new Web services model. While not all are fully defined standards, they are maturing quickly with broad industry support. An educational institutions digital library environment will likely encompass both local collections and externally provided resources from such sources as subscription services and other libraries. There is often a desire to structure this blend of internal and external resource as a unified collection from the user's point of view, with a single gateway and a comprehensive set of support services.

The first organizations to build large-scale digital libraries encountered many challenges in organizing, funding, managing and ensuring the long-term maintenance of the digital library environment. These challenges and shared experience of the early adopters may help others to avoid pitfalls and take advantage of evolving best practices. The funding issue is probably the single largest barrier to digital library development; this is why most existing collections are essentially pilot projects or R&D activities.

"The challenge of mounting a large-scale digitization effort, encoding appropriate metadata to ensure ease of discovery and use and making a commitment to long term preservation can be daunting to libraries already struggling to pay for existing activities. Some institutions like Harvard University have been able to generate start-up funding with the philosophy of" "built it and they will come". (Arms, 2000b)

METADATA: ELEMENTS AND STANDARDS

Metadata is an integral part of any digital objects as it provides information that a) allows discovery of collections or objects through the use of search tools, and b) provides sufficient context for understanding what has been found. When collections become large or when searching multiple collections (such as over the Internet) the discovery of objects of interest becomes a "needle in a haystack" exercise. Without agreed-upon metadata standards and the discipline of capturing and storing appropriate descriptive metadata, all but the smallest digital collections would be useless.

Metadata for individuals objects varies by the type of object but would include such things as its title, what it is, who created it, contributors, language, when it was Created, where it is located, the subject, etc. At the collection level users should be able to determine the scope, ownership, any access restrictions and other important characteristics that would assist in understanding the collection. Probably the best-known descriptive metadata standards for libraries is MARC (Machine Readable Catalog) used for cataloging books and other publications.

MARC has served the traditional library well, but was not designed for describing images, sound files and other new media types. An important emerging descriptive metadata standard for images and other multimedia objects is Dublin Core, a group of 15 items of information designed to be simple to understand and use. Dublin Core was designed to provide a very widely accepted mechanism to allow discovery, but with the option for different communities of users to adapt and customize it by adding more fields of particular importance to the community. In this way, the same base standards can be used for wide variety of purposes and business models.

Metadata is of following types:

Structural Metadata

The second type of metadata is structural metadata. This describes the associations within or among related individual information objects. A book, which consists of pages and chapters, is one of the most straightforward examples of structural metadata. The structural metadata would explain how individual page images make up individual chapters, and how chapters make up the book. There could also be individually imaged figures, and structural metadata could also relate these to chapters or to a list of all figures in the book. Structural metadata aids the user in navigating among individual objects that comprise a compound object.

Administrative Metadata

Administrative metadata facilitates access, management, and preservation of the digital resource. It can describe the viewer or player necessary to access the object, automatically opening that viewer or player when a user selects that resource. It can describe attributes such as image resolution, file size, or audio sampling rate. It can provide a record of how and when an object was created as well as archival and rights management information.

An important emerging standard for interoperability of digital collections is the Metadata Encoding and Transmission Standards (METS), which provides a uniform framework for managing and transmitting digital objects. The making of America II project ("Making of America," n.d.) developed an encoding format for descriptive, administrative, and structural metadata for textual and image-based works. Supported by the Digital Library Federation and the Library of Congress, METS builds upon the work of MOA2. It provides a format for encoding metadata necessary for both management of digital library objects within a repository and exchange of such objects between repositories (or between repositories and their users).

DIGITAL RIGHTS MANAGEMENT

Traditionally, libraries have purchased physical objects for their collections and permitted these to be used as allowed by copyright law and best practices. Many electronic resources, on the other hand, are maintained by publishers, venders, or others designated by them, and libraries or individuals can obtain rights of access through custom or mass-market licenses.

As libraries increasingly focus on building gateways that direct patrons both to the library's own content and to networked digital resources owned or controlled by other entities, rights management becomes a major concern. "In constructing a digital library service environment, the library becomes responsible for configuring access to a world of information of which it owns or manages only a part," says the California Digital Library's Dan Greenstein." (Greenstein, 2000) Accordingly, the digital library is known less for the extent and nature of the collections it owns than for the networked information space it defines through a range of online services.

A library's readers then access the works through high-speed information networks. A library's electronic resources licenses generally permit reader a broad range of educational, research, and personal uses, and, increasingly, the book and journal suppliers promise, in the licenses, to deliver ongoing ("Perpetual") access or to give the institution a residual "Product" should the publisher or vendor discontinues the work, sell it to another supplier, or leave the business altogether.

The traditional regime of copyright, enshrined in the copyright laws creates for libraries (institutions that at least the last century have been designated as holders of materials for the public good, materials that they then make freely available to the reading public) a role that now appears to be challenged if not attacked outright.

In this type of cooperative resource sharing environment, mechanisms for identifying information users and their access privileges are essential. With increased use of the Internet to buy, sell or license the use of documents, images, video and other copyrighted content in digital form, comes the need to protect that content from unauthorized use once it is outside the control of the publishers or distributor.

As libraries generally shift towards a service rather than a collection orientation, and as the economics and technologies of publishing (particularly for digital materials) make it harder for libraries to own their materials, the concept of freely accessible information, at least to the academic and public library user at the point of use, may well be at risk.

Nonetheless, this new business and (non) ownership model raises many questions for libraries and for society. What future, if any, is there for the largest research libraries in an era when, increasingly, materials that readers want are available without going to the library? More importantly, when libraries or other entities do not have contractual rights to archive and preserve electronic content, can they develop adequate archival and preservation mechanisms for electronic materials? These questions speak to large and vital questions of societal well-being.

DIGITAL PRESERVATION

Libraries place high value on preserving the irreplaceable contents of their collections, making the historical and cultural artifacts of our civilization available for future generations. Stanford University's Michael Keller comments, "Libraries are communications devices from preceding generations to succeeding generations. Preservation of scholarly publications is tremendously important." Fire prevention systems, environmental controls, and microfilming initiatives guard against catastrophic loss of irreplaceable items. Even the move from acid to alkaline paper in publishing has worked for long-term retention of printed items.

In 1991, the American Library Association published a preservation policy outlining the responsibilities of the library profession for preserving access to information of all forms. In 2001, that policy was updated to reflect changes brought about by the Internet. The preamble of the revised policy states: "Librarians must be committed to preserving their collections through appropriate and non-damaging storage, remedial treatment of damaged and fragile items, preservation of materials in their original format when possible, replacement or reformatting of deteriorated materials, appropriate security measures, and life-cycle management of digital publications to assure their usefulness for future generations." (http://www.ala.org/ala/mgrps/divs/alcts/resources/preserv/01alaprespolicy.cfm.

With digitized resources, it would seem that preservation would be much easier to achieve, especially since an unlimited number of copies can be created of the individual object. There are, however, a number of issues that complicate the maintenance of digital objects over long periods of time:

- Deterioration of media: Stone tablets have a considerable advantage over today's digital media for long-term storage. The problem of deterioration limit the useful life of today's digital media to between 5 and 50 years, while librarians debate how to retain the artifacts of our civilization for thousands of years to come.
- Evolution in type and format of media: In addition to the concerns of physical deterioration of media, we must be aware of the challenges posed by changes in media type and format. In the relatively recent history of personal computer use, we have seen an evolution from 5-1/4" floppy disks to higher density 3-1/2" diskettes to high-density zip disks, all requiring different physical disk drives and reader software. Optical storage technology is next, and there will undoubtedly be continual change in storage technologies.
- Changes in applications and operating systems: New software constantly appears on the horizon,

- Rendering older versions obsolete. The hardware required by applications and operating systems software also changes over time. Any information stored in a given software/hardware environment will eventually be rendered obsolete through technological obsolescence, most likely before deterioration of the actual storage media occurs. Today, locating a system capable of reading 20-year-old VisiCalc spreadsheet files or MultiMate word processing files is a difficult proposition; in 50 years' time it will likely be impossible.

- Preservation of processing results: Some digital resources exit only fleetingly as a program runs and cannot be preserved a static objects. Preservation of such resources requires maintenance of the program and the surrounding operating environment in operable form. Of course, not all digital resources have the same preservation requirements. "We are more concerned about persistence and authenticity of the collection of images than the long-term preservation of the surrogate," explains David Bearman, Director of the Art Museum Image Consortium (AMICO). "Museums are in the business of preserving the real thing." The skill set of the archivist, establishing criteria for selection of content as the amount of digital content expands. (http://www.mcn.edu/conference/MCN98/sessions_thursday.html

Today, most digital libraries follow a schedule of copying archived digital resources to address the issue of media deterioration. As organizational standards for formats and applications evolve, many libraries also convert the objects over time to maintain readability. Specific preservation policies and best practices, however, are not well developed. The Research Libraries Group (RLG) is an international member alliance, including universities and colleges, national libraries, archives, historical societies, museums and independent research collections, and public libraries dedicated to "improving access to information that supports research and learning." (www.**rlg.org**)

The National Library of Australia sponsors an initiative called "Preserving Access to Digital Information" (PADI) with the goal of providing mechanisms that help ensure that digital information is managed with appropriate consideration for preservation and future access. PADI recommends the strategies for long-term preservation of digital collections (Anderson, 2002).

The migration of digital information from one hardware/software configuration to another or from one generation of computer technology to a later one offers one method of dealing with technological obsolescence.

1. Adherence to standards will assist in preserving access to digital information.
2. Technology emulation potentially offers substantial benefits in preserving the functionality and integrity of digital objects.
3. Encapsulation, a technique of grouping together a digital object and anything else necessary to provide access to that object, has been proposed by a number of researchers as a useful strategy in conjunction with other digital preservation methods.
4. It is universally agreed that documentation is an important tool to assist in preserving digital material. In addition to the metadata necessary for resource discovery, other sorts of metadata, including preservation metadata, describing the software/hardware and management requirements of the digital material will provide essential information for preservation.

DIGITAL LIBRARY SERVICES

Deployment of portal technology has occurred side-by-side with digital collection development and access. As libraries create, license, or negotiate access to more and more digital content, the need for an easy-to-use interface becomes increasingly important. Library portals typically include an online catalog of materials as well a gateways to collections of digital resources accessible to the user.

Broadcast search tools allow library users to search all of these sources simultaneously with a single query. Portals may include electronic reference services ("ask a librarian"), personalization features ("my bookshelf," custom intelligent search), and other research tools. Enriched content, such as author biographies and book reviews, tables of contents, and jacket images can be provide to supplement the online catalog. Some libraries have built interactive features into their portals, allowing development of virtual communities.

The resulting nonprofit organization, the Art Museum Image Consortium (AMICO) now includes more than 35 major museums in the United States, Canada, and the UK. As the museums grew their digital collections and usage increased, they found that the task of dealing with requests by students and faculty took increasing amounts of time. AMICO provides a more efficient means of dealing with the work of rights management and access by clearing a licensed set of rights and delivering access to the consolidated collections through a variety of distribution mechanisms. (http://www.amico.org/)

More than three million AMICO Library subscribers access not only the images, but also find detailed provenance information, curatorial text, multiple views, and other related multimedia for many of the works. AMICO maintains the half-terabyte master repository in a custom-developed relational database that is growing by 20,000 works per year. Current challenges include expanding the multimedia items in the collection. Clearing digital right for works sought for inclusion in the AMICO Library also remains a continuing challenge.

The University of California at Berkeley has been in the forefront of digital library innovation for many years. Projects begun at Berkeley included the creation of specifications for encoding electronic finding aids that are used to access special collections and archives. These specifications later evolved into the XM-based Encoded Archival Description (EAD). Current work involves development of a modular object management environment, called Gen DL (for "Generic Digital Library"). Gen DL includes three components that can be thought of as three separate systems ("University of California, Berkeley", n.d.).

- The Web-based content management system, where creation and maintenance of the digital content is controlled. Descriptive, administrative, and structural metadata is created and linked to digitized or born-digital content. The resulting digital library objects are then encoded to the METS standard.
- The preservation repository (a joint project with the California Digital Library), where the digital content is managed to ensure its integrity and longevity.
- The access system, which is used to discover, display, and navigate objects that may have complex internal organizations (i.e., structural metadata).

Having undertaken one of the world's most aggressive digitization programs, Cornell library has been a developer of best practices and a leader in the field of digital libraries. As a Sun Center of Excellence for Digital Libraries, Cornell has served as a co-developer with Endeavor Information Systems for the product "ENCompass," a specially tailored multimedia management system intended for library implementations. Although Cornell has gained international recognition for its computer science advances in digital library technology, this university also recognizes the value of off-the-shelf products. (http://www.library.cornell.edu/)

Cornell has attained recognition for the substantial digital collections it has developed. One of the best known is the "Making of America" collection, a multi-institutional digitization initiative making available primary sources of 19th century American culture and history, including popular magazines like Harper's, Atlantic Monthly, and Scientific American. To date, more than 900,000 pages, which are full-text searchable and freely accessible over the Internet, are in the collection. More than 40 other digital collections have been established, ranging from audio recordings of rare birdcalls to digital facsimiles of essential works in the literature of witchcraft and demonology, drawn from Cornell University's Rare Book Collection.

There are several strategic digital library priorities. One is to establish a central repository for all information resources deemed worthy of long-term maintenance. The repository's aim is to support the total lifecycle of those materials. Harvard University has a very large and decentralized library system including more than 100 libraries and 35 major research collections. There is no hierarchy tying these libraries into a single organizational group.

Harvard's digital library activities are designed to provide a common technology infrastructure, consulting assistance, and guidance on policy issues to all of the Harvard libraries. Unlike many universities, Harvard has established major funding to support the development of a comprehensive infrastructure for digital libraries. The $12 million, 5-year program is called the "Library Digital Initiative," deliberately emphasizing the library orientation of the program. The goal of centrally funding this initiative to serve the decentralized network of libraries is to create incentive for participation in a common, standardized solution featuring a robust production. It environment and common practices for digitizing, reformatting,

metadata creation, digital licensing, preservation, and migration of objects, etc. (Flecker, 2000)

The central Oracle repository supports all types of multimedia objects and a set of catalogs. A Portal sits over the catalogs, allowing cross-catalog searching. Although born digital information is at the heart of the program, a program of internal grants has also been established to foster additions to the collection. It is expected that there will be a lot of activity devoted to the interface with learning systems in the future. There will also be increased emphasis on scholarly communication and the libraries' role in capturing the university's intellectual output.

The Problems associated with storing back issues of printed journals and locating articles of interest in those back issued led to the creation of JSTOR, an electronic archive of scholarly journals. JSTOR began as a pilot project sponsored by the Andrew W. Mellon Foundation in 1990. Ten journals in economics and history were selected in initially, and all back issues were digitized. High-resolution images of each page were captured and linked to a text file generated with optical character recognition software. (www.jstor.org)

Table of contents indices were developed as well, to provide search and retrieval of journal content of interest. When five test libraries showed enthusiasm about the space savings and ease of access, JSTOR was born. In 1995 JSTOR was established as an independent non-profit organization with the goals of providing a trustworthy archive of important scholarly journals, reducing the cost of accessing these materials, and assuring their long-term preservation. JSTOR now provides 1,100 user institutions worldwide access to 169 journals. Originally written in Perl, the Web interface has been ported to Java. Java's object-oriented approach makes it easier for JSTOR's geographically distributed developers to quickly write small pieces of reusable code. More than five million requests per month are satisfied through three sites at Princeton, the University of Michigan, and the University of Manchester. 12

The entire JSTOR archive requires 2.2 tera-bytes of storage for more than eight million pages of journal content. Usage has been growing at a rate of 50% per year, with rapid growth among international users. There is also increasing emphasis on allowing access to the JSTOR archive by secondary schools and public libraries. The University of Maryland has opportunistically grown its unique digital collections, beginning with the Performing Arts Library and the Broadcasting Archives. Both were highly motivated to make their holdings more accessible and usable.

A 1996 implementation of a commercial multimedia management platform had mixed results, due to the difficulty of integrating the product into the existing environment and the lack of specific library functionality. The University of Maryland has since taken a different.

Stanford University is well known for its pioneering work in digital library development and electronic publishing. Stanford has participated in both phase of the NSF Digital Library Initiative, provided online publishing services to nearly 100 scholarly societies, developed extensive digital collections, and is currently implementing an advanced digital repository. Stanford has entrusted the responsibilities of University Librarian, Publisher of the University Press, Publisher of the High Wire Press, and Director of Academic Computing to a single individual at Stanford.

DIGITAL REVOLUTION AND SCHOLARLY COMMUNICATION

The past brought recognizable information formats such as books' journals, film and other fixed media. Many electronic information resources, however, are brand-new creations that resemble traditional media less and less. They include the millions of Web pages and databases produced and government agencies. These creations represent a variety of information types, including descriptive materials, corporate report datasets, educational offerings theses and dissertations, and many more.

But along with these recognizable publication types are many new kinds of publications beyond anything anyone has kinds of publications beyond anything anyone has ever imagined in terms of size, scale, complexity, and function .These resources spring out of the energy and creativity of society's best minds out of the energy and creativity will only increase. For example, Corbis offers a huge collection of digital images derived from traditional photo foundation collects thousands and integrates them with related materials.

Microsoft's Teraserver project, collaboration with the U.S. Geological Survey, is a collection of satellite photos of many parts of the United States and selected parts of the rest of the world. The project, which is freely available and offers high-quality information, is an experiment in managing a very large database for public access. It is impossible to describe any of these projects in traditional terms that would allow comparing their collections to items, although they are fully analogous to and might well substitute for, library holdings. Even resources that seem to be more traditional, such as the research projects fostered by the Institute for Advanced Technology in the Humanities(IATH) at the University of Virginia, challenge traditional expectations by virtue of their constant state of flux. terraserver-usa.com/default.aspx

The institute's Web site contains no single stable artifact to "collect"-it is very much a work in progress Arts and Letters Daily (A&LD) is a Web site that goes one step further. In appearance, it is a daily "newspaper "who's content is cultural. But all that the editors provide is a front page with short descriptions and links to content found on hundreds of other freely available sites, many of them well-known resources in their own right. The repackaging accomplished by linking articles intelligently to a single site makes A&LD a hugely popular and highly useful site.

Long-established standard newspapers are avoiding links to material from other sources (for legal reasons, possibly); many of the newer newspapers and magazines, however, are filled with links to other sites. Preserving the news nowadays requires collecting not just the specific news source, but also the content of links to other Web spaces. The nation is investing significant sums to advance research in scientific areas, investments that will bear fruit in many directions now little surmised. Both the Los Alamos Genome Database are collective works that bring together new extraordinary power to advance and build scientific research.

It is entirely reasonable to imagine that, particularly in scientific and technological fields, such initiatives after only an inkling of what is to come .As the committee was deliberating, initiatives such as Pub Med Central (sponsored by the National Institutes of Health) and the Department of Energy initiative Pub SCIENCE were set to be scaled up in the very near future. Other resources are the electronic equivalents of printed information.

The electronic mode makes it possible to deliver the information wherever the reader may be (for instance to his or her computer in the home or workplace or by wireless technology, to any place),to present information that cannot be captured in print (such as video attachments, tables that can be manipulated, and so an),and to facilitate use of the information through quality interfaces and search capabilities. Some of the world publishing industry can be captured by briefly considering two well-established publishing formats-journals and books.

ONLINE ELECTRONIC JOURNALS

There is no truly reliable or single source of information on the growth of electronic announcement list NewJour reveals that in 1989, fewer than 10 e-journals were available. They were created in basic ASCII (.txt) form and had to be distributed in small chunks, lest they crash the mailboxes of subscribers. Today, many large publishers around the world, both for-profit and not-for-profit, maintain Web sites that make available their full collections of print journals (with only limited back-file runs, so far) to subscribers.

Given this penetration of new technologies into scholarly, scientific and popular journal and magazine publication, a list such as NewJour will one day soon no longer be needed. In this decade (or even half-decade), most print magazines and journals will have a Web version, if they do not already have one. Furthermore although for the moment it is convenient to think of print and Web versions as providing the same or identical information, the two styles are already beginning to pull apart and will only diverge further.

Not only will the same name ultimately denote collections of content that are in fact very different, but some of the e-journals also will evolve into new genres. The prevailing vision is that this wealth of journal literature will be linked through indexing services and this vision is rapidly being realized. For as long as print versions continue to be published, tracking and collecting will be much more difficult. The most significant problem for ubiquitous electronic access is that of long-term achievability and preservation, a not to maintain costly parallel print and electronic systems.

So far, very few electronic journals (or any other resource) have had to survive on the internet for even one decade. While some experts say that long-term sustainability is a trivial matter. Studies suggest high costs and tremendous uncertainties. Fundamental to these uncertainties is matter of ownership, which libraries rarely have, given that electronic information produces no fixed artifact for characterizes scholarly and research journals, the committee found similar or even faster growth in the even broader universe of all continuing publications that includes popular magazines, series and newspapers as well as annual reports, directories, series, and so on.

Standard periodical indexing and abstracting services began to become available electronically in the 1970s through specialized vendors such as Dialog and BRS, whose proprietary systems required the mediation of expert easy-to-use Web interfaces for any licensed subscriber. Thus it is no surprise that the journal articles cited by these sources would become quickly available online. However, books-such as novels and scholarly monographs, for example-have seemed far less susceptible to electronic transformation.

While some books are consulted in bits and bytes(for particular facts or small sections),many(the argument goes) need to be deliciously savored and contemplated from beginning to end, and an online screen is hostile to such prolonged congenial or intense reading. "You can't take it to bed or to the beach or onto the plane with you," is the oft-heard lament .The vision now being articulated by many players in the book publishing industry and its partners(in printing, distribution, and software) is that the full text of all published books, at least from mainstream publishers, will exist on vast electronic information servers, there to be channeled to the output of the reader's choice: traditional print formats or digital formats (by accessing a local copy on a PC or portable device or by viewing a remote copy through the Web).that is, the authoritative source file of many books may soon be an electronic version that can generate various derivative versions.

The e-book may be on the verge of acceptance and success because of the convergence of large computer servers, big network pipelines, rapid progress in developing e-book standards, rapid progress in developing e-book standards, and the increasing sophistication and utility of handheld book-reading devices, as well as business partnerships to take advantage of all this .Like e-journals, e-books also have a history that goes back to the 1980s.

In the mid-1990s, an entrepreneur making a car trip with his wife had a vision of "the world's largest bookstore," a virtual shop in which the discerning reader could obtain every book-or nearly every book-currently in print. Jeff Bezos, founder and CEO of amazon.com, Time Magazine's person of the year for 1999, achieved his dream: situating bookselling at the core of e-commerce and radicalizing the bookstore concept, to say nothing of notions of business success. Through the Web, the Amazon.com shopper fills a virtual shopping cart with the desired books, which are delivered a day or two or three later to the reader's address of choice.

Through Amazon.com, large collections of books have come one step nearer to their readers-and no library has played a part in this dramatic convergence of reader and book. In the case of the virtual superstore, the reader controls the atmosphere, which need not be as public as a library or bookshop and may be as comfortable as reading in a lounge chair wearing fuzzy slippers and a dressing gown. Most significantly, the rise of the book superstore has implicitly changed the overall economics of access to books and information.

Where once a good public library was the best and most accessible source of materials for many, if not most, communities, bookstores of similar size may be a few doors down the block, open longer hours, and with enough copes of popular titles to satisfy almost all comers. And, most libraries and physical bookstores are dwarfed by online bookstores. These book superstores offer a remarkably wide range of library-like services-lectures, discussion groups, ready access to books, a sense of community. What they do not yet offer is information service-labor-intensive; predict that they will not continue to expand their range.

For now, it is most noticeably the information navigation functions of the library-the instruction in finding, filtering, and evaluating information from a welter of available sources-and in provision of historical depth that the bookstores make the least attempt to supplant. Borders began its career with claims about the literacy and helpfulness of its staff, all of whom had to pass a test to demonstrate their book lore as a condition of employment despite this, the library is less than ever a primary supplier of access to new and current books. Libraries continue however, to be strong in providing access to both older and more specialized material.

Another implication of the shift in the economy of information is that collecting and storing materials are arguably somewhat less the jobs of the library than before. The current emphasis is on services. Indeed, many public libraries have always had this bias, retaining from among older book only those of continuing interest to their readers, while clearing out shelf space for what a current generation demands.

In any case, the superstores and Amazon.com have by no means reached the end state of the publishing industry's book-to-reader vision, nor do libraries seem to have much of a role in that next vision either. The concept of books on demand has been in gestation for some time. For example, in the early 1990s, Xerox partnered with a few large publishing houses in an OD experiment. The products were acceptable, but computer servers and network pipelines were less capacious that today and so the results were slow. The need to resolve right and permissions issues also posed a significant challenge. The concept needed time to ripen, and ripen it has.

Most individuals, organizations and publishers agree that at the very least the traditional book format is facing competition from formats that do some things better. In 1999, the American Historical Association announced an electronic book prize to be awarded annually for several years to half a dozen brilliant dissertations in various fields of history. Dissertations that take full advantage of the converging can offer and books cannot. The results will enliven the books, attract readers, promote the new medium as a viable one for serious scholarship and give young scholars a leg up.

DIGITAL CONVERGENCE AND RISING COSTS

Traditional libraries are most often conceived of as repositories of textual artifacts. High culture constructs itself around artifacts that can be managed and cataloged in particular ways. But the technological changes of the last two decades have posed a challenge. The technical convergence of data desktop (or palmtop) through a single network connection, is encouraging consumers to think first of data and only secondarily of media.

Libraries are being challenged to decide whether and to what extent their traditional focus on textual or mostly textual artifacts fulfills their responsibility. At the very least, libraries in the year 2000 are actively assessing the possibility of whole classes of artifact quite unlike what they owned before, placing very different demands on their various skills.

Formally published online information resources are expensive to license, often costing more than one would expect to pay for print. Start-up costs for both sellers and purchasers of information are higher than the costs of maintaining traditional print information:

- Information providers are investing in new technologies and skills and a database or subscription price attempts to recover many, if not all, of the start-up costs over time;
- Institutions are developing their own technological and human capabilities, also with significant new costs; and
- Libraries and publishers are maintaining parallel information systems and resources in traditional and electronic media.

These additional costs will not disappear for some time. But the primary barrier to the use of online information resources is the cost of licensing the electronic resources marketed by publishers and vendors. Most libraries are funded on a model for the acquisition of fixed-format materials. License agreements, or even specialized CD-ROM products and services, are being offered at prices that encourage many libraries to consider cooperative purchasing. Furthermore, the new model for library acquisitions must consider not only the cost of access to the information, but also the cost of maintaining the technical capability (hardware, software, personnel) required to make these resources available to readers.

Various contemporary students of the economics of information have asserted that the only financial survival option of libraries is to scale up into efficient, cooperating entities. The large consortia that build national catalogs-the large utilities such as Research Libraries Group (RLG) and OCLC-clearly have a part to play in organizing any such meta-system. Although librarians and publishers have, as yet, little quantitative data or user analysis to show how much or even how electronic information resources are used, there is no question that usage, to the extent it can be measured, is shooting up with every passing month.

Research regularly demand more and more such resources and protest loudly if online access to any index, dictionary encyclopedia, text or collection is removed, even if the reasons are seemingly good ones-for example, if a library or institution believes the price is too high or the usage too small to justify continuance. This reaction is no surprise and from the reader's point of view makes perfect sense. Because we live in an age of intense national, institutional, and personal competition, information is essential, and meeting the need for knowledge is an indisputable requirement.

SCHOLARLY COMMUNICATION

The multitude of electronic databases, the rapid growth of Web sites, the increase in the number of electronically available print journals, and the availability of numerous full-text resources such as reports, dissertations, and electronic books all represent a dramatic change in the dissemination of scholarly and cultural content. The history of this revolution is short and there is still much to learn, on all levels and in all areas. Not a great deal has been published about how the great libraries are transforming themselves to greet the electronic age, although Maurice B Line (12) notes that three factors have caused an almost ceaseless questioning of the roles and futures of national libraries:

1. Automation, information, and communications technology;
2. The intrusion of the private sector into areas formerly sacred to libraries; and
3. The globalization of libraries.

Libraries have accordingly begun to move aggressively in the direction of becoming hybrid libraries (i.e., libraries that embrace information in numerous formats, now including electronic formats). The transformation of library cultures and practice by adoption of information technology continues apace. An increasing emphasis on service and a decreasing emphasis on collection have already been noted. Libraries are incorporating electronic technologies and services into the everyday work of all staff by doing a number of things:

- Working for the broadest possible access for readers in the electronic environment. Not only are libraries seeking technological standards' and presentation of resources in forms accessible to the broadest range of readers, but they are also lobbying to advance the public policy debate in ways that support broad access for the good of society as a whole.
- Reallocating an increasing and visible portion of collections budgets to the electronic resources needed by their readers. For

example, ARL Supplementary Statistics indicate that in FY98/99, 29 ARL member libraries spent more that $1 million of their collections budgets for licensing electronic databases, 41 representing anywhere from 6 to 22 percent of their library materials budgets.

- Building collections of digital resources that, while not yet rivaling traditional collections in scope and bulk, are substantial, of high value, and integrated in the traditional patterns of collection and use.

- Working to shape and support initiatives such as community education, online course support, Web page design, teaching-specialist electronic resources, and digitizing of materials for these programs-all with a view to making educational opportunities as broad, rich, and accessible as possible. Lifelong learning is the opportunity and the goal, and "distance learning" us the current buzzword for the tactics librarians seek to support.

- Finding new ways to measure the usage patterns and behaviors of readers, so as to anticipate and support their needs, bringing the right resources into play for readers. The digital environment facilitates such measurement and, accordingly, such feedback, giving a better allocation of resources than has ever been possible with print media.

- Devoting increasing effort to more sophisticated reader services associated with single and multiple electronic resources. Librarians are more often than ever teachers of how to use electronic resources, and readers spend less time pursuing simple factual information at traditional reference desks.

- Cooperating with other libraries in setting up networks that make libraries effectively a single virtual (through the locator tool of interoperable online catalogs) institution

that can deliver physical materials, via advanced interlibrary loans and document delivery, to more and more readers more effectively -and more cost-effectively -than ever.

- Delivering physical materials by electronic means. As physical materials become increasingly deliverable at a distance, libraries are putting more and more electronic delivery services into operation.

- Partnering with other participants in the creations and dissemination of knowledge. Libraries can for example, work with individual authors, organizations, publishers (commercial and noncommercial), booksellers, and software companies to create and make available functional and well used online resources.

- Digitizing and making available to readers materials already in library collections and special collections. Such materials would include, in particular out-of-copyright material, image collections, sheet music, maps, and other traditional library treasures.

- Subscribing to online services that provide statistical data. Libraries would help readers learn to manipulate services containing anything from historical census data to financial market data.

- Creating multimedia servers for music, film, and other media. At the same time, thorny questions of access and permitted use must be addressed, and the technological capability to handle significant quantities of such material must be developed.

- Using the new generation of library management systems as a springboard not only for integrating forms of access to a wide range of materials and formats but also for reengineering the entire workflow and back-office processes of traditional librarianship. The technical services of libraries are becoming increasingly business-like, streamlined, and closely managed, with closer links than ever to vendors through electronic data interchange (EDI) and other forms of electronic interaction that work to the advantage of all parties.

- Working to understand the technical demands, possibilities, and long-term costs and responsibilities of digital media as instruments for the preservation of library information, including material from traditional print media (e.g., the contents of books printed on acid-based paper) and material created in digital form. When we fully understand the challenges of moving digitally preserved information from format to format, from one hardware and software systems to a new hardware and software system, we will have made great progress in solving what many think is the biggest remaining problem in establishing truly functional and satisfactory digital libraries.

- Working through the issues that must be faced in deciding which kinds of resources are best maintained locally, library by library, and which resources are best maintained elsewhere, whether by publishers, vendors, library consortia, or third parties. Traditional librarianship achieves security and preservation by having redundant physical copies: the challenge now is to balance redundancy (and thus security) with optimal efficiency and to avoid unnecessary duplication of effort.

- Understanding evolving legal regimes such as copyright and licensing. In this arena, librarians seek not only to understand but also to shape and influence developments, thus securing agreements that offer reader's high-quality, reliable, and permanent access to resources.

- Exercising responsible stewardship of library resources, which are usually purchased with public funds or from not-for-profit institutional budgets. Such

stewardship requires keen understanding of the business models and economics of the new information sources in an environment in which libraries find themselves increasingly offered not ownership but access not a once-for-all price but something closer to annual subscription or by-the-drink pricing.

- Cultivating an expertise in technology matters. The technological infrastructure of a library now faces a new degree of volatility and continuing costs as equipment and software need upgrading. The marketplaces makes it literally impossible to choose not to play the upgrade game: in a very short time, a library's information would simply become unavailable if it persisted in using even slightly outmoded operating systems or software.

- Continuously upgrading human resources and skills. The librarians and support staff at this time of transformation must undergo no less arduous a series of "upgrades." As in other sectors of our economy, it is impossible in the library sector for staff to acquire and practice skills and then use them for a lifetime; instead, they must grow and adapt, and there are real and substantial costs for supporting the necessary training and for paying a more highly skilled staff.

- Seeking new funding sources and opportunities. Traditional funding sources-annual budgets doled out by the government or not-for -profit organization with a tiny annual increase-no longer suffice.

Librarians are increasingly engaged in entrepreneurial efforts, whether soliciting research and development funding from granting agencies, developing partnerships with other entities in the library sector, or participating in cost-recovery projects with the commercial sector that serves and interacts with the library community.

CHALLENGES

The challenge in utilizing digital technology for enhanced access is the need to secure that investment, and guarantee long-term access to that information. The role of digital technologies as a preservation strategy is a contentious issue, with the traditional school of library preservation clinging to microfilm as the preferred reformatting medium for long term archival storage. The challenge is to react pro-actively, to look forward to consider ways of minimizing identified future risks associated with new media, and to look back into the past to understand the nature and development leading to their creation.

Digital information and electronic resources have transformed academic research fundamentally. As the price of print materials, such as scholarly journals continues to rise, the accessibility and functionality of electronic versions become more attractive, and libraries invest more heavily in new technologies. A related issue in the need to preserve digital resources' is a growing reliance of libraries as service providers on digital technology, which must impact on our institutional goals. Digital technologies find their place in the preservation strategies of research libraries in the opportunities presented to such goal in improved public access to on-line digital surrogates. Digitization is now a mainstream activity of several libraries.

The improvements in storage media are so great as to drive market forces. Longevity of a floppy disk common until a year or two ago, can be estimated at between one and ten months. CD longevity is estimated between 10 and 100 years. Other advantages can be found in the aggregation of larger quantities of information to facilitate data management. 650Mb of data can be stored on a CD.

CHALLENGE OF OBSOLESCENCE

The most serious problems facing managers of digital collections, is not unstable media, but data

format and software obsolesce. Transforming information from one digital format to another, migration is an essential strategy for persistent adherence to international standard format. Infrastructure risks include the presence or lack of persistent institutional support in terms of funding, hardware, software and staff to manage the repeated migration of digital collections. Emulation of software and hardware platforms aims to use the power of present computer technology to function as if it were the technology of a previous generation.

Long term preservation of digital resources is feasible through the implementation of sound polices at the inception and in the development of digital libraries. The challenge lies in the need for libraries to move pro-actively in establishing digital collection development programmed in an electronic environment that is conducive to preservation. The collaboration of a wide community of information professionals was responsible for developing new strategies for data management and shortage for the preservation of digital information resources.

By differentiating between the storage of the bits that comprise the digital object and the related information carried by the metadata it is possible to create and infrastructure for life cycle management for digital preservation. In fact, information products, like electronic documents and digital objects are particularly important because they represent that purest form of Electronic Commerce. Indeed Electronic Commerce, with its greatly reduced cost of production and distribution makes may new knowledge businesses practical that were previously impractical. For example, a fully realized infrastructure for Electronic Commerce would make it practical for authors to charge pennies for paragraphs and still make a profit because the author can reach millions world-wide over the internet, who can pay and download the paragraph at little or no cost to the author. Electronic Commerce does not completely address collaborative design and manufacturing activities, although they do share may of the same sorts of activities. The publication of compelling electronic catalogs, advertisements, and product information requires the same set of electronic publishing tools, as the author of an electronic document or digital object for a digital library.

In the information age, a large percent of the commerce will never be embodied physically. Information products are enabled by information technology and not just distributed more efficiently by it. These products can consist not just of electronic publications, catalogs, videos and the like, but can include interactive video games, software programs, electronic keys and tokens, customized design specifications, even electronic keys that can open to hotel rooms, cars, storage compartments, and airport boarding gates.

Furthermore, these information products are not just created entirely by the service provider, but can be designed or customized by the customer, adding a customer driven activity call "design" to the purchase cycle. Indeed, information products can be continuously added to modified, and morphed, as they pass along a chain of users. It is also likely that for these products ordering, billing, payment, and distribution would likely all happen simultaneously. Some micro payment schemes for use over the internet have been proposed that are significantly weaker than those being proposed for the more traditional payment schemes.

There are however, a number of standardized services that are needed to fully realize their complete potential. Most of these services are common to many different applications, including electronic commerce and digital libraries. Most of the current solutions being prototyped over the Internet, all vary in their approach to security and privacy, their ability to handle micro-payments, and their applicability to various types of transactions. They also differ in their business models- for example, in their pricing strategy and in their assumptions as to who bears the risk in case of insufficient funds or disputes.

A truly interoperable common infrastructure, for applications such as electronic commerce and digital libraries, would allow parties to conduct their transactions in private, without paying any fees to intermediaries unless they provide some real added values, such as credit or search services. This infrastructure would make it easier for any and all interested persons to become services providers as well as consumers. The infrastructure must be based on a common set of services and standards that ensure interoperability. Preferably, these services and standards can be used as standard building blocks that service providers and application designers can combine, enhance, and customize.

CONCLUSION

Current information needs are being provided in electronic form with varying success in public, college and research libraries around the world. Research libraries have only begun to take on the provision, organization and preservation of information with the same long-term commitment they have made for print materials. It is an expensive, uncharted and difficult task. But until the long-term commitments are undertaken, many currently proposed solutions will have only temporary effects. The ability of the scholarly community to give serious weight to electronic information depends upon their trust in such information being dependably available, with authenticity and integrity maintained. Changes in scholarly publishing to help alleviate the serials crisis, for example, are usually thought to be bound up with the prestige of electronic journals in the academic tenure process. The ability of the academy to count on long-term, secure existence of electronic scholarly work will be an important determinant of the success of academic electronic publishing. Libraries and universities have a stake in helping electronic publishing to succeed, and therefore have an interest in establishing secure digital research libraries. Users' needs will continue to be what they long have been.

The locus of information may be called the electronic storage repository. Over time, we will learn how collection development plays out in an access environment as well as in an ownership environment. It is sometimes loosely proposed that libraries need not acquire electronic information, for it will be available somewhere on the network. Such proposals ignore the obvious truth that some institution must still, in the end, take responsibility for the information. That has always been a definition of the library responsibility.

There will be many electronic storage repositories, responding both to requirements of redundancy and to the individual needs of institutions. In contrast to print collections, it is unlikely that there will be a high degree of content duplication across many electronic repositories, since for most purposes existence in a single place allows world-wide access.

REFERENCES

Anderson, J. (2002). The New-Look PADI: The National Library of Australia's Subject Gateway. *Gateways*. Retrieved from http://www.nla.gov.au/pub/gateways/archive/60/p20a01.html

Arms, W. (2000). *Digital Libraries*. Cambridge, MA: MIT Press.

Art Museum Image Consortium. (n.d.). Retrieved from http://www.amico.org/

Bearman, D. (n.d.). *Issues facing the Art Museum Image Consortium*. Retrieved from http://www.mcn.edu/conference/MCN98/sessions_thursday.html

Cornell University Library. (n.d.). Retrieved from http://www.library.cornell.edu/

drtc.isibang.ac.in/bitstream/1849/232/1/paperY_Malik.pdf (n.d.).

Flicker, D. (2000). *Harvard's Library Digital Initiative: Building a First Generation Digital Library Infrastructure*. Retrieved from http://www.dlib.org/dlib/november00/flecker/11flecker.html

Greenstein, D. (2000). Digital Libraries and Their Challenges. *Library Trends*, *49*(Fall), 290–303.

Hedstrom, M. (2004). Digital preservation: A time bomb for digital libraries. *Computers and the Humanities*, *31*(3), 189–202. doi:10.1023/A:1000676723815

http://www.ala.org/ala/mgrps/divs/alcts/resources/preserv/01alaprespolicy.cfm

http://www.rlg.org (n.d.).

ILA Preservation policy. (n.d.). Retrieved from

JSTOR. (n.d.). Retrieved from http://www.jstor.org

Lancaster, F. W. (1978). *Toward Paperless Information Systems*. New York: Academic Press.

Lynch, C. (1994). The Integrity of Digital Information: Mechanics and Definitional Issues. *Journal of the American Society for Information Science American Society for Information Science*, *45*(10), 737–744. doi:10.1002/(SICI)1097-4571(199412)45:10<737::AID-ASI4>3.0.CO;2-8

Making of America. (n.d.). Retrieved from http://quod.lib.umich.edu/m/moagrp/

National Science Foundation. (n.d.). Retrieved from http://www.nsf.gov

Sun Microsystems. (n.d.a). Retrieved from http://www.sun.com

Sun Microsystems. (n.d.b). White Paper. Retrieved from http://www.sun.com/software/whitepapers/wp.../wp-dhbrown99.pdf

TerraServer-USA. (n.d.). Retrieved from terraserver-usa.com/default.aspx

University of California. *Berkeley*. (n.d.). Retrieved from http://berkeley.edu/

Wiseman, N., Rusbridge, C., & Griffin, S. M. (1999). The Joint NSF/JISC International Digital Libraries Initiative. *D-Lib Magazine, 5*(6). Retrieved from **http://**www.dlib.org/dlib/june99/06wiseman.html

40

Chapter 3
Digitisation:
Methods, Tools and Technology

Jagdish Arora
INFLIBNET, Ahmedabad, India

ABSTRACT

This chapter provides a practical approach to digital libraries. The authors present a comprehensive picture of digitization and explains the process of digitization in a step-by-step approach. The chapter also describes different file formats and alternatives to digitization.

INTRODUCTION

All recorded information in a traditional library is analogue in nature. The analogue information can include printed books, periodical articles, manuscripts, cards, photographs, vinyl disks, video and audio tapes. However, when analogue information is fed into a computer, it is broken down into 0s and 1s changing its characteristics from analogue to digital. These bits of data can be re-combined for manipulation and compressed for storage. Voluminous encyclopaedias that take-up yards of shelf-space in analogue form can fit into a small space on a computer drive or stored on to a CD ROM disc, which can be searched, retrieved, manipulated and sent over the network. One of the

most important traits of digital information is that it is not fixed in the way that texts printed on a paper are. Digital texts are neither final nor finite, and are not fixed either in essence or in form except, when it is printed out as a hard copy.

Flexibility is one of the chief assets of digital information. An endless number of identical copies can be created from a digital file, because a digital file does not decay by copying. Moreover, digital information can be made accessible from remote location simultaneously by a large number of users.

Digitisation is the process of converting the content of physical media (e.g., periodical articles, books, manuscripts, cards, photographs, vinyl disks, etc.) into digital format. In most library applications, digitisation normally results in documents that are accessible from the web site of a library and thus, on

DOI: 10.4018/978-1-61520-767-1.ch003

the Internet. Optical scanners and digital cameras are used to digitise images by translating them into bit maps. It is also possible to digitise sound, video, graphics, animations, etc.

Digitisation is not an end in itself. It is the process that creates a digital image from an analogue image. Selection criteria, particularly those which reflect user needs are of paramount importance. Therefore, the principles that are applicable in traditional collections development are applicable when materials are being selected for digitisation. However, there are several other considerations related to technical, legal, policy, and resources that become important in a digitisation project.

Digitisation is one of the three important methods of building digitised collections. The other two methods include providing access to electronic resources (whether free or licensed) and creating library portals for important Internet resources.

DIGITISATION: BASICS

Definition

The word "digital" describes any system based on discontinuous data or events. Computers are digital machines because at their most basic level they can distinguish between just two values, 0 and 1, or off and on. All data that a computer processes must be encoded digitally as a series of zeroes and ones.

The opposite of digital is analogue. A typical analogue device is a clock in which the hands move continuously around the face. Such a clock is capable of indicating every possible time of the day. In contrast, a digital clock is capable of representing only a finite number of times (every tenth of a second, for example).

As mentioned before, a printed book is analogue form of information. The contents of a book need to be digitised to convert it into digital form. Digitisation is the process of converting the content

of physical media (e.g., periodical articles, books, manuscripts, cards, photographs, vinyl disks, etc.) to digital formats.

Digitisation refers to the process of translating a piece of information such as a book, journal articles, sound recordings, pictures, audio tapes or videos recordings, etc. into bits. Bits are the fundamental units of information in a computer system. Converting information into these binary digits is called digitisation, which can be achieved through a variety of existing technologies. A digital image, in turn, is composed of a set of pixels (picture elements), arranged according to a pre-defined ratio of columns and rows. An image file can be managed as a regular computer file and can be retrieved, printed and modified using appropriate software. Further, textual images can be OCRed so as to make its contents searchable.

Needs of Digitisation

Digitising a document in print or other physical media (e.g., sound recordings) makes the document more useful as well as more accessible. It is possible for a user to conduct a full-text search on a document that is digitised and OCRed. It is possible to create hyperlinks to lead a reader to related items within the text itself as well as to external resources. Ultimately, digitisation does not mean replacing the traditional library collections and services; rather, it serves to enhance them.

A document can be converted into digital format depending on the objective of digitisation, end user, availability of finances, etc. While the objectives of digitisation initiatives differ from organization to organization, the primary objective is to improve the access. Other objectives include cost savings, preservation, keeping pace with technology and information sharing. The most significant challenges in planning and execution of a digitisation project relate to technical limitations, budgetary constraints, copyright considerations, lack of policy guidelines and lastly, the selection of materials for digitisation.

While new and emerging technologies allow digital information to be presented in innovative ways, the majority of potential users are unlikely to have access to sophisticated hardware and software. Sharing of information among various institutions is often restricted by the use of incompatible software.

One of the main benefits of digitisation is to preserve rare and fragile objects by enhancing their access to multiple numbers of users simultaneously. Very often, when an object is rare and precious, access is only allowed for a certain category of people. Going digital could allow more users to enjoy the benefit of access. Although, digitisation offers great advantages for access like, allowing users to find, retrieve, study and manipulate material, it cannot be considered as a good alternate for preservation because of ever changing formats, protocols and software used for creating digital objects.

There are several reasons for libraries to go for digitisation and there are as many ways to create the digitised images, depending on the needs and uses. The prime reason for the digitisation is the need of the user for convenient access to high quality information. Other important considerations are:

Quality Preservation

The digital information has potential for qualitative preservation of information. The preservation-quality images can be scanned at high resolution and bit depth for best possible quality. The quality remains the same inspite of multiple usage by several users. However, caution need to be exercised while choosing digitised information as preservation media.

Multiple Referencing: Digital information can be used simultaneously by several users at a time.

Wide Area Usage: Digital information can be made accessible to distant users through the computer networks over the Internet.

Archival Storage: Digitisation is used for restoration of rare material. The rare books, images or archival material are kept in digitised format as a common practice.

Security Measure: Valuable documents and records are scanned and kept in digital format for safety.

SELECTION OF MATERIAL FOR DIGITISATION

To begin the process of digitisation, first of all, we need to select documents for digitisation. The proccess of selection of material for digitisation invloves identification, selection and prioritization of documents that are to be digitized. If an organization generates contents, strategies may be adopted to capture data that is "borne digital". If documents are available in digital form, it can be easily converted into other formats. If the selected material is from the external sources, IPR issues need to be resolved. If material being digitised is not available in public-domain then it is important to obtain permission from the publishers and data suppliers for digitisation. Moreover, decision may be taken whether to OCR the digitized images. Documents selected for digitisation may already be available in digital format. It is always economical to buy e-media, if available, than their conversion. Moreover, over-sized material, deteriorating collections, bound volumes of journals, manuscripts, etc. would require highly specialized equipment and highly skilled manpower.

The documents to be digitised may include text, line art, photographs, colour images, etc. The selection of document need to be reviewed very carefully considering all the factors of utility, quality, security and cost. Rare and much in demand documents and images are selected as first priority without considering the quality. Factors that may be considered before selecting different media for digitisation include:

Audio: The sound quality has to be checked and require corrections made together by the subject expert and computer sound editor.

Video: The video clippings are normally edited on Beta max tapes which can be used for transferring it on digital format. While editing colour tone, resolution is checked and corrected.

Photographs: The selection of photographs is very crucial process. High resolution is required for photographic images and slides. Especially the quality, future need and the copyright aspects have to be checked.

Documents: Documents which are much in demand, too fragile to handle, and rare in availability are reviewed and selected for the process. If the correction of literary value demands much input, then documents are considered for publication rather than digitisation.

STEPS IN THE PROCESS OF DIGITISATION

The following four steps are involved in the process of digitisation. Software, variably called document image processing (DIP), Electronic Filing System (EFS) and Document Management Systems (DMS) provides all or most of these functions:

Scanning

Electronic scanners are used for acquisition of an electronic image into a computer through its original that may be a photograph, text, manuscript, etc. An image is "read" or scanned at a predefined resolution and dynamic range. The resulting file, called "bit-map page image" is formatted (image formats described elsewhere) and tagged for storage and subsequent retrieval by the software package used for scanning. Acquisition of image through fax card, electronic camera or other imaging devices is also feasible. However, image scanners are most important and most commonly used component of an imaging system for the transfer of normal paper-based documents.

Steps in the Process of Scanning using a Flatbed Scanner

Step 1. Place picture on the scanner's glass
Step 2. Start scanner software
Step 3. Select the area to be scanned
Step 4. Choose the image type
Step 5. Sharpen the image
Step 6. Set the image size
Step 7. Save the scanned image using a desirable format (GIF or JPEG)

Indexing

If converting a document into an image or text file is considered as the first step in the process of imaging, indexing these files comprises the second step. The process of indexing scanned image involves linking of database of scanned image to a text database. Scanned images are just like a set of pictures that need to be related to a text database describing them and their contents. An imaging system typically stores a large amount of unstructured data in a two file system for storing and retrieving scanned images. The first is traditional file that has a text description of the image (keywords or descriptors) along with a key to a second file. The second file contains the document location. The user selects a record from the first file using a search algorithm. Once the user selects a record, the application keys into the location index finds the document and displays it.

Most of the document imaging software packages through their menu drive or command driven interface, facilitate elaborate indexing of documents. While some document management system facilitate selection of indexing terms from the image file, others allow only manual keying in of indexing terms. Further, many DMS packages provides OCRed capabilities for transforming the images into standard ASCII files. The OCRed text then serve as a database for full-text search of the stored images.

Store

The most tenacious problem of a document image relate to its file size and, therefore, to its storage. Every part of an electronic page image is saved regardless of the presence or absence of ink. The file size varies directly with scanning resolution, the size of the area being digitized and the style of graphic file format used to save the image. The scanned images, therefore, need to be transferred from the hard disc of scanning workstation to an external large capacity storage devices such as an optical disc, CD ROM / DVD ROM disc, snap servers, etc. While the smaller document imaging system may use offline media, which need to be reloaded when required, or fixed hard disc drives allocated for image storage. Larger document management system use auto-changers such as optical jukeboxes and tape library systems. The storage required by the scanned image varies and depends upon factors such as scanning resolution, page size, compression ratio and page content. Further, the image storage device may be either remote or local to the retrieval workstation depending upon the imaging systems and document management system used.

Retrieve

Once scanned images and OCRed text documents have been saved as a file, a database is needed for selective retrieval of data contained in one or more fields within each record in the database. Typically, a document imaging system uses at least two files to store and retrieve documents. The first is traditional file that has a text description of the image along with a key to the second file. The second file contains the document location. The user selects a record from the first-file

using a search algorithm. Once the user selects a record, the application keys into the location index finds the document and displays it. Most of the document management system provides elaborate search possibilities including use of Boolean and proximity operators (and, or, not) and wild cards. Users are also allowed to refine their search strategy. Once the required images have been identified their associated document image can quickly be retrieved from the image storage device for display or printed output.

DIGITISATION: INPUT AND OUTPUT OPTIONS

A document can be converted into digital format depending on the objective of digitisation, end user, availability of finances, etc. There are four basic approaches that can be adapted to translate from print to digital:

Scanned as Image Only
OCR and Retaining Page Layout
Retaining Page Layout using Acrobat Capture; and
Re-keying the Data

Scanned as Image Only

Image only is the lowest cost option in which each page is an exact replica of the original source document. Several digital library projects are concerned by providing digital access to materials that already exists with traditional libraries in printed media. Scanned page images are practically the only reasonable solution for institutions such as libraries for converting existing paper collection (legacy documents) without having access to the original data in computer processible formats convertible into HTML / SGML or in any other structured or unstructured text. Scanned page images are natural choice for large-scale conversions for major digital library initiatives. Printed text, pictures and figures are transformed into computer-accessible forms using a digital scanner or a digital camera in a process called document imaging or scanning. The digitally scanned images are stored in a file as a bit-mapped page image, irrespective of the fact that a scanned page contains a photograph, a line drawing or text. A bit-mapped page image is a type of computer graphic, literally an electronic picture of the page which can most easily be equated to a facsimile image of the page and as such they can be read by humans, but not by the computers, understably "text" in a page image is not searchable on a computer using the present-day technology. An image-based implementation requires a large space for data storage and transmission.

Capturing page image format is comparatively easy and inexpensive, therefore, it is a faithful reproduction of its original maintaining page integrity and originality. The scanned textual images, however, are not searchable unless it is OCRed, which in itself, is highly error prone process specially when it involves scientific texts. Options of technology for converting print to digital are given separately.

Since OCR is not carried out, the document is not searchable. Most scanning software generate TIFF format by default, which, can be converted into PDF using a number of software tools. Scan to TIFF / PDF format is recommended only when the requirement of project is to make documents portable and accessible from any computing platform. The image can be browsed through a table of contents file composed in HTML that provides link to scanned image objects.

Optical Character Recognition (OCR) and Retaining Page Layout

The latest versions of both Xerox's TextBridge and Caere's Omnipage incorporate technology that allow the option of maintaining text and graphics in their original layout as well as plain ASCII and word-processing formats. Output can also include HTML with attributes like bold, underline, and italic which are retained.

Retaining Layout after OCR

A scanned document is nothing more than a picture of a printed page. It can not be edited or manipulated or managed based on their contents. In other words, scanned documents have to be referred to by their labels rather than characters in the documents. OCR (Optical Character Recognition) programs are software tools used to transform scanned textual page images into word processing file. OCR or text recognition is the process of electronically identifying text in a bit-mapped page image or set of images and generate a file containing that text in ASCII code or in a specified word processing format leaving the image intact in the process.

Retaining Page Layout Using Acrobat Capture

The Acrobat Capture 2.0 provides several options for retaining not only the page layout but also the fonts, and to fit text into the exact space occupied in the original, so that the scanned and OCRed copy never over- or under-shoots the page. Accordingly, it treats unrecognizable text as images that are pasted in its place. Such images are perfectly readable by anyone by looking at the PDF file, but will be absent from the editable and searchable text file. In contrast, ordinary OCR programs treat unrecognized text as tilde or some other special character in the ASCII output. Acrobat Capture can be used to scan pages as images, image +text and as normal PDF, all the three options retain page layout.

Image Only: Image only option has already been described in option 1.

Image + Text: In image+text solutions, OCRed text is generated for each image where each page is an exact replica of the original and left untouched, however, the OCRed text sits behind the image and is used for searching. The OCRed text is generally not corrected for errors since, it is used only for searching. The cost involved is much less than PDF Normal. However, the entire page is a bitmap and neither fonts nor line drawings are vectorised, so the file size of Image + Text PDFs is considerably larger than the corresponding PDF Normal files and pages will not display as quickly or cleanly on screen.

PDF Normal: PDF normal gives the clear view on-screen display. It is searchable, with significantly smaller file size than Image+Text. The result is not, however, an exact replica of the scanned page. While all graphics and formatting are preserved, substitute fonts may be used where direct matches are not possible. It is a good choice when files need to be posted on to the web or otherwise delivered online. If during the Capture and OCR process, a word cannot be recognized to the specified confidence level, Capture, by default, substitutes a small portion of the original bitmap image. Capture "best guess" of the suspect word lies behind the bitmap so that searching and indexing are still possible. However, one cannot guarantee that these bitmapped words are correctly guessed. In addition, the bitmap is somewhat obtrusive and detracting from the 'look' of the page. Further, Capture provides option to correct suspected errors left as bit-mapped image or leave them untouched.

Re-Keying

A classic solution of this kind would comprise of keying-in the data and its verification. This involves a complete keying of the text, followed by a full rekeying by a different operator, the two keying-in operation might take place simultaneously. The two keyed files are compared and any errors or inconsistencies are corrected. This would guarantee at least 99.9% accuracy, but to reach 99.955% accuracy level, it would normally require full proof-reading of the keyed files, plus table lookups and dictionary spell checks.

TECHNOLOGY OF DIGITIZATION

Digital images, also called "bit-mapped page image" are "electronic photographs" composed or set of bits or pixels (picture elements) represented by "0" and "1". A bit-mapped page image is a true representation of its original in terms of typefaces, illustrations, layout and presentation of scanned documents. As such information or contents of "bit-mapped page image" cannot be searched or manipulated unlike text file documents (or ASCII). However, an ASCII file can be generated from a bit-mapped page image using an optical character recognition (OCR) software such as Xerox's TextBridge and Caere's OmniPage. The quality of digital image can be monitored at the time of capture by the following factors:

1. Bit depth / dynamic range
2. Resolution
3. Threshold
4. Image enhancement

Terminology associated with technological aspects of digitisation described below is given in the keywords. Students are advised to understand the terminology, specially bit, byte and pixel before going through the unit.

Bit Depth or Dynamic Range

The number of bits used to define each pixel determines the bit depth. The greater the bit depth, the greater the number of gray scale or colour tones that can be represented. Dynamic range is the term used to express the full range of total variations, as measured by a densitometer between the lightest and the darkest of a document. Digital images can be captured at varied density or bits pixel depending upon i) the nature of source material or document to be scanned; ii) target audience or users; and iii) capabilities of the display and print subsystem that are to be used. Bitonal or black & white or binary scanning is generally employed in

Table 1. No. of bits used for representing shades in colour and gray-scale scanning

Sl. No.	No. of Bits	No. of bits/ shades	No. of shades	No. of Shades / pixel
1	2	2	$2^2=4$	$4^3 = 64$
2	4	3	$2^3=8$	$8^3 = 512$
3	8	4	$2^4 = 16$	$16^3 = 4096$
4	16	5	$2^5 = 32$	$32^3 = 32768$
4	32	6	$2^6 = 64$	$64^3 = 262144$
5	64	7	$2^7 = 128$	$128^3=2097152$
6	128	8	$2^8= 256$	$256^3=16777216$

libraries to scan pages containing text or the drawings. Bitonal or binary scanning represents one bit per pixel (either "0" (black) or "1" (white). Gray scale scanning is used for reliable reproduction of intermediate or continuous tones found in black & white photographs to represent shades of grey. Multiple numbers of bits ranging from 2-8 are assigned to each pixel to represent shades of grey in this process. Although each bit is either black or white, as in the case of bitonal images, but bits are combined to produce a level of grey in the pixel that is, black, white or somewhere in between.

Lastly colour scanning can be employed to scan colour photographs. As in the case of grey-scale scanning, multiple bits per pixels typically 2 (lowest quality) to 8 (highest quality) per primary colour are used for representing colour. Colour images are evidently more complex than grey scale images, because it involves encoding of shades of each of the three primary colours, i.e. red, green and blue (RGB). If a coloured image is captured at 2 bits per primary colour, each primary colour can have 2^2 or 4 shades and each pixel can have 4^3 shades for each of the three primary colours. Evidently, increase in bit depth increases the quality of image captured and the space required to store the resultant image. Generally speaking, 12 bits per pixel (4 bits per primary colour) is considered.

minimum pixel depth for good quality colour image. Most of today's colour scanner can scan at 24-bit colour (8 bit per primary colour).

Resolution

The resolution of an image is defined in terms of number of pixel (picture elements) in a given area. It is measured in terms of dot per inch (dpi) in case of an image file and as ratio of number of pixel on horizontal line x Number of pixel in vertical lines in case of display resolution on a monitor. Higher the dpi is set on the scanner, the better the resolution and quality of image and larger the image file.

Regardless of the resolution, image quality of an image can be improved by capturing an image in greyscale. The additional gray-scale data can be processed electronically to sharpen edges, file-in characters, remove extraneous dirt, remove unwanted page strains or discoloration, so as to create a much higher quality image than possible with binary scanning alone. A major drawback in gray scale is that there is large amount of data capture. It may be noted that continuing increase in resolution will not result in any appreciable gain in image quality after some time, except for increase in file size. It is thus important to determine the point where sufficient resolution has been used to capture all significant detail present in the source document.

The black and white or bitonal images (textual) are scanned most commonly at 300 dpi that preserve 99.9% of the information contents of a page and can be considered as adequate access resolution. Some preservation projects scans at 600 dpi for better quality. A standard SVGA/VGA monitor has a resolution of 640 x 480 lines while the ultra-high monitors have a resolution of about 2048 x 1664 (about 150 dpi).

Threshold

The threshold setting in bitonal scanning defines the point on a scale, usually ranging from 0 - 255, at which grey values will be interpreted as black or white pixels. In bitonal scanning, resolution and threshold are the key determinants of image quality. Bitonal scanning is best suited to high-contrast documents, such as text and line drawings. Gray scale or colour scanning is required for continuous tone or low contrast for documents such as photographs. In grey scale/colour scanning both resolution and bit depth combine to play significant roles in image quality.

In Line art mode, every pixel has only two possible values. Every pixel will either be black or white. The Line art Threshold control determines the decision point about brightness determining if the sampled value will be a black dot or a white dot. The normal Threshold default is 128 (the midrange of the 8-bit 0 - 255 range). Image intensity values above the threshold are white pixels, and values below the threshold are black pixels. Adjusting threshold is like a brightness setting to determine what is black and what is white.

Threshold for text printed on a coloured background or cheap-quality paper like newsprint has to be kept at lower range. Reducing threshold from 128 to about 85 would greatly improve the quality of scan. Such adjustments would also improve the performance of OCR software.

Image Enhancement

Image enhancement process can be used to improve scanned images at a cost of image authentic-

ity and fidelity. The process of image enhancement is, however, time consuming, it requires special skills and would invariably increase the cost of conversion. Typical image enhancement features available in a scanning or image editing software include filters, tonal reproduction, curves and colour management, touch, crop, image sharpening, contrast, transparent background, etc. In a page scanned in grey-scale, the text /line art and half tone areas can be decomposed and each area of the page can be filtered separately to maximize its quality. The text area on page can be treated with edge sharpening filters, so as to clearly define the character edges, a second filter could be used to remove the high-frequency noise and finally another filter could fill-in broken characters. Grey-scale area of the page could be processed with different filters to maximize the quality of the halftone.

COMPRESSION

Image files are evidently larger than textual ASCII files. It is thus necessary to compress image files so as to achieve economic storage, processing and transmission over the network. A black & white image of a page of text scanned at 300 dpi is about 1 mb in size where as a text file containing the same information is about 2-3 kb. Image compression is the process of reducing size of an image by abbreviating the repetitive information such as one or more rows of white bits to a single code. The compression algorithms may be grouped into the following two categories:

Lossless Compression

The conversion process converts repeated information as a mathematical algorithm that can be decompressed without loosing any details into the original image with absolute fidelity. No information is "lost" or "sacrificed" in the process of compression. Lossless compression is primarily used in bitonal images.

Lossy Compression

Lossy compression process discards or minimize details that are least significant or which may not make appreciable effect on the quality of image. This kind of compression is called "lossy" because when the image that is compressed using "Lossy" compression techniques is decompressed, it will not be an exact replica of the original image. Lossy compression is used with grey-scale / colour scanning.

Compression is a necessity in digital imaging but more important is the ability to output or produce the uncompressed true replica of images. This is especially important when images are transferred from one platform to another or are handled by software packages under different operating system.

Uncompressed images often work better than compressed images for different reasons. It is thus suggested that scanned images should be either stored as uncompressed images or at the most as lossless compressed images. Further, it is optimal to use one of the standard and widely supported compression protocols than a proprietary one, even if it offers efficient compression and better quality. Attributes of original documents may also be considered while selecting compression techniques. For example ITU G-4 is designed to compress text where as JPEG, GIF and ImagePAC are designed to compress pictures. It is important to ensure migration of images from one platform to another and from one hardware media to another. It may be noted that highly compressed files are more prone to corruption than uncompressed files.

Compression Protocols

The following protocols are commonly used for bitonal, gray scale or colour compression:

TIFF-G4

International Telecommunication Union (ITU Group 4) is considered as de facto standard compression scheme for black & white bitonal images. An image created as a TIFF and compressed using ITU-G4 compression technique is called a Group-4 TIFF or TIFFG4 and is considered as defacto standard for storing bitonal images. TIFF G-4 is a lossless compression scheme. Joint Bi-level Image Group (JBIG) (ISO-11544) is another standard compression technique for bitonal images.

JPEG (Joint Photographic Expert Group)

JPEG (Joint Photographic Expert Group) is an ISO-10918-I compression protocol that works by finding areas of the image that have same tone, shade, colour or other characteristics and represents this area by a code. Compression is achieved at loss of data. Preliminary testing indicates that a compression of about 10 or 15 to one can be achieved without visible degradation of image quality.

LZW (Lenpel-Ziv Welch)

LZW compression technique uses a table-based lookup algorithm invented by Abraham Lempel, Jacob Ziv, and Terry Welch. Two commonly-used file formats in which LZW compression is used are the Graphics Interchange Format (GIF) and Tag Image File Format (TIFF). LZW compression is also suitable for compressing text files. A particular LZW compression algorithm takes each input sequence of binary digit of a given length (for example, 12 bits) and creates an entry in a table (sometimes called a "dictionary" or "codebook") for that particular bit pattern, consisting of the pattern itself and a shorter code. As input is read, any pattern that has been read before the results in the substitution of the shorter code effectively compresses the total amount of input to something smaller. The decoding program that uncompresses the file is able to build the table itself by using the algorithm as it processes the encoded input.

OCR (Optical Character Recognition)

OCR (Optical Character Recognition) programs are software tools used to transform scanned textual page images into word processing file. OCR or text recognition is the process of electronically identifying text in a bit-mapped page image or set of images and generate a file containing that text in ASCII code or in a specified word processing format leaving the image intact in the process. The OCR is performed in order to make every word in a scanned document readable and fully searchable without having to key-in everything in the computer manually. Once a bit-mapped page image has gone through the process of OCR, a document can be manipulated and managed by its contents, i.e. using the words available in the text.

OCR does not actually convert an image into text but rather creates a separate file containing the text while leaving the image intact. There are four types of OCR technology that are prevailing in the market. These technologies are: matrix matching, feature extraction, structural analysis and neural network.

    i.   Matrix / Template Matching: Compares each character with a template of the same character. Such a system is usually limited to a specific number of fonts, or must be "taught" to recognize a particular font.

    ii.   Feature Extraction: Can recognize a character from its structure and shape (angles, points, breaks, etc.) based on a set of rules. The process claims to recognize all fonts.

    iii.   Structural analysis: Determines characters on the basis of density gradations or character darkness.

    iv.   Neural Networking: Neural networking is a form of artificial intelligence that attempts to mimic processes of the human mind. Combined with traditional OCR techniques plus pattern recognition, a neural network-based system can perform text recognition and "learn" from its success and failure. Referred to as "Intelligent Character Recognition", a neural network-based system is being used to recognize hand-written text as well as other traditionally difficult source material. Neural network ICR can contemplate characters in the context of an entire word. Newer ICR combines neural networking with fuzzy logic.

Several software packages now offer facility of retaining the page layout after it has been OCRed. The process for retaining the page layout is software dependent. Caere's Omnipro offer two ways of retaining page layout following OCR. It calls them True Page Classic and True Page Easy. True Page Classic places each paragraph within a separate frame of a word processor into which the OCR output is saved. If one wish to edit anything subsequently, then the relevant paragraph box may need to be resized. However, Easy Edit facilitates editing of pages without the necessity of resizing the boxes although there are greater chances of spillage over the page. Xerox Text Bridge offers similar feature called DocuRT which is broadly equivalent to True Page Easy edit. The process of OCR dismantle the page, OCR it, and then reassemble it in such a way that all the component parts such as tabs, columns, table, graphics can be used in a text manipulation package such as word processor.

There is a little doubt about the fact that OCR is less accurate than rekeying-in the data. At an accuracy ratio of 98%, a page having 1800 characters will have 36 errors per page on an average. It is therefore, imperative to cleanup after OCR unless original scanned image will be viewed as a page and OCR is being used purely to create a searchable index on the words that will be searched via a fuzzy retrieval engine like Excalibur, which is highly tolerant to OCR errors.

Another possibility for cleaned-up OCR is use of specialist OCR system such as, Prime Recognition. With production OCR in mind, Prime OCR licenses leading to recognizing engine and passes the data through several of them using voting technology along with artificial intelligent algorithms. Although it takes longer initially, but saves time in long run and prime contends that it improves the result achieved by a single engine by 65 – 80%. The technology is available at a price depending upon number of search engine that one would like to incorporate. Michigan Digital Library production services used Prime OCR for placing more than two million pages of SGML – encoded text and the same No. of page images on the web.

FILE FORMATS AND MEDIA TYPES

A defined arrangement for discrete sets of data that allow a computer and software to interpret the data is called a file format. Different file formats are used to store different media types like text, images, graphics, pictures, musical works, computer programs, databases, models and designs video programs and compound works combining many type of information. Although, almost every type of information can be represented in digital form, a few important file formats for text and images typically applicable to a library-based digital library are described here. However, every object in a digital library needs to have a name or identifier which distinctly identifies its type and format. This is achieved by assigning file extensions to the digital objects. The file extensions in a digital library typically denote formats, protocols and right management that are appropriate for the type of material.

Text and image-based contents of a digital library can be stored and presented as i) simple text or ASCII (American Standard Code for Information Interchange; ii) unstructured text; iii) Structured text (SGML or HTML or XML); iv) page description language and v) page image formats. Textual and image formats are dealt elaborately in the section on "Technical Infrastrcuture of Digital Library".

TOOLS OF DIGITIZATION

Digital imaging is an inter-linked system of hardware, software, image database and access sub-system with each having their own components. Tools used for digitisation include several core and peripheral systems. An image scanning system may consist of a stand-alone workstation where most or all the work is done on the same workstation or as a part of a network of workstation with imaging work distributed and shared amongst various workstations. The network usually includes a scanning station, a server and one or more editing, retrieval stations. A typical scanning workstation for a small, production-level project could consist of the following:

- Hardware (Scanners, computers, data storage and data output peripherals)
- Software (image capturing and image editing)
- Network (data transmission)
- Display and Printing technologies

Chapter would concentrate on scanners and scanning software as important components of the scanning system.

Scanners

Digital scanners are used to capture a digital image from an analogue media such as printed page or a microfiche / microfilm at a predefined resolution and dynamic range (bit range). There are two types of image scanners: vector scanner and raster scanners. The vector scanners scan an image as a complex set of x,y coordinates. Vector images are generally used in geographical information systems (GIS). The display software for the vector image interprets the image as function of coordinates and other included information to produce an electronic replica of the original drawing or photograph. Vector images can be zoomed in portion to display minute details of a drawing or a map. Maps, engineering drawings, and architectural blueprints are often scanned as vector images. Raster images are captured by raster scanners by passing lights (laser in some cases) down the page and digitally encoding it row by row. Multiple passes of lights may be required to capture basic (as a set of bits known as bit map) colours in a coloured image. Raster scanners are used in libraries to convert printed publications into electronic forms. Majority of electronic imaging system generate raster images. The scanners used for digitizing analogue images into digital images come in a variety of shapes and sizes.

How Scanner Works?

Scanners are equipped with a lamp that moves with the scanner head to light-up the object being scanned. Most scanners use a cold cathode florescent lamp or a xenon lamp. The scan head is made up of the mirrors, lens, filter, and charge-coupled devices (CCD) array. A belt that is connected to the stepper motor makes the scan head move. A stabilizing bar prevents wobbling during the pass. The mirrors reflect what is being scanned into the lens and the image is then focused through a filter on the CCD array. Three smaller images of the original are made by the lens. These images then go through a color filter and onto a section of the CCD array. The data is then combined into a single image.

While selecting a scanner, one should consider resolution, sharpness, and rate of image transfer.

The resolution is measured in dots per inch (dpi). The average scanner has at least 300x300 dpi. The number or sensors in a row of the CCD array determines a scanners dpi. Sharpness depends on how bright the lamp is and the quality of the lens. Image transfer depends on the connection used to connect the scanner to the computer. The slowest is the parallel port. Universal Serial Bus or USB scanners are affordable, easy to use, and have decent speed.

The hardware required for a scanner is a connector such as a USB. The software required is a driver. The driver is needed to communicate with the scanner. TWAIN is the language spoken by scanners. Any program that supports TWAIN can acquire a scanned image.

There are the Following Types of Scanners

- Flatbed Scanners – right angle, prism and overhead flatbed
- Sheet-Feed Scanners
- Drum Scanners
- Digital Cameras
- Slide Scanners
- Microfilm Scanner
- Video Frame Grabber
- Hand-held scanners

The type of scanner selected for an imaging project would be influenced by the type, size and source of documents to be scanned. Many scanners can handle only transparent material, whereas others can handle only reflective materials.

Flatbed Scanners

Flatbed scanners are most common, and widely used scanners that look like a photocopier and are used in much the some way. Source material in a flatbed scanner is placed face down for scanning. The light source and charge-coupled devices (CCDs) move beneath the platen, while the document remains stationary as in the case of photocopying machine. Flatbed scanner comes in various models like right-angle, prism and planetary/overhead to handle bound volumes and books. Flatbed scanner can scan a document at 600 dpi. Many flatbed scanners offer higher resolution.

Sheet Feed Scanners

In a sheet-feed scanner, as is indicated in the name, document is fed over a stationary CCD and light source via roller, belt, drum, or vacuum transport. In contrast to a flat-bed scanner, sheet-feed scanner have optional attachment to auto feed uniform-sized stacks of documents to be scanned.

Drum Scanners

Source material in a drum scanner is wrapped on a drum, which is then rotated past a high-intensity light source to capture the image. Drum scanners offer superior image quality, but require flexible source material of limited sized that can be wrapped around the photosensitive drum. Drum scanners are specially targeted for graphic art market. Drum scanners offer highest resolution for grey scale and colour scanning. Drum Scanner use Photo-Multiplier (Vacuum) Tubes (PMTs) instead of CCDs, which offer a greater bit depth (12 to 16 bits).

Digital Cameras

Digital cameras mounted on copy cradle resemble microfilming stand. Source material is placed on the stand and the camera is cranked up or down in order to focus the material within the field of view. Digital cameras are most promising scanner development for library and archival applications.

Slide Scanner

Slide scanners have a slot in the side to accommodate a 35mm slide. Inside the box, the light passes through the slide to hit a CCD array behind the slide. Slide scanners can generally scan only 35mm transparent source materials.

Microfilm Scanner

Specially targeted to library/archival application, microfilm scanners have adapters to convert roll film, fiche, and aperture cards in the same model.

Video Frame Grabber or VideoDigitizer

Video digitizers are circuit boards placed inside a computer and attached to a standard video camera. Any thing that is filmed by the video camera is digitized by the video digitizer.

Hand-held Scanners

Hand-held scanners are used for scanning selective sections of data. It may require multiple pass to capture large area. Moreover, a user should have a steady hand while moving the scanner over the document to be scanned.

Software for Digitization

The software required digitizing analogue media into digital formats can broadly be categorized into following three types:

Scanning Software

The scanning software is used for scanning the image and capturing it in the computer. This software is provided by the manufacturer of the product to the buyers. These drivers translate the instructions into commands, which the scanner understands.

Figure 1. Scanning using a flatbed scanner

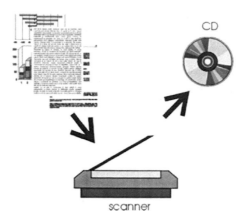

Image Editing Applications

Image editing applications are used once the process of scanning the image is over and the image is available in the computer for further manipulation. Most image editing software offer features like image editing, sharpening, filter, cropping, colour adjustments, forms conversion, resizing, etc. Most of the image editing software can also be used for capturing the images.

Digitisation of Audio and Video

The song or speeches that we generally listen from tape recorders or radio are in an analogue form. The analogue sound and video tracks are required to be digitized in order to import it into the computer so as to play, edit, and convert them into different formats or inserted into a file.

Devices specifically designed for audio digitizing or video digitizing can be used for this purpose. The mBox by DigiDesign is a choice as an audio-only solution. A less expensive audio-only solution is the UA-1D USB Digital Audio Capture. To plug a cassette player into any of these devices or an audio capture card, a special cable is required that has a 1/8" stereo plug (like a headphone jack) on one end, and two RCA audio plugs at the other end (usually one red and one white). The audio files can be saved as .wav, mp3, midi, etc. MP3 format is highly compact and the sound quality is better in comparison to other formats. Audio files can be further processed using noise reduction software.

Like audio, video capture also requires a video capture card with input from video cassette player (VCP / VCR), TV antenna, cable or movie camera. The digitised files can be saved as .mov, .avi, .mpg file formats. Several different types of video digitizers are on the market. Dazzle converters by Pinnacle Systems are popular.

Figure 2. Two file system in a image retrieval system

Figure 3. Rekeying is an option for digitisation

ORGANIZING DIGITAL IMAGES

A disc full of digital images without any organization, browse and search options may have no meaning except for one who created it. Scanned images need to be organized in order to be useful. Moreover, images need to be linked to the associated metadata to facilitate their browsing and searching. The following three steps describes the process of organizing the digital images:

Organize

the scanned image files into disc hierarchy that logically maps the physical organization of the document. For example, in a project on scanning of journals, create a folder for each journal, which, in turn, may have folder for each volume scanned. Each volume, in turn, may have a subfolder for each issue. The folder for each issue, in turn, may contain scanned articles that appeared in the issue along with a content page, composed in HTML providing links to articles in that issue.

Figure 4. Setting bit depth in Precisionscan Pro scanning software

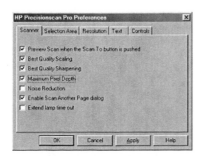

Name

the scanned image files in a strictly controlled manner that reflects their logical relationship. For example, each article may be named after the surname of first author followed by a volume number and an issue number. For example, file name "smithrkv5n1.pdf" conveys that the article is by "R.K. Smith" that appeared in volume 5 and issue no.1. The file name for each article would, therefore, convey a logical and hierachial organization of the journal.

Describe

the scanned images file internally using image header and externally using linked descriptive metadata files. The following three types of metadata are associated with the digital objects:

i. Descriptive Metadata: Include content or bibliographic description consisting of keywords and subject descriptors.

Figure 5. Setting up resolution manually

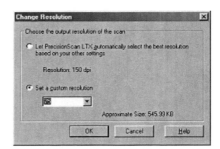

Figure 6. Threshold setting in bitonal scanning

 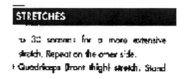

Threshold Setting = 128   Threshold Setting = 85

Figure 7. Sharpening an image using HP Precisionscan Pro

Figure 8. The image scanner optically captures text images to be recognized. Text images are processed with OCR software and hardware. The process involves three operations: document analysis (extracting individual character images), recognizing these images based on i) their template stored in the OCR database, ii) structure and shape (angles, points, breaks, etc.) iii) density gradations or character darkness and iv) contextual processing. The output interface is responsible for communication of OCR system that results to the outside world.

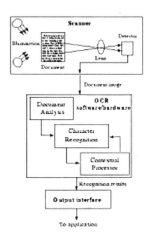

Figure 9. Flatbed scanner

ii. Administrative or technical Metadata: Incorporates details on original source, date of creation, version of digital object, file format used, compression technology used, object relationship, etc. Administrative data may reside within or outside the digital object and is required for long-term collection management to ensure longevity of digital collection.

iii. Structural Metadata: Elements within digital objects facilitates navigation, e.g. table of contents, index at issue level or volume level, page turning in an electronic book, etc.

iv. Identification Metadata: Used for tracking different versions and editions of same digital work, i.e. pdf, HTML, PostScript, MS Word, etc. and TIFF, JPG, BMP, etc. in case of images.

The simplest and least effective method for providing access is through a table of contents and links each item to its respective object / image. Content pages of issues of journals done in HTML would offer browsing facility. Full-text search to HTML pages or OCRed pages can be achieved by installing one of the free Internet search engines like Oingo Free Search (http://www.oingo.com/oingo_free_search/products.html); Swish-E (http://www.berkeley.edu/SWISH-E/); WhatyoUseek (http://intra.whatuseek.com/); Excite (http://excite.com/) and Google (http://www.google.com).

Figure 10. Sheet feed scanner

Figure 11. Drum scanners

Large scanning projects would, however, require a back-end database storing images or links to the images and metadata (descriptive / administrative). Back-end database used by most document management system holds the functionality required by most web applications. Important management systems like FileNet have now integrated their database with HTML conversion tools. These databases entertain queries from users through "HTML forms" and generate search results on the fly. Several digital library packages are now available as "open source" or "free-ware" that can be used not only for organzing the digital objects but also for their search and retrieval. Open source digital library software are elaborated in details in the section on "Components of Digital Library".

SUMMARY

Digitisation is the process of converting the content of physical media (e.g., periodical articles, books, manuscripts, cards, photographs, vinyl disks, etc.)

Figure 12. Digital camera

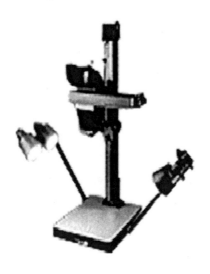
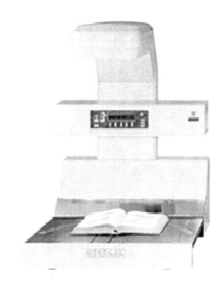

Figure 13. Slide scanner

into digital format. In most library applications, digitisation normally results in documents that are made accessible from the web site, and thus are available on the Internet. Optical scanners and digital cameras are used to digitise images by translating them into bit maps. It is also possible to digitise sound, video, graphics, animations, etc.

Digitisation is the first step in the process of building digital libraries. Digitisation is also used for achieving preservation and archiving although it is not considered as good option for preservation and archiving. It is highly labour-intensive and cost-intensive process that involves several complexities including copyright and IPR issues. However, digital objects offer numerous benefits in terms of accessibility and search. The documents to be digitised may include text, line art, photographs, colour images, etc. The selection of document need to be reviewed very carefully considering all the factors of utility, quality, security and cost. Rare and much in demand documents and images are selected as first priority without considering the quality.

The process of digitisation involves four steps, namely scanning, indexing, storage and retrieval. A scanned document is nothing more than a picture of a printed page. It can not be edited or manipulated or managed based on their contents. In other words, scanned documents have to be referred by their labels rather than charac-

Figure 14. Microfilm scanner

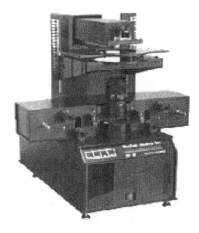

Figure 15. Video graber

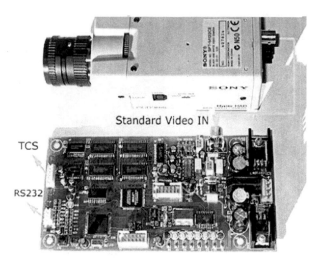

Standard Video IN

TCS

RS232

ters in the documents. OCR (Optical Character Recognition) programs are software tools used to transform scanned textual page images into word processing file. OCR or text recognition is the process of electronically identifying the text in a bit-mapped page image or set of images and generates a file containing text in ASCII code or in a specified word processing format leaving the image intact in the process.

The quality of digital image can be monitored at the time of capture by four factors, namely i) bit depth / dynamic range; ii) resolution; iii) threshold; and iv) image enhancement. This section describes these parameters in detail. Image files are evidently larger than textual files. It is thus necessary to compress image files. Image compression is the process of reducing size of an image by abbreviating the repetitive information such as one or more rows of white bits to a single code. The compression algorithms may be grouped as lossless compression and lossy compression. The section describes compression technology and protocols.

An image scanning system may consists of a stand-alone workstation where most or all the work is done on the same workstation or as a part of a network of workstation with imaging work being

distributed and shared amongst various workstations. The network usually includes a scanning station, a server and one or more editing and retrieval stations. A typical scanning workstation for a small production-level project, could consist: Hardware (scanners, computers, data storage and data output peripherals); Software (image capturing and image editing); Network (data transmission) and Display and Printing technologies. This section describes hardware and software requirement for digitizing analogue media into digital media and process of organizing digital images.

REFERENCES

Arms, W. Y. (1995 July). Key concepts in the architecture of the digital library. *D-lib Magazine*.

Arms, W. Y. (2000). *Digital libraries*. Cambridge, MA: The MIT Press.

Haigh, S. (1996). Optical Character Recognition (OCR) as a Digitization Technology. *Network Notes*, 37.

IMLS. *A Framework of Guidance for Building Good Digital Collections*. (n.d.). Retrieved from http://www.imls.gov/pubs/forumframework.htm

Jantz, R. (2001). Technological discontinuities in the library: Digital projects that illustrate new opportunities for the librarian and the library. *IFLA Journal, 27*, 74–77. doi:10.1177/034003520102700207

Kenney, A. R., & Chapman, S. (1996). *Digital imaging for libraries and archives*. Ithaca, NY: Dept. of Preservation and Conservation, Cornell University Library.

Kessler, J. (1996). *Internet digital libraries: The International Dimension*. Boston: Artech House Publishers.

Lesk, M. (1997). *Practical digital libraries: books, bytes and bucks*. San Francisco: Morgan Kaufmann Publishers.

Noerr, P. (2000). *Digital library tool kit*. Sun Microsystems. Retrieved from http://www.sun.com/products-n-solutions/edu/libraries/digitaltoolkit.html

Northeast Document Conservation Center. (n.d.). *NEDCC Handbook for digital projects: A management tool for preservation and access*.

Ostrow, S. (1998 February). *Digitizing historical pictorial collections for the Internet*. CLIR. Retrieved from http://www.clir.org/pubs/reports/ostrow/pub71.html

Rosenfeld, L., & Morville, P. (1998). *Information architecture*. Cambridge, MA: O'Reilly.

Townsend, S., et al. (n.d.). *Digitising history*. Retrieved from http://hds.essex.ac.uk/g2gp/digitising_history/index.html

Tyson, J. (2003 December). *How Scanners Work*. How Stuff Works. Retrieved from http://www.howstuffworks.com

KEY TERMS AND DEFINITIONS

ASCI: American Standard Code for Information Interchange or ASCI is a standard coding technique for representing computer information.

Analogue: A term used to describe a signal, such as the human voice and electric current, whose value varies continuously with time or transmission method, such as the traditional telephone network, which carries source signals as electrical waves. Compared with digital systems, an analogue telephone line carries data at low speed; it also requires a modem to convert the computer's digital output into a form (analogue) which it can handle.

Bit and Byte: Bit is short term for binary digit, the smallest unit of information on a machine. A single bit can hold only one of two values: 0 or 1. More meaningful information is obtained by combining consecutive bits into larger units. A byte is composed of 8 consecutive bits.

Bit Depth: The number of bits used to represent each pixel. The greater the bit depth, the more colours or grey-scales can be represented. For example, a 24-bit colour scanner can represent 2 to the 24th power (16.7 million) colours.

Bitonal: Each pixel in a bitonal image is represented by a single bit, i.e. black and white. Textual documents and line drawings are scanned in bitonal, i.e. a pixel is either black or white whereas each pixel for a picture (black and white or colour) may contain 2-8 bit per primary colour.

Capture: A term used in document imaging for scanning of a document or any other artefact.

Crop: The process of elimination of a portion of a picture, illustration or photograph that contain unnecessary material or to highlight a certain area of the image.

Digitisation: The process of converting data and information into digital format is called digitisation. It is synonymous with scanning, it is the conversion from printed paper, film, or some other media, to an electronic form where the page is represented as either black and white dots, or color or grayscale pixels.

Document Scanning: Document scanning is the process by which print and film documents are fed into a scanner and converted into electronic documents. During the scanning process documents can be OCRed and indexed to insure quick retrieval at a later date.

Dots Per Inch (DPI): Dots per inch (dpi) indicates the resolution of images or printers. The more dots per inch, the higher the resolution.

Dynamic Range: The number of colours or shades of grey that can be represented by a pixel. Dynamic range is a measurement of the number of bits used to represent each pixel in a digital image. 1-bit or bitonal means that a pixel can either be black or white. Bitonal imaging is good for black and white images, such as line drawings and text. However, scanning in grey-scale rather than bitonal may produce a better looking image. 8-bit color or 8-bit grey-scale means that each pixel can be one of 256 shades of colour or one of 256 shades of grey. 24-bit colour means that each pixel can be one of 16.8 million colours.

Halftone: A method of generating an image that requires varying densities or shades to accurately render the image. This is achieved by representing the image as a pattern of dots of varying size. Larger dots represent darker areas, and smaller dots represent lighter areas of an image.

Image Sharpening: Scanned images can be adjusted to increase edge contrast and artificially enhance the overall quality of image. Most paint and colour manipulation programs have special tools to selectively sharpen isolated areas of an image.

Metadata: Data about data, or information known about the image in order to provide access to the image. Usually includes information about the intellectual content of the image, digital representation data, and security or rights management information.

Optical Character Recognition (OCR): The OCR refers to the process of scanning text using a scanning device from a printed page into an image and translate it into a computer processible format, i.e. an ASCII file. OCR systems include an optical scanner for reading text and sophisticated software for analyzing images.

Pixels: The term "pix" means "part of a picture" and "el" means "from element". In bitonal (black and white) display, each pixel can have only one bit, i.e. either black or white, whereas in a gray-scale display, each pixel can have three numerical values for three colour, i.e. Red, Green, Blue (RGB) to represent the colour. These three RGB components can be represented by three 8-bit numbers for each pixel. Three 8-bit bytes (one byte for each of RGB) is called 24 bit colour. Each 8 bit RGB component can have 256 possible values, ranging from 0 to 255. For example, three values like (250, 165, 0), meaning (Red=250, Green=165, Blue=0) to denote one Orange pixel. The pixels are most commonly used to represent images as a computer file. Pixel are of a uniform size and shape.

Portable Document Format (PDF): Portable Document Format is a type of formatting that enables files to be viewed on a variety computers regardless of the program originally used to create them. PDF files retain the "look and feel" of the original document with special formatting, graphics, and colour intact. A special program or print driver (Adobe Distiller or PDF Writer) is used to convert a file into PDF format. The Acrobat Reader program available free from the Adobe site.

PostScript: A page description language developed and marketed by Adobe Systems. PostScript can be used by a wide variety of computers and printers, and is the dominant format used for desktop publishing. Documents in PostScript format are able to use the full resolution of any PostScript printer, because they describe the page to be printed in terms of primitive shapes which are interpreted by the printer's own controller. PostScript is often used to share documents on the Internet because of this ability to work on many different platforms and printers.

Primary Colour: Colours that are basis for all other colour combinations. Primary colours are red, green and blue (RGB).

RGB: Red, Green and Blue (RGB) are the colours that are basis for all other colour combinations. They are called primary colours.

Resolution: Resolution refers to the number of pixels contained on a display monitor, printers and bit-mapped graphic images. In the case of printers and images, it is indicated the number of dots per inch. For graphics monitors, the screen resolution signifies the number of dots (pixels) on the entire screen. Resolution generally refers to the sharpness and clarity of an image.

Scanner: An optical input device that uses light–sensing equipment to capture an image on paper or some other subject. The image is translated into digital signals that can then be manipulated by optical character recognition (OCR) software or graphics software. Scanners come in a number of types, including flatbed (scan head passes over a stationary subject), feed (subject is pulled across a stationary scan head), drum (subject is rotated around a stationary scan head), and hand-held (user passes device over a stationary subject).

TIFF: Tag Image File Format (TIFF) is a common format for exchanging raster (bitmapped) images between application programs. Usually identified with the ".tiff" or ".tif" filename extension, the format was developed in 1986 by an industry committee chaired by the Aldus Corporation (now part of Adobe). One of the more common image formats, TIFFs are common in desktop publishing, faxing, and medical imaging applications.

Threshold: The minimum level at which a signal of any kind can be detected, either by the human senses or by using any electronic instrumentation. In image processing, threshold is a specified grey level used for producing a binary image.

Chapter 4
Tools and Techniques for Digital Conversion

Pravin Kumar Choudhary
DLF Limited, India

ABSTRACT

In the last two decades, significant theoretical work has been done in the area of electronic conversion of documents. There are different methods, tools and techniques to carry on digitization activities. This chapter tries to bridge the gap between theory and practice by presenting generalized tools that link digitization and electronic document management practices. This connection can be understood most readily at the organization process level where workflow, information flow, and service delivery come together, i.e. Electronic Document Management Goals. The detailed tools and techniques which need to be integrated into the system design process, and result in the identification of technology specifications and opportunities for improving performance through improved access to documents has been incorporated. Different products and technology options have also been discussed. The content discussed in this chapter can form the models for action: Practical approaches to Electronic Records Management and Preservation. It also presents practical tools that seamlessly integrate into the system design process and result in the identification of technical specifications and opportunities for improving performance through improved access to records. At the end different considerations with regard to the tools also identify critical management and policy factors which must be in place to support a full system implementation have been discussed.

DOI: 10.4018/978-1-61520-767-1.ch004

DEFINING THE PROCESS OF DIGITIZATION

Digitization is the process of converting any physical or analogue item into an electronic representation. In the context of this chapter, digitization refers to the creation of digital images from paper books or documents by means of scanning or digital photography Digital imaging is the process of converting paper documents including text, graphics, or pictures into digital images. The image can be made accessible over electronic networks.

A digital image, in turn, is composed of a set of pixels (picture elements), arranged according to a pre-defined ratio of columns and rows. An image document file can managed as regular computer file and can be retrieved, printed and modified using appropriate software. Further, textual images can be OCRed so as to make its contents searchable. Digital imaging is an inter-linked system of hardware, software image database and access sub-system with each having their own components.

Digital image is also named as "bit-mapped page image" are "electronic photographs" composed or set of bits or pixels (picture elements) represented by "0" and "1". A bitmapped page image is a true representation of its original in terms of typefaces, illustrations, layout and presentation of scanned documents. As such information contents of "bit-mapped page image" cannot be searched or manipulated unlike text file documents (or ASCII). However, an ASCII file can be generated from a bit-mapped page image using an optical character recognition (OCR) software such as Xerox's TextBridge and Caere's OmniPage.

GOALS AND OBJECTIVE

Before starting digitization activity, the organization must be clear about its objective and goals which it wants to achieve. There may be different objectives and goals for example faster retrieval of required documents, backup of documents, gain competitive edge over related organization.

From Digital Information Centre Points of View

The digital conversion of documents/ digital library/information may include:

- Achieving faster retrieval of information;
- Improve access to information, by;
- Greater sharing of information; and
- The reduction of the storage space required for paper records.

From Organizational Point of View

The goal may be in terms of

- Bring the documents/ record to the forefront of system design activities: Managing document associated reference with business process plays a vital role in system design considerations The maintenance and ongoing accessibility of documents has been established to the forefront of the system design and development process.
- To identify electronic documents/records functionality as part of system design: The organizational requirements that underlie the document management requirements drive the selection of appropriate supporting technologies. The tools consider ongoing internal and external secondary access to documents, aids the selection of suitable technologies, and take care system migration related issues.
- To create electronic documents, which support organizational requirement: It also aids the identification of all authenticity requirements tied to a business process including legal admissibility. It emphasized that how authenticity and evidentiary needs cannot

only be addressed by technology but must be supported by appropriate management practices and organizational policies.

- To integrate different document forms and formats into records. The tools help organizations identify the different forms and formats that a system must accommodate and facilitate the choice of technical strategies, that can be used to ensure that the required forms and formats are integrated into a documents and are accessible over time.

  - To identify need for internal and external primary and secondary access to records. The tools help identify access needs from the perspective of internal users during a business transaction, as well as internal and external access needs after a transaction has been completed. The questions are designed to identify the components of information/documents required by each of these user types as well as their preferred or required mechanisms for accessing them. The tools, therefore, help ensure that the value of information collected and maintained during a business process will be maximized across all user groups and over time.

  - To create electronic documents which are accessible over time. It identifies the specific information/document components that must be captured at each step during the course of a transaction. The considerations associated with ongoing access to documents over time, and identify technology, management, and policy strategies to ensure that records are adequately captured and will remain accessible for both current and future use.

Organizations need to create and maintain record centre/information/documents/records to fulfill its carry out their responsibilities. The responsibility may be in relation to business activities, document support for business actions and decisions. Organizations are increasingly relying upon electronic information to manage work and make decisions because of timely and easy accessibility of documents. Many transactions that were once paper-based are now being performed electronically, as networked computer systems that once played a purely supportive role have moved to center stage. However, with the shift from paper to digital information, many organizations find that their current electronic records are not sufficient to support the evidentiary needs of their business functions. Others face the problem of linking documents created in different forms and formats for organizational need. Many organizations are in danger of losing access to information stored in personal computers, e-mail boxes, or personal local area network directories. From an archival perspective, focused on the long-term societal and organizational need for records, these problems result in partial or complete loss of records of enduring value. In view of all these challenges organizations are increasingly moving towards digital document system.

SCOPE OF THE CHAPTER

Printed books/documents exist in a variety of formats including maps, plans, photographs and other documents of various colours, paper types and sizes. The chapter includes digitization recommendations that are broad enough to apply to the majority of paper records. In some cases, particular characteristics of different types of paper may call for different technical parameters and approaches from those included here, and the same is to be considered at operation level by the professional.

EXCLUSIONS

The conversion of other analogue records, such as video or audio recordings, into a digital form is outside the scope of this chapter. The chapter does not include advice on high-quality digitization of historical documents for preservation purposes.

APPROACHES TO DIGITAL CONVERSION OF PRINTED DOCUMENTS

The emerging digital imaging technology gives us a number of choices for digitization of documents. The required technologies can be adopted based on the objective of scanning, end user, availability of finances, to mention few options. There are three basic approaches that can be adapted to translate documents from print to digital:

- Scanned as Image
- OCR and Retaining Page Layout
- Re-keying the Data

Scanned as Image

In this approach printed documents are scanned with the help of scanner of our choice and requirement. Scanning is done at 100 to 150dpi, depending on the quality of image. This is the lowest cost option in which each page is an exact replica of the original source document. Since OCR is not carried out, the document is not searchable. Most scanning software generates tiff format by default, which, can be converted in to pdf and other required format using a number of software tools. Scan to tiff/pdf format is recommended only when the requirement of digitization is to make documents portable and accessible from any computing platform. The image can be browsed through a table of contents/metadata fields file composed in html that provides link to scanned image objects.

OCR and Retaining Page Layout

In this case scanning of documents should be done at 300 dpi. This is recommended in view of better recognisition of character, retaining layout and minimizing the junk character which appears during OCR. This step can be discussed under following two headings:

Optical Character Recognition (OCR)

Optical Character Recognition (OCR) is a software dependent process that recognizes printed text as alphanumeric characters. Intelligent Character recognition (ICR) is also a software dependent process and pattern based character recognition that recognizes handwritten and printed text as alphanumeric characters. Zone OCR is ideal, where same forms are repeatedly processed. Zone OCR enables automated document indexing that reads certain regions (zones) of a document and then places information into the appropriate index template fields. In this way it reduces data entry time and demands on system memory.

The latest versions of both *Xerox's TextBridge* and *Caere's Omnipage* incorporate technology that allow the option of maintaining text and graphics in their original layout as well as plain ASCII and word-processing formats. Output can also include html with attributes like bold, underline, and italic is retained.

It is important to note that no OCR is error free and there are always chances of junk character and defective content after OCR. The error/ junk character can be minimized by using authentic OCR software and scanning the documents at appropriate dpi. The fixation of dpi for scanning is objective and experience based decision.

Retaining Layout after OCR

The process for retaining the page layout is software dependent. Many software packages now offer facility of retaining the page layout after it has been OCRed. Caere's Omnipro offer two ways of (True Page Classic and True Page Easy) retaining page layout following OCR.

- True Page Classic places, each paragraph within a separate frame of a word processor into which the OCR output is saved. If one wishes to edit anything subsequently, then the relevant paragraph box may need to be resized.
- Easy Edit, facilitates editing of pages without the necessity of resizing the boxes although there is a greater chance of spillage over the page.

Since OCR is not 100 percent accurate, it is therefore, imperative to cleanup the image after OCR. OCR of documents is being used purely to create a searchable index on the words that will be searched via a fuzzy retrieval engine like Excalibur which is highly tolerant to OCR errors.

Re-keying of the Data

This process comprise of keying-in the data and its verification. This involves a complete keying of the text, followed by a full re-keying by a different operator, the two keying-in operation might take place simultaneously. The two-keyed files in this case are compared and any errors or inconsistencies are corrected. This would guarantee at least 99.9% accuracy, but to reach 99.955% accuracy level, it would normally require full proof-reading of the keyed files.

TECHNOLOGIES FOR DIGITIZATION

The basic tools of digitization and digital information system management include:

- Digital systems include:
  - Hardware (Scanners, computers data storage and data output peripherals)
  - Software (image capturing, data compression)
  - Network (data transmission)
  - Display technologies
  - Disaster Management (Archiving and Data backup in particular)

STEPS IN THE PROCESS OF DIGITIZATION

The following four steps are involved in the process of digitization.

1. Scanning
2. Document image processing (DIP),
3. Electronic Filing System (EFS) and
4. Document Management Systems (DMS) provides all or more of these functions:

Scanning

It is the process of converting hardcopy data (as per our scope of this chapter) into digital form. The scanning produces a raster (picture) image that can be stored on a computer. The scanner should preferably have both *flat bat* and *ADF* (Automatic Document Feeder). The process of scanning involves acquisition of an electronic image through its original that may be a photograph, text, manuscript, etc. into the computer using an electronic image scanner.

An image is scanned at a predefined resolution and dynamic range. The resulting file, called "bitmap page image" is formatted (image formats describes elsewhere) and tagged for storage and subsequent retrieval by the software package used for scanning. Acquisition of image through fax card, electronic camera or other imaging devices is also feasible. However, image scanners are most important and most commonly used component of an imaging system for transfer of normal paper-based documents.

There are a number of challenges in ensuring that digitized paper records remain accessible and useable. It is advisable that the digitization program should be carefully planned to meet appropriate standards and avoid the need to repeat work. Consideration must also be given to the categorization and storage of the original paper documents that are digitized i.e. codification and classification. The important digitization issues regarding accessibility and usability of digitized paper records including file formats, image qualities, the way the image files are stored and the process that is adopted to accomplish the digitization.

It is advisable to have high level of understanding of the technical aspects of scanning within the organization prior to implementing a digitization program. The quality of digital image can be monitored at the time of capture by the following factors:

A. Resolution
B. Bit depth
C. Compression
D. Threshold
E. File format

Resolution

Resolution denotes the number of dots spread over an area. This is measured in dots per inch (dpi), which is shortly termed as "DPI". Pixel or dots form technically the images. When the resolution is increased, the images appear darker. *Pixels (or the picture element),* can be considered the building blocks of all digital images. These are square cells of a single colour or shade. Pixels arranged in a regular grid pattern, form the digital image. The resolution of a digital image is the density of pixels (measure per inch) that make up the image

pixels per inch (PPI). Occasionally, an image will be described by using its pixel dimensions rather then pixel density. By determining the source material dimensions in inches and using the provided horizontal and vertical pixel totals, the pixel density of the image can be discovered.

Scanning at 150/200 dpi is done generally and if the image quality is poor the standard recommended maximum limit can be upto 600dpi. It is important to note here that the memory size increases with the increase of dpi. Therefore decision related to scanning at judiciously decided dpi for different kinds of documents should be done in order to optimize memory. Some preservation projects scan at 600 dpi for better quality.

A standard SVGA/VGA monitor has a resolution of 640 x 480 lines while the ultra-high monitors have a resolution of about 2048 x 1664 (about 150 dpi). For example, a 1024 x 768 image displayed full screen on a 17" monitor (viewing size 13" x 10") has a resolution of approximately 80 PPI.

Recommended Resolutions

DPI is a measure of printing resolution; in particular the number of individual dots of ink a printer or toner can produce within a linear one-inch space. Due to the similarity with other measurements of graphical resolution, the DPI measurement is frequently misused, for instance, to specify a scanner's sampling resolution or the number of pixels per inch in a computer display. Using DPI measurement in these cases is generally considered to be inaccurate and misleading, though the intended meaning is usually clear based on context. In these cases, a measure given in DPI can be taken as the number of pixels per inch.

Bit Depth

Bit depth is the possible number of colour combinations of the colours. The number of bits used to define each pixel determines bit depth. The greater the bit depth, the greater the number of

Table 1.

Document Type	Page Size	Resolution
Standard text documents	Up to A3	200 PPI
Oversized documents, e.g. maps	Larger than A3	200 PPI
Photographs	6"x4" 7"x5" 9"x6"	600 PPI 430 PH 300 PPI

gray scale or colour tones that can be represented. The term dynamic range is used to express the full range of total variations, as measured by a densitometer between the lightest and darkest of a document.

Consideration With Regard To Digital Images:

Digital images can be captured at varied density or bits pixel depending upon i) the nature of source material or document to be scanned; ii) target audience or users; and iii) capabilities of the display and print subsystem that are to be used.

Bitonal or black & white or binary scanning represents one bit per pixel (either "0" (black) or "1" (white) is generally employed in libraries to scan pages containing text or the drawings. In Gray scale scanning, multiple numbers of bits ranging from 2-8 are assigned to each pixel to represent shades of grey in this process is used for reliable reproduction of intermediate or continuous tones found in black & white photographs to represent shades of grey.. Although each bit is either black or white, as in the case of bitonal images, but bits are combined to produce a level of grey in the pixel that is black, white or somewhere in between. Lastly in colour scanning, typically 2 (lowest quality) to 8 (highest quality) per primary colour are used for representing colour that can be employed to scan colour photographs. As in the case of grey-scale scanning, multiple bits per pixels. Colour images are evidently more complex than grey scale images, because, it involves encoding of shades of each of the three primary colours, i.e. red, green and blue (RGB). If a coloured image is captured at 2 bits per primary colour, each primary colour can have 2 or 4 shades and each pixel can have 4 shades for each of the three primary colour. Evidently, increase in bit depth increases the quality of image captured and the space required to store the resultant image. Generally speaking, 12 bits per pixel (4 bits per primary colour) is considered minimum pixel depth for good quality colour image.

Recommended Bit Depths

A "bit" is the fundamental unit of computer information having two possible values, either 0 or 1.

Table 2.

Document type	Bit Depth
Black and white text only	1-bit bi-tonal
Text with some colour	8-bit colour
Text with shades of grey	8-bit grey
Colour drawings I presentations I graphics	8-bit colour
Black and white photographs	8-bit grey
Colour photographs	24-bit colour

Bit depth is the number of bits used to describe the colour of each pixel. Greater bit depth allows a greater range of colours or shades of grey to be represented by a pixel. Using multiple bits increases choice and variety, at the expense of increased file size. For example, using only 1-bit pixels gives 2 colours, usually either black or white. Using 4 bits gives 16 colour choices (i.e. 2 x 2 x 2 x 2). Typical bit depths are described below.

Compression and File Size (Calculating File Size)

Compression:

Image compression is the process of reducing the size of an image by abbreviating the repetitive information such as one or more rows of white bits to a single code.

Image files are evidently larger than textual ASCII files. A black & white image of a page of text scanned at 300 dpi is about 1 mb in size where as a text file containing the same information is about 2-3 kb it is thus necessary to compress image files so as to achieve economic storage, processing and transmission over the network.

The compression algorithms may be grouped into the following two categories:

- Lossless Compression: The conversion process converts repeated information as a mathematical algorithm that can decompressed without loosing any details into the original image with absolute fidelity. No information is "lost" or "sacrificed" in the process of compression. Lossless compression is primarily used in bitonal images.

- Lossy Compression: Lossy compression process discards or averaged details that are least significant or which may not make appreciable effect on the quality of image. This kind of compression is called "lossy" because when the image compressed using "Lossy" compression techniques, is decompressed; it will not be an exact replica of the original image. Lossy compression is used with gray scale/colour scanning and in particular with complicated images where merely appreciating the information will not result in any appreciable file savings.

Recommendation

Compression is a necessary in digital imaging but more important is the ability to output uncompressed true replica of images. This is especially important when images are transferred from one platform to another or are handled by software packages under different operating system.

Uncompressed images often work better than compressed images for different reasons. It is thus suggested that scanned images should be either stored as uncompressed images or at the most as lossless compressed images.

As indicated in the previous sections, the total number of pixels used to make up an image affects file size. Additionally, the colour depth of each of those pixels has a multiplying effect on the file size. In the example used earlier, an A4 page was digitized at 300 PPI giving a total of 8 700 867 pixels. The following table shows the number of bits that make up this image at varying colour depths and resolutions, and shows approximate file sizes.

Threshold

The threshold defined in bitonal scanning is the point on a scale, usually ranging from 0.255, to which gray values will be interpreted as black or white pixels. In bitonal scanning, resolution and threshold are the key determinants of image quality. Bitonal scanning is best suited to high-contrast documents, such as text and line drawings. For continuous tone or low contrast documents such as photographs, gray scale or colour scanning is

Table 3. Uncompressed file sizes for an A4 page digitized at different pixel depths and resolutions

Color depth	Resolution (PPI)	Total bits	Uncompressed file size (Mb)
1 bit bi-tonal	300	8 700 867	1.04
1 bit bi-tonal	600	34803468	4.15
8 bit grey or colour	300	69 606 936	8.30
8 bit grey or colour	600	278,427,744	34.00
24 bit colour	300	208 820 808	24.89
24 bit colour	600	835,283,232	101.96

required. In gray scale/colour scanning both resolution and bit depth combine to play significant roles in image quality.

Image Enhancement

Image enhancement process is used to improve scanned images at the cost of image authenticity and fidelity. The process of image enhancement requires special skills and is time consuming. It invariably increases the cost of conversion. Typical image enhancement features available in image editing software include, filters, tonal reproduction, curves and colour management, touch, crop, image sharpening, contrast, transparent background, etc. In a page scanned in grayscale, the text/line art, and half tone areas can be decomposed and each area of the page can be filtered separately to maximize its quality. For example the text area on page can be treated with edge sharpening filters so as to clearly define the character edges, to remove the high-frequency noise, a second filter could be used and finally another filter could fill in characters. Gray scale area of the page could be processed with different filters to maximize the quality of the halftone.

File Formats

The digitally scanned images are stored in a file as a bit-mapped page image. The scanned image can be formatted and tagged in different formats to facilitate easy storage and retrieval, depending upon the scanner and its software. National and international standards for image-file formats and compression methods exist to ensure that data will be interchangeable amongst systems. An image file format consists of three district components, i.e. header which stores information on file identifier and image specifications such as its size, resolution, compression protocols, etc.; Image data consisting of look-up table and image raster and lastly footer that signal file termination information.

File formats encode information into a form which is intended for processing and use by specific combinations of hardware and software. Fortunately, the current technology trends of interoperability and compatibility have led to many file formats being supported on a variety of hardware and software platforms. This trend applies to image file formats with many image processing and viewing programs available for Windows, UNIX, and Apple computer systems.

The five file formats most commonly used for digitization are

i. Joint Photographic Experts Group (JPEG) File Interchange Format (JFIF)

This format of images is commonly used on the World Wide Web (WWW) and in digital photographic equipment best to photographs and complex graphics with continuous tones to minimize file sizes.

ii.   Tagged Image File Format (TIFF)

TIFF (Tagged Image File Format) is the most commonly used file format and is considered de facto standard for bitonal scanning. TIFF is a truly multi-platform protocol and is a good for scanning projects. Some image formats are proprietary, developed and supported by a commercial vendor and require specific software or hardware for displaying the printing scanned images. The TIFF format was developed in 1986 by Microsoft and Aldus and is currently maintained by Adobe.

TIFF files are used in desktop publishing, faxing, 3-0 applications and medical imaging applications. The sub-formats within the TIFF specification are. TIFF CCITT Group 3 and Group 4 which are the most widely used format in document imaging most fax transmissions are in TIFF Group 3 format. Other sub formats of TIFF support grayscale, colour depths of up to 64-bit and offer compression choices.

TIFF 6.0, was launched in 1992. The baseline version of TIFF 6.0 is fully compatible with applications designed to read earlier TIFF images and a number of additional features were added that require software to be specifically tailored to support the newer version. JPEG compression was included in the TIFF 6.0 specifications, and despite a technical revision in 1995 to overcome serious design flaws, there still remain problems with the use of this lossy compression within TIFF files. The draft TIFF version 7.0 specification appeared in 1997, is still to be released is expected to feature a more stable implementation of JPEG compression amongst other new features.

iii.   Graphics Interchange Format (GIF)

Graphics Interchange Format (GIF) is a widely used image format introduced in 1987 by CompuServe. In the early years of the WWW, developers adopted GIF for its efficiency and widespread familiarity. A large proportion of the images on the Web are presented in GIF format, and virtually all Web browsers that support graphics can display GIF files.

The GIF format supports a maximum 256 palettised colours or shades of grey so is most suited to discrete images, such as illustrations, black and white images, logos and line drawings rather than photographs.

iv.   Portable Network Graphics (PNG)

Portable Network Graphics (PNG) is a lossless, portable, well-compressed storage format for images. The open-source and patent free PNG format was designed to replace the proprietary GIF format and, to some extent, the much more complex TIFF format. The second edition of PNG is an ISO standard - ISO/IEC 15948:2003 (E). The PNG format was designed specifically for use in online viewing applications such as the WWW, and the format offers a range of attractive features that should eventually make PNG the most common graphic format.

v.   Portable Document Format (PDF)

The PDF format was created by Adobe to provide a standard storing and editing documents. Portable Document Format (PDF) is a widely used proprietary file format. The PDF format was released in 1993 and is based on the Adobe Postscript printing language.

JPEG and PNG are non-proprietary formats while TIFF and PDF are proprietary formats which have freely available specifications.

CONSIDERATIONS FOR DIGITIZING MULTI-PAGE DOCUMENTS

TIFF is the only image format described here that is able to capture more than one image in a single file. This enables storage of individually scanned pages of a multi-page document into a single file.

Table 4. Image formats compared

Name and Current Version	TIFF 6.0	GIF BSa	JPEG JFIF	PNG 1.2	PDF 1.4
Extension	.tif	gif	.jpg	.png	.pdf
Bit-depth(s)	1-bit bi-tonal: 4-or 8-bit grayscale or palette colour Up to 64-bit colour	1-8 bit bi-tonal, grayscale, or colour	8-bit grayscale 24-bit colour	1/2/4/8-bit palette colour or grayscale 16-bit grey-scale,24/48 –bit true colour	4-or 8-bit greyscale or palette colour Up to 64-bit colour support
Compression	Uncompressed Lossless: ccii G3/G4, LZW, Packbits, JPEG	Lossless: LZW	Lossy: JPEG	Lossless: Deflate, an LZ77 derivative	Uncompressed Lossless: cdT, LZW. JBIG Lossy: JPEG
Standard Proprietary	Defacto standard, 12W com-pression may require license	De facto standard, 12W compression may require license	JPEG:ISO 10918-1/2 JFIF: de facto standard	ISO 15948	ISO 15930-1:2001. De facto standard
Web Support	Plug-in or external application	Native since Microsoft® Internet Explorer 3	Native since Microsoft® Internet Explorer 2	Native since Microsoft® Internet Explorer 4	Plug-in or external application
Metadata Support	Basic set of labeled tags	Free-text com-ment field	Free-text comment field	Basic set of labeled tags plus user-defined tags.	Basic set of labeled tags

The other image formats described here can only deliver a single image per file. If these formats are used for digitization of multi-page documents, image management software or other systems are required to provide the linkage and sequencing required to represent multiple images making up the pages of digitized document as a single entity.

Some systems, and high volume scanning software, require that a multi-page format, typi-cally TIFF or PDF, be used for image storage so that a single file is capable of representing several scanned pages of a document. This should be viewed as a software limitation rather than best practice, and if organizations are forced to use TIFF or PDF solely due to their support for multiple paged documents, they should do so with caution after thoroughly investigating all options.

While TIFF is widely regarded as the standard file format to use when capturing documents as bi-tonal images, it lacks the compression and bit depth combinations to suit other document types, particularly grayscale and colour documents. If no compression or the inefficient *packbits* compres-sion is used to capture multiple page grayscale or colour documents as a single TIFF file, file sizes can become very large, affecting the accessibility and storage of the file.

To overcome this file size issue, some vendors have chosen to implement JPEG compression within the TIFF file format, providing a higher rate of compression, but with the data loss inherent of this compression scheme. There is no agreed standard for the implementation of JPEG compres-sion within the TIFF format. Using non-standard formats for the storage of digitized records may create compatibility problems with other software, such as preventing the images from being viewed or printed

Table 5. File format recommendations

Document Type	File Format
Black and white text only	TIFF G3 I G4 PNG Bi-tonal
Text with some colour	GIF colour PNG 4- or 8-bit colour TIFF (LZW)
Text with shades of grey	GIF grey PNG 4- or 8-bit grey TIFF (LZW)
Colour drawings I presentations / graphics	GIF PNG 4- or 8-bit TIFF (LZW)
Black and white photographs	JPEG 8-bit grey PNG 8-or 16-bit grey TIFF (JPEG)
Colour photographs	JPEG 24-bit (high quality compression 10:1) PNG 24-bit TIFF (high quality JPEG compression 10:1)

RECOMMENDED FILE FORMATS

The table below lists the document types file formats recommended for digitizing different images cropped or incomplete

- Missing pixels or scan lines
- Poor quality dithering

RECOMMENDED QUALITY CHECKS POINTS

It is recommended that digital images should be inspected and checked against the attributes listed below, in addition to standard records management quality checks.

Attributes to check include:

- Image size
- Image resolution
- Bit depth: bitonal, greyscale or appropriate colour depth
- Too light or too dark
- Too low or too high contrast

- Lack of sharpness
- Too much sharpening, unnatural appearance and halos around dark edges
- Image orientation
- Skewed or not centred
- Obvious use of lossy compression
- Necessary derivatives produced
- Have procedures for the disposal of the original paper record been followed? Has the equipment been calibrated correctly?

Following issues should also be checked

- File format
- File size
- Appropriate security applied
- Incomplete or incorrect profile information I metadata

WORKFLOW OF SCANNING OPERATION

A generalized workflow of scanning activity can be discussed under following heads

Figure 1. Workflow pictographic representation

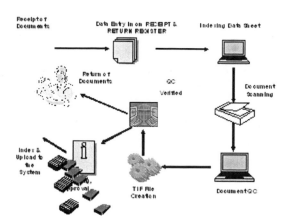

- Receipts of Documents
- Recording of data in master issue receipt file- This step complete the issue of document from repository
- Preparation of indexing data
- Document preparation for scanning
- Scanning of Documents
- Quality checking of images in terms of image quality and completeness
- Storage of files in agreed format3in this case tiff format)
- Quality check at second level in order to avoid human error at first level of check
- Indexing and uploading the scanned images on the system
- Recording the complete process at different level for quality monitoring & other purposes.
- Return of documents to document repository

The pictorial view of the workflow is depicted as follows.

TOOLS OF DIGITIZATION

An image scanning system may consists of a stand-alone workstation, or as a part of a network of workstation with imaging work is distributed and shared amongst various workstations. The network usually includes a scanning station, a server and one or more editing, retrieval stations. A typical scanning workstation for a small, production level project could consist of the following:

i. Computer System
ii. Scanner and Scanning Software
iii. Storage System
iv. Network
v. Display System
vi. Printer

Here we will concentrate on scanners and scanning software as important components of scanning tool.

Scanners

Digital scanners are used to capture a digital image from an analogue media such as printed page or a microfiche / microfilm at a predefined resolution and dynamic range

(Bit range). There are two types of image scanners:

a. vector scanner and
b. raster scanners.

Vector Scanning

The vector scanners scan an image as a complex set of x,y coordinates. The display software for the vector image interprets the image as function of coordinates and other included information to produce an electronic replica of the original drawing or photograph. Vector images can be zoomed in portion to display minute details of a drawing or a map, engineering drawings, and architectural blueprints are often scanned as vector images. Vector images are generally used in geographical information systems (GIS).

Raster Scanner

Raster images are captured by raster scanners by passing lights (laser in some cases) down the page and digitally encoding it row by row. Multiple passes of lights may be required to capture basic (as a set of bits known as bit map) colours in a coloured image. The scanners used for digitizing analogue images into digital images come in a variety of shapes and sizes. Raster scanners are used in libraries to convert printed publications into electronic forms. Majority of electronic imaging system generate raster images.

Figure 2. Flatbed scanners HP ScanJet 6300C, Ricoh IS420

There are following categories of Scanners:

a. Flatbed Scanners: It looks like a photocopier and is used in much the some way. Source material, in a flatbed scanner is placed face down for scanning. The light source and CCD move beneath the platen, while the document remains stationary as in the case of photocopying machine. Flatbed scanner comes in various models right angle, prism and overhead flatbed.

Product Examples: HP ScanJet 6300C, Ricoh IS420

b. Sheet-Feed Scanners: It is fed over a stationary CCD and light source via roller, belt, drum, or vacuum transport. In contrast to be flat-bed scanner, sheet-feed scanner has optional attachment to auto feed uniformed-sized stacks of documents to be scanned.

Product Example: Kodak 500S, Tangent CCS300-SF

c. Drum Scanners: In a drum scanner is wrapped on a drum, which is then rotated past a high-intensity light source to capture

Figure 3. Sheet-feed scanners

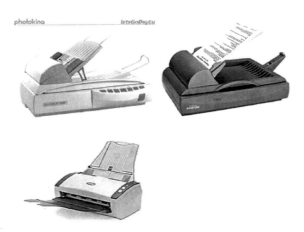

Figure 4. Drum scanners Juno CP-4000, scan graphics ScanMate 5000, ColorGetter

the image. Drum scanners are specially targeted for graphic art market. Drum scanners offer highest resolution for grey scale and colour scanning Product Example: Juno CP-4000, Scan graphics ScanMate5000, ColorGetter.

d. Digital Cameras: Source material is placed on the stand and the camera is cranked up or down in order to focus the material within the field of view. Digital cameras are most promising scanner development for library and archival applications.

Product Example: Zeutschel OminiScan 3000, Minolta PS 3000.

e. Slide Scanners: Slide scanners have a slot in the side to accommodate a 35mm slide. Inside the box the light passes through the slide to hit a CCD array behind the slide. Slide scanners can generally scan only 35mm transparent source materials.

Product Example: Kodak PCD Scanner 4045, Nikon LS3510, Leaf Systems Leafscan 45.

f. Microfilm Scanner: Specially targeted to library/archival application, microfilm scanners have adapters to convert roll film, fiche, and aperture cards in the same model.

Product Example: Mekel M500XL, SunRise SRI-50, Lenzpro 2000 Multimedia

g. Video Frame Grabber: Video digitizers are circuit boards placed inside a computer, attached to a standard video camera. Anything that is filmed by the video camera is digitized by the video digitizer

h. Book Eye Scanners

Figure 5. Slide scanners Kodak PCD scanner 4045

Figure 6. Book Eye scanners

ORGANIZATION OF DIGITAL IMAGES

A disc full of digital images without any organization, browse and search options may have no meaning except for one who created it. Scanned images need to be organized in order to be useful. Moreover, images need to be linked to the associated metadata to facilitate their browsing and searching. The following three steps describe process of organizing the digital images:

Organize

Store

Retrieve

Organize

the scanned image files into disc hierarchy that logically maps the physical organization of the document. For example, in a project on scanning of journals, create a folder for each journal, which, in turn, may have folder for each volume scanned. Each volume, in turn may have a subfolder for each issue. The folder for each issue, in turn, may contain scanned articles that appeared in the issue along with a content page, composed in HTML providing links to articles in that issue.

Document Image Processing (DIP): Indexing

The process of indexing scanned image involves linking of database of scanned images to a text database. Scanned images are just like a set of pictures that need to be related to a text database describing them and their contents. The document management software (DMS) packages, through their menu drive or command driven interface, facilitate elaborate indexing of documents. While some document management system facilitate selection of indexing terms from the image file, others allow only manual keying in of indexing terms. Further, many DMS packages provides OCRed capabilities for transforming the images into standard ASCII files. The OCRed text then serves as a database for full-text search of the stored images.

Store

The scanned image files in a strictly controlled manner that reflect their logical relationship.

For example, each article may be named after the surname of first author followed by volume number and issue number. The file name for each article would, therefore, convey a logical and hierarchical organization of the journal.

Electronic Filing System (EFS): Store

Every part of an electronic page image is saved regardless of present or absence of ink. The size of the files depends directly with scanning resolution, the size of the area being digitized and the style of graphic file format used to save the image. The scanned images, therefore, need to be transferred from the hard disc of scanning workstation to an external large capacity storage devices such as an optical disc, CD ROM / DVD ROM disc, snap servers, Cartridges etc. the smaller document imaging system use offline media, which need to be reloaded when required, or fixed hard disc drives allocated for image storage, larger document management system use auto-changers such as optical jukeboxes and tape library systems. The storage required by the scanned image varies and depends upon scanning specifications factors such as scanning resolution, page size, compression ratio and page content. Further, the image storage device may be either remote or local to the retrieval workstation depending upon the imaging systems and document management system used.

Retrieve/Search

Document Management Systems (DMS): Retrieve

Once scanned images and OCRed text documents have been saved as a file, a database is needed for selective retrieval of data contained in one or more fields within each record in the database. An imaging system typically stores a large amount of unstructured data in a two file system one for storing and another for retrieving scanned images. The first is traditional file that has a text description of the image along with a key to a second file. The second file contains the document location. The user selects a record from the first file using a search algorithm. Once the user selects a record, the application keys into the location index, finds the document and displays it. Most of the document management systems provides elaborate search possibilities including use of Boolean and proximity operators (and, or, not) and wild cards. Users are also allowed to refine their search strategy. Once the required images have been identified their associated document image can quickly be retrieved from the image storage device for display or printed output.

The schematic sketch of the overall process can be depicted as follows

Search Process Start
User
Search algorithm

Record Selection

Application Key

Location Index
Document Display

These three processes are controlled through software based processes which are being discussed as follows.

HYBRID SOLUTION

It would be imperative to consider producing a more reliable media like microfilm simultaneous to the process of digitization if archival preservation is one of the objectives. The process of microfilming produces high-resolution images on the microfilm / microfiche that equates to approximately 1000 dpi in digital binary scanning. In comparison, a bitonal digital image can at best be scan at 600 dpi for archival storage. The microfilm / microfiche can be used for conversion to electronic image format. Moreover, future improvements in scanning technology can be utilized by rescanning a microfilm to obtain high-resolution images. It is expected that ultimately electronic scanning will reach or exceed photographic quality. Durability and reliability of computers and storage media and formats used for electronic image files may also increase and stabilize.

DIGITAL PRESERVATION

Preservation in the digital world is a challenging task for libraries and archivists. Protocols, strategies and technologies involved in digital preservation have now been well defined and understood. Digital preservation is a cost-intensive activity of continuing nature. Digitization with long-term preservation and storage of research collections requires deep and continuing commitment by the parent institution. Digital resources, undoubtedly have several advantages over its analogue counter part, however, preservation is definitely not onc of them. The fact that the risk of loss of data in digital form is much greater than any other physical form is well understood and addressed to. Failure to address to the digital preservation issues may result in loss of valuable digital data resulting in exorbitant costs for recovery, if at all possible

The basic principles of preservation digital data are

- Longerty
- Selection
- Quality
- Integrity
- Accesses

Digital Preservation of Metadata

Administrative or technical metadata is needed to manage a digital object througout its life cycle and is required for long-term collection management. It is a subset of metadata that describes attributes of digital resources essential for its long term accessibility. It escribes and record information needed to manage the preservation of digital resources. A subset of administrative metadata design to assist in the management of technical metadata for continuing access to the digital content. It stores technical details on the format, structure and use of the digital content. The information recorded includes

- Original source
- Date of capture/creation
- Scanning resolution
- Initial Capture Settings
- Version of digital object
- File Format
- Compression technology used
- Object resolution used etc.

The hardware and software used for capturing contents automatically generate the administrative or technical metadata. The administrative metadata also record legal and financial aspects of access to the object such as: rights management, costs, authorization, authentication etc.

Microfilming and Digital Preservation: A Hybrid Solution

The high-resolution microfilm masters can be safely archived and retrieved when needed to generate new high-use, highly accessible digital version.

The process also serves to circumvent the problems with digital technology, i.e. constant migration; new digital files in successive software generations could be created as required from the microfilm master.

DIGITAL PRESERVATION STRATEGIES

We need to adopt clear-cut strategies to preserve digital data. The strategies may be in relation to short term, long term, investment considerations, alternative strategies or combination of two or more.

Short-term Strategies: here following considerations are required to be taken care of

Bit-stream Copying

Refreshing

Replication

Technology Preservation or Computer Museum

Backwards Compatibility and Version Migration

Bit-Stream Copying

It is known as "backing up data"; making an exact duplicate of a digital object.

It is remote storage guard against disastrous event. Minimum maintenance strategy for even the most lightly valued, ephemeral data are required. It is not a long-term preservation strategy.

Refreshing

Refreshing helps in copying digital information from one long-term storage medium to another with no change in the bit-stream. It addresses both decay and obsolescence issues related to the storage media. It doesn't address the issue of obsolescence of encoding and formatting schemes. Longeivity of media does not guarantee availability of hardware / software required to read the stored format. The backward compatibility and interoperability are serious threat to longevity of digital information.

Replication

- Replication is used to represent multiple digital preservation strategies.
- Bit-stream copying is a form of replication.
- LOCKSS (Lots of Copies Keeps Stuff Safe) is a consortia form of replication, while peer-to-peer data trading is an open, free-market form of replication.
- Objective is to enhance the longevity of digital documents while maintaining their authenticity and integrity through copying and the use of multiple storage locations.

Technology Preservation

- Also called the "computer museum" solution.
- Rely on preserving the computer, operating systems, original application software, media drives, etc.
- Applicable for neglected digital objects.
- Assumes that media has not decayed beyond readability.
- Limitation: No obsolete technology can be kept functional indefinitely.
- Requires a considerable investment in equipment and personnel.

Backwards Compatibility and Version Migration

- Current versions of software can interpret and present digital material created with previous versions of the same software.
- Option for version migration converts documents into the current format.
- MS Word, Excel and Access applications, allow previous versions of their file formats to be transformed and resaved in a new version
- Option not to be available for all types of objects.

The process of migration is likely to introduce unwanted changes to a document incrementally if used over many generations

Medium- to Long-Term Strategies

Here following considerations are required to be taken care of

1. Migration
2. Viewers and Migration at the Point of Access
3. Canonicalization
4. Emulation

Migration

- Periodic transfer of digital materials from one hardware / software configuration to another or from one generation of computer technology to subsequent generations.
- Migration may include conversion of data to avoid obsolescence not only of the physical storage medium, but of the encoding and format of the data.
- Digital objects will have to be constantly migrated and converted to new formats, computing devices, storage media and software to ensure they are not left behind on obsolete system.

Viewers and Migration at the Point of Access

- An alternative to recurring migration. Involves use of viewers, software tools that provide accessibility at the time of access, using the original data stream.
- Example: The "migration on request" approach has been developed in CEDARS and CAMILEON projects that use a software tool to record method of access.
- Google's Google Docs
- Limitations i) viewers not be available for all formats; ii) Viewers may represent some, but not all; iii) the gap between the original format and the prevailing technologies

at the time of access may be too much to tackle.

Canonicalization

- Technique designed to determine maintenance of essential characteristics of a document through conversion from one format to another.
- Canonicalization relies on the creation of a representation of a digital object that conveys all its key aspects.
- Once created, this form could be used to algorithmically verify that a converted file has not lost any of its essence.

Emulation

Emulation uses a special type of software, called an emulator, to translate instructions from original software to execute on new platforms. It eliminates the need to keep old hardware working. Emulation requires the creation of emulator programs that translate code and instructions from one computing environment so it can be properly executed in another.

INVESTMENT STRATEGIES

1. Restricting Range of Formats and Standards
2. Reliance on Standards
3. Data Abstraction and Structuring
4. Encapsulation
5. Software Re-engineering
6. Universal Virtual Computer
7. Alternative strategies
8. Analogue Backups
9. Digital Archaeology or Data Recovery

Restricting Range of Formats and Standards

- Preservation programmers may decide to only store data in a limited range of formats and standards.
- All digital objects within an archival repository of a particular type can be converted into a single chosen file format that is thought to embody the best overall compromise amongst characteristics such as functionality, longevity, and preservability.
- For, example most of the textual and graphical information can be converted into PDF format.
- The strategy does not solve the access problem of obsolescence of formats and standards

Reliance on Standards

- Advocates use of well-recognized standards and discarding proprietary or less-supported standards.
- Backward compatibility for older formats would maintain if it is widely used as a standard.
- For example, if JPEG2000 becomes a widely adopted standard, the sheer volume of users will guarantee that software to encode, decode, and render JPEG2000 images will be upgraded to meet the demands of new operating systems, CPUs, etc.

Data Abstraction and Structuring

- Data abstraction involves analyzing and tagging data so that the functions, relationships and structure of specific elements can be described.
- Using data abstraction, the representation of content can be liberated from specific software applications and be achieved using different applications as technology changes.

- The technique requires extensive development of tools and methods for analysis and processing in order to correctly represent and tag each type of data.

Encapsulation

- Technique of grouping together digital objects and metadata necessary to provide access to that object.
- The grouping process lessens the possibility that any critical component necessary to decode and render a digital object will be lost.
- Appropriate types of metadata to encapsulate with a digital object include reference, representation, provenance, and fixity and context information. Encapsulation is considered a key element of emulation.

Software Re-Engineering

- Software reengineering may offer a number of strategies for transforming software as technologies change.
- Adjustment and re-compiling of source code for a new platform;
- Re-coding of the software from scratch, or re-coding in another programming language; and
- Translation of compiled binary instructions for one platform directly into binary instructions for another platform.
- Requires source code. Porting to other platforms requires considerable time and effort.

Universal Virtual Computer

- A form of emulation.
- Requires development of a computer program independent of existing hardware or software that could simulate the basic architecture of every computer.

- Users could create and save digital files using software of their choice, but all files would be backed up in a way that could be read by the universal computer.
- Reading a file in future would require only a single emulation layer—between the universal virtual computer and the computer of that time.

Alternative Strategies

- No single digital preservation strategy can serve as a practical solution to the problem of technological obsolescence for digital materials.
- No single solution that is appropriate for all data types, situations, or institutions
- It is, therefore, reasonable for preservation programmes to look for multiple strategies, especially if they are responsible for a range of materials over extended periods.
  - The long-term strategies that are being practiced for digital preservation includes:
    - Use of standards for data encoding
    - Structuring and description
    - Emulation of obsolete software or hardware
    - Migration of data from one operating technology to another.
  - None of them have proven themselves against unknown threats over centuries of change.
  - Most of these strategies are, however, being used in the management of data, and it is likely that combinations of the will continue to be researched and proposed for large-scale, long-term preservation.

Analogue Backups

- Combines the conversion of digital objects into analogue form, e.g., taking high-quality printouts or the creation of microfilm.
- An analogue copy of a digital object can, in some respects, preserve its content and protect it from obsolescence.
- Technique makes sense for documents whose contents merit the highest level of redundancy and protection from loss.

Digital Archaeology

- Rescue content from damaged media or from damaged hardware and software
- An emergency recovery strategy involves specialized techniques to recover data from unreadable media, either due to physical damage or hardware failure.
- Carried out by data recovery companies
- Given enough resources, readable bit-streams can often be recovered even from heavily damaged media (especially magnetic media)

CONCLUSION

Digital conversion of documents is a worldwide phenomenon. The easy portability and data backup of digital documents are two important driving forces for it. The important challenges in this direction are technological changes, redundancy of information, data integrity, statutory status and digital storage of documents. It is important to decide upon different organization policies before going for digitization of documents.

REFERENCES

(2003). Western States Digital Standards Group. Accessed March 2005 at http://www.cdpheritage.org/digital/scanning/documents/WSDIBP_v1.pdf.

Adobe Systems Inc. (1992). *TIFF Revision 6.0.* Retrieved March 2005, from

Adobe Systems Inc. (2005). *Adobe PDF.* Retrieved March 2005, from

and Information Resources. Retrieved March 2005, from

Archives. Retrieved March 2005, from

at http://www.tasi.ac.uk/advice/creating/quality.html

Brown, A. (2003). *Digital Preservation Guidance Note 1: Selecting File Formats for Long-*

Canadian Heritage Information Network. (2002). *Creating and Managing Digital Content.*

Cunningham A. Metadata Standards in Australia – An Overview. 2005. Presentation at Queensland State Archives March 2005. National Archives of Australia. Creating and Managing Digital Content. 2002. Canadian Heritage Information Network. Accessed March 2005 at http://www.chin.gc.ca/English/Digital_Content

Cyberspace Law and Policy Centre, University of New South Wales. Accessed March 2005 at http://www.bakercyberlawcentre.org/ddr/

Data Dictionary—Technical Metadata for Digital Still Images. (2003). National

Digital Imaging for Archival Preservation and Online Presentation: Best Practices. (2001). Michigan State University. Retrieved March 2004 at

Digital Preservation and Storage. (2004). Technical Advisory Service for Images.

digitisation on demand. National Archives of Australia. Retrieved March 2005, from

Digitization Disposal Policy. *Policy on the authorization of the early disposal of original paper records after digitization.* (2006). Queensland State Archives. Retrieved April 2006, from http://www.archives.qld.gov.au/government/ddp.asp

Electronic Records Management Guidelines. (2004). Minnesota State Archives. Accessed

Engineering, Monash University. Retrieved March 2005, from

File Formats and Compression. 2004. Technical Advisory Service for Images. Accessed March 2005 at http://www.tasi.ac.uk/advice/creating/fformat.html#ff2

Formats. 2002. *Digital Preservation Coalition.* Retrieved March 2005, from

Frey, F. (2000). *Guides to Quality in Visual Resource Imaging.* Council on Library and.

2005 from

2005 from http://www.bakercyberlawcentre.org/ddr/

2005 from http://www.phototechmag.com/sample/sharma.pdf

2005 from http://www.statelib.lib.in.us/www/isl/diglibin/techmeta.pdf

General Guidelines for Scanning. (1999). *Colorado Digitization Project.* Retrieved March.

Gillespie, J., Fair, P., Lawrence, A., & Vaile, D. (2004). Coping when Everything is Digital? *Digital Documents and Issues in Document Retention – White Paper.* Baker & McKenzie

Glossary of Archival and Recordkeeping Terms. 2004. Queensland State Archives. Accessed March 2005 at http://www.archives.qld.gov.au/downloads/GlossaryOfArchivalRKTerms.pdf

Governments. 2003. Ohio Electronic Records Committee. Retrieved March 2004 at

Guidelines for management, appraisal and preservation of electronic records. (1999).

Hilton, D., & Warr, P. (2004). *Unlocking Queensland's Picture Heritage – Picture Queensland Digital Imaging Workshop Course Notes*. State Library of Queensland.

Horton, S. (2004). *Web Style Guide 2nd Edition: PNG Graphics*. Retrieved March 2004 at http://www.webstyleguide.com/graphics/pngs.html

How To Fix Bad Scans. (2004). Dixie State College of Utah. Retrieved March 2005, from http://cit.dixie.edu/vt/vt2600/bad_scans.asp

http://chnm.gmu.edu/digitalhistory/links/cached/chapter3/link3.45.CD

http://cit.dixie.edu/vt/vt2600/bad_scans.asp

http://partners.adobe.com/asn/developer/pdfs/tn/TIFF6.pdf

http://www.adobe.com/products/acrobat/adobepdf.html

http://www.archives.gov/research_room/arc/arc_info/techguide_raster_june2004.pdf

http://www.archives.qld.gov.au/publications/PublicRecordsAlert/PRA105.pdf

http://www.archives.qld.gov.au/publications/PublicRecordsAlert/PRA205.pdf

http://www.cdpheritage.org/digital/scanning/documents/WSDIBP_v1.pdf

http://www.clir.org/PUBS/archives/ensuring.pdf

http://www.ctie.monash.edu.au/EMERGE/multimedia/JPEG/COMM03.HTM

http://www.dpconline.org/graphics/medformedia.html

http://www.historicalvoices.org/papers/image_digitization2.pdf

http://www.jasc.com/tutorials/scantip.asp

http://www.library.cornell.edu/preservation/tutorial/quality/quality-01.html

http://www.library.cornell.edu/preservation/tutorial/quality/quality-02.html

http://www.naa.gov.au/Publications/corporate_publications/digitising_TLing.pdf

http://www.naa.gov.au/recordkeeping/dirks/dirksman/dirks.html

http://www.nationalarchives.gov.uk/electronicrecords/advice/pdf/procedures2.pdf

http://www.niso.org/standards/resources/Z39_87_trial_use.pdf

http://www.ohiojunction.net/erc/imagingrevision/revisedimaging2003.html

http://www.pcworld.idg.com.au/index.php/id;1170029196;fp;2;fpid;1585691688

http://www.prepressure.com/formats/tiff/fileformat.htm

http://www.prov.vic.gov.au/vers/standard/standard

http://www.slq.qld.gov.au/__data/assets/file/5449/sd1_meta_v1.2.doc

http://www.slq.qld.gov.au/__data/assets/file/6289/How_of_Metadata.doc

http://www.slq.qld.gov.au/__data/assets/word_doc/32645/sd2_current.doc

Image Quality Working Group of ArchivesCom. (1997). *Technical Recommendations for Digital Imaging Projects*. Retrieved March 2005, from http://www.columbia.edu/acis/dl/imagespec.html

Imaging Best Practices. (2003). University of California, Berkley. Retrieved March 2005, from http://www.lib.berkeley.edu/digicoll/bestpractices/image_bp.html

Indiana Digital Library. (2004). *Suggested Technical Metadata Elements.* Retrieved March.

Information Resources. Retrieved March 2005, from http://lyra2.rlg.org/visguides/

Information Standards Organization and AIIM International. Retrieved March 2005, from

Jasc Software Inc. (1999). *Scanning Tips and Techniques.* Retrieved October 2004, from http://www.jasc.com/tutorials/scantip.asp

JPEG Image Coding Standard. (1998). Centre for Telecommunications and Information

Leurs, L. (2001). *The TIFF file format.* Retrieved March 2005, from

Library of Congress. (1998). *Manuscript Digitization Demonstration Project.*

Moving Theory into Practice: Digital Imaging Tutorial. 2003. Cornell University Library/Research Department. Accessed March 2005 at http://www.library.cornell.edu/preservation/tutorial/quality/quality-01.html

Moving Theory into Practice: Digital Imaging Tutorial. 2003. Cornell University Library/Research Department. Accessed March 2005 at http://www.library.cornell.edu/preservation/tutorial/quality/quality-02.html

Ling, T. (2002). *Taking it to the streets: why the National Archives of Australia embraced digitisation on demand. National Archives of Australia. Accessed March 2005 at http://www.naa.gov.au/Publications/corporate_publications/digitising_TLing.pdf*

LZW Patent Information. 2005. Unisys Corporation. Accessed March 2005 at http://www.unisys.com/about__unisys/lzw/

March 2005, from http://tasi.ac.uk/advice/delivering/metadata.html

March 2005, from http://www.w3.org/Graphics/PNG/

March 2005, from http://www.mnhs.org/preserve/records/electronicrecords/erguidelinestoc.html

March 2005, from http://www.tasi.ac.uk/advice/creating/fformat.html#ff2

Mendham, S. (2005). JPEG 2000. *IDG Communications.* Retrieved March 2005, from

Metadata and Digital Images. 2004. Technical Advisory Service for Images. Accessed March 2005 at http://tasi.ac.uk/advice/delivering/metadata.html

Moving Theory into Practice. (2003). *Digital Imaging Tutorial.* Cornell University.

Moving Theory into Practice. (2003). *Digital Imaging Tutorial.* Cornell University.

National Archives and Records Administration (US). (2004). *Technical Guidelines for Digitizing Archival Materials for Electronic Access.* Retrieved March 2005, from

Cyberspace Law and Policy Centre, University of New South Wales. Accessed March 2005 at http://www.bakercyberlawcentre.org/ddr/

PNG (Portable Network Graphics). (2004). *World Wide Web Consortium.* Retrieved.

Pscanningguidelines.html.

Public Record Office, The National Archives (UK). Retrieved March 2005, from

Public Record Office Victoria. (2004). *Management of Electronic Records PROS 99/007* (Version 2). Retrieved March 2005, from

Public Records Alert No 1/05: Day batching of records. (2005). Queensland State

Public Records Alert No 2/05: Understanding and applying recordkeeping metadata.

Quality Assurance. (2004). *Technical Advisory Service for Images*. Retrieved March 2005

Queensland. Retrieved March 2005, from

Queensland. Retrieved March 2005, from

2005 Queensland State Archives. Retrieved March 2005, from

Queensland State Archives March 2005. National Archives of Australia.

Recordkeeping in Brief No. 11: Digital Imaging and Recordkeeping. 2003. State Records New South Wales. Accessed March 2005 at www.records.nsw.gov.au/publicsector/rk/rib/rib11.htm

Revised Digital Imaging Guidelines for State of Ohio Executive Agencies and Local

Roelofs, G. (2005). *Multiple-image Network Graphics*. Retrieved March 2005, from http://www.libpng.org/pub/mng

Rothenberg, J. (1999). *Ensuring the Longevity of Digital Information*. Council on Library.

Sharma, A. (2001). *Digital Noise, Film Grain. Digital Photo Techniques*. Retrieved March.

Standard, D. (2003). *1 – Cataloguing and Metadata for Digital Images*. State Library of.

Standard, D. (2003). *2 – Digital capture, format & preservation*. State Library of.

Tanner, S. From Vision to Implementation – strategic and management issues for digital collections. 2000. The Electronic Library – strategic, policy and management issues seminar. Accessed March 2005 at http://heds.herts.ac.uk/resources/papers/Lboro2000.pdf

Term Preservation. National Archives (UK). Retrieved March 2005, from http://www.nationalarchives.gov.uk/preservation/advice/pdf/selecting_file_formats.pdf

The DIRKS Manual: A Strategic Approach to Managing Business Information. (2003).

The Preservation Management of Digital Material Handbook, Chapter 5: Media and

Thornely J. The How of Metadata: Metadata Creation and Standards. 1999. 13th National Cataloguing Conference, October 1999, Accessed March 2005 at http://www.slq.qld.gov.au/__data/assets/file/6289/How_of_Metadata.doc

Chapter 5
Building Digital Libraries:
Role of Social (Open Source) Software

Kshema Prakash
Dayalbagh Educational Institute, India

Jason A. Pannone
Harvard University, USA

K. Santi Swarup
Dayalbagh Educational Institute, India

ABSTRACT

Blogging is a relatively recent phenomenon, and its use in academic libraries is in nascent stage. The authors of this chapter use blogs as part of their outreach to patrons, though in slightly different contexts and for slightly different purposes. Blogging can be an important component of digital libraries, one that allows for timely two-way communication of news, information, bibliographic instruction, and the like. While challenges have been raised to the worth and value of academic library blogs (e.g., Gorman, 2005), the authors believe, based on the research and their experience, that blogging is a useful tool for academic librarians and digital libraries.

INTRODUCTION

The use of blogging by academic librarians is a relatively recent development (Bar-Ilan, 2007; Zhuo, 2006). Unsurprisingly, there is debate over the use and value of blogging by academic librarians, and of blogging in general. Some see blogging as passé, a fad whose time has come and gone, e.g., Boutin, 2008, and now largely superseded by social networking sites such as Facebook and Twitter. There have been sharp criticisms of blogging, such as Gorman's editorial (Gorman, 2005).

Others counter that blogging can be a useful and effective means of interacting with patrons (Coulter & Draper, 2006), and that librarians should work to promote an environment where traditional and emerging forms of communication like blogging can coexist peacefully (Gordon, 2005).

The authors of this chapter embrace the view that blogging can be a useful and effective means to communicate with patrons, but academic librarians have not fully exploited that potential to date. Blogging is one valuable way among many to reach distance education students, provide reference services, notify patrons of new materials, offer bibliographic instruction, and so forth.

DOI: 10.4018/978-1-61520-767-1.ch005

The authors have several objectives in this chapter. First, we will provide a short history of and potential applications for blogging in academic libraries based on our literature review. Next, we will examine two case studies from our experiences as bloggers; the first will look at the use of blogging as part of daily interactions with patrons, while the second will look at blogging as part of distance library services. Then, we will investigate the challenges, limitations, and objections to blogging, followed by a section in which we respond to these issues. After that, we will offer several proposals for would-be bloggers, and, finally, give our conclusions.

Let us turn now to a history of blogging, to show how blogging in academic libraries has grown in a relatively short period.

HISTORY OF BLOGGING IN ACADEMIC LIBRARIES

Any history of blogging in academic libraries must take into account the development of two related concepts: Web 2.0, or Social Software, and Library 2.0. We will outline these concepts in the next two sections.

Web 2.0 or Social Software

The concept of Web 2.0 originated as a list of characteristics of successful web properties. Among these are the Read/Write web, the web as platform, the Long Tail[1], harnessing of collective intelligence, network effects, core datasets from user contributions, and lightweight programming models. Web users of the web engage many of these properties on a daily basis.

The benefits of the principles of Web 2.0 and its technology are that they offer libraries many opportunities to serve their patrons better and reach out beyond the walls and websites of the institution to reach potential beneficiaries where they are, and in association with the task they happen to

be undertaking. It is worth appreciating the level of integration and interoperability of Web 2.0 and Library 2.0 that are designed into the interface of a library portal or intranet.

Taking a cue from the Libraries and Social Software in Education (LASSIE) Project Report (Secker, 2008), we will use the term 'social software' for Web 2.0 tools and technologies, as these terms are broadly synonymous. As is evident from its overall characteristics, social software is more about user-created content than content created by an organization. Social software also includes development of user profiles and the use of 'folksonomies,' or tagging, to attach keywords users create to items to help them retrieve information. Examples of key technologies that underpin the concept of social software are RSS feeds; blogs; wikis; social bookmarking and resource sharing, sites such as CiteULike, Del.icio.us; social networking sites, including MySpace, Facebook, and LinkedIn; media sharing sites such as YouTube, PhotoBucket, Flickr; and virtual worlds. The majority of these technologies are non-proprietary and accessible to all.

Library 2.0

The emergence of the Library 2.0 paradigm follows upon the emergence of Web 2.0. Because of the widespread use of Web 2.0 services, there are cultural changes affecting library users' information-seeking behaviors, communication styles, and expectations. As a result, the term 'Library 2.0' has been introduced into the professional language of librarianship as a way to discuss these changes, though what Library 2.0 is and what it means are still under discussion in the world of librarian blogging, the so-called 'biblioblogosphere.' Library 2.0 is a concept wherein users are not only information consumers, but also content creators. It is a library without any boundaries and with the fullest participation of users as architects.

In terms of the history of the use of the term 'Library 2.0,' Michael Casey first introduced it in September 2005 (Library 2.0, 2009). The British Integrated Library Software (ILS) vendor, Talis, took an early interest in promoting the term (Miller, 2005; Chad & Miller, 2005; Miller, 2006). Michael Stephens exposed a wider audience to the term when he discussed Library 2.0 on the American Library Association's (ALA) Techsource Blog (Stephens & Casey, 2005; ALA Techsource Blog Library Technology Reports, n/d, a; ALA Techsource Blog Library Technology Reports, n/d, b).

Some of the popular definitions of Library 2.0 include the notions that

i.   Library 2.0 is the application of interactive, collaborative, and multimedia web-based technologies to web-based library services and collections (Maness, 2006).

ii. The heart of Library 2.0 is user-centered change. It is a model for library service that encourages constant and purposeful change, inviting user participation in the creation of both the physical and the virtual services they want, supported by consistently evaluating services. What makes a service Library 2.0? Any service, physical or virtual, that successfully reaches users, is evaluated frequently, and makes use of customer input, is a Library 2.0 service. Even older, traditional services can be Library 2.0 if certain criteria are met. Similarly, the mere fact of being new is not enough to make a service Library 2.0 if it fails to meet these criteria (Casey & Savastinuk, 2006).

iii. Library 2.0 is a concept of a very different library service, which operates according to the expectations of today's library users. In this vision, the library makes information available wherever and whenever the user requires it (Chad & Miller, 2005).

Given the above, we can describe Library 2.0 as a subset of library services designed to meet user needs caused by the direct and peripheral effects of Web 2.0 services, and leveraging concepts of the Read/Write Web, the Web as Platform, The Long Tail, harnessing of collective intelligence, network effects, core datasets from user contributions, and lightweight programming models (Library 2.0, 2009; Habib, 2006).

This definition understands that Web 2.0 precipitates changes in user needs and that Library 2.0 services arise to meet these needs. The definition includes all implementations of Web 2.0 methodologies and technologies by libraries; however, this concept is not about replacing traditional technologies already in use, but rather about adding functionality. Figure 1 illustrates the key principles governing Library 2.0.

Library 2.0 is a service model. The heart of Library 2.0 is user-centred change. It is a model for library service that encourages constant and purposeful change, inviting user participation in the creation of both physical and virtual services. It also attempts to reach new users and better serve current ones through improved customer-driven offerings. Each component by itself is a step towards better serving users. However, it is through the combined implementation of all of these components that Library 2.0 can be fully realized. The information environment within which libraries find themselves is changing, probably faster than ever before, which offers great opportunities for progressive libraries to reach out far beyond the boundaries of their buildings and websites, and to engage with an increasingly literate body of information consumers. The library domain has repeatedly evolved to embrace new technologies and to adapt in line with changing expectations, and it will doubtless continue to do so.

Social Software and Academic Library 2.0

Michael Habib (Habib, 2006), who wrote his master's dissertation on Library 2.0, sees it as occupying the virtual space between academic (Virtual Learning Environments [VLEs] and

Figure 1. Academic Library 2.0 (Habib, 2006). Licensed under Creative Commons.

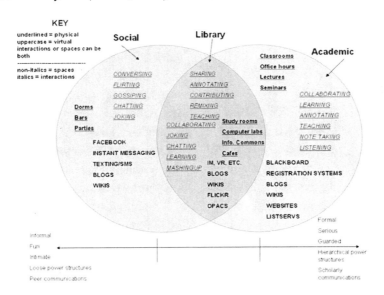

course management systems) and social spaces (Facebook, MySpace, etc.). This very much reflects his view of the physical library as being both a social and academic physical space, as illustrated in the figure below.

Blogging and Academic Libraries

Habib's model features blogs as one of the major social software platforms of Academic Library 2.0, which relies heavily on digital technology. Blogs are probably the most popular and best-known examples of social software. Jorn Berger coined the term "weblog" on 17 December 1997, but they have come to be known, most commonly, "blogs." People maintained blogs long before the term was coined, but blogging gathered momentum with the introduction of automated publishing system. There has been a good deal of interesting litera-ture generated on blogs and libraries in general and their application for academic libraries in particular. Laurel A. Clyde's book, *Weblogs and Libraries* (Clyde, 2004), provides an extensive overview of the concept and process of blogging, lists a plethora of resources, and discusses various

types of blogging software, strategies and tools for finding weblogs, and a detailed planning process for creating and maintaining weblogs, among other things. Sauers, 2006 and Casey & Savastinuk, 2007 are also helpful resources.

What Makes Academic Library Blogging Valuable?

One of the most valuable aspects of a blog is that it can act as a Content Management System (CMS) to provide a platform for disclosure of informa-tion relevant in e-learning contexts. Academic librarians can assume the role of managing that content and be active in discovering and disclos-ing information relevant to academics, students, and the university community in general. Coulter and Draper, 2006, note another valuable aspect, arguing for the potential value of weblogs as community-building and learning tools in higher education, and reporting their use of blogs as a supplement to face-to-face information literacy instruction and as the sole means of library out-reach to graduate distance learners. Zhuo, 2006, discusses the application of blogs in education in general and in academic libraries in particular, highlighting the contribution of blogs in imparting library instruction.

Blogs as Tool for Communication and Training

Caldwell, 2005 notes that blogging is an excellent way for library staff to communicate with each other and spread their message to a wider audience. Her interviews with some pioneers of academic library blogging suggested many positive outcomes, such as community building and breaking down the 'us versus them' barrier between librarians and patrons. The bloggers noted that the informal nature of blogging can contribute to the library community culture and that a library website is the perfect place to host blogs, especially for universities. Most importantly, blogging is a tangible way of demonstrating to the campus at large the commitment the library has to intellectual freedom and freedom of speech. Similarly, Schrecker, 2008, 127, concludes that

"Blogs, or web logs, are versatile platforms for presenting information to academic library patrons. When combined with academic library web sites, as well as specific web sites for curriculum resource centers, they are capable of enhancing existing web presence and providing opportunity for conversation and communication."

Likewise, Bell, 2005, thinks that blogs have real potential for promoting library services to a community. Given that library users have literally thousands of blogs to choose from, how to draw readers back regularly to the library blog is a challenge he answered by suggesting that the academic library blog be hosted through a Content Management System/Learning Management System. At first, Bell, concerned about students needs, was doubtful of the utility of library blogs postings. He studies, with faculty consent, 20

courses at Philadelphia University to determine whether the students really wanted, needed, and cared about library blog postings. During the spring semester of 2005, postings were added to the Gutman Library blog, "Get It at Gutman," on a regular basis. At the end of the semester, he created a 12-question survey instrument, and 97 students responded. His survey revealed that a vast majority of students (75%) found the library posts useful and indicated that the library should continue to provide this content to the course sites.

As blogging software has grown increasingly user-friendly, many libraries are employing blogs to make their web presence as inviting and interactive as their brick-and-mortar counterparts, according to Brookover, 2007. Libraries are reaping the rewards, too. Well-written, frequently updated public blogs help librarians relate to their patrons, generate support for new building initiatives, and market programs, collections, and services. As we noted above, internal staff blogs can also foster improved staff communication and camaraderie.

It is evident from the extensive literature published in the context of academic library blogging that this initiative contributes to promoting and marketing library services and resources in the digital age. Fichter, 2003, for instance, discusses the use of blogs for promoting and marketing library services. While librarians have seized the opportunities to market libraries in the real world via traditional media like newsletters, brochures, pathfinders etc., they can use blogs for similar purpose. By following simple principles like updating regularly, posting relevant information, and keeping posts short and crisp, librarians can maintain their blogs and promote their library events, resources, and services while ensuring that readers return to their blogs on a regular basis.

Bar-Ilan, 2007, details the use of blogs by libraries and librarians by compiling a list of blogs from data obtained from several lists/directories. After conducting a multifaceted content analysis, the results, in general, indicated that blogs have an impact on information professionals. Blogs are a novel information channel for transferring information to other professionals as well as to non-professionals. Bar-Ilan concludes that librarians use blogs to disseminate information, and to market library events and resources. An example of information dissemination comes from Wilson and Yowell, 2008. They report an effort to help raise awareness about the need for disaster planning in health sciences libraries, undertaken by emergency response planners at the University of Virginia's Claude Moore Health Services Library. These planners considered how best to promote the idea and provide a forum for gathering and exchanging information while maintaining control over content, in order to keep the focus and the quality of the entries consistent. The blog they created has been successful in providing much-needed assistance to hospital and other libraries, both large and small, as well as for individuals and organizations worldwide.

Another use for blogs, in terms of marketing and service promotion, is to raise awareness of library services to on- and off-campus users. Many of the academic library blogs maintained at universities such as the University of Minnesota's UThink Blogs (UThink Blogs, 2009), Fairfield University's Your Voice Counts! (20082008Your Voice Counts! 2008!!), Georgia State University's University Library Blogs (University Library Blogs, 2009) deliver current awareness service. Similarly, Tom Roper, information resources development coordinator for the B&S, at Falmer, Sussex, UK, runs a blog (Roper, 2009) focusing on current state of medical trends that was developed initially for the medical school, but is now hosted by the Higher Education Academy Subject Centre for Medicine, Dentistry and Veterinary Medicine as a national service.

Another area in which blogs can serve as potential tools is in delivering digital current awareness service. A blog is a tool through which communities of information-seekers and information providers can collaborate. Blogs act as organizers of data; each element in a blog is a standard data object that can be referenced. Completeness and accuracy are the traditional measures of success of the reference transaction. The advantage of blogs in this respect, according to Pomerantz & Stutzman, 2004, is that they are a community exercise. If an individual posts inaccurate information, there is a community of readers who are in a position to correct that inaccuracy. In this way, the thread increases in value as, over time, it also comes to be more accurate.

Blogs may also revolutionize the reference function of libraries. Reichardt & Harder, 2005, for example, discuss reference work blogging. They suggest that reference desk blogging is one alternative that can help keep reference team members informed of developments at the reference desk. Likewise, Pomerantz & Stutzman, 2004, explored the use of blogs as a platform for providing reference services, and discussed using Lyceum, an open source software project from ibiblio.org, for this purpose. They claimed that, blogs were not being used by library reference services at all, only by a few online reference services unaffiliated with libraries. In their exploration of the evolution of libraries' uses of blogs, the advantages of conducting the reference transaction as a collaborative effort and the use of blogs as an environment that fosters collaboration, they argued that blogs may be used to good effect in reference services.

Blogs can also be a tool for providing information literacy instruction. For example, Stuart Boon and Sheila Webber, both of the Department of Information Studies at the University of Sheffield, set up the Information Literacy blog (Boon & Webber, 2009). What the blog offers is evident from its title, and the posts are targeted to a wide audience, including librarians, faculty, and non-academics. Boon believes that blogs sit at the heart of the librarian's role (Caldwell, 2005).

Blogging as Part of Alterative Models of E-Learning

From the literature, we see that blogs can be used for promoting and supplementing e-learning. Although social software tools like blogs are not created primarily for educational purposes, they can be easily adapted to support learning. Using social software can help facilitate an approach to e-learning, which differs from using a Learning Management System (LMS), as Dalsgaard, 2006, notes. The personal tools and social networks support a self-governed, problem-based, and collaborative learning process.

According to Glogoff, 2005, instructional blogging operates as a knowledge-centred instructional tool. In this model, the instructor involves students in research activities, engages them in discussion with practitioners, and leads them through developmental concepts of the discipline's knowledge domain. As a valuable e-learning tool, blogging can be used in a number of ways to engage students in discussion, exploration, and discovery. It is appropriate for both hybrid and fully online courses. In his article, Glogoff, 2004 explains that blogging is a simple and adaptable technology that can be used to construct learning environments that work well with receptive, directive, and guided discovery instructional techniques.

Through their empirical study, Williams & Jacobs, 2004, conclude that blogs have the potential, at least, to be a truly transformational technology in that they provide students with a high level of autonomy while simultaneously providing opportunity for greater interaction with peers. They suggest that blogging tools would be a valuable addition to any LMS. Likewise, Hall & Davison, 2007, report an investigation of blog technology's potential for encouraging interaction among students, and its consequences in terms of peer learning and support on a module of an accredited LIS degree programme. Content analysis of the collected data revealed that blogs offer comparable and additional benefits to students'

projects designed to encourage reflective engagement with teaching materials, such as learning journals. Instead of being merely an option for providing online information, they recommend that blogs should be seen as learning tools in their own right.

Blogging as Part of Effective Knowledge Management and Sharing

Röll, 2004, states that weblogs serve as personal publishing tools for knowledge workers in the digital world and support the process of knowledge work. Besides being personally beneficial to the knowledge worker, blogging also helps in disseminating knowledge throughout an organization. Basing his assessment of knowledge work processes on the Framework of Knowledge Work analysis developed by Efimova, 2004, Röll quotes a relevant passage from her article, which is very much relevant to the functions mostly performed by the academic librarians in the digital world: "Much of the work of finding, interpreting and connecting relevant pieces of information, negotiating meanings and eliciting knowledge in conversations with others, creating new ideas and using them to come up with a final product, happens in the head of a knowledge worker or as a part of communication or doing work." (Efimova, 2004, 3). Röll concludes that blogs support knowledge work by providing a space to capture information, annotate it, reflect on it, get feedback, share, discuss and network with others. They also provide organizational benefits. Blogging can facilitate corporate/organizational story telling, an ace leadership and motivational technique and a powerful concept for knowledge sharing in organizations. Since blogs have a human voice, they encourage interaction with the author and other readers, as well as providing context a point well noted by Nichani & Rajamanickam, 2001.

In light of all this research, we maintain that the research and literature provide a substantial base for the assumption that academic librarians are equivalent to knowledge workers, and that blogging helps organize their work to better manage and share knowledge.

Blogging as a Means of Reaching Out to Distance Learners

Today's increasingly e-learning culture collapses the boundaries between regular on-site students and off-campus, external programme students, i.e., distance learners. Hence, academic librarians are playing the roles of instructors and knowledge workers by reaching out to them with the help of social networking tools like blogs.

There is a body of literature and research that demonstrates that blogging is an excellent means of reaching out to distance learners. Secker & Price, 2007, for example, describe a recent project funded by the University of London to explore how social software of Web 2.0 technologies can enhance the use of libraries by distance learners. LASSIE, funded by the Centre for Distance Education, University of London, was a 9-month project completed in December 2007. The project addressed concerns at the University of London that the external programme students, i.e., their distance learners around the world, were not making full use of electronic library resources. The reasons for this were thought to be varied, including low awareness of how to access library resources and information literacy issues. The project explored how the provision of appropriate social software might impact the use of library services by distance learners. Their exploration was a four-step project plan:

1. Conduct a literature review on physical libraries as social spaces;
2. Explore the current use of social software in libraries;
3. Evaluate the potential of social software in libraries;
4. Identify specific external programme courses to pilot social software tools and evaluate their impact on student learning, using an email questionnaire and interviews to gather qualitative data.

The LASSIE Project performed an extensive literature review that focused on topics such as libraries and distance learners, libraries as social spaces, Web 2.0, Library 2.0, overview of Web 2.0 technologies, and libraries using social software. Based on different social software being used in libraries, case studies for each of its uses were developed and dealt with online reading lists; social bookmarking; podcasts and screencasts; blogging as a social software; and, finally, the use of Facebook by libraries. Of special interest to the authors of this chapter is the fourth case study, which explored libraries and blogging. This study provides good practice guidance for librarian bloggers and discusses the set up, maintenance, and role of several different blogs, and showed that a blog to support distance education could be used successfully.

Another supporter of using blogs in distance education is Todd Bryant (Byrant, 2006). In his paper, Bryant discusses the application and implications of blogging for educational purposes. For Bryant, a blog is the first tool that comes to mind when thinking about social software. He strongly supports blogging as a tool for reaching out to students and faculty in order to fulfill their information needs.

In spite of the research cited here, it is evident from the literature that there is lack of targeted library services for distance learners. Despite the mammoth growth of distance education, very few academic institutions have a distance education librarian or a librarian for extending distance library services. In a fast-growing economy like India, this initiative would be desirable and of utmost importance, given the increasing number of distance learning institutions.

Developing social software for blogging will highly benefit off-campus users by helping them access library resources remotely. Much as learning environment are changing in on-campus programmes, where students and faculty are increasingly employing virtual and e-library services on their desktops and laptops, the same technology can be used and adapted for distance learners.

Indeed, we suggest that distance learning institutions should begin to think along these lines and consider providing effective library support to distance learners. The possibility of maximizing the use of social software in a developing country such as India provides some fascinating alternatives. Though guidelines for providing library services to distance learners exist, whether from Association of College and Research Libraries (ACRL), American Library Association (ALA), Commonwealth of Learning (COL) topical guide (Watson, 2003) and the Indian Library Association (ILA), we argue that precise policies need to be laid down for initiating and implementing them.

For example, the COL Topical Guide on Developing Library and Information Services for Distance Education mentions the most important distance library service considerations to be timeliness of service; high level and quality access to distance library materials; and, where possible, to initiate and maintain personal contact with students and faculty. We argue that these considerations can be addressed largely by embracing social software in providing distance library services, and by blogging in particular. Blogging, as a web-based technology, addresses the issue of timeliness as well diminishing physical barriers. An experienced librarian who is an effective blogger can fulfill the information needs of distance learners and ensure the quality of information posts, references, and referrals. Furthermore, blogs, by being a collaborative tool that allow discussions among and contributions from many, can satisfy information needs. Finally, blogs offer a human touch, encourage conversation, and provide context. All of this

addresses the personal contact factor listed in the COL topical guide.

Summary

We have looked at a number of items in this section. First, we discussed the concepts of Web 2.0 and Library 2.0. Then we examined social software and its relations to Library 2.0, especially Academic Library 2.0. Next, we looked at a high-level overview of blogging and academic libraries, and the value of blogs in a number of contexts. After that, we outlined several examples of how blogs are used in academic libraries, whether as new tools to offer traditional services, as part of alternative models of e-learning, an element of effective knowledge management and sharing, and as a means of reaching out to distance learners. Our hope, in our review of the research and literature, is that we have shown that blogging is a valuable tool for academic librarians.

CASE STUDY – BLOGGING AS PART OF DAILY INTERACTION WITH PATRONS

Robbins Library Notes (Pannone, 2007-2009), which you can access at http://blogs.law.harvard.edu/pannone/ was begun in August 2007 in response to three needs. First, was the need to deliver timely and relevant information to patrons; second, to counter the prevalent false perception about the paucity of philosophically related resources at Harvard; and third, to be in line with department expectation of an increase in the use of technology for pedagogical and research purposes.

As noted above, the first reason that led to the creation of Robbins Library Notes was a desire to use an alternative way to deliver timely and relevant information to patrons about electronic and print resources, and bibliographic instruction. Offering print pathfinders and creating static web pages was found to be of little use or help, to patrons, and there was relatively little interest in bibliographic instruction, in spite of heavy marketing on the author's part.

The second reason was to counter a prevalent false perception about the paucity of philosophically related resources at Harvard. Many patrons complained that the few databases of which they were aware did not contain articles and resources they needed. Despite attempts to educate patrons in a variety of formats about available databases and resources, these efforts were bearing little fruit.

Third, the Department of Philosophy chair is strongly encouraging faculty to embrace technology (e.g., personal web sites, course web sites, and the like) as part of their teaching and research efforts. Thus, blogging makes sense as a way to fulfill this expectation.

Using a Blog in Daily Patron Interaction

Robbins Library Notes are used for a variety of purposes. A few examples of these uses follow

Several early posts focus on the most relevant databases for philosophy-related research, to educate patrons about the various electronic resources they might want to consult when doing research. These Database Overviews highlight what the respective database is, its strengths and weaknesses, tricks and ways to maximize its use, and in what contexts it is most valuable. Sample searches are included with each overview, along with updates to the databases as they become available.

The author created several cheat sheets, distilling best practices for searching, and posting them on a special "Bibliographic Instruction" page. These cheat sheets cover the basics of searching, using search limiters, thinking differently about searching, and so forth, and can be easily accessed from the blog home page. Related to bibliographic instruction, the Notes often features a "Question of the Week," based on a complicated reference question that was received during the week. The

process for resolving the question is outlined, step-by-step, so that readers can incorporate the process in their research strategies. These posts have been popular and helpful, and readers often post alternative strategies to find information, which benefits everyone.

Blogging can be a useful place to highlight a book, journal, or item of interest for patrons, whether a table of contents or a review. A good number of posts have focused on these items. On occasion, the author publishes an editorial on technology, the future of libraries, and the like. This can be a place to make the case for maintaining a physical library space, and to promote the value of libraries and librarians. Robbins Library Notes has contained posts that debate the value and future of e-books, the ubiquity of Google, and the place of Wikipedia in academic research.

Robbins Library Notes, from time to time, also incorporates humorous posts, which is appropriate on an academic library blog, if they are not excessive or in poor taste. The humor posts on Robbins Library Notes generally, though not always, have a philosophical bent, fitting for a philosophy department library blog. Including these posts helps to prevent the blog from getting stale and stodgy; they also can be used to promote certain services, e.g., a video of the "first IT call" to promote bibliographic instruction.[2] We hope that the above will give some indication as to why an academic librarian might set up a blog, and how it might be used to interact with patrons.

CASE STUDY – BLOGGING FOR REACHING OUT TO DISTANCE LEARNERS

Dayalbagh Educational Institute has its roots in the field of education beginning in 1917 and was conferred Deemed University status in 1981. Imparting education till Ph.D. level in disciplines including the sciences, arts, social sciences, education, commerce, and engineering, the Institute has Memorandum of Understanding (MoU) with various institutes and universities of global repute such as IITs in India, University of Maryland (College Park, USA), and the University of Waterloo (Canada), to name a few. The Institute ventured into the field of distance education in the year 2004, offering educational programmes to those unable to matriculate on campus due to physical location or lack of funding, to facilitate flexi-time, flexi-place learning to all, at their doorstep, imparted on par with on-site education. Programmes are currently available in vocational skills, and at the undergraduate levels, and are operational at 71 study centres in India and abroad. For more information about the Institute, please visit http://www.dei.ac.in.

After four successful years in distance education, the academic administrators of the Institute felt there was a strong need for the Institute to extend library support to the study centres. Accordingly, a coordinator for extending these services was identified. Generally, distance learners, removed from direct teaching and devoid of face-to-face teaching and interaction, occupy an ambiguous space and are often unsure of how to find additional information resources. Any effort by the librarian to reach out to such learners would definitely be welcomed. Once the librarian bridges this gap with distance learners through electronic/digital media, such as through e-mail, instant messaging, discussion forums and listservs, which are not constrained by time, they can be at ease in utilizing the resource to seek out information.

Developing the Blog

Given the above, interacting with distance learners over a blogging platform becomes an effective and simple alternative. Hence, in September 2008 a blog, Distance Library Services (Prakash, 2008-2009), which can be accessed at http://kshema-distancelibraryservices.blogspot.com was initiated. The objectives for creating this blog were to

- Provide a common platform for the distance learners to interact with the coordinator for their information needs. It was intended to serve as a common platform to share information and support peer learning for the students.
- Create awareness related to library and information resources among distance learners.
- Initiate and promote library instruction and information literacy among distance learners.
- Provide information resources to distance learners through electronic/digital media.

The potential target groups for the blog were the students in the undergraduate, post–graduate, and diploma programmes. Though students in the vocational programmes were not the potential audience, the author of the blog posted useful reading materials for course coordinators, developers, and mentors and facilitators who served as teaching mediators at the study centres.

The blog initiative was given wide publicity through emails to faculty, staff, and students. Good response was received from course coordinators, developers, administrative and academic functionaries at several study centres, and some post-graduate students. Of the responses received from students, the majority were from those earning a post-graduate diploma in theology.

Challenges, Uses, and Opportunities

The librarian blogger has limited time to devote to updating and maintaining the library blog. Sometimes a mere 10 to 15 minutes is sufficient, but with a growing readership and an increasing number of topics to cover, time management is becoming an increasingly important and necessary skill. Additionally, care is taken to post only relevant, authentic and quality information, following Institute's guidelines about posting in electronic/digital media.

Other challenges include the fact that blogs cannot target all audiences regularly. Getting target readers to the blog is another challenge. And unless there is regular response from the target audience, communication remains one-directional. Regular responses, or the lack thereof, affect the momentum of the blog. In fact, we argue that the overall success of a blog can be measured by patron interaction. While a stat-counter is an effective way to measure the number of hits and visits a blog receives, patron interaction remains the more reliable indicator of its success.

There are many other potential uses of the Distance Library Services blog. Not only does blogging help to reach out to distance learners but it will also be useful to communicate with the administrators of various distance learning centres. When an academic institution initiates a distance learning programme, the study centres are also expected to maintain libraries, though small, at their respective centres for the convenience of the students registered with the centre. If the centre is located in an already operating academic location, setting up and/or maintaining the centre's libraries does not pose too much of a problem to the centre administrators. If the administrators are new to the field, they may face problems in providing learning and information support to the centres' students. In such instances, the librarian(s) at the main branch can help support them in establishing and maintaining libraries at the centres. They can adopt various modern electronic/digital methods to interact with the centres' administrators, such as e-mail, instant messaging, being available by telephone, and so forth, so that the job can be done in a timely and accurate fashion. Blogs are particularly useful in this case. Because of the versatile features of such methods, the librarian can easily and effectively interact with the centres and offer solutions and services efficiently and effectively. With the availability of various collaborative software tools like e-snips, slideshare, and embeddable media tools, the librarian can now host a range of instructional materials, audios, videos, podcasts etc., by which to instruct and assist administrators in setting up their own libraries.

The author of Distance Education Services, inspired by the LASSIE project success, plans to implement social bookmarking and resource sharing tools, online reading lists, and short screencasts and podcasts about library topics of interest to the readers and academic staff at the study centres in the future. As more programmes targeted at various levels are launched by the University in the near future, there is a positive opportunity for growing reader base and response. The blog will be particularly useful for providing information resources to researchers.

CHALLENGES, LIMITATIONS, AND OBJECTIONS TO BLOGGING

The authors concur there are four challenges for the librarian blogger: daily posting, relevancy, marketing, and being the "public face" of the department.

Posting on a blog daily is difficult, especially when it has to be fit in among other job responsibilities. Writing a good post rather than a slapdash, mediocre post, takes time and effort and must be part of the daily schedule. In addition, the blogger needs to be constantly thinking ahead the next topics.

Relevancy is also a major issue. For example, the topics, philosophers, resources, bibliographic instruction, and such that appear on Robbins Library Notes must be relevant to the patrons' needs and research interests. Moreover, writing well – clearly and concisely, especially in a department full of logicians – with wit and style, to keep the readers interested, is a major part of keeping posts relevant. Similarly, in the case of Distance Library Service, posting information relevant to the students of several different programmes is a challenge, with the problem being the variety in the academic backgrounds and educational levels of learners. All of which makes writing posts targeting specific reader groups tricky. Finally, given the sheer number of blogs in existence now, avoiding being lost in the information overload is a major issue. How to be a recognized voice among many clamoring for patrons' attention is an issue shaping the writing of both blogs.

Connected with relevancy is the issue of marketing. Random Internet searches will not usually turn up little-known blogs. Thus, it is very important to inform patrons early and often about a blog, whether that be through e-mail, e-mail signature, a link on a web site or sites, or some other vector.

Finally, and very importantly, those who write blogs should remember that they are the "public face" of their department or library.

Yet, these challenges are not the only ones would-be academic librarian bloggers face. There are a number of objections to blogging in the literature. Indeed, some have offered sharp criticisms of and strong objections to blogging. Gorman, 2005, for example, has stated that, from his observations, many blogs post poorly written, unedited, and ungrammatical content. His remarks raised a strong response from librarians, the blogging community, and technophiles (Fialkoff, 2005), partly because they interpreted Gorman's comments, as the then-president-elect of ALA, as adding to a perceived negative perception of librarians as anti-technology and obsolete in the digital age. Nevertheless, Gordon, 2005, Fialkoff, 2005, and other senior professionals have expressed their views on how to counter this perception.

Similar negative sentiments on blogging are echoed by Blaise Cronin, Dean and Rudy Professor of Information Science at the School of Library and Information Science, Indiana University at Bloomington, on the school's website. He writes,

Admittedly, some blogs are highly professional, reliable and informative, but most are not. What prompts this kind of digital exhibitionism? The present generation of bloggers seems to imagine

that such crassly egotistical behavior is socially acceptable and that time-honoured editorial and filtering functions have no place in cyberspace. Undoubtedly, these are same individuals who believe that the free-for-all communication approach of Wikipedia is the way forward. Librarians, of course, know better. (Cronin, 2005)

One can argue that there is some truth in what is written by Cronin, Gorman, and others who are unfavorably disposed to blogging. Nonetheless, the authors do not believe these challenges, limitations, and objections to be insurmountable. Indeed, we argue that they can be met with good planning and thoughtfulness, as we will outline in the "Answering Challenges" section, next.

ANSWERING THE CHALLENGES, LIMITATIONS, AND OBJECTIONS

How have the four challenges facing Robbins Library Notes and Distance Library Services – daily posting, relevancy, marketing, and being the "public face" of the department – been answered?

In terms of daily posting, the authors have found that scheduling specific times during the workday to research and write blog posts to be beneficial. We have also assured our respective superiors that we will cut back on or cease blogging if posting begins to interfere with other job responsibilities. These simple steps help minimize the pressure of daily posting, and makes us responsive to readers as well as administration. Relevancy remains a difficult challenge, though a surmountable one. In the case of Robbins Library Notes, the consensus is that the blog does deliver relevant library-related information in a more timely, interactive, and interesting format to patrons, based on the ad hoc feedback. As for Distance Library Services, based on ad hoc feedback, readers have commented that the blog is well written, organized, interesting, and informative. Additionally, readers found it to be very useful both for distance learners and for regular students. Moreover, while the students found it to be a useful source of information, the faculty enjoyed the posts and expressed that it was helpful to have relevant information provided conveniently in one place. Overall, the feedback received for the blogging initiative has been encouraging.

The authors find that being able to offer a variety of formats and media -- text, video, and images, for example -- is helpful. Furthermore, they have also discovered that blogging is also a great vector for offering bibliographic instruction, to be able to outline the method of searching in a precise format, something that audience at all levels could appreciate.

Marketing is also something of a challenge. The author of Robbins Library Notes has had difficulty in getting patrons to actually read the blog, and, even more so, to comment. As the old cliché says, you can lead a horse to water, but you can't make him drink. In spite of an increase in hits and viewings from the blog's launch in 2007 to the end of 2008, it is unclear if this increase is the result of new viewers or aggressive spambots. More frustrating are the reports of patrons who claim to be unaware of Robbins Library Notes, despite having received marketing materials from the author about its existence. Nonetheless, marketing has raised awareness and visibility of Robbins Library Notes, and the hope is that continued publicity will continue to do so in the future. In the case of Distance Library Services, in spite of encouraging initial feedback, getting readers to comment on the posts has been a challenge. At this point, Distance Library Services is something of a one-way conversation. As we noted in the case study for this blog, the success of a blog is scalable and measurable only with responses or discussions and conversations through reader comments. However, given that academic library blogging is nascent in India, it might take time to increase the reader base and encourage them to interact with the blogger. This fact suggests that

there is huge need for marketing and promoting the service.

Finally, in terms of being a "public face," this means making sure that all posts are of high quality and relevance, and reflect well on the Department or the University. It means avoiding topics and views on both blogs that have the potential for reflecting badly on the Department or the University, even inadvertently. An academic library blog should display itself as one of the many valuable services offered to patrons by the library. Thus, the authors do not address contentious political issues or controversies, nor do they express personal views on irrelevant topics. In this way, the blog becomes part of the many attractive features of the department, rather than a detriment. In addition, doing so goes a long way in countering the objections of Gorman, Cronin, and others who perceive blogs as being of little value.

The authors want to remind their readers that blogging is a relatively recent development in academic libraries. As such, it faces a number of growing pains and developmental issues, as it were, while academic librarians experiment and develop best practices for the medium. Supervisors, managers, and other senior staff should work actively with would-be academic librarian bloggers as they experiment and develop policies, to ensure the success of these blogs. Furthermore, policies and guidelines around language, content, frequency, audience, and so forth should be developed. In the interim, would-be academic librarian bloggers should seek clear guidelines about blogging from their respective parent institutions. Lastly, would-be bloggers should take time to consider and plan the content, organization, widgets, tools, and feeds on the blog, so that their target audience will be drawn back to the blog and be encouraged to leave comments and join in the conversation.

PROPOSALS

There are five proposals we offer to would-be academic librarian bloggers. The first is obvious – blogging is hard work. Do not underestimate the time that will be spent planning, setting up, and maintaining a blog. However, while blogging is a lot of work, it is also a lot of fun. One will learn a great deal from blogging, whether in terms of developing one's writing skills, researching a post, interacting with readers, or making new connections inside and outside the library. Thus, it is important to keep the element of fun in place.

The second proposal is to get approval from your superior and determine the interest of your patrons before you start blogging. Make sure to lay out your case, to see if they think a blog is something that will be of benefit to them and to you. Making your case will help in planning how to incorporate a blog into your daily work routine. By getting permission and determining interest, you will generate good will, excitement, and publicity for the blog. Finally, it will help to set limits on what the blog will and will not cover, aiding in being the "public face" of library.

The third proposal is to leave room for failure and learning. Mistakes and failures can be good learning experiences, so do not be afraid to commit them as you go about blogging.

Fourth, and connected with the third proposal, is to tinker with the blog. Always think of new ways to present content. Ask constantly, "What sort of things might my readers be interested in? Is there a new widget for your blog that may perk it up? Is the format helpful, or distracting?" Ask your readers, too, for feedback on things they would like to see, formatting issues, and so forth. They will give feedback, which helps to establish rapport with them.

Finally, have no regrets about blogging. In other words, view blogging as an experiment: if it cannot be made to work, take what can be learned from the experience and walk away, without regret. Doing so helps to keep a sense of perspective and a sense of humility, as well as a sense of detachment.

CONCLUSION

We have tried to argue in this chapter that blogging is a useful and effective means of communication with patrons that has not fully been exploited by librarians. In looking at the history of blogging in academic libraries, and in outlining the challenges, limitations, and objections to blogging, and responding to them, we have tried to show that, in spite of the difficulties, blogging is a worthwhile practice for academic librarians. Through commenting on the research and offering our own experiences, we have tried to illustrate how blogging can be a fruitful part of the work of an academic librarian. We hope that our work will encourage other academic librarians to start their own blogs.

ACKNOWLEDGMENT

Dr. Kshema Prakash and Dr. K. Santi Swarup would like to acknowledge with thanks Prof. V.G. Das, Director, and Prof. V.B. Gupta, Coordinator, Distance Education, Dayalbagh Educational Institute (Deemed University), Dayalbagh for kindly permitting to publish the work.

Mr. Jason Pannone, the author of Robbins Library Notes, would like to acknowledge with thanks Dr. Michael Hemmett, Harvard University, for extending an invitation to present material that laid the foundation for the Notes case study at the 24 September 2008 Plug n' Play meeting at Harvard University.

Finally, the authors would also like to thank Ms. Ann Bledsoe for her valuable suggestions in preparing the chapter.

REFERENCES

Bar-Ilan, J. (2007). The use of Weblogs (blogs) by librarians and libraries to disseminate information. *Information Research, 12*, Paper 323. Retrieved October 17, 2008, from http://InformationR.net/ir/12-4/paper323.html

Bell, S. (2005). Where the Readers Are. *Library Journal*, 8-12. Retrieved February 17, 2009, from http://nrs.harvard.edu/urn-3:hul.eresource:abiinfor

Boon, S., & Webber, S. (2009). *Information Literacy Blog*. Retrieved February 18, 2008, from http://information-literacy.blogspot.com/

Boutin, P. (2008). Twitter, Flickr, Facebook Make Blogs Look So 2004. *Wired Magazine*. Retrieved December 3, 2008, from http://www.wired.com/entertainment/theweb/magazine/16-11/st_essay

Brookover, S. (2007). Why We Blog. *Library Journal, 132*, 28-31. Retrieved 2/18/2009, from http://nrs.harvard.edu/urn-3:HUL.ejournals:sfx954921392997

Bryant, T. (2006). Social Software and academia. *EDUCAUSE Quarterly, 2*, 61–64.

Caldwell, T. (2005). Pen a Blog Buster. *Information World Review*, 16-17. Retrieved 2/17/2009, from http://nrs.harvard.edu/urn-3:hul.eresource:abiinfor

Casey, M. E., & Savastinuk, L. C. (2006). Library 2.0: Service for the next-generation library. *Library Journal*. Retrieved 2/18/2009, from http://www.libraryjournal.com/article/CA6365200.html

Casey, M. E., & Savastinuk, L. C. (2007). *Library 2.0: A Guide to Participatory Library Service*. Newark, NJ: Information Today, Inc.

Chad, K., & Miller, P. (2005). *Do Libraries Matter? The Rise of Library 2.0*. Retrieved February 19, 2008, from http://www.talis.com/applications/resources/white_papers.shtml

Clyde, L. A. (2004). *Weblogs and Libraries*. Oxford, UK: Chandos Publishers, Ltd.

Coulter, P., & Draper, L. (2006). Blogging It into Them: Weblogs in Information Literacy Instruction. *Journal of Library Administration, 45*(1/2), 101–115. doi:10.1300/J111v45n01_06

Cronin, B. (2005). *Dean's Notes: BLOG: see also Bathetically Ludicrous Online Gibberish*. Retrieved February 19, 2008, from http://www.slis.indiana.edu/news/story.php?story_id=958

Dalsgaard, C. (2006). Social Software: E-learning beyond learning management systems. *European Journal of Open, Distance and E-learning*. Retrieved February 18, 2008, from http://www.eurodl.org/materials/contrib/2006/Christian_Dalsgaard.htm

Efimova, L. (2004). *Discovering the iceberg of knowledge work: A weblog case*. Paper presented at the OKLC 2004. Retrieved January 25, 2008, from https://doc.telin.nl/dscgi/ds.py/Get/File-34786

Fialkoff, F. (2005). The Power of Blogs. *Library Journal, 130*(6), 8–8.

Ficther, D. (2003). Why and How to Use Blogs to Promote Your Library's Services. *Information Today, 17*. Retrieved October 17, 2008, from http://www.infotoday.com/mls/nov03/fichter.shtml

Glogoff, S. (2005). Instructional Blogging: Promoting Interactivity, Student-Centred Learning, and Peer Input. *Innovate: Journal of Online Education, 1*. Retrieved February 19, 2008, from http://innovateonline.info/

Gordon, R. S. (2005). Revenge of the NextGen People. *Library Journal, 130*(9), 78–78.

Gorman, M. (2005). Revenge of the Blog People! *Library Journal, 130*(3), 44–44.

Habib, M. (2006). *Toward Academic Library 2.0: Development and Application of a Library 2.0 Methodology.* Unpublished Master's Dissertation, University of North Carolina, Chapel Hill.

Hall, H., & Davison, B. (2007). Social software as support in hybrid learning environments: The value of the blog as a tool for reflective learning and peer support. *Library & Information Science Research, 29*(2), 163–187. doi:10.1016/j.lisr.2007.04.007

Library 2.0. (2009, February 6). Wikipedia, The Free Encyclopedia. Retrieved February 19, 2009, from http://en.wikipedia.org/w/index.php?title=Library_2.0&oldid=268990356

Maness, J. M. (2006). Library 2.0 Theory: Web 2.0 and Its Implications for Libraries. *Webology, 3.* Retrieved February 18, 2009, from http://www.webology.ir/2006/v3n2/a25.html

Miller, P. (2005). Web 2.0: Building the new library. *Ariadne, 45.* Retrieved February 19, 2008, from http://www.ariadne.ac.uk/issue45/miller/intro.html

Miller, P. (2006). *Library 2.0 - the challenge of disruptive innovation.* Retrieved February 19, 2008, from http://www.talis.com/applications/resources/white_papers.shtml

Nichani, M., & Rajamanickam, V. (2001). Grassroots KM through Blogging. *Elearningpost.com.* Retrieved January 4, 2009, from http://www.elearningpost.com/features/archives/001009.asp

Pannone, J. (2007-2009). Robbins Library Notes. Retrieved November 6, 2008, from http://blogs.law.harvard.edu/pannone/

Pomerantz, J., & Stutzman, F. (2004). *Lyceum: A Blogsphere for Library Reference.* Retrieved February 17, 2009, from http://www.ibiblio.org/fred/pubs/Lyceum.pdf

Prakash, K. (2008-2009). *Distance Library Services.* Retrieved November 6, 2008, from http://kshema-distancelibraryservices.blogspot.com/

Reichardt, R., & Harder, G. (2005). Weblogs: Their use and application in science and technology libraries. *Science & Technology Libraries, 25,* 105-116. Retrieved February 18, 2009, from http://nrs.harvard.edu/urn-3:HUL.ejournals:sfx958480310487

Röll, M. (2004). *Distributed KM – Improving knowledge workers' productivity and organizational knowledge sharing with weblog-based personal publishing.* Paper presented at the Blog Talk 2.0, "The European Conference on Weblogs.

Roper, T. (2009). *Tom Roper's Weblog.* Retrieved February 18, 2009, from http://tomroper.typepad.com/

Sauers, M. P. (2006). *Blogging and RSS: A Librarian's Guide.* Newark, NJ: Information Today.

Schrecker, D. L. (2008). Using Blogs in Academic Libraries: Versatile Information Platforms. *New Library World, 109*(3/4), 117–129. doi:10.1108/03074800810857586

Secker, J. (2008). *Case Study 4: blogging and libraries.* Retrieved February 17, 2009, from http://clt.lse.ac.uk/Projects/Case_study_four_report.pdf

Secker, J., & Price, G. (2007). Libraries, social software and distance learners: blog it, tag it, share it! *New Review of Information Networking, 13*(1), 39–52. doi:10.1080/13614570701754536

Stephens, M., & Casey, M. E. (2005). *Where Do We Begin? A Library 2.0 Conversation with Michael Casey.* ALA Techsource Blog. Posted to http://www.alatechsource.org/blog/2005/12/where-do-we-begin-a-library-20-conversation-with-michael-casey.html

Techsource Blog, A. L. A. Library Technology Reports. (n.d.a.). *Review of Web 2.0 and Libraries: Best Practices for Social Software.* Retrieved 2/20/2009, from http://www.alatechsource.org/ltr/web-20-and-libraries-best-practices-for-social-software

Techsource Blog, A. L. A. Library Technology Reports. (n.d.b). *Review of Web 2.0 & Libraries, Part 2: Trends and Technologies.* Retrieved February 20, 2009, from http://www.alatechsource.org/ltr/web-20-libraries-part-2-trends-and-technologies

University Library Blogs. (2009). Retrieved February 18, 2009, from http://homer.gsu.edu/blogs/library/

UThink Blogs. (2009). Retrieved February 18, 2009, from http://blog.lib.umn.edu/uthink/start.phtml

Voice Counts, Y. (2008). Retrieved February 18, 2009, from http://blog.fairfield.edu/summerreading2008/

Watson, E. F. (2003). *Developing Library and Information Services for Distance Education.* Retrieved February 18, 2009, from http://www.col.org/resources/publications/trainingresources/knowledge/Pages/library.aspx

Williams, J. B., & Jacobs, J. (2004). Exploring the use of blogs as learning spaces in the higher education sector. *Australasian Journal of Educational Technology, 20*(2), 232–247.

Wilson, D. T., & Yowell, S. S. (2008). Resourceful Blogging: Using a blog for information sharing. *Medical Reference Services Quarterly, 27*(2), 183–210. doi:10.1080/02763860802114660

Zhuo, F. (2006). Blogs in American Academic Libraries: An Overview of Their Present Status and Possible Future Use. In L. Feng et al. (Eds.), Proceedings of Web Information Systems – WISE 2006 Workshops WISE 2006 International Workshops, Wuhan, China, October 23-26, 2006 (Vol. 4256, pp. 145-152). Heidelberg: Springer.

Chapter 6
Web 2.0 and Social Web Approaches to Digital Libraries

Arun Kumar Chakraborty
Bose Institute, India

ABSTRACT

The Chapter begins with a definition of digital library approaches and features, examines ways in which open source and social software applications can serve to fill digital library roles. In order to incorporate Web 2.0 functionality effectively, digital libraries must fundamentally recast users not just as content consumers, but as content creators. This chapter analyzes the integration of social annotations – uncontrolled user-generated content – into digital collection items. The chapter briefly summarizes the value of annotations and finds that there is conceptual room to include user-generated content in digital libraries, that they have been imagined as forums for social interaction since their inception, and that encouraging a collaborative approach to knowledge discovery and creation might make digital libraries serve as boundary objects that increase participation and engagement. The chapter concludes with a review of positive and negative outcomes from this approach and makes recommendations for further research.

INTRODUCTION

Public awareness of the Net as a critical infrastructure in the 1990s has spurred a new revolution in the technologies for information retrieval in digital libraries. The chapter discusses the development and usage of new information technology for substantial collections. (Schatz, and Chen, 1999).

What are digital libraries, how should they be designed, how will they be used, and what relationship will they bear with "libraries"? It is hard to answer all these critical questions in this short chapter, we do hope to argue, and in some small enumerate to shape, the dialog among computer

DOI: 10.4018/978-1-61520-767-1.ch006

scientists, librarians, and other interested parties out of which answers may arise. Our involvement here is to make unambiguous, and to question, certain assumptions that motivate current digital library efforts. We will squabble that current efforts are limited by a largely unexamined and unintended commitment to an idealized analysis of what libraries have been, rather than what they in reality are or could be. Since these limits come from current ways of thinking about the problem, rather than being inherent in the technology or in social practice, expanding our conception of digital libraries should serve to expand the scope and the utility of development efforts. This chapter also discusses the use of social software applications in digital library environments. It finds the use of blogging software as an interface to digital library content stored in a separate repository. (Mitchell, and Gilbertson, 2008).

A significant portion of digital library literature focuses on issues such as document/technology heterogeneity and the relationship of users and communities in digital libraries [Borgman, 1996; Lagoze, Krafft, and Payette, 2005; Renda, and Straccia, 2005].

There are a number of possible approaches to using social software in digital library environments. Downloadable applications such as MediaWiki or WordPress blogging software lend themselves to data and interface customization. Other sites, such as Flickr, support data storage and application programming interface functions that could be used to create a digital library application.

Digital libraries are complex sociotechnical artifacts that are much more than searchable electronic collections. Even initial definitions in the literature were fairly broad; Borgman, (1999) bisects the conceptions of digital libraries into those of researchers (content collected on behalf of user communities) and librarians (digital libraries as institutions or services). At that time, digital library literature was understandably concerned with mapping the boundaries of the field, and

Lesk (1999) identifies an inadequate focus on user needs in digital library research.

Social institutions today look enormously different from what they did even five years ago. An array of forces, most specifically economic changes and technological progress, have reshaped and redefined our notions of what constitutes a bank, a service station, or a bookstore.

This chapter is an attempt to facilitate library professionals to comprehend some of the changes in relation to Web 2.0 and social web approaches to digital libraries. These changes are affecting libraries in the approaching years, and prompt library professionals need to consider seriously about how to deal with these changes.

The chapter begins by outlining the far-reaching changes involving different types of institutions. It then reviews how technological trends have been affecting library services, and focuses on the implications of an increasing dependence on resources not controlled by the local library. The chapter then lays out a set of key areas that will challenge libraries in an online age, before discussing a number of the hazards that libraries will face.

This chapter highlights the idea of Web 2.0 to a sociological audience as a key example of a process of cultural digitization that is moving faster than our ability to analyse it. It offers a definition, a schematic overview and a typology of the notion as part of a commitment to a renewal of description in sociology. It provides examples of wikis, folksonomies, mashups and social networking sites and, where possible and by way of illustration, examines instances where sociology and sociologists are featured. The chapter then identifies three possible agendas for the development of a viable sociology of Web 2.0: the changing relations between the production and consumption of internet content; the mainstreaming of private information posted to the public domain; and, the emergence of a new rhetoric of 'democratisation'. The chapter concludes by discussing some of the ways in which we can engage with these new web applications and go about developing sociological understandings of the new online culture as they become increasingly significant in the mundane routines of everyday life. Viewing digital libraries as sociotechnical systems, networks of people and technology interacting with society. (Beer, and Roger,2007).

ISSUES, CONTROVERSIES AND PROBLEMS IN SHIFTING SOCIO-ECONOMIC DEVELOPMENT

Technology and economics are shifting all our institutions, particularly those that shape our towns and cities. The substitution of local grocery stores (specially in high rise building and housing societies in urban areas of big cities in India) by chain supermarkets over the past few years has been supplanted by a movement to ever larger superstore markets (such as Pantaloons, Bigbazar, Superstores etc.) and warehouses. These mega-discount stores now account for good amount of grocery and other different item sales by volume.

This recontextualization, consolidation, and movement to larger, less-personal institutions are also affecting the institutions we rely upon for culture. The cinema hall has given way to the mall-based multiplex. Repertory cinemas have almost disappeared, and access to older films is now primarily through video stores. Local independent bookstores are disappearing. The proliferation of chain bookstores and also moving toward superstores.

Our whole social setting is shifting. Institutions that were a dependable part of our social setting for decades are becoming unrecognizable, and services are becoming like commodities -- detached from any particular domain and shifted from one institution to another. Libraries are not immune to these kinds of changes.

TECHNOLOGY TRENDS TRANSFORM LIBRARY SERVICES: SOLUTIONS TO PROBLEMS

Since the 1980s each new step in library automation has revolutionized library services. In observation we could see a number of trends, among them: access from several locations, making additional resources accessible, making information presented in rawer forms, and the role of intermediaries. These trends have been enabled by technological developments in the areas of networking, file storage, and more graphic user interfaces (Besser 1997). They have also been enabled by agreements on standards and protocols (such as Z39.50) which permit the linking together of resources from disparate sources.

Usage from Several Locations

A key outcome of automation was to make access more convenient to library users. In the days of card catalogs, library systems often strained users to travel to a central catalog or multiple branches just to ascertain holdings. Today those users can check with all holdings from workstations throughout the system (and often from home). A split-up library service from a physical location provokes intense disparity in what a library is.

Building a System to Access More Resources

For many years library automation systems were thought of as merely ways of delivering only bibliographic records (essentially online card catalogs). But over time these systems have been greater than before with more services. Many library automation systems currently carry indexing and abstracting services. And on a number of college / university / research campuses offer non-library information services (such as phone listings, course descriptions, class schedules, pre-enrollment capabilities) that are being delivered through the same system delivering library automation.

Making Information Available in Cruder Forms

The types of information available to users in digital form has continued to proliferate. If we consider a bibliographic record to be a "representation" of an original book or article, then over the past decade we have been providing users with more and more truer representations (i.e. representations that are closer and closer to the original raw material).

Thinning Roles for Mediators

The success of library automation has meant that users increasingly interact with online systems, and have less reliance upon library staff. Many of today's systems allow users to check circulation information without ever contacting the circulation department. Many ILL experiments let the user request a work without ever interacting with a library staff member.

Implications of Library Focus on Remote Resources

We are already seeing a change in the world of libraries. Libraries are becoming less important for the materials they collect or house, and more important for the kind of material they can obtain in response to user requests. This movement from collecting material "just in case" someone will need it, to delivering material from elsewhere "just in time" to answer a user's needs, is a profound shift for the library as an institution. This shift is a direct result of the recent proliferation of digital networking in an environment where standards for description were already well established.

Best-Seller Phenomenon

Economies-of-scale makes mass-distributed information cheap and available, and can lead to an environment where smaller-audience information is more expensive and harder to find (Besser, 1995d). Over time this may well lead to the favoring of electronic delivery of entertainment over delivery of information (Besser 1994a).

Consolidation of Electronic Information Distributors

As corporate mergers, buy-outs, and consolidations leave us with fewer and fewer independent information providers, how will that change what information people get? Will large conglomerates with interests in many different types of industries begin to treat their information distribution divisions the same way they treat all their other commodity distribution divisions?

Privacy

As people begin to pay for the information they receive electronically, what kind of privacy issues does this raise? Will reading and buying habits be traced and sold as demographic data? Can libraries continue to take their strong traditional privacy stand when providing pay-per-view information?

Access

Who will guarantee access in an era when someone must pay for each byte of information that is accessed? Can libraries continue to provide free (or subscription-fee) access to all their constituents in a pay-per-view era? Will society become divided between information *haves* and *have-nots?*

Enriching and Economic Diversity

Will the world of online digital information lead to more or less variety in that information? Will the best-seller phenomenon take hold and make available only *least-common-denominator* information (as in broadcast television)? Will the information needs of the less affluent be met in ways that they can afford?

WEB 2.0: ISSUES, PROBLEMS AND CONTROVERSIES

While the term is widely defined and interpreted, "Web 2.0" was reportedly first conceptualized and made popular by Tim O'Reilly and Dale Dougherty of O'Reilly Media in 2004 to describe the trends and business models that survived the technology sector market crash of the 1990s (O'Reilly, 2005). As O'Reilly (2005) observes in what is often cited as the seminal work on Web 2.0, personal web-pages are evolving into blogs, encyclopedias into Wikipedia, text-based tutorials into streaming media applications, taxonomies into "folksonomies," and question-answer/email customer support infrastructures into instant messaging (IM) services.

The implications of this revolution in the Web are enormous. Librarians are only beginning to acknowledge and write about it, primarily in the "biblioblogosphere" (weblogs written by librarians). Journals and other more traditional literatures have yet to fully address the concept, but the application of Web 2.0 thinking and technologies to library services and collections has been widely framed as "Library 2.0" (Miller, 2005a; 2005b; 2006a; 2006b; Notess, 2006).

Within 15 years the Web has grown from a group work tool for scientists across the globe into a global information space with more than a few billion users. Currently, it is both returning to its roots as a read/write tool and also entering a new, more social and participatory phase. These trends

have led to a feeling that the Web is entering a 'second phase'—a new, 'improved' Web version 2.0. But how justified is this perception?

The different reports establish that Web 2.0 is more than a set of 'cool' and new technologies and services, important though some of these are. It has, at its heart, a set of at least six powerful ideas that are changing the way some people interact. Secondly, it is also important to acknowledge that these ideas are not necessarily the preserve of 'Web 2.0', but are, in fact, direct or indirect reflections of the power of the network: the strange effects and topologies at the micro and macro level that a billion Internet users produce. This might well be why Sir Tim Berners-Lee, the creator of the World Wide Web, maintains that Web 2.0 is really just an extension of the original ideals of the Web that does not warrant a special moniker. However, business concerns are increasingly shaping the way in which we are being led to think and potentially act on the Web and this has implications for the control of public and private data. Indeed, Tim O'Reilly's original attempt to articulate the key ideas behind Web 2.0 was focused on a desire to be able to benchmark and therefore identify a set of new, innovative companies that were potentially ripe for investment.

As with other aspects of university life the library has not escaped considerable discussion about the potential change afforded by the introduction of Web 2.0 and social media. There needs to be a distinction between concerns around quality of service and 'user-centred change' and the services and applications that are being driven by Web 2.0 ideas. This is particularly important for library collection and preservation activities and some of the key questions for libraries are: is the content produced by Web 2.0 services sufficiently or fundamentally different to that of previous Web content and, in particular, do its characteristics make it harder to collect and preserve? Are there areas where further work is needed to be done by researchers and library specialists? (Anderson, Paul, 2007)

'Web 2.0' or 'Web 1.0'?

Web 2.0 is a slippery character to pin down. Is it a revolution in the way we use the Web? Is it another technology 'bubble'? It rather depends on who you ask. A Web technologist will give quite a different answer to a marketing student or an economics professor. The short answer, for many people, is to make a reference to a group of technologies which have become deeply associated with the term: blogs, wikis, podcasts, RSS feeds etc., which facilitate a more socially connected Web where everyone is able to add to and edit the information space. The longer answer is rather more complicated and pulls in economics, technology and new ideas about the connected society. To some, though, it is simply a time to invest in technology again—a time of renewed exuberance after the dot-com bust.

For the inventor of the Web, Sir Tim Berners-Lee, there is a tremendous sense of *déjà vu* about all this. When asked in an interview for a podcast, published on IBM's website, whether Web 2.0 was different to what might be called Web 1.0 because the former is all about connecting people, he replied: *"Totally not. Web 1.0 was all about connecting people. It was an interactive space, and I think Web 2.0 is of course a piece of jargon, nobody even knows what it means. If Web 2.0 for you is blogs and wikis, then that is people to people. But that was what the Web was supposed to be all along. And in fact, you know, this 'Web 2.0', it means using the standards which have been produced by all these people working on Web 1.0."1* (Laningham,Ed.2006).

To understand Sir Tim's attitude one needs look back at the history of the development of the Web, which is explored in his book *Weaving the Web* (1999). His original vision was very much of a collaborative workspace where everything was linked to everything in a 'single, global information space' (p. 5), and, crucially for this discussion, the assumption was that 'everyone would be able to edit in this space'. The first development was Enquire, a rudimentary project management tool, developed while Berners-Lee was working at CERN, which allowed pages of notes to be linked together and edited. A series of further technological and software developments led to the creation of the World Wide Web and a browser or Web client that could view *and edit* pages of marked-up information (HTML).

However, during a series of ports to other machines from the original development computer, the ability to edit through the Web client was not included in order to speed up the process of adoption within CERN (Berners-Lee, 1999). This attitude to the 'edit' function continued through subsequent Web browser developments such as ViolaWWW and Mosaic (which became the Netscape browser). Crucially, this left people thinking of the Web as a medium in which a relatively small number of people published and most browsed, but it is probably more accurate to picture it as a fork in the road of the technology's development, one which has meant that the original pathway has only recently been rejoined. The term 'Web 2.0' was officially coined in 2004 by Dale Dougherty, a vice-president of O'Reilly Media Inc. (the company famous for its technology-related conferences and high quality books) during a team discussion on a potential future conference about the Web (O'Reilly, 2005a). The team wanted to capture the feeling that despite the dot-com boom and subsequent bust, the Web was 'more important than ever, with exciting new applications and sites popping up with surprising regularity' (O'Reilly, 2005a, p.1).

Core Point of Web 2.0

There are a few core points that we should hold on to when thinking about Web 2.0 and how it might impact on education: firstly, that Web 2.0 is more than a set of 'cool' and new technologies and services, important though some of these are. It is actually a series of at least six powerful ideas or drivers that are changing the way some people interact. Secondly, it is also important to acknowledge that these ideas are not necessarily the preserve of 'Web 2.0', but are, in fact, direct or indirect reflections of the power of the network: the strange effects and topologies at the micro and macro level that a billion Internet users produce. This might well be why Sir Tim Berners-Lee maintains that Web 2.0 is really just an extension of the original ideals of the Web which does not warrant a special mention; but the fact that business concerns are starting to shape the way in which we are being led to think and potentially act on it means that we need to at least be more aware of these influences. For example, many of the Web 2.0 services are provided by private, often American companies. Start-up companies tend to either fail or be bought out by one of a triumvirate of corporates: Google, Yahoo and Microsoft. This raises questions about the ownership of the user data collected. May be delineating Web from Web 2.0 will help us to do that. And finally, there are profound intellectual property debates ahead as individuals, the public realm and corporations clash over ownership of the huge amounts of data that Web 2.0 is generating and the new ways of aggregating and processing it. This chapter elaborates that integrating Web 2.0-type social annotations into digital libraries can serve the larger goals of supporting users' information seeking needs and practices, and encourage increased exploration and engagement. Imagining students, researchers and the public interacting around a digital library collection item via social annotations is an attractive idea. An unobtrusive list of social annotations associated with digital library collection items would allow alternative views of digital content, and create a sense of collaborative endeavor.

EDUCATIONAL AND INSTITUTIONAL: PROBLEMS AND ISSUES

There is significant debate over the alleged advantages and disadvantages of incorporating social software into mainstream education. This is compounded by the fact that there is very little reliable, original pedagogic research and evaluation evidence and that to date, much of the actual experimentation using social software within higher education has focused on particular specialist subject areas or research domains (Fountain, 2005). Indeed, JISC recently announced an open call to investigate the ways that this technology is being used by staff and students and identify opportunities for integration with existing institutional IT systems. In this section focus is on the following four areas: learning and teaching, scholarly research, academic publishing, and libraries.

Teaching

One of the most in-depth reviews undertaken in the UK of the potential impact of social software on education has been carried out by the Nesta-funded FutureLab. Their recent report, *Social Software and Learning* (Owen et al. 2006), reviews the emerging technologies and discusses them in the context of parallel, developing trends in education. These trends tend towards more open, personalised approaches in which the formal nature of human knowledge is under debate and where, within schools and colleges, there is a greater emphasis on lifelong learning and supporting the development of young people's skills in creativity and innovation.

Within higher education, wikis have been used at the University of Arizona's Learning Technologies Centre to help students on an information studies course who were enrolled remotely from across the USA. These students worked together to build a wiki-based glossary of technical terms they learned while on the course (Glogoff, 2006). At the State University of New York, the Geneseo Collaborative Writing Project deploys wikis for students to work together to interpret texts, author articles and essays, share ideas, and improve their research and communication skills collectively. Using wikis in this way provides the opportunity for students to reflect and comment on either their work or others.

Learning

Alexander, (2006) describes social book marking experiments in some American educational research establishments. Alexander also believes that wikis can be useful writing tools that aid composition practice, and that blogs are particularly useful for allowing students to follow stories over a period of time and reviewing the changing nature of how they are commented on by various voices. In these scenarios, education is more like a conversation and learning content is something you perform some kind of operation on rather than 'just' reading it.

Scholarly Research

Tim Berners-Lee's original work to develop the Web was in the context of creating a collaborative environment for his fellow scientists at CERN and in an age when interdisciplinary research, cutting across institutional and geographical boundaries, is of increasing relevance, simple Web tools that provide collaborative working environments are starting to be used. The open nature of Web 2.0, its easy-to-use support for collaboration and communities of practice, its ability to handle metadata in a lightweight manner and the nonlinear nature of some of the technology (what Ted Nelson once called *intertwingled*) are all attractive in the research environment (Rzepa, 2006) and there are four specific technology areas which have seen uptake and development:

Academic Publishing

Speed of communication in fast-moving disciplines is also a benefit offered to academic publishing, where social software technologies increasingly 'form a part of the spectrum of legitimate, accepted and trusted communication mechanisms' (Swan, 2006). Indeed, in the long run, the Web may become the first stage to publish work, with only the best and most durable material being published in paper books and journals, and some of this may introduce a beneficial informality to research (Swan, 2006; JISC Technology and Standards Watch, Feb. 2007).

Such developments are obviously closely tied up with the Open Access debate and the need to free data in order to provide other researchers with access to that data: these datasets will need to be open access before they can be mashed. Those involved in the more formal publishing of research information are actively working on projects that make use of Web 2.0 technologies and ideas. For example, Nature is working on two developments: Open Text Mining Interface (OTMI) and Connotea, a system which helps researchers organize and share their references. Some publishers are also experimenting with new methods of a more open peer reviewing process (Rogers, 2006). Once again, Nature is devoting resources to a system where authors can choose a 'pre-print' option that posts a paper on the site for anyone to comment on, whilst in the meantime the usual peer-reviewing processes are going on behind the scenes. Another website, arXiv, has also been providing pre-publication papers for colleagues to comment on. In addition, the SPIRE project provides a peer-to-peer system for research dissemination.

Libraries, Repositories and Archivings

As with other aspects of university life the library has not escaped considerable discussion about the potential change afforded by the introduction of Web 2.0 and social media (Stanley, 2006). Berube, (2007) provides a very readable summary of some of the implications for libraries and there have been debates about how these technologies may change the library, a process sometimes referred to as 'Library 2.0' a term coined by Mike Casey (Miller, 2006). Proponents argue that new technologies will allow libraries to serve their users in better ways, emphasise user participation and creativity, and allow them to reach out to new audiences and to make more efficient use of existing resources. Perhaps the library can also become a place for the production of knowledge, allowing users to produce as well as consume? Others worry that the label is a diversion from the age-old task of librarianship. However, what is interesting about many of these debates is that they are very broad, sometimes contradictory, and much of the discussion can often be seen in the context of the wider public debate concerning the operation of public services in a modern, technology-rich environment in which user expectations have rapidly changed (Crawford, 2006), rather than Web 2.0 *per se*. For example, comparison has been made between Amazon's book delivery mechanisms and the inter-library loans process (Dempsey, 2006). People worry that library users expect the level of customer service for inter-library loans to be comparable to Amazon's, and while this is obviously an important aspect of what Amazon provides, it is not one of its Web 2.0 features. This is not to say that there is no genuinely Web 2.0-style thinking going on within the Library2.0 debate (for example, in the USA, the Ann Arbor public library online catalogue utilises borrowers' data to produce an Amazon-style, 'readers who borrowed this book, also borrowed' display feature64 and John Blyberg's Go Go Google Gadget, which uses data mash-ups to provide a personalised Google homepage with library data streams showing (http://blogs.nature.com/wp/nascent/2006/04/web_20_in_science.html) popular lendings, only

that it might be helpful for librarians, in terms of thinking about the future of libraries, to separate out the Web 2.0 ideas, services and applications from the technology and more general concerns about 'user-centred change'.

Mark Hepworth (2007) argues that tagging is a form of indexing, blog track backing is similar to citation analysis, blog-rolling echoes chaining and RSS syndication feeds can be considered a form of 'alerting'—all recognised concepts within discussions of IR. This is not to say that they are necessarily the same: whereas traditional IR normally works with an index based on a closed collection of documents, Web searching involves a different type of problem with an enormous scale of documents/pages, a dynamic document base, huge variety of subject domains and other factors (Levene, 2006). However, we can say that the thinking and discussion that has taken place within IR both in traditional systems and more recently in the context of the Web in general (Gudiva et.al., 1997) will have some bearing on an understanding of Web 2.0 services and applications. It may even be the case that Web 2.0 ideas and applications can contribute solutions to some of the recognised existing problems within IR with regard to user behaviour and usability issues (Hepworth, 2007), and even that the newer Web technologies such as RIA may be harnessed to help the user or learner to organise and view data or information more effectively. Another reason why it may be important to think about the ideas behind Web 2.0 is in the issue of the archiving and preservation of content generated by Web 2.0-style applications and services.

LIBRARY 2.0: PROBLEMS, ISSUES AND CONTROVERSIES

According to Miller, (2005a), "Library 2.0" is a term coined by Michael Casey on his Library Crunch blog. Though his writings on Library 2.0

are ground breaking and in many ways authoritative, Casey, (2006a) defines the term very broadly, arguing it applies beyond technological innovation and service. In addition to Casey, other blogging librarians have begun conceptually exploring what Library 2.0 might mean, and because of this disparate discussion with very wide parameters, there is some controversy over the definition and relative importance of the term.

A theory for Library 2.0 could be understood to have these four essential elements:

- It is user-centered. Users participate in the creation of the content and services they view within the library's web-presence, OPAC, etc. The consumption and creation of content is dynamic, and thus the roles of librarian and user are not always clear.
- It provides a multi-media experience. Both the collections and services of Library 2.0 contain video and audio components. While this is not often cited as a function of Library 2.0, it is here suggested that it should be.
- It is socially rich. The library's web-presence includes users' presences. There are both synchronous (e.g. IM) and asynchronous (e.g. wikis) ways for users to communicate with one another and with librarians.
- It is communally innovative. This is perhaps the single most important aspect of Library 2.0. It rests on the foundation of libraries as a community service, but understands that as communities change, libraries must not only change with them, they must allow users to change the library. It seeks to continually change its services, to find new ways to allow communities, not just individuals to seek, find, and utilize information. (Gawrylewski, 2008)

Application of Libraries 2.0: Recommendations and Solution to Problems

"We're in this Google age and people just want to type something in and get results with limited effort," says Marcus Banks, manager of education and information services at the University of California, San Francisco, library. "That frustrates librarians because in some cases it's not that much more effort to get a much better result." Most librarians today have a graduate degree in information or library sciences. And librarians like Osterbur, who has a genetics PhD, often possess degrees in their specialty, such as biology.

Science librarians of today can scope out particular resources for researchers and give lab scholars a tutorial session on special database searching, or hunt down ancient and obscure citations. Here are better ways to get and manage information from popular databases, plus top tips from science librarians on how to make the most of your university and the Internet resources. It is beyond the limited scope of a TechWatch report to do real justice to the wide-ranging debate over of the pedagogical issues but it is perhaps important to point out some of the implications that these issues will have for education in the same way as other sectors:

- There is a lack of understanding of students' different learning modes as well as the 'social dimension' of social software. In particular, more work is required in order to understand the social dimension and this will require us to really 'get inside the heads of people who are using these new environments for social interaction' (Kukulska- Hulme, 2006).
- Web 2.0 both provides tools to solve technical problems and presents issues that raise questions. If students arrive at colleges and universities steeped in a more socially networked Web, perhaps firmly entrenched in

their own peer and mentoring communities through systems like MySpace, how will education handle challenges to established ideas about hierarchy and the production and authentication of knowledge?

• How will this affect education's own efforts to work in a more collaborative fashion and provide institutional tools to do so? How will it handle issues such as privacy and plagiarism when students are developing new social ways of interacting and working? How will it deal with debates over shared authorship and assessment, the need to always forge some kind of online consensus, and issues around students' skills in this kind of shared and often non-linear manner of working, especially amongst science/engineering students (Fountain, 2005). One area where this is already having an impact is the development of Virtual Learning Environments (VLEs). Proponents of institutional VLEs argue that they have the advantage of any corporate system in that they reflect the organisational reality. In the educational environment this means that the VLE connects the user to university resources, regulations, help, and individual, specific content such as modules and assessment. The argument is that as the system holds this kind of data there is the potential to tailor the interface and the learning environment (such as type of learning resources, complexity of material etc.) to the individual, particularly where e-learning is taking place, although so far relatively little use has been made of, for example, usage statistics of VLEs or tailored content to substantiate these claims. However, others now question whether the idea of a Virtual Learning Environment (VLE) even makes sense in the Web 2.0 world.

Collecting and Preserving the Web

'The goal of a digital preservation system is that the information it contains remains accessible to users over a long period of time.' Rosenthal, (2005), section 2. *'The most threatened documents in modern archives are usually not the oldest, but the newest.'* Brown and Duguid, 2000 p. 200. The Web is an increasingly important part of our cultural space and for this reason the archiving of material and the provision of a 'cultural memory' is seen as a fundamental component of library work (Tuck, 2007), and there has been considerable discussion, debate and research work undertaken in this area ((Tuck, 2005a ; Lyman, 2002). At the British Library it is the policy that 'the longer term aim is to consider web-sites [*sic*] as just another format to collect within an overall collection development policy' (Tuck, 2005a). However, there are many issues to consider with regard to the archiving and preservation of digital information and artefacts in general, and there are also issues which are particularly pertinent to the archiving and preservation of the Web (Mesanès, 2006). Currently, the only large-scale preservation effort for the open Web is the Internet Archive, although there are a number of small-scale initiatives that focus on particular areas of content (e.g. the UK Web Archive (JISC Technology and Standards Watch, Feb. 2007).

Consortium, which focuses on medical, Welsh, cultural and political materials of significance. Within the UK, the UK Web Archiving Consortium (UKWAC) is engaging with the technical, standards and IPR related issues for collection and archiving of large scale parts of the UK Web infrastructure (Tuck, 2005b). This work has included the initial use of archiving software developed in Australia (Pandas), the development of a Web harvesting management system (Web Curator Tool) and investigation work into the longer-term adoption new standards, such as the emerging WARC storage format for Web archiving (Beresford, 2007). There have also been a number of reports considering the issue of preservation of the Web. In 2003, for example, JISC and the Wellcome Trust prepared a report on general technical and legal issues (Day, 2003) and UKOLN recently developed a general road-map for the development of digital repositories, which should be considered when reviewing the difficulties of preserving newer Web material (Heery, and Powell,2006).

The Day report (2003) outlined two phases to the process of preserving Web content: collection and archiving. Collection encompasses automatic harvesting (using crawler technologies); selective preservation, which uses mirror-sites to replicate complete websites periodically; and asking content owners to deposit their material on a regular basis. Secondly, there is the process of archiving where a respected institution creates a record of the material collected and provides access for future users.

However, part of the problem for the process of preservation is that the Web has a number of issues associated with it which make it a non-trivial problem to develop archiving solutions (Masanès, 2006; Day,2003; Lyman, 2002; Kelly, 2002).

The Web is Transient

The Web is growing very rapidly, is highly distributed but also tightly interconnected (by hyperlinks) and on a global scale. This makes the overall topology of the Web transient and it becomes extremely difficult to know what's 'out there'—its true scope. In addition, the average life span of webpages is short: 44 days in Lyman (2002, p. 38) and 75 days in Day (2006, p. 177). Dealing with this ephemerality is difficult, especially when combined with the fact that the Web can be considered an active publishing system Masanès, (2006) in that content changes frequently and can be combined and aggregated with content from other information systems.

Web Technologies are Not Always Conducive to Traditional Archiving Practices

Problems with archiving the Web are inherently caught up with technology issues. At a very basic level, as with all digital content, Web content is deeply entangled with or dependent on technology, protocols and formats. For example, the average page contains links to five sourced objects such as embedded images or sound files with various formats: GIF, JPEG, PNG, MPEG etc. (Lyman, 2002). These protocols and formats evolve rapidly and content that doesn't migrate will quickly become obsolete. In addition, information is always presented within the context of a graphical look and feel which 'evokes' a user experience (Lyman, 2002) and content may even be said to exhibit a 'behaviour' (Day, 2006). This varies according, in part, to the particular browser/plug-in versions in use and it is often argued that preservation should attempt to retain this context. It is the difference between what Clay A consortium of Wellcome, British Library and National Library of Wales (JISC Technology and Standards Watch, Feb. 2007).

Shirky calls 'preserving the bits' and 'preserving essence'. With this in mind, how do we go about migrating not only the data but also the manner in which it was presented? However, technology issues also go much deeper. Web content's *cardinality* (an important concept in preservation) is not simple. A webpage's cardinality might be considered to be one, as it is served by a single Web server and its location is provided by the unique identifier, the URL. Masanès, (2006) argues this means that, in archiving terms, it is more like a work of art than a book and is subject to similar vulnerabilities, as the server can be removed or updated at any time. However, this is further complicated by the fact that a webpage's cardinality can be considered one and it can be many, at the same time. A large, perhaps almost unlimited, number of visitors can obtain a 'copy' of the page for display within their browser (an *instantiation*) and the actual details of the page that is served may well vary each time. This complex cardinality is an issue for preservation in that it means that a webpage permanently depends on its unique source (i.e. the publisher's server) to exist.

In addition, they way HTTP works poses problems for archiving as it provides information on a request-by-request basis, file by file. It cannot, unlike FTP, be asked to provide a list of the whole set of files on a server or directory. This means that there is an extra layer of effort involved as the extent of a website has to be uncovered before it can be archived. This problem can be extrapolated to the whole of the Web.

The main method for gathering this information about the extent of a website, either for search engine indexing or for archiving, is to follow the paths of links from one page to another (so-called 'crawling') and there are two main issues with this:

- Websites can issue 'politeness' notices (in robots.txt files on the server) using the Robots Exclusion Protocol (Levene, 2006). These notices issue instructions about the manner in which crawling can be carried out and might, for example, restrict which parts of a site can be visited or impose conditions as to how often a crawl can be carried out.

- Robot crawlers may not actually reach all parts of the Web and this leaves some pages or even whole websites un-archived. There are two main reasons for this: to some websites are never linked to anything else to a large proportion of the Web cannot be reached by crawling as the content is kept behind password-protected front-ends or is buried in databases in what is known as the 'deep', 'hidden' or 'invisible' Web (Levene, 2006). Levene estimates that the size of this hidden Web is perhaps 400 to 550 times the extent of standard web pages. Content in the 'hidden Web' needs a specific set of user interactions in order to access it and such access is difficult to automate. Some, limited, headway has been made with this problem by attempting to replicate these human actions with software agents that can detect HTML forms and learn how to fill them in, using what are known as hidden Web agents (Masanès, (2006)).

In simple terms the number of instances (or copies) of each work that are available to deal/work with. In the traditional case of a book, a number of copies, maybe 2,000 of each edition are published, printed and distributed (each of which is the same in terms of content). There is no need for an archive to use a particular one of these copies in order to preserve a representation of that edition. In this instance, the book's cardinality would be 2,000. A simple example: Many website homepages graphically display the current time and date. If we take a copy of that page then it is unique on the date and at the time shown, but will not be the same on the next visit. (JISC Technology and Standards Watch, Feb. 2007). One alternative requires direct collaboration with a site's owner, who agrees to expose the full list of files to an archive process through a protocol such as OAI-MHP. Another alternative, which saves the site's owner from setting up a protocol and which is useful for websites that offer a database gateway which holds metadata about a document collection, is to extract (*deep mine*) the metadata directly from the database and archive it, together with the documents, in an open format. In effect, the database has been replaced, at the archive, by an XML file. This is the approach being facilitated by the deepArc tool that is being developed by the Bibliothèque Nationale de France as part of the International Internet Preservation Consortium (IIPC).

Legal Issues Pertaining to Preservation and Archiving are Complex

Day, (2003) argues that another major problem that relates to Web archiving is its legal basis. In particular, there are considerable intellectual property issues involved in preserving databases (as opposed to documents) which are compounded by general legal issues surrounding copyright, lack of legal deposit mechanisms, liability issues relating to data protection, content liability and defamation that pose problems for the collection and archiving of content.

Preserving Content Produced Through Web 2.0 Services and Applications

As we have seen, there are considerable issues around the long-term preservation of the Web, but how do these issues change with the introduction of Web 2.0 ideas and services? Material produced through Web 2.0 services and applications is clearly dynamic, consisting of blog postings, data mash-ups, ever-changing wiki pages and personal data that have been uploaded to social networking sites. Some would argue that much of this content is of limited value and does not warrant significant preservation efforts. On the other hand, Web 2.0 material is still part of the Web and others argue that since the Web is playing a major role in academic research, scientific outputs and learning resources there is a strong case for preserving at least some of it (Day, 2003) and a clear argument is now developing for the preservation of blogs and wikis (Swan, 2006). Blogs in particular clearly form part of a conversation that is increasingly part of our culture. From the point of view of education, increasingly, published academic research will make reference to Web 2.0-type material, for example, a peer group wiki focused on an experiment. There are two key questions one can ask of Web 2.0 with regard to preservation. Firstly,

to what extent does Web 2.0 content form part of the hidden Web? Most Web-based archiving tools make use of crawler technology and the issue here is whether the Web is evolving towards an information architecture that 'resists traditional crawling techniques' (Masanès, (2006)). Getting at the underlying data that is being used in a wide variety of Web 2.0 applications is a major problem: many Web 2.0 services and mash-ups use layered APIs which sit on top of very large dynamic databases. Unfortunately, technology to allow the preservation of data from a dynamic database is only just beginning to be developed. This might involve the development of some kind of 'way-back machine' that reconstructs a database's state at a specific time (Rosenthal, 2006). In addition, the APIs used by many of the Web 2.0 systems are often described as open, but they are, in fact, proprietary and subject to change; much of Web 2.0 is in perpetual beta and Open Archive Initiative Metadata Harvesting Protocol.

CHANGING TRENDS IN LIBRARY AND INFORMATION CENTRE

Library and Information centers resources and services are changing with the advent of technology. Some of the changes are as follows:

Physical Collection and Online Collection

Along with the changes in libraries as institutions have come changes in the roles of librarians. With the explosion of networked digital information, the librarian's role is changing from custodian of a physical collection to someone who identifies resources in collections housed elsewhere.

This is currently evident in major research libraries where librarians spend much of their time generating (World Wide Web-based) electronic indicator to resources on the Internet. Efforts like this are likely to greatly increase in the anticipated future. These trends entail less in-person intervention by library staff (as clients access information directly), but more of a behind-the-scenes intermediary role in selection and creating annotated/evaluative guides to peripheral resources. This also means a greater role for library staff as instructors, trouble-shooters, and guides.

Splitting libraries and their services from physical collections raises serious issues. Libraries that need to provide access to materials that they don't themselves own and control should worry about assurances that they will be able to access that material far into the future. This problem is particularly acute with WorldWide Web resources.

Print Resources and Web Resources

At this point in time libraries need to be careful about becoming too dependent upon WorldWide Web resources. Web resources often change location, and until location-independent naming schemes replace URLs, updating a library's links to external resources is likely to be a serious problem. Few information providers have the kind of commitment to long-term information maintenance that libraries have; libraries need to be concerned that the creators of the key resources they link to today may soon tire of updating these resources. Finally, libraries need to avoid relying too heavily upon external information resources which are free today but may become expensive some time in the future.

Libraries that shift their focus from acquisition to access need to realize its implication for other parts of their operation. This often requires a significant investment in equipment and training. It requires the development of an infrastructure to support document delivery. And the process of selection can become even more time-consuming for a library that is pointing users to remote materials than for a library that is buying its own materials. (This is particularly true on the WorldWide Web where pointers have to be constantly maintained,

and where there are fewer clues as to the reliability of information sources.)

Blogs and Publishing

Blogs and wikis are fundamentally 2.0, and their global proliferation has enormous implications for libraries. Blogs may indeed be an even greater milestone in the history of publishing than webpages. They enable the rapid production and consumption of Web-based publications. In some ways, the copying of printed material is to webpages as the printing press is to blogs. Blogs are HTML for the masses.

The most obvious implication of blogs for libraries is that they are another form of publication and need to be treated as such. They lack editorial governance and the security this provides, but many are nonetheless integral productions in a body of knowledge, and the absence of them in a library collection could soon become unthinkable. This will, of course, greatly complicate collection development processes, and the librarian will need to exercise a great deal of expertise and fastidiousness when adding a blog to a collection (or, perhaps, an automated blog-collection development system). Or, perhaps the very notions of "reliable" and "authoritative", so important to collection development, will need to be rethought in the wake of this innovation.

Wikis and Encylopedia

Wikis are essentially open web-pages, where anyone registered with the wiki can publish to it, amend it, and change it. Much as blogs, they are not of the same reliability as traditional resources, as the frequent discussions of Wikipedia (an online encyclopedia where any registered user can write, amend or otherwise edit articles) in the library world well note; but this of course does not eliminate their value, it merely changes librarianship, complicates collection development and information literacy instruction. The lack of peer review and editorship is a challenge to librarians, not in that users should avoid wikis, but only in that they should understand and be critical in depending on them. Wikis as items in a collection, and the associated instruction of users in the evaluation of them, are almost certainly part of the future of libraries.

In addition, a library wiki as a service can enable social interaction among librarians and patrons, essentially moving the study group room online. As users share information and ask questions, answer questions, and librarians do the same within a wiki, a record of these transactions is archived perhaps for perpetuity. And these transcripts are in turn resources for the library to provide as reference. Furthermore, wikis and blogs will almost certainly evolve into a more multi-media environment as well, where both synchronous and asynchronous audio and video collaborations will take place. Blogs are new forms of publication, and wikis are new forms of group study rooms.

Ultimately, blogs and wikis are relatively quick solutions for moving library collections and services into Web 2.0. thinking skills of information literacy are paramount to all other forms of learning.

Synchronous Messaging and Reference Service

This technology has already been embraced quite rapidly by the library community. More widely known as instant messaging (IM), it allows real-time text communication between individuals. Libraries have begun employing it to provide "chat reference" services, where users can synchronously communicate with librarians much as they would in a face-to-face reference context.

Many might consider IM a Web 1.0 technology, as its inception predates the technology market crash and it often requires the downloading of software, whereas most 2.0 applications are wholly web-based. It is here considered 2.0 as it is consistent with the tenets of Library

2.0: it allows a user presence within the library web-presence; it allows collaboration between patrons and librarians; and it allows a more dynamic experience than the fundamentally static, created-then-consume nature of 1.0 services. It is also considered 2.0 as it is becoming a more web-based application, and the software used by chat reference services is usually much more robust that the simplistic IM applications that are so popular (they often allow co-browsing, file-sharing, screen-capturing, and data sharing and mining of previous transcripts).

Streaming Media and Collection Creation

The streaming of video and audio media is another application that many might consider Web 1.0, as it also predates Web 2.0 thinking and was widely employed before many of the following technologies had even been invented. But for reasons similar to synchronous messaging, it is here considered 2.0. Certainly, for libraries to begin maximizing streaming media's usefulness for their patrons, 2.0 thinking will be necessary.

As mentioned, library instruction delivered online has begun incorporating more interactive, media-rich facets. The static, text-based explanation coupled with a handout to be downloaded is being supplanted by more experiential tutorials.

Another implication of streaming media for libraries is more along the lines of collections instead of services. As media is created, libraries will inevitably be the institutions responsible for archiving and providing access to them. It will not be enough to simply create "hard-copies" of these objects and allow users to access them within the confines of the library's physical space, however. Media created by the Web on the Web belongs on the Web, and libraries are already beginning to explore providing such through digital repository applications and digital asset management technologies. Yet these applications are generally separate from the library's catalog, and this fracture will need to be mended. Library 2.0 will show no distinction between or among formats and the points at which they may be accessed.

Social Networks and Library Networks

Social networks are perhaps the most promising and embracing technology discussed here. They enable messaging, blogging, streaming media, and tagging, discussed later. MySpace, FaceBook, Del.icio.us, Frappr,(2006) and Flickr are networks that have enjoyed massive popularity in Web 2.0. LibraryThing enables users to catalog their books and view what other users share those books. The implications of this site on how librarians recommend reading to users are apparent. LibraryThing enables users, thousands of them potentially, to recommend books to one another simply by viewing one another's collections. It also enables them to communicate asynchronously, blog, and "tag" their books.

It does not require much imagination to begin seeing a library as a social network itself. In fact, much of libraries' role throughout history has been as a communal gathering place, one of shared identity, communication, and action. Social networking could enable librarians and patrons not only to interact, but to share and change resources dynamically in an electronic medium.

Tagging and Cataloguing

Tagging essentially enables users to create subject headings for the object at hand. As Shanhi, (2006) describes, tagging is essentially Web 2.0 because it allows users to add and change not only content (data), but content describing content (metadata). In Flickr, users tag pictures. In LibraryThing,(2006) they tag books. In Library 2.0, users could tag the library's collection and thereby participate in the cataloging process.

Tagging simply makes lateral searching easier. Of course, tags and standardized subjects are not mutually exclusive. The catalog of Library 2.0 would enable users to follow both standardized and user-tagged subjects; whichever makes most sense to them. In turn, they can add tags to resources. The user responds to the system, the system to the user. This tagged catalog is an open catalog, a customized, user-centered catalog. It is library science at its best.

RSS Feeds and Publishing Content

RSS feeds and other related technologies provide users a way to syndicate and republish content on the Web. Users republish content from other sites or blogs on their sites or blogs, aggregate content on other sites in a single place, and ostensibly distill the Web for their personal use. Such syndication of content is another Web 2.0 application that is already having an impact on libraries, and could continue to do so in remarkable ways. Already libraries are creating RSS feeds for users to subscribe to, including updates on new items in a collection, new services, and new content in subscription databases. They are also republishing content on their sites. Varnum, (2006) provides a blog that details how libraries use RSS feeds for patron use. But libraries have yet to explore ways of using RSS more pervasively.

Mashups and Information Retrieval

Mashups ostensibly hybrid applications, where two or more technologies or services are conflated into a completely new, novel service. Users search for images by sketching images. In some ways, many of the technologies discussed above are mashups in their very nature. Another example is WikiBios, a site where users create online biographies of one another, essentially blending blogs with social networks.

Library 2.0 is a mashup. It is a hybrid of blogs, wikis, streaming media, content aggregators, instant messaging, and social networks. Library 2.0 remembers a user when they log in. It allows

Figure 1. DELOS digital library resource domain concept map (DELOS, 2007)

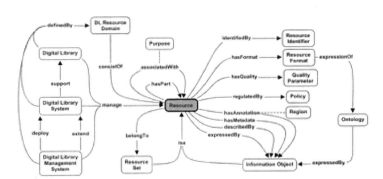

the user to edit OPAC data and metadata, saves the user's tags, IM conversations with librarians, wiki entries with other users (and catalogs all of these for others to use), and the user is able to make all or part of their profile public; users can see what other users have similar items checked-out, borrow and lend tags, and a giant user-driven catalog is created and mashed with the traditional catalog.

Library 2.0 is completely user-centered and user-driven. It is a mashup of traditional library services and innovative Web 2.0 services. It is a library for the 21st century, rich in content, interactivity, and social activity. Digital collection items can also be boundary objects, even if those conversations take place asynchronously.

Can social annotations fit into current digital library architecture? Two concept maps in the DELOS,(2007) reference model, in the Resource (Figure 1) and User (Figure 2) domains, suggest that they can. Giving users write-access to collections essentially means they would be creating a new resource type, one that need not append content directly to the item record, but may populate a separate table with an associative link. Figure 1 shows that according to the DELOS conceptual model, a Resource can have a "has Annotation" relationship with an Information Object that is conceptually equivalent to other metadata.

Similarly, the DELOS 2007 User domain concept map (Figure 2) shows that an End-user can have roles of Librarian, Content Consumer or

Figure 2. DELOS digital library users domain concept map (DELOS, 2007)

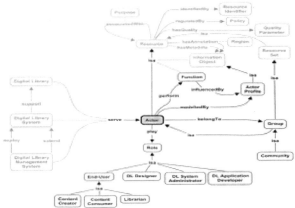

Content Creator. Starting from the more general Actor node, there is a direct conceptual relationship with the Resource node; the Actor "is a" Resource, in the same sense as a collection item.

One promising application of Web 2.0-type collaborative annotation of digital collection items can be found in the PennTags project (Day 2006). Designed as both a personal resource and as a toolkit for collaboration around digital objects, PennTags allows social book marking and annotation of OPAC items as well as Web URLs and journal article database items (though the latter are available only within the University of Pennsylvania community).

This brief review suggests that there is conceptual room for users as both interactors and content creators in digital libraries, and that annotations have been a historically valid form of user-generated content. Web 2.0 has provided an infrastructure within which users can participate, and when given the chance, they have done so enthusiastically. This leads to the research question driving this article: Can social computing functionality in the form of social annotation translate well to a digital library? To address this question, the results of a long-term participant observation of a Web 2.0 social question and answer site are analyzed, resulting in eight decision points that should be considered when deciding how or whether to incorporate social annotation in a digital library environment.

FUTURE RESEARCH DIRECTIONS

Firstly, folksonomies are starting to be used in scientific research environments. One example is the CombeChem work at Southampton University which involved the development of a formal ontology for laboratory work which was derived from a folksonomy based on established working practices within the laboratory. However, there is, to put it mildly, some debate about the role and applicability of folksonomies within formal

knowledge management environments, not least because of the lack of semantic with researchers of all disciplines in order to engage in peer debate, share early results or seek help on experimental issues (Skipper, 2006). However, it has had no serious review of its use in higher education (Placing et al., 2005). Butler, (2005) argues that blogging tends to be used by younger researchers and that many of these make use of anonymous names to avoid being tracked back to their institutions. Some disciplines are so fast-moving, or of sufficient public interest, that this kind of quick publishing is required (Butler cites climate change as one example).

There has also been a trend towards collective blogs (Varmazis, 2006) such as Science Blogs and Real Climate, in which working scientists communicate with each other and the public, as well as blog-like, peer-reviewed sites such as Nature Protocols. These tools provide considerable scope to widen the audience for scientific papers and to distinction between the use of tags. A recent JISC report *Terminology services and technology* (Tudhope, Koch, and Heery, 2006) reviewed some of the characteristics of 'social tagging' systems and the report notes that 'Few evaluative, systematic studies from professional circles in knowledge organisations, information science or semantic web communities have appeared to date' (p. 39). Issues raised by the JISC report include the obvious lack of any control over the vocabulary at even the most basic level (for example, word forms – plural or singular – and use of numbers and transliteration) and goes on to highlight shortcomings related to the absence of rules in the tagging process, for example, on the granularity or specificity of tags.

Some researchers are, however, beginning to investigate whether it could be fruitful to combine socially created tags with existing, formal ontologies (Al-Khalifa, and Davis, 2006). Tagging does provide for the marking up of objects in environments where controlled indexing is not taking place, and as the tagging process is strongly 'user-centric', such tagging can reflect topicality and change very quickly. (JISC Technology and Standards Watch, Feb. 2007).

Secondly, although evidence is only anecdotal, blogging seems to be becoming more popular assist in the process of public understanding of science and research (Amsen, 2006). Indeed, Ashlin, and Ladle, (2006), argue that scientists need to get involved in the debates that are generated across the blogosphere where science discussions take place. These tools also have the potential to facilitate communication between researchers and practitioners who have left the university environment.

Thirdly, social tagging and bookmarking have also found a role in science (Lund, 2006). An example of this approach is CiteULike a free service to help academics share, store, and organise the academic papers they are reading. Finally, there have also been developments in scientific data mash-ups and the use of Web Services to link together different collections of experimental data (Swan, 2006). Examples include AntBase and AntWeb, which use Web Services to bring together data on 12,000 ant species, and the USA-based water and environmental observatories project (Liu et.al., 2007).

This corresponds to moves in recent years to open up experimental data and provide it to other researchers as part of the process of publication (Frey, 2006) and the Murray-Rust Research Group is particularly well known for this. The E-bank project is also looking at integrating research experiment datasets into digital libraries. However, opinion is divided over the extent to which social software tools are being used by the research community. Butler, (2005) for a recent article in Nature, conducted interviews with researchers working across science disciplines and concluded that social software applications are not being used as widely as they should in research, and that too many researchers see the formal publication of journal and other papers as the main means of communication with each other.

Though designed as systems for knowledge discovery, the majority of digital libraries operate from the traditional expert model. Subject experts create content, digital library experts provide access to it, and individual users consume it. Very few systems have been built with an architecture that encourages users to create content, associate it with collection items, or share their impressions with other users. Providing digital library users read-access to collections is the traditional finish line. Providing them write-access – the ability to append content to that in a digital collection – is something else entirely.

CONCLUSION

In an era of changing institutions, libraries need to examine what their missions have been in the past, and how they can concentrate on the part of their core mission that is not repetitive of what other institutions do. Librarians need to find the parts of their core mission that will be sustainable in a changed environment.

The library is an integral part of the society that surrounds it. It is shaped and changed by many of the same forces that shape other types of institutions. Librarians need to recognize the changes that have already taken place in libraries, and to be aware of the ways in which broader societal changes are affecting other institutions. Then (rather than sitting idly by and passively observing the evolution of the library as an institution) they need to use this knowledge to actively reshape the library. If librarians do not become involved in this reshaping, key principles from librarianship may disappear in the library of the future.

Because many library functions will migrate to other environments (and because libraries are affected by the society around them), librarians must resist the types of changes that threaten basic principles such as equal access to information and fair use. They need to realize the disadvantages of mass delivery of library services and be wary of moving services outside the local arena. And they need to be concerned about issues such as pay-per-use, privacy, cultural diversity, and the consolidation of electronic content owners and distributors.

Certainties about the future are nearly impossible, however, technology will play a large role in the library of the future. And there are many ways that the library can use technology to advance its mission. But before plunging ahead, some perspective should be placed on our so-called "Age of Information."

The library's collection will change, becoming more interactive and fully accessible. The library's services will change, focusing more on the facilitation of information transfer and information literacy rather than providing controlled access to it. It is virtual reality of the library, a place where one can not only search for books and journals, but interact with a community, a librarian, and share knowledge and understanding with them.

Despite this change fitting so well with the history of libraries and their mission, it is still a major paradigmatic shift for librarianship to open not just access to their catalogs and collections, but access to their control.

Finally, rest assured that print resources will not disappear. They are too extensive, authoritative and well organized. Librarians love to show students how to save 20 minutes in the library with just an hour or two of searching on the Web.

Social computing, or Web 2.0, operates in much the same way. Whether via links, tags, social bookmarks, comments, ratings or other means, providing users the means to create, share and interact around content typifies the Web 2.0 approach. Most instances of Web 2.0 operate from a model of aggregate peer authority. Most critically, knowledge discovery and transfer is no longer restricted to a model of one expert creator to many consumers. In Web 2.0, consumers are creators, who can add their voices to both expert and non-expert claims. Users get the benefit of multiple

perspectives and can evaluate claims in the best tradition of participative, critical inquiry.

This chapter has covered a lot of ground. It has looked at Web 2.0, tried to separate out some of the sense from the sensational, reviewed the technologies involved and highlighted some of the issues and challenges that this poses to higher education. This is a complex and rapidly evolving area and this chapter can, perhaps inexorably, seem to raise as many questions as it answers.

Libraries are not untouchable to the community forces re-shaping other institutions. Library rapidly evolves into something that looks quite different than it did just a few decades ago, it is significant that librarians not only become aware of this advancement, but that they actively mediate to help adapt the institution in ways that are steady with the core operation of libraries. Changes to libraries are certain, and if librarians do not get actively involved in shaping those changes, it is likely that the new age library will carry very few of the core missions and values that have historically been associated with libraries.

REFERENCES

Abram, S. (2005). Web 2.0—huh?! library 2.0, librarian 2.0. *Information Outlook, 9*(12), 44–46.

Al-Khalifa, H. S., & Davis, H. C. (2006). Harnessing the wisdom of crowds: how to semantically annotate Web resource using folksonomies. In *Proceedings of IADIS Web Applications and Research 2006 (WAR2006)*. Retrieved from http://eprints.ecs.soton.ac.uk/13158/

Alexander, B. (2006, March/April). Web 2.0: A new wave of innovation for teaching and learning. *EDUCAUSE Review, 41*(2), 32–44.

Amsen, E. (2006). Who Benefits from Science Blogging? *Hypothesis Journal, 4*(2).

Anderson, C. (2006). *The Long Tail: How endless choice is creating unlimited demand.* London: Random House Business Books.

Ashlin, A., & Ladle, R. (2006). Environmental Science Adrift in the Blogosphere. *Science, 312*(5771), 201. doi:10.1126/science.1124197

Beer, D., & Roger, B. (2007). Sociology and of and in Web 2.0: Some Initial Considerations. *Sociological Research Online, 12*(5). Retrieved from http://www.socresonline.org.uk/12/5/17.html.

Beresford, P. (2007). Web Curator Tool. *Ariadne,* 50.

Berners-Lee, T. (1998). Realizing the potential of the Web. In Lloyd, P., & Boyle, P. (Eds.), *WebWeaving.* London: Butterworth-Heinemann.

Berners-Lee, T., Hall, W., Hendler, J., Shadbolt, N., & Weitzner, D. (2006). Creating a science of the Web. *Science, 313*(5788), 769–771. doi:10.1126/science.1126902

Berube, L. (2007). *On the Road Again: The next e-innovations for public libraries?* Retrieved from http://www.bl.uk/about/cooperation/pdf/einnovations.pdf

Besser, H. (1995d). From Internet to Information SuperHighway. In Brook, J., & Boal, I. A. (Eds.), *Resisting the Virtual Life: The Culture and Politics of Information* (pp. 59–70). San Francisco: City Lights.

Borgman, C. (2003). Personal digital libraries: creating individual spaces for innovation. In *NSF/JISC Post Digital Library Futures Workshop,* June 15-17, Cape Cod, Massachusetts. Retrieved from http://www.sis.pitt.edu/~dlwkshop/paper_borgman.html

Borgman, C. L. (1996). *Social aspects of digital libraries.* Retrieved November 2, 2006, from http://is.gseis.ucla.edu/research/dl/UCLA_DL_Report.html

Borgman, C. L. (1999). What are Digital Libraries? Competing Visions. *Information Processing & Management, 35*(3), 227–243.

Breeding, M. (2006). Web 2.0? let's get to web 1.0 first. *Computers in Libraries, 26*(5), 30–33.

Butler, D. (2005, December 1). Science in the web age: Joint efforts. *Nature, 438,* 548–549. doi:10.1038/438548a

Butler, D. (2006, March 14). *The scientific Web as Tim originally envisaged.* Tutorial session on Web 2.0 in Science, Bio-IT world Conference.

Casey, M. (2006a, January 3). Born in the biblioblogosphere. *LibraryCrunch.,* 2006.

Casey, M. (2006b). *LibraryCrunch: bringing you a library 2.0 perspective.*

Crawford, W. (2006). Library 2.0 and 'Library 2.0.' *Cites and Insights,* 6. Retrieved from http://cites.boisestate.edu/civ6i2.pdf

Day, M. (2003). *Collecting and Preserving the World Wide Web, Version 1.0.* JISC: Bristol, UK. Retrieved from http://www.jisc.ac.uk/uploaded_documents/archiving_feasibility.pdf

DELOS. (2007). *The DELOS Digital Library Reference Model: Foundations for Digital Libraries, version 0.96.* Retrieved from http://www.delos.info/files/pdf/ReferenceModel/DELOS_DLReferenceModel_096.pdf

Dempsey, L. (2006, April). Libraries and the Long Tail: Some Thoughts about Libraries in a Network Age. *D-Lib Magazine, 12*(4). Retrieved from http://www.dlib.org/dlib/april06/dempsey/04dempsey.html. doi:10.1045/april2006-dempsey

FaceBook. (n.d.). Retrieved from http://www.facebook.com/

Flickr. (n.d.). Retrieved from http://www.flickr.com/

Fountain, R. (2005). *Wiki Pedagogy*. Dossiers Pratiques, Profetic. Retrieved from http://www.profetic.org:16080/dossiers/dossier_imprimer.php3?id_rubrique=110

Frappr. (2006). Retrieved from http://www.frappr.com/

Frey, J. G. (2006). *Free The Data*. WWW 2006 Panel Discussion, Edinburgh, UK, March 25, 2006. Retrieved from http://eprints.soton.ac.uk/38009/

Gawrylewski, A. (2008). *Library 2.0: Secrets from science librarians that can save you hours of work*. Retrieved from http://www.the-scientist.com/2008/11/1/82/1/

Glogoff, S. (2006). The LTC wiki: experiences with integrating a wiki in instruction. In Mader, S. L. (Ed.), *Using Wiki in Education*.

Gudiva, V., Raghavan, V., Grosky, V., & Kasana-gottu, R. (1997). Information Retrieval on the World Wide Web. *IEEE Internet Computing, 1*(5), 58–68. doi:10.1109/4236.623969

Guy, M. (2006). Wiki or Won't He? A Tale of Public Sector Wikis. *Ariadne, 49*. Retrieved from http://www.ariadne.ac.uk/issue49/guy/.

Habib, M. (2006). Conceptual model for academic library 2.0. *Michael Habib's weblog on library and information science*. Retrieved from http://mchabib.blogspot.com/2006/06/conceptual-model-for-academic-library.html

Herry, R., & Powell, A. (2006). Digital Repositories Roadmap: looking forward. *UKOLN*. http://www.ukoln.ac.uk/repositories/publications/roadmap-200604/rep-roadmap-v15.pdf

JISC Technology and Standards Watch. (2007). *Web 2.0*. Retrieved from http://www.blyberg.net/2006/08/18/go-go-google-gadget/

Kelly, B. (2002). Archiving the UK domain and UK websites. In Proceedings of Web-archiving: managing and archiving online documents and records, London, March 25, 2002.

Kukulska-Hulme, A. (2006). Learning activities on the move. In *Handheld learning conference*, 12th Oct 2006, London. Podcast retrieved from http://www.handheldlearning.co.uk.

Lagoze, C., Krafft, D., & Payette, S. (2005). What is a digital library anyway? Beyond search and access in the nsdl [Electronic Version]. *D-Lib Magazine*. Retrieved from doi:10.1045/november2005-lagoze

Laningham, S. (Ed.). (2006). *Tim Berners-Lee*. Podcast retrieved from http://www-128.ibm.com/developerworks/podcast/

Leonard, G. D. (1993). *Multiculturalism and library services*. New York: Haworth Press.

Levy, S., & Stone, B. (2006). The New Wisdom of the Web. *Newsweek*. Retrieved from http://www.msnbc.msn.com/id/12015774/site/newsweek/page/5/

Library 2.0 Theory: Web 2.0 and Its Implications for Libraries. (n.d.). Retrieved from http://www.webology.ir/2006/v3n2/a25.html

LibraryThing. (2006). Retrieved from http://www.librarything.com/

Liu, Y., Myers, J., Minsker, B., & Futrelle, J. (2007). *Leveraging Web 2.0 technologies in a Cyberenvironmnt for observatory-centric environmental research*. Presented at The 19th Open Grid Forum (OGF19), Jan 29th – Feb 2nd 2007, North Carolina, USA. Retrieved from http://www.semanticgrid.org/OGF/ogf19/Liu.pdf

Masanes, J. (2006). *Web Archiving*. Berlin: Springer-Verlag. doi:10.1007/978-3-540-46332-0

Miller, P. (2005a). *Do libraries matter?: The rise of library 2.0* [White Paper]. Talis. Retrieved from http://www.talis.com/downloads/white_papers/DoLibrariesMatter.pdf

Miller, P. (2005b, October). Web 2.0: building the new library. *Ariadne, 45*. Retrieved from http://www.ariadne.ac.uk/issue45/miller/.

Miller, P. (2006, January 31). *Introducing the Library 2.0 gang.* Recorded telephone conference as part of the Talking with Talis podcast series. Retrieved from http://talk.talis.com/archives/2006/02/introducing_the.html

Miller, P. (2006a). Coming together around library 2.0: a focus for discussion and a call to arms. *D-Lib Magazine, 12*(4). Retrieved from http://www.dlib.org/dlib/april06/miller/04miller.html. doi:10.1045/april2006-miller

Miller, P. (2006b). *Library 2.0 - the challenge of distruptive innovation* [White Paper]. Talis. Retrieved from http://www.talis.com/resources/documents/447_Library_2_prf1.pdf

Mitchell, E., & Gilbertson, K. (2008). Using Open Source Social Software as Digital Library Interface. *D-Lib Magazine, 14*(3/4). doi:10.1045/march2008-mitchell

MySpace. (n.d.). Retrieved from http://www.myspace.com/

Notess, G. R. (2006). The terrible twos: web 2.0, library 2.0, and more. *Online, 30*(3), 40–42.

O'REILLY. T. (2003, April 6). The Architecture of Participation. *ONLamp.com.* Retrieved from http://www.oreillynet.com/pub/wlg/3017

Owen, M., Grant, L., Sayers, S., & Facer, K. (2006). *Social Software and Learning.* Bristol, UK: FutureLab. Retrieved from http://www.futurelab.org.uk/research/opening_education/social_software_01.htm

Placing, K., Ward, M., Peat, M., & Teixeira, P. (2005). *Blogging Science and science education.*

Renda, M. E., & Straccia, U. (2005). A personalized collaborative digital library environment: A model and an application. *Information Processing & Management, 41*(1), 5. doi:10.1016/j.ipm.2004.04.007

Rogers, A. (2006, September). Get Wiki with it. *Wired, 14*(9), 30–32.

RSS. *(file format).* Wikipedia. Retrieved from http://en.wikipedia.org/wiki/RSS_(protocol)

Schatz, B. R., & Chen, H. (1999). Digital Libraries: Technological Advances and Social Impacts (Guest Editors' Introduction). *IEEE Computer, 32*(2), 45–50. doi:.doi:10.1109/2.745719

Shanhi, R. (2006). Web 2.0: data, metadata, and interface. Retrieved from http://www.rashmisinha.com/archives/05_08/web2-data-metadata-interface.html

Skipper, M. (2006). Would Mendel have been a blogger? *Nature Reviews. Genetics, 7,* 664. doi:10.1038/nrg1957

Stanley, T. (2006). *Web 2.0: Supporting Library Users.* QA Focus, UKOLN. Retrieved from http://www.ukoln.ac.uk/qa-focus/documents/briefings/briefing-102/briefing-102-A5.doc

Star, S. L., & Griesemer, J. R. (1989). Institutional Ecology, 'Translations' and Boundary Objects: Amateurs and Professionals in Berkeley's Museum of Vertebrate Zoology. *Social Studies of Science, 19,* 387–420. doi:10.1177/030631289019003001

Swan, A. (2006). Overview of scholarly communication. In Jacobs, N. (Ed.), *Open Access: Key Strategic, Technical and Economic Aspects.* Oxford, UK: Chandos Publishing.

Tuck, J. (2005b.) *Creating Web Archiving Services in the British Library*. DLF Fall Forum, Nov 9, 2005. Retrieved from http://www.diglib.org/forums/fall2005/ presentations/tuck-2005-11.pdf.

Tuck, J. (2005a, November 24). *Collection Development and Web Publications at the British Library*. PowerPoint presentation at Digital Memory, Tallin. Retrieved from http://www.nlib.ee/html/yritus/digital_mem/24-2-tuck.ppt

Tuck, J. (2007). Author's notes. In *Memories for Life: the future of our pasts*, British Library, London, Dec 12th 2006. Retrieved from http://www.memoriesforlife.org/events.php

Tudhope, D., Koch, T., & Heery, R. (2006). *Terminology Services and Technology: JISC state of the art review*. UKOLN/JISC: Bristol, UK. Retrieved from http://www.ukoln.ac.uk/terminology/JISC-review2006.html

Van der Wal, T. (2005). *Folksonomy definition and Wikipedia*. Retrieved from http://www.vanderwal.net.

Varmazis, C. 2006. *Web 2.0: Scientists Need to Mash It Up*. BIO-IT World.com. http://www.bio-itworld.com/newsitems/2006/april/04-06-06-news-web2

Varnum, K. (2006). *RSS4Lib: Innovative ways libraries use RSS*. Retrieved from http://blogs.fletcher.tufts.edu/rss4lib/

WikiBios. (n.d.). Retrieved from http://www.wikibios.com/

Wikipedia. (n.d.). Retrieved from http://www.wikipedia.com/

Chapter 7
Information Preservation and Information Services in the Digital Age

Manisha Saksena
Independent Scholar, USA

ABSTRACT

In the digital world, library services need to be transformed utilizing the advancements possible due to that automation and machine-to-machine communication of information. In this chapter prime focus is laid upon the need of digitization and how to achieve it effectively and appropriately. The strategies for digitization have also been discussed at reasonable length. The issues debated are digital decay as against paper decay, accessibility interpretation in digital world, utility of e-journals, gray content boom, problems of access to excess, human dependence of information sharing and collaboration, dis-intermediation. In this chapter adequate care has been taken to visualize the importance of traditional conservation as well. The main emphasis is on the spirit of collaboration and skill to take initiative for digitization project. It has been repeatedly mentioned that institutional collaborations at national and international level have given more fruitful results in the area of digitization. This chapter shows the changed picture of librarianship in digital environment along with the change in user perspectives and service perspective.

INTRODUCTION

As developed for more than 200 years, academic libraries have generally been designed first and foremost as a place to collect, access and preserve print collections. To enter and use them was considered privilege. Despite their handsome exteriors

the interior spaces were often dim and confining. The buildings were difficult to navigate and specialized services and collections were inaccessible to all but the serious scholar. Building planning and design of these libraries were primarily devoted to the preservation and security of materials and to the efficiency of the library collection services. Prime space was routinely reserved for processing materials.

DOI: 10.4018/978-1-61520-767-1.ch007

Information today is being produced in greater quantities and with great frequency than at any time in history. The ease with which electronic information can be created and published makes much of what is available today. Digital is now often the first choice for creating, distributing and storing contents from text to motion pictures to sound. As a result digital content embodies more and more of the world's intellectual, social and cultural history. And the preservation of such content has become a major challenge for society. (Glister, 1997)

Libraries collect and preserve books and other materials for future generations to ensure that every citizen has equal access to information. With the advent of the internet and World Wide Web libraries can extend their reach unbound by time and space. The internet had made shared knowledge and technical collaborations across national boundaries a viable endeavor. This is a defining moment for libraries.

Technological innovation and the ubiquity of communication tools, economic uncertainty, changes in workplace and educational structures, the globalised economy, generational differences, the blurred distinction between the production and consumption of information and heightened national security are just some of the factors affecting the creation of digital library programs. In addition, there is an almost insatiable demand for content to meet the needs of the more than six billion internet users worldwide. And libraries no longer have market concerned on information services. Studies have shown that todays' students first turn to internet and that many library patrons are willing to settle for less, convenience over comprehensiveness.

Academicians, students or researchers, all have a craving for information. Digital library is being renamed to library itself because everything in this library is stored electronically and digitally. Digital libraries are sets of electronic resources and associated technical capabilities for creating, searching and using information. In a sense they are an extension and enhancement of information storage and retrieval systems that manipulate digital data in any medium [text, images, sounds, static or dynamic images] and exist in distributed networks. The content of digital libraries includes data, metadata, that describes various aspects of the data and metadata that consists of links or relationship to other metadata, whether internal or external to the digital library (Caplan, 2008).

DIGITAL LIBRARIES

Digital libraries are constructed- collected and organized by a community of users and their functional capabilities support the information needs and the uses of that community. They are a component of communities in which individuals and groups interact with each other using data, information and knowledge resources and systems. In this sense they are the extension, enhancement and integration of variety of information institution as a physical place where resources are selected and collected and organized, preserved and accessed in support of user community. Implicit in its definition digital library is a broad conceptualization of library collection.

The meaning of digital library is less transparent than one might expect. The words conjure up images of cutting edge computer and information science research. They are invoked to describe what some assert to be radically new kinds of practices for the management and use of information.

According to Digital Library Federation, "Digital libraries are organizations that provide the resources, including the specialized staff, to select, structure, offer intellectual access to, interpret, distribute, preserve the integrity of, and ensure the persistence over time of collections of digital works so that they are readily and economically available for use by a defined community or set of communities."

Of course, the concept of digital library has multiple senses that one might invoke in various contexts. For example, the concept may refer simply to the notion of collection without reference to organization, intellectual accessibility or service attributes. This extended sense seems to be in play, for example, when we hear the World Wide Web described as a digital library. The concept might also refer to the organization underlying the collection, or even more specifically to the computer-based system in which the collection resides.

This definition germinates the themes of library activities. One theme is that digital library encompasses the full information life cycle: capturing information at the time of creation, making it accessible, maintaining and preserving it in forms useful to users, community and sometimes disposing of information. With physical collections users discover and retrieve contents of their interests; their use of that material is independent of library systems and services. With digital collections users may retrieve manipulate and contribute content. Another theme implicit in the definition is the expanding scope of content that is available. Content now readily available in digital form includes primary sources such as remote sensing data, census data and archival documents. Distinction between primary and secondary sources are problematic or controversial, however as they vary considerably by discipline and by context. Some sources may be primary for some purpose and secondary for others. One more theme is the need to maintain coherence of library collections.

Karen Draberstoff briefs:

- The digital library is not a single entity.
- The digital library requires technology to link the resources of many libraries and information services.
- Transparent to end users are the linkage between the many digital libraries and information services.

- Universal access to digital libraries and information services is a goal.
- Digital libraries are not limited to the document surrogates, they extend to digital artifacts that cannot be represented or distributed in printed formats.

Purpose

Amply has been argued about why to digitize and what to digitize. The main cause for it is optimum access and accurate use. Though there is wide and huge scope of debate on the purpose of digitization many libraries across the globe have adopted this culture. These libraries have seen something very beneficial and lucrative about such project and decided to go with it. And most of the goals achieved through digitization have ensured availability, identity, understandability, Fixity, authenticity, viability and renderability of digital information.

Availability- A library that wants to preserve digital images it created in a scanning project is likely to have preservation masters in its possession, perhaps offloaded to tape or on DVDs. A library that wants to preserve the intellectual output of a university will have much harder time and may need to work with the faculty and administration to establish institutional repository. Deposit agreements, license negotiated to provide a library with an archival copy and contracts with publishers are all ways to get copies of published materials. Depending on the materials and circumstances getting a copy of the objects may be long or quite difficult.

Identity- if the end of digital preservation is long term access and usability, the digital objects must be described in sufficient detail and should carry descriptive metadata within them. Many contemporary file formats support embedded metadata, but only if object creators take advantage of their capabilities. Whether the metadata is internal or external there are no separate standard for descriptive metadata for preservation.

Understandability - A repository must ensure that the preserved information in independently understandable to its user community. For example descriptive metadata may tell us that a dataset represents the results of a certain pre lection poll, but unless we have the codebook we won't know what questions were ask and how the answers are represented in the file. The repository is responsible for providing and preserving enough information as metadata documentation and related objects to enable future users to understand the presented objects.

Fixity- Preservation systems must protect digital objects form unauthorized changes, whether deliberate or inadvertent. Industry standard computer security regimes are the best defense against both malicious and careless behavior. This includes virus protection, firewall, tight authentication, intrusion detection and immediate attention to security alerts. Media degradation may also cause bitstream corruption and is prevented by sound storage management practices, including climate control and media refreshment.

Authenticity- A preservation program may not be able to guarantee that all the digital objects it handled are authentic, but preservation treatment should not compromise the authenticity of the object in any way. There must be policies and procedures to endure data integrity and to ensure that the chain of custody and all authorized changes are documented. The event history pertaining to a digital object is known as its "digital provenances" and is a critical part of preservation metadata.

Viability- Viability is a quality of being readable from media. Media deterioration and media obsolescence are threats to viability and both of these are experienced by most of us in our everyday lives. Viability of a digital file is easily ensured when the files are actively managed, as digital data, then unlike analog data can be copied without loss. Files should be copied periodically to new media and back up copies should be stored on different physical devices.

Digital Storage and Preservation Strategies

Digital files can provide extra ordinary access to information. They can make the remote accessible and hard to see visible. Digital surrogates can bring together reserve materials that are widely scattered about the globe allowing viewers to conflate collections and compare items that can be examined side by side solely by virtue of digital representation. Digital technology can also make available powerful teaching materials for students who would not otherwise have access to them. Among the most valuable types of materials to digitize from classroom perspective are these from special collections of research institutes including rare books, manuscripts, musical scores and performances, photographs and graphic materials and moving images. Often these items are extremely rare, fragile, or in fact unique and gaining access to them is difficult. Digitizing these types of primary sources offers teachers at all levels unheard of opportunities to expose to their students.

Image processing – the manipulation of images after initial digital capture can greatly expand the capacity of the researcher to compare and contrast details that the human eye cannot see unaided. Images can be enhanced in size sharpness of detail and color contrast. Through image processing a badly faded document can be read more easily, dirty images can be cleaned up and faint pencil marks can be made legible.

While we know that the daily number of hits at the site of Wikipedia is greater than the number of readers who visit the library reading room each day, we have very little data now as to how much these types of online images are used and for what purpose. Some large libraries are attempting to compile and analyze usage statistics, but this intensive task presents quite a challenge. We need more user studies before we can assert confidently what may seem self evident to us now. Adding digitized special collections to the mass of information available on the internet is in public interest and enhances education. We also need to ensure that libraries are working collaboratively in their efforts to digitize materials so that together they can create a mass of research sources that are complementary and not duplicative and they begin to fulfill the promise of coordinated digital collection building. However at present there is no central depository providing information of what has been digitized and with what processes, as there is for titles that have been microfilmed for preservation.

Some of the drawbacks of digital technology for access, as for preservation stem from the technology's uncanny ability to represent the original in a seemingly authentic way. Working with digital surrogates can distort the research experience somewhat by taking research materials out of context of the reading room. The nature of computer display makes only serial viewing possible, very different indeed for example from spreading photographs in their original sizes around a flat surface and looking at them simultaneously and in different groupings. Every page, every object is mediated by the screen which automatically flattens the images and removes their contexts. And a digital image no matter how high the resolution and sensitive the display monitor is always presented through the high density of information of the computer screen compromising the high density nature of analog materials which can be artificial for assessing some visual evidence.

Digital raw materials on the web are not as raw as they might appear to be. Many of the items that may be viewed on the websites of renowned institutions come from special collections that are large, often catalogued only at the collection level and often unedited with few descriptions that aid a scholar. The amount of physical preparation and intellectual control work that is needed for every digital project is very large. Scanning is very expensive process, and most of the cost occurs before the item is being laid on the scanner. Part of that is physical preparation of research into and

description of an item. The collections that are on the web are in an real sense publications accompanied as they are by a great deal of descriptive information created in order to make the items understandable in the context of the internet.

Access

Despite high cost of digital conversion many institutions have taken ambitious projects in order to find out for themselves what the technology can do for them. The impact of digitizing projects on an institution, its way of operating its traditional audience and its core functions are often hard to anticipate. The challenge of selecting the parts of large collection that will be scanned is, for some novel task that calls into question principle of collection development and access policies. Making information available on the internet removes the very barriers from use that we take for granted in physical collection. (Lankes, Collins, and Kasowitz, Ed., 2000) There are ways to build in electronic barriers to access for all or portions of site, using much of the same technology that commercial entities use in granting fee based access. However constructing these barriers add a layer of administrative complexities to manage the site that libraries and archives may not be prepared to take on, even if the technology does exist. Only when digitization is viewed specifically as a form of publishing and not simply as another way to make resources available to researchers are the thornier issues of selection for conversion put into an editorial context that provides a strong intellectual and ethical basis for imaginative selection of complex materials.

Ownership

Many of the collections that may be of the highest research and teaching value will not be digitized for web access because of the structure of copyright that may apply. For this reason library websites these days contain a disproportionate amount of public domain material which distorts the nature of the source base for research restricted to the web.

Strategies

Preservation strategies can be thought of as falling into two categories. The methods in the first category address the goals of fixity and viability and include techniques such as copying data to new media of the same type, copying data to the newer media, and maintaining multiple, frequently verified copies of data. These activities are often referred to as "bit level "or "passive" preservation. The methods in the second category attempt to address the goals of renderability and authenticity and are unique to the preservation realm.

Format migration and emulation are often touted as the two main strategies for digital preservation. In fact numbers of different strategies are available to preservationists and multiple approaches are often used together to good effect. When strategies addressing renderability are employed it is called "full" or "active" preservation.

So the main strategies for preservation include, Technology preservation, Emulation, Universal Virtual Machine, Universal virtual computer, Format Migration, Format Normalization.

Technology Preservation-- Often called the "computer museum approach" technology preservation is familiar to anyone who still owns a record player for listening to vinyl LPs. If a format depends upon a particular combination of hardware and software for rendering, it should be possible to preserve at least a few working examples of the obsolete platform. Technology preservation is generally considered an interim approach at best because it is not scalable. However preserving old technologies can provide historical information about genuine behaviors of obsolete application. There is a fairly strong consensus that technology preservation is probably impractical as a digital preservation strategy, largely because the number

of hardware components requiring preservation would soon grow to unmanageable levels while the cost of maintaining preserved hardware in working order would become increasingly expensive as the hardware aged. Moreover hardware as a physical object requires physical space for storage which would significantly increase the cost of preservation. On top of this there would be additional costs involved in preserving the software intended to run on the preserved hardware as well as digital objects the preserved hardware and software are intended to support.

In short technology preservation requires the preservation of every component of the original computing environment along with the archived content itself. While in some cases it is desirable – for example a museum exhibit designed to offer visitors an authentic computing experience from earlier times- the costs are too high to warrant serious consideration of technology preservation as a strategy for maintaining access to digital objects over long period of time. (Mcclure et.al., 2002)

Emulation-- It involves the use of hardware and/ or software that allow computer instructions written for one platform to be run on another platform. Emulation has been in use in the computer industry for years to extend the life of programs written for earlier models of machine. Today emulation is widespread, particularly to allow programs written for one microcomputer operating systems to run on any other. Emulation as a strategy for long term digital preservation however is still largely experimental.

Many experts consider that of all digital preservation strategies, emulation harbors the highest potential costs. First a library of emulators must be developed and maintained- of course the greater the number of formats supported by the repository, the larger the library of emulators needed. Second the software environment for the archived digital objects i.e. operating systems and application program, need to be preserved as digital objects in their own right, with all of the associated costs of doing so. And finally the emulators themselves represent digital object subject to the vagaries of an ever-changing technological environment: as current technologies are eventually displaced and become obsolete. New emulators must be written that are compatible with whatever new environment emerges. (Hughes, 2004)

Universal Virtual Machine-- Universal virtual machine behaves as intermediate layer between the emulator and the current platform isolating the emulator from the technology changes. One of the problems with simple emulation is that modern computer technology is moving target- not only does an emulator has to be written for each obsolete platform, but emulators must be updated or rewritten as a current platform change. Although the UVM itself may require updating or rewriting for new platform, it is presumably less work to update one UVM than dozen of emulators.

Universal virtual computer--Raymond Lorrie of IBM expanded the concept of a Universal Virtual Machine to that of a Universal virtual computer for preservation. In this approach, files of a given format are translated to a simpler Logical Data View by a "decoder" program written to run on the Universal Virtual Computer. The original file, the Logical Data View and a schema describing the Logical Data View are all archived together. In the future, files in the format can be rendered by the first building a UVC emulator to run on then current hardware then executing the decoder to generate the Logical Data View and finally writing a viewer to render the Logical Data View according to the schema. National Library of the Netherlands has been a leader in exploring the use of the UVC in a production preservation environment.

Format Migration-- Format migration is also called "forward migration" that creates a version of a source file in a different format that is considered to be a successor format. This is routinely done by common desktop application such as Microsoft Word or excel, which can open a file written by an earlier version of the program and save it in the current format. In some cases

the successor to one format may be an entirely different format. One concern about the use of format migration for digital preservation is the likely need for successive migration over time. Since any format transformation could potentially lose or even add information, it is possible that successive migrations would accumulate errors leading to results less and less like the original. A counter strategy is to save the original and write programs to migrate directly from the original to the current format. In particular format migration involves an alteration in the way the 'ones and zeroes' of a digital object are encoded usually in order to make the object's bit streams accessible and interpretable by contemporary software/hardware environments.

The cost of format migration hinges on a number of factors, including the frequency of occurrence, the availability of standardized tools for carrying out the migration, and the tolerance of information loss sustained as a byproduct of the migration process. Clearly, the more frequent the need to migrate archived objects to new formats, the greater the cost. Unfortunately this factor is largely outside the repository's control, and lies instead in the hands of the pace of innovation and user expectations. Standardized tools limit the costs of migration, and repositories can control this factor, to the extent that they can choose formats for which such tools exist: however the flexibility of choices in this regard may again be limited by the expectations of users. Similar reasoning applies to the degree of tolerable information loss, which can be inversely related to the costs of migration, but also governed by the expectations of the user community.

Format Normalization-- The process of format normalization creates a version of a source object in a preferred format while maintaining the essential properties of the original. For example textual documents in proprietary word processing formats could be converted to Rich Text Format or to an open XML based format. Some preservation systems, particularly those designed for archival materials, normalize all incoming documents on ingest. This has an advantage that there are fewer formats for the repository to support and maintain over time. The disadvantage is that normalization can be loss and unless the original is also preserved, the initial decision as to what properties must be maintained is critical. Normalization can impact structure, appearance and functionality in widely differing ways, depending on the original format of the object.

Advantages of Digitization

In recent years, a growing understanding of the costs of digitization, in terms of both time and financial resources, has placed a greater focus on developing digitization initiatives and pro-grammes that will realize tangible and strategic benefits for the institution and its users, rather than opportunistic or short term projects that are limited in their scope or focus. Consequently, it has been necessary to articulate clearly the concrete benefits of running digitization projects at the outset. Digitization is a complex process, and there are concrete benefits to be realized from many types of digitization projects. These can be summarized as Access, Support of preservation activities, Collection development, Institutional and strategic benefits, and Research and education.

Access--The primary and usually the most obvious advantage of digitization is that it enables greater access to collection of all types. All manner of material can be digitized and delivered in electronic form and the focus of the content that is selected for digitization varies across institutions. Digital materials can be made available to a broader audience than those who have the resources or ability to travel to see the analogue collections and access can be expanded to non- traditional audiences such as lifelong learners. Audience can access the collection for often unanticipated and broad-ranging research interests. Whatever the audience, their access to the materials is enhanced by the advantage of the digital format. With the

application of the right technological tools, and careful attention to the design of the user interface, it is possible to search, browse and compare materials in useful and creative ways. Patrons may scroll or browse through thumbnails of the materials in image catalogues, including images of materials that were previously inaccessible, such as glass plate negatives, or over sized or fragile materials. Digital images or texts can be integrated with, and linked to other materials, to provide an enriched archive of materials.

Support of preservation activities-- Developing a digital surrogate of a rare or a fragile original object can provide access to users while preventing the original from damage by handling or display. This was the motivation behind the digitization of many priceless artifacts. Often, the fragile condition of collections prevents or reduces their use. Digitization is not a substitute for traditional preservation microfilming however. The digital format is too unstable and issues related to the long-term preservation of digital media have not yet resolved.

Collection development--The provision of digital materials can overcome gaps in existing collections. Primarily, there is an opportunity for collaborative digitization initiative to allow the re-unification of disparate collections. It is often the case that materials that were originally part of a complete collection are now held in far-flung locations, and there is a growing desire to present at least a virtual sense of what the entire collection would look like. Many projects have been motivated by the goal of virtually 're-unifying' such materials.

Digitization is a means of creating resources that can be re-purposed for unforeseen uses in the future. Changing research trends may alter the demand for items in a collection: the development of new fields of study means that collections once perceived as ephemeral or of low research value are now heavily researched. Similarly collections of items that were once in high demand are now banished to offsite storage for lack of use. Furthermore, libraries are increasingly under pressure to provide access to materials in response to user requests, and are transitioning policies from collecting material 'just in case' someone will need it, to one of developing relationship which allow the library to deliver material from elsewhere 'just in time' to answer a user's need.

Institutional and strategic benefits-- There is no doubt that digitization programs can raise the profile of an institution. Projects to digitize priceless national treasures or valuable scholarly materials, if done well, can bring prestige to the whole institution. Raising the profile of an organization by showcasing digital collections can be useful public relation exercise. Digital collection can also be used as leverage with benefactors and funders by demonstrating an institutional commitment to education, access, and scholarship. Certain funding opportunities exist for digitization and it may be expedient for an institution to use them as an opportunity to accelerate a digitization program.

Developing digital projects can have long-term benefits for the institution, although it may take many years to realize these benefits fully. Such initiatives may create an opportunity for investment in the technological infrastructure and can create an opportunity to develop the overall technological skill base among staff. Staff members may benefit from access to digitization programs that give them an opportunity to learn about new technologies, that way it gives tremendous opportunities for staff development. Many funding opportunities are contingent on collaborations and partnerships between several institutions, so this can be an excellent opportunity to develop strategic liaisons with other institutions.

Research and education-- Digitization of cultural heritage materials can have tremendous benefits for education. Many institutions present educational 'modules' on their websites, presenting 'packages' of educational material based around their collections. Museums have been particularly successful in this respect, as

most organizations have in-house educational departments, which have been charged with developing materials that will exploit the potential of technology for delivering educational resources to all levels of learners.

The advantages to academic research and advanced scholarship are equally impressive and the potential of networked technologies to create a dynamic reading and scholarly environment is driving digitization initiatives at many institutions. Digitization can also be the first step in conducting advanced research on historical materials. Ancient documents present a prime candidate for digitization because of their historical import, combined with centuries of exposure and degradation. (Gorman, 2003)

REFERENCE AND INFORMATION SERVICES IN DIGITAL ENVIRONMENT

The motto of providing information services is not at all changed. But as the environment is switched to the digitization, the service staff is required to be trained accordingly. The digital library offers users the prospect of remote, around-clock access to electronic resources. There is serious need for bringing service perspectives and traditions of the physical library to the digital library. Human assistance in the digital environment is badly needed, as users lack the most basic skills using web-based catalogs, indexes, circulation, reserves and ILL systems search engines and databases. This new digital service environment requires that we radically change our perspectives on user needs and transform the ways in which we organize roles of reference staff to serve these needs. There are some workable progressive reference trends to implement in digital library service atmosphere as: tiered service, roving librarians, growth of research consultation activities, increasing number of professionals working outside of the library, use of more paraprofessionals etc.

The terms public services and technical services are ingrained in our collective culture. These two terms certainly embody a dichotomy. This mild opposition has been rendered even milder by recent coinage such as "access services", "information delivery services' and interpretative services. The two services have been psychologically divided for many years and this has been detrimental for services to users and for the quality of work life of librarians. " Public services " seems to imply groups of people who are uniquely suited to interaction with the users of the library, whereas "technical services" denotes a group of secretive, hidden librarians, devoted to the area of cataloguing and the dark world of systems.

However library collections are defined, they are either inert or randomly used without the human interaction that we call reference service. Person to person reference service is on its way out that will go the way the Library of Congress catalogue card and readers' advisory services. As with many other predictions concerning "virtual libraries" and the like, forecasting the death of face to face reference seems to ignore the manifest advantages and popularity of service, it seems that one has to have extremely strong argument to facilitate or allow the demise of a service that is both expected and appreciated by a wide range of library users.

Knowing the reference collection well is important to good reference work, but so is an intimate knowledge of the wider collections. If we can use technology and electronic collections to enhance this complex structure, then so much the better for all. There are those who propose that technology can be employed to provide a satisfactory alternative to the nuances of the interaction between librarian and user, the librarian's familiarity with range of the recorded knowledge and information, and the subtleties of information and knowledge seeking. Though reference librarian is not always directly involved in preservation of the records of civilization, he is vitally concerned about the totality of the record. As far as electronic

resources are concerned, the reference librarian has a duty to view them in the light of all other resources. This means using them when they are the best source and eschewing them when they are not. Good reference librarians are aware of and value the whole world of recorded knowledge and information- from books to maps, videos, electronic resources and everything in between. They are concerned for all resources of all kinds and their onward transmission to posterity. They cannot therefore be indifferent to the fact that the inchoate nature of electronic resources and their mutability poses a preservation problem unlike anything in the last 500n years. There is a very real chance that much of what is available electronically will not be available in few years. By unavailable means lost forever, not just difficult to find. This is a sea change in the history of communication or rather a reversion.

Skill Requirements

The proliferation of knowledge of IT in general and computer science in particular has reached a mad level over last two decades that most of LIS courses incorporated too much of it in their curricula without matching provision for wards to acquire skills. The academic and theoretical aspects like history of computers, generations of computers, etc. were taught on par with any computer science course and the utility of which in practice was found negligible. Interestingly some concepts and techniques of librarianship have again surfaced with new names in the latest IT and electronic world. For example, push or feed technology is conceptually same as SDI and Meta data is same as bibliographic data or surrogates of information sources. One undesirable feature in the training of LIS professionals in the areas of classification and cataloguing till 70s and in the areas of IT or computer science during last two decades is that there has been lopsided emphasis on specific schemes, systems, soft wares or languages, and general underlying principles, concepts and techniques are not given due importance. It is very unfortunate that even principles and techniques are enunciated as corollaries to a given scheme or system.

The electronic environment of 21st century will encompass a wide range of technologies including computer, communication, storage, recognition and other technologies. As such it is easy to say that knowledge and operating skills in all these areas are required by future LIS professionals. As mentioned earlier, as for as breadth and scope of required skills are concerned, LIS professionals must have technical skills, IT skills and managerial skills. Before getting into these three broad groups of skills, we may note that skills are not generally acquired by self study or listening to lecturer. What are called 'practical sessions' in the traditional schools of library and information science also hardly impart skills. At the best, they arouse curiosity for knowledge. Secondly, when we discuss skill requirements that too in alien areas like management and IT, it is necessary to be clear about the level or depth of the skills expected of LIS professionals.

As far as IT related skills required by new LIS professionals in the electronic world in the near future are concerned, we can identify different levels of skills. Firstly LIS professionals should have skills required for handling IT products, particularly, keyboard, operating system, softwares, physical handling of gadgets, telecommunication products, DBMS, data and file management, DTP, word processing, generation of reports, etc. The next level skills include skills required to apply IT for service management in general and information processing, search and retrieval in particular. This involves collection and organization of data in electronic form, indexing techniques, selection and evaluation of sources, searching techniques, updating techniques, etc. Information retrieval skills include online searching as well as searching CD-ROM databases. This level should incorporate skills required for query formulations as well as query interpretation. The advanced level skills

include internet skills and skills required for accessing networked resources as well as marketing of electronic information. A lot more can be said about skills expected for electronic publishing, electronic commerce and electronic marketing. Hence advanced skills can be considered as a sort of specialization.

Other IT related skills expected of new LIS professionals are skills required for evaluation of search results including modification of query for bettering the results and ranking of hit records and all that comes under post search processing and presentation of data/information. The post search processing is closely related to the personal information system (PIS) discussed earlier in the sense that customers should be trained to enable them to upload the data to the PIS. Hence PIS and post-search processing are also to be treated as enabling technologies and services. This aspect not only expects appropriate skills on LIS professionals but also presupposes ability to impart the same skills to customers. (Pace, 2003)

CONCLUSION

The preservation of the written heritage in whatever format it s being produced is of crucial significance to civilized society. Given that it is so important and that there are many strategic factors and costs which need to be established and predicted for the long term, it is an area where there are uncertainties. Digitization of cultural heritage materials is changing the ways in which collections are used and accessed. Many materials are amenable to digitization, including scarce, fragile and ephemeral materials, as well as the whole spectrum of moving image and audio materials. All can be safely used by wider audience in digital form. Research and interrogative tools for digitized source materials can also make digital surrogates more amenable to certain types of interpretation, such as full-text searching and indexing, as well as comparison of materials for multiple sources.

Many factors will come into play when evaluating the value of digital resources, but these factors may help in assessing when digitizing collections can be cost effective. Valuable digital resources which will bring prestige to the institutions that create and maintain them will be those to support scholarship without any loss of the benefits of working with originals. When evaluating materials for digitization and evaluating whether or not the time is right for an institution to embark on such an initiative, it is important to consider the experimental nature of digital projects. Much work that will be undertaken in the completion of digitization programmes will be at the bleeding edge of new technologies. This concept is relative: for institutions that have never worked with electronic resources before, all aspects of technology implementation can be traumatic. It will be necessary to ascertain the willingness and preparedness of institutions to embrace a certain degree of risk and experimentation and to understand whether or not such experimentation is acceptable or indeed necessary.

Developing understanding of the information that will be needed to preserve digital content has been an impressive co-operative effort on an international scale. It is an ongoing task and technology is not standing still while we figure it out. However great gains have come and will continue to come from sharing expertise throughout the digital archiving community. Cooperative efforts including metadata, standards, metadata extraction and conversion tools and format registries offer the hope of a longer life for digital content worldwide.

REFERENCES

Caplan, P. (2008). *The Preservation Of Digital Materials; Expert Guides To Library Systems And Services*. Chicago, IL: American Library Association.

Council on Library and Information Resource. (2005). *CLIR Publication No. 129.*

Deegan, M., & Tanner, S. (Eds.), *Digital Preservation*. London: Facet Publishing.

Glister, P. (1997). *Digital Literacy*. Hoboken, NJ: John Wiley And Sons Inc.

Gorman, M. (2003). *Enduring Library*. Chicago, IL: American Library Association.

Hughes, L. M. (2004). *Digitizing Collections. Strategic Issues for The Information Manager*. London: Facet Publishing.

Lankes, D. R. (Eds.). (2000). *Digital Reference Services in the New Millennium; Planning Management and Evaluation*. New York: Neal Schuman Publishers Inc.

Mcclure, C. R. (2002). *Statistics, Measures And Quality Standards For Assessing Digital Reference Library Services: Guidelines And Procedures*. Syracuse, NY and Tallahassee, FL: Syracuse University and Florida State University.

Pace, A. K. (2003). *The Ultimate Digital Library; Where the New Information Players Meet*. Chicago, IL: American Library Association.

Chapter 8
Digital Preservation Challenges, Infrastructures and Evaluations

David Giaretta
Science and Technology Facilities Council, UK

ABSTRACT

To preserve digitally encoded information over a long term following the OAIS Reference Model requires that the information remains accessible, understandable and usable by a specified Designated Community. These are significant challenges for repositories. It will be argued that infrastructure which is needed to support this preservation must be seen in the context of the broader science data infrastructure which international and national funders seek to put in place. Moreover aspects of the preservation components of this infrastructure must themselves be preservable, resulting in a recursive system which must also be highly adaptable, loosely coupled and asynchronous. Even more difficult is to be able to judge whether any proposal is actually likely to be effective. From the earliest discussions of concerns about the preservability of digital objects there have been calls for some way of judging the quality of digital repositories. In this chapter several interrelated efforts which contribute to solutions for these issues will be outlined. Evidence about the challenges which must be overcome and the consistency of demands across nations, disciplines and organisations will be presented, based on extensive surveys which have been carried out by the PARSE.Insight project (http://www.parse-insight.eu). The key points about the revision of the OAIS Reference Model which is underway will be provided; OAIS provides many of the key concepts which underpin the efforts to judge solutions. In the past few years the Trustworthy Repositories Audit and Certification: Criteria and Checklist (TRAC) document has been produced, as well as a number of related checklists. These efforts provide the background of the international effort (the RAC Working

DOI: 10.4018/978-1-61520-767-1.ch008

Group http://wiki.digitalrepositoryauditandcertification.org) to produce a full ISO standard on which an accreditation and certification process can be built. If successful this standard and associated processes will allow funders to have an independent evaluation of the effectiveness of the archives they support and data producers to have a basis for deciding which repository to entrust with their valuable data. It could shape the digital preservation market. The CASPAR project (http://www.casparpreserves.eu) is an EU part funded project with total spend of 16MEuros which is trying to faithfully implement almost all aspects of the OAIS Reference Model in particular the Information Model. The latter involves tools for capturing all types of Representation Information (Structure, Semantics and all Other types), and tools for defining the Designated Community. This chapter will describe implementations of tools and infrastructure components to support repositories in their task of long term preservation of digital resources, including the capture and preservation of digital rights management and evidence of authenticity associated with digital objects. In order to justify their existence, most repositories must also support contemporaneous use of contemporary as well as "historical" resources; the authors will show how the same techniques can support both, and hence link to the fuller science data infrastructure.

INTRODUCTION

Much work has been undertaken in the area of digital preservation. It has been said National Science Foundation Cyberinfrastructure Council, 2007) that "the Open Archival Information System OAIS,(2002), now adopted as the 'de facto' standard for building digital archives". The work presented here is firmly based on OAIS.

OAIS REFERENCE MODEL

The OAIS Reference Model provides a number of models for repositories including a Functional Model, to which is relatively easy to map an existing archive system, an Information Model, which is rather more challenging, an Information Packaging Model and federation models, plus preservation perspectives including types of migration and a variety of software related processes. A number of overall strategies, processes and supporting infrastructures may be derived from these.

OAIS Information Model

The Information Model provides the concepts to support the long-term understandability of the preserved data. This introduces the idea of Representation Information.

The UML diagram in Error! Reference source not found. means that

- An Information Object is made up of a Data Object and Representation Information
- A Data Object can be either a Physical Object or a Digital Object. An example of the former is a piece of paper or a rock sample.
- A Digital Object is made up of one or more Bits.
- A Data Object is interpreted using Representation Information

Representation Information is itself interpreted using further Representation Information.

This figure shows that Representation Information may contain references to other Representation Information. When this is coupled with the fact

Figure 1. OAIS information model

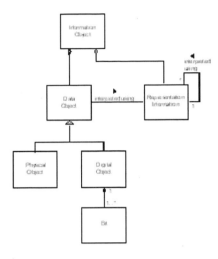

that Representation Information is an Information Object that may have its own Digital Object and other Representation Information associated with understanding each Digital Object, as shown in a compact form by the .interpreted using. association, the resulting set of objects can be referred to as a Representation Network. The question of where this recursion ends is answered by the concept of Designated Community, which is touched on further in sections 2.3.1.1 and 2.3.

The types of Representation Information are very diverse and it is highly likely to be discipline dependent, although there will be some commonalities.

Role of Significant Properties

At this point it is worth comparing the concept of Significant Properties with that of Representation Information. The former is widely used in the library community but it is hard to see how it applies to, for example, science data.

Clearly Significant Properties focus on those aspects of digital objects which can be evaluated in some way and checked as to whether they have been preserved. In particular after a transformation of the digital object this is an important consideration. However, the meaning associated with a Significant Property is nowhere defined. Therefore it must be the case that the Significant Properties,

Figure 2. shows more details and in particular breaks out the semantic and structural information as well as recognising that there may be "other" representation information such as software.

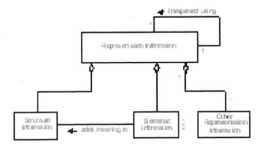

while useful, do not contribute to Understandability. For example it a Significant Property might be that a text character is red, however the meaning of that redness is not defined.

The question then is what is their significance. Giaretta (2009) argues that the role that Significant Properties play is more closely related to authenticity. Essentially the data curator will check that the selected Significant Properties are unchanged after a transformation in order to assure him/herself that the new transformed version, to his/her satisfaction, may be used as an authentic copy.

This view of significant properties allows the concept to be included in the revision of OAIS which is being prepared, and related to Representation Information. It also allows Significant Properties of scientific data to be clearly defined; however that is the topic of another paper.

OAIS Conformance

The mandatory responsibilities that an organization must discharge in order to operate an OAIS archive are likely to change, in the review which is coming to a close, to:

- ○ Negotiate for and accept appropriate information from information Producers.
- ○ Obtain sufficient control of the information provided to the level needed to ensure Long-Term Preservation.
- ○ Determine, either by itself or in conjunction with other parties, which communities should become the Designated Community and, therefore, should be able to understand the information provided, thereby defining its Knowledge Base .
- ○ Ensure that the information to be preserved is Independently Understandable to the Designated Community. In other words, the

community should be able to understand the information without needing the assistance of the experts who produced the information.
- ○ Follow documented policies and procedures which ensure that the information is preserved against all reasonable contingencies, including the demise of the archive, ensuring that it is never deleted unless allowed as part of an approved strategy - there should be no ad-hoc deletions,
- ○ Make the preserved information available to the Designated Community and enable the information to be disseminated as copies of, or as traceable to, the original submitted Data Object., with evidence supporting its Authenticity.

In addition a conforming OAIS must support the OAIS Information Model.

OAIS Concepts Applied to Usability and Testability

As a precursor to discussing its preservation, one may begin by asking what the definitions of information or data might be - how restrictive do we need to be? OAIS provides a very general definition of Information, namely: Any type of knowledge that can be exchanged. In an exchange, it is represented by data.

Information clearly includes data as well as documents, and covers behaviour, performance and explicit, implicit and tacit information.

Data is defined as: A reinterpretable representation of information in a formalized manner suitable for communication, interpretation, or processing.

Preservation and Testability

We need first some methodology by which to test the basic claim that someone is preserving some digitally encoded information; without such a test this is a meaningless claim. OAIS introduces the, quite reasonable, test that the digital object must somehow be useable and understandable in the future. However by itself this is too broad - are we to be forced to ensure that the digitally encoded designs of a battleship are to be understood by everyone, for example a 6 year old child? In order to make this a practical test the obvious next refinement is to describe the type of person - and more particularly their background knowledge - by whom the information should be understandable. Thus OAIS introduces the concept of Designated Community, defined as an identified group of potential Consumers who should be able to understand a particular set of information. The Designated Community may be composed of multiple user communities. Note that a Designated Community is defined by the repository and this definition may change/evolve over time.

Bringing these ideas together we can then say, following OAIS, that preserving digitally encoded information means that we must ensure that the information to be preserved is Independently Understandable to (and usable by) the Designated Community.

We are clearly concerned about long term preservation, but how long is that? OAIS defines Long Term as long enough to be concerned with the impacts of changing technologies, including support for new media and data formats, or with a changing Designated Community. Long Term may extend indefinitely.

The recursion in Representation Information leads to the question of how and where this recursion ends. Given the definitions one can see that the natural end of the recursion lies with what the Designated Community knows i.e. the Knowledge Base, defined as a set of information, incorporated by a person or system, that allows that person or system to understand received information, of the Designated Community. Once again, experience shows that any such Knowledge Bases changes over time, the changes ranging from the introduction of new theories to drift in vocabularies.

Definition of the Designated Community
An important clarification is needed here, namely that the definition of the Designated Community is left to the preserver. The same digital object held in different repositories could be being preserved for different Designated Communities, each of which could consist of many disjoint communities. In such a case each repository could require different sets of Representation Information.

The quid pro quo is that those funding or entrusting digital objects to the repository can judge whether the definition of the Designated Community is appropriate for their needs.

Preservation and Current Use

Bringing usability and understandability into the discussion of preservation, with the implication that Representation Information needs to be collected, has additional ramifications. In addition to the future users, who are the focus of preservation efforts of a digital object, there are current users who may also wish to understand and use those same digital objects. Current users will also require appropriate Representation Information.

The tools and techniques which are needed for preservation are therefore also of use in making digital objects usable to a wider audience. This point will be expended in section 0.

THREATS AND CHALLENGES

What Can Change?

We can consider some of the things can change over time and hence against which an archive must safeguard the digitally encoded information.

Hardware and Software Changes

Use of many digital objects relies on specific software and hardware, for example applications which run on specific versions of Microsoft Windows which in turn runs on Intel processors. Experience shows that while it may be possible to keep hardware and software available for some time after it has become obsolete, it is not a practical proposition into the indefinite future, however there are several projects and proposals which aim to emulate hardware systems and hence run software systems.

Environment Changes

These include changes to licences or copyright and changes to organisations, affecting the usability of digital objects. External information, ranging from name resolvers such as the DNS to DTDs and Schema, vital to the use and understandability, may also become unavailable.

Changes in What People Know

As described earlier the Knowledge Base of the Designated Community determines the amount of Representation Information which must be available. This Knowledge Base changes over time.

Termination of the Archive

Without permanent funding, any archive will, at some time, end. It is therefore possible for the bits to be lost, and much else besides, including the knowledge of the curators of the information encoded in those bits. Experience shows that much essential knowledge, such as the linkage between holdings, operation of specialised hardware and software and links of data files to events recorded in system logs, is held by such curators but not encoded for exchange or preservation. Bearing these things in mind it is clear that any repository must be prepared to hand over its holding – together with all these tacit pieces of information – to its successor(s).

Threats to Preservation

Surveys have been undertaken by PARSE. Insight Project and members of the Alliance for Permanent Access (http://www.alliancepermanentaccess. org/), investigating creation, re-use, preservation and publication of digital data. These surveys show a substantial demand for a science data infrastructure which is consistent across nations, continents and over a remarkably wide range of disciplines. There has been time for only an initial analysis of the results. The results of most immediate interest revolve around a collection of "threats" to digital preservation which are based on prior analyses of the domain and which are pertinent to data re-use also. It is worth noting that similar lists can be found in most project proposals related to digital preservation.

The major threats are as follows:

1. Users may be unable to understand or use the data e.g. the semantics, format, processes or algorithms involved
2. Non-maintainability of essential hardware, software or support environment may make the information inaccessible
3. The chain of evidence may be lost and there may be lack of certainty of provenance or authenticity
4. Access and use restrictions may make it difficult to reuse data, or alternatively may not be respected in future
5. Loss of ability to identify the location of data
6. The current custodian of the data, whether an organization or project, may cease to exist at some point in the future
7. The ones we trust to look after the digital holdings may let us down

The preliminary survey results show that between 50% and 70% of responses indicate that all the threats are recognized as either "Important" or "Very Important", with a clear majority supporting the need for an international preservation infrastructure.

Another clear message is that researchers would like to (re-)use data from both their own and other disciplines and that this is likely to produce more and better science. However more than 50% report that they have wished to access digital research data gathered by other researchers which turned out to be unavailable.

EFFECTIVENESS OF PRESERVATION EFFORTS

Background

The Need for Trusted Repositories

The Preserving Digital Information report of the Task Force on Archiving of Digital Information [Garrett, and Waters, Ed., 1996] declared.

- A critical component of digital archiving infrastructure is the existence of a sufficient number of trusted organizations capable of storing, migrating, and providing access to digital collections.
- A process of certification for digital archives is needed to create an overall climate of trust about the prospects of preserving digital information.

The issue of certification, and how to evaluate trust into the future, as opposed to a relatively temporary trust which may be more simply tested, has been a recurring request, repeated in many subsequent studies and workshops.

Audit and Certification of Digital Repositories

Section 1.5 of OAIS (Road map for development of related standards) included an item for accreditation of archives, reflecting the long-standing demand for a standard against which Repositories of digital information may be audited and on which an international accreditation and certification process may be based. It was agreed that RLG and NARA take a lead on this follow-on standard. This they did, forming a closed panel which produced Trustworthy Repositories Audit & Certification: Criteria and Checklist [TRAC, 2007].

TRAC was based on two documents, namely the OAIS Reference Model [OAIS, 2002] and the Report on Trusted Digital Repositories: Attributes and Responsibilities [RLG-OCLC, 2002]. The former lays out fundamental requirements for preservation, while the latter focussed on the administrative, financial and organisational requirements for the body undertaking the preservation activities.

Other, separate, work includes the nestor Catalogue of Criteria for Trusted Digital Long-term Repositories [Nestor Working Group Trusted Repositories-Certification, 2006], which is also based on OAIS, and DRAMBORA (Digital Repository Audit Method Based on Risk Assessment) [DRAMBORA] developed jointly by the Digital Curation Centre (DCC) and Digital Preservation Europe [DPE].

Development of an ISO Accreditation and Certification Process

The next step was to bring the output of the RLG/NARA working group back into CCSDS. This has been done and the Digital Repository Audit and Certification (RAC) Working Group has been created, the CCSDS details are available from http://cwe.ccsds.org/moims/default.aspx#_MOIMS-RAC, while the working documents are available from http://wiki.digitalrepositoryauditandcertification.org. Both may be read by anybody but, in order to avoid hackers, only authorised users may add to them. The openness of the development process is particularly important and the latter site contains the notes from the weekly virtual meetings as well as the live working version of the draft standards.

Besides developing the metrics, which started from the TRAC document, the working group also has been working on the strategy for creating the accreditation and certification process. Review of existing systems which have accreditation and certification standard processes it became clear that there was a need for two documents

- Metrics for Audit and Certification of Digital Repositories
- Requirements for Bodies Providing Audit and Certification of Digital Repositories.

The first document lists the metrics against which a digital repository may be judged. It is anticipated that this list will be used for internal metrics or peer-review of repositories, as well as for the formal ISO audit process. In addition tools such as DRAMBORA could use these metrics as guidance for its risk assessments.

It must be recognised that the audit process cannot be specified in very fine, rigid, detail. An audit process must depend upon the experience and expertise of the auditors. For this reason the second document sets out the system under which the audit process is carried out; in particular the expertise of the auditors and the qualification which they should have is specified. In this way the document specifies how auditors are accredited and thereby helps to guarantee the consistency of

the audit and certification process. For this reason the RAC Working Group refers to accreditation and certification processes.

At the time of writing both documents are in an advanced state of preparation; the aim is to submit these documents for ISO in the late Spring or early Summer of 2009. While the reviews are underway further preparations for the accreditation and certification processes will be undertaken. It should be noted that the OAIS reference Model has also been undergoing revision and the new version is expected to be submitted for ISO review at around the same time. Because of the close links between the metrics and OAIS concepts and terminology it is important that the two remain consistent, and cross-membership of the working groups will ensure this.

In addition to the "central" accreditation body there will be an eventual need for a network of local accreditation and certification bodies.

REQUIREMENTS FOR A SCIENCE DATA INFRASTRUCTURE

We base the requirements for the preservation/re-use/access infrastructure on a broad analysis of the threats described in section 0 and an initial set of solutions.

ROADMAP OF SOLUTIONS

A set (not an exhaustive list) of services which satisfying the above requirements and which could

Table 1.

Threat	Requirements for solutions
Users may be unable to understand or use the data e.g. the semantics, format, processes or algorithms involved	Ability to create and maintain adequate Representation Information
Non-maintainability of essential hardware, software or support environment may make the information inaccessible	Ability to share information about the availability of hardware and software and their replacements/substitutes
The chain of evidence may be lost and there may be lack of certainty of provenance or authenticity	Ability to bring together evidence from diverse sources about the Authenticity of a digital object

Table 2.

Access and use restrictions may make it difficult to reuse data, or alternatively may not be respected in future	Ability to deal with Digital Rights correctly in a changing and evolving environment
Loss of ability to identify the location of data	An ID resolver which is really persistent
The current custodian of the data, whether an organisation or project, may cease to exist at some point in the future	Brokering of organisations to hold data and the ability to package together the information needed to transfer information between organisations ready for long term preservation
The ones we trust to look after the digital holdings may let us down	Certification process so that one can have confidence about whom to trust to preserve data holdings over the long term

be provided as the basis for a 'generic' science data infrastructure is as follows:

- A set of tools and services, supported over the long term, which make it easier to create adequate Representation Information, and maintain it particularly after active work on the dataset has ceased or slowed.
- A set of services which make it easier to exchange information about obsolescence of hardware and software and techniques for overcoming these.
- A set of standards and tools through which a user in the future can be provided with evidence e.g. provenance, on which he/she may judge the degree of Authenticity which may be attributed to a digital object.
- Registry of/Clearinghouse for rights information and dark archive of licensing tools
- A persistent identifier system for locating and cross-referencing digital objects which has adequate organisational, financial and social backing for the very long term which can be used with confidence
- A system which will allow organisations which are no longer able to fund the preservation of a particular dataset is able to find an organisation willing and able to take over the responsibility. The ultimate fallback could be the European Storage Facility
- An internationally recognised accreditation, audit and certification process (for preservation aspects of repositories) with a well defined and long-lived support organisation, with appropriate tools and best practice guides.

In addition we must of course encourage and support disciplines to define their metadata/Representation information, and groups of discipline to work on interdisciplinary usage; data in the system will only be usable by aficionados if this is not done.

Supporting these are a number of considerations about policy, organisation and finance.

Possible Organisational Infrastructure Concepts and Components

It is clear that a number of the infrastructure components described above are themselves archives which need to preserve digital information over the long term and which therefore themselves require the support of that very preservation infrastructure. For example any of these components must themselves be able to be handed over to another host

Figure 3. shows a possible preservation infrastructure, in the context of a broader e-research infrastructure

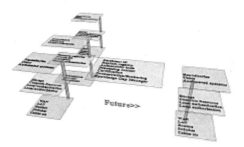

organisation, and the Persistent Identifiers must support such a move and resolve correctly.

An initial organisational setup could be supported by a government-level organisation, for example a component of the EU, however the commitment to provide a service for an indefinite time tends not to be popular. Therefore in the long term the responsibility could be handed over to an arms-length or consortium based organisational structure, and here the Alliance for Permanent Access is bringing together key stakeholders and may play a key role. Even this may need to be underpinned by governmental guarantee in order to provide real confidence in the infrastructure's longevity.

Possible Financial Infrastructure Concepts and Components

It seems difficult to avoid the conclusion that the initial funding to develop these infrastructure components must be provided by, for example, the EU in the first instance, together with major stakeholders such as the members of the Alliance for Permanent Access. However given that there is also significant commercial need for digital preservation, although this tends not to be for the indefinite future, there may be options to create a self-funding set of services, especially where the service does not scale with the amount of data needing preservation.

The Registry of Representation Information, the Knowledge gap manager, the Authenticity tools, the licence tool dark archive, the brokerage systems and the certification system, described in section 0, do not necessarily suffer the problem of scaling with the amount of information being preserved. For example one piece of Representation Information may be used to describe 1 billion data objects.

The Storage Facility on the other hand would grow with data growth, although the declining cost of storage means that this does not imply a simple linear cost relationship. Nevertheless such a facility may be able to supply added value services such as disaster recovery and integrity checking.

Cost/benefit analyses are likely to be very highly instance specific yet some common models are essential if judgments are to be made about what can be afforded. A common framework for at least collecting the information would be useful if a good understanding of the important parameters is to be gained.

Possible Policy Infrastructure Concepts and Components

There are a number of broad policies or statements of intents about preservation, re-use and (open) access. Although it is not clear when or whether these will converge, it is clear that there is almost

Figure 4. CASPAR information flow

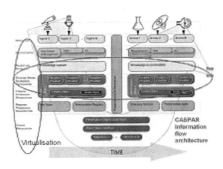

certainly be a variety of such policies for the foreseeable future. The preservation infrastructure must be able to operate in this environment. Nevertheless alignment of policies will undoubtedly make the task simpler, for which co-ordination at national and international levels, including EU and transnational consortia of key stakeholders such as the Alliance, would be essential.

This is an area which needs further investigation and planning, as is being done by the PARSE. Insight project (PARSE)

Preservation Infrastructures

Analogy is drawn with the network infrastructure which links islands of connectivity (e.g. the EU funding of GEANT). The network supplies services to isolated organisations, each with its own resources such as CPU and storage. Additional infrastructure such as the EU's EGEE project, and the UK's various GRID project, connect these. Similarly infrastructure components connect the repositories which use the lower levels of functionality.

In the future there should be some similar interconnected repositories and we need to transfer information from the "now" to the future.

CASPAR/DCC APPROACH

Regarding the OAIS mandatory responsibilities the CASPAR project [CASPAR D1201: Concep-

tual Model-Phase 1, 2007] one can derive a number of requirements for information flow. For example an archive needs to identify/capture

1. The access and digital rights management (DRM) associated with a digital object
2. The Representation Information – shown in Figure 4
3. The Designated Community
4. An appropriate storage mechanisms
5. An infrastructure to support preservation over the long term

In addition, the artifacts, such as the DRM and Representation Information, must themselves be preserved over the long term.

Further details of CASPAR are available from the CASPAR web site http://www.casparpreserves.eu and the DCC [Digital Curation Centre] web site.(http://www.dcc.ac.uk)

There are a number of ways in which, for example, Representation Information, may be captured, and a number of strategies must be examined. The following section illustrates some of these strategies.

CASPAR CONCEPTUAL MODEL

Much of what is reported in this paper follows on from the CASPAR Conceptual Model [Giaretta, June 2007], which is of great importance to the project's approach to digital preservation, because it brings together the key concepts which

Figure 5. contains a number of information flows; some sequences of these flows making up workflows important for digital preservation and two of these are described next.

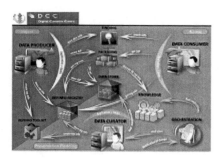

shape CASPAR, namely those to do with digital preservation, guided by the OAIS Reference Model and supplemented by the ideas of automation and discipline independence. The latter set of concepts helps to highlight those areas which can form a broadly applicable infrastructure to support digital preservation in a cost-effective manner.

Another important concept is that of recursion. This appears time and again within CASPAR and through the Conceptual Model. It means that components which appear at one level of granularity re-appear in a finer grained view, within the detailed breakdown of those or other components. An example is Representation Information, which itself needs its own Representation Information to be understandable; the recursion stops at the

Knowledge Base of the Designated Community. (These terms are taken from OAIS.)

It is evidently true that the components of a preservation infrastructure themselves need to be preservable: for example a Registry which supports OAIS-type archives must itself be an OAIS-type archive in that it must be relied upon to preserve its (Representation) Information objects over the long term. The Conceptual Model aims to provide an overall view of the way in which the project sees preservation working. It is provided primarily as a project-internal high level overview, and has been designed to:

• Help the members of CASPAR ensure integration and consistency across the project;
• Help people outside the project understand the fundamental ideas behind the design.

Figure 6. Use of registry/repository of representation information

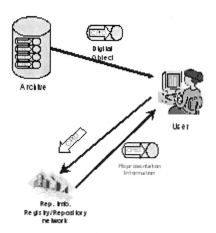

Figure 7. Represents information dependencies

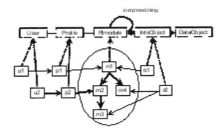

The model discusses the different levels of application of OAIS. It identifies what components of a CASPAR-based archival system are required, their functions and how they must interoperate at a high level. These components include for example a Representation Information Toolbox, a Virtualisation Assistant and a Preservation Orchestration Manager. The Conceptual Model also surveys the key underlying technologies of knowledge management and virtualisation that underpin the entire CASPAR approach. It touches on all aspects of the CASPAR approach to the preservation of digitally encoded information, and is reflected in the CASPAR architecture.

PRESERVATION WORKFLOWS

A number of other workflows arise from the support components identified by CASPAR, which may be summarized in Figure 5.

Workflows for Use of Digital Objects

The following workflow, extracted from Figure 3, illustrates the way in which digital objects may be used and understood by users.

Identifiers (called here Curation Persistent Identifiers - CPID) are associated with any data object, which point to the appropriate Representation Information in a Registry/Repository, as illustrated in Figure 6. The Representation Information returned by the Registry/Repository itself is a digital object with its own CPID.

The above is not meant to imply that there must be a single, unique, Registry/Repository, nor even a single definitive piece of Representation Information for any particular piece of digitally encoded information.

Workflows for Maintaining the Representation Network

The Registry/Repository is supplemented by the Knowledge Manager – more specifically a Representation Information Gap manager which identifies gaps which need to be filled, based on information supplied to the Orchestration component.

Of course the information on which this is based does not come out of thin air. People (initially) must provide this information and the Orchestration Manager collects this information and distributes.

Support for automation in identifying such "gaps", based on information received, is illustrated in Figure 7 which shows users (u1, u2…) with user profiles (p1, p2… – each a description of the user's Knowledge Base) with Representation Information {m1, m2,…) to understand various digital objects (o1, o2…).

Take for example user u1 trying to understand digital object o1. To understand o1, Representation Information m1 is needed. The profile p1 shows that user u1 understands m1 (and therefore its dependencies m2, m3 and m4) and therefore has enough Representation Information to understand o1.

When user u2 tries to understand o2 we see that o2 needs Representation Information m3 and m4. Profile p2 shows that u2 understands m2 (and therefore m3), however there is a gap, namely m4 which is required for u2 to understand o2.

For u2 to understand o1, we can see that Representation Information m1 and m4 need to be supplied.

This illustrates on of the areas in which Knowledge Management techniques are being applied within CASPAR, in addition to the capture of Semantic Representation Information.

CONCLUSION

Digital preservation is not a one-off activity; the variety of continuing threats and challenges, as outlined in this paper, must be addressed. The approach taken by OAIS has several benefits including providing the basis for certifying archives and showing how a preservation infrastructure is intimately connected with a general data infrastructure. This paper has expanded on these ideas and also described how the standard for audit and certification of digital repositories is being developed.

Further detail may be found at http://www. casparpreserves.eu; full documentation of the deliverables may be downloaded at http://www. casparpreserves.eu/publications/deliverables The software may be found at http://developers. casparpreserves.eu:8080/. Many strategies must be considered and appropriate infrastructures are needed to share the effort of preservation.

ACKNOWLEDGMENT

The work reported in this paper could not have been done without the help of colleagues in the CASPAR and PARSE.Insight projects and also colleagues in the CCSDS working on OAIS and the Repository Audit and Certification Working Group.

REFERENCES

1Alliance for Permanent Access. (n.d.). Retrieved from http://www.alliancepermanentaccess.org/

CASPAR D1201. *Conceptual Model – Phase 1.* (2007). Retrieved from http://www.casparpreserves.eu/Members/cclrc/Deliverables/caspar-guidelines/at_download/file

Digital Curation Centre (DCC). (n.d.). Retrieved from http://www.dcc.ac.uk

Digital Preservation Europe. (n.d.). Retrieved from http://www.digitalpreservationeurope.eu/

DRAMBORA. (n.d.). Retrieved from http://www.repositoryaudit.eu/

Garrett, J., & Waters, D. (Eds.). (1996). *Preserving Digital Information, Report of the Task Force on Archiving of Digital Information commissioned.* The Commission on Preservation and Access and The Research Libraries Group. Retrieved from http://www.ifla.org/documents/libraries/net/tfadi-fr.pdf

Giaretta, D. (June 2007). The CASPAR Approach to Digital Preservation. *IJDC 2*(1), 2007. Retrieved July 25, 2008, from http://www.ijdc.net/ijdc/article/view/29/32

Giaretta, D. (2009). Significant Properties, Authenticity, Provenance, Representation Information and OAIS. Paper in iPRES, San Francisco, 5&6 October 2009.

National Science Foundation Cyberinfrastructure Council (NSF). (2007). *Cyberinfrastructure Vision for 21st Century Discovery.* Retrieved from http://www.nsf.gov/pubs/2007/nsf0728/nsf0728.pdf

Nestor Working Group Trusted Repositories – Certification. (2006). *Catalogue of Criteria for Trusted Digital Repositories*. Retrieved from http://edoc.hu-berlin.de/series/nestor-materialien/8en/PDF/8en.pdf

OAIS. (2002). *Reference Model for an Open Archival Information System*. Retrieved July 25, 2008, from http://public.ccsds.org/publications/archive/650x0b1.pdf

PARSE. *Insight project.* (n.d.). Retrieved from http://www.parse-insight.eu

RLG-OCLC. (2002). *Report on Trusted Digital Repositories: Attributes and Responsibilities.* Retrieved from http://www.oclc.org/programs/ourwork/past/trustedrep/repositories.pdf

TRAC. (2007). *Trustworthy Repositories Audit & Certification: Criteria and Checklist.* Retrieved from http://www.crl.edu/PDF/trac.pdf

Chapter 9
Managing Change in Reference and Information Services in Digital Environment

Shantanu Ganguly
TERI New Delhi, India

Shweta Pandey
Indus World School of Business (IWSB), India

ABSTRACT

Libraries and librarians are no longer the sole providers of reference and information services. Reference services have traditionally played a crucial role in the delivery of library services both in the public and academic spheres. However, developments in Web technologies have seen the emergence of online or digital reference services, which many initially feared sought to replace the traditional library-based personalized service. A digital library is not merely a means of access to information over the network. As long as "library" word is attached to the concept, a digital library does and should care about users and communities that are in need of information and services just like conventional libraries. "Services", therefore, should be one of the crucial aspects of digital libraries. In the recent trend, reference services have taken a central place in library and information services. Sometimes, they are also regarded as personalized services since in most cases a personal discussion takes place between a user and a reference librarian. The librarian point to the sources that are considered to be most appropriate to meet the specific information needs of the user. Since the Web and digital libraries are meant for providing direct access to information sources and services without the intervention of human intermediaries, the pertinent question that appears is whether we need reference services in digital environment, and, if so, how best to offer such services. This chapter looks at the inevitable change taking place in the platform of reference services.

DOI: 10.4018/978-1-61520-767-1.ch009

INTRODUCTION

Library is the richest information treasure of human knowledge and cultural wealth, and should be able to meet effectively the challenges of the new technology revolution. However, the developments in advanced technology have provided good opportunities for the survival and development of traditional libraries of different types. The library, as a traditional information institution, is undergoing radical changes in its information service in the new era. With more and more digital materials available to the reader, the library no longer simply collects printed materials only but provide access resources 24x7. As for library users, their reading habits and usage of reading materials have also changed. The increased use of computers and especially expansion of internet based resources has led to some modifications in the methods of academic work, such as undertaking research, writing articles, and producing teaching materials. Developing an efficient digital library cannot be "the" answer for the digital user community, but providing an effective digital library services can only suffice the requirements. For this reason, both before and after developing a digital library, user studies are helpful in both improving the library system's performance and user satisfaction.

Recent changes in computer and communication technologies, especially the introduction and development of the Internet and its associated Web technologies in the course of the past decade have significantly influenced both the way libraries provide information services to their patrons and the way patrons choose to access information. For example, a large number of Web-based reference services have appeared over the past few years. While dotcom companies provide most of these services, some libraries and library consortia have also introduced Web-based reference and information services. Such services are termed "virtual" or "digital" reference services. Digital reference services in India are slowly picking up the race to compete.

Functionality, Usability, and Accessibility in the Digital Library Context

Functionality, usability, and accessibility testing of digital library information services and products are essential for providing high quality services to a broad and diverse population of users. A number of specific methods, as shown in this paper, can be readily developed to provide such evaluations. In this paper, specific goals guide the presentation of the development through time of the methods and instruments created, tested, refined, and operationalized in functionality, usability, and accessibility testing by the researchers. The goals of this paper are to:

- Demonstrate the potential roles of multiple, iterative evaluation strategies in the development and refinement of digital libraries;
- Detail the methodologies that focus on how the services meet the needs of users; and
- Encourage further discussion of the uses of these multiple evaluation approaches in assessing these libraries.

Functionality, usability, and accessibility are methodologies that provide different data regarding the ability of a digital library to meet the needs of users. More specifically:

- Functionality testing determines the extent to which a digital library, in whole or in part, is able to perform desired operations (e.g., basic search, multiple languages).
- Usability testing determines the extent to which a digital library, in whole or in part, enables users to intuitively use a digital library's various features.
- Accessibility testing determines the extent to which a digital library, in whole or in part, provides users with disabilities the ability to interact with the digital library.

Rather than focus strictly on technological aspects, this combination of methodologies places emphasis on how well the digital library serves its community of users on the whole (see Table I). Such methodologies account for key points of library service from the perspective of providing service where: information and services must be comprehensible for all users; features and functions necessary to provide library services must be present and always operate properly; and the needs of a diverse population of users within a library's community, which includes those with special access needs must be considered.

Moreover, the combination of all three of these techniques provides a composite picture that is far more comprehensive and robust than any of these evaluation strategies can provide individually. Further, by employing this combination of approaches in an iterative fashion, evaluations of digital libraries can be used to continually refine and improve the services of these libraries. More specifically, this multi-method approach to evaluating the digital services and resources of libraries enables researchers, library managers, and funding agencies to understand the extent to which:

- A library's networked environment meets desired user system features – e.g. search and retrieve functions, information access displays (for immediate download, location and availability, format, language);
- The design of the library is intuitive and overall enables users to navigate with ease; and
- Users with various disabilities (e.g. visual, auditory, mobility) can engage services and resources for information seeking and retrieval processes.

Together, therefore, this combination of evaluative data provides multiple and powerful perspectives on the operation and use of a digital library.

Information Literacy in Digital Environment

The internet has had a major impact on modern life by facilitating direct interaction between the individual and government, businesses, organisations and other people. The direct nature of this communication has bypassed many of the traditional intermediaries in a multitude of human interactions. New business models capitalise on the ability to interact directly with the customer. Whilst there have been some costly failures, there have been many successes. Furthermore, we can all now become entrepreneurs in the digital economy by using sites such as www.ebay.co.uk to sell direct to other users of networked communications technology.

As ever more communication and delivery of services takes place within a digital environment, there is increasing pressure for citizens of those nations that would like to describe themselves as information societies to be prepared to interact with this medium. This can be empowering, but it can also be bewildering. The online environment is a relatively new phenomenon, which continues to evolve. Martin describes the current state of online interactions as being in transition but as moving towards becoming mainstream, everyday "e-activities" (Martin, 2004). To operate effectively in this online environment, to be able to learn, work, communicate with others, interact with government, shop and for entertainment, we will need a set of skills that will allow us to function with sufficient competence to achieve our goals. Bundy has identified a number of areas that require a new kind of literacy in information intensive societies:

- Participative citizenship;
- Social inclusion;
- The creation of new knowledge;
- Personal empowerment; and
- Learning for life (Bundy, 2004).

Information Literacy: an Evolving Concept

Literacy (derived from Latin *litteratus*) is a concept that has been evolving over time and has had a variety of meanings, to include the skills needed to perform well in society. The simplest form of literacy involves the ability to use language in its written form: a literate person is able to read, write and understand his or her native language and expresses a simple thought in writing (Bawden, 2001, p. 220).

The literature offers several definitions, explanations and clarifications of what information literacy is. The term "information literate" was first introduced in 1974 by Zurkowski (the then President of the US Information Industry Association), in a submission to the US National Commission on Libraries and Information Science, to identify people "trained in the application of information resources to their work" (Carbo, 1997). He put forward recommendations to the US government that it should establish a national programme, aimed at achieving widespread, work-related information literacy (Webber and Johnston, 2000a). Zurkowski used the term "information literacy" to address a goal within an information policy, to accommodate the transformation of traditional library services into innovative private sector information provision, for the new information industry that was emerging. In his perspective, information literacy was associated with the effective use of information within a working environment, specifically for problem solving (Bawden, 2001).

According to American Library Association Information literacy is a set of abilities that enables an individual to "recognize when information is needed and have the ability to effectively locate, evaluate, and use the needed information." The American Library Association was the first organisation to formulate a widely accepted criterion for what characterizes an information literate person (ALA, 1989).

Today in the digital divide it is necessary to make the users more literate, it was the time when the users were introduced with library orientation programs, as the shift is taking place in the forms of resources simultaneously instructional programs, contents and mode are also transforming.

These are the common characteristics which are related to Information Literacy:

- Literacy is deliberately taught and consciously and deliberately learned.
- It is the ability to read write impacts considerably on a person's potential.
- Communicate and learn

Information Literacy encompasses the following "literacies":

- Tool literacy (software, networks)
- Resource literacy (information resources)
- Socio-structural literacy (knowledge of how information

Is created and socially placed)

Bawden (2001), in his review on information literacy and digital literacy, attempts to clarify related concepts and a multiplicity of terms, which are often used synonymously. Some of these are:

- Information literacy;
- Library literacy;
- Media literacy;
- Computer literacy (synonyms – IT/information technology/electronic/electronic information literacy);
- Network literacy (synonyms – Internet literacy, hyper-literacy); and
- Digital literacy (synonym – digital information literacy).

(Bawden, 2001) argued that library literacy, media literacy and computer literacy are skills-based literacies that emerged to meet the needs of an evolving and increasingly complex landscape of information resources, with new technologies and a wider variety of media and services. In this context, library literacy refers to competencies in the use of libraries (collections and services), the ability to follow a systematic search strategy to locate and evaluate the most relevant information on a given topic (Humes, 1999). Media literacy refers to critical thinking in assessing information made available through television, radio, newspapers, magazines and increasingly the Internet (Bawden, 2001). In turn, Hancock (2002) quoting the Second Cox Report states that: "Media education seeks to increase children's critical understanding of the media… How they work, how they produce meaning, how they are organized and how audiences make sense of them". Computer literacy is usually associated with technological know-how to manipulate computer hardware and software (Humes, 1999).

Other definitions of the information literate person tend to cover the same elements, but expand them in one way or another (Langford, 1999). Meanwhile, Webber and Johnston (2000b) point out that the majority of definitions of information literacy put forward tend to include the following elements:

- Competency in selecting and interacting with the most appropriate source of information, whether that be in print, electronic or another person;
- Feeling comfortable with the tools needed for that interaction;
- Communicating information effectively and appropriately;
- Taking an intelligently critical approach to information in whatever form (e.g. paper, electronic, other people) and appreciating the changes in information economy that affect what is presented;
- Using and managing information effectively in a personal and work context;

- Developing a sense of oneself as an information literate person.

In this context, the same authors (Webber and Johnston, 2001) propose a broad definition: "Information literacy is the adoption of appropriate information behaviour to obtain, through whatever channel or medium, information well-fitted to information needs, together with critical awareness of the importance of wise and ethical use of information in society".

In summary, to deal with the complexities of the current information environment requires a comprehensive and much broader form of literacy – information literacy – which embraces all forms of skill-based literacies, but cannot be restricted to any of them or to any particular form of technology and requires "understanding, meaning and context" (Bawden and Robinson, 2001).

STAKEHOLDER'S PERSPECTIVES

The context for planning digital reference services is best understood by briefly reviewing the perspectives of the stakeholders – students, faculty, and library staff.

Student as Stakeholder

The student perspective, whether that of distance learners or otherwise, has been shown to value convenience and, often, the path of least resistance. This is a powerful force in student decision making, sometimes resulting in a willingness to place convenience before quality. Network access can exacerbate these inclinations. Lynch,(1994) observes a phenomenon where "… electronic information resources are too successful and too convenient. Users view them as defining the totality of available information". Given this, the challenge for the library would be to conveniently locate high quality resources and services in the paths of users. In planning reference services, the question becomes *Where and when in the networked environment, are the points of need?* And then to position references services accordingly to that appropriate need.

Faculty as Stakeholder

The faculty perspective can be prescient about the changing learning environment and this has resulted in an outright challenge to the digital library and librarians. The e-learning modules have opened a new dimension for the faculty members. Faculty not only enjoy the federated search of vast resources available in digital form, but also they want using advance Information and Communication Technology (ICT) streaming videos of lectures, presentations etc using open source software such social networking software like Youtube, VCASMO, DRUPAL etc. Here, faculty that teach distance courses are most often the same that teach on-campus courses. In fact, in the e-learning environment the usage of interactive television or live Internet streaming technologies, faculty often deliver instruction to a classroom of students and a geographically distributed number of students simultaneously such as streaming videos can be easily synchronized with power point presentations. It has become increasingly clear that distance and on-campus learning programs are on a path of convergence.

Library Professionals as Stakeholder

The perspective of library staff must be considered in the context of the overall environment and organization. If the small branch libraries are located at different places in India, then all these can be integrated with one main-campus to one "platform-one window" using powerful broadband technology and web-based federated search application. Exchange of resources among the branch libraries with the main-campus libraries is a common phenomenon. Some of the help operations in the libraries are also streamlined such as

acquisition of resources, cataloguing of resources, digital reference services from one "window-one platform". These integrated systems have found to be most effective, in terms of sharing of print and electronic resources, sharing of skilled manpower resources, and also duplication of efforts etc. This concept of "one-window one-platform" is an extremely cost effective mechanism.

LITERATURE REVIEW ON DIGITAL REFERENCE SERVICES

While doing a literature survey, it was felt that several papers are published in the field of Digital Library but a little attention has been paid to the service aspects of the digital library in previous studies. The few studies that dealt with service aspects mainly focused on adopting new technologies and providing new software to digital library users. In addition to a search tool and various features, a digital library should include some types of information services to support an interaction between materials and users' needs, and to promote learning using its collections. Librarians play a major role in providing services in the context of users' information seeking process. They assist and interact with users by answering questions about materials, instructing them on how to use information, help them for research purposes. Such conventional services are essential in a digital library environment as well.

Libraries and librarians are no longer the sole providers of reference and information services. Arms (2000) forecasts the creation of fully automated libraries that can substitute IT for staffing in the performance of tasks that at present require human intellectual ability such as provision of reference services. He argues that computers have massive power that can outperform humans in some tasks that require speed and accuracy. At the same time he notes that machines "lack the power not of being inclusive, but selective". This means that machines cannot employ judgement, an important element of any reference and information service. Rudner (2000) suggests that patrons have become more independent in their information seeking attitudes, but the quality of their findings is poor due to their inability to select the best information sources. In a recent conference well-known experts discussed the current state of Digital Reference Services (DRS) and areas that would be useful for further exploration. Turender (2002) discusses some of these issues, including the essential infrastructure needed to provide advanced reference services such as "live librarians", the cost implications, the technologies that are available, and the need to identify the audience.

A digital library is not merely a means of access to information over the network. As long as "library" is attached to the concept, a digital library does and should care about users and communities that are in need of information and services just like conventional libraries. Services, therefore, should be one of the crucial aspects of digital libraries. Till date, a major emphasis on digital library development and implementation was given to technology which is an important organ such as technical architecture, digitization, and techniques of how to build a digital library with respect to a system architecture, digital object creation and management, and so on (Chowdhury,.2002; Chowdhury, and Chowdhury,2003; Marchionini, and Fox,1999; Sloan, 1998; Arms,Blanchi, and Overly,1997; Chen, 2000; Cleveland, 1998; McCray, and Gallagher, 2001; Marchionini, and Fox, 1999) pointed out four dimensions in designing a digital library: community, technology, services, and content. According to them, services reflect the functionality afforded by systems serving the community of users. Such services include access, reference and question answering, on-demand help, fostering of citizenship and literacy, and mechanisms to simplify participatory involvement of user communities. Borgman,(1999) also viewed digital library as combination of a service,

architecture, a set of information resources, and a set of tools to retrieve information resources. However, most digital library projects so far mainly focused on offering search mechanism and tools for information retrieval.

In addition to a search tool and various features, a digital library should include some types of information services to support an interaction between materials and users' needs, and to promote learning using its collections. Librarians played a major role in providing services in the context of users' information seeking process. They assist and interact with users by answering questions about materials, instructing them on how to use information, help them for research purposes. Such conventional services are essential in a digital library environment as well.

Many experts (Fox,and Urs, 2002; Harter,1996; Marchionini, and Komlodi, 1998; Noerr, 2003) that suggested services can be divided into two broad categories of services:

- Traditional services and
- Services unique to the digital environment.

Harter, (1996) advocated that traditional library services such as ready reference, help with search tools, access to and assistance with commercial search services, and so forth should be included in a digital library. Marchionini, and Komlodi, (1998) provided a list of service types to be offered in a digital library, that is, search services, reference and question answering services, filtering and SDI (MyLibrary service), and instruction. Fox, and Urs, (2002) offered some examples of unconventional services including personalized digital reference services. An emerging trend in digital libraries to support users' specific information needs and preferred search and retrieval strategies is the personalization service. Based on users' interest and characteristics, information in a digital library is automatically filtered and delivered to users via a personalized interface. Cohen, S.(2000) reported a personalized electronic service project, MyLibrary, in the Cornell University Library. With the service, students, faculty, and staff can collect and organize resources for private use, and stay informed of new resources provided by the library. Jayawardana, Hewagamage, and Hirakawa,(2001a, b) introduced a framework for personalized information environment (PIE) in which users can build personalized views on library materials based on their interests and are able to organize the collected information, annotate, modify, and integrate library sources as part of their knowledge construction.

Many terms are used to describe digital reference (Lankes, 2004). Wasik, (1999) defined digital reference services as "Internet-based question-and-answer services that connect users with experts in a variety of subject areas." A digital library can put such digital reference services in place since it is built on the networking system. Sloan, (1998) and Janes, (2003) described a number of experiments with extending reference services into the networked world. Examples of this are e-mail reference, live chat reference, instant messaging, desktop videoconferencing, and so on. Tenopir, (2001) and Tenopir, and Ennis, (2001) also showed current practices of digital reference services in academic libraries.

One of the ways for information dissemination used in traditional libraries is current awareness such as distribution of the table of contents for all journals in their collection to users. The main objective of current awareness is to provide users with up-to-date information. With many technological features like mailing list software, such services can be offered to users (Chu, and Krichel, (2003). Chu, and Krichel,(2003) and Cruz, Kritchel, and Trinidad, (2003) reported a model for current awareness service.

RISING ISSUES IN DIGITAL REFERENCE AND INFORMATION SERVICES

Why to Develop This Service?

Libraries have made efforts to better serve users with information and value-added services. They provide services both in a traditional way and in an innovative way by applying ICT. Digital reference services and some advanced services for personalization and interactivity have been implemented in libraries and other organizations. While access services have been central in digital library development and projects for personalization and interactivity have been implemented in digital environments, less attention has been paid to other reference and information services. With the evolution of new environments, a digital library should redefine digital library services. Such services need to include both conventional and innovative types of services. With well-designed services, digital libraries will be able to better serve their users and community. Campbell, (1992) has questioned the overall performance and economic viability of reference services as they currently exist, and has identified three major forces that will change reference services, whether libraries participate or not:

1. The migration of learning into the asynchronous environment;
2. The emergence of the web-based generation, and
3. The arrival of commercial forces into the education marketplace, which will not hesitate to eliminate irrelevant services (Campbell,2000).

Ferguson, and Bunge, (1997) in their paper lay the conceptual foundation for transformative change in the delivery of reference services. They assert that the evolution of the digital library must include the "metamorphosis of the library's core user services, particularly reference and instruction, in ways that enable delivery over the network in order to achieve a high degree of user independence, anywhere the network goes and at any time the user chooses". More recently, Ferguson, (2000) proposes a reference service model and blueprint that substantially integrate services to on-site and remote users.

What is so Important in the Design of Digital Reference Services?

Kasowitz, Bennett, and Lankes, (2000) suggest that the enduring quality standards of traditional reference services should guide the development of digital services. Many call for sensitization to new aspects of users that are becoming evident in the digital environment. Drabenstott, K.M.(1994) states that the digital library comprises linkages between multiple libraries and information services, and that these linkages must be transparent to the user. Also, user-librarian interaction in the research and learning process must also be preserved. Through studies of social interactions involving library users in physical settings, Twidale, Nichola, and Paice,(1997) have identified a number of traits, many involving forms of collaboration between the user and the information provider that should be transferred to the digital environment.

A common thread in many papers on electronic service design is the need to migrate the interpersonal element and qualities of human touch which are hallmarks of traditional reference services. Abels, (1996), Tibbo,(1995) and Straw, (2000) provide key observations and strategies involving the translation of the reference interview into the digital service environment.

CHANGE IN SCHOLARLY PUBLISHING

It is clear that a significant shift in academic publishing has occurred away from print to digital, although the difference in degree of shift between subject areas and types of publication is quite marked. With this shift towards digital come two important side-effects that have notable implications for strategy and management. Typically, when a library pays for a printed resource it becomes the owner and may retain it forever or dispose of it as it wishes. When a library pays for a digital resource it does not acquire that resource, but obtains a licence to use it, for a given period and for access by a given number of people, usually within a given organisation, building or institution. This clearly has important implications for financial planning, and future access and preservation. The financial implications of paying for a license for many users who may or may not use a resource, as opposed to buying a resource for a fixed fee can be serious. Secondly, there is a shift underway from holding the resource in one's own library, towards accessing it on the supplier's site. This has its advantages and disadvantages. We no longer have to manage the resources in-house, whether digital or printed, and might need fewer new buildings and staff to handle collections, but we have to be much better organised in finding information, linking to it and ensuring that those links persist. We need good quality portals and enhanced skills of assessment and evaluation of resources in order to help our users.

However, there is also a paradox here in Indian perspective. Each library's service is becoming in part a menu of distributed electronic resources to which users are given access. From the library point-of-view we have a highly distributed model (a "virtual library") but from the point-of-view of each respective resource it has become highly centralized. The publisher no longer providing copies of the resource but simply maintains a central database, possibly mirroring it in two or three other places around the globe. The publisher has tighter control and the publisher, not the library, now has control over resources for which the library pays. This is a clear threat, not only for the preservation of the academic record, but to the future capability of institutions to pay in what is in effect a monopolistic situation. Commercial publishers whose main motivation is profit may tend to exploit this situation at the expense of their customers, despite the fact that evidence has been produced to argue that current pricing policies in monopoly situations could be self-defeating (Jeon-Slaughter, Herkovic, and Keller, 2005).

E-Journals

In the digital library decade e-journals have emerged most quickly as the dominant component of the digital library. Despite a number of difficulties, usually concerned with pricing policies and digital rights management, publishers and libraries have negotiated themselves into a position whereby large quantities of e-journals are available for licensing in electronic form if the library wishes and can afford the cost. In 2005, *Ulrich's Periodicals Directory* reported almost 30,000 online journals, of which about 12,000 were scholarly and refereed. In the biomedical, natural and exact sciences (with the possible exception of mathematics), as far as western language journals are concerned, critical mass has now been achieved in the publication of e-journals to the extent that libraries can adopt strategies of preferring e-resources for access to current research, where possibly more than 95 per cent of users' needs can be satisfied electronically; this is indeed a fundamental change (Montgomery, 2002). Moreover, the non-subscription costs of electronic journals compared with those of paper journals have been shown to be lower (Schonfield et.al., 2004)).

E-Books

The situation with e-books is rather more complicated. In the first place the term "e-book" can mean different things to different people. Most commentators agree that the term can embrace a variety of things:

- A digital object (or collection of objects) designed to be read (or listened to) on a special device;
- A digital object (or collection of objects) that can be read with special software on a PC; and
- Any linear digital text that can be read on a computer.

Of these, the first two are generally thought of as being e-books in the narrow sense and the third in a broader sense. A valuable discussion of the issues surrounding e-books and their future is contained in a paper by Lynch, (2001). From a strategic point-of-view it may still be too early for many libraries to have significant e-book activity as it is not clear what libraries or their users want in this regard and there may be very little relevant material available in a particular domain. A perfectly good strategy could be simply to watch and wait for developments to become clearer. In any event it seems unlikely that libraries would want to invest in special devices on any significant scale for normal use. That would seem like substitution of the physical book by a physical device with little apparent strategic gain.

Secondary Services

Production of secondary services such as indexes, abstracts, collections, reference sources, and databases in electronic form is nothing new and pre-dates what we define as the digital library, but should obviously be included in our inventory of developments in the publishing world that are relevant to our theme of change. In the context of the digital library we should now add the proliferation of portals and linking services that have become important in finding our way around global digital library resources. Highly performing navigation services are now an essential part of any digital library. We note, however, that various studies have shown that students now use Google and other internet search engines as a first (and sometimes only) resort in their information seeking behaviour (Griffiths, and Brophy, 2005). This is despite the many warnings from librarians that it is unsafe to rely only on these channels for proper literature searching.

E-Learning

Over the last few years there has been much discussion about forthcoming changes in the world of education as a result of technology and globalization. Many commentators believe that significant change is to be expected. Most universities and higher education organizations are active in innovation in teaching and learning, usually involving trials and testing of new technologies, ideas and approaches. However, it is also the case that if you look at what is going on internally in universities the level of structural change appears to be quite low. By structural we mean formally agreed and persistent changes to the structure of educational programmes and the relationship between teachers and students through use of e-learning, as opposed to projects and experiments of a temporary nature. Even when successful, it is common for innovation projects not to be continued on into full-scale implementation.

As far as the market for electronic learning materials is concerned there have been a few ambitious enterprises in the arena of global higher education partnerships that have failed, or at least failed to deliver. There are comparisons to be made here with the general collapse of the dot. com bubble. However, it is safe to say that many educational publishers have e-learning and innovative products high on their agenda.

The problem is that the introduction of e-learning is considerably more complex than the introduction of e-journals. Strategic aspects are still unclear and it is difficult therefore for librarians to predict the way forward. Part of this may be to do with the fact that e-learning and distance learning can get confused. A number of trends, however, seem to be generally agreed. It is expected that student-centered learning will develop, whereby students work in a more independent, investigative and co-operative way, as opposed to passively receiving information transmission from teachers. Teachers will operate more as facilitators and advisors than instructors. Naturally, students will spend a proportionately greater amount of their time working with electronic sources, products and courseware. The way, in which library and staff will support, students will change and the skills required for the staff will have to be enhanced (Roes, 2001).

WEB-ENABLED REFERENCE SERVICES

A number of reference and information services are now available on the Web. Interestingly, many of these services are provided by non-library and commercial organisations. While some are free, others need payment. Detailed discussions on such services are available in a number of publications (see for example, Chowdhury, and Chowdhury, (2001a, 2001b); Lankes, Colliins, and Kasowitz, (2000); Sherman, (2000); McKiernan, (2001) maintains a site that provides categorised listing of libraries that offer real-time reference services using chat software, live interactive communication tools, bulletin board services and other Internet technologies. Most of these services are designed for registered users of the libraries concerned.

Chowdhury, and Chowdhury, (2001b) categorised online reference and information services into three broad groups:

1. Reference and information services from publishers, database search services, and specialised institutions;
2. Reference services provided by libraries and/or experts through the Internet; and
3. Reference and information services where users need to conduct a search and find information through the Web.

Chowdhury, and Chowdhury, (2001a) discussed several online information services that belong to the first category mentioned above. They have listed various current awareness and SDI services such as:

- The contents page service from commercial publishers, such as Elsevier's Contents Direct Service;
- Information on new books available free from publishers and vendors, such as the Amazon.com;
- SDI services from online search service providers, such as Dialog (*Dialog Alerts*);
- *Current Contents* and *ISI Alerting Services* from ISI, and so on.

Some of these services, particularly the contents page services from publishers of journals, are free, while for others, such as *Dialog Alerts* or *Current Contents* from ISI, users need to register and pay.

There are also some Web-based reference services where users need to conduct a search for a reference query. Such services provide free access to various online reference sources, and allow users either to select a specific source or conduct a search on a range, or all, of the reference sources. Examples of such services include the following:

- Internet Public Library (http://www.ipl. org).
- Infoplease (http:www.infoplease.com).
- Britannica (http://www.britannica.com).

- Bartleby Reference (http:www.bartleby. com/reference).
- Internet Library for Librarians (http://www.itcompany.com/inforetriever/).
- Electric Library (http://ask.elibrary.com/refdesk.asp).
- Mediaeater Reference Desk (http://www.mediaeater.com/easy-access/ref.html).
- ReferenceDesk (http://www.referencedesk.org/).
- Xrefer (http://www.xrefer.com/).

While most of these Web-based reference services are available free, some charge a small fee.

Next-Generation

Impacted by the rapid development of cutting-edge technologies and emerging technologies, we can clearly foresee the next generation web-based library user services. No doubt, the next generation of the internet will become the backbone of the future information dissemination and exchange in the digital age.

Based on the Next-Generation Web-based Client/Server Library Information Architecture displayed in Figure 1, library users at the frontend (Tier 1), can use desktops, notebooks, tablets, personal digital assistants (PDAs), handheld computers, hi definition televisions (HDTVs) and cell phones to access, locate, convert, and disseminate library information resources, services, and instructions via the next generation internet and broadband wireless services. Also, JavaScript, Extensible Stylesheet Language (XSL), Extensible Hypertext Markup Language (XHTML), and Extensible Markup Language (XML) will be widely used to define web page contents, data manipulation, data mining and data management. At the Tier 2, the middleware such as web services and document object model (DOM) will handle server-side processes. At the Tier 3, Object Relational Database Management Systems

Figure 1. Next-generation web-based client service library information architecture

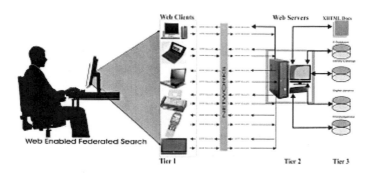

(ORDBMS) will become primary repository tools to build e-databases and digital libraries.

Specialized Web-Enabled Reference Services

Although Ask Jeeves, as shown Figure 2, is basically a search engine, many researchers also see it as a Web-based information service because of two reasons:

1. Users can ask a question in Ask Jeeves, and in many cases can get an answer right away; and

2. Users can ask a question on a given topic, and Ask Jeeves comes up with a list of questions on the same or similar topics; the user can select any of the those predefined questions,

and then Ask Jeeves provides answers to that.

Ask Jeeves is a unique question-answering system that allows users to ask questions in plain English, and then delivers the answer. As one of the most sophisticated navigation systems on the Internet, Ask Jeeves combines a unique natural language engine with a proprietary knowledgebase. Taken together, this mechanism processes the meaning and grammar of real questions in plain English; provides intelligent responses for user confirmation; links directly to relevant, high-quality answers; and, perhaps most exciting of all, becomes more intelligent as its knowledgebase expands with each question asked and each answer delivered.

The site further says that Ask Jeeves processes each query syntactically (to analyse the grammar)

Figure 2. www.askjeeves.co.uk

and semantically (to determine meaning), and then Ask Jeeves' answer-processing engine provides the question template response (the list of questions that users see after they ask a question). When the user clicks on a response, the answer-processing engine retrieves the answer template that contains links to the answer locations. Thus, Ask Jeeves helps users select a query from a pre-defined set of queries on a given topic. However, there is a debate on whether the kind of service provided by Ask Jeeves matches reference services provided by libraries. The Ask Jeeves site can be accessed at (www.AskJeeves.co.uk). Many argue that it is the sheer volume of information available on the Web confronting unprecedented numbers of new users that has created the need for digital reference services. Chowdhury, (2002) notes that librarians have a crucial service role to play in digital environments, not least in providing structure to what can seem chaotic. He argues, in terms of Marchionini and Fox, that online reference is required to facilitate users becoming a real part of online communities. There is then, a general consensus about the need for reference services in the digital environment though many commentators have identified important ways in which they differ from those offered traditionally.

The Virtual Reference Desk (VRD) Network, a Web-based support service to digital reference services, has developed 11 facets of quality which can be used to aid the development or improvement of such a service (Virtual Reference Desk, 2000a). These range from accessibility to response policy and timescales and cover training, privacy, access and regular review of the service. The fourth facet relates to the interactive nature of the service, particularly the provision of a reference interview, allowing users to provide the service with relevant information in order to facilitate an accurate response to the query. A further facet relates to how instructive the service is. The network argues that users should not simply be furnished with answers but aided in information literacy.

OPEN SOURCE SOFTWARE AND REFERENCE SERVICE

The exponential growth and popularity of online information gathering tools has challenged libraries to demonstrate and publicise the ways they can add value to the user experience. A new generation of online tools known as Web 2.0 or social software is increasingly presented as the solution to this problem. Under the umbrella of this term come tools like blogs, really simple syndication (RSS) feeds, wikis, photo-sharing applications and discussion forums. Social software has the potential to make library services much more interactive. Social software tools not only give users access to content, they also allow users to easily contribute their own content, develop communities and share their knowledge with the library community. Social software may be a new concept, but it is already making a major impact. These tools continue to receive a lot of attention in the library community; at conferences, in blog postings and in practitioner journals.

Development of the Concept

In 2005, Tim O'Reilly published an article entitled "What is Web 2.0" (O'Reilly, 2005). In this piece, O'Reilly described a range of popular web services and characterized them by the fact that they offered users the ability to communicate interactively online and to create and share content. He argued that these popular web services belonged to a second generation of web tools (blogs, wikis and RSS feeds among them) that all shared the same underlying goal of enabling collaboration, community and participation. O'Reilly called these software tools Web 2.0 tools (2005). Librarians were quick to see the potential of these web services as they applied to libraries and to begin discussing them. The idea of providing online services that were more user-centred, collaborative and community-focussed was and still is a compelling one for public libraries, because many librarians think of them as a natural extension of traditional library services. For example, (2007) saw social software as "a technology-enhanced progression of traditional library services and goals".

The Conceptual Impact of Social Software

An established body of literature uses the term Library 2.0 to discuss the positive change that social software tools could bring to the library environment. The librarian Michael Casey coined the term Library 2.0 in 2005 to describe social software services as they applied to libraries. He argued that, using these technologies, libraries could create a new model of library service that encouraged "constant and purposeful change, inviting user participation in the creation of the both physical and the virtual services they want" (Casey, and Savastinuk, 2006). The term Library 2.0 has often been used to frame arguments about how libraries should use social software to strategically position themselves for continued relevance in a technological future (Miller,2005; Chad, and Miller, 2005; Stephens, 2006; Casey, and Savastinuk, 2006; Maness, 2006).

The term Library 2.0 has been used by both by the representatives of library system vendors and by librarians themselves (Casey, and Savastinuk, 2006; Stephens, 2006) to support their cause. Several of the early papers on how social software could be used in libraries were written by the representatives of library system vendors (Miller,2005; Chad, and Miller, 2005). These papers argued that if a library was to be innovative and customer responsive, it must embrace the concept of Library 2.0 (by embracing a specially designed new library system that incorporated participative elements). Some librarians without vendor affiliations also shared the view that libraries must experiment with technological innovations in order to remain relevant in today's society (Casey, and Savastinuk, 2006). Those who saw technological innovation as synonymous with relevance stood opposed to those who argued that innovation in libraries did not necessarily involve technology (Crawford, 2006).

Literature on Library 2.0 included arguments about the place of technology in libraries (Stephens,2006), the future role of librarians (Chowdhury, Poulter, and McMenemy, 2006), and the philosophy that should underpin library service as it moved into the twenty-first century (Casey, and Savastinuk, 2006. Crawford, 2006) clarified this debate by giving an overview and critique of literature on Library 2.0. He pointed out that the term Library 2.0 itself implied a power relationship between a better Library 2.0 and a lesser "Library 1.0" which libraries were moving from. In this way, use of the term implicitly criticised those libraries that do not use social software. Crawford also usefully drew a distinction between Library 2.0 as "the movement or bandwagon" (Crawford, 2006, p. 2) and Library 2.0 as the positive concept that concentrated on "building on today's best and improving for the future" (Crawford, 2006, p. 1).

Of all those who have contributed to the debate on social software in libraries, Maness, (2006) has provided one of the most developed critical perspectives. Maness developed many of the more ephemeral ideas on the subject of Library 2.0, arguing that "a more exact definition and theory for Library 2.0 is necessary to focus discussion and experimentation within the community" (Maness, 2006, p. 3). He proposed a new definition of Library 2.0 as "the application of interactive, collaborative, and multi-media web-based technologies to web-based library services and collections" (Maness, 2006, p. 3).

Major Attributes of Using Open Source Software "Library 2.0"

The major attributes which impacted on the Library system are (Rutherford, (2008):

- Creating communities around the library;
- Reaching users where they are;
- Attracting new users;

- Opening the channels of communication;
- Redressing the power imbalance;
- Measuring usage; and
- Measuring value.

Creating Communities Around the Library

It has the potential to create online communities of people who can share recommendations for books, advice on how to research their family history, review recent library events, etc.

Reaching Users Where They Are

The ability to reach physically distant users was the most important advantage of social software instead of forcing them to come into the physical building.

Attracting New Users

The ability to reach users wherever they are geographically has the obvious benefit of attracting new users to the library service. This social software could attract users who did not feel comfortable using the physical library, as well as those who were unable to use the physical library due to barriers of distance or lack of mobility.

Opening the Channels of Communication

One of the often-cited characteristics of social software is that it enables virtual communication. All the social software had indeed improved communication between users and library staff.

Redressing the Power Imbalance

The reasons for implementing social software, and what hoped to achieve by doing this. Reasons included allowing users opinions to be heard more clearly, creating more convenient services for users

and fostering a sense of community and ownership in the library. All of these goals seemed to be very user focused, and to share a theme of giving users more power to shape their libraries, it is a true symbol of user-oriented approach.

Measuring Usage

Talking about measuring the usage of social software is a difficult issue, as each separate tool has different possibilities for measuring use. The most commonly used method of measuring usage was by gathering usage statistics.

Measuring Value

Two of the respondents talked about the issues associated with determining the value to users of implementing social software. One raised the problem of measuring value, mentioning that she/he felt it would be easier to evaluate by "qualitative measures".

MARKETING DIGITAL RESOURCES

Which ever approach is taken, the question of definition is paramount. "Virtual library," "digital library," "electronic library" are all terms to used describe library and information services delivered via the Internet, but they can mean different things to different users. Therefore the issue of marketing these services is problematic since, as LIS professionals we must ask what exactly are we trying to market and to whom? Are we marketing a collection of digitized material that belongs to a physical library, that is, a hybrid library? Or are we marketing the library's services via the web? The growth of digital libraries makes one wonder if, in the zealous drive to digitise and make collections available as widely as possible, we have not created a monster!

Due to the growth in services which focus on a client-orientated approach (rather than product delivery or sale), and the increasing use of the Internet for marketing, marketers have turned to relationship marketing (RM) techniques. Relationship marketing could be one approach LIS professionals take when marketing digital library services. Thus, the purpose of this issue's column is to raise some of the issues LIS professionals may have to consider when marketing digital collections in this way.

Relationship Marketing and Digital Collections

Relationship marketing is to identify and establish, maintain and enhance and when necessary also to terminate relationships with customers and other stakeholders, at a profit, so that the objectives of all parties are met and this is done by mutual exchange and fulfilment of promises. (Grönroos, 1994)

In order to be sure that they are providing the best, and most appropriate services to customers, it is essential that libraries know who their customer (or potential customer) is. This can be achieved through the organisation of personal data and its storage in a central database – in line with data protection regulation. This information can then be used for market segmentation, in which the user population is divided into groups according to similar characteristics.

This may be done on the basis of demographic details, such as age, ethnic origin, gender, occupation; or according to borrowing characteristics, the library services they use, their interests, the time they visit the library – or more likely a combination of the two (De Saez, (1993). This data can be used to ascertain to what extent the services currently offered are appropriate to the customer and can be used to make decisions about the creation of new services and the termination of existing ones.

The population can then be further segmented, at a customer level, by personalising services to customers (Goldsmith, 1999). This would involve

using their personal data to make predictions about their individual needs, and offering services to them or making recommendations about the services they already use – for example, using data on their book borrowing to suggest books they might like to read. This approach can be taken when the library has the data available and knows who its customers are. Segmentation can help libraries target particular user groups via RM techniques.

The benefits of relationship marketing are:

* No costs of acquiring new customers
* Less need to offer incentives to customers
* Less price sensitive (loyal customers are pleased with the service)
* Loyal satisfied customers will recommend the service to others

RM has largely developed due to the use of IT as part of the marketing function. New technology has allowed organizations to implement Customer Relationship Management (CRM) systems to manage the RM function. It is via CRM systems that libraries could promote digital services to users, by using data from existing library management systems to target particular customers and promote specific services. Libraries have been doing this for years, making the customer the focus of service delivery. However, now the Internet can be used to target customers more effectively.

The transition from printed to digital versions of reference works has important consequences not only for those materials as collections of resources, but also for the ways in which libraries select and use those materials. Users are attracted by the benefits of online tools: remote access, around the clock access, access to multiple copies, and improved searching features. Librarians are aware of the drawbacks: the absence of some content, technical complexity, higher costs, and risks that arise when leased access replaces ownership. Database purchasing decisions may bypass the expertise of subject bibliographers, while aggregators, consortia and grant-makers play new roles in defining the content of library collections. The technical and mechanical problems associated with databases present new challenges to reference desk staff, and introduce systems staff as partners. Successful engagement with change includes an appreciation of users' expectations, and a positive attitude.

PRACTICE AND PROBLEMS IN REFERENCE SERVICES

In one of the in-house survey, during the interviews with library staff, we have tried to understand the problems librarians face and to discuss initiatives or directions for potential future developments. We investigated how DRS function within established in-house reference services, how librarians respond to patrons' queries electronically, how the work load is handled, what software libraries use and what improvements they would like to see in the provision of service in a digital environment.

Reference in Practice

Staff in libraries explained how the traditional enquiry desks operate on a daily basis. The enquiry desk staff that also receive and answer enquiries via e-mail. Some of these library staff are also responsible for maintaining the library's Web pages. Some librarians keep certain answers in their personal computer files, though these are not shared. There are separate enquiry services in the education faculty and law libraries, the latter attracting a notably large amount of enquiries for a single department service.

For example Chowdhury and Margariti (2004) mentioned in their paper of Glasgow University Library (GUL) that most enquiries are answered on the spot. A few of the more detailed telephone enquiries are recorded on enquiry sheets and filed for future reference. Subject librarians answer

queries that relate to their areas of expertise as they are passed to them from general enquiries. In GUL, the enquiry team deals with traditional face-to-face reference enquiries but also with many enquiries by telephone or e-mail. Queries can be of an in-depth, academic nature or simply about operational procedures. Furthermore, enquiries are received not just from members of the university – it is not unusual to receive a significant flow of enquiries from patrons outside the university. Although staff work on the front desk and answer enquiries on the spot where possible, if necessary (for example if the queries are more subject specific), they are passed to "subject" librarians through an e-mail. There is also a special section in the library that deals specifically with maps and official publications, and some queries may be passed on to this section. Alternatively, patrons may contact this section directly.

Reference Service Problems

Many librarians pointed out that DRS in academic libraries will typically process a large volume of enquiries, but they also say that the electronic enquiry desk lacks enquiry management software which could help manage such a large volume of enquiries. Library staff suggested that the use of software that could automatically distinguish between unique or demanding reference questions and repetitive, simple queries might solve a great deal of problems. This would help librarians concentrate on answering queries that require more research. However, it is obvious that no such ideal software tool currently exists.

Because librarians do not have software to record the volume of DRS enquiries, these are for the most part manually recorded on paper instead. An alternative is to add "original" patron questions to FAQs pages, a time-consuming activity. Original texts need manual editing before doing so, since patrons tend to include personal information that has to be removed. There is clearly a potential role for time-saving software to be introduced to address these problems.

Cost Implications: Acquisition of Digital Material to Support DRS

In any academic library, the most heavily used items are available in the short-loan collection in multiple copies. However, this is not always enough to satisfy the need for certain high demand titles and multiple networked access to electronic text seems to offer a way of addressing the need for multiple access to highly popular material. DRS similarly require an ample supply of such digital material to form the basis of virtual interactions with users. If electronic books seem to provide a good solution for such problems, it is worth querying why provision of electronic reference book material has not yet expanded to levels commensurate with the hard copy monograph provision in many libraries. An issue of prime importance is economics: the costs of e-book provision must be adequately dealt with if the medium is to expand. Digital provision of the entire text of many high quality student or reference books is expensive, not least because many such e-books are made available on a subscription basis as part of large "compulsory purchase" multi-title services. These replicate many of the cost disadvantages of the worst type of all-in-one, subscription-only e-journal service, whose enormous market dominance, inflexibility, complex pricing structures and spiralling expense have earned much disapproval from librarians world-wide.

However, at the time of writing the availability (or rather lack of availability) of digital reference material is a limiting factor on the spread of digital reference. Issues such as the models of pricing for e-book services are one of a number of factors which need to be addressed if this problem is to be solved.

FUTURE DIRECTIONS: RESEARCH

Current digital libraries research focus more on access to, and retrieval of, digital information. There are two more important components where lot of thrust is given towards different stakeholder's perspective such as information literacy, and social networking, social community development using open source software.

CONCLUSION

Today there is tremendous change in services earlier we use to make users to visit libraries or centers frequently but through the advantages of ICT we are taking libraries to their desk tops, this is what today user's demands is. The challenge exists before today's reference librarian is to use the web to deliver appropriate service at the right time in the right format, particularly in support of the library's extensive service.

Building on our own experiences and relations hope we can better understand and anticipate the users and enhance the services and products which best suited with their requirements and needs. By enhancing skills, knowledge and working practices on software's and building the customer relationships we will sure move our reference desk to their desktops.

As libraries adjust to an increasingly digital environment and a clientele that is more widely distributed and not confined to the physical library building itself, they need to assess more traditional library services to determine those which can and should be transmigrated meaningfully into the new environment. Allowing for clients to ask questions of a knowledgeable human being with the expectation that the questions will either be answered directly or that information will be provided to guide the clients' own searches is a respected traditional service within librarianship; its usefulness and value to clients is reflected in the number and range of libraries providing this service. This type of service provides an important safety net for clients who often face daunting problems in tasks associated with using information systems, such as framing queries, devising adequate search strategies, and evaluating the desired information. The libraries that have implemented variations of DRS need to continue to look at its implementation within their institutions to insure that they are marrying the old values and benefits with the evolving capabilities of the new environment.

Reference librarians need to shift their focus from providing technical assistance on using library resources to user education, thus assisting students in developing information literacy skills to identify when information is needed, and to locate, evaluate and use the needed information effectively. Today through many Learning management software's we can instruct our users by integrating those software e.g. web tutorials, face to face class instructions, chats in our libraries resources.

REFERENCES

Abels, E. (1996). The e mail reference interview: electronic mail library queries. *RQ, 35*(3), 345-58.

American Library Association. (1989). *Final Report, Presidential Committee on Information Literacy*. Retrieved from http://www.ala.org/acrl/nili/ilit1st.html

Arms, W. Y. (2000). Automated digital libraries: how effectively can computers be used for the skilled tasks of professional librarianship? *D-Lib Magazine, 6*(7/8). Retrieved from http://www.dlib.org/dlib/july00/arms/07arms.html. doi:10.1045/july2000-arms

Arms, W. Y., Blanchi, C., & Overly, E. A. (1997). An Architecture for information in Digital libraries. *D-Lib Magazine, 3*(2). Retrieved April 28, 2009, from http://www.dlib.org/dlib/february97/cnri/02arms1.html

Bawden, D. (2001). Information and digital literacies: a review of concepts. *The Journal of Documentation, 57*(2), 218–259. Retrieved from http://gti1.edu.um.es:8080/jgomez/hei/intranet/bawden.pdf. doi:10.1108/EUM0000000007083

Bawden, D., & Robinson, L. (2001). Training for information literacy: diverse approaches. In Graham, C. (Ed.), *Online Information 2001: Proceedings* (pp. 87–90). Oxford: Learned Information.

Borgman, C. L. (1999). What are digital libraries? Competing visions. *Information Processing & Management, 35*(3), 227–243.

Bundy, A. (2004). One essential direction: information literacy, information technology fluency. *Journal of eLiteracy, 1*(1). Retrieved December 22, 2004 from www.jelit.org/archive/00000006/

Campbell, J. D. (1992). Shaking the conceptual foundations of reference: a perspective. *RSR. Reference Services Review, 20*(4), 29–35. doi:10.1108/eb049164

Campbell, J. D. (2000). Clinging to traditional reference services. *Reference and User Services Quarterly, 39*(3), 223–227.

Carbo, T. (1997). *Mediacy: knowledge and skills to navigate the information highway. Paper present at the Infoethics conference*. Monte Carlo.

Casey, M., & Savastinuk, L. C. (2006). Library 2.0. *Library Journal, 131*(14).

Chad, K., & Miller, P. (2005). *Do Libraries matter?* Retrieved at March 15, 2009, from http://www.talis.com/downloads/white_paper/DoLibraries-Matter.pdf

Chen, H. (2000). Introduction to the special topic issue: part 2. *Journal of the American Society for Information Science American Society for Information Science, 51*(4), 213–215. doi:10.1002/(SICI)1097-4571(2000)51:3<213::AID-ASI1>3.0.CO;2-R

Chowdhary, G., & Margariti, S. (2004). Digital reference services: a snapshot of the current practices in Scottish libraries. *Library Review, 53*(1), 50–60. doi:10.1108/00242530410514793

Chowdhary, G., Poulter, A., & McMenemy, D. (2006). Public Library 2.0. *Online Information Review, 30*(4), 454–460.

Chowdhury, G. (2002). Digital libraries and reference services: present and future. *The Journal of Documentation, 58*(3), 258–283. doi:10.1108/00220410210425809

Chowdhury, G. G., & Chowdhury, S. (2001a). *Searching CD-ROM and Online Information Sources*. London: Library Association Publishing.

Chowdhury, G. G., & Chowdhury, S. (2001b). *Information Sources and Searching on the World Wide Web*. London: Library Association Publishing.

Chowdhury, G. G., & Chowdhury, S. (2003). *Introduction to Digital Libraries*. London: Facet Publishing.

Chu, H., and Krichel, T. (2003).NEP: current awareness service of the RePEc Digital Library. *D-Lib Magazine, 9*(12). Retrieved

Cleveland, G. (1998). *Digital Libraries: Definitions, Issues and challenges*. Retrieved April 20, 2001, from www.ifla.org/VI/5/op/udtop8/ udtop8.html

Cohen, S. (2000). My Library: personalized electronic services in the Cornell University Library. *DLib Magazine, 6*(4). Retrieved April 05, 2009, from www.dlib.org/dlib/april00/mistlebauer/04 mistlebauer.html

Crawford, W. (2006). Library 2.0 and Library 2.0. *Cities and Insights, 16*(2). Retrieved March 12, 2009, from http://cities.boisestate.edu/civ6i2.pdf9

Cruz, J. M. B., Kritchel, T., & Trinidad, J. C. (2003, September). *Organizing current awareness in a large digital library*. Paper presented at the Conference on Users in the Electronic Information Environments, Espoo.

De Sàez, E. E. (1993). *Marketing concepts for Libraries and Information services*. London: Library Association Publishing.

Drabenstott, K. M. (1994). *Analytical Review of the Library of the Future*. Washington, DC: Council on Library Resources.

February 15, 2009, from www.dlib.org/dlib/december03/chu/12chu.html

Ferguson, C. (2000). Shaking the conceptual foundations, too: integrating research and technology support f or the next generation of information service. *College & Research Libraries, 61*(4), 300–311.

Ferguson, C., & Bunge, C. (1997). The shape of services to come: values-based reference service for the largely digital library. *College & Research Libraries, 58*(3), 260.

Fox, E., & Urs, S. (2002). Digital libraries. *Annual Review of Information Science & Technology, 36*, 503–589. doi:10.1002/aris.1440360113

Goldsmith, R. E. (1999). The personalized marketplace: beyond the 4Ps. *Marketing Intelligence & Planning, 17*(4), 178–185. doi:10.1108/02634509910275917

Griffiths, J. R., & Brophy, P. (2005). Students searching behavior and the web: use of academic resources and Google. *Library Trends, 53*(4), 539–554.

Gronroos, C. (1994). Relationship marketing: strategic and tactical implications. *Management Decision, 34*(3), 5–14. doi:10.1108/00251749610113613

Hancock, A. (2002). Notes on information literacy. In *WSIS Focus - World Summit on the Information Society*. Retrieved from http://www.ideography.co.uk/wsis-focus/positions/hancock_01.html

Harter, S. (1996, September). *What is a digital library? Definitions, content and issues*. Paper presented at KOLISS DL '96: International Conference on Digital Libraries and Information Services for the 21st Century, Seoul.

Humes, B. (1999). *Understanding Information Literacy*. Retrieved from http://www.ed.gov/pubs/UnderLit/

Janes, J. (2003). *Introduction to Reference Work in the Digital Age*. New York: Neal-Schuman.

Jayawardana, C., Hewagamage, K. P., & Hirakawa, M. (2001 a). Personalization tool for active learning in digital libraries. *Journal of Academic Media Librarianship, 8*(1). Retrieved March 28, 2009, from wings.buffalo.edu/publications/mcjrnl/v8nl/active.html

Jayawardana, C., Hewagamage, K. P., & Hirakawa, M. (2001 b). A personalized information environment for digital libraries. *Information Technology and Libraries, 20*(4), 185–197.

Jeon-Slaughter, H., Herkovic, A. C., & Keller, M. A. (2005). Economics of scientific and biomedical journals: where do scholars stand in the debate of online journal pricing and site license ownership between libraries and publishers? *First Monday*. Retrieved June 28, 2006, from http://www.firstmonday.org/issues/issue10_3/jeon/index.html

Kasowitz, A., Bennett, B., & Lankes, R. D. (2000). Quality standards for digital reference consortia. *Reference and User Services Quarterly, 39*(4), 355–364.

Lankes, D., Collins, J. W., & Kasowitz, A. S. (2000). *Digital Reference Service in the New Millennium: Planning, Management, and Evaluation*. New York: Neal-Schuman.

Lankes, R. D. (2004). The digital reference research agenda. *Journal of the American Society for Information Science and Technology, 55*(4), 301–311. doi:10.1002/asi.10374

Lynch, C. (2001). The battle to define the future of the book in the digital world. *First Monday, 6*(6). Retrieved March 10, 2009, from http://www.firstmonday.orh/issues/issues6_6/lynch/index.html

Lynch, C. A. (1994). Rethinking the integrity of the scholarly record in the networked information age. *Educom Review, 29*(2). Retrieved April 28, 2009, from http://www.educause.edu/pub/er/review/reviewArticles/29238.html

Maness, J. M. (2006). Library 2.0 theory: Web 2.0 and its implications for libraries. *Webology, 3*(2), 25. Retrieved March 10, 2009, from www.webology.ir/2006/v3n2/a25.html

Marchionini, G., & Fox, E. A. (1999). Progress toward digital libraries: augmentation through integration. *Information Processing & Management, 35*(3), 219–225.

Marchionini, G., & Komlodi, A. (1998). Design of interfaces for information seeking. *Annual Review of Information Science & Technology, 33*, 89–12.

Martin, A. (2004). *What is eLiteracy?* IT Education Unit, University of Glasgow, Glasgow. Retrieved from http://www.iteu.gla.ac.uk/eliteracy/whatiseliteracy.html

McCray, A. T., & Gallagher, M. E. (2001). Principles for digital library development. *Communications of the ACM, 44*(5), 49–54. doi:10.1145/374308.374339

McKiernan, G. (2001). *LiveRef(Sm), a registry of real-time digital reference services.* Retrieved March 15, 2009, from http://www.public.iastate.edu/~CYBERSTACKS/Liveref.htm

Miller, P. (2005). Web 2.0: building the new library. *Ariadane, 45.*

Noerr, P. (2003). *The Digital Library Toolkit* (3rd Ed.). Sun Microsystems, Inc. Retrieved January 16, 2009, from www.sun.com/products-n-solutions/edu/whitepapers/digitaltoolkit.html

O' Reilly, T. (2005). *What is Web 2.0? Design patterns and business models for the next generation of software.* Retrieved February 13, 2009, from http://www.oreillynet.com/pub/a/oreilly/tim/news/2005/09/30/what-is-web-20.html

Roes, H. (2001). Digital libraries and education: trends and opportunities. *D-Lib Magazine, 77*(8). Retrieved March 20, 2009, from http://dlib.org/dlib/july01/07roes.html

Rudner, L. (2000). Who is going to mine digital library resources? And how? *D-Lib Magazine, 6*(5). Retrieved from http://www.dlib.org/dlib/may00/runder/05runder.html. doi:10.1045/may2000-rudner

Rutherford, L. L. (2008). Building participative library services: the impact of social software use in public libraries. *Library Hi Tech, 26*(3), 411–423. doi:10.1108/07378830810903337

Schonfield, R. C., King, D. A., Okerson, A., & Fenton, G. (2004). Library periodicals expenses: comparison of non-subscription costs of print and electronic formats on life cycle basis. *D-Lib Magazine, 10*(1). Retrieved February 28, 2009, from http://www.dlib.org/dlib/january04/schonfeld/01schonfeld.html

Sherman, C. (2000). Reference resources on the Web. *Online, 24*(1), 52–56.

Sloan, B. G. (1998). Service perspectives for the digital library remote reference services. *Library Trends, 47*(1), 117–143.

Stephens, M. (2006). Exploring Web 2.0 and libraries. *Library Technology Reports, 42*(4), 8–14.

Straw, J.E (2000).A virtual understanding: the reference interview and question negotiation in the digital age. Reference & User Services Quarterly, 39(4), 376-9.

Tenopir, C. (2001). Virtual reference services in a real world. *Library Journal, 126*(12), 38–40.

Tenopir, C., & Ennis, L. A. (2001). Reference services in the new millennium. *Online, 2*(4), 40–45.

Tibbo, H. R. (1995). Interviewing techniques for remote reference: electronic versus traditional environments. *The American Archivist, 58*(3), 294–310.

Turender, H. (2002). Digital reference: trends, techniques and changes. *Library Hi Tech News, 19.* Retrieved from http://masetto.emeraldinsight.com/v1=9380369/cl=29/nw=1/rpsv/cw/mcb/07419058/v19.

Twidale, M. B., Nicholas, D. M., & Paice, C. D. (1997). Browsing is a collaborative process on online systems, example of ARIADANE. *Information Processing & Management, 33*(6), 761–783. doi:10.1016/S0306-4573(97)00040-X

Virtual Reference Desk. (2000). *Facets of quality for digital reference services* (Version 4). Retrieved January 12, 2009, from www.vrd.org/facets-10-00.shtml

Wasik, J. M. (1999). Building and maintaining digital reference services. *ERIC Digest.* Retrieved March 15, 2009, from http://www.ed.gov/databases/ERIC_Digests/ed427794.html

Webber, S., & Johnston, B. (2000a). Conceptions of information literacy: new perspectives and implications. *Journal of Information Science, 26*(6), 381–397. doi:10.1177/016555150002600602

Webber, S., & Johnston, B. (2000b). *The information literacy class at Strathclyde University.* Paper presented at the SCONUL Conference 2000. Retrieved from http://dis.shef.ac.uk/literacy/sconuljuly.pdf

Chapter 10
Digital Library and Repositories:
An Indian Initiative

Bharat Kumar
Management Development Institute, India

ABSTRACT

This chapter discusses digital libraries and repositories. The purpose of this research is to identify digital libraries and repositories in India available in the public domain. It highlights the state of digital libraries and repositories in India. The digital libraries and repositories were identified through a study of the literature, as well as internet searching and browsing. The resulting digital libraries and repositories were explored to study their collections. Use of open source software especially for the creation of institutional repositories is found to be common. However, major digital library initiatives such as the Digital Library of India use custom-made software.

INTRODUCTION

Nowadays, libraries exist in many forms and are of many types. Recent developments in information and communication technologies (ICT), especially computers and the internet, have brought significant changes in the way we generate, distribute, collect, access and use information. Digital technologies and their applications have also come into every part of our daily life. It is accepted that we are now living in a digital world.

The history of digital libraries can be characterized as short and volatile. The digital library is a new form of managing the knowledge record and cultural heritage. Thousands of digital collections have been, and will continue to be, created around the world. Large amounts of research effort and money have been devoted to digital library research throughout the world over the past decade (Chowdhury and Chowdhury, 2003; Arms, 2000). Digital collections

DOI: 10.4018/978-1-61520-767-1.ch010

such as institutional repositories, cultural heritage curated digitally and a variety of versions of digital libraries are blooming worldwide. However, many organizations have found that the pool of information professionals with the expert knowledge and skills to create and manage digital collections is very small. But there is still shortage of supply, a lack of information professionals with the right combination of skills, for specialist areas such as digital librarians (Fisher, 2002; Wilder, 2002). There an urgent need to develop suitable education programs to train and equip new librarians and information professionals who will be capable and comfortable in working in a digital environment. Digital library education can be inducted as the programs or courses specific to the training and educating of students who will be able to build and manage digital libraries after graduation. The combination of social trends and technology is here the push for educational developments for creation and management of digital libraries (Saracevic and Dalbello, 2001).

THE GLOBAL PICTURE

These days, digitization is taking place on a global scale. All organizations, large and small, around the world from many different sectors (museums, archives, libraries, art galleries, government and commercial) are creating or converting resources into digital form for a wide range of patrons. Many of these projects have made significant contributions to preserve and increase access to the knowledge / cultural heritage of a nation.

Developments in digital technologies and interoperability of systems enable cross-sectoral participation and harvesting of metadata, while the internet provides the delivery mechanism. National and overseas major funding opportunities for digitization have encouraged organizations to create digital material and convert existing material into digital format.

HISTORICAL OVERVIEW

Digital libraries have a short yet turbulent and explosive history. A number of early visionaries, such as Lickhder (1965), had a notion of libraries in the future being highly innovative and different in structure, processing, and accessing information through heavy applications of technology. But, besides visionary and futuristic discussion and highly scattered research and development experimentation, nothing much happened in the next two decades. By the end of 1980s digital libraries (under various names) barely a part of the landscape of librarianship, information science or computer science. But just a decade later, by the end of 1990s, research, practical developments and general interest in digital libraries exploded globally.

Borgman's (1999), discussion of computing vision for digital libraries is a good beginning and understanding the forces and players involved.

Digital Library?

A digital library is a computer based system for acquiring, storing, organizing, searching, and distributing digital materials for end user access. It is not network based but designed to attach a network. A digital library is not just a collection of material in electronic form; it includes a browser interface and perhaps a virtual space and society. It requires less space and the data can be made available through communication networks to anyone, anywhere, while facilitating searches with speed. The digital library is not a single entity and as such it is linked to the resources of many such collections.

The term digital library was used first time in print may have been in 1988 report to the Corporation for National Research Initiatives. The term digital library was first popularized by the NSF / DARPA / NASA Digital Libraries Initiative in 1994.

In Wikipedia digital library has been defined as "a digital library is a library in which collections are stored in digital formats (as opposed to print, microform, or other media) and accessible by computers."

"Welcome to a special issue on information and how to digitize it, manipulate it, find it, it, store it, protect it and oh yes share it with the rest of world. We can call this digital libraries", said Daine Crawford (Kaul, 1998, p 173). The growth of digital libraries involve: digitization of existing library materials; connectivity to the patrons in the world online and offline; integration with networking; and availability on the World Wide Web (WWW).

WHY DIGITAL LIBRARIES?

The fundamental (Arms, 2001) for building digital libraries is a belief that they will provide a better delivery of information than was possible in the past. Traditional libraries are part and a basic necessity of a society, but they are not perfect. Can we do better? Technology has developed and changed to facilitate the develop digital of libraries. In some disciplines, a professional is better served by sitting at a personal computer (PC) connected to network than by making a visit to the library. From a PC, the patrons are able to consult materials that are available in digital format around the world. But printed documents are very important part of civilization that their dominant role in storing and conveying information can not be changed except gradually.

A SHIFT FROM TRADITIONAL LIBRARY TO DIGITAL LIBRARY

The development is already taking place. The traditional closed access libraries are shifting towards open access library. The open access libraries are shifting towards automated libraries,

the automated one towards the electronics, the electronics to digital and finally to digital library. The truth is that nobody knows what will be the future of libraries.

FACTORS OF CHANGE IN DIGITAL LIBRARIES

The limited buying power of libraries, complex nature of recent documents, storage problems etc are some of the common factors which are influencing change to digital mode, some other factors are

i.   Rapid growth in information;
ii. Developments of new ICT technologies;
iii. Reducing cost of technology; and
iv. Inter disciplinary research
iv. Expectations of the patrons.

DIGITAL LIBRARY SOFTWARE

The creation of digital libraries and repositories involves the use of suitable software, hardware and content. While selection and acquisition of hardware is not a major concern today (considering the decreasing cost and increasing capabilities of computer hardware), the selection and implementation of digital library and repository software has been a problem area. The digital library and repository software available can be broadly classified into:

i.   Open Source Software (OSS), such as DSpace, ePrints, Fedora, ARNO, i-TOR, CDSware, and Greenstone Digital Library (GSDL). In a global survey (Jose, 2007) on adoption of OSS in this area, identified some 20 OSS packages, with DSpace being the most popular followed by ePrints, GSDL and Fedora.
ii. Commercial software, such as DigiTool from ExLibris, and digital library software by VTLS Inc, etc.

iii. Custom-made software. Major digital library initiatives in India, such as the Kalasampada (www.ignca.nic.in/dlrich.html) and Digital Library of India (http://dli.iiit.ac.in/), are using custom-made software or OSS that has been highly customized. The Indian Institute of Information Technology and Management (IIITM), Trivandrum, has developed some digital library software known as ACADO. Commercially available off-the-shelf digital library solutions are not known to be popular among libraries for the creation of digital libraries and repositories in India. This differs from the situation with library management systems (LMS) where a number of commercial LMS packages are used such as LibSys and Alice for Windows.

ADVANTAGES OF DIGITIZATION

Traditional libraries are limited by storage space; digital libraries have the potential to store much more information, simply because digital information requires very little physical space to contain it. As such, the cost of maintaining a digital library is much lower than that of a traditional library.

A traditional library must spend large sums of money paying for staff, book maintenance, rent, and additional books. Digital libraries do away with these fees. Both types of library require cataloguing input to allow patrons to locate and retrieve material. Digital libraries may be more willing to adopt innovations in technology providing patrons with improvements in electronic and audio book technology as well as presenting new forms of communication such as wikis and blogs; conventional libraries may consider that providing online access to their OPAC catalogue is sufficient. An important advantage to digital conversion is increased accessibility to patrons. There in also availability to individuals who may not be traditional patrons of a library, due to geographic location or organizational affiliation.

i. No Physical Boundary: A patron of a digital library need not to go to the library physically; people from all over the world can gain access to the same information, as long as an internet connection is available.

ii. Round the Clock Availability: A major advantage of digital libraries is that patrons can access to the information at any time, night or day.

iii. Multiple Accesses: A resources can be used simultaneously by a number of patrons.

iv. Information Retrieval: The patrons are able to use any search term (word, phrase, title, name, and subject) to search the entire collection. Digital libraries can provide very user-friendly interfaces, giving clickable access to its resources.

v. Information can be Shared: Placing information in digital format on networks makes it available to everybody.

vi. Structured Approach: Digital library provides access to much richer content in a more structured manner i.e. we can easily move from the catalog to the particular book then to a particular chapter and so on.

vii. Space: Whereas traditional libraries are limited by storage space, digital libraries have the potential to store much more information, simply because digital information requires very little physical space.

viii. Added Value: Certain characteristics of objects, primarily the quality of images, may be improved. Digitization can enhance legibility and remove visible flaws such as stains and discoloration (Gertz, 2000).

ix. Cost: The cost of maintaining a digital library is much lower than that of a traditional library. A traditional library must spend large sums of money paying for staff, book maintains, rent, and additional books. Digital libraries do away with these fees.

REASONS FOR DIGITIZATION

Documents are available in diverse physical formats. Some documents are rarely available to the patrons in spite of constant demand. Our cultural and knowledge resources are available in the various forms and formats and can be made available and accessible to the patrons, if digitized. The reasons (Deegan and Tanner, 2004) for digitations of documents are as:

i.   The ability to republish out-of-print documents;
ii. Access to documents available remotely;
iii. Potential to display documents that are in inaccessible formats, for instance, large volumes or maps;
iv. 'Virtual reunification'—allowing dispersed collections to be brought together;
v.   The ability to enhance digital images in terms of size, sharpness, color contrast, noise reduction, etc.;
vi. The potential for integration into teaching documents;
vii. Enhanced searchability, including full-text;
viii. Integration of different media (e.g., images, sounds, video); and
ix. The potential for presenting a critical mass of documents for analysis or comparison.

The learning objects, like, self-learning study materials, tutorials, exercises, assignments, case studies, project reports, dissertations, theses, articles, seminar presentations, conference papers, audio-visual materials, etc are essentially used by the open and distance learners in their learning process. These materials can be made available to this section of the users, if these learning objects are digitized and stored in a learning objects repository or in a digital library. Some other reasons for digitizing learning objects, apart from the list provided by (Deegan and Tanner, 2004) are as:

i.   The qualitative learning objects can be shared by learners of different programs within open and distance learning (ODL) institution;
ii. The qualitative learning objects can be shared by learners of different ODL institutions within or outside the country;
iii. The learning objects would be made available to the cross sections of the learners;
iv. The learning objects would be made available to learners of different ODL institutions;
v.   Duplication of efforts of preparing self-learning study materials can be minimized;
vi. Duplication of final projects, dissertations, theses of learners can be restrained;
vii. Creativity and innovation of the learners can be ignited when they see others' works; and
viii. Visibility and prestige of the ODL institutions, which initiate learning objects repositories, would be increased.

DIGITIZATION OF SCHOLARLY DOCUMENTS

If a document is created in digital environment and available in a digital format, it can be called a 'born-digital' object. On the other hand, if the document is only available in physical format, it can be converted into digital format through the process of digitization or through re-keying the texts. Similarly, if a learning object is not electronically available, but already available in the form of analogue format, can be digitized through digitization program. An ODL institution has to plan a digitization project of learning materials that aims to establish a learning objects repository with a robust architecture and structure. The Figure 1 shows different stages, processes and flows of digitization of learning materials. The selection of types of documents is foremost step of digitization. After identifying types of documents to be digitized, appropriate tools and technologies can be adopted. For examples, for textual documents

Figure 1. Digitization workflow for documents

Selection of Documents for Digitization
↓
Textual Objects/ Images/ Microfilms/ Slides/ Audio Objects/ Video Objects/ Multimedia Objects
↓
Selection of Metadata Element Sets Appropriate to Particular Document
↓
Convert Analogue Document into Digital Formats Using Digital Conversion Tools and Technologies
and Save in Appropriate File Formats
↓
Edit the Digital Masters and Remove Errors/ Noises/ Inaccuracies
↓
Provide Metadata Information to Describe and to Identify the Content of Every Learning Object
↓
Check the Quality of the Digital Document and Metadata, and Make Necessary Corrections
↓
Integration of Metadata of Document into Searchable Indexes, Tables of Contents
↓
Integrate All Types of Documents into a Learning Object Repository/ Institutional Repository/ Digital
Library
↓
Deliver the Learning Objects to the Distance and Open Learners through Internet/ Intranet/ CD-ROMs
↓
Allow Metadata Harvesters and Search Engines to Index the Contents of Repository, if it is delivered
through Internet

and images, document scanner will be required; for microfilmed documents, microfilm scanner will be required; for audio materials, sound converter will be required; and so on. After converting analogue objects into digital objects, there will be a need of quality control that may check quality of digital masters. The digital masters can be edited to remove inaccuracies, inconsistencies, errors and noises. The digital masters should be stored in appropriate file formats and should use appropriate feature (e.g. resolution, size, etc.). Metadata elements are required to describe different attributes of a document. Metadata helps to describe and to identify a document. Metadata creation is another important aspect in the digitization process. Metadata elements should be appropriate to the types of documents. For example, some metadata element sets for journal articles can be different from metadata element sets for dissertations or audio materials. Metadata also helps to search

and retrieve a document from a digital repository. After metadata creation, the learning objects are to be integrated into a learning objects repository or into a digital library. This digital repository can be made accessible through online mode using internet or Intranet technologies or can be made available through offline mode using CD-ROM technology. If it is made accessible through internet, metadata harvesters and search engines should be allowed to index the contents of learning objects. This would increase the visibility of the digital repository, promote interoperability and flexibility of search. Figure 1 illustrates an outline of workflow in a digitization project that can be elaborated further in each stage.

The digitization of documents, particularly textual and image documents should adhere to certain guidelines. The guideline helps to maintain standards and quality of digital objects as well as digital repositories. A number of guidelines have been prepared by different agencies, which are the guiding principles to digitization initiatives abroad. Most digitization projects in India either adopt international digitization guidelines or follow the norms as per international practice. In India, a few guidelines are also available for digitization of certain types of documents. Recently, University Grants Commission has drafted a guideline for electronic theses and dissertations. National Mission for Manuscripts has prepared a guideline for digitization of manuscripts. This guideline can be used in other digitization initiatives that involve digitization of visual materials. On the other hand, Digital Library Federation and Research Libraries Group of the United States have drafted several guidelines of digitization for maintaining quality in imaging projects. Some of the national and international guidelines of digitization are shown in Table 1.

DIGITIZATION FRAMEWORK

The digitization framework (Hollwy, 2004) consists of the following elements:

- Inventory of digitization projects;
- Creating awareness of digitization;

- Training and upgradation of skills of staff involved in digitization activities;
- Developing networks, collaborations and relationships for digitization activities;
- Obtaining funding to support digitization;
- Instigating digitization projects;
- Enhancing the IT infrastructure; and
- Strategic planning and policy development.

FEATURES

Digital libraries have attracted almost all the developed and developing countries due to its features and the opportunities it extends to the information providers and information seekers. Digital library has information in electronic form and electronic media facilitates the access to information available in digital form at different places. It offers new levels of access to broader audiences of users and new opportunities for library and information science field to advance both theory and practice. They contain information collections predominantly in digital or electronic form. Electronic publications have some special problems of management as compared to printed document. They include infrastructure, acceptabil-

Table 1. List of some guidelines for digitization

India	International
1 Guidelines for Digitization of Manuscripts (National Mission for Manuscripts, 2005) http://namami.nic.in/DigiStds.htm 2 Electronic Thesis Online (India): UGC (Submission of Metadata and Full-text of Doctoral Theses in Electronic Format) Regulations, 2005: Current Scenario, Major Issues, Data Standards and Implementation Process (University Grants Commission, 2005) <http://www.ugc.ac.in/new_initiatives/etd_hb.pdf>	1 Guides to Quality in Visual Resource Imaging Guide 1: Planning an Imaging Project Guide 2: Selecting a Scanner Guide 3: Imaging Systems: the Range of Factors Affecting Imaging Quality Guide 4: Measuring Quality of Digital Masters Guide 5: File Formats for Digital Masters (Digital Library Federation and Research Libraries Group, 2000) www.rlg.org/visguides/ 2 General Guidelines for Scanning (Colorado Digitization Project, 2002) www.cdpheritage.org/resource/scanning/std_scanning.htm 3 Standards and Guidelines for Digitization Projects (Canadian Digital Cultural Content Initiative, 2001) www.pch.gc.ca/cdcci-icccn/pubs.htm

ity, access restrictions, readability, standardization, authentication, preservation, copyright, user interface etc. But still the advantages are more and therefore the importance of digital libraries has been recognized by all nations of the world. India has indeed recognized the importance of digital libraries and lots of initiatives have been taken by various libraries / institutes / organizations.

Digital libraries do enable the creation of local content, strengthen the mechanisms and capacity of the library's information systems and services. They increase the portability, efficiency of access, flexibility, availability and preservation of content. Digital Libraries can help move the nation towards realizing the enormously powerful vision of 'anytime, anywhere' access to the best and the latest of human thought and culture, so that no classroom, individual or a society is isolated from knowledge resources. Digital library brings the library to the user, overcoming all geographical barriers.

TECHNOLOGICAL ISSUES

A digital library can be built around specific repository software. The best known examples of this are DSpace, Eprints, Fedora, dLibra (Poland), and Greenstone Digital Library Software.

The main technological issues (Liu, 2004), problems and concerns for libraries that are digitizing collections concern methods for capturing printed information for use in a digital setting. Much attention focuses on the reliability of equipment and software.

The process should simple with minimum steps and the equipment should be easy to use. The bindings should not have to be removed from books. The image processing software should allow for curvature correction and tidying of the image created, meaning the book remains in original condition. There is increased use of scaled-back and "simplified" photo imaging software applications, such as Paint Shop Pro and "limited" versions of

Adobe PhotoShop. There is a trend toward using mounted digital cameras for digitizing, rather than flatbed scanners. A major technological issue is deciding on the size of the digital images on the library's Web site. Larger images take more time for the customer to download. Another issue surrounds the storage of thousands of image files on the library's internal servers.

PROJECT MANAGEMENT

Digital projects are extremely complex, and effective project management – including managing budgets, staffing, workflow, determining technical specifications, and metadata creation – is vital for a successful digitization project. Several authors provide guidelines for managing digital projects. Chapman (2000) discusses three phases of a digital project – setting goals, planning and budgeting, and managing workflow – and he discusses various issues and tasks in each phase. Grout and others (2000) discuss management issues involved in creating digital resources, and they provide guidelines for such aspects of a digital project as project planning, preparation for data creation, resource delivery, and archiving and preservation. Cervone (2005) outlines a process for digital library project teams to use in the important task of decision making, including the use of an option assessment matrix.

Drawing on his experience of managing a digitization project at the University of Nevada, Las Vegas, Eden (2001) presents guidelines for managing such projects. He discusses identifying best practices, designing the web site, and choosing a metadata scheme, as well as the importance of communication, collaboration, and quality control for a successful project. Hull and Dreher (2001) report on the design of a management system to track the various tasks involved in a project at Temple University to digitize photographs and a collection of World War I and II posters. The authors state that the tracking database helped maintain efficiency and control of the project, and was used for statistics, report generation, and documentation of the project.

THE STUDY

Scope

A number of digital library and repository initiatives have been reported in India, the number of digital libraries available in the public domain are less than operational. Increased awareness, training facilities and, availability of required technology at affordable cost and internet are motive for setting up digital libraries and repositories using OSS. More and more libraries are using OSS rather than commercial or custom-made software. A number of digital collections have been developed using OSS with the purpose of restricted use, or use on the intranet of the institution. This study takes into account only those initiatives that are available for access in the public domain.

Methodology

The digital libraries and repositories in India were identified from the literature, the internet and open access registries. The Registry of Open Access Repositories (ROAR) (http://roar.eprints. org/) and the web sites of respective digital library software sites, such as DSpace, ePrints and GSDL, were visited to identify the digital libraries and repositories using OSS in India. The URLs obtained were followed to reach the home page of the digital library. In case URLs were not working, Google searches were made to locate the digital library directly and / or through the institutional web site. The type of collection on the web sites of the digital libraries was noted and, in cases where it was not given, it was attempted to locate from internet. Some initiatives identified through the foregoing methodology

could not be accessed despite several repeated attempts at different intervals during the study period and these have been reported here without the relevant details.

DIGITAL LIBRARIES AND REPOSITORIES IN INDIA

Globally, digital library and repository initiatives began in the mid-1990s and before the arrival of the twenty-first century a few digital libraries had come into being. With regard to India, a few institutions undertook research and development activities but there were no digital libraries as of the year 2001 (Kalra, 2001). Kalra (2001) discussed the efforts towards digitization of libraries in India along with the problems and prospects and noted that despite the negative attitude of the authorities, lack of precedents and standards, and other associated handicaps, some of the better informed library professionals have been able to develop electronic resources and services. Bhattacharya (2004) and Jain and others (2006) made more comprehensive studies on digital library initiatives in India. In recent years, OSS has stormed into the world of proprietary software and today many of the OSS, such as Linux, has established themselves by their ubiquitous presence and widespread use. It was found in the study that DSpace, GSDL and Eprints are becoming common solutions for the creation of digital libraries and repositories in India. DSpace is the most popular, with forty one libraries identified by the study.

DSpace

DSpace is freely available as open source software. It is a digital repository system that captures, stores, indexes, reserves, and redistributes an organization's research data. It was jointly developed by MIT Libraries and Hewlett-Packard

Table 2. Libraries in India using DSpace

S No	Name of Institute	URL	Type of Items
1	Aryabhatta Research Institute of Observational Science, Nainital	http://202.141.125.171:8080/jspui/handle/123456789	Information not available
2	Asia Pacific Institute of Management Studies	http://www.dspace.org/www.asiapacific.edu/	Information not available
3	Bangabondhu Shekh Mujib Medical University	http://sunzi1.lib.hku.hk/hkuto/index.jsp	Information not available
4	Bangalore Management Academy, Bangalore	http://www.bma.ac.in:8080/dspace/	Faculty members and institute publications
5	Bharathidasan University	http://dspace.bdu.ac.in/	Faculty members publication
6	Central Drug Research Institute, Lucknow	http://dkr.cdri.res.in:8080/dspace-oai/request	Research outputs of the institute
7	Central Institute of Medicinal and Aromatic Plants	http://kr.cimap.res.in/index.jsp	Journal articles, conference proceeding articles, Technical reports, thesis, dissertations, etc
8	Cochin University of Science and Technology, Cochin	http://dspace.cusat.ac.in/dspace/	Article, preprints, technical reports, theses, previous years question papers, images, etc
9	Delhi College of Engineering, Delhi	http://202.141.12.109/dspace	Publications of faculty members and students
	Dyuthi, Cochin University of Science and Technology	http://dyuthi.cusat.ac.in/dspace/	Journal and conference articles and theses, etc
10	GB Pant University of Agriculture & Technology, Pant Nagar	http://dspace.irri.org:8080/dspace/	Information not available
11	Guru Gobind Singh Indraprastha University, Delhi	http://dspace.ipu.ernet.in:8080/	Information not available
12	Indian Institute of Astrophysics, Bangalore	http://prints.iiap.res.in/	Archival collection, theses, newspaper clippings, in-house journal,
13	Indian Institute of Management, Kozhikode	http://dspace.iimk.ac.in	Conference proceedings, working papers, IIMK publications
14	Indian Institute of Science, Bangalore	http://etd.nsci.iisc.ernet.in	Theses and Dissertation
15	Indian Institute of Technology, Delhi	http://eprint.iitd.ac.in/dspace/	Theses, research publications, dissertations
16	Indian Institute of Technology, Kanpur	http://172.28.64.70:8080/dspace	Theses and dissertations
17	Indian Institute of Technology, Mumbai	http://dspace.library.iitb.ac.in/jspui/	Institute and faculty publications
18	Indian Statistical Institute, Bangalore	http://library.isibang.ac.in:8080/dspace	Publication of the institute
19	Indira Gandhi Institute of Development Research, Mumbai	http://oii.igidr.ac.in:8888/dspace	Information not available
20	Indira Gandhi National Open University (IGNOU), New Delhi	www.egyankosh.ac.in	Distance Learning Materials, Courseware
21	Information and LIBrary NETwork Centre, (INFLIBNET), Ahmedabad	http://inflibnet.dspace.ac.in	Library related literature
22	Institute of Chartered Financial Analyst (ICFAI) Business School, Ahmedabad	http://202.131.96.59:8080/dspace	Knowledge repository of faculty and research fellows of ICFAI Business School, Ahmedabad

continued on following page

Table 2. continued

S No	Name of Institute	URL	Type of Items
23	Institute of Petroleum Management, Gandhinagar	http://203.77.192.116:8080/dspace/index.jsp	Government order
24	Librarians' Digital Library (LDL) at Documentation Research Training Centre, Bangalore	https://drtc.isibang.ac.in	Information not available
25	M N Dastur & Company Pvt Ltd, Kolkata	http://e-lib.dasturco.in:8080/dspace	Information not available
26	Mahatma Gandhi University,	http://www.mgutheses.org/	Theses
27	Management Development Institute, Gurgaon	http://dspace.mdi.ac.in/dspace/	Institutional news and articles published by faculty members
28	National Center for Antarctic Research (NCAOR)	http://dspace.ncaor.org:8080/dspace/	Information not available
29	National Centre for Antarctic & Ocean Research	http://dspace.ncaor.org:8080/dspace/index.jsp	Information not available
30	National Chemical Laboratory,	http://dspace.ncl.res.in	Theses, Research Papers, Articles, Reports, etc.
31	National Chemical Laboratory, Pune	http://dspace.ncl.res.in/dspace/index.jsp	Patents, project reports, research publications, theses
32	National Institute of Oceanography, Goa	http://drs.nio.org/drs/index.jsp	Journal articles, conference proceedings articles, technical reports, theses, dissertations, etc
33	National Institute of Science Communication and Information Resources, National Science Digital Library, New Delhi	http://nsdl.niscair.res.in/	Research journals published by the institute
34	National Institute of Science Communication and Information Resources, Online Periodicals Repository, New Delhi	http://nopr.niscair.res.in	Information not available
35	National Institute of Technology, Rourkela	http://dspace.nitrkl.ac.in/dspace	Journal articles, pre-prints, conference papers authored by NITR researchers
36	Raman Research Institute, Bangalore	http://dspace.rri.res.in	Research publications of faculty members and students, collected papers of C V Raman and historical records of the institute
37	Sarai Multimedia Digital Archive, Delhi	http://archive.sarai.net/dspace/	Audio, video, scripts, etc
38	Thapar University, Patiala	http://dspace.tiet.ac.in/dspace	Theses, newsletter, research documents, minutes of meetings
39	University of Delhi, Delhi	http://library.du.ac.in/dspace/	Information not available
40	University of Hyderabad, Hyderabad	http://202.41.85.207:8080/dspace/index.jsp	Information not available
41	University of Mumbai	http://dspace.vidyanidhi.org.in:8080/dspace/	Information not available
42	Vidyanidhi Digital Library, E Scholarship Portal	http://dspace.vidyanidhi.org.in:8080/dspace/	Doctoral theses
43	World Health Organization Southeast Asian Region Digital Repository	http://repository.searo.who.int/	Information not available

Labs, the software platform serves a variety of digital archiving needs.

The DSpace Community manages the code base and releases new versions of the software. An active community of developers, researchers and users worldwide contribute their expertise to the DSpace Community.

Forty three initiatives in India were identified form the searches. However, fifteen URLs returned error messages and so those web sites could not be accessed. It is possible that either the URLs have changed or the access is not available to external users or the initiative has been shelved. Table - 2 gives the details of the libraries in India using DSpace.

E-Prints

E-Prints is a flexible platform for building quality, value repositories, recognized as the easiest and fastest way to set up repositories of research literature, scientific data, student theses, project reports, multimedia artefacts, teaching materials, scholarly collections, digitized records, exhibitions and performances. The software was developed at Southampton University in the UK (Simpson, 2006) and used for creating digital repositories.

It enables research literature to be accessible to all, and provides the foundation for all academic institutions to create their own research repositories (www.eprints.org). Sixteen initiatives in India were identified form the searches. Seven URLs returned error messages and so those web sites could not be accessed. It is possible that either the URLs have changed or the access is not available to external users. The institutions using Eprints along with observations are given in Table – 3.

Sixteen initiatives identified using Eprints, which is essentially used for creating institutional repositories. The most prominent repository is the Indian Institute of Science (IISc), Bangalore predominantly research papers emanating from the Institute. The National Aerospace Laboratories,

Bangalore is also a major repository using Eprints. The OpenMed of the National Informatics Centre, New Delhi is an initiative using Eprints, which allows any author to self-archive publications in medical and allied sciences, thus being an exception as other institutional repositories was found to be restricted to the institution concerned only. The Indian Institute of Management, Kozhikode is a leading institution in India using and also propagating the cause of GSDL in not only India, but the South Asian region.

GSDL

GSDL has been developed and distributed in co-operation with UNESCO and the Human Info Non-Governmental Office in Belgium. Its developers received the 2004 Namur award of the International Federation for Information Processing (IFIP) for "contributions to the awareness of social implications of information technology, and the need for a holistic approach in the use of information technology that takes account of social implications" (www.greenstone.org/factsheet).

Use of GSDL software in India, it was found that there have been a few initiatives using GSDL for the creation of digital libraries and repositories in India. The Central library of IIT Roorkee is experimenting with archival collection and once it is completed it will be available on the internet. The Archives of Indian Labour preserves all kinds of resources on issues relating to labour, including records of the Ministry of Labour, National Commissions on Labour and other Government agencies. It is reported that features like automated hyperlinking and metadata generation were used efficiently to activate the archive both in terms of form and content, thereby not limiting the endeavourer to being just a mere library collection of material. A model of a digital library has been developed by IIM, Kozhikode. Table 4 lists the digital libraries using GSDL in India.

Table 3. Libraries in India using E-prints

S No	Name of Institute	URL	Type of Items
1	Bangalore University, Bangalore	http://smart.ncsi.iisc.ernet.in	Scholarly publications of faculty
2	Indian Academy of Science	http://smart.nsci.iisc.ernet.in	Research output and scholarly publications of IAS follows
3	Indian Institute of Information Technology, Allahabad	http://eprints.iiita.ac.in	Research papers
4	Indian Institute of Management, Kozhikode	http://eprints.iimk.ac.in	Information not available
5	Indian Institute of Science, Bangalore	http://eprints.iisc.ernet.in	Information not available
6	Institute of Mathematical Sciences, Chennai	https://www.imsc.res.in/eprints	Information not available
	Institute of Minerals and Materials Technology, Bhubaneswar	http://eprints.immt.res.in/	Articles, reports, these and patents, etc
7	Medknow Eprints	http://eprints.medknow.com	Information not available
8	National Aerospace Laboratories, Banglore	http://nal-ir.nal.res.in	Journal articles, conference papers, technical reports, presentations / lectures, preprints, images, theses, etc
9	National Centre for Catalysis Research, Chennai	http://203.199.213.48/	Scholarly material on catalysis produced by NCCR and NCI
10	National Informatics Centre, MEDLARS Centre	http://openmed.nic.in	Self archives of authors in medical and allied sciences
11	National Institute of Immunology, New Delhi	http://eprints.nii.res.in/cgi/oai2	Information not available
12	National Knowledge Commission	http://roar.eprints.org/	
13	One World South Asia	http://open.ekduniya.net	Material on aspects of ICT enabled development in global and local contexy
14	Sardar Vallabhai National Institute of Technology, Surat	http://eprints.svnit.ac.in/	Information not available
15	School of Biotechnology, Madurai Kamaraj University	http://eprints.bicmku.in/	Information not available
16	University of Delhi, Delhi	http://eprints.du.ac.in	Research publications and theses of the university

Custom-Made Software

Besides the digital libraries and repositories using open source software reported so far, there are some other digital library initiatives that have either used custom-made software or the nature of software used is not immediately known to the authors of the present study. The data regarding such digital libraries are given in Table 4.

Kalasampada

Some of the more successful digital library projects have apparently been developed using custom-made software. Kalasampada, the digital library holding resources of Indian cultural heritage, facilitates the scholars (users) to access and view materials of rare books, rare photographs, audio and video along with highly researched publications of the Indira Gandhi National Centre for the Arts (IGNCA) from a single window. Multimedia computer technology has been used for the de-

Table 4. Libraries in India using GSDL

S No	Name of Institute	URL	Type of Items
1	Archives of Indian Labour	www.indianlabourarchives.org	Prime repository of labour related records
2	Computer Science and Engineering Department, IIT, Kanpur	http://www.cse.iitk.ac.in/sdl/cgi-bin/library	Report, project reports, theses
3	Indian Institute of Management, Kozhikode	www.iimk.ac.in/gsdl/cgi-bin/librray	E-books in various disciplines, IIMK publications
4	Indian Institute of Technology, Mumbai	http://etd.library.iitb.ac.in	Theses and dissertations

velopment of a software package that integrates a variety of cultural information accessible in one place. The digital corpus includes over 50 lakhs folios of manuscript, over one lakh slides, 4,000 photographs, IGNCA published books, Kalakalp (IGNCA's journal), Vihangama (IGNCA's newsletter), over 4,000 hours of audio and video and approximately 50 walk-throughs. A retrieval application is stated to have been developed and the majority of these materials are available for online access on IGNCA Intranet. Searching is available in both English and Hindi (Devanagari) and users are given the option to select the material of their interest either from a specific type of collection like books, manuscripts, slides, audio, video etc., or from the entire collection (Kalasampada Product

Brochure, 2007). Perhaps this is one of the largest collections in a digital library in India; however, the facility is stated to be currently available only on an intranet and Figure 2 shows the opening page of the web site.

Traditional Knowledge Digital Library

The Traditional Knowledge Digital Library (TKDL) is another collaborative initiative project between Council of Scientific and Industrial Research (CSIR), Ministry of Science and Technology and Department of AYUSH, Ministry of Health and Family Welfare, and is being implemented at CSIR. An inter-disciplinary team of Traditional Medicine (Ayurveda, Unani, Siddha

Table 5. Libraries in India using custom-made software

S No	Name of Institute	Purpose	URL	Status / Remark
1	Indira Gandhi National Centre for Arts, N Delhi	Kalasampada (Digital library on resources of Indian cultural heritage)	http://ignca.nic.in	Operational. Partial access available on internet
2	National Library, Kolkatta	Digitization of rare and brittle documents onto CD	http://nlindia.org/index2.html	Internet access not yet available
3	Traditional Knowledge Digital Library	Protect the traditional knowledge	http://tkdl.gov.in	Access to 5000 ayurvedic formulations available
4	Mobile Digital Library (Dware Dware Gyan Sampada)	C-DAC, Noida, Department of Information Technology, aims to bring one million e-books to people in India	http://mobilelibrary.adacnoida.in/index.html	105 e-books available for download
5	Digital Library of India	Aims to create a "free to read" searchable collection of one million books predominantly in India languages available to everyone over internet	http://new.dli.ernet.in/http://dli.iiit.ac.in	Information not available

Figure 2. Opening page of Kalasampada the digital library

and Yoga) experts, patent examiners, IT experts, scientists and technical officers are involved in creation of TKDL for Indian Systems of Medicine. A collection of 80,000 formulations in Ayurveda, 1,000,000 in Unani and 12,000 in Siddha had already been put in the TKDL, and is being made available in five languages — English, German, French, Spanish and Japanese. In 1999, the Department of Ayurveda, Yoga & Naturopathy, Unani, Siddha and Homoeopathy-(AYUSH), erstwhile Department of Indian System of Medicine and Homoeopathy (ISM&H) constituted an inter-disciplinary Task Force, for creating an approach paper on establishing a Traditional Knowledge Digital Library (TKDL). The project TKDL was initiated in the year 2001.

Digital Library of India

Since time immemorial, India has possessed a rich traditional knowledge of ways and means practiced to treat diseases afflicting people. This knowledge has generally been passed down by word of mouth from generation to generation. A part of this knowledge has been described in ancient classical and other literature, often inac-cessible to the common man and even when ac-cessible rarely understood. Documentation of this existing knowledge, available in public domain, on various traditional systems of medicine has become imperative to safeguard the sovereignty of this traditional knowledge and to protect it from being misappropriated in the form of patents on non-original innovations, and which has been a matter of national concern.

The Digital Library of India (DLI) is a success-ful, fast-paced digital library, the mission of which is to create a portal which will foster creativity and free access to all human knowledge, Figure 4. A pilot project to scan around 10,000 books was initiated at Carnegie Mellon University and then followed up at the Indian Institute of Science, Bangalore, the Indian Institute of Information Technology, Hyderabad and other organizations. The vision is to use ICT to preserve all the knowl-edge of the human race in digital form and make that content searchable, independent of language and location. So far, more than 289,000 books have been scanned, of which nearly 170,000 are in Indian languages. More than 84,000 books (25 million pages) are available on the DLI web site hosted by the Indian Institute of Science (www. new.dli.ac.in/), and more than 149,000 books (43 million pages) are available on the DLI web site,

Figure 3. Web page of traditional knowledge digital library

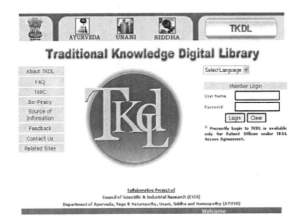

which is hosted by the International Institute of Information Technology (http://dli.iiit.ac.in/). The link to other partner sites is also provided through www.new.dli.ernet.in/. Contents between the two sites overlap in order to ensure fail-safe availability. The books can be accessed from either of these web sites. All the tools and technologies used by DLI are open source, technologies like Linux, Apache web server etc. Technology for the deployment of information retrieval in Indian languages has been demonstrated by the development of the OmSe search engine using the off-the-shelf open source software Greenstone search engine (2006Balakrishnan and others, 2006!; Ambati and others, 2006).

DIGITAL LIBRARY DEVELOPMENT ISSUES IN INDIA

There are umpteen numbers of problems the Digital Library development teams face in India while they embark on the digital library development as well as during the progress phase. Some of the prominent and predominant among them include the following:

i.   Lack of proper Information & Communication Technology (ICT) Infrastructure
     ◦   Digital Libraries demand cutting edge IT and Communication infrastructure such as: High end and

Figure 4. Web page of digital library of India

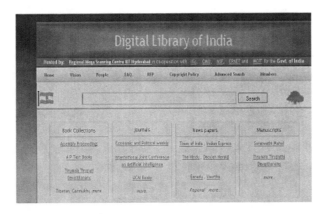

powerful Servers; Structured LAN with Broadband Intranet facilities, ideally optical fibre based Gigabit networks;

○ Required number of Workstations capable of providing online information services, computing and multi-media applications;

○ Internet connectivity with sufficient bandwidth, capable of meeting the informational; and

○ Computational requirement of the user community; There are many more related facilities / services which are highly essential in an ideal digital library environment. It is observed that the ICT infrastructure in most of the Institutions / Organizations, barring exceptions, is not up to the desired level so as to run advanced digital library services to the optimum level.

ii. Lack of Proper Planning and Integration of Information Resources

Presently the library acquisitions in India are either paper based and electronic. In most of the libraries, paper based documents outnumber the electronic subscriptions and acquisitions. Some of the libraries need retro-conversion and digitization of library holdings too. Literature on related studies show that there is a severe lapse on the libraries with regard to proper planning of their information resources which are conducive for developing digital libraries. Also, the electronic resources penetrate to the libraries in a multiplicity of complex formats and with different access terms and conditions. These information resources are scattered and distributed across a wide variety of publication types and a vast number of publishers. There is a dire need for proper planning and a meticulously framed content integration model which is achieved and implemented through world standard digital library technologies.

iii. Rigidity in the Publishers' Policies and Data Formats

Having successfully installed and configured a digital library does not qualify a library to automatically populate all its digital collection into the digital library. One has to obtain publisher's consent and copyright permissions for the same. Digital library softwares usually accept and process all popular and standard digital formats such as HTML, Word, RTF, PPT, or PDF. Most of the publishers put their materials in their own proprietary e-book reader formats, from which the text extraction becomes almost impossible. A vast majority of the scholarly content rests in journal literature and due to copyright issues they cannot be easily (almost impossible) find its way into the local repositories of the digital library.

iv. Lack of ICT Strategies and Policies

A vast majority of the libraries in India do not have laid down policies on ICT panning and strategies to meet the challenges posed by the technology push, the information overload, as well as the demand pull from the users.

v. Lack of Technical Skills

The Human Resources available in the libraries need time-to-time professional enrichment inputs and rigorous training on the latest technologies which are playing around in the new information environment. The kind of training programs being imparted in India at the moment is not able to meet the demand in terms of quantity as well as quality.

vi. Management Support

For the provision of world class information systems, resources and services the libraries need the wholehearted support from the respective management. Institutional support in terms of proper funding, human resources and IT skills enrichment are prerequisites for the development and maintenance of state-of-art digital library systems and services. There are many more pressing problems being faced by the libraries in India in its pursuit of building digital libraries.

vii.   Copyright / IPR Issues

Issues of copyright, intellectual property and fair use concerns are posing unprecedented array of problems to the libraries and librarians are struggling to cope with all these related issues in the new digital information environment.

PROBLEMS AND PROSPECTS

The problems for digital library development are manifold in India. But there are many constraints that have to be overcome to mature services to international standards. The main hurdles in the digital library development in a developing country are:

i.   The lack of interest on the part of parent institutions and the absence of action plans or priorities to that extent is the major hindrance.

ii.   Though ICT infrastructure and reducing is improving in the country considerably in the country, their availability for information work is not appreciated in many organizations. Many times librarians fail to convince the management in many institutions, thereby eclipsing their role in strategic planning.

iii.   How are copyrights transferred and handled in the digital environment? Institutions, individuals or private publishers have rights over content, and motivating these owners to ease their rights to other entities for electronic access provision (when the former are not inclined to do so) will be the main

bottleneck. But these issues can be resolved by entering into collaborations between the owner of copyright and institution performing the digitization.

iv.   Another aspect to be considered simultaneously is how the access rights are implemented. What mechanisms are used to impose restrictions on access? When hosted as a paid facility, how are charges levied from users? How are login and password access strictly ensured? If provided as a free facility, how are funds needed to set up the infrastructure and continue the operations generated? How far can the facility be subsidized with the help of advertisements and sponsorships? Levying charges for access is a distant proposition, due to the specific nature of usage and the fact that these contents, such as journals, are not attracting much personal subscription now. Instead, sponsorships from institutions, government bodies and library suppliers can be explored as viable means to bring in money for this task.

v.   Even when content is accessible free, enough security mechanisms like firewalls, filtering routers and encryption–decryption must be put on the server side to prevent any trespassing by hackers. Threat perceptions from the vulnerable areas of the internet layer, routing infrastructure, domain name server and network management (Atkinson, 1997) have to be addressed from the technical, administrative and operational angles.

vi.   The advent of ICT and the its boom engulfing the country has changed the way information is collected, organized and delivered in the country. As a result, sweeping changes are happening in different disciplines, and selecting useful content requires careful review and selection by subject experts. Digitization will only help to preserve the information, and careful selection of content is thus required for enhanced and continued access.

vii. Sufficient internet bandwidth should available in the country for faster access of Web content. Though a lot of institutions have designed content for hosting on the Web, most of the time users have to wait rather impatiently to access it. Agarwal (1999) mentions efforts of VSNL to create a bandwidth of 155 Mbps in four metros, Bangalore and Pune. Internet (Ghosh, 2000) connections in India have exceeded 1.2 million (from 20,450 on September 30, 2000, a 50% growth rate in three months (Dikshit, 2000)) and they are expected to cross 10 million in the next three years. The hope is that initiatives like VSNL's six gateways, the Dishnet DSL submarine cable between Singapore and Chennai, the landing point of FLAG (Fibre optic Loop Around the Globe) and other international undersea links like SEA-ME-WE (III) (South East Asia, Middle East and Western Europe) and SAFE (South Africa Far East) optic fiber submarine cable will soon improve the internet bandwidth in the country.

viii. Financial support for developing digital library prototypes is very desirable. Thus funding agencies, research councils and institutions should offer monetary support, especially for augmenting the existing infrastructure, for content leasing and for staff honorarium. The success and experience gained in these projects is most important for further digitization projects.

ix. Proper documentation, retrieval and access of indigenous knowledge have gained more prominence in recent days, as has preserving the IPRs in the emerging philosophy of free trade and liberalization.

x. The professional staff members working in many libraries in developing countries are engrossed in administrative and routine jobs related to library operation and administration. Many institutions need not demand that their professionals pursue such aggressive

roles. There are also problems of lack of ability, lack of incentives, and lack of role model initiatives.

xi. Even in places where infrastructure is available, there is an acute shortage of competent personnel to take up the task of digitizing local content and evolving digital information repositories. The students, faculty, curriculum and training methodology at the disposal of our library schools have to be visibly improved to meet this challenge. Coupled with this, steps should be taken for continuing education programs for retraining the existing staff.

The increasing interest in library website development and migration of information sources and services to the Web should be treated as stepping stone in digital library development. The internet facilities existing in the premier education and research institutions can be trapped for building digital kiosks as storage and service centers for all online information available at those sites. The digital resources thus accessed will contribute a lot to the research activities in the country by reducing some of the existing barriers of present information communication channels like time and space. The software boom engulfing the country, as a result of the big leap in computer penetration, sudden rise in proficient manpower and sizable improvement in communication infrastructure should also be treated as an asset and taken advantage of by authorities and information professionals to create and maintain digital information facilities to usher in the new information age.

CONCLUSION

Digital libraries and repositories in India are developing with a rapid pace. Open source software, especially DSpace, is increasingly being used for the creation of digital repositories. However, considering that India has a large number of education and research institutions, the number of digital libraries and repositories available today is still fairly low. The collection size in all the digital libraries put together are minuscule when considering the fact that India is abound with volumes of information that can be digitized and made available in digital libraries. The Digital Library of India is one major initiative that is striving to create a truly digital library. Awareness of the creation of institutional repositories is essential and funding agencies should have open access mandates so that creation of institutional repositories or depositing publications to open access repositories becomes compulsory.

REFERENCES

Agarwal, P. K. (1999). India's national internet backbone. *Communications of the ACM, 42*(6), 53–58. doi:10.1145/303849.303862

Ambati, V., Balakrishnan, N., Reddy, R., Pratha, L., & Jawahar, C. V. (2006). The Digital Library of India project: process, policies and architecture. In *Proceedings of the International Conference on Digital Libraries*, New Delhi, December 5 - 8, 2006.

Arms, W. Y. (2001). *Digital libraries.* Cambridge, MA: MIT Press.

Association of Research Libraries. (n.d.). *Definition and purpose of digital libraries.* Retrieved June 5, 2009, from http://sunsiteberkeley.edu/ARL/definition.html

Atkinson, R. J. (1997). Towards a more secure internet. *IEEE Computers, 30*(1), 57–61.

Bhattacharya, P. (2004). Advances in digital library initiatives: a developing country perspective. *The International Information & Library Review, 36*(3), 165–175. doi:10.1016/j.iilr.2003.10.008

Borgman, C. L. (1997). What are digital libraries? *Information Processing & Management, 35*(3), 227–243.

Cervone, H. (2001). Making decisions: methods for digital library project teams. *OCLC Systems & Services, 21*(1), 30–35. doi:10.1108/10650750510578127

Chapman, S. (2000). Considerations for project management. In Sitts, M. K. (Ed.), *Handbook for digital projects: a management tool for preservation and access* (pp. 31–42). Andover, MA: Northeast Document Conservation Center.

Chowdhury, G. G., & Chowdhury, S. (2003). *Introduction to digital library.* London: Fate.

Coleman, A. (2002). The road ahead for education in digital libraries. *D-Lib Magazine, 8* (7/8). Retrieved June 18, 2009, from http://www.dlib.org/dlib/july02/coleman/07coleman.html

Das, A. K., Sen, B. K., & Dutta, C. (2005). *Digitization of scholarly materials in India for distance and open learners.* Paper presented ICDE International Conference, New Delhi. Retrieved June 15, 2009, from http://openmed.nic.in/1217/01/Anup_Kumar_Das_ICDE_Conference_05.pdf

Deegan, M., & Tanner, S. (2004). Conversion of primary sources. In S. Schreibman, R. Siemans, & and J. Usworth (Ed.), A companion to digital humanities. Oxford: Blackwell Publishing.

Digital library. (n.d.). LIS Wiki. Retrieved June 05, 2009, from http://liswiki.org/wiki/Digital_library#Definition

Digital Library. (n.d.). Wikipedia: the free encyclopedia. Retrieved June 5, 2009, from http://en.wikipedia.org/wiki/Digital_library

Digital Library of India. (n.d.). Retrieved July 1, 2009, from http://dli.iiit.ac.in/

Dikshit, S. (2000, December 10). Growth in Internet connections lopsided. *The Hindu*. Retrieved from http://www.hindu.com/2000/12/10/stories/0210000t.htm

Directory of Open Access Repositories - Open-DOAR. (n.d.). Retrieved June 30, 2009, from http://www.opendoar.org/

DSpace. (n.d.). Retrieved May 18, 2009, from http://www.dspace.org

Eden, B. (2001). Managing and directing a digital project. *Online Information Review, 25*(6), 396–400. doi:10.1108/14684520110412948

EPrints. (n.d.). Retrieved May 18, 2009, from http://www.eprints.org

Fisher, W. (2003). The electronic resources librarian position: a public services phenomenon. *Library Collections, Acquisitions & Technical Services, 2*(1), 3–17. doi:10.1016/S1464-9055(02)00303-2

Gertz, J. (2000). Selection for preservation in the digital age. *Library Resources & Technical Services, 44*(2), 97–104.

Ghosh, A. (1997). Internet bandwidth: India needs a backbone. Retrieved May 22, 2009, from http://www.ieo.org/backbone.html

Grout, C., Purdy, P., & Rymer, J. (2000). *Creating digital resources for the visual arts: standards and good practice*. Oxford: Oxbow Books.

Holley, R. (2004). Developing a digitization framework for your organization. *The Electronic Library, 22*(6), 518–522. doi:10.1108/02640470410570820

Hull, R., & Dreher, S. (2001). Into the middle of the thing (with apologies to Horace), developing a system to manage a grant-funded digital collection project. *Collection Management, 26*(3), 29–38. doi:10.1300/J105v26n03_04

Jain, P. K., Jindal, S. K., & Babbar, P. (2006). Digital libraries in India. *The International Information & Library Review, 38*(3), 161–169. doi:10.1016/j.iilr.2006.06.003

Jeevan, V. K. J. (2004). Digital library development: identifying sources of content for developing countries with special reference to India. *The International Information & Library Review, 36*, 185–197. doi:10.1016/j.iilr.2003.10.005

Jose, S. (2007). Adoption of open source digital library software packages: a survey. In M. K. Kumar (Ed.), *Proceedings of CALIBER 2007: 5th International Convention on Automation of Libraries and Research Institutions*, Punjab University, Chandigarh. Retrieved June 6, 2009, from http://eprints.rclis.org/8750/1/Sanjojose.pdf

Kalasampada Product Brochure. (n.d.). Retrieved July 2, 2009, from http://ignca.nic.in/kalasampada.pdf

Kalra, H. P. S. (2004). Efforts towards digitization of libraries in India: problems and prospectus. *The International Information & Library Review, 33*(2/3), 197–204.

Kaul, H. K. (1998). *Library resource sharing and networks*. New Delhi: Virgo.

Licklder, J. C. R. (1965). *Libraries of the future*. Cambridge: MIT Press.

Liu, Y. Q. (2004a). Is the education in digital libraries adequate? *New Library World, 105*(1196/1197), 60–68. doi:10.1108/03074800410515273

Liu, Y. Q. (2004b). Best practices, standards and techniques for digitizing library materials: a snapshot of library digitization practices in the USA. *Online Information Review, 28*(5), 338–345. doi:10.1108/14684520410564262

Loptin, L. (2006). Library digitization projects, issues and guidelines: a survey of literature. *Library Hi Tech, 24*(2), 273–289. doi:10.1108/07378830610669637

Mittal, R., & Mahesh, G. (2008). Digital libraries and repositories in India: an evaluative study. *Program: Electronic Library and Information Systems*, *42*(3), 286–302. doi:10.1108/00330330810892695

Saracevic, T., & Dalbello, M. A. (2001). A survey of digital library education. In. *Proceedings of American Society for Information Science*, *38*, 209–223.

Sharma, R. K., & Vishwanathan, K. R. (2001). Digital libraries: developments and challenges. *Library Review*, *50*(1), 10–15. doi:10.1108/00242530110363190

Traditional Knowledge Digital Library. (n.d.). Retrieved from http://www.tkdl.res.in/tkdl/langdefault/common/Home.asp?GL=Eng

Traditional Knowledge Digital Library (n.d.). Wikipedia: the free encyclopedia. Retrieved July 1, 2009, from http://en.wikipedia.org/wiki/Traditional_Knowledge_Digital_Library

Wilder, S. J. (2002). New hires in research libraries demographic trends and hiring priories. *ARI*, *221*(5).

Wilson, W. (2003). Building and managing a digital collection in a small library. *North Carolina Library*, *61*(3), 88–97.

Yongqing, M., Clegg, W., & O'Brien, A. (2006). Digital library education: the current status. In *JCDL '06. Proceedings of the 6th ACM/IEEE-CS Joint Conference on Digital Libraries, 2006* (pp. 165–74). Retrieved June 15, 2009, from http://ieeexplore.ieee.org/stamp/stamp.jsp?arnumber=04119115

Chapter 11
Collaborative Digital Library Development in India:
A Network Analysis

Anup Kumar Das
Jawaharlal Nehru University, India

B.K. Sen
New Delhi, India

Chaitali Dutta
Jadavpur University, India

ABSTRACT

Digital library provides an excellent opportunity to widely disseminate our documentary heritages and greatly increases access to library collections of rare documents as well as current research literature. Indian digital library initiatives aim at producing a vast amount of digitized documents pertaining to different forms of recorded human knowledge, ranging from the rare manuscripts to current research literature. Digitized documents are made accessible in online information systems either through intranet or Internet channels. However, maintaining an Internet-based online digital library system has several problems such as availability of web server for 24X7 timeframe, robust broadband connectivity, efficient retrieval engine, ownership of digitized documents, etc. This chapter tries to address and document some of the prevailing social networking issues affecting Indian digital library initiatives, particularly the collaboration patterns among participating institutions as well as funding agencies. This chapter also tries to identify social relationships amongst the networked institutions in terms of nodes and ties.

DOI: 10.4018/978-1-61520-767-1.ch011

Nodes are the individual actors within the networks, and ties are the relationships between the actors. This chapter shows how social networks in the collaborative digital libraries play a critical role in determining the way problems are solved, organizations are run, and the degree to which individual projects succeed in achieving their goals. Digital Library of India (DLI) is the largest digitization initiative in India spreading across states of India and involving over ninety organizations to ensure several thousands of rare books written in Indian languages as well as non-Indian languages are accessible through Internet channel. This chapter critically appraises the formation of a formal social network in the DLI project embracing local memory institutions across the states of India as well as the funding agencies. Similarly, this chapter also critically analyses and elaborates another collaborative digital library initiative in India, namely, Traditional Knowledge Digital Library (TKDL).

INTRODUCTION

India is a country where cultural diversity and cultural pluralism are coexisting for their centuries. Over the time Indian cultural institutions became the repositories of rich collections of cultural heritage resources embracing culturally and linguistically diverse communities across states of India. While traditional knowledge of linguistically diverse communities is largely undocumented, there were several attempts to collate them. Systematic documentation of traditional knowledge is centuries old practice of scholars and researchers to make the knowledge re-usable by future generations. These documentation initiatives ended up with producing literature of various kinds. On the other hand, some of the documentary heritage resources available with Indian institutions are on the verge of extinction due to lack of preservation and conservation initiative at the institutional level.

As a member country of UNESCO, India became de-facto signatory of the *UNESCO Universal Declaration on Cultural Diversity*, adopted unanimously by the General Conference at its 31st session held on 2 November 2001. This is an international standard-setting legal instrument which raises cultural diversity to the rank of "common heritage of humanity" (India, Ministry

of Communication and Information Technology 2004; UNESCO, 2001). The Declaration attempts to respond to two major concerns: (i) to ensure respect for cultural identities with the participation of all people in a democratic framework, and (ii) to contribute to the emergence of a favourable climate for the creativity of all, thereby making culture a factor of development.

Article 6 of the *UNESCO Universal Declaration on Cultural Diversity* emphasizes on equitable access to culturally diverse multilingual contents with help of digital technologies. Modern information and communication technologies (ICT), including internet technologies, have tremendous potential to act as enabler for intercultural dialogue through digital dissemination of cultural information, particularly with culturally diverse contents. Cultural informatics can also bridge linguistically diverse contents through translations and adaptations. Thus, cultural informatics can help in making culture a factor of development.

Networked knowledge societies give priorities in protecting documentary and cultural heritages by establishing documentary repositories. Digital library provides an excellent opportunity to widely disseminate our documentary heritages and greatly increases access to library collections of rare documents as well as current research literature. Indian digital library initiatives aim at producing a vast amount of digitized documents pertaining to different forms of recorded human knowledge, ranging from the rare manuscripts to current research literature. When establishing digital library with a large collection, collaboration is inevitable. Indian digital library projects are no exception as funding agencies or implementing agencies do not necessarily possess physical collections that need to be digitized and disseminated through digital library systems. Thus, they need to collaborate with source institutions having rich collections of documentary heritage. On the other hand, outreaching digitized documentary heritage collections require another level of collaboration with possible stakeholders, so that digital library system and its collections get noticed by target audience.

This chapter attempts to study national and international collaboration patterns, with special reference to two important collaborative digital library initiatives, namely, Digital Library of India (DLI) and Traditional Knowledge Digital Library (TKDL). DLI project is a large-scale digital library in India having collaboration with more than 100 institutions across the country. TKDL is widely publicized and recognized digital library initiative from India having international collaboration mainly at the outreach level.

DIGITAL LIBRARY OF INDIA (DLI) PROJECT

The Digital Library of India (DLI) is large scale digital library initiative in South Asia, spreading all over the country and establishing a network of four mega scanning centres and many scanning centres, which feed the digital contents into the digital library systems. Dr. A.P.J. Abdul Kalam, the former President of India, launched the portal of Digital Library of India on 8 September, 2003. Digital Library of India project is a part of the Universal Digital Library (UDL) or Million Book Project, coordinated by the Carnegie Mellon University in United States of America.

Although the original UDL project has already been concluded and successfully implemented in the United States, the DLI project still ripples around with much acclamation.

The vision and mission statements of DLI are similar to that of parent Universal Digital Library project, except some local variations. As perceived by project document, two major benefits of Digital Library of India project are (i) To supplement the formal education system by making knowledge available to anyone who can read and has access; and (ii) to make locating the relevant information inside books far more reliable and much easier (Balakrishnan, 2005; Balakrishnan et.al., 2006).

Positioning Digital Library of India Initiative in Global Context

The Digital Library of India project is an essential part of Universal Digital Library project that aims at providing access to million plus books. Universal Digital Library is a global initiative of four nations, namely, the United States of America, India, China and Egypt, for disseminating centuries-old indigenous knowledge of mankind, spreading in the sub-continents of the countries.

Figures 1 and 2 illustrate the international dimension of UDL project, with an indication of availability of associated UDL portals that disseminate million plus digitized books in different languages. Table 1 specifies that Digital Library of India initiative is a subset of Universal Digital Library project. Other subsets of the UDL project are (i) China-US Million Book Digital Library

Figure 1. Universal digital library - collaborative countries

Figure 2. UDL portals maintained by collaborative countries

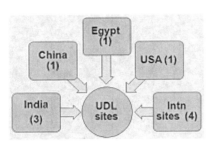

Project, hosted by Zhejiang University, China (ii) Digital Assets Repository, hosted by Bibliotheca Alexandrina, Egypt and (iii) The Universal Library, hosted by Carnegie Mellon University, USA. Each subset of this global initiative is responsible for digitizing important literature produced in the respective country or sub-continent. A vast amount of oriental literature in different Indian languages produced in Indian sub-continent is thus digitized and hosted in DLI portals. National portals of DLI have country-specific identity, similar to other three member countries.

Founded in 1897, Zhejiang University is one of China's oldest and most prestigious institutions of higher education. Zhejiang University hosts China-US Million Book Digital Library Project, which is the Chinese partner of UDL project.

Bibliotheca Alexandrina, the national library of Egypt, is a wonderful reincarnation of the famed ancient library of Alexandria. Bibliotheca Alexandrina is the Egyptian partner of UDL project and hosts Digital Assets Repository (DAR), another partner site of UDL. In India, UDL project partners maintain three associated portals in the name of Digital Library of India sites.

Figure 3 indicates the contribution of different countries in the UDL portal in terms of available digitized books (Das, 2008). This shows UDL portal has received maximum number of digitized books from Chinese partner (75.48%), whereas Indian partner stands second (22.21%) and Egyptian partner third (2.31%) in terms of contributions. This pie chart also discloses that Chinese, Indian and Egyptian partners of UDL are solely responsible for content creation through large-scale digitization initiatives at the national level, whereas UDL partner in USA is only responsible for strategic planning and hosting of digitized contents.

Structure of DLI Project

Digital Library of India was initiated at the national scale to digitize significant collections of old and rare documents available with important

Table 1.

UDL Portals
Universal Digital Library – 1 International Portal http://www.ulib.org 3 Mirror Sites in China North, China South and India
United States – 1 National Portal http://tera-3.ul.cs.cmu.edu/
China – 1 National Portal, i.e., China – US Million Book Digital Library (CADAL) http://www.cadal.zju.edu.cn/IndexEng.action
Egypt – 1 National Portal i.e., Digital Assets Repository (DAR) http://dar.bibalex.org/
India 3 National Portals, i.e., Digital Library of India (DLI) [REMOVED HYPERLINK FIELD] http://dli.iiit.ac.in/ http://www.dli.cdacnoida.in

Figure 3. Country-wise contribution of digitized books in the UDL portal (as of 3 July, 2008)

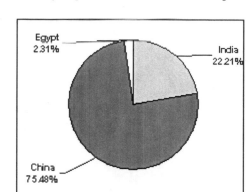

libraries and cultural institutions across India. DLI project maintains a decentralized structure, where Indian Institute of Science Bangalore (IISc) acts as National Coordinator of this project and as international collaborator with the UDL partners abroad. IISc is also a research partner of UDL project, responsible for development of applications software related to the project, in close collaboration with another research partner International Institute of Information Technology Hyderabad (IIIT Hyderabad). For maintaining whole country coverage, DLI project established

four Regional Mega Scanning Centres (RMSCs) across India, three in different metropolitan cities and one in a big city. RMSCs also maintain decentralized structure where local scanning centres carry out digitization activities at their end, in partnership with source libraries situated in close proximity of the respective scanning centre. Figure 4 illustrates a schematic structure of Digital Library of India project. This picture also depicts functional hierarchy of each individual entity within the whole DLI partner institutions. Rolling of responsibilities can also be visualized

Figure 4. Schematic structure of digital library of India project

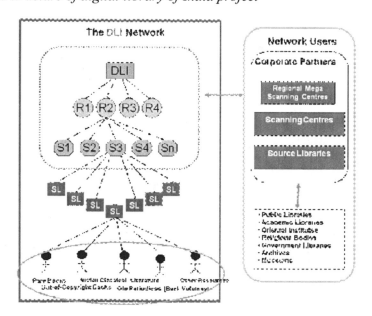

in this figure as National Coordinator IISc takes care of activities in the RMSCs. Similarly, each RMSC coordinates activities in local scanning centres, and each scanning centre secures continuous supply of physical documents from source libraries. On the other hand, captured digitized documents are being transferred from scanning centres to respective regional mega scanning centre in the specified formats. Then RMSC undertakes rigorous quality checking processes and uploads both metadata and digitized contents into the respective DLI portal. RMSCs in Kolkata and Allahabad again transfer captured digitized contents to DLI national office in Bangalore for uploading into DLI portal in IISc. The ERNET India is the backbone of DLI project, providing ICT infrastructural supports to the DLI partner institutions, including high storage web servers and high speed broadband Internet connectivity. Figure 5 illustrates a layer of ICT connectivity provided by ERNET India that makes out a backbone to the DLI project. Having a dedicated broadband connectivity provided by ERNET India in different centres of DLI project, data flow from one level to next higher level becomes robust as shown in Figure 6. This Figure also depicts data transfer process within DLI partner institutions.

Spreading of DLI Project Sites Across the Country

Digital Library of India project sites spread over India through an array of scanning centres and source libraries, coordinated by four RMSCs and

Figure 5. ICT infrastructure provided by ERNET India

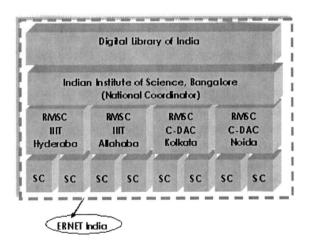

Figure 6. Data flow diagram within DLI project partners

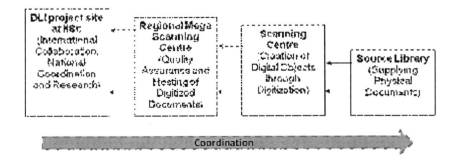

Figure 7. Participating centeres of DLI project across the country

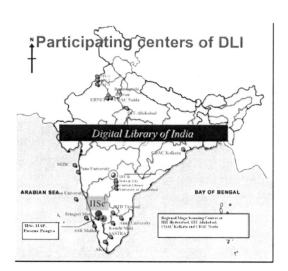

a national coordinator. Figure 7 illustrates nation-wide spread of DLI project sites (Balakrishnan, 2005; Balakrishnan et.al., 2006). This is only an indicative map as on 17 May 2007. Few other DLI partners were added later. This map indicates that DLI project sites are located in many states of India, particularly where resourceful libraries and institutions are located. DLI project partners also ensure that geographical representation should be reflected during the book selection process. For example, scanning centres in West Bengal ensure digitization of rare books of Bengali literature and culture.

Funding Sources of DLI Project

Digital Library of India project is primarily funded by two national and one overseas agencies, namely Ministry of Communication and Information Technology (MCIT), Government of India; Office of the Principal Scientific Advisor to the Government of India; and the National Science Foundation, United States of America. Initially the Universal Digital Library project was funded by the National Science Foundation (NSF), a research funding agency in United States of America. NSF provided seed money to Indian UDL partners for

the procurement of high performance book scanners and development of essential digitization software, when UDL project extended to India. Using NSF fund, first few book scanners were procured in India for the first few DLI scanning centres. The Office of the Principal Scientific Advisor to the Government of India has provided financial support to Indian Institute of Science, Bangalore for the establishment and maintenance of national project coordination centre there. Indian Ministry of Communication and Information Technology (MCIT) is funding many DLI-linked projects at various partner centres of the Digital Library of India, including RMSCs and local scanning centres. Since the initiation of DLI project in 2002, MCIT has been generously providing financial supports to DLI project partners in different phases of DLI project cycle. MCIT is the major contributor for development and maintenance of ICT infrastructure in DLI project sites across India. ICT infrastructure in DLI project includes terabyte web servers for hosting DLI portals, broadband connectivity, local servers and workstations at the scanning centres and RMSCs. Figure 9 identifies that financial supports received by DLI-linked projects vis-à-vis other digitization projects in the country (India, Ministry of Communication and

Figure 8. Funding sources of DLI project

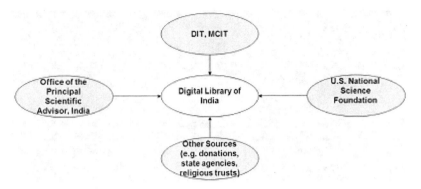

Information Technology, 2009). Seventeen (85%) DLI-linked projects received MCIT financial assistance compared to three (15%) other digitization projects. This also signifies that National Digital Libraries Cell of MCIT stands very favorable to the Digital Library of India initiative, than any other digital library initiatives in the country.

The RMSCs and local scanning centres of DLI are free to generate their additional resources for the self-sustainability of the project by collaborating with the state authorities and non-government trusts including religious trusts and industrial agencies. Some scanning centres, in collaboration with private vendors, also undertake out-sourced digitization activities from the overseas clients as a spin-off of the project. DLI project also accepts donations from individuals and institutions. Donations are used for activities such as selection and acquisition of books, packing and shipping costs,

and quality assurance of the digitized contents. Figure 8 indicates that DLI secures multi-stake funding sources for implementation of this project across the country.

Partnership Pattern in DLI Project

Digital Library of India project is a flagship project in India that began with international collaboration. Over the time, this project built up successful multi-stake partnership, where different kinds of agencies joined hands to develop synergies in building up large scale digital library of collective wisdom. The partners were drawn from academic institutions, cultural institutions, research agencies, religious institutions, government agencies and industrial agencies. Universities and colleges represent academic institutions, whereas museums, archives, public

Figure 9. MCIT-supported digitization projects

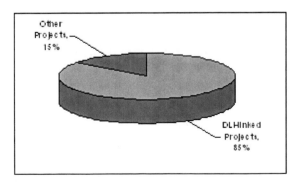

Figure 10. Partnership pattern in DLI project

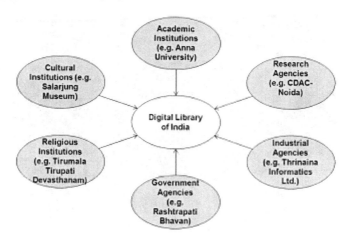

libraries represent cultural institutions. Religious institutions consist of religious bodies and trusts such as Tirumala Tirupati Devasthanam and Sri Sringeri Sharada Peetham. The Centre for Development of Advanced Computing (C-DAC) and Academy of Sanskrit Research (ASR) represent research agencies that became active partners of the DLI project. Many government agencies are also participating in this project. The Rashtrapati Bhavan (President's House), Raj Bhavan (Governor's House), West Bengal State Legislative Assembly are the examples of highly prestigious government offices taking part in this project. This project also expands partnership with corporate houses and industrial agencies such as Microsoft India, Thrinaina Informatics Limited and PAR Informatics Limited. DLI project successfully adopted public-private partnership (PPP) model for digitizing a large volume of literature. This project also helped in formation of a new industry segment to deal with outsourced digitization services, both from Indian and overseas organizations. Many enthusiastic entrepreneurs established companies to handle digitization activities at DLI scanning centres across India, as these newly established scanning centres were designed to be operated through third-party vendors for achieving operational efficiency. While professional librarians in

the host institutions carefully evaluate metadata of each scanned document, data-entry operators and scanning assistants, provided by the third party vendors, are engaged in activities such as scanning, image editing and metadata entry. Thus, this project also helped in capacity building of private enterprises in India, who later on participated in many digitization projects across India, even overseas.

Outreaching DLI Portals at Remote Locations Through Mobile E-Library

DLI contents are disseminated globally through DLI and UDL portals. Many content aggregators in cyberspace, index and disseminate DLI contents to their respective end-users. C-DAC Noida has initiated a mission-mode project titled *Digital e-Library* (Dware Dware Gyan Sampadaa/ Providing Books at Your Doorsteps) in bringing the million books, available with the DLI and UDL portals, to the doorsteps of common citizens located at remote locations. Its Mission is "Internet enabled Mobile Digital Library brought to use of the common citizen for promoting literacy". Different places such as schools in villages and other remote areas are covered under this programme to promote literacy and demonstrate the use of

Figure 11. Knowledge dissemination and outreach model

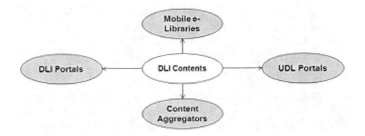

technology for masses, particularly in close proximity to the National Capital Region (NCR) and in particular states in northern and central India such as Delhi, Uttar Pradesh, Haryana, Madhya Pradesh, Himachal Pradesh, Uttarakhand, Punjab, Rajasthan, and Bihar. The schools, adult learning centres, public libraries or local panchayats can invite this mobile digital library for accessing resources and services attached with the mobile unit. This initiative makes use of a mobile van with satellite connection for Internet connectivity. The van is fitted with necessary accessories for providing bound books to the end user from a single point. The mobile van is equipped with:

- Dish Antenna for Internet Connectivity
- Multimedia Laptop
- Laser Printer
- Scorer and Cutter
- Automatic Book Binder

Other than books available in DLI portals, some full-text e-books are also made available locally in through portal in either one of DJVU, PDF and DOC formats. Some of the books are meant for neo-literates in spreading functional literary and lifelong learning in remote areas. The locally available e-books are written in Hindi language, as this initiative is covered in Hindi-speaking states only.

Figure 11 indicates knowledge dissemination and outreach pattern of DLI contents across different regions. While DLI portals, UDL portals,

content aggregators have global reach, mobile digital library bridges the digital divide in remotely located villages in some states of India.

Research Issues in DLI Project

The technological needs and challenges arising out of DLI project have inspired much multidisciplinary research activities covering areas such as image processing and document analysis, information retrieval, cross-lingual issues in information access, data compression techniques, multimedia and Indian language computing. One of the major objectives of DLI project is to become a repository of public domain Indian language books. Thus, a significant volume of Indian language books were digitized across the scanning centres in India. DLI portals become most resourceful digital library of Indian language books, having several million scanned pages in Indian languages.

As several million scanned pages in Indian languages are available with the DLI scanning centres and RMSCs, DLI became a test-bed for many Indian language applications, spearheaded by DLI research partners – Indian Institute of Science Bangalore (IISc), International Institute of Information Technology Hyderabad (IIIT Hyderabad) and Centre for Development of Advanced Computing (C-DAC). These institutions also have collaborated with Technology Development for Indian Languages Programme (TDIL) of Ministry of Communication and Information Technology (MCIT) for development of software applications

Figure 12. Indian language applications developed by DLI research partners

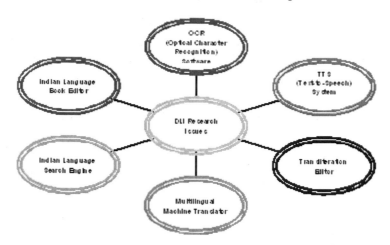

for Indian language computing and spreading Indian language applications to the cross-section of people.

Some of the Indian language applications developed by DLI research partners and described in different research papers (Balakrishnan, 2005; Balakrishnan et.al., 2006; Ganapathiraju et.al., 2005; Prahallad, and Black, 2005; Prahallad, Prahallad, and Ganapathiraju, 2005; Seethalakshmi et al., 2005; Shukla, Arora, and Gugnani, 2004) are:

- OCR (Optical Character Recognition) Software for Indian languages, e.g., Kannada OCR.
- TTS (Text-to-Speech) Software for Indian languages.
- Example-based Multilingual Machine Translator for Indian languages, e.g., Saraswati Machine Translation Tool.
- Transliteration Tool for Indian languages, e.g., OM Transliteration Editor.
- Indian Language Search Engine, and
- Indian Language Book Reader.

Figure 12 provides a graphical overview of Indian language applications, developed by DLI research partners from DLI datasets.

Benefits of DLI Initiative at the National Scale

Digital Library of India initiative provides many opportunities to all segments of learners and readers, including persons located in remote places but having access to ICT facilities at their neighbourhoods. Some of the benefits have already been achieved by the DLI. The benefits achieved are described below as well as indicated in Figure 13:

- DLI supplements the formal education system by making knowledge available to anyone who can read and has access;
- Makes available the out-of-print, out-of-circulation, out-of-copyright and un-copyrighted books, magazines, reports and other useful documents, originated from Indian subcontinent;
- Makes available the classic literature – originated from Indian subcontinent and beyond;
- Supplements collections of small libraries such as public libraries, school libraries and mobile libraries;
- Supplements national libraries in the subcontinent which have very large collections, but citizens do not have online access to those collections;

Figure 13. Benefits of digital library of India

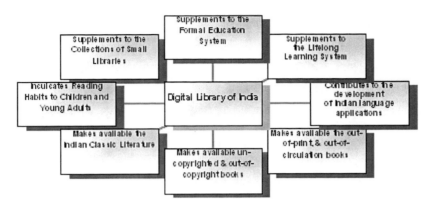

- Supplements the community learning centres, village knowledge centres and community e-centres with substantive e-contents and knowledge resources;
- Helps self-learners, lifelong learners and neo-literates increasing their skills, knowledge and expertise;
- Helps researchers in different disciplines through online literature search and retrieval facility;
- Inculcates reading habits to school children and young adults, who have access to and can interact with digital world in a meaningful way;
- Makes locating the relevant information inside of books far more reliable and much easier;
- Increases visibility and availability of Indian books published by Indian institutions and publishers;
- Encourages other resourceful South Asian institutions to digitize and disseminate their knowledge resources through online portals;
- Creates significant base of South Asian knowledge resources available, searchable and retrievable online; and finally

Makes significant contributions in the development of Indian language applications and tools such as OCR (optical character recognition) software, TTS (text-to-speech) software, machine translation tool, transliteration tool, search engines, book-readers, etc.

TRADITIONAL KNOWLEDGE DIGITAL LIBRARY (TKDL)

Traditional Knowledge Digital Library (TKDL) is well-known Indian digital library initiative, being implemented by the Council of Scientific and Industrial Research (CSIR). TKDL aims at preventing the misappropriation of traditional knowledge of India and some other South Asian countries through an appropriate arrangement with national and foreign patent offices (Das, Dutta, and Sen, 2007; India, Council of Scientific and Industrial Research 2009). TKDL is available in five official languages of the United Nations, namely, English, Japanese, German, French and Spanish. TKDL targets codified information on the Indian systems of medicine, namely, Ayurveda, Unani, Siddha, Yoga, Naturopathy and tribal medicine. TKDL has already documented traditional medicinal formulations comprising 13 million A4 size pages of data on transcribed 62,000 formulations in Ayurveda, 60,000 formulations in Unani, and 1,300 formulations in Siddha (Das, 2008). TKDL is now documenting more formulations from different Ayurvedic, Unani and Siddha texts, whereas formulations from other Indian systems of medicine, e.g. Yoga, Naturopathy, tribal medicine, etc. will be added in near future.

At the core of TKDL project is the innovative approach in the form of Traditional Knowledge Resource Classification (TKRC) that enables structured classification for the purpose of systematic arrangement, dissemination and retrieval of formulations described in classical texts of Ayurveda, Unani and Siddha, into patent compatible format, compatible to the International Patent Classification (IPC) code. TKRC has evolved for about 5000 sub-groups against earlier one sub-group in International Patent Classification.

TKDL has been receiving wide international coverage. This has been publicized most as compared to other digital library initiatives in India. TKDL is widely acknowledged by the World Intellectual Property Organization (WIPO) and its member countries. The International Patent Offices have direct access to TKDL for preventing the misappropriation of traditional knowledge of India. The SAARC Documentation Centre in New Delhi is also currently engaged in the establishment of TKDL for SAARC nations.

Partnership Pattern in TKDL Project

TKDL project is a flagship project for digitization of documented traditional knowledge, more particularly on Indian systems of medicine, in order to prevent bio-piracy and misappropriation of traditional knowledge. Over the time, this project has built up successful multi-stake partnership, where different kinds of agencies joined together to develop synergies in building up a digital library on Indian systems of medicine. The project was initiated by the Council of Scientific and Industrial Research (CSIR), in collaboration with the Department of Ayurveda, Yoga & Naturopathy, Unani, Siddha and Homoeopathy (AYUSH), erstwhile Department of Indian System of Medicine and Homoeopathy (ISM&H). As main target audience of this project is the examiners of Patents and Geographical Indications, partnership was extended

to the Controller General of Patents Design & Trade Marks (CGPDTM) of India and regional patent offices across the country. In this project, subject experts are consulted from different central councils and research institutions, viz., Central Council of Indian Medicine, Central Council for Research in Ayurveda & Siddha (CCRAS), Central Council for Research in Unani Medicine (CCRUM) and Central Council for Research in Yoga & Naturopathy (CCRYN). This project was initially coordinated and implemented by the National Institute of Science Communication and Information Resources (NISCAIR) located at New Delhi. Later, the project was relocated at CSIR headquarters. SAARC Documentation Centre (SDC), located at NISCAIR also participated in this endeavor for awareness raising across the SAARC countries through training programmes. National level partnership pattern is depicted in Figure 14, where all active partners are shown. This multi-stakeholder collaboration resulted in building up considerable good amount of documented traditional knowledge into the digital library system as depicted in Figure 15.

This Figure also indicates content creation process, which starts with documentation of the traditional knowledge available in public domain from the existing literature related to Ayurveda, Unani, Siddha and Yoga. Then TKDL initiates aggregation of information on traditional medicines, with compositions, effects and diseases, methods of preparations, mode of administration, etc. After the process of classification of selected contents based on Traditional Knowledge Resource Classification (TKRC), the contents get digitized and hosted in TKDL web-server.

Outreaching TKDL Across the World Through International Patent Offices

TKDL contents are disseminated globally through TKDL portal. TKDL collaborates with national and international patent offices of different countries for providing access to TKDL by establishing

Figure 14. National level partnership pattern in TKDL project

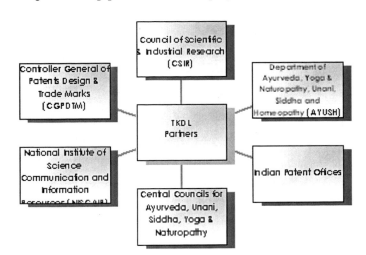

TKDL Access Agreement. TKDL has already established *TKDL Access Agreement* with European Patent Office (EPO), United States Patent and Trademark Office (USPTO), Japan Patent Office (JPO), beside many other member countries of the World Intellectual Property Organization (WIPO). Thus, full access to TKDL contents is presently available only for patent examiners attached in patent offices across the world in some of their official languages as depicted in Figure 16. As the target audience is specifically patent examiners, TKDL does not provide full access to its contents to other interested users. However, partial content, i.e., about 500 formulations, is accessible to the users across the world who do not have login rights.

CONCLUSION

This chapter illustrates how Indian digital libraries have evolved in collaboration with national and international entities. Given the globalized nature of ICT-enabled projects, targeting global

Figure 15. Centralized content creation process in TKDL

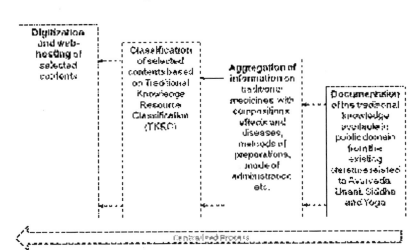

Figure 16. Knowledge dissemination model: Geographically and language-wise

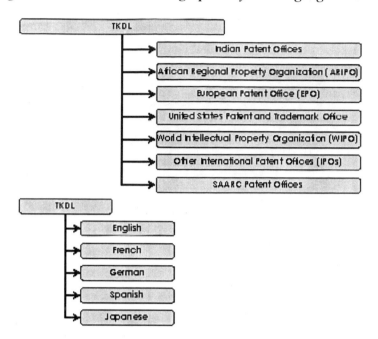

Table 2. Collaborative digital library initiatives in India, attempting access for all to cultural diversity

Name of the Initiative	Implementing Agency	Funding Agency	URL
Digital Library of India (DLI)	Indian Institute of Science; IIIT Hyderabad; C-DAC	Ministry of Communication and Information Technology (MCIT) and many others	http://www.new.dli.ernet.in/; http://dli.iiit.ac.in/; http://www.dli.cdacnoida.in/
Traditional Knowledge Digital Library (TKDL)	Council of Scientific and Industrial Research (CSIR)	Department of Ayurveda, Yoga & Naturopathy, Unani, Siddha and Homoeopathy (AYUSH)	http://www.tkdl.res.in/
Kalasampada: Digital Library Resources for Indian Cultural Heritage (DL-RICH)	Indira Gandhi National Centre for the Arts (IGNCA)	MCIT	http://www.ignca.nic.in/dlrich.html
Cultural Heritage Digital Library in Hindi	IGNCA	MCIT	http://tdil.mit.gov.in/CoilNet/IGNCA/welcome.html
National Databank on Indian Art and Culture	IGNCA	MCIT	http://ignca.nic.in/ndb_0001.htm
Kritisampada: National Database of Manuscripts	National Mission for Manuscripts, IGNCA	Ministry of Culture	http://www.namami.org/pdatabase.aspx
Muktabodha Online Digital Library	Muktabodha Indological Research Institute	Self-funded	http://muktalib5.org/digital_library.htm
Archives of Indian Labour	V. V. Giri National Labour Institute & Association of Indian Labour Historians	Ministry of Labour	http://www.indialabourarchives.org/

Figure 17. Source library having membership of multiple networks

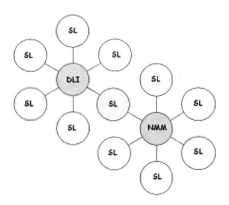

audience necessitates multi-stakeholders' supports both financially and technically. Different kinds of stakeholders are involved in development and dissemination of Indian digital library initiatives as observed in DLI and TKDL project initiatives. These two digital library projects have instances of international collaboration with varying degrees. Table 2 provides another set of digital library projects. Most of them have minimal overseas collaboration, with an exception of 'Muktabodha Online Digital Library'.

Over the time Indian institutions, involved in development of large and medium-scale digital library projects, have developed commendable infrastructural facilities. After completion of these projects, these institutions should be ready to further collaborate and share their infrastructural facilities and latest digital library technologies for wider participation of community level institutions having potential resources. Utilization of existing infrastructural facilities will be resulted in development of connectivity in multiple networks, having similar objectives of dissemination of culturally-diverse indigenous knowledge. This aspect is depicted in Figure 17.

The digital library initiatives in India have tried to contribute towards achieving multicultural and cross-cultural dialogs in a democratic society, in addition to making the endangered documentary resources digitally available. Digitization of documentary heritage collections in a culturally rich

and diverse country is a major challenge to the ICT professionals and policymakers, due to nature of vastness versus available financial resources and institutional frameworks. Thus, scaling up is real concern in India that needs to involve all possible stakeholders as well as end users.

REFERENCES

Balakrishnan, N. (2005). Universal Digital Library – Future Research Directions. *Journal of Zhejiang University. Science, 6A*(11), 1204–1205. doi:10.1631/jzus.2005.A1204

Balakrishnan, N., Reddy, R., Ganapathiraju, M., & Ambati, V. (2006). Digital Library of India: a testbed for Indian language research. *TCDL Bulletin, 3*(1).

Das, A. K. (2008). *Open Access to Knowledge and Information: Scholarly Literature and Digital Library Initiatives – the South Asian Scenario.* New Delhi: UNESCO. Retrieved February 1, 2009, from http://dlist.sir.arizona.edu/2281/01/Open%5FAccess%5FBook.pdf

Das, A. K., Dutta, C., & Sen, B. K. (2007). Information Retrieval Features in Indian Digital Libraries: A Critical Appraisal. *OCLC Systems & Services: International Digital Library Perspectives, 23*(1), 92–104. doi:10.1108/10650750710720793

Ganapathiraju, M., Balakrishnan, M., Balakrishnan, N., & Reddy, R. (2005). Om: One tool for many (Indian) languages. *Journal of Zhejiang University. Science, 6A*(11), 1348–1353. doi:10.1631/jzus.2005.A1348

Indian Council of Scientific and Industrial Research. (2009). *About TKDL*. Retrieved February 1, 2009, from www.tkdl.res.in/tkdl/langdefault/common/AboutTKDL.asp

Indian Ministry of Communication and Information Technology. (2004). *Digitization of Culture - Background Note for Asia IT Ministers' 2nd Summit, Hyderabad*. Retrieved February 1, 2009, from http://www.asiaitsummit.nic.in/Digitisation.pdf

Indian Ministry of Communication and Information Technology. (2009). *National Digital Libraries Cell: List of Projects and Current Status including Achievements*. Retrieved February 1, 2009, from http://www.mit.gov.in/default.aspx?id=325

Prahallad, K., & Black, A. (2005). A text to speech interface for Universal Digital Library. *Journal of Zhejiang University. Science, 6A*(11), 1229–1234. doi:10.1631/jzus.2005.A1229

Prahallad, L., Prahallad, K., & Ganapathiraju, M. (2005). A simple approach for building transliteration editors for Indian languages. *Journal of Zhejiang University. Science, 6A*(11), 1354–1361. doi:10.1631/jzus.2005.A1354

Seethalakshmi, R. (2005). Optical character recognition for printed Tamil text using Unicode. *Journal of Zhejiang University. Science, 6A*(11), 1297–1305. doi:10.1631/jzus.2005.A1297

Shukla, V. N., Arora, K. K., & Gugnani, V. (2004). *Digital library: language centered research, test beds and applications*. Retrieved May 15, 2008, from www.cdacnoida.in/technicalpapers/PaperICDL1.pdf

UNESCO. (2001). *Universal Declaration on Cultural Diversity*. Retrieved February 1, 2009, from http://www.un-documents.net/udcd.htm

Chapter 12
Intellectual Property Rights

Jaideep Sharma
Indira Gandhi National Open University, India

ABSTRACT

This chapter explains the concept of IPR. The author throws light on the global problem of copyright violation and software piracy and discuss the legal measures to control these at international level as well as in India. The authors also discuss the scenario of digitization of information and the digital measures to overcome copying and ensure IPR.

INTRODUCTION

The desire of human beings to own is natural. It provides a sense of security and satisfaction. It is true of tangible and intangible things. The temptation to own, forces one to do it by fair or unfair means, by the educated and uneducated alike. A study conducted on global trends in software piracy by Business Software Alliance and the IDC, reports that 36% of the software in the world is not licensed, amounting to a heavy loss to the software industry. The economic implications reveal that for every purchase of software for 2 dollars, software worth 1 dollar is procured illegally. Another estimate puts the amount spent in 2003 on software purchase as

$50 billion, implying a loss of $30 billion to the software industry. China tops the list of countries in piracy rates with 92% and the United States lies at the bottom with 22% piracy. (Sharari, 2006). Moorthy and Karisiddappa (2005) inform that Indian music and film industry lost Rs. 350 crores due to piracy of films and video records in comparison to Rs. 6073 crores lost by the Indian music industry in 2001. The practice of illegal copying in the print industry is also quite common. Chemical impregnation of paper and the change of type faces that are not visible to the naked eye are some measures taken to prevent copying from paper to paper (Cornish, 2005). But these could not find use due to the exorbitant costs involved to implement. Digital Rights Management (DRM) technologies have been developed to prevent illegal copying

DOI: 10.4018/978-1-61520-767-1.ch012

and controlling the use of digital contents. The technologies include cryptography, watermarking, digital signatures, tagging, Secured Digital Music Initiative (SDMI) for digital music and Content Scrambler System for DVD. (Moorthy, 2006).

Advances in digital information have changed drastically the scenario of information access. It enables anyone to produce digital copies of works that are as good as original. Parts of works can be easily copied to create new documents due to digital technology. An individual's efforts behind creating something need to be protected. Law has come to the rescue of creators of knowledge. It protects their creations in recorded form. Such rights are termed as Intellectual Property Rights (IPR), provided to the creators/inventors of intellectual works. IPR are divided into copyright, patents, service and trade marks and design rights. It includes copyright for literary, graphical, musical and other artistic works; patents, trademarks, layout designs of integrated circuits. IPR comprise moral rights and economic rights. Moral rights help preserve the integrity of the work and attribution of the work to the author. Economic rights provide economic benefits to the creator. Their scope is explained by Ebersole (1994) as the right to: reproduce/copy, prepare derivative works, distribute its copies publicly, do public performance and public display. IPR also limits rights of libraries to reproduce, loan out to other libraries and also of individuals to make limited copies for use or archiving in the context of fair use.

PATENT

Patent is granted for an invention. It may be a process showing a new way of doing something or for a product created that is new. Novelty is important in the product or process for the patent to be granted. The criteria for an invention to be granted a patent is:

i.   It should be novel.
ii. It should have inventive step or it must be non-obvious.
iii. It should be capable of industrial application.
iv. It should not fall within the provisions of section 3 and 4 of the Patents Act 1970".

Certain subjects are not patentable e.g., methods for medical treatment, scientific theories or discoveries of natural elements. Patents are beneficial to the society as they promote creativity and innovation. Patents have a long history. Edison got a patent for electric bulb. "Patent protection for inventions is older than copyright. The earliest patents giving the exclusive right to exploit an invention were awarded in Italy in the 1400s. In England the Crown awarded patents giving inventors a monopoly to exploit their inventions in the same way it gave printers monopolies to print books." Hofman (2009).

TRADEMARK

Trademark is a "word, phrase, symbol or design, or a combination of words, phrases, symbols or designs, that identifies or distinguishes the source of the goods of one party from those of others" (United States. Patent and Trademark Office). A more elaborate definition of trademark "is a visual symbol which may be a word signature, name, device, label, numerals or combination of colours used by one undertaking on goods or services or other articles of commerce to distinguish it from other similar goods or services originating from a different undertaking" (India. Controller General of Patents, Designs and Trademarks. Office of the Registrar of Trademarks).

It identifies a product or an organization and helps the consumer to decide for buying it. It is granted at different levels, i.e., local, national and international level for different time periods in different countries. At the international level, it is administered by the Madrid System for the International Registration of Marks established by the Madrid Agreement, 1891 and the Madrid Protocol, 1989. (Agnew, 2008). The Madrid System allows for registration in multiple jurisdictions. Trademark is administered in India by the Trade Marks Registery according to the Trade Mark Act 1999. A trade mark should be:

- Capable of being represented graphically (that is in the paper form).
- Capable of distinguishing the goods or services of one undertaking from those of others.
- Used or proposed to be used mark in relation to goods or services for the purpose of indicating or so as to indicate a connection in the course of trade between the goods or services and some person have the right to use the mark with or without identity of that person. (India. Controller General of Patents, Designs and Trademarks. Office of the Registar of Trademarks).

DESIGN

Design "means only the features of shape, configuration, pattern or ornament or composition of lines or colour or combination thereof applied to any article whether two dimensional or three dimensional or in both forms, by any industrial process or means, whether manual, mechanical or chemical, separate or combined, which in the finished article appeal to and are judged solely by the eye, but does not include any mode or principle or construction or any thing which is in substance a mere mechanical device, and does not include any trade mark, as define in clause (v) of sub-section of Section 2 of the Trade and Merchandise Marks Act, 1958, property mark or artistic works as defined under Section 2(c) of the Copyright Act, 1957." In India it is registered under the Designs Act 2000 and granted for a pe-

riod of 10 years that can be extended for 5 years more on application. (India. Controller General of Patents, Designs and Trademarks.Department of Industrial Policy and Promotions. Ministry of Commerce and Industry).

COPYRIGHT

Copyright gives the creator, the right to protect his/her creation.Protection does not mean that access to the creation is forbidden. If it so happens, it will hamper further growth of knowledge since creation of knowledge requires information as an ingredient. It is aptly stated by Ahuja (1996, 7-8), "It is important to note that a copyright exists in form and not in idea. For instance, if a person were to write a classical love story based on the idea, in the settings of the early 18th century, it is not that nobody can use the said idea and write another novel, but it is merely, that the novel of the first writer should not be copied." Thus, copyright is assigned to documents or recorded work and not to ideas. It can be assigned to individuals or to organizations. An example of an organization earning a copyright is when its employee works and produces a document pertaining to its policies, objectives, functioning, etc. An author may transfer copyright to his/her publisher for reproducing copies of the work. But that does not imply that the ownership of the work is transferred to the publisher. In this case the author has transferred exploitation/economic rights to the publisher but the moral rights remain with him/her. He/she has all rights to be acknowledged for the work and not to permit changes and mutilation to the work. Any copyrighted work should have:

- "A means of identifying each work and its copyright status;
- A means for assuring that conversion via scanning results in a digital form that includes the identity of the work, the copyright status and whether permission for a conversion has been granted;

- A means for authenticating each work;
- A means for protecting each work so that only an authorized recipient can receive and perceive it;
- A means for controlling, and setting limits on, specific uses (e.g., display only, print one copy, and no downloading);
- A means for right protection of right protection for each work so it cannot be altered;
- A means for metering usage;
- A means for electronic contracting for access and use;
- A means for billing and collecting payment;
- A means for establishing the perimeters of authority for software agents, including, for example, limiting the amount that can be obligated in electronic contracting conducted by software agents; and
- A means for assuring that copyright identification and some means of control stay with every portion of the work when it is downloaded or otherwise transferred in digital form, or when it is printed." (Ebersole, 1994).

Software Piracy

Software is also protected under copyright but then it is quite common to see people using software acquired illegally. Sharari (2006) has stated 10 ways in which software can be pirated:

1. Soft lifting- Buying one licensed copy of software and loading on several machines for use against the agreement is called soft lifting.
2. Unrestricted Client Access- Occurs when one buys single use license software and loads on a server accessible to clients on a server.
3. Hardware loading- Selling of illegally acquired software loaded on the hardware sold by the vendor is called hardware loading.

4. OEM privacy/ Unbundling- Some software are sold along with the hardware under contract with the software publisher. Some vendors copy and sell this software separately against the contract which is illegal. Some software are sold as a bundle, however people sell these separately after unbundling that is illegal.
5. Commercial use of non-commercial software- Some software are for educational and other non-commercial purposes. Selling of these is also reported commercially which is illegal.
6. Counterfieting- It involves selling copies of software duplicated in an unauthorized way.
7. CD-R piracy- Copying software by CD-R technology and selling copies illegally has also been quite common.
8. Internet piracy- Copied and pirated software is available for sale on the Internet which is illegal.
9. Manufacturing plant sale of overruns and scraps- Mass production of software is done on CDs at CD-ROM production plants under strict supervision of the publisher on the number of copies to be produced for sale. Some plants produce these in excess and sell illegally. Sometimes, even the number of CDs produced is as instructed but some remainders are sold by the plant owners as pirated copies.
10. Renting- Acquiring a licensed copy of the software and later providing it for fees to others on rent is also a practice followed that is illegal.

Copyright Violation: Why

It is worth probing why do people violate copyright. It is important in view of the fact that these industries are important to the economy of a nation. It contributes 5.06% to the GNP in India and 5.8% to that of the U.S.A. It employs about 3%

workforce in the developing countries. (Alikhan and Mashelkar, 2004*quoted in* Moorthy and Karisiddappa, 2005). Ignorance of the copyright laws is one major reason for their violation. Cost is another reason why people copy in developing countries, where people are dependent upon books published from the developed world. Ananda and Raveendra (1996) have enumerated reasons for libraries violating copyright as: limited and shrinking budgets, non-availability of books (out of print books), delay in supply and procurement of books and journals, high cost of books and journals, ignorance of IPR and due to language for translation. Sharari (2006) gives reasons for software piracy as economic, availability of such software on the Internet, increased transmission speeds enabling sending and downloading of heavy files easier and absence and poor enforcement of online copyright laws.

Copyright: Terms and Conditions

Copyright need not be registered, it is provided automatically to the creator, the time period of the right provided varies from country to country as per their copyright laws. TRIPS mentions as, till 50 years after the death of the creator as a general criteria. Digital Management of Copyright Act (DMCA) assigns copyright till after 70 years of the death of the author. It is for lifetime of an individual and 60 years after his/her death in India whereas it is 70 years after the death of the author in the European Union. Compilations like directories, databases, bibliographies etc. are not copyrightable for as long as creations deemed original thoughts are. Database is copyrightable for a period of 15 years every time it is updated. A broadcaster is assigned copyright for 20 years after the broadcast whereas live performances are granted copyright for 50 years after the performance to the performer and the producer. Moral rights are awarded for different time periods in the legislation of different countries. Generally the right to the integrity of the work lasts till the author/creator is alive whereas the right of attribution lasts till the time period of the copyright. (Calson, 2007*in*Agnew, 2008)

International Copyright Law

Copyright laws of countries did not provide cover to authors of other countries. It resulted in publishers printing books of authors from other countries and selling them in their countries. Even renowned authors like Charles Dickens and Mark Twain suffered on this account when their works were printed and sold by publishers in the US and Canada respectively. This led nations to think of protecting the works of authors of other countries. To quote Hofman (2009) "In the 1800s the author Charles Dickens drew attention to the problem of cheap foreign editions when he objected to his works being published without his permission both in the United States and in British colonies. Later it was an American author, Mark Twain, who objected to his works being published in Canada without his permission. Countries began to deal with problems of this sort by entering into bilateral treaties. These treaties required each country to give the citizens of the other country the same copyright protection their own citizens enjoyed." It resulted in the International Convention for the Protection of Artistic and Literary Works popularly known as Berne Convention held in 1886 (revised number of times later) when 10 member countries agreed to protect the rights of authors in the member countries. The credit for the movement goes to Victor Hugo, the French author who initiated it by forming an association Association Littéraire et Artistique Internationale (ALAI) for the cause. Berne Convention later gave birth to the World Intellectual Property Organisation (WIPO), in fact it is now administered by WIPO.

Article 2 of the Convention states "Authors who are subjects or citizens of any of the countries of the Union, or their lawful representatives, shall enjoy in the other countries for their works, whether published in one of those countries or unpublished, the rights which the respective laws do now or may hereafter grant to natives." (Hofman, 2009). The Berne Convention provides basic guidelines for copyright protection that the signing countries can adapt keeping in view the conditions in their country. An example is the time period for copyright protection that has been laid down as a minimum of 50 years after the death of the author. It varies from 50 to 70 years in the member countries. The Convention has simplified procedures in that an author for copyright protection need not to register for it or to give a proof of authorship, the appearance of his/her name at the appropriate place in the work is sufficient for it. Granting moral rights to authors under copyright is another contribution of the Berne Convention as it was not provided earlier in copyright laws of countries e.g., United States.

UNESCO played its part in copyright by formulating the Universal Copyright Convention, Geneva 1952 and Paris 1971. It brought into fold countries not part of the Berne Convention by making registration for copyright mandatory and also introducing the copyright symbol for copyright protected works. To overcome the Western bias in the Berne Convention as felt by some countries, it recommended member nations to accord equal treatment to authors of other countries as that of their own countries.

Trade Related Aspects of Intellectual Property Rights (TRIPS) 1995 is another important effort in internationalizing intellectual property law under the auspices of World Trade Organization (WTO). For any country to be a member of WTO compliance with TRIPS is necessary. TRIPS has integrated IPR with trade agreement on other commodities. It incorporates the Berne Convention except for the moral rights of authors.

WIPO also formulated the WIPO Copyright Treaty (WCT) that builds on the provisions of Berne Convention. It was signed in Geneva in 1996. It includes compilations and computer programs for copyright protection. Another provision in WCT is protecting legally, authors, for using measures that disallow infringing use of their works. It has received criticism as it allows for measures against the use of works before their use as well as after copyright period.

WCT incorporates the three step test for allowing exceptions to copyright that was part of Berne Convention 1967 but finds no mention in the 1971 text. The following act as guidelines in case of exceptions to copyright:

"Exceptions to copyright (1) must therefore be for special cases rather than for normal use of resources, (2) must not conflict with normal exploitation of the work and (3) must not unreasonably prejudice the legitimate interests of the author" (Agnew, 2008, 16).

When there is an international agreement on copyright, it is a binding on the countries to follow. When the countries formulate legislation on the lines of the international agreement, it is a binding on the individuals of the countries to follow. According to the International Copyright Order 1958 of the Government of India, a work published in any of the countries that is a member of the Berne Convention or the Universal Copyright Convention will be copyright protected as any work published in India (Ananda and Raveendra, 1996, 18).

Copyright in India

To quote Menon (1996), a legal expert, "India today has one of the fair and purposive copyright law very much in tune with the world opinion and international standards on the subject. There may be justifiable criticisms on the level of enforcement, which cannot be helped given the overall level of efficiency of the administration in what is called a 'soft state'. There is scope for improvement in administrative efficiency which the state will have to necessarily address given the commitment for globalization and technological upgradation."

Ahuja (1996) elaborates copyright as stated in Section 14 of the Indian Copyright Act 1957 as:

- To reproduce the work in any material form including the storing of it in any medium by electronic means;
- To issue copy of the works to the public, not being copies already in circulation;
- To perform the work in public or to communicate to the public;
- To make any cinematograph film or sound recording in respect of the work;
- To make any translation of the work;
- To make any adaptation of the work.

However Clause (o) and (p) of Section 52 provide some relaxation for libraries. Clause (o) permits a public library to make not more than three copies of a book for use in the library if it is not available in India. Clause (p) permits anyone to reproduce a work for personal use for research, available for access in a public institution. It also allows an author to use, under the fair use doctrine, an unpublished work in research only after proper acknowledgement (Ahuja, 1996). It also allows one to make use of copyrighted material without the permission of the copyright owner if it is used for: personal study or research, teaching, criticism or review, quotation, or judicial proceedings. Indian Copyright Law, 1957 amended at regular intervals, latest in 1999, provides protection to the following types of works:

1. Original literary works, newspaper articles, lyrics, manuals, computer programs and databases;
2. Original dramatic, musical and artistic works including drawings and technical drawings, photographs, maps, paintings, sculpture and other such forms;
3. Audio, video, broadcast and other musical programmes; and
4. Architectural works (Das, 2003).

Anyone violating copyright law can face imprisonment of 6 months to 3 years and a fine of 50,000 – 2 lakhs when violated for the first time and for subsequent times an imprisonment of 1year – 3 years and a fine of 1 lakh – 2 lakhs.

Digital Rights Management (DRM)

DRM has been used interchangeably with Electronic Management System (EMS) and Electronic Copyright Management System (ECMS) that refers to the use of digital technology for protecting copyright. DRM is defined as the "digital management of rights pertaining to the access and use of digital materials" (Agnew, 2008, 1). It includes under its scope, the creator, resource and the user. DRM comprises policies, practices and technologies that enable legal use of resources. The aim of any DRM is to provide integrated, seamless access to information, assuring privacy of the entities involved in the process. The entities include the creator/owner of the information, the content as well as the license for use. Saha et al (2006) have stated the objective of such systems as, to: identify the item and its attribution, control access to it and track its usage.

IPR laws of different nations refer to these as technological measures to control use to digital documents. The large number of options available which is on the increase has resulted in experts suggesting different ways of classifying them. Reported by Fernandez-Molina(2003), Schlachter (1997) classifies these as: pre-infringement, metering and post-infringement that refer to measures taken to: prevent infringement; measure, use made of the document and; improve upon methods used to prevent infringement. She further explains the differentiation between these measures as those that: identify and protect the work, have control of access to the work and control the use of the work. She concludes by favouring the different types of technological measures suggested by Oman(1998), Vinje(1999), Koelman and Helberger (2000) and Koskinen-Olsson(2001). It classifies these as the one: controlling access, controlling use, protecting the integrity and ensuring economic benefits for the use of the work. Access control is done at various levels, e.g, in case of online services the control is at the origin and use is made by means of a password. The criteria for an information security system that has been given by the Information Technology Security Council (ITSEC) applies equally well to any DRM system. It is:

- "Confidentiality prevention of the unauthorized disclosure of information
- Integrity prevention of the unauthorized modification of information
- Availability prevention of the unauthorized withholding of information or resources." (European Commission, 1991)

DRM prevents unauthorized use of literature adopting either of the following:

- Deterrence- It makes unauthorized copying of copyright material cumbersome by introducing a factor of nuisance in terms of resources incurred e.g., time and finances. But it is successful if the cost of the resource is reasonable.
- Prevention- Use of technologies to prevent unauthorized use and copying of material is another approach of DRM.
- Detection- Some resources are freely available on the Internet for controlled use. Detection technologies enable the owner to detect unauthorized use. In case of networked information services, it is important that the identity and privacy of the user and his/her request is secured and also the integrity of the information is preserved during transmission. The technologies adopted for deterrence, prevention and detection include encryption, digital certificates, watermarking, digital signatures, fingerprints, and timestamps, simple marks,

licenses, trusted systems, secured hardware and secured transmission protocols.

Encryption

Encryption scrambles the content to make it unintelligible to use until it is decrypted by someone having the decryption key. An example of a scrambling system commercially developed by Matsushita and Toshiba is the Content Scrambling System used to encrypt files. The problem with these systems is that their decryption solutions are freely available on the net. Encryption can be broadcast, public or private. In broadcast encryption the content is broadcast to a wide audience which introduces an element of risk as it introduces uncertainty over controlled use. To counter the problem, time bound keys are used that provide access for a limited time. Public encryption and private encryption differ in access control available to many or only to two participants. Public encryption makes use of two keys, public and private key. Public key is known to a wide audience whereas the private key is known only to the owner of information. Public key enables the user to decrypt information and encryption is in the hands of the owner only through the private key thus maintaining the integrity of the information. It involves the use of asymmetric key techniques that are difficult to hack. But still there are instances where these have been decoded and modified by hackers. Reverse engineering is used to illegally decrypt information. The system of encryption is so designed to make reverse engineering uneconomical to use and thus avoid illegal use (Moorthy and Karisiddappa, 2000). Steganography is another method of sending information in a concealed way in a carrier file. It may be a text or an image file though the latter is generally preferred due to its large size. It differs from cryptography that it is invisible. Cryptography hides the content but steganography hides the content as well as the sender (Wikipedia).

Digital Watermarking

Digital watermarking is widely used for control in the use of information. Watermarks are signals, patterns, or logos containing information about the owner, sender, recipient, copyright permission information and the watermark detector decoder. Two types of watermarks are used, the visible and invisible marks. The visible marks do not hamper the use of information. It controls the use of information by establishing and providing information regarding its use helping to ascertain source and copies of illegal use (Moorthy et al, 2001). It also discourages illegal copying as these copies do not bear the watermarks in the form of a bar code which is placed on the first page of the article. It shows that the copy is an illegal copy. Invisible watermarks also perform the functions of a watermark except for the fact that its presence does not affect the use of the information.

A watermark should imperceptible, robust, reversible and secure. Imperceptibility is important so that the watermark does not affect the readability and use of the information. Visible watermarks help to reveal ownership and other details of the information for preview and selection. Robustness in a watermark provides it the capability to withstand attempts to edit and alter the information and thus maintain its originality. The feature of reversibility in a watermark helps to remove it, if desired by authorized users and maintain its originality. Security as a feature is most important in watermark as it may affect its functioning. Only authorized users should be able to access and remove the watermark. (Agnew, 2008).

Open Access (OA)

The exorbitant cost incurred in access to information led to the open access movement. Its philosophy is to unshackle the barriers to accessing knowledge and make it democratically available free of cost. It started as a movement launched by Free Software Foundation with the availability of software free along with the source code also with the permission to change it for modification use and distribution. It has conditions to give credit to the first author and to the modifier for subsequent modifications and also to make it available as open source.

OA publishing is quite popular today. There are three OA models from the point of view of copyright. These are: copyright residing with the author, residing with the author and partly with the publisher, and share it with the publisher. Different OA journals follow either of these approaches. Electronic Journal of Comparative Law allows the author to retain copyright while allowing use for educational purposes. There is an obligation on the author that while publishing the article somewhere else to mention the OA journal as the original source. The British Medical Journal is an example of the second type of model where the moral rights of the article remain with the author and the journal has the economic rights. (Saha etal., 2006). OA has made use of literature free of legal complexities. Economic aspects to sustain publishing need to be stabilized.

CONCLUSION

There is ample proof of IPR violations in the society. Digitisation has enabled one to easily copy and reproduce information as good as the original. Internet has provided a channel to access and transmit unlimited information. Computer enables to alter information in any way. Technology is a facilitator; it helps to improve standards of the society. IPR violations cannot be ascribed to developments in technology. Technology has come to the fore again to prevent IPR violations. DRM technologies is an example, they help to control these violations. Anti-circumvention technology is also progressing. Software piracy is a matter of concern for the software producers as well as for the public at large. Producers loose revenue but loss to the public is indirect as it results in rising costs of software, less research and development and decreased job avenues in the IT sector. Collaborative efforts are required to be put in by international bodies, non-governmental organizations, and individuals including software designers and developers, journalists and businesses. (Sharari, 2006). Important role can be played here by library and information scientists, teachers, lawyers and parents. The reasons for violation of IPR are, people doing it knowingly and unknowingly. Those who do it knowingly have to be discouraged from doing so by introducing deterrents in the form of stricter laws that need to be enforced regularly and uniformly. The law enforcement agencies feel a handicap due to the intangible nature of the laws as well as the intangible property, the intellectual property to which these need to be applied. To add to these, interpretation of these laws is no easy due to the fragile digital medium and the Internet.

There have been persistent efforts both at national and international levels towards creating awareness of IPR laws in the public. WTO and IFLA along with governments of different countries have played a laudable role in this regard. There are detailed websites informing the, what and how of IPR. One can clear doubts and also know procedures for filing and obtaining IPR. Ministry of Information Technology, Ministry of Industry, their departments, special divisions and organizations like Patent Facilitating Centre, Technology Information Forecasting Cell (TIFAC), and Federation of Indian Chambers of Commerce of India (FICCI) are some such examples that can be cited from India. There are journals and other literature on IPR, e.g. Journal of Intellectual Property Rights published by the Council of Scientific and Industrial Research (CSIR).

Libraries have an important role to play in creating awareness of IPR. Information Literacy (IL) skills include ability to use information ethically. Programmes to inculcate such skills need to be designed in such a way that they are meaningful and practical. Public libraries can play a more important role here. Old habits die hard. If children are taught to paraphrase and cite information it will go a long way with them. Librarians in collaboration with teachers and parents can play a role in developing informed citizenry towards IPR.

REFERENCES

Agnew, G. (2008). *Digital Rights Management: A Librarian's Guide to Technology and Practice*. Oxford: Chandos.

Ahuja, A. (1996). Chaining the Unchained Books: Copyright as an Infringement on the Philosophy of Library Science. *DESIDOC Bulletin of Information Technology, 16*(6), 5–10.

Alikhan, S., & Mashelkar, R. (2004). *Intellectual Property Rights and Competetive Strategies in the 21st Strategies*. The Hague: Kluwer Law International.

Ananda, T. B., & Reddy, R. B. (1996). Copyright in the Information Age: Librarian's Viewpoint. *DESIDOC Bulletin of Information Technology, 16*(6), 17–19.

Caslon Analytics. (2007 February). *Moral Rights. Caslon Analytics Intellectual Property*. Braddon, ACT, Australia: Caslon Analytics. Retrieved from http://www.caslon.com.au/ipguide18.htm

Controller General of Patents. Designs and Trademarks. (n.d.). *Frequently Asked Questions*. Department of Industrial Policy and Promotions, Ministry of Commerce and Industry. Retrieved from http://www.patentoffice.nic.in/

Controller General of Patents. Designs and Trademarks. (n.d.). *Frequently Asked Questions*. Office of the Registrar of Trademarks. Retrieved from http://ipindia.nic.in/tmr_new/default.htm

Cornish, G. P. (2005). Electronic Information Management and Intellectual Property Rights. *Information Services & Use, 25,* 59–68.

Das, J. (2003). Copyright in Library. In *Knowledge Management in Special Libraries, XXIV All India Conference of IASLIC,* Dehradun (pp. 255-260).

Ebersole, J. L. (1994). *A Review of Protecting Intellectual Property Rights on the Information Superhighway.* Washington, DC: Information Industry Association.

European Commission. (1991). *Information Technology Security Evaluation Criteria (ITSEC): Provisional Harmonised Criteria, Version 1.2 Document COM (90) 314.* Brussels: European Commission. Retrieved from http://www.ssi.gouv.fr/site_documents/ITSEC/ITSEC-uk.pdf

Fernandez-Molina, J. C. (2003). Laws Against the Circumvention of Copyright Technological Protection. *The Journal of Documentation, 59*(1), 41–68. doi:10.1108/00220410310458000

Hofman, J. (2009). *Introducing Copyright: A Plain Language Guide to Copyright in the 21st Century.* Vancouver, Canada: Commonwealth of Learning.

Koelman, K. J., & Helberger, N. (2000). Protection of Technological Matters. In *Copyright and Electronic Commerce: Legal Aspects of Electronic Copyright Management* (pp. 165–227). The Hague: Kluwer Law International.

Koskinen-Olsson, T. (2001). *Secure IPR Content on the Internet.* Paper presented in the Second International Conference on Electronic Commerce and Intellectual Property, Geneva, 19-21 September. Retrieved from http://www.ecommerce.wipo.int/meetings/2001/conference/presentations/pdf/Koskinen.pdf

Lakshmana Moorthy, A. (2006). Copyright Issues in Digitization Era. In Moorthy, A. L., & Laxman Rao, N. (Eds.), *Technology Managemnt in Libraries: Festchrift Volume in Honour of Dr. E Rama Reddy.* New Delhi: Allied.

Lakshmana Moorthy, A., & Karisiddappa, C. R. (2000). Copyright in networked environment. In R. Vengan, H.R. Mohan & K.S. Raghavan (Ed.), *CALIBER-2000: Seventh National Convention on Information Services in a Networked Environment* (pp. 4.18--4.30). Ahmedabad, India: INFLIBNET Centre.

Lakshmana Moorthy, A., & Karisiddappa, C. R. (2005). *Copyright Issues in Digital Environment.* Paper presented in the Seminar on Perspectives in Intellectual Property Rights, 13-14th August, 2005, Dharwar (pp. 32-52). Retrieved from http://drtc.isibang.ac.in:8080/xmlui/bitstream/handle/1849/362/Copyright-Hubli.pdf?sequence=1

Lakshmana Moorthy, A., Prahalada Rao, M., & Karisiddappa, C. R. (2001). Intellectual property rights of electronic information in the age of digital convergence. In *NACLIN 2001: Networking of Digital Resources for National Development: Papers of the Fourth National Annual Convention on Library and Information Networking* (pp.583-589). New Delhi, India: DELNET.

Menon, M. (1996). Copyright Problems in Library Services. Guest Editorial. *DESIDOC Bulletin of Information Technology, 16*(6), 3.

Oman, R. (1998). From Scourge to Savior: How Digital Technology will Save Authorship in the Age of the Internet. In WIPO Internet Forum on the Exercise and Management of Copyright and Neighbouring Rights in the Face of the Challenges of Digital Technologies, Sevilla, 14-16 May (pp. 207-26). Geneva: WIPO.

Saha, N. C. (2006). Copyright Implications in Open Access Environment. In *XXII National Seminar of IASLIC* (pp. 193–200). Kolkota.

Schlachter, E. (1997). The Intellectual Property Renaissance in Cyberspace: Why Copyright Law Could be Unimportant on the Internet. *Berkley Technology Journal, 12*(1). Retrieved from http://www.law.berkeley.edu/journals/btlj/articles/vol12/Schlachter/html/reader.html

Sharari, S. A. (2006). Intellectual Property Rights Legislation and Computer Software Piracy in Jordan. *Journal of the Social Sciences, 2*(1), 7–13. doi:10.3844/jssp.2006.7.13

United States Patent and Trademark Office. (n.d.). *Trademark, Copyright or Patent*. Washington, DC: USPTO. Retrieved from http://www.uspto.gov/web/offices/tac/doc/basic/trade_defin.htm

Vinje, T. (1999). Copyright Imperiled. *European Intellectual Property Review, 21*(4), 197–207. Retrieved from http://www.eblida.org/ecup/publica/vinje.rtf.

Wikipedia. (n.d.). *Steganography*. Retrieved from http://en.wikipedia.org/wiki/Steganography

Chapter 13

Facilitating Access to Indian Cultural Heritage:
Copyright, Permission Rights and Ownership Issues vis-à-vis IGNCA Collections

Ramesh C Gaur
Indira Gandhi National Centre for the Arts (IGNCA), India

ABSTRACT

It is estimated that India possesses more than five million manuscripts on varied subjects lying scattered or fragmented in India and foreign collections. This invaluable and unique pool of knowledge is under threat. Recognizing the need to encompass and preserve this knowledge resource and to make these accessible to scholars and researchers, Kala Nidhi Division of Indira Gandhi National Centre for the Arts (IGNCA) initiated a microfilming of manuscripts programme of private and public institutions in 1989. IGNCA has, so far, microfilmed over 250000 manuscripts in 20,600 microfilm rolls, out of that 14,400 rolls have been digitized. National Mission for Manuscripts (NMM) established in February 2003 seeks to unearth and preserve the vast manuscript wealth of India. The digitization of over 25000 manuscripts under NMM, IGNCA and also under project mode by Cultural Informatics Laboratory (CIL), IGNCA makes largest repository of copies of manuscripts at IGNCA. Besides, IGNCA is also having a unique collection of 2500 rare books, about 1,0,5000 slides, 2000 paintings, 3000 photographs, more than 3000 hours of video recordings, art objects, 10 personal collections of eminent scholars such as Dr. Suniti

DOI: 10.4018/978-1-61520-767-1.ch013

Kumar Chatterjee, Prof. Hazari Prasad Dwivedi, Dr. Kapila Vatsyayan and Prof. Maheswar Neog, photo documentation work on Rock Art, and various museums in India etc. Many of these collections such as rare books, photographs etc are well covered and some are not covered under copyright laws. However, there are issues such as ownership rights, permission rights and access rights etc, which do not allow open access to these collections. As per the existing arrangements, consultation to all collections at IGNCA is allowed to all, 25% copies of the material are also allowed on cost basis. However, to get a copy of the material, user need to approach the concerned library (from where the copies have been obtained) to seek permission. This chapter attempts to describe factors considered as hindrance to providing access to Indian cultural heritage material. Lack of proper policy guidelines especially on copyright issues and intellectual property rights concerning both cultural heritage materials in original as well as in digital form are an obstacle. Open access initiatives worldwide are advocating access to even current information. Cultural heritage belongs to the humanity worldwide, therefore, access should be given to all. These issues, which may not be solved at individual level or institutional level, require debate, deliberations and formulation of policy framework at the highest level.

INTRODUCTION

The term cultural heritage denotes all kind of archival material related to cultural traditions of various civilizations of the world. It refers to knowledge created by the people associated with Art, culture and allied areas. cultural heritage may be classified as tangible cultural heritage and intangible cultural heritage. Tangible cultural heritage may be further divided as immoveable and natural heritage. Moveable heritage includes work of arts, books, manuscripts, artifacts, art objects, artwork etc. Immoveable Heritage refers architecture, monuments, archeological sites and buildings to historical significance. Natural heritage may include the record of the countryside, natural environment, flora and fauna, forests, etc.

According to the 2003 UNESCO Convention for Safeguarding of the Intangible Cultural Heritage, the intangible cultural heritage (ICH) – or living heritage – is the mainspring of our cultural diversity and its maintenance a guarantee for continuing creativity. Oral traditions and expressions including language as a vehicle of the intangible cultural heritage; Performing arts (such as traditional music, dance and theatre); Social practices, rituals and festive events; knowledge and practices concerning nature and the universe; traditional craftsmanship; water management, tradition healings. Intangible Heritage includes those knowledge resources, which are not formally documented and may not be available in form of a material. Government of India has ratified the UNESCO Convention for safeguarding of intangible cultural heritage. It also agreed to contribute to the "Fund for the Safeguarding of the Intangible Cultural Heritage" at least every two years.

INDIAN CULTURAL HERITAGE

The glorious past of Indian culture lies in ancient manuscripts. These are the basic historical evidence and have great research value, which led to recognize its need and importance internationally. It is estimated that India possesses more than five million manuscripts, making her the largest repository of manuscript wealth in the world. They are written on different kinds of material like birch bark, palm leaf, cloth and paper. These manuscripts are in the custody of different institutions like libraries, museum, mutts and individuals.

Table 1. Heritage wealth of India

Total number of manuscripts in India	5,000,0000
Indian manuscripts available in European countries	60,000
Indian manuscripts in South Asia and Asian countries	1,50,000
Number of manuscripts recorded in catalogue	1,000,0000(approx.)
Percentage of manuscripts recorded in catalogue	67%
Other Indian languages	25%
Arabic/Persian/Tibetan	8%

An estimate of heritage wealth of India is as under:

Source:http://asiaitsummit.nic.in/digitisation. pdf. Though our ancestors had tried to preserve these manuscripts, thousands of such valued unpublished Indian manuscripts on varied subjects are lying scattered or fragmented in India and foreign collections and some of these are no longer accessible to research scholars. This invaluable and unique pool of knowledge is under threat and manuscripts are disappearing at an alarming rate.

Apart from IGNCA, Asiatic Society at Kolkata and Mumbai, Khuda Bakhsh Oriental Public Library at Patna, Rampur Raza Library at Rampur are institutions of national importance in possession of great Indian cultural knowledge resources. In a city like Kolkata, it is estimated that item are 200000 manuscripts and Rare Books.

Khuda Bakhsh Oriental Public Library, Patna http://kblibrary.bih.nic.in/

The Rampur Raza Library http://razalibrary.org/ The Asiatic Society of Bombay, Mumbai http://www.asiaticsociety.org/ The Asiatic Society, Kolkata http://www.asiaticsocietycal.com/

A large amount of intangible cultural heritage is lying scattered with many individuals and institutions. Keeping this in view, in year 2006 Ministry of Culture, Government of India announced the launch of a National Mission on Intangible Cultural Heritage with Indira Gandhi National Centre for Arts as a nodal Agency. However the mission is still in files only as after this announcement, IGNCA is still waiting for funds and other necessary instructions from the Government of India.

THE COPYRIGHT ACT 1957 AND CULTURAL HERITAGE

The ownership rights of copyright holders in case of tangible cultural heritage materials except Indian ancient manuscripts are well covered in Indian copyright act 1957 as amended in 1995. The explanations for such works as given in the above act is as given below:

- Work of architecture means any building of structure having as artistic character or design, or any model for such building or structure;
- Artistic work: a painting, a sculpture, drawing (including a diagram, map, chart or plan), an engraving or a photograph, whether or not any such work possesses artistic quality
- A work of architecture and any other work of artistic craftsmanship.
- Cinematograph film means any work of visual recording on any medium produced through a process from which a moving image may be produced by any means and

includes a sound recording accompanying such visual recording and cinematograph shall be construed as including any work produced by any process analogous to cinematography including video films.

- Engravings include etchings, lithographs, woodcuts, prints and other similar works, not being photographs.
- Musical work means a work consisting of music and includes any graphical notation of such work but does not include any words or any action intended to be sung, spoken or performed with the music.
- Photograph includes photolithograph and any work produced by any process analogous to photography but does not include any part of a cinematograph film.
- Plate includes any stereotype or other plate, stone, block, mould, matrix, transfer, negative duplicating equipment or other device used or intended to be used for printing or reproducing copies of any work, and any matrix or other appliance by which sound recording for the acoustic presentation of the work are or are intended to be made.
- Sound recording means a recording of sounds from which such sounds may be produced regardless of the medium on which such recording is the method by which the sounds are produced.

Ownership of Copyright as Given in Copyright Act 1957

First owner of copyright:- subject to the provisions of the Act, the author of a work shall be the first owner of the copyright therein; in the case of a photograph taken, or a painting or portrait drawn or an engraving or a cinematograph film made, for valuable consideration at the instance of any person such person shall in the absence of any agreement to the contrary, be the first owner of the copyright therein.

Term of Copyright as per Copyright Act 1957

Term of copyright in published literary, dramatic, musical and artistic works:- Except as otherwise hereinafter provided, copyright shall subsist in any literary, dramatic, musical or artistic work(other than a photograph) published within the lifetime of the author until sixty years from the beginning of the calendar year next following the year in which the author dies.

- The making of sound recordings in respect of any literary, dramatic or musical work, if
  ◦ Sound recordings of that work have been made by or with the licence or consent of the owner of the right in the work.
  ◦ The person making the sound recordings has been given a notice of his intention to make the sound recordings, has provided copies of all covers or labels with which the sound recordings are to be sold, and has paid in the prescribed manner to the owner of right in the work royalties in respect of all such sound recordings to be made by him, at the rate fixed by the copyright Board in this behalf.
- The making or publishing of a painting, drawing, engraving or photographs of a work of architecture or the display of a work of architecture.
- The making or publishing of a painting, drawing, engraving or photograph of a sculpture, or other artistic work falling under sub-clause (iii) of clause (c) of section 2 if such work is permanently situate in the public place or any premises to which the public has access.
- The inclusion in a cinematograph film of: -Any artistic work permanently situate in a public place or any premises to which

the public has access; or Any other artistic work, if such inclusion is only by way of background or is otherwise incidental to the principal matters represented in the film;

• The reconstruction of a building or structure in accordance with the architectural drawings or plans by reference to which the building or structure was originally constructed. Provided that the original construction was made with the consent or licence of the owner of the copyright in such drawings and plans.

INFORMATION TECHNOLOGY ACT 2000 VIS-À-VIS DIGITAL PRESERVATION AND ACCESS TO DIGITAL INDIAN CULTURAL HERITAGE

Indian IT Act 2000 does not cover issues concerning digital preservation and access to Indian cultural heritage. There is a brief mention about "access", "information", "electronic record" etc but all in different contexts and connotations. Some of the terms as defined in above act are as given below:

(1) In this Act, unless the context otherwise requires, —
   (a) "Access" with its grammatical variations and cognate expressions means gaining entry into, instructing or communicating with the logical, arithmetical, or memory function resources of a computer, computer system or computer network;
   (r) "Electronic form" with reference to information means any information generated, sent, received or stored in media, magnetic, optical, computer memory, microfilm, computer generated microfiche or similar device;
   (t) "Electronic record" means data, record or data generated, image or sound stored, received or sent in an electronic form or microfilm or computer generated microfiche;
   (v) "Information" includes data, text, images, sound, voice, codes, computer programmes, Software and databases or microfilm or computer generated microfiche:

DIGITAL PRESERVATION: LEGAL ISSUES

Copyright protects the rights of copyright owner. There is a relationship between preservation and access in both the traditional and digital forms. Copyright provides safeguard to protect the original work from copying and reproduction. Digitization deals with conversion of material from print or non-print to digital form. So, it may be termed as reproduction of the original work. Digital preservation deals with issues concerning "refreshing", "migration" and "emulation" of contents from one form to other or one media to other. This copying process has raised many legal issues. Both copyright Act 1957 and Indian IT act 2000 are silent on these emerging issues. It needs to have a fresh look and strategy to deal with issues concerning digital preservation.

Many countries have legal deposit acts for digital material. Books Delivery Act, which has provisions of deposition of books at National Library of Kolkata and Delhi Public Library, New Delhi also needs a revision. A new act as per present demands, which may cover both the provisions of books and digital deposits, is required soon. It may demand a fresh look at Indian Copyright Act and IT Act also. The legislation for deposit of digital material may help in protection of IPR and related rights.

BARRIERS TO ACCESS TO CULTURAL HERITAGE

Cultural heritage in India is unique, vulnerable and voluminous. The benefits of cultural heritage, traditional knowledge and monuments etc are not shared equally amongst all. Our cultural heritage should be accessible not just to eminent class of scholars but also to everyone whosoever wants to use it. Some of the key issues regarding access to cultural heritage are as given below:

1. Collect, store and organize for long term preservation
2. Select, digitize, organize and validate content to create an effective archiving system for users.
3. It should be accessible to all users, irrespective of the technology they use or their disabilities, including navigation, content, and interactive elements.
4. Access systems should be user-centered, as per the needs of users, relevance and ease of use.
5. It should take care of multi-linguality. Access in more than one language should be provided.
6. It should use interoperable systems within cultural networks to enable users to easily locate the content and services that meet their needs.
7. Copyright, ownership rights and other legal issues should be clearly defined and protected.

There are certain initiatives for preservation of cultural heritage but access to cultural heritage has remained restricted to certain group or groups of elite class. Most Indian cultural heritage is hard to access. The rules of various libraries, museums and archives pertaining access to such material are harder for users who are not either graduate students or faculty. It is difficult even for students and faculty. Non-availability of catalogue, proper organization of material, closed access, and bad physical condition of such material are common barriers in access to such resources in all institutions in India.

The museums and other cultural institutions in India are in a dilemma with regard to facilitate of dissemination and access to the cultural material available with them. Many of these institutions even do not have proper storage space for the material available with them. The majority of cultural heritage material available with them is still not catalogued. Digitization has been started by some of these institutions, however access to digitized material is still a dream.

There are many barriers in free and fair access of Indian Cultural Heritage not only to common people but also to the scholarly community. Some of such barriers to access to Indian cultural heritage are discussed below.

Technological Barriers

Technology acts both as a barrier as well as a catalyst in enhancement of access to information and knowledge. It also helps in the preservation of Cultural Heritage. How technology is a barrier in access to information is discussed below:

Lack of Basic Infrastructure

The lack a basic infrastructure with many cultural institutions in India is well known fact. Infrastructure such as telephone, computers, Internet, Intranet, availability of trained IT manpower is still beyond the reach of many cultural institutions in India. Hence the digital is increasing.

Lack of Technological Vision

In recent years a number of initiatives have been taken up for introduction of IT applications at various cultural institutions. A number of digitization projects initiated with financial support from Ministry of Information and Communication Technologies and Ministry of Culture have resulted in digitization of manuscripts and other various cultural knowledge resources such as manuscripts, photographs, paintings, and audio video material at various institutions. Some of the digitization work has also been undertaken by institutions themselves like IGNCA etc. Some institutes have digitized the material with the help of National Informatics Centre, C-DAC etc and with the funding support from Ministry of Information and Communication Technology and other funding agencies. However, most of this digitized material is lying in form of CD/DVDs or file server. There is no technological vision for access this material. There is no comprehensive plan or guidelines prepared by any institution in relation to following objectives:-

- Digital preservation
- Digital archiving
- Digital repository.
- Meta data standard

International Standards

Incompatibility of metadata standards to describe cultural heritage objects, and lack of other standards for the cultural heritage sector are some of the barriers to access to Indian cultural heritage.

Lack of Digital Archiving Software

India is considered as IT super power, however, Library Automation and digital library initiatives in India are not supported by good quality softwares.

Economic Barriers

Without adequate financial resources neither cultural heritage can be preserved nor access can be provided. Unlike resources in science and technology, it is expected that access to resources in the field of Cultural Heritage should be made free of charge. However, there is cost involved in it. This cost need to be taken care of either Government or other stakeholders. Therefore, appropriate funds are required for making provisions for faster access to cultural heritage resources. But situation is otherwise. As Art and Humanities are not considered a priority sector and is not having sufficient budget available for preservation and access to cultural resources.

Language Barriers

India is a country with many languages and scripts. The cultural heritage material particularly manuscripts are available in different languages and scripts. There are 18 official recognized languages in India. There are more than 400 different languages existing in India. About 50 different languages are being taught in schools in India. India has newspapers in 87 different languages, Radio programmes in 71, and films in 15 languages. The scholars are not available to read and translate many ancient languages and scripts. So language is a barrier to access to Indian cultural heritage material. Many inscriptions available in India are not being translated on account of their language.

Technological Obsolescence

Many of the audiovisual cultural heritage material are still not integrated into traditional library activities. Old gramophones, spool tapes, VHS and many more old forms of audio visual material are facing problem of technological obsolescence as players for many of these equipments are not available. Conversion of these materials into new form of multimedia technologies is very expensive. The digital version of such material also requires large storage space. Multimedia technologies are also facing problem of current technological obsolescence as technologies are changing at very faster pace.

CULTURE HERITAGE IGNCA

The Indira Gandhi National Centre for the Arts (IGNCA), established in 1987 as an autonomous institution encompassing the study and experience of all forms of the arts-each from with its own integrity, yet within a dimension of mutual view of the arts, integrated with, and essential to the large matrix of human culture. The IGNCA's view of the arts encompasses a wide area of studies, such as creative and critical literature, written and oral; the visual arts, ranging from architecture, sculpture, paintings and graphics to general material culture; photography and film; the performing arts of music, dance and theatre in their broadcast connotation; and all else in festivals, fairs and in lifestyles that has an artistic dimension. It is on the Centre's agenda to explore, study and revive the dialogue between India and her neighbors, especially in the South and South East Asia, in areas pertaining to the arts. The uniqueness of the IGNCA's approach to the arts lies in the fact that it does not segregate the folk and classic, the oral and the aural, the written and the spoken and the old and the modern. Here the emphasis is on the connectivity and the continuity between the various fields that ultimately relate human-to human and human-to-nature. The IGNCA manifests its academic and research work in its publications, international and national seminars, conferences, exhibitions and lecture series. The schools and other education institutions are within the focus of the outreach programme of the IGNCA. Government of India has designated IGNCA as the model agency for all matters relating to the settings up a national data bank on arts, humanities and cultural heritage.

Kala Nidhi Division of the IGNCA is a National Information System and a Data Bank of the arts, humanities, and cultural heritage with a fully supported reference library of multimedia collections. It has a large collection of primary and secondary material in the broad areas of humanities and the arts. Material relating to different genres in the original and in the other forms of copies is collected, classified and catalogued in the cultural archives of the Centre. The archives are enriched by personal collection, ethnographic collections documentation and cultural exchange. Many scholars, artists and art enthusiasts, over the last decades, have carefully and dedicatedly collected materials of their interest ranging from literature and personal histories, recitation, painting, music to folklore and tribal arts. Some of these rare collections of ethnography and audio/visual documentation of old masters and rare arts forms have been acquired by the archives. Ethnographic collections constitute core collections consisting of originals, reproductions and reprographic formats used as basic resource material in the projects of lifestyle studies. In-house documentation includes video and film documentations of various events of the Centre. Emphasis is also given to researched audio and video documentation in various studies sponsored by the Centre. A major collection of the archives comprises cultural material obtained through cultural exchange and research in area studies. The archival collections are conserved, documented and made available for the purposes of research and dissemination.

Some of the IGNCA collections and various issues concerning copyright, ownership rights and permission rights are discussed below:

Rare Books

Rare books are crowning jewels of any library and the illustrations in these add to its antiquity. IGNCA has a good collection of 2500 rare books, some more than 200 years old. IGNCA is making all efforts to identify such books that are held by a large number of institutions and individuals all over the country, to further develop this important collection. All these books are out of copyright as per copyright Act 1957.

Personal Collections

Another unique feature of the Kala Nidhi reference library is the holding of personal collections of eminent scholars and artists. Already 10 such personalities such as Dr. Suniti Kumar Chatterjee, Prof. Hazari Prasad Dwivedi, Dr. Kapila Vatsyayan and Prof. Maheswar Neog etc. have gifted their personal collections, which they had collected painstakingly over a period of time, to the library. These collections have helped to enrich the reference library substantially. Copyright Issues dealt as per copyright Act 1957.

Cultural Archives Collections

The Cultural Archives focuses on the collection, classification and cataloguing of personal collections of scholars/artists who have devoted a life time in collecting materials pertaining to their fields of interest or discipline. It consists of more than 36 personal collections of eminent scholars in the field of photography, music, paintings, video recording of some living legends, slides, masks, artifacts, sculpture, art objects, and textiles etc. Some of these are as listed below:

Sahitaya (Literature)

- Dr. R.C.Rangra collection –41 audio collections
- Voice of Tagore collection – 20 audio spools
- Akhilesh Mittal collection – 21 audio spools

Vastu Silpa (Architecture)

- Lance Dane collection 998 art objects.
- Benoy Behl collection – 675 colour slides (35mm)
- Shambunath Mitra collection – 15,189 black and white negatives

Chayapata (Photographs)

- Raja Lala Deen Dayal collection –2700 glass plate negatives, over 2700 contact prints, 200 original prints
- Henri Cariter- Bresson collection –107 black &White photographs
- DRD Wadia collection – 8000 black &white prints, 4141 black and white negatives (35and 12mm), 9 framed photographs, 39 equipment items and scrap books.
- David Ulrich collection – 25 black & white mounted prints
- Jyoti Bhatt and Raghava Kanerria collection – 50 mounted prints
- Snil Janah collection – 50 mounted prints
- Shambhu Saha collection – 61 Black & white un-mounted prints.
- Ashvin Mehta collection – 985 digital images, 15 colour photographs, 10 black & white photographs

Sangita (Music)

- S. Krishnaswami collection – 599 photographs, 1300 negatives, 784 black & white slides, 369 sketches
- S.Natarajan collection – 363 audio spools
- V.A.K.Ranga Rao collection – 608 music records (78 rpm)
- Ranganayaki Ayyengar collection – 57 music records
- Dr. S.Venkatesan collection – 116 music records (78 rpm)

Other Collections:-

- Elizbeth Brunner paintings – 1751 colour slides (35mm), 852 paintings
- Coorg constumes and Jewellery – 43 pieces of jewellery and 2 sets of wedding costumes, and video cassette on coorgi wedding.

- Abdul Majid Ansari collection – 9 clay surahis
- Prof. R.P.Mishra collection – 63 maps
- Ananda Coomaraswamy collection – 48 books, 1097 journals 115 letters, 703 music discs, 486 glass slides, 227 photographs, (more being added)
- UNESCO Posters – 44 colour plastified photographs

Masks

Total number of masks – approx. 1000
  Digitized status all to be digitized.
  Photographs are allowed

Copyright Issues

Some material such as photographs, music, paintings, slides, artifacts are covered under copyright Act 1957. Some intangible cultural heritage material has not been covered under copyright laws. IGNCA has signed MOUs with most of these donors / collectors and the terms and conditions of these MOUs are guidelines for all reproduction. IGNCA has all rights for display, reproduction for its own academic purpose, exhibitions, reference of scholars at IGNCA, and publications.

Some of the Terms and Conditions of MOUs Signed by IGNCA for Acquisition of Personal Photographic Collections

i.   The copyright and all other rights in respect of the collection are hereby transferred and assigned by the Depositor to the IGNCA free from any claim, encumbrance, lien or charge whatsoever.

ii. The Depositor hereby declares that the Depositor is the sole and absolute owner of the collection to be supplied and delivered to the IGNCA as provided in this agreement and that the collection is free from any claim or ownership or possession of the collection

or reprographic copies thereof or any right, title or interest in respect of the same or otherwise relating thereto is hereafter made by any right, title or interest in respect of the same or otherwise relating whatsoever, it shall be the sole responsibility and liability of the Depositor to settle such claim from time to time to save, defend and deep harmless and indemnified the IGNCA from and against all actions, causes, suits, proceedings, accounts, claims and demands, whatsoever or otherwise which are IGNCA may incur, sustain or suffer in consequence or by reason of the supply and delivery by the Depositor of the collection to the IGNCA as aforesaid and against all damages, costs, charges and expenses and other sums of money incurred in respect thereof. The Depositor shall give an undertaking and an indemnity to the IGNCA in such form and in such manner as may be required by the IGNCA in relation to the Agreement.

iii. The Depositor shall be given due acknowledgement whenever reprographic copies of the photographic material furnished by the Depositor are given out by the IGNCA for reproduction in publications of scholarly work.

iv. The users will be allowed reference to the material from the collection during specified hours of working days of the week in the premises of IGNCA.

v.   Subject to the provisions of the copyright act 1957 copies of the photographic material from the collection shall be given to the users on such terms and conditions as may from time to time be prescribed by the rules and regulations made and the proceedings held by the IGNCA for the purpose.

vi. Subject to the provisions of the copyright act 1957 copies of the collection hereby supplied and delivered by the Depositors shall not be given by the IGNCA in its entirely or in substantial part thereof to any research institution, archives or other similar organizations so as to give the collection the status of an asset exclusive to the Trust.

vii. The Depositor shall not give any copies of the collection hereby supplied and delivered IGNCA Trust to any person.

Some of the Terms and Conditions Related Copyright and Permission Rights as Per Mous Signed by Ignca for Gifted Digital Collections

i. The donor shall have the right to see the consult his material as per the rules and regulations of IGNCA and get digital copies free of cost as an when desired by the donor for academic or reference use.

ii. The copyright of the donors work would vest during his lifetime with him and thereafter with the legal inheritor of his assets. However, IGNCA will be having all rights to make use of donated material for access to users or its library and also to outside scholars for academic and research activities.

iii. The IGNCA shall not have the right to make commercial use in any of the images given by the donor to IGNCA by commercial use in meant the use of photo or any other material in the collection for promoting any product or Institutions or company there than IGNCA.

iv. The IGNCA shall have the right to make copies of the donor's material for purpose of preservation of cataloguing and dissemination for academic/research purposes.

v. The IGNCA shall have the right to display some of the selected works in its website for users information.

Manuscripts Collections

Recognizing the need to encompass and preserve this knowledge resource and to make these accessible to scholars and researchers,

IGNCA in year 1989 has initiated the most important manuscript-microfilming programme. The IGNCA has approached many of the private and public institutions and individuals who are in possession of valuable manuscripts preferably in Sanskrit Language and has signed Memorandum of Understanding with each of them for microfilming of their manuscripts. The IGNCA has, so far, microfilmed over 250000 lakh manuscripts. Out of the total of over 20,600 microfilm rolls, 17087 rolls have been digitized and 13803 rolls duplicated. Some of the reprographic material of various primary and secondary texts has also been obtained from many foreign institutions including Bibliotheque Nationale (Paris), Cambridge University Library (Cambridge, UK), Staatsbibliothek (Berlin), INION (Russia), and Wellcome Institute for the History of Medicine (London), and India Office Library & Records (London).

National Mission for Manuscripts, IGNCA

The National Mission for Manuscripts(NMM) is the other important programme at IGNCA for preservation and documentation of Manuscripts. The Ministry of Tourism and Culture, Government of India established the National Mission for Manuscripts in February 2003. A unique project in its programme and mandate, the Mission seeks to unearth and preserve the vast manuscript wealth of India. Working with specially identified Manuscript Resource Centres (MRC-s) and Manuscript Conservation Centres (MCC-s) in states all over the country, the Mission collects data on manuscripts located in a variety of places, from universities and libraries to temples, mathas, madrasas, monasteries and private collections. It also brings manuscripts and the knowledge they house to the public through lectures, seminars, publications and specially designed programmes for school children and university students.

Table 2. The details of the repository collection are as under

Sl. No.	Name of the Projects	Total Mss.
1	Advaita Ashram Mayavati, Pithoragarh	91
2	Anand Ashram Samsthan, Pune	949
3	Maulana Abdul Kalam Azad Arabic & Persian Research Institute, Tonk	988
4	Asiatic Society of Mumbai, Mumbai	7
5	Atomba Research Centre, Imphal	33
6	Bharat Kala Bhawan, Banaras Hindu University, Varanasi	72
7	Bhandarkar Oriental Research Institute, Pune	18572
8	Bharat Itihas Samsodhak Mandal, Pune	881
9	Bombay University, Mumbai	9
10	Dhinachandra Singh Memorial Mss. Library, Imphal	273
11	Dr. U.V. Swaminathan Iyer Library, Chennai	3294
12	Government Museum, Alwar	1
13	Government Oriental Mss. Library & Research Centre, Chennai	46806
14	Guru Sangolsem Kalidaman Singh Collection, Imphal	67
15	Hijam Romani Singh Collection, Imphal	2
16	Juma Masjid Of Bombay Trust, Mumbai	141
17	Kamrupa Anusandhan Samiti, Guwahati	82
18	Keladi Museum and Historical Research Bureau, Keladi	111
19	Khuda Bakhsh Oriental Public Library, Patna	800
20	L.D.Institute. of Indology, Ahmedabad	1987
21	Maharaja Sawai Man Singh-II Museum, Jaipur	38
22	Manipur State Archives, Imphal	110
23	Manipur State Kala Academy, Imphal	556
24	Manipur State Museum, Imphal	52
25	Mutua Museum, Imphal	15
26	Nagpur University, Nagpur	22
27	Natuam Sangeeta Academy, Imphal	38
28	Oriental Research Instt. & Manuscripts Library,Thiruvananthapuram	5426
29	Oriental Research Institute, Mysore	10249
30	People's Museum, Kakching, Imphal	516
31	Pt. Chandra Singh Memorial Library, Imphal	204
32	Padamshree N. Khelchandra Singh Collection, Imphal	599
33	Rajasthan Oriental Research Institute, Alwar	3237
34	Rajasthan Oriental Research Institute, Jodhpur	2466
35	Rajasthan Oriental Research Institute, Udaipur	633
36	Rama Krishan Mission, Chennai	70
37	Rampur Raza Library, Rampur	142

continued on following page

Table 2. continued

Sl. No.	Name of the Projects	Total Mss.
38	Sahitya Sanstha Rajasthan Vidyapeeth, Udaipur	93
39	Sankara Mutt, Kancheepuram	3232
40	Saraswati Bhawan Library, Varanasi	111339
41	Scindhia Oriental Research Institute, Ujjain	4190
42	Shri Chaitanya Research Institute, Calcutta	170
43	Shri Ranbir Sanskrit Research Institute, Jammu	5437
44	Sree Jagadguru Mooru Savira Math, Hubli	442
45	Sri Rama Verma Government Sanskrit College, Tripunithura	3661
46	Thanjavur Maharaja Sarfoji Saraswati Mahal Library, Thanjavur	13042
47	Vaidika Samsodhana Mandala, Pune	14393
48	Vrindaban Research Institute, Vrindaban	142
49	Yumnam Dhananjai Singh Collection, Imphal	42
	External Collection	255722

Kritisampada: The National Database of Manuscripts

The Mission's main aim is to create an electronic database of manuscripts. The database contains information of various kinds on India's manuscripts-titles, themes, authors, commentaries, scripts, languages, conservation status and much more. The database all contains information on existing catalogues. The Mission endeavors to provide complete and valid information about each manuscript. This database can be searched at http://www.namami.org/pdatabase.aspx

Access to IGNCA Manuscripts Collection and Copyright Issues

There is no copyright in relation to ancient manuscripts. Only ownership rights are involved. IGNCA has singed MOU between concerned libraries that copies of the manuscripts will not be provided to any user without their permission. Scholars and researchers can access this microfilm/microfiche collection at the IGNCA.

They can also obtain copies, subject to certain restrictions, and indeed the conditions spelt out in the MOUs signed between IGNCA and concerned manuscript Library. Access is free to all at IGNCA. As a general practice, one need to seek permission of concerned library to obtain a copy of the manuscript from IGNCA Collection. Copies are being made available in Digital / Microfilm / Print formats on some reproduction cost basis. The consultation to all above manuscripts at IGNCA Reference Library is open to all without any charges. Online catalogue of these manuscripts will be made available soon.

- IGNCA has approached these libraries for transfer of permission rights to IGNCA as a result of which three institutions have given their consent. Seeking permission from the others is still in the process.

Some of the terms and conditions in relation to permission rights as listed MOUs signed by IGNCA for microfilming of manuscripts with various Institutions is as given below:

i.   In consultation with the concerned Manuscripts Library, authorities, IGNCA will identify the Manuscripts, which are to be microfilmed.

ii. All the Manuscripts will be microfilmed by IGNCA in the premises of the concerned Manuscripts Library by Kala Nidhi Reprography Unit of IGNCA.

iii. IGNCA will prepare one set of Master Negative Roll and two more sets (Positive) of each roll.

iv. While IGNCA will retain the Master Negative Roll for archival storage in their repository, one set of roll will be given to the concerned Manuscripts Library (free of cost). The other set of MF Roll will be kept in the Reference Library of IGNCA for consultation.

v.   The copies of manuscripts will not be given to any one outside IGNCA without the permission of the concerned library.

vi. The microfilm rolls of the Manuscripts will be used for Academic & Research and not for commercial purpose.

vii. Publication of these Manuscripts, if any, by IGNCA will be done with due acknowledgement and credits to the concerned Manuscripts Library. Publication of manuscripts may also be done on equal sharing of cost and copyright, when done by mutual consultation.

Slide Collection

IGNCA has a collection of over 100000 slides on subject such as Indian arts, paintings, sculpture, architecture, illustrated manuscripts and the performing arts. Over the years it has acquired and generated carefully selected slides from 17 centres in India and 15 abroad. Notable among such acquisitions from museums abroad are the important slide collection from the Victoria & Albert Museum (UK) and the Chester Betty Collection through the courtesy of INTACH (Charles Wallace bequest). In addition to this, the American Association of South Asian Art has also gifted a complete set of 8,000 slides. Besides slides, the Unit also has a collection of more than 1,700 photo-negatives. All slides have been digitized.

- British Library, London -27671
- Chester Beatty Library, London-3441
- British Museum, London – 574
- Victoria and Albert Museum, London 6419
- Staatliche Museum, Berlin 156
- Ashmolean Museum, Oxford – 100
- Slides from Yugoslavia – 216
- American Committee for Sought Asian Art (ACSAA) – 16222
- Picture of Records (USA) – 253
- Asian Culture Centre for UNESCO (ACCU) – 978
- Prof. Kuchertz of Frieie University Berlin – 7
- Virginia Museum of Fine Arts, Virginia, USA – 1
- Staats Bibliothek Presussischer Kulturbesitz, Berlin – 51
- Los Angeles Country Museum, California – 1
- Catherine B Asher, University of Minnesota, collection – 383
- American Committee for South Asian Art (ACSAA) – 3023
- Raza Library Rampur – 2483
- Gita Govinda – 2090
- Festival of India – 5251
- India International Puppetry Festival – 1059
- IGNCA Seminars and fucntion – 2063
- Dr. Ranjit Makkuni collection – 57
- Bandarkar Oriental Research Institute, Pune – 199
- Archaeological Survey of India, New Delhi – 103
- Kashmir Miniature painting – 343
- Balisattra Bhagavata Purana, Assam – 96
- National Museum Sculpture, New Delhi – 85

- Himalayan Scenery – 107
- Illustrated Rare Book, IGNCA 1537
- Madhumalti paintings – 15
- Exhibition on Bhutan – 103
- Thankas of Ladakh – 80

Copyrights, Permission Rights and Ownership Rights

i.   IGNCA is having copyright on part of collection.
ii.   Access at IGNCA is open to all without any charges.
iii. To obtain a copy, user need to seek permission from the concerned library from where slides have been acquired. Some libraries charge some access fee.
iv.   Re-production copies are available at present on charge basis in any format i.e. slide, digital or print for academic and research purpose.
v.   There are different charges and rules for commercial use and it depand on the purpose of the use.

IGNCA is also engaged in photo-documentation of various museums in India. Some of the terms and conditions of MOUS Signed by IGNCA for Photo Documentation of Museum collections are as given below:

i.   In consultation with the concerned Museum (authorities), IGNCA will identify the artifacts to be photo documented.
ii.   The equipment necessary for photo documentation will be provided by the IGNCA.
iii. The artifacts will be documented by IGNCA in the premises of the concerned Museum.
iv.   IGNCA will prepare two sets of slide documentation of each object. IGNCA will retain one set of slides for archival storage in their repository, and provide one set of slides to the concerned Museum.

v.   This will be a no profit no loss project and copyright will be shared. Any publication by IGNCA will be done with due acknowledgement and credit to the concerned Museum.
vi.   Low resolution images of the artifacts along with textual data many be made available.

PROBLEMS IN ACCESS TO CULTURAL HERITAGE AT IGNCA

Most of the above collection available at IGNCA has been obtained from various individuals and institutions from India and abroad. Some of these acquisitions are in form of gifts and some have been acquired on payment basis. However, most of these cultural heritage materials have been acquired under certain agreements. These agreements have put various conditions in relation to outside access and reproduction. One of the major condition in these agreements is that copies of these materials may not be available to any outside user without permission from concerned individual or library. This condition is a big obstacle in free and open access to cultural heritage at IGNCA. Some of the major problems faced by the users are as described below:-

i.   As per the existing arrangements users need to seek permission directly from the owner of the cultural heritage, which some time is granted, and some time no response is received. In many cases particularly in relation to manuscripts the response received is very late, therefore, there is a delay in providing the copies of the material to the users.
ii.   Although, majority of cultural heritage material at IGNCA has been digitized but due to various restrictions this digitized material cannot be put on Internet for access to worldwide scholarly community.
iii. Open access versus restricted access is a debate going on at IGNCA since long. Still no decision has been taken about access to cultural heritage at IGNCA under open access environment.

iv. There is no complete catalogue of all the cultural heritage under available at IGNCA. Most of the archival material housed in Cultural Archives and in Divisions other than Reference Library of IGNCA is still un-catalogued. So non-availability of comprehensive catalogue is obstacle in locating the material in particular area of interest. The catalogue is also not available on Internet. Some efforts are being made to fulfill these requirements.

v. More than 60% of non-print material at IGNCA has been digitized. However, there is no centralized archiving system or online digital library in plan. Many of these materials are available in either CD/DVDs or digital in form of TIFF and JPEG files. Millions of pages of digital material have been stored in different files. There is no PDF or searchable PDF file to read particular manuscript or other multiple page document.

vi. Lack of comprehensive Metadata for all digitized material is also a big hurdle in access to digitized material.

vii. IGNCA also not having any well-drafted digital preservation policy for long term preservation of digitized material.

viii. IGNCA is leader in digitization of cultural heritage, however it does not have well placed IT infrastructure. There is no Intranet and lack of trained IT manpower also affects the various digital Library initiatives.

ix. Indian cultural heritage at IGNCA is under utilized. Therefore, an awareness regarding availability of such material is also need to be created for the benefit of the scholars.

WHAT NEEDS TO BE DONE AT GOVERNMENT LEVEL

Various barriers to access to cultural heritage faced by IGNCA and other cultural institutions as discussed above need a comprehensive well drafted strategy at the highest level. Most of the manuscripts and other cultural heritage material are available either with Government institutions or institutions supported by various State and Central Government. Many of the manuscripts Libraries, Museums and Archives are part of various Universalities in India, which is also controlled by University Grants Commission, body of Government of India. There are no copyright restrictions on many of cultural heritage resources. Individuals and institutions themselves have laid down most of these restrictions. There are various reasons for these restrictions. It may includes mindset, fear of loosing control and avenues for revenue generation etc. Instructives from Government of India at the level of Ministry of Culture in collaboration with Ministry of HRD and other concerned Ministries may lead to some solution. A directive from Government of India may open these cultural heritage materials to all its users.

OPEN ACCESS TO CULTURAL HERITAGE

At present access to cultural heritage of India is available with in the boundaries of libraries, museum and archives only. Open access to Indian cultural heritage resources is still a beautiful dream. To fulfill this dream into reality, some hard decisions are required to be made. Cultural Resources belongs to humanity, so its access to all should be made available. Copyrights, ownership rights and permission rights need to be re-looked.

CONCLUSION

In India there is Copyright Act, Information Technology Act and Book Delivery Act to deal with issues concerning information and knowledge. Many initiatives in the form of National Mission on Manuscripts, National Mission on Intangible Cultural Heritage, National Mission on Education and proposed National Mission on Libraries have been started for preservation and access to Indian Cultural Heritage resources. Ministry of Information and Communication Technology is also supporting digitization of Indian cultural heritage. National Digital Preservation Programme (NDPP) is a good beginning to have a National Digital Preservation Policy for India. However, there dose not seem any coordination and linkages amongst these initiatives. Ministry of Culture is also planning revision of Books Delivery Act (The delivery of Books and Newspapers (Public Libraries Act) and other acts are also being revised from time to time. But there is nothing about Indian Traditional Knowledge Systems in these acts. Like other countries India will also be needing legislation for legal deposit of digital material. In such a Scenario proposed National Mission on Libraries under consideration of Ministry of Culture, Government of India seems to be the best choice to work on a comprehensive legislation in relation to safeguarding, access and preservation of Indian cultural heritage resources.

REFERENCES

Brakker, N., & Kujbyshev, L. (1994). Information resources on cultural heritage: some problems of integration. *INSPEL, 33*(4), 199–208.

Caplan, P. (2004). Building a digital preservation archive: tales from the front. *The Journal of Information and Knowledge Management Systems, 34*(1), 38–42.

Gorman, M. (2007). The wrong path and the right path: the role libraries in access to, and preservation of, cultural heritage. *New Library World, 108*(11-12), 479–489. Retrieved from http://www.emeraldinsight.com/0307-4803.htm. doi:10.1108/03074800710838236

Kansa, E., & Schultz, J. (2004 1st August). *Perspectives on cultural heritage and intellectual property.* Alexandria Archive Institute.

Klang, M. (2008). Open access barriers: an action research. In Avgerou, C., Smith, M. L., & van den Besselaar, P. (Eds.), *Social Dimensions of Information and Communication Technology Policy* (pp. 335–348). doi:10.1007/978-0-387-84822-8_23

McDaniel, L. M. (2000, August 18). *Barriers and recommendations to the implementation and use of advanced technology in native American communities.*

Minerva Europe. (2004). *Cultural Website Quality Principles: Celebrating European cultural diversity by providing access to digital cultural content.* Retrieved from http://www.minervaeurope.org/publications/tenqualityprinciples.htm

SPRI Museum & Archives: access policy and plan (2006-2009). (2008). Retrieved from http://www.spri.cam.ac.uk/museum/policy/access.html

UNESCO. (2002). *Memory of the World: general guidelines to safeguard documentary heritage. CII-95/WS-11rev February 2002. Heritage Collections Committee of the Cultural Ministers Council. (1995). National conservation and preservation policy for movable cultural heritage.* Canberra, Australia: Department of Communications and the Arts.

Universal's encyclopedia of important central acts and rules (Vol. 6). (2004). New Delhi: Universal Law Publishing.

Chapter 14
Harnessing Technology for Providing Knowledge for Development:
New Role for Libraries

M. Ishwara Bhatt
Birla Institute of Technology and Science, India

ABSTRACT

Rural poor people particularly in developing countries do not get the knowledge and information which they need for their day to day living. Yet, there are no mechanisms for making this knowledge available. This marginalized sector includes small farmers, fishermen, micro-entrepreneurs, small businessmen, unemployed youth etc. They need information for day to day life, such as daily weather forecast, market prices of agricultural produce, how to treat a crop disease, where to get application for the police-men's vacancies, addresses of local masonry persons, etc. Local content is what is most important. Many times, such information is available freely, but the needy person does not get it because of lack of awareness. Such information has to be collected on daily basis from the right sources such as agricultural departments, meteorology offices, bank branches, primary health centers or wholesale markets. The information has to be disseminated through the fastest media such as Internet, community radio, loudspeakers, community newspapers or interactive meetings. Libraries need to work closely with the various agencies, both in government and private sectors and the civil society in order to find out the knowledge requirements of the poor and research into how to package it and deliver efficiently. The chapter gives examples of successful knowledge initiatives for the poor in five countries: Bangladesh, Ethiopia, India, Nepal, and Malawi.

DOI: 10.4018/978-1-61520-767-1.ch014

INTRODUCTION

Importance of knowledge for development is increasingly being stressed for the past more than a decade. One of the first comprehensive publications to appear on this subject was *Knowledge for Development* brought out by World Bank in the year 1999 (World Bank, 1999). The theme of the book is that the major cause of poverty in the present day is lack of access to knowledge by the poor. The book gives numerous examples of how the lives of millions of poor people changed with improved access to knowledge.

This paper is about knowledge needs of rural poor and how libraries can play an effective role. I have given a few case studies to illustrate the point. I have selected this topic because South Asia is home to a half of the world's poor and about 70% of South Asians live in rural areas (World Bank, 2009; "SAARC Regional Poverty Profile (RPP)," 2003).

In this context it is relevant to describe the Millennium Development Goals set by UN and how libraries can play an active role in this. Millennium Development Goals are spelt out below:

i.   Eradicate extreme poverty and hunger;
ii.   Achieve universal primary education;
iii. Promote gender equality and empower women;
iv.   Reduce child mortality;
v.   Improve maternal health;
vi.   Combat HIV/AIDS, malaria and other diseases;
vii. Ensure environmental sustainability;

viii. Develop a global partnership for development.

(United Nations, 2005)

The UN has set specific and measurable objectives for each of the above objectives which are to be achieved by 2015.

LIBRARIES VIS-À-VIS DEVELOPMENT AGENDA

Though libraries provide knowledge to the people, their role in the development process is in the indirect way. The primary role of our libraries in socio economic development of a country is through literacy advancement and therefore, the effect is in the long run. This is because the libraries are planned to meet the needs of literate population whereas the knowledge and information needs of illiterate and poor sector are not integrated in the library setup. Libraries contain generic information which are mainly used by students, academics, professionals or general public. Our libraries do not contain dynamic information which are required by the poor people of developing countries. Let us take for instance, the information requirements of a farmer.

These are the kinds of information which a poor person needs for his/her day to day living. The information changes on day to day basis (sometimes even on hourly basis) and therefore, it is dynamic. A poor farmer's or fisherman's or laborer's earning for the day is decided by the above kind of information. Though there are many agencies in the governmental/non governmental sector which

Table 1.

Information requirements of farmers - examples
Meteorological information relating to local area; Market prices for produces; Government schemes for the poor; Cattle and feeds; Agricultural information (Disease control; Paddy cultivation methods); Availability of vaccines and medicines in health centers; Wages fixed by government; Rules and regulations of employment exchanges; Yellow pages (addresses of doctors, government officials, carpenters, masonry people etc); Bus timings; Availability of food grains in the fair price shop; Fish segregation over the coast etc.

produce the above information, it does not reach the poor because of ineffective dissemination methods. No wonder, for critical information, the villager depends on friends or traders or social circles, though the information one gets often is not accurate. Many times, the information made available by the governmental agencies cannot be used since they are not presented in a way which can be understood by a layman. Farmers or villagers do not use reference style libraries even though village libraries are available in some of our states (Devi & Surachand, 2008).

In case libraries have a serious intention to help this sector, information of the above kind have to be collected from various agencies and made available to this needy user in the language and form which is understandable to him/her.

Thus, the traditional library services are of little use to a poor person. Mismatch occurs in several ways:

i.   *All our libraries put together, including the Internet, the Open Archives and emerging digital libraries serve only a small fraction of human kind* (Arunachalam, 2002). There are physical and distance barriers. Libraries are found in urban or semi urban areas whereas major population of ours live in rural areas.

ii.   *Poor people, in their struggle to keep body and together, they cannot think of information and libraries* (Arunachalam, 2002). What they want is solution to their day to day crisis situations and libraries are never their first choices.

iii. Information our libraries contain is outdated and is not of much use to the poor. The focus in our libraries is on printed information sources which contain generic information; most of the publications get revised after long gaps.

iv.   Information we have, cannot be understood by the poor and illiterate Even the language cannot be understood, leave alone the textual

matter. This is because, our books are brought out keeping in view the needs of educated public.

v.   There are procedural barriers too, such as membership requirements, payment of fees, caution deposit etc which all make our libraries beyond a poor person's reach.

vi.   Most of the information our libraries contain is irrelevant to a poor person. Even the much talked about Internet contains material which is useful for the western countries. As pointed out by Alfonso Gumucio Dagron, ' the content of the web is 90% irrelevant to the needs of 90% of the people in poor countries' (Arunachalam, 2002). No wonder, use of ICT and internet is also poor in rural areas as indicated by studies (Shukla & Gautam, 2008).

Given below are a few successful experiments which challenged the information problems of the poor. These examples show how the information centers need to be planned in order to help the poor earn their livelihood. The first one is an example of pure ICT applications in village knowledge centers and it illustrates the innovative range of services which libraries have to integrate in their scheme in order to meet development needs of the villages. The other four examples are that of libraries which have built relevant content and provided effective outreach services using technology.

DEVELOPMENT FOCUSED KNOWLEDGE CENTERS

Village Knowledge Centers (VKC), Pondicherry, South India

Set up by M S Swaminathan Research Foundation ("MS Swaminathan Research Foundation," n.d.), the VKC Research Project was started in the year 1998. The project aims at building a model

Figure 1. Daily announcement of wave heights over public address system. The information from the US Navy website is downloaded and interpreted by the scientists at the Villianur hub and announced in all the village knowledge centers for the benefit of the fishermen. Source: http://www.utsc.utoronto. ca/~chen/istb01readings/ICTenabledknowledge.pdf Accessed on 3.4.2009

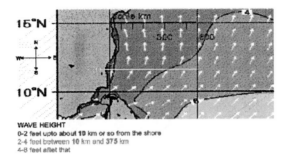

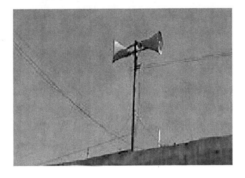

for the use of Information and Communication Technology (ICT) not only to meet the knowledge and information requirements of the rural people, but also to link it to the 'means ' of its use. The project is also known by the name, 'Information Village'.

VKC network has connected 10 villages through hybrid – wired and wireless network - consisting of PCs, telephones, VHF duplex radio devices, Spread Spectrum and email connectivity through dial-up telephone lines or VSAT – that facilitates both voice and data transfer, which enables the villagers to get information they need to improve their lives (Senthilkumaran et al., 2003). The use of multimedia technology with voice facilities enables even illiterates get the information or understand the messages. Solar power back up is available to meet the sporadic electricity.

VKC network works on a 'hub and spokes' model. There is hub at Villianur which functions as a value addition center and the other nine VKC nodes are connected to the hub. Villianur hub serves as headquarters of the network and is run by the project staff of MSSRF (two social scientists and one computer professionals). The Villianur hub has six computers, two telephone lines, and a dial up connectivity to two Internet Service Providers (ISPs). The other VKCs have offline wireless access to email and Internet through the hub at Villianur. VHF duplex radio devices facilitate voice transfer among the centers. Each VKC is equipped with three or four computers, telephones, a printer, wireless device and a solar panel (to meet power breakdowns). One of the computers is dedicated to communication with the main server at Villianur. The other computers are used by the community for typing, learning, etc.

Information needs are identified at each center and transmitted to the hub by email across the wireless network. The staff at Villianur collect the required information from the Internet and other sources and send it to the centers by email. For instance, information about weather is downloaded from the images obtained from U S Navy website twice a day, interpreted and transmitted to the VKCs. For the benefit of illiterate persons, information such as prices of agricultural products and inputs, weather reports are announced over loudspeakers located in the VKCs.

The VKCs provide locale specific information that directly benefit the villagers and this is given free of cost. The types of information include prices of agricultural input (seeds, fertilizers, pesticides), agricultural produces (rice, vegetables, fruits etc), markets (potential for export), entitlements (schemes of governments and banks for the poor), health care (availability of doctors and medical facilities in the nearby hospitals), diseases (both humans and cattle), transport (road conditions, bus schedules), weather reports (appropriate time of sowing, harvesting, catchments for fish, wave heights at sea (Bhatnagar et al., 2009).

One of the distinctive features of the project is local content creation. More than 100 databases have been created that provide updated information on issues ranging from crop prices to government programs (Bhatnagar et al., 2009). The contents of the database relate to the daily needs of the local people. Examples of databases are: Cattle and feeds; Agricultural Information; Educational Information; Health Information; Current Information etc. These databases are updated very regularly (sometimes even twice daily). Knowledge from external agencies such as government, universities and banks are compiled and edited to make them simple and ready to use. Information such as examination results, wave heights, employment news and information from Government of India is downloaded from the Internet. Most of the enquiries are answered by using locally compiled sources (Senthilkumaran et.al., 2003).

Rural yellow pages compiled by the VKCs enable the villagers to find out who rents agricultural equipment in the region, names of cattle agents, carpenters or availability of materials (bricks, pesticides, jute bags etc). This helps enhancement or rural income.

The VKCs bring out an online daily news bulletin, *Farmer's Dairy* which provides information on technologies relevant to agriculture and animal husbandry, with emphasis on sustainable approaches such as Integrated Pest Management, Integrated Crop Management and Integrated Nutrition Management Practices. Printouts are taken daily and displayed on notice boards of the VKCs. Besides, the VKCs bring out a free printed newspaper, *Nammavur Seithi* twice a month (Senthilkumaran et.al., 2003).

The VKC has a bottom-up approach and the villagers are responsible for its maintenance though MSSRF provides guidance and support. Villages provide resources for the basic infrastructure, such as office space and identify volunteers to manage the VKCs. MSSRF provides the necessary equipment and training to the volunteers. Most of the operations are carried out by local women who become instrumental in influencing the programs. Women volunteers collect information from different sources, feed it into an intranet type network, and provide access through the VKCs. These volunteers are given three months' training in operation of computers, use of data and voice network, website construction, handling information queries, and management basics. Abundant use of local language (Tamil) and multimedia enable illiterate users participate in the program apart from availing the benefits.

The VKCs also spare the computer facilities to the school students for preparing slides, downloading examination results etc. They do organize periodic computer training programs for students.

VKCs have become hub of social gatherings where people meet and share knowledge. As a result of knowledge sharing, women get empowered. VKCs facilitate the formation of Self Help Groups (SHGs) in order to generate income generating schemes in the villages. As the MSSRF project staff say, "after all, information is only one element in the development process. To get optimal results and reap the benefit of synergy we need to integrate it with other key factors" (Senthilkumaran et.al., 2003).

In a short time, close relationship developed with government departments which came forward to offer help of various kind, including financial support. The VKCs became channels through which the Government departments disseminated information to the villages on regular basis. Through the VKCs, National Remote Sensing Agency provides information about the fish aggregation over the coast. In order to follow up suggestions emerging in meetings, VKCs send letters to governments with copies to political representatives.

Before designing the project, the project staff held several interactive sessions with the villagers in order to identify their information requirements. It was found that the villagers were most interested in 'dynamic' and customized information, which needs to be accurate and provided quickly. They are not desperately in need of technological information. Meetings continue to be held every month where the village community and the MSSRF project staff discuss the information services required for the village.

Prior to the project—according to MSSRF studies covering 10 percent of the resident families—the predominant sources of commercial information were the local shopkeepers, the market place and the input suppliers. Now close to 90 percent of the information needs of the villagers have been met by the knowledge centers (Express Computer, 2003).

The project is funded by International Development Research Center (IDRC) and Canadian International Development Agency with support from Pondicherry Government. Close to 50000 people living in the 10 villages are benefited by the VKC program.

READ Foundation, Nepal

Established in 1991, the Rural Education and Development Foundation of Nepal (READ Foundation) has built a network of 43 libraries, some in very remote, mountainous villages. Through libraries and literacy development, READ aims at socio-economic development in rural Nepal. The libraries are initiated and owned by the community and each library has its own income generating schemes which sustain its operations. Often revenues generated by the libraries not only support the library, but have funded additional community development projects such as child care centers, health clinics, literacy centers and a workable river bridge.

These libraries conduct many community development programs apart from providing reading materials. According to READ website, "Each library has several thousand books in Nepali, furniture, a card catalogue, a children's section and a trained librarian and a sustaining project to support operations" ("ReadNepal," n.d.). Many of them have computers and multimedia centers with internet access wherever possible.

Those who cannot read, watch videos or listen to audio tapes to acquire knowledge or learn income generating opportunities, for example, microfinance schemes.

The libraries also bring out local contents in the form of wall newspapers, newsletters and online bulletins that are used to share information across villages on cultural, agricultural and community issues.

Libraries also serve as social hubs for child care, medical assistance, literacy training, women discussion groups, AIDS awareness programs, and farming and animal husbandry workshops. These social services are provided in partnership

Figure 2. Boat libraries of Bangladesh specifically designed boat libraries which provide ventilation and natural light. The covered roof protects the library from inclement weather even during the height of monsoon. Flat plant floors allow boats to glide through the shallow canals and even to travel through flooded lands. Source: Shidhulai website, http://www.shidhulai.org/ourwork.html. Accessed on 2.4.2009

with social welfare providers, university libraries, Nepal National Library, Asia Foundation and Unesco. By direct involvement in the development of the community, these libraries have become active community centers. In some communities, women's groups have started microfinance programs for local families that further strengthen the local economy. Libraries serve as platforms for women to meet and discuss problems within their areas and come up with solutions through dialogue with concerned agencies.

The community run, income generating projects are paramount to READ's success. Each library has its own income generating project, which suits the local situation. Examples of projects are: ambulance service, furniture factory, telephone booths, rickshaw service, office rentals, x-ray services, stationery store, grain mill, fish pond, printing press, handicraft manufacture and so on. These enterprises provide the much needed infrastructure and jobs in the villages, apart from supporting the libraries.

READ gets involved when the community shows willingness to support projects administratively and economically. The READ website says, "Each library costs approximately $30,000, which covers READ's portion of the costs to purchase the land, construct a building, purchase and catalog 5,000 books, train the librarian and management committee, build a sustaining project to support the library after it's finished and oversee the project. The community investment is at least 20% of the total project cost".

READ Foundation Nepal received the 2006 Access to Learning Award from the Bill and Melinda Gates Foundation.

Boat Libraries in Bangladesh

Boat libraries working in Natore, Pabna and Sirajganj districts of Bangladesh are excellent examples of how libraries can brighten the lives of poor by taking books and information to their doorsteps which otherwise remain cut off from the mainland because of lack of infrastructure and communication. The boat libraries are run by Shidhulai Swanirvar Sangstha (2008), which was founded in the year 1998 with a mission to assist the communities in northwestern Bangladesh to develop livelihoods through education, training and information service This remote region of Bangladesh is home to some of the poorest and most marginalized communities of Bangladesh. Road access is extremely difficult with boats being the only dependable means of transport, especially in the monsoons which is often heavy

Figure 3.

and spreads over 5-6 months in a year. Access to education is limited and it is difficult even to find teachers because of lack of transport and the schools get flooded in monsoons. Shidhulai found a novel way to circumvent the absence of education facilities by starting schools, libraries and computer training centers working on boats and these are run successfully. Boat libraries started working in 2002.

Covering a radius of 240 kilometers of rivers, streams and wetlands, Shidhulai runs 21 boat libraries (besides 5 boats for agricultural training, 4 boats for evening educational shows, 5 boats for healthcare and 7 boats for workshop, transportation and waste management) touching the lives of 88,000 families ("Shidhulai Swanirvar Sangstha," 2008).

Flat plank floors allow the boats to glide in shallow waters and the side windows provide the natural light and air for the readers. Each library has about 1500 books, 50 periodicals, 5 newspapers and a wide range of information and computer training materials. Also there are 5-6 computers with cellular modems and high antennae for internet access, DVD/CD players, printer, digital projectors and screens. The boat libraries work for 6 days in a week. On a typical day, a boat library makes two halts and spends two hours in each place. The libraries are managed by well trained volunteers. Library staff teach the users how to use the technology to retrieve the information.

The boats are powered by solar powered batteries and lightweight generators.

Locally produced content on Human Rights, Women's Rights, Biodiversity, Environment etc are made available in libraries. Information materials on agriculture, crop management, modern farming, pest management, fisheries, commodity prices are also made available. Contents are tailored to both literates and illiterates. Multimedia programs are available for the benefit of illiterates. Internet access provided in the libraries help them stay in touch with the outside world. The libraries screen film shows in the evenings on topics such as water management, pest control and use of pesticides, disease prevention etc. Shidhulai has tie up with various universities, voluntary organizations, government departments and international organizations in order to arrange the educational programs. The farmers send their agricultural problems by email which are answered by specialists. Women are now able to visit libraries which come to their doorsteps and this was not possible hitherto since in Bangladesh, the religious and cultural values restrict women's mobility.

Shidhulai has established community networks in order to bring long term benefits to the villagers. Prominent among them are Water User Association, Girl Children's Right Association and Micro Enterprise Groups. These groups meet regularly, identify the problems and solve those problems using the boat library resources.

Studies reveal that on account of improved access to up to date information, the farmers have been able to increase their income by 45% on average, and the average use of synthetic pesticides has decreased by 60%, with about one third of them eliminating its use altogether (The Ashden Awards for Sustainable Energy, 2007).

Shidhulai received the Bill and Melinda Gate Foundation's 2005 Access to Learning Award.

Chiwamba Information Resource Centre (CIRC), Malawi

Chiwamba is situated 45 kilometers east of Lilongwe, capital of Malawi in Africa. The development information activities were designed after an assessment of the community needs study (Information Provision for Rural Development - INFORD1) was carried out between 1990 and 1992 which was funded by IDRC, Canada (Mchombu, 1996). The study identified that rural development information needs fall into two categories: information needs common to all rural communities and needs that are location specific. For example, common information needs included information on: income generation, community leadership, education and literacy support, basic economics, government policies on rural development, soil conservation and health matters. Location specific needs are more specific to the situation of a particular rural community, and varied from place to place. (Mchombu, 1996). For example, specific information needs identified in Chiwamba were: Agriculture (Tobacco – modern farming, marketing) and Health and Sanitation (Malaria prevention, hygienic handling of local brews etc). The services began in 1993 as a collaborative project between Malawi National Library Services and Chiwamba community under the sponsorship of IDRC Canada ("International Development Research Centre," n.d.). The following services were offered:

- Reading and borrowing of materials relating to formal education, income generation, adult literacy and entertainment.
- Video shows relating to development information.
- Community newsletter by name, Village News Sheet (*Nkhani za Kumudzi*) which was widely distributed.
- Literacy classes.
- Community events such as graduation celebrations.
- Talks and discussions with experts in the area of agriculture, community development and health.
- Games and cultural activities. CIRC facilitated games and cultural activities in its premises to meet the entertainment needs of the community. Drama, Youth and Women's Clubs were created for organizing the cultural events.
- Events to preserve local culture and traditions.

An evaluation of the project which was carried out during 1995-1999 (INFORD 2) found that the information received from the CIRC benefited them in several ways:

i. Health information had raised the awareness of HIV/AID and other sexually transmitted diseases, family planning, hygiene and sanitation and maternal and child care.

ii. Agricultural information helped improve farming techniques, livestock breeding and fertilizer applications, employ crop rotation methods, manage soil erosion and understand deforestation.

iii. Education and academic information supported literary skills and provided better understanding of the need to keep children in school. Curriculum related books served as supplementary study materials.

Overall, the community were of the view that the CIRC created a learning environment in the community and increased respect for Malawian culture through discussions and reflections on their own culture and traditions (Mchombu, 1999). CIRC was taken over by Malawi National Library Service once the IDRC ended (Mchombu & Cadbury, 2006).

Illubabor Community Libraries and Information Centers

Illubabor is a district in southwest Ethiopia. As a part of Oxfam Canada's Horn of Africa Capacity Building Program ("*Oxfam Canada*," n.d.). twelve slightly dilapidated government reading rooms in rural Ethiopia were revitalized and transformed into vibrant community library and information centers. Previously, the libraries used to provide only printed materials for adults and children (IConnect, 2002). Local communities wanted the libraries to interlink their activities with the socioeconomic development of the region and start various extension activities which will benefit all sections of the community, including semi-literate population.

The partnership between the Oxfam and the Illubabor community aimed at harnessing information and knowledge to drive community development. The specific objectives were to:

- Increase the use of new information and knowledge to help rural people manage social changes, improve their agricultural production, and learn better health practices to protect themselves and their families from disease;
- Nurture the ability of people to innovate and spread the innovations locally;
- Support rural people to become increasingly independent and regain their dignity;
- Increase the capabilities of rural people to identify, evaluate and use their deep and rich indigenous knowledge that had

become marginalized (Mchombu & Cadbury, 2006)

The capacity building program provided by Oxfam helped the Library Management Committees to meet regularly, share their experience, identify the needs of the community, liaise with both government and private funding agencies and develop the services. Training was provided in skill development which included strategic planning, accountability, community participation and the exploration of the role of information for development, moving from the previous role of serving as mere reading rooms. The capacity building enabled the Library Management Committees to use the information to tackle pressing social problems such as family planning, HIV/AIDS, food security, social economic development of the community and the need to harness indigenous knowledge and local culture in designing the community library system.

Apart from providing books and promoting a reading culture, the libraries started holding various outreach programs which included: Meetings and Debates on various social issues, Workshops on agriculture and health, Literary activities like drama and poetry performances, Television and Video Screening, Cultural events and Quizzes. Information centers became hubs of social action by forming a vibrant civil society which came up with activities for dialogue, local development forums and exchange of ideas. Libraries served as platforms for nurturing traditional knowledge by sharing knowledge about local handicrafts and artifacts, traditional medicine, village stories and proverbs. Reading materials were published in local language, *Oromifa.* ICTs such as community radio, photocopying, Fax and computers were introduced step by step. Libraries launched revenue generation programs such as selling coffee/tea on the premises, fee for watching video programs, tree plantation etc. Illubabor Community Information Centers are excellent examples of libraries directly involving in the development agenda.

LESSONS FROM THE SUCCESS STORIES

Many lessons can be learnt from the above success stories. Community development could be achieved by the information centers by providing a good blend of outreach and extension activities along with traditional library service. Mere providing of books and reading materials benefits primarily a certain class of society, which is the literate population while the underprivileged society is being left out. Therefore, the knowledge has to be made available using an integration of various kinds of resources and be disseminated using the right kind of media, which appeals to all sections of the community. For example, in Pondicherry, the use of traditional loudspeakers was most effective in keeping the people informed about the wave heights in the Bay of Bengal. On the other hand, for expert advice on medical or agricultural problems, video conferencing and email chat was more suitable and it was used. ICTs have to be introduced only when people are ready for it.

What poor people need mostly is the local content such as information relevant to market, health, agriculture, employment opportunities, government schemes for the poor or weather conditions. This is in contrast to the generic information contained in our library books. Locally relevant information is generated in various government departments, universities, banks, business chambers, hospitals etc. But, because of poor dissemination system, the information does not reach the poor and needy. To make them usable, intermediaries are required whose job is to collect, verify, interpret and disseminate in the most effective way.

When libraries turn out to be hub of development activities, they cease to be silent, serious reading/learning centers. Libraries become 'knowledge sharing' as against 'knowledge finding' centers. Meetings and discussion programs are bound to disrupt many of our physical arrangements such as shelving, displays, seating etc. Even the routine work schedule of library staff will be affected in the process of organizing development oriented programs.

The wide range of extension activities and outreach services cannot be organized by librarians alone. We need to involve people from the various walks of life and also other professionals. Librarians need to work closely with the civil society who are experienced in developmental work.

Development information activities cannot succeed unless they are 'owned' by the people. Programs which are imposed from outside will not yield the results unless the beneficiaries are actively involved in the planning, execution and running them. There has to be a 'bottom up' approach.

Apart from change in outlook, librarians need to be multi skilled. They need to develop many additional skills such as presentation, liaison work, editing, web authoring, writing, events management, fundraising, marketing etc. They must remain in the continuous process of researching into the information needs of the poor and sources of information.

ROLE OF LIBRARIES

Higher Education (HE) libraries need to take the lead in development information work by taking up suitable Community Information projects. Research needs to be carried out on information requirements of the poor and how to package the information for their benefit. Here, 'one size fits all' principle will not work since the information needs vary from place to place. Librarians are specialists in organizing and dissemination of information. However, for effective community development, mere providing of information is not enough. Institutional linkages need to be established in order to avail the benefits which will change the lives of the poor people. This calls for a synergy of various agencies such as

Education, Health, Forestry department, Public Libraries, Rural Banks, World Bank, IT networks, etc. Librarians, by virtue of their knowledge and position, are better placed to take a leadership in this area. Training programs and workshops are to conducted by libraries which will provide a boost to development information activities. Close working relationship with the civil society is important in order to improve service delivery.

CONCLUSION

Development information work provides new opportunities for the librarians to involve in the uplifting of poor and the needy. Role of knowledge and information in the day to day living of the rural poor is as crucial as that for any other citizen In fact, any critical information provided to them will make a quick difference in their lives. But, this type of information needs to be collected from various agencies, interpreted and disseminated in most usable way. Materials found in printed or online resources are not of much use to them. What is required is more of local content creation which forms a major part of the rural community information activity. Besides, knowledge sharing has to be promoted in the information centers by organizing extension and outreach activities. Technology chosen has to be inexpensive and relevant and at the same time, it has to be efficient. Librarians have to work closely with various stakeholders in order to make service delivery effective.

REFERENCES

Arunachalam, S. (2002). *ICT-enabled knowledge centers for the rural poor – a success story from India.* Retrieved February 4, 2009, from http://www.utsc.utoronto.ca/~chan/istb01/readings/ICTenabledknowledge.pdf

Bhatnagar, S., et al. (2009). *M. S. Swaminathan Research Foundation's Information Village Research Project (IVRP), Union Territory of Pondicherry.* Retrieved February 4, 2009, from http://siteresources.worldbank.org/INTEMPOWERMENT/Resources/14654_MSSRF-web.pdf

Devi, P., & Surachand Singh, K. L. (2008). Information needs of the rural people. In Dhawan, S. M. (Eds.), *Shaping the future of special libraries* (pp. 115–124). Delhi: Ane Books.

Express Computer. (2003, October 6). *Swaminathan using IT for rural development.* Retrieved February 4, 2009, from http://www.expresscomputeronline.com/20031006/indiacomputes01.shtml

IConnect Online. (2002). Retrieved February 4, 2009, from http://www.iconnect-online.org/Stories/Story.import4612

International Development Research Centre. (n.d.). Retrieved April 2, 2009, from http://www.idrc.ca/en/ev-1-201-1-DO_TOPIC.html

Mchombu, K. (1996). *Impact of information technology on rural development: background, methodology and progress.* Retrieved February 4, 2009, from http://archive.idrc.ca/books/focus/783/mchombu.html

Mchombu, K. (1999). *Information provision for rural development 2: measuring the impact of information on rural development.* Retrieved February 4, 2009, from http://idrinfo.idrc.ca/archive/corpdocs/115513/finalrep.99.pdf

Mchombu, K., & Cadbury, N. (2006). *Libraries, literacy and poverty reduction: a key to African development.* Retrieved February 4, 2009, from http://www.bookaid.org/resources/downloads/Libraries_Literacy_Poverty_Reduction.pdf

MS Swaminathan Research Foundation. (n.d.). Retrieved April 3, 2009, from http://www.mssrf.org

Oxfam Canada. (n.d.). Retrieved April 2, 2009, from http://www.oxfam.ca/

ReadNepal. (n.d.). Retrieved April 3, 2009, from http://www.readglobal.org/nepal.asp

Regional Poverty Profile, S. A. A. R. C. *(RPP).* (2003). Retrieved April 3, 2009, from http://www.saarc-sec.org/data/pubs/rpp2005/pages/frameset-2.htm

Senthilkumaran, S., et al. (2003). *Using ICTs in development: Information village research project, Pondicherry.* Paper presented at World Congress – Engineering and Digital Divide, at Tunis, 12-19 October 2003.

Shidhulai Swanirvar Sangstha. (2008). Retrieved April 3, 2009, from http://www.shidhulai.org/

Shukla, S., & Gautam, J. N. (2008). Role of ICTs in rural development. In Dhawan, S. M. (Eds.), *Shaping the future of special libraries* (pp. 125–132). Delhi: Ane Books.

The Ashden Awards for Sustainable Energy. (2007). *Case Study: Shidhulai Swanirvar Sangstha, Bangladesh.* Retrieved from http://www.ashdenawards.org/winners/shidhulai

United Nations. (2005). *Millennium Development Goals.* Retrieved February 4, 2009, from http://www.un.org/millenniumgoals (Accessed on 2.4.2009)

World Bank. (1999). *World development report 1998/99: Knowledge for development. Oxford, UK: World Bank.* Oxford: University Press.

World Bank. (2009). *South Asia: Data, Projects and Research.* Retrieved April 3, 2009, from http://web.worldbank.org/WBSITE/EXTERNAL/COUNTRIES/SOUTHASIAEXT/0,pagePK:158889~piPK:146815~theSitePK:223547,00.html

Chapter 15

Digital Library And E-Governance:
Moving Towards Sustainable Rural Livelihoods

Pradip Kumar Upadhyay
National Informatics Centre, India

Madaswamy Moni
National Informatics Centre, India

ABSTRACT

Rural Connectivity is the lifeline of Indian economy. India is a land of diversity with different types of terrain, various agro-climatic conditions, different levels of socio-economic conditions, and varied levels of regional development. At the beginning of the new millennium, 260 million people in the country did not have incomes to access a consumption basket, which defines the poverty line. Sustainable livelihood is a multi-faceted concept. Rural India thus desires to take advantage of "knowledge-intensive" techniques for its sustainable development and sustainable consumption. Grassroots level Information access (Contents) and Grassroots level access to Information (Networking) are the two essential components for grassroots level development strategies through ICT. Community Information and Communication Centres (CICC), as a concept and model, aim to "boost efficiency and enhance market" integration through Internet/ Intranet technologies for sustainable remote/regional development at grassroots level. Libraries can play an important role and participate in community action and enhance their function as proactive catalysts

DOI: 10.4018/978-1-61520-767-1.ch015

of social change. Community Information & Communication Networks in India empower disadvantaged community for effective information & communication, in view of the stated pronouncement of "India to become Knowledge Society", and also facilitate "social inclusion" of marginalised rural poor to access knowledge and information. There are about 56000 Public Libraries (which include 51000 at village level), 400000 School Libraries, 11000 University/College Libraries, 13000 R&D Libraries, 28 State Libraries, and 526 District Libraries in India. Only 8.4% of the Villages have access to Public Libraries in India. Rural Public Libraries are a part of this revolution and will serve as the backbone for "literacy mission and poverty alleviation". There are empirical evidences to support that rural digital libraries will sustain Community Information & Communication Centres (e-Community Centres). Granthalaya, a Sanskrit word means 'Library'. This chapter deals with "e-Granthalaya: a digital agenda of library automation and networking" facilitating "rural digital libraries" and promoting "local contents" through UNICODE and interoperability capabilities of XML. Networked Library environment play an important role in rural revitalization, as libraries have emerged as a sunrise industry due to globalization and liberalization at regional level, and decentralization trends at grassroots level.

VIABLE SOCIETY IN A RURAL SPACE: AN EPITOME FOR RURAL LIVELIHOODS

India is a land of diversity with different types of terrain, various agro-climatic conditions, different levels of socio-economic conditions, and varied levels of regional development. There have been concerns about persistent rural poverty, unemployment and inequality, and resulting social tensions at grassroot level in India. The strategies and policies developed by the planners and policymakers, adopted two approaches: one focusing on the overall economic development (through percolation, trickle down and spread effect), and the other poverty alleviation (direct intervention). Though these two approaches reinforce each other, there has been no effect to integrate them. The most important sectors for sustainable national development are Agriculture, Education, Healthcare, Water and Energy.

As per 10th Five Years Plan Document (Planning Commission, Government of India: Five Years Plan, 2002-2007), at the beginning of the new millennium, 260 million people in the country did not have incomes to access a consumption basket, which defines the poverty line. Of these,

75 per cent were in the rural areas. Agricultural wage earners, small and marginal farmers, casual workers engaged in non-agricultural activities, rural women (especially women-headed households), among the others, constitute the bulk of the rural poor. The growing populations need food, clothing, shelter, fuel and fodder for their livestock.

As market oriented economic development proceeds, Indian farmers in rural areas continue to experience great disparity in income compared to other sectors. They revert to natural resources as the most accessible sources of livelihood. Degradation of natural resources is a key threat to socio-economic development, and to global environment (e.g., climate change and loss of biodiversity). After decades of limited success in eliminating rural poverty, new ideas about rural development (i.e. viable society in a rural space, livelihood approach, sustainable livelihood approach, sustainable agricultural and rural livelihood approach, sustainable community concept, Multiple Livelihood Opportunities, etc) are emerging so as to reduce the vulnerability of the rural poor. Poverty Alleviation, Livelihood Opportunities and Gainful Employment are closely linked.

Since the Rio Earth Summit in 1992, agriculture remains high on the international agenda because it brings together critical issues like water, poverty, hunger, and health. Rural families in developing countries make a living by engaging in diverse activities, which range from farming, to rural trade, to migration to distant cities and even abroad (Frank Ellis, 2000). Multiple Livelihood Opportunities (MLO), if developed at the farm / community level, help to increase the number of employment days, diversify activities, enhance total income and minimize risks.

Science and Technology (S&T) offers tremendous opportunities in simultaneous achievements of the goals of sustainable agriculture and improving the rural livelihoods (World Bank, 2003). "Doubly Green Revolution" talks about "growth in agricultural production (GAP)" and "improved livelihoods" through:

- Access to land, capital and knowledge;
- Dissemination and sharing of knowledge and technologies (IPRs);
- Improvement of user training and qualification;
- Affordable and accessible technologies;
- Gender equity; and
- Improve/Enable risk/benefit assessment at national, institutional and private level.

Experience shows (Acharya, 2004) that rural livelihoods can be improved in a sustainable way if the following conditions hold true: -

- Availability of appropriate technology;
- Availability of inputs, services and credit to farmer and rural families;
- Availability of market support to farmers and rural households;
- Adequate local institutions and social capital;
- Security of tenure or rights to resources;
- Absence of poor non-friendly macro policies; and

- Good governance.

Sustainable livelihood is thus a multi-faceted concept as against sustainable food security, which is a uni-dimensional concept (Maxwell, and Franken Berger, 1992).

ICT DIFFUSION AND INFUSION: QUINTESSENTIAL FOR SUSTAINABLE GRASSROOTS DEVELOPMENT IN DEVELOPING COUNTRIES

There have been both national and international efforts (DOT Force of the UN, the UN/ESCAP Committee on Poverty Reduction, the Millennium Development Goals, PovertyNet of the World Bank, etc) to improve information flows and communication services to eliminate poverty (ICT for Poverty Reduction). Information, knowledge and communication are the lifeblood of economic and social interaction. Developing appropriate ICTs (i.e. a framework) for sustainable development and sustainable livelihoods is, therefore, essential. These deprivations are compounded at the societal level. The poor lack:

- Access to information that is vital to their lives and livelihoods:
  - About market prices for the goods they produce,
  - About health,
  - About the structure and services of public institutions;
  - About their rights.
- Political visibility and voice in the institutions and power relations that shape their lives;
- Access to knowledge, education and skills development that could improve their livelihoods;
- Access to markets and institutions, both governmental and societal, which could provide them with needed resources and services;

- Access to, and information about, income-earning opportunities.

Information and Communications Technologies (ICTs) catalyze fundamental changes in the world's economies and societies, toward Knowledge Economy (KE) and Information Society (IS). A national 'knowledge economy' can be achieved only if the population is transformed into a 'knowledge society' (Raslan Ahmad, 2000). But the problem of the digital divide stands in the features of the 'knowledge society'. ICT diffusion and infusion to overcome "divides" should induce developments, in the areas of:

- Physical connectivity to bridge distances;
- Electronic connectivity to increase communication;
- Knowledge connectivity to provide information, technology, and increased understanding;
- Market connectivity to link rural products to markets.

"Networking of People" and "Networking of Information" are essential. Informatics Networks, besides Computer Networks, are increasingly considered as development tools for achieving:

- Reaching the Unreached: Public Services
- From Digital Divide to Digital Opportunities for sustainable development and economic growth.
- Fostering agricultural growth, poverty reduction and sustainable resources use.
- Sustainable Development & Earth Care Policies (Bhoovigyan Vikas Foundation, 2002) - Water, Energy, Education, Health, Agriculture & Rural Development, Biodiversity
- A Cluster of Villages - Sustainable Societies in Viable Rural Space

One of the major problems of using ICT for poor is language barrier. Content development in local languages (*more than 22 official languages and more than 1000 dialects spread over 6.25 thouasand* villages) is challenging task ahead. Grassroots level Information access (Contents) and Grassroots level access to Information (Networking) are the two essential components for grassroots level development strategies through ICT. Indian grassroots are about 6.25 thousand villages and about 230 thousand Panchayats (i.e. grassroots level governance institutions).

Indian village is a cognizable unit located in a specific agro-ecological and sociological environment. Its potentials and constraints for development are well known and documented elsewhere. As of today, the development planning is a highly compartmentalized activity managed by atomized government departments handling agriculture, rural enterprises, forests, fisheries, water, health, education, culture, technology and livelihoods - almost in isolation of each other through different projects that rarely converge. Village problems are inter-related and the resources (natural and human) are integrated. People are both the "end and means" of development and also bound by a common space, history, culture and know-how. Indian villages are still complex, intertwined and multi-faceted.

Abdul Kalam, (2005) visualizes establishment of Village Knowledge Centers (VKCs) in 2.30 Panchayats to empower the villagers with the knowledge and to act as a nodal center for knowledge connectivity for the villagers, and also identifies a "Village Information Officer" to be "the extended eyes and ears of the villagers to the world of knowledge". The benefits of e-governance, tele-education, tele-medicine, e-commerce and e-judiciary initiatives should be reaped at, through these Knowledge centres.

Rural India thus desires to take advantage of "knowledge-intensive" techniques for its sustainable development and sustainable consumption.

Community Information and Communication Centres (CICC) or e-Community Centres, as a concept and model, aim to "boost efficiency and enhance market" integration through Internet/ Intranet technologies for sustainable remote/regional development at grassroots level. In India, NICNET based "Community Information Centres (CIC)" in grassroots level in the North Eastern States (Arunachal Pradesh, Assam, Manipur, Meghalaya, Mizoram, Nagaland, Tripura), Sikkim and Jammu & Kashmir, aim to "boost efficiency and enhance market integration" through Internet/Intranet through VSATs, for sustainable development at block level.

Community Information & Communication Networks in India empower disadvantaged community for effective information & communication, in view of the stated pronouncement of "India to become Knowledge Society" and also facilitate "social inclusion" of marginalised rural poor to access knowledge and information. Through e-Community centres, rural people can obtain necessary information and knowledge that can improve their livelihoods and lead to their empowerment. However, building e-Community Centre is not only about providing ICT equipment, it is also about understanding the needs of the people who will use them, and providing locally useful content and applications in local languages (i.e. information related to inputs, services and credit to farmers and rural families, etc).

DIGITAL DEVELOPMENT AT GRASSROOTS: A JOURNEY STARTED IN 1985 WITH THE ESTABLISHMENT OF NICNET IN DISTRICTS OF INDIA

In India, "district" is the basic administrative unit at the sub-state level and also consistent with the decentralized planning process prevailing at the grass-root. With the establishment of NICNET in districts numbering about 439 in 1985-87, National Informatics Centre (NIC) has launched its "district information system (DISNIC)" (DISNIC) in about 27 sectors viz., agriculture, animal husbandry, education, health, industries, rural development, micro-level planning, etc., as an informatics tool for development planning and responsive administration. In the era of e-Governance at grassroots, the relevance of the DISNIC Programme has been felt necessary even now, and hence the Planning Commission has desired to re-establish the DISNIC-PLAN Project, with institutional linkages of grassroots level organizations, to provide continuous support to development agencies in districts, during 2004-07. The National Task Force on Information Technology and Software Development (1998) recommended that "*DISNIC-PLAN programme should be made widespread and the database updated online should be made available to the public, the Panchayat among others*" under the Section "*Citizen IT Interface - Empowering people through the use of IT and information availability: Decentralised Planning and Implementation*".

The DISNIC-PLAN new initiative will support building up databases (spatial and non-spatial), decision support systems, and communication systems to facilitate: sustainability of resources, poverty alleviation, and empowerment of women, full employment, production systems planning, infrastructure planning, and habitat planning. Production potentials of village through "circular-flows" and "chain-effect" should be understood. The Informatics Blueprint includes, among the others, parameters related to the following sectors at village level:-

- Village Identification and Location
- General Characteristics
- Public Utilities
- Meteorology
- Geology
- Soil conditions
- Environmental Problems
- Bio-Resources & Forestry
- Household Details

- Agriculture and its constraints
- Livestock and Animal Husbandry
- Fisheries
- Industry & Craft
- Irrigation Potentials
- Agricultural Machinery & Implements
- Transport & Communication
- Power & Energy
- Agricultural & Rural Marketing
- Financial Institutions
- Education facilities
- Health & Family Welfare
- Public Distribution System
- Drinking Water Supply System & Sanitation features
- Cooperatives
- Water Resources
- Development Schemes

The Draft dataset is available at http://disnic.nic.in .

Generic Models of e-Government (broadcasting/ wider dissemination model, Critical flow Model, Comparative Analysis Model, e-Advocacy Model, Integrated Services Model, etc) will be the expected deliverables. After successful implementation in pilot districts, it will be scaled up to cover all the districts of the Country. The key to sustainability of e-Community Centre is to ensure that the information and facilities that these centres provide, met with the needs of the Community / Citizen.

WARANA WIRED VILLAGE EXPERIMENT IN 1990S: TRUE REFLECTION OF A PUBLIC-PRIVATE-PARTICIPATORY (PPP) MODEL OF NIC AND WARANA NAGAR COOPERATIVE SOCIETY IN THE STATE OF MAHARASHTRA

Another pro-poor initiative is the Warana Wired Village (National Information Centre, 1998) in Maharashtra State, which has set up information kiosks in 70 villages to enable villagers to access agricultural, medical and educational information through the Internet. About 20 farmers visit each kiosk daily to access information on crop cultivation practices and schedules, quantities harvested and sold net income due to them, pest and disease control, and marketing, among other topics. All information is being provided in the local language (i.e. in Marati).

The WARANA Experiment shows that for farmers, the Internet is a better source of information than traditional sources such as traders, field officers, television, radio and the print media. By providing neutral information, this ICT service also minimizes cheating by unscrupulous traders quoting the prices of farm products. This experiment has also proved that Community-based Telecentres offered a way of providing affordable access to ICT services in rural areas.

FACETS OF A CITIZEN: A DIFFERENTIAL STUDY

Emergence of Information Technology on the national agenda and announcement of Information Technology (IT) Policies by various state governments have recognised the "Convergence of Core Technologies (Information Technology, Communication Technology and Broadcasting Technology) and E-Governance" as the tool for sustainable development and globalisation of economy. Introduction of e-governance is considered as a high priority agenda in India, as it is considered to be the only means of taking IT to the "Citizen".

A "Citizen" is defined as a member of a country, state, and a district etc. "Citizen" play the role of a "common public", "children", "woman", "mother", "farmer", "employee", "dealer", "trader", "business man", "industrialist", "vendors", "voter", "fisherman", "entrepreneurs", "unemployed", "youth", "sportsman", 'NGO", "senior citizen", "widow", "destitute", "teacher", "poor", "socially backward", "tribal", "driver", "income tax payer", "permit holder", "builder", "exporter", "importer", "manufacturer", "tenant", "freedom fighter", "ex-service man", "orphan", "pensioner", "handicapped", "land owner", "property owner", "employer", "consumer", "travel agent", "passport holder", "Non Resident Indian", "BPL Family", "doctor", "lawyer", etc. Both the central government and state governments implement various development schemes with special reference to target groups and also location specific.

A study was undertaken by Moni, (2002) to find out what type of services, as given below, to citizen is appropriate for ICT applications in governments so as to facilitate good governance at grassroots level. ICT applications in the following areas, wherein interactions between Citizen and Government (Central and State) are higher, reinforce commitment for good governance:

(a) Issue of Certificates (a partial list)
  ○ Age Proof certificate
  ○ Allotment of residential plots
  ○ Arms license
  ○ Birth & Death Registration Certificate
  ○ BPL Certificate
  ○ Bus Conductor license
  ○ Caste Certificate
  ○ Certificate of Widow of Ex-Service Man
  ○ Destitute Pension Certificate
  ○ Election Commission Identity Card
  ○ Encumbrance Certificate
  ○ Family Income Certificate
  ○ Fertiliser Dealer License
  ○ Freedom fighters Pension Identify Card
  ○ Handicapped Person Certificate
  ○ Income Tax Permanent Account Number
  ○ Kerosene Dealer License
  ○ Legal heir Certificate

  ○ License for Cinema and Entertainment related
  ○ License for Fair Price shops
  ○ License for oil mills
  ○ License for running Hotels
  ○ License for selling and storing explosives
  ○ Marriage Certificate
  ○ Nationality Certificate
  ○ Nativity Certificate
  ○ Old Age Pension Certificate
  ○ Orphan Certificate
  ○ Passport
  ○ Permanent Resident Certificate
  ○ Permission for cutting trees
  ○ Permission for small savings agent
  ○ Permit for leasing ponds for fishing
  ○ Permit for stamp paper selling
  ○ Pesticide Dealer License
  ○ Pharmaceutical Dealer License
  ○ Property Registration
  ○ Ration card
  ○ Road Transport Driving license
  ○ Sales Tax Registration No.
  ○ Seed Dealer License
  ○ State Excise Registration No.
(b) Developmental Schemes
  ○ Central Sector Schemes
  ○ Centrally Sponsored Schemes
  ○ MP LAD Schemes
  ○ MLA/MLC LAD Schemes
  ○ State Sector Schemes
  ○ District Sponsored Schemes under Untied Funds
  ○ PRI Schemes
  ○ NABARD Development Plan
(c) Resources Information
  ○ Infrastructure Details
  ○ Socio-Economic
  ○ Agro-economic
  ○ Natural resources
(d) Agriculture
  ○ Agricultural Extension Services
  ○ Agricultural Inputs

- ◦ Agricultural Commodities Prices
- ◦ Agri-Business
- ◦ Crop Insurance
- ◦ Production System Planning
- ◦ Region and Crop Specific Agronomic Practices
- ◦ Soil Health Card
- ◦ Credit distribution to farmers by Primary Agricultural Credit Societies
- ◦ Kisan Credit Card

(e) Animal Husbandry & Veterinary Services
  - ◦ Animal Disease Information and Advisory Services
  - ◦ Breed and Husbandry Practices
  - ◦ Milk Price

(f) Fisheries
  - ◦ Potential Fishing Zone Information

(g) General Administration
  - ◦ Public Grievances Redressal
  - ◦ Citizen's Charter
  - ◦ Pay-slip for Government Employees
  - ◦ Service Register of Government Employee
  - ◦ Government Employees Personnel Information
  - ◦ Government Pension Payment
  - ◦ Government Tenders
  - ◦ Application Forms and Procedures of Government Departments, Public sector and Cooperative sector

(h) Financial Resources
  - ◦ Payment of Customs Duty, Central Excise, State Excise, VAT etc
  - ◦ Payment of Direct Taxes (Income Tax, Wealth Tax, Corporate Tax, etc)
  - ◦ Payment of Municipal Taxes (Property Tax, Property Assessment, etc)
  - ◦ Payment of Utility Charges (Electricity charges, Water bill, Telephone Bill)

(i) Rural Economy through Cooperative Development
  - ◦ E-Commerce applications in Cooperative Banks to strengthen agro and rural industries
  - ◦ E-commerce applications in Primary Agricultural Credit Societies
  - ◦ Registration of cooperative societies

(j) District Revenue Administration
  - ◦ Revenue Recovery
  - ◦ Land Acquisition
  - ◦ Land Ownership Details
  - ◦ Electoral rolls

(k) Industries
  - ◦ Intellectual Property Rights related information to SMEs
  - ◦ Agro and Rural Industries information
  - ◦ Wholesale and Retail Price Details of Products

(l) Labour
  - ◦ Networking of Industrial Training Institutes
  - ◦ Employment Exchanges Computerisation

(m) Home Finance and Insurance
  - ◦ General Insurance Schemes
  - ◦ Life Insurance Schemes
  - ◦ Postal Life Insurance Schemes
  - ◦ Private and MNCs Insurance Schemes
  - ◦ Home Finance Institutions Schemes

(n) Shares Markets Information

(o) Tour and Travel
  - ◦ Integrated reservation of multiple Airlines, Railways, Waterways, and Roadways

Various published documents of the Department of Information Technology (DIT) (Parliament of Information Technology, 2008) of the Indian Union Government show features of e-Governance framework, as given below:-
  - ◦ Setting up of a common minimum infrastructure;
  - ◦ Creation of data centres & repository of data with necessary computerization / data entry;

○ Implementation of process architecture for resource use;

○ Reaching of remote areas;

○ Electronic delivery of information and services;

○ Digital contents to support back-end processes for integrated delivery of information and services through portals;

○ Undertaking Business Process Re-Engineering;

○ Rapid prototyping and rolling out of e-Governance applications;

○ Delivery chain of community based service Centres;

○ Projects of promoting empowerment;

○ Data architecture for implementing standards and security procedures; and

○ Replicating best practices and projects that made an impact.

The DISNIC Programme of National Informatics centre (NIC) envisaged development of information system on 27 sectors and initiated an "information system revolution" in districts (Moni, and Vijayaditya, 1990) throughout the Country. Each Indian State has, now, its own model for implementing e-governance initiatives since 1995, but the basket of services offered remains identical across states. A good approach towards implementation of e-governance is to combine short-term projects and long-term goals (i.e. AGMARKNET, AGRISNET etc).

COMMUNITY INFORMATION & COMMUNICATION CENTRE (CICC)/E-COMMUNITY CENTRES: SUSTAINABILITY ISSUES

A Community is defined (World Book Encyclopedia, Pp245) as "people or a group of people living in a particular local area with day-to-day problem solving and with participation in the democratic process". Information sources of relevance to them will relate to any topics that affect/impact the life of the community. John B. Rose,(2005) defines Community Information & Communication Centre (CICC) as "a shared community facility, capable of servicing most of the information and the ICT (information and communication technology) requirements of the local population." It may also be called: "Community TeleService Centre", "Virtual Village Hall", "Telecottage", "Multipurpose Community Telecentre" (MCT), Community Multimedia Centre (CMC), Community Knowledge Centre, Community Learning Resource Centre, Community Technology Learning Centre (CTLC), etc.

To establish successful e-community centers, it is necessary to build awareness among local government policy makers and rural communities regarding the important role that ICT can play for rural development. Asian Development Bank Institute,(2004) suggested what e-Community centre could be used for, included:

• As a tool for distance learning

• For medical and health care – including diagnosis and training

• For agriculture – enabling farmers to access markets as well as information on markets, crops and climate

• For enabling greater participation of isolated communities in local, regional and national decision making through e-governance, and

• For income generation – by enabling rural communities to sell their crafts and products online to national and international buyers.

Turning easy accessibility into a reality, the two separate programmes of e-*Setu* and CIC (Community Information Centre) have more than made up for the lack of a 'real bridge' between the Majli island (State of Assam) and its the mainland (http://www.teriin.org/terragreen/issue53/feature. htm). With the advent of e-*Setu*, digital opportunities initiative supported by the Government of India and UNDP (United Nations Development Programme) on the island, hazardous and time-consuming journeys to avail basic government services have been drastically reduced. The case studies related to regional knowledge sharing projects for agriculture, national projects targeted specifically at bring information to the poor, and private-public partnerships aimed at using ICT to generate not just knowledge, but income in local communities by enabling them to set up local franchises. John B. Rose,(2005) identifies the following applications as "key applications" of "Community Information and Communication Centre":

- Public libraries and access to databases
- Education and e-learning
- Health services to citizens
- Services to economic agents (such as farmers)
- E-government & Citizen participation

Developments in Information Technology are bringing about a second industrial revolution, but the new drivers are information, data, computer and connectivity and not iron and coal. Library Technology is poised to become the new sunrise sector with digital libraries dominating the information service sector while content generation is expected to boom. Information Technology, Biotechnology and Library Technology (IT-BT-LT) revolution would be the route to economic progress for developing countries. Libraries must change from "collection" orineted institution to "service" oriented organisation. The World Information report (1997-98) observes, with respect to South Asia that:

- Bulk of the population is not information dependent in day-to-day work and living;
- A large proprotion of the population cannot

consume information, especially if it is delivered in written form;
- The vast majority of the population does not have the means to access information;
- People, in general, are not accustomed to pay, cannot pay, or unwilling to pay for information. In fact, information does not appear in their list of wants.
- The existing pattern of economic activities does not favour a growth in information consumption;
- The countries do not have sufficent capacity to invest in infrastructure development;

Converting "traditional' Library into "digital" is essential for self sustainaed growth. The future is undisputedly "digital" and concern has been expressed elsewhere on the effects of digital restructuring in deepening economic, political and social inequalities (Crow, and Longford, 2000). Rural poor are now being treated as a resource, whose ideas and experiences form an integral part of the development strategy Rajiv Theodore,(2005). According to Dr. Julius Nyerere, the former President of United Republic of Tanzania, "Knowledge is not a way to escape poverty. It is a way of fighting it"(The Hindu, December 4, 2001).

LIBRARY: A COMMUNITY INFORMATION & COMMUNICATION CENTRE AT GRASSROOTS LEVEL: A MUCH NEEDED STARTEGY

Libraries are considered as the pillars of the democracy and society's memory. Libraries preserve the culture and knowledge of the country. They serve communities as cultural and educational centers – known as 'knowledge institutions'. The cities and urban areas are well identified by the modern library buildings. There are about 400 thousand School Libraries, 11000 University/College Libraries, and 13,000 R&D Libraries, 56000 Public Libraries (which include 51000 at village level), 35 State Libraries and about 526 District Libraries functioning in India. This means that only 8.4% of the villages have Pubic Libraries in India. Networking of these Government Libraries and converting them into "digital Libraries" will be the step towards India becoming a Knowledge Society (Moni, 2002). These Libraries should take the shape of "Community Information Centres", which should serve as the backbone of "Literacy Mission and Poverty Alleviation". The need of the Library Science is to "empower the people" to improve their working cultures for better their livelihood. Mehra. and Srinivasan, (2007) suggests a library-community convergence framework (LCCF) to extend the role of all libraries to participate more fully in community action and enhance their function as proactive catalysts of social change, as compared to a sometimes perceived role of bystanders and highlights deliberations about the involvement of public libraries in their local communities.

Indian Libraries and Information sectors can be divided into five sub-sectors: national, academic, special, government and public. It is a fact that both the government and public librray sectors are responsible for library and information sector development. According to International Fedration of Library Associations and Institutions (IFLAI), there should be a one public Library for every 3000 persons (Bhattacharjee, 2002). Rural Libraries lagged behind in the application of ICT. But the Library technology is poised to become the new sunrise sector with digital libraries dominating the information services sector, while content generation is booming. Rural Public Libraries are also a part of this revlotuion. Rural Libraries, as a concept, exist in India. Professor Chatopadhyay Committee on National Policy on Library and Information system (NAPLIS) (1985) recommended to establish, maintain and strengthen "free public libraries" and in particular, "the rural public library". There have been noteworthy developments for "Libraries and Information Systems Development for Rural Areas" in India, since its independence:

- Advisory Committee for Libraries, 1957
- Public Library Acts in States
- Establsihment of Raja Rammohan Roy Library Foundation
- National level Associations:
  - Indian Library Association (ILA)
  - Government of India Library Association (GILA)
  - Indian Association of Special Libraries and Information Centres (IASLIC)
  - Indian Association of Teachers of Library and Information Science (IATLIS)
  - Society for Information Science (SIS)
  - Association for Government Librarians and Information Specialists (AGLIS)
  - Medical Library Association of India (MLAI)
  - Association of Agricultural Librarians and Documentalists in India (AALDI)
  - State Level Associations (A.P Library Association, bengal Library Association, etc)
  - Joint Council of Library associations in India (JOCLAI)
- Delhi Public Library (1951)
- Delivery of Books (Public Libraries) Act 1954 – A mandatory provision for all publishers to send one copy each of their publications to national Library at Kolkata, Connemera Library at Chennai, Asiatic Society Library at Mumbai (and the fourth one was to be delivered to Central Reference Library at Delhi)
- Chatopadhyay Committee on National Policy on Library and Information System (NAPLIS).
- National Knowledge Commission (NKC)

Various Organisations, who played a prominent role in building the rural Library movement in the country, include:

- Raja Rammohan Roy Library Foundation
- Rajiv Gandhi Foundation
- Indian Library Association
- Indian Public Library Association
- Andhra Pradesh Library Association
- Bengal Library Association

Indian Parliament Library (New Delhi) with ISO-9002 certification and with the knowledge contents of about 3 Million publications and facilitation for reference, research and information services, is not available for "common man" due to physical security problems. A US Government Report (1999) indicated a widening in the gap between "information rich" and "information Poor" with the division based on education, income and ethnicity in that country. Public Libraries have the potential to play a key role in tackling social exclusion (Muddiman, 2001). Internet Resources is considered to be the biggest library in the Planet Earth: Webs sites, Portals, Vertical portals on subjects, problems, issues, location specific issues, lifestyles, etc.

A framework for building Community Information Networks in India combining Public Libraries will empower the Community for effective information communication, in view of the stated pronouncement of "India to become Knowledge Society". This will facilitate "social inclusion" of marginalised rural poor to access knowledge and information. Rural Digital Libraries will sustain Community Information & Communication Centres, as citizens, business, local governments, and public institutions like schools and libraries take part in the information economy. The goal is to increase the capacity of the community to adapt to a rapidly changing 21st century society and to use technology to solve increasingly complex community challenges. There has been popular suggestions that the public libraries in urban as well as rural areas should be converted to modern community information centers, which could serve as the backbone of Literacy Mission and Poverty Alleviation. The basic infrastructure for rural ICT initiatives includes: electricty, telephony and network connectivity.

DIGITAL LIBRARY SERVICES: A PARADIGM SHIFT & A STEP TOWARDS SUSTAINABLE RURAL LIVELIHOODS

Digital information needs to be achieved and preserved for future use. Digital Libraries are not the "Digital Equivalents" of the present day library. Digital Library is a new instrument, which can spread the knowledge nearly at the speed of light. The concept of "digital library" is evolving over time. Moreover different communities are active in the area of 'digital libraries". Borgman, (1999) defines "digital Library" as:

a. "content collected on behalf of users", and
b. "institutions providing a range of services in a digital environment".

While most of the digital library projects falls into (a), the speculation about the future developments concentrates on (b). This is an acceptable definition, as it talks about an institution. Digital Library involves not only automation of traditional services and activities, but also calls for redfinition of services, new groupings of services or replacements of groups of services with other solutions. Digital Library breaks time, space and langauage barrrers. However, it requires a great need for adopting "standards and best practices" to build interoperable digital libraries.

Convergence of print medium, databases and telecommunication has led to the advent of the electronic content industry. The Content industry has come to mean various commercial and non-commercial activities relating to the bibliographic, textual and statistical databases as well as the information, education and entertainment materials in the electronic form including audio, video and multimedia forms. Considering the vast global and domestic market, the content industry has a potential to grow to a size comparable to the computer software industry with enormous opportunities for income and employment generation. Content development being an integral part of any information system, the content industry is recognised as a priority sector for lending and according the same benefits for purposes of promotion and development as given to the software sector.

India has rich information relating to literature, music, traditional system of medicine and science embedded in palm leaves. In February 2003, the Government of India launched the (Indira Gandhi National Cenre for Arts) National Mission for Manuscripts, aimed at preserving the valuable manuscripts in India. The IT Action Plan (Part III) of the Long Term National IT Policy (1998) of India emphasized on "content creation and content industry". This Policy also considered that the Government of India would give priority for promoting this human-resource intensive industry extensively in the country. The Government and its associated organizations are the largest producers of socio-economic and statistical information. Abdul Kalam, (2004) urges to create a "Knowledge Management Grid" with the Central Digital Library Data Center equipped with the comprehensive Virtual Digital Library and Knowledge Management System into which all the participating organizations are connected with broadband along with Internet connectivity.

Connectivity is strength, connectivity is wealth, and connectivity is progress. For enabling knowledge connectivity, in rural areas, it is necessary to have a comprehensive plan for developing new infrastructure for extending the digital library services in regional languages. Large and effective digital libraries are to be built during the 21st century to make "India, a Knowledge Society". Upadhyay, Moni, and Vijayaditya (2004) felt necessary to accelerate content creation and development industry in India, and discussed key issues in digital content development and management (viz., migration from traditional to digital, maintenance, interoperability, universal access, localisation, private participation, sustainability, legal & copyright issues, digital divide, standards & formats, and meta data).

Digital Content Management System is the most complex and advanced forms of information systems because it involves collaboration support, digital document preservation, distributed database management, hypertext, information filtering, information retrieval, instructional modules, intellectual property rights management, multimedia information services, question answering and reference services, resource discovery, and selective dissemination of information. The use of metadata standards facilitates interoperability. Digital Library design should facilitate "one-stop-shop". Dempsey et al., (1996) proposed the following standards for use in digital Library projects:

- User Interface: Common Web Browser
- Data handling and Interchange
  - Graphic Formats: JPEG, TIFF, GIF, PNG, Group 4 Fax, CGM
  - Structured Documents: SGML, HTML, XML
  - Moving Pictures / 3D: MPEG, AVI, GIF89A, Quicktime, Real Video, ViviActive, VRML
- Metadata
  - Resource description: Dublin Core, WHOIS++, Templates, US-MARC, TEI Headers, Other Open Source and Domain Specific Standards.
  - Resource identification: URN, PURL, DOI, SICI
- Security, Authentication and payment Services
  - Emerging e-Commerce Standards.

Most of schools and colleges are located across the country in rural areas. They lack better communication and transportation infrastructure. These institutions turn out thousands of students every year. Majority of the students are not even capable of purchasing reference basic textbooks and are mostly dependent on the obsolete/old textbooks. The teachers are really handicapped with the current knowledge due to lack of accessibility to knowledge source. There is need to equitable development of the country through uniform distribution of the Natural and ICT resources. These difficulties can be overcome if the Indian libraries (Viz., 400 thousand School Libraries, 11000 University/College Libraries, and 13,000 R&D Libraries, 56000 Public Libraries (which include 51000 at village level), 35 State Libraries and about 526 District Libraries) become the part of "digital library" movement and form the nodes of "Knowledge Management Grid" of India. These Virtual Libraries provide extensive information and instant access to users through information networks.

Digital libraries and knowledge management are innovations, the implementation of which is still nascent in developing countries. However, they hold the promise of becoming key technologies for knowledge creation and management in the future. The Long Term Policy (1998) has also envisaged a "National Internet Centre of Excellence (NICE)", to promote standards, assist digital content development in India, devise standards for content building and delivery, and research new technologies. For enabling knowledge connectivity in our rural areas, Upadhyay, Moni, and Vijayaditya (2004) stressed the need to have a comprehensive plan for developing new infrastructure (viz., development of OCR Software in all the Indian languages, language independent operating system, database servers, search engines, web servers and messaging servers) for extending the digital library services in regional languages. This will enable the digital library initiative to percolate to the rural masses in the form of e-governance, tele-education and tele-medicine.

For India, a national inventory of all digital library initiatives (*Viz., Vidyanidhi (Mysore University, Karnataka), Nalanda Digital Library (NIT, Kozhikode), IGNCA Digital Library (GOI), Digital Library of India Project (Department of Information Technology and CMU - USA), Digital Library on Indian System of Medicines (Department of Indian System of Medicines & Homeopathy and CSIR), etc*) is a high priority, apart from putting in place, an enabling system to develop digital skills in academia, government institutions, NGOs and the private sectors. The International Conference on Digital Libraries (ICDL, 2004) in New Delhi has suggested following guidelines:

- Bridge knowledge gaps between developing and developed countries
- Initiate capacity building activities in digital libraries
- Evolve a road map for the digitization of archives, manuscripts, and libraries
- Provide a forum for facilitating interaction amongst participants
- Formulate recommendations on digitization technologies, Acts, and policies

The Joint Conference on Digital Libraries (JCDL) is a major international forum focusing on digital libraries and associated technical, practical, and social issues. XML is a core document technology that is starting to revolutionize the way data and documents are managed and produced on the web and elsewhere by bringing years of text-encoding experience to bear on document representation and management. Metadata is simply "data about data" and a methodology and language for describing on-line learning resources that will facilitate effective searching. The Dublin Core is a 15-Metadata Element set (*Title, Subject, Description, Source, Language, Relation, Coverage, Creator, Publisher, Contributor, Rights, Date, Type, Format, and Identifier*) intended to facilitate discovery of electronic resources (Dublin Core).

E-GRANTHALAYA: A DIGITAL AGENDA FOR LIBRARY AUTOMATION AND NETWORKING

According to International Federation of Library Associations and Institutions (IFLA), for every 3000 persons, there should be one public library. With more than 1.2 billion population, there is a requirement of over 330,000 libraries in India. A large majority of the population does not have access to free public libraries and rural areas have been neglected compared with urban areas. There is a need to integrate the functioning of rural libraries with information centres. School Libraries and Public Libraries in villages can function as public libraries where an information facilitation centre can be established; and this integrated infrastructure can take the shape of a digital library (Venkatasubramaian, 2002). There is a widespread belief that rural information centres with computer networks can create new roads for knowledge, services, money etc., to travel from one node to other one even across long distances. However, there is a need to create appropriate S&T based digital sources in rural areas (i.e. soil map to help the farmer to correctly depicting land capability or land suitability, etc).

In order to make "India A Knowledge Based Society", it is essential to network the 60000 Public Libraries in India for Internet Access. In view of the importance of bibliographic informatics services, as a knowledge input to S&T services, NIC proposes to undertake programmes for establishing "digital library", strengthening of Bibliographic Services Programme, networking of Libraries of Ministries/Departments of the Central Government, and networking of 35 State Libraries and 526 District Libraries, to enrich "bibliographic informatics" programme in the country. In view of economic importance

and social relevance to facilitate "libraries" to become "knowledge centres", NIC has envisaged a digital agenda "e-Granthalaya" (which means "electronic book house", in other words "digital library") during the eleventh plan. The objectives of this mission are as follows:-

- Automation and Networking of Government Libraries and Information Centers;
- Automation and Networking of Public Libraries and Information Centers;
- To provide marginalized villagers their opportunity to access knowledge;
- To serve as an integrated Information Center model by creating cost effective and economically viable model to the masses in a timely period;
- Impacting Information Technology on the G2C interface; and
- Providing platform for self-employment.

To strengthen this movement, NIC has developed a library automation package "e-Granthalaya" http://egranthalaya..nic.in) to suit the needs the requirements of different classes of libraries. Figure-1 exhibits various functions and modules of e-Granthalaya Software. This Software is operational in many Government Libraries, Educational Institutions, R&D Libraries, and Public Libraries.

A "Consortium" of Libraries, which are under Ministry of Communications and Information Technology, Government of India (http://mcit-consortium.nic.in) has been formed to share the available library resources and also create a digital library. This is a stepping stone for visualizing a "consortium of digital libraries" in Government sector. Development of an e-Granthalaya Network (Community Information & Communication Centre Network) is conceptualized as in Figure

Recent advances in ICT have made it possible to develop e-Granthalaya Network for functioning as "Rural Digital Library" which will provide

Figure 1. Functions and modules of e-Granthalaya software

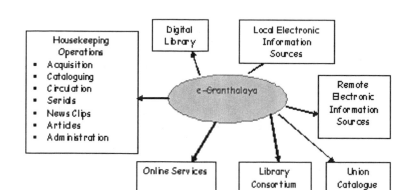

"electronic services" to common citizen of India at grassroots level. There is an immense scope for creating content in Indian languages through UNI-CODE and interoperability capabilities of XML at e-Granthalaya Nodes. These e-Granthalaya Nodes facilitate quickening the pace of knowledge and transfer of power to the masses. This will enable the digital library initiative to percolate to the rural masses in the form of e-governance, tele-education and tele-medicine. Networked Library environment play an important role in rural revitalization, as libraries have emerged as a sunrise industry due to globalization and liberalization at regional level, and decentralization trends at grassroots level.

LIBRARIES AND E-GOVERNANCE SYNERGY

Authors have already mentioned the library technologies and their involvement in ongoing eGovernance programmes in the sections 7, 8 and 9 of this article. However to strengthen the advocacy of libraries in eGovernance programme it will be better to focus on more critical areas.

Libraries are society's memory. These are physical and intellectual custodians of the human memory. The need of the library science is to empower the people to improve their working culture for better livelihood. It is very difficult to educate the people without books. Libraries are the source of information on various fields. The cities and urban areas are well identified by the modern library buildings. The people always regarded libraries as the temples of knowledge, which represents the community's aspirations. These are widely used by the learned and academicians who are the drivers of the knowledge based society.

Information acts as catalyst for productivity and hence access to it will definitely lead to economical gains to users at Rural Population. Community Involvement and Cultural Integration of Rural Digital Libraries is another big challenge. It is witnessed time and again that "an educated citizen can only earn his/her livelihood using his/her enlighted brain power" and e-Granthalaya will emerge as a tool in the "education cycle" of the rural Indian citizen for their livelihood. This will be facilitated to have "access to" books of primary school level, National Council of Educational Research and Training (NCERT) and National Book Trust (NBT), Newspapers and Agro-industry based information in regional language and multi-media capabilities. e-Granthalaya will emerge as the backbone of Village Knowledge Centres, as there is a compelling argument for providing Digital Library Services to Rural India. A part of

Figure 2. E-Granthalaya network at micro level

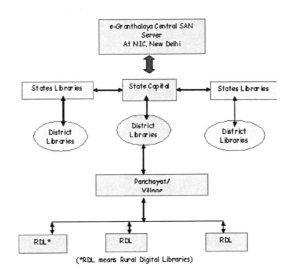

the Education Cess collected by the Union Government may be utilized to setup Rural Digital Libraries.

According to GARTNER (A leading information technology research and advisory company) content archiving is characterized by siloed platforms that deal with application-specific or process-specific archiving needs. By 2010, leading-edge enterprises will consolidate their disparate architectures for unstructured content. Today, there are different technologies offered by a variety of vendors that handle different forms of fixed content — documents, files, images, records and e-mail. Over time, these siloed archiving applications will converge into an integrated content archiving platform.

Government of India has approved the National e-Governance Programme (NeGP) with the cost of estimate of Rs. 23,000 Crores on 18th May 2006 and all measures are underway to accelerate the pace of implementation of its various components. e-Governance/e-Government programmes mean "dealing with digital resources of 0s and 1s", and "citizen-centric".

Library Sciences Curriculum is embracing advancements of Computer Sciences, whereas the Computer Science Curriculum is not doing vice versa. The buzzwords in computer science viz. metadata, information infrastructure, information management, ontology, etc have already deep roots in library science. Even today also they are at matured research level and in practice in library science. For example, what is metadata in computer science is the metaphor of cataloguing and ontology is nothing but the decades old topic "indexing and classification" in library science. Ranganathan has given concept of chain indexing, which may be the firm basis for organizing information on the web sites. Thousands of Government web sites today are lacking the skill of organizing information in a scientific way, that may adopt the strength of traditional librarianship and canons of Ranganathan (Ranganathan). The most far reaching effect of Ranganathan's contribution flows from his formulation of the Five Laws of Library Science.

- *Books are for use*
- *Every reader his/her book*
- *Every book, its reader*
- *Save the time of the reader*
- *A library is a growing organism*

These laws are even relevant today for web content management and citizen-centric eGovernance services. Various ongoing digital library efforts in India are important steps toward preserving the history. This is an essential aspect to include the power of library science when we move towards e-Governance/e-Government (that is digital governance – governance through digital resources. Access to information is prime component in the development of society and in this context, Library and Information Centres are playing dynamic role in provision of needed information. Education and Knowledge Centres have an integral relationship. According to Kothari Commission on Education System (1964-65), the knowledge centre increases research output by providing the following:-

- To provide resources necessary for research;
- To aid the faculty keeping abreast of new developments in the new field;
- To provide facilities and services for success in all formal programmes of instructions;
- To open the door to the wide field of resources;
- To bring resources, users and scholars together;

National Knowledge Commission, submitted to the Hon'ble Prime Minister of India in 2006, in relation to the Library Segment. The Theme title of the Report is "People's Access to Knowledge can transform India". The Key recommendations of the NKC 2006 run as follows:-

- Set up a National Commission on Libraries
- Prepare a National census on all Libraries
- Revamp Library & Information Science Education, Training & Research
- Re-Assess staffing of Libraries
- Promote ICT applications in all Libraries

- Set up a Central Library Fund
- Facilitate donation and maintenance private collections
- Encourage Private-Public-Partnership (PPP) in LIS development
- Modernize Library Management and Encourage Community Participation in Library Management

In the recommendation of the NKC 2006, it is important to underline the theme "People's Access to Knowledge can transform India". This shows a future for Indian Libraries to facilitate "People's Access to Knowledge which can transform India". Rural India thus desires to take advantage of "knowledge-intensive" techniques for its sustainable development and sustainable consumption. Grassroots level Information access (Contents) and Grassroots level access to Information (Networking) are the two essential components for grassroots level development strategies through ICT. Community Information and Communication Centres (CICC), as a concept and model, aim to "boost efficiency and enhance market" integration through Internet/ Intranet technologies for sustainable remote/regional development at grassroots level.

Community Information & Communication Networks in India empower disadvantaged community for effective information & communication, in view of the stated pronouncement of "India to become Knowledge Society and also facilitate "social inclusion" of marginalized rural poor to access knowledge and information. There are about 56000 Public Libraries (which include 51000 at village level), 400000 School Libraries, 11000 University/College Libraries, 13000 R&D Libraries, 28 State Libraries, and 526 District Libraries in India. Only 8.4% of the Villages have access to Public Libraries in India. Networking of these Government Libraries and converting them into "digital Libraries" will be the step towards India becoming a Knowledge Society. Rural Public

Libraries may be made a part of eGovernance programme to serve as the backbone for "literacy mission and poverty alleviation". There are empirical evidences to support that rural digital libraries will sustain Community Information & Communication Centres (e-Community Centres). Networked Library environment play an important role in rural revitalization, as libraries have emerged as a sunrise industry due to globalization and liberalization at regional level, and decentralization trends at grassroots level.

"Digital Library Science" is to be brought out. To achieve, "SEMANTIC Technologies and Networking to enable e-LEARNING and Global Knowledge ACCESS", Digital Library Science is the need of the HOUR. Digital Library Science = Library Science + Library Technology + Computer Science + Computer Engineering + Computer Technology. This will usher in PROFOUND RETURN ON INVESTMENT (ROI) for the e-Governance Programme in any Country.

CONCLUSION

To reach the un-reached in the Information Technology evolution and to bridge the divide between Information-rich and Information-poor, e-Granthalaya will play a lead role in creation of an Information Society. It is not an easy task. Problems like content in local language, network bandwidth, reliable storage medium, affordable access, user-friendly interface for IT literate people and ease-of-use interface for illiterate people like touch screens are expected to arise, but the outcome envisaged in the project out-weigh these problems. In the process of converting the Information–starved people into a knowledgeable society, e-Granthalaya will not only generate job opportunities at the local level, but it will act as a catalyst in harnessing the human intellect in more innovating manner. Networked Library environment play an important role in rural revitalization,

as libraries have emerged as a sunrise industry due to globalization and liberalization at regional level, and decentralization trends at grassroots level. Rural India requires an "e-Granthalaya" on a mission mode for facilitating sustainable livelihoods: Poverty Alleviation, Livelihood opportunities and gainful employment. The 'e-Granthalaya' acts as 'wheels of transformation' of the rural people through information facilitator vehicle - NICNET.

Libraries across the country should be developed as Knowledge Kendras / Centres and all Library Resources should be digitized and shared across the country". Ministry of Culture and National Informatics Centre may undertake as a "Mission Mode" project under the NeGP of the Ministry.

Since most higher education and research institutions in India are funded and controlled by the central and state governments, national plans and polices are on their way for infrastructure, standards, metadata, interoperability, multi-lingual databases, training, co-ordination, copyright, and archiving and preservation methods, so that heritage of knowledge and culture can overcome the ravages of time, and present and future generations can benefit and be guided by them.

SPECIAL LIBRARIES and INFORMATION CENTRES are relevant today for acting as "bridge" between the COMMON PUBLIC and the e-Governance/e-Government Programmes. All the Stakeholders of the e-Governance/ e-Government programmes are required to be exposed to Digital Library Science, which will facilitate "design and development" of "Knowledge Management" in the e-Governance/e-Government Programmes

ACKNOWLEDGMENT

The Authors acknowledge various technical papers available on Internet while writing this article.

REFERENCES

Abdul Kalam, A. P. J. (2004). Inaugural Speech, "Digital Library and its Multidimensions." In *International Conference on Digital Libraries (ICDL-2004)*, 24-27 February 2004, New Delhi.

Abdul Kalam, A.P.J. (2005). *Address to the Nation by the President of India.* Delivered on the eve of 56th India's Republic Day – 2005.

Acharya, S. S. (2004). Sustainable Agriculture and Rural Livelihoods. In Sundaram, K. V., Moni, M., & Jha, M. M. (Eds.), *Natural Resources management and Livelihood security: Survival Strategies and Sustainable Policies.* Delhi: Concept Publishing Company.

Ahmad, R. (2002, December). Forging a Sustainable Development Model: The Malaysian way. *Development, 45*(4), 74–79. doi:10.1057/palgrave.development.1110409

Asian Development Bank Institute. (2004). *Proceedings of the Regional Workshop on Building e-Community Centres for Rural Development,* Bali/Indonesia.

Bhattacharjee, R. (2002*). Public Libraries Section, Country Report: India.* International Federation of Library Associations and Institutions. Retrieved September 30, 2008, from http://www.ifla.org/VII/s8/annual/cr02-in.htm

Bhoovigyan Vikas Foundation. (2002). *International Conference on Sustainable Agriculture, Water Resources Development and Earth Care Policies.* New Delhi (India).

Borgman, C. L. (1999). What are digital Libraries? Competing Versions. *Information Processing & Management, 35*(3), 227–243.

Crow, B., & Longford, G. (2000). Digital Restructuring: gender, class and citizenship in the information society in Canada. *Citizenship Studies, 4*(2), 207–230. doi:10.1080/13621020050078096

Dempsey, L., et al. (1996). *eLIB Standards Guidelines version 1.0, Feb. 1996.* Retrieved from: http://www.ukoln.ac.uk/services/elib

Department of Information Technology. (n.d.). Retrieved September 30, 2008, from http://mit.gov.in

DISNIC. (n.d.). Retrieved September, 30, 2008 from http://disnic.nic.in

Dr. S. R. Ranganathan. (n.d.). Retrieved September, 30, 2008 from http://drtc.isibang.ac.in/DRTC/srr/index.html

Dublin Core: (n.d.). Retrieved September, 30, 2008 from http://dublincore.org/

Ellis, F. (2000). *Rural Livelihood Diversity in Developing Countries: Analysis, Policy, Methods. School of Development Studies/University of East Anglia.* Oxford, UK: Oxford University Press.

Gartner. (n.d.). Retrieved September, 30, 2008 from http://www.gartner.com/

ICDL. *2004.* (2004). Retrieved September, 30, 2008 from http://www.teriin.org/events/icdl/icdl2004rprt.htm

Indira Gandhi National Centre for Arts. (2002). *National Mission for Manuscripts.* Retrieved September 30, 2008 from http://ignca.nic.in/nl002203.htm

Joint Conference on Digital Libraries. (n.d.). Retrieved September, 30, 2008 from http://www.jcdl.org.

Maxwell, S., & Franken Berger, T. R. (1992). *Household Food Security: Concepts, Indicators and Measurement.* New York: UNICEF.

Mehra, B., & Srinivasan, R. (2007). The Library-Community Convergence Framework for Community Action: Libraries as Catalysts of Social Change. *Libri, 57,* 123–139. doi:10.1515/LIBR.2007.123

Moni, M. (2002). *Digital Libraries in Rural India: A digital opportunity for sustainable development.* Invited talk on the National Technology Day, May 11, 2002.

Moni, M. (2002). *Digital Opportunities for Responsive Administration in India: Electronic Administration of Services to Citizens.* Internal Note sent to e-Governance Division of Department of Information Technology, 2002.

Moni, M., & Vijayaditya, N. (1990). *DISNIC – A NICNET Based District Government Informatics Programme in India.* Hyderabad, India: Indian Computing Congress.

Muddiman, D. (2001). Open to all? The Public Library and Social exclusion: Executive Summary. *New Library World, 102*(1163/1164), 154–157. doi:10.1108/03074800110390626

National Informatics Centre. (1998 June). *Project Proposal For Wired Village Project at Warana Nagar, Maharashtra.* Retrieved September, 30, 2008 from http://www.mah.nic.in/warana/

Parliament of India Library. (n.d.). Retrieved September 30, 2008, from http://parliamentofindia.gov.in Planning Commission, Government of India: *Five Year Plans. 10th Plan (2002-2007).* Volume 2, Chapter 3.2. Retrieved September, 30, 2008 from http://planningcommission.nic.in/plans/planrel/fiveyr/10th/volume2/v2_ch3_2.pdf.

Rose, J. B. (2005). Community Telecentres: Assessing their impact and viability. In *The National Symposium on «Information and Communication Strategies for Grassroots development,* 4-5 March, University of Madras, Chennai, India.

Theodore, R. (2005 January). Rural development. *Yojana.*

Upadhyay P. K., Moni M., & Vijayaditya N. (2004). Digital Library Initiatives in India. *Libraries, Information & Knowledge, 21(1).*

Venkatasubramaian, K. (2002). *Presidential Address.* Delivered at the Seminar on Electronic Libraries in Rural India, 11 May 2002.

Venkatasubramanian, K. (2001, December 4). Education & Poverty. *The Hindu.* Retrieved June 30, 2006 from http://www.hinduonnet.com/the-hindu/op/2001/12/04/stories/2001120400060100.htm

World Bank. (2003). Multi-Stakeholder Regional Consultation for International Assessment on Role of Agricultural Science and Technology in reducing hunger, improving rural livelihoods and stimulating environmentally sustainable economic growth. Organized by The World Bank, 12-13 May 2003, New Delhi.

World Book Encyclopedia. (n.d.). Community. In World Book Encyclopedia (Vol. 4., pp. 245). Chicago: World Book.

Chapter 16
Bridging the Digital Divide:
A Review of Critical Factors in Developing Countries

Leila Nemati Anaraki
Islamic Azad University, Iran

Azadeh Heidari
Islamic Azad University, Iran

ABSTRACT

Recent developments in Information and Communication Technologies (ICT), while making our life easier, created a social divide that is known as the digital divide. The global information gap is likely to widen the North – South divide and this global digital divide raises many issues for discussion that will be explored and reviewed further in this research. This chapter provides a brief overview of digital divide and the effects of some critical factors on it. Unequal investment of Information and Communication Technologies (ICTs), the potential of the Internet, the important role of education, literacy, education, e-governance, librarians, libraries and also digital libraries etc. are some discussed factors in this chapter. It concludes that paying attention to all so called critical factors can bridge and decrease this global digital divide.

INTRODUCTION

Although in recent years the information environment has greatly improved in many developed and developing countries, there is no indication that the digital divide is decreasing. Access to information and communication technologies is the crucial issue to a sustainable agenda of socio-economic development. Access to new technologies will furnish vital knowledge inputs into the productive

DOI: 10.4018/978-1-61520-767-1.ch016

measures of developing countries, especially those who are rural and poor.

For the last ten years the term 'digital divide' has become a familiar way of expressing the wide variations in access to information and communication technologies (ICTs) across the world. While there may be some disagreement over what the expression actually means, and what indicators should be used to map it, there is no doubt that developing countries, lag far behind industrialized countries in their take-up of new digital technologies, especially the Internet. The emphasis in early accounts of the digital divide was on inequalities in infrastructural provision and access to technology. Many countries have devised information strategies, taking for granted the relationship between ICT diffusion and economic development, in an attempt to close the gap. These have generally focused on infrastructural improvements: policies in education, for example, have concentrated on hardware provision with much less attention paid to the issues of how new technologies are used.

There is no doubt about the fact that there are many benefits associated with ICTs, but still significant barriers to its effective use exists in both developed and developing countries. Some of these barriers may be endemic(e.g. the generation gap, learning processes and gaining in ICTs, poor telecoms infrastructure, poor computer and general literacy, and so on).Information and communication technologies (ICTs) can be considered as an important weapon in the war against world challenges. When used effectively, it offers huge potential to empower people in developing countries and disadvantaged communities to overcome obstacles, address the most important social problems they face, strengthen communities, democratic institutions, a free press, and local economies and maybe above all, facilitate information flow with which real information society can come true. But, a digital divide separates those who can access and use ICT to gain these benefits, and those who either do not have access to such technology or who are unable to use it for one reason or another. The digital divide has become a common metaphor originating from now nearly obsolete phrases such as "information haves and have not's" and "information rich and information poor".

There are numerous approaches that libraries can and have taken in diminishing this divide. Libraries can play a vital role in bridging the digital divide by providing access to computer and the internet to those who do not have such facilities, but it is not a job that can be done single-handedly. It is a challenge that must be dealt with in partnership among the various public and private sectors of society, such as the telecommunications industry, educational systems, policy makers, and community organizations.

As a result, the present article focuses on some of several dimensions of the digital divide and discusses about some key factors which have an impressive role in digital divide.

Definition of Digital Divide

Digital divide is a familiar and dynamic concept which has evolve over time. There is not a single divide, but multiple divides: for instance, within countries, between men and women, between the young and the elderly, different regions etc. (World Information Society Report, 2007)

The Internet has profoundly changed many things in our world. The "have" versus "have not" distinction traditionally refers to "the great divide" in our world, between people who have health, wealth and opportunity versus those who have not. The same distinction can be made about people who have access to the new information and communication technologies (ICTs) versus those who have not, and this is referred to as "the digital divide" and globally, there is a gaping digital divide between the "information rich" and "information poor". (The digital divide, n.d.)

The digital divide has been frequently defined. Here, some definitions relevant to our discussion are considered as follows:

- The lack of access to information and communication technologies to segments of the community. The digital divide is a generic term used to describe this lack of access due to linguistic, economic, educational, social and geographic reasons (Scrutiny of Acts and Regulations Committee, 2005). The gap between those people and communities who can access and make effective use of information technology and those who can not

- The growing gap between those parts of the world which have easy access to knowledge, information, ideas and works of information through technology and those who do not.
- A term used to describe the discrepancy between people who have access to and the resources to use new information and communication tools, such as the Internet, and people who do not have the resources and access to the technology.(Mutula, 2007)

According to Alextbox the "digital divide" refers to the fact that certain parts of the population have substantially better opportunities to benefit from the new economy than other parts of the population. Most commentators view this in purely economic terms. However, two other types of divide will have much greater impact in the years to come. (Alextbox, 2006)

Literature Review

In order to understand the digital divide in related literature one must pay attention to how the concept was introduced, how has it been influenced by some factors, and how it is identified. Doubtless, this may lead to overcoming the digital divide.

In association with access rate, Foulger, (2001) declares that: People who live in digital countries have greater access to a variety of communication media and information. While Internet access may or may not be ubiquitous, it is certainly set up in most schools, companies, and communities in order that people who want Internet access can get it. Therefore, the digital divide is really a continuum of choice. The choice is a fundamental issue informed by psychological and social concerns, not just economic concerns. Some people choose to make extensive use of digital resources. Others do not. Most people fall somewhere in between. (Foulger, 2001)

A number of studies have examined the relevance of ICT and the internet technology in particular with regard to the socio- economic development of developing countries.

For instance "ICT, education and digital divide in developing countries", by Tahereh Saheb is an article which has analysed how ICT and digital revolution have influenced education system by focusing on the advantages of new system of learning that has been produced by new information and communication technologies. At the end, she has elucidated digital divide and key factors to bridge the digital divide between developing and developed countries. (Saheb, 2005)

"The knowledge explosion and the knowledge divide" presents frames of reference to examine the prospects for the development of science and technology in developing countries during the first two decades of the 21st century. This paper concludes by drawing out main directions for developing countries and implications in the post-Baconian age. (The knowledge explosion and the knowledge divide, 2001)

"Managing information and technology: critical roles for librarians in developing countries" is an article which tries to provide a critical overview of the contribution of information technology to the current shift from information to knowledge processing. It situates that shift in the context of management challenges for librarians from the developing countries. (Omekwu, 2006)

Noh and Yoo in their papers provide new findings about the impact of Internet adoption and the income inequality on economic growth. Analytical insights are suggested within a framework of a pure-exchange overlapping generations model. A panel data set for 60 countries for the period 1995–2002 was assembled to test the analytical investigations. The panel estimation shows that the implied effect of Internet adoption on growth is negative for countries with high income inequality because the digital divide hinders economic growth incurred by the Internet. From a policy standpoint, this result implies that the positive impact of Internet on growth will be reinforced by the income redistribution. (Noh,, and Yoo, 2008)

"Bringing lost sheep into the fold: questioning the discourse of the digital divide" is an article which tries to critique the discourse of the digital divide and to propose ways of responding to digital inequalities. The research consisted of 47 semi-structured interviews and action research involving designing an e-literacy curriculum and running a course based on it. Findings indicate that a discourse of missed opportunities and "being left behind", present in policy statements and popular media, leads to objectifying non-users of information and communication technologies (ICT) as "others". This discourse is often internalized by non-users, but it does not necessarily lead to positive actions, leaving some feeling inadequate. So far initiatives seeking to address the digital divide have had moderate success. To respond to digital exclusion we need to oppose the unchecked spread of e-services, and help non-users of ICT to become users or (if they choose to) informed of it. Initiatives aiming to facilitate people ought sustainable and meaningful use of ICT to draw on individual and community resources. A curriculum should be determined by learners' experiences and their expressions of needs, and go beyond IT skills. (Klecun, 2008)

AIMS AND OBJECTS OF THE STUDY

The aim of the present study is to review and analyze special factors which have affects on digital divide in developing countries, like access to the Internet as basic infrastructure for information search and dissemination. Thus the study has the following objectives:

- How unequal investment on Information and Communication Technologies (ICTs) affects of developing countries?
- How e-governance and private institutions have affected digital divide?
- The relationship between human development, learning and digital divide. And how

well specialized libraries and digital libraries and also skilled librarians have a role on delivering reliable and special information to special user.

THE INTERNAET, IT, ICT, AND THE ROLE OF INFRASTRUCTURE

The Role of Internet and the Digital Divide

The internet is a communication technology with a wide spread use all over the world. As with other ICTs, the internet provides a potentially powerful means of accessing information. In developing countries the internet offers a cheap and versatile mechanism of connecting users with a global repository of information. (Grace, 2004)

Application of internet technology has transcended all fields of human development in recent years. It has had a wider application in the educational development of all nations, of both the developed and developing world. The new communication technology is said to provide access to global knowledge resources, since it allows users to share their knowledge, resources and experiences of different people. The internet, through the World Wide Web, offers efficient access to research information anywhere, anytime and in any form; which is of paramount use in the conduct of scientific and technological research in developing countries.

The Internet acts like an integrator (due to its transcended national boundaries and influences cross border flow of education, health and trade services) and divider (due to its disparities in access). The digital divide becomes more important because the Internet is not only a communication medium, but also a market place. The Internet gives value to the customer, enhances profit for producer and eliminates middlemen. The Internet continues has to become more popular and at present has turned into an economic activity.

The five areas that need to be given priority for bridging digital divide and converting into digital dividends are distance education, telemedicine, job matching, local development and market reach.

Internet and other computer networks emerged rather unexpectedly. They took on a life and a complexity of social action that governments and most other power structures never predicted their use, for many years, was limited to such a small portion of the population that their social significance was generally not realized until long after the fact of their establishment and unchecked growth (Harris, 1996).

The Internet users account for only 6% of world's population and out of that 85% of them are in developed countries where 90% of all Internet hosts are located. This is the essence of global digital divide that needs to be transformed into global digital opportunity. For the Internet to be a true mass medium, it will have to achieve harmony among all consumer segments. There are different dimensions to digital divide such as economic level of individuals, economic prosperity of nations, ethnicity, age (young/old), rural/urban, gender, geographic location, quantitative and qualitative aspects, dial-up and broadband access.

The facts about digital divide based on global perspective reveals an estimated 429 million people are online globally (represents 6% of world population) and out of that, percentage wise, 41 in North America (USA and Canada), 27 in Europe, the Middle East and Africa and 20 in Asia Pacific. Even among highly developed nations, there exists a vast difference in the availability of home Internet access. Sweden ranks the highest (61%) home Internet connections where as Spain has lowest (20%) homes connected. Also, 57% of those not online in the USA have no intention of going online; worldwide, this figure accounts to 33%. (Foundation, 2002)

Potentially the effect of the Internet in broadening and enhancing access to information and communication may be greatest in poorer nations. The Internet also offers promise in the delivery of basic services like education and health infor-

Figure 1. Average diffusion of internet use, by income inequalities. Note: Each measures, respectively, average internet users of low income inequality countries, low middle income inequality countries with upper middle income countries and high income inequality countries.
Source: International Telecommunication Union

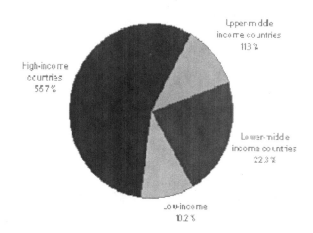

Distribution of Internet usage by income group of countries

mation to far-flung regions. Distance learning can widen access to training and education. The Internet promises to level the playing field and strengthen the voice of the voiceless in the developing world.

In the last few years, international agencies like the World Bank, United Nations Development Programs (UNDP) and etc., have expressed growing concern that the explosion of the Internet may leave many nations far behind, producing growing disparities between advanced industrialized and developing societies. As a result, poorer societies can become increasingly marginalized at the periphery of communication networks. (Norris, 2000)

One of the key challenges facing development practitioners today is how to utilize information and communication technology (ICT) tools to provide service to this underserved segment with the objective of decreasing human poverty and improving livelihoods. (Information have`s and have not`s, 2007)

Internet Usage

There are differences between developed countries, where broadband is growing rapidly, and developing countries, where narrowband dial-up is still relatively prevalent:

In many developed counties, the growth of broadband is largely due to competition and declining prices, but is also made possible thanks to available infrastructure; In low-income developing countries, expanding broadband infrastructure such as cable and optical fiber connections outside urban areas tends to be very costly; Wireless technologies can help circumvent the cost of infrastructure for remote or rural areas. Vietnam, for example, is using the cutting-edge technology Wimax (worldwide interoperability for microwave access, which offers much higher speeds and wider range than wi-fi or wireless fidelity) to bring broadband Internet to rural areas; Developing countries are catching up with developed countries in terms of overall Internet usage. In 1997, nearly three-quarter of the world's population lived in developing countries but accounted for only 5% of the world's Internet users. By 2006, the share of developing countries in total Internet usage had risen to over 30%.

Distribution of internet usage by income group of countries.

In terms of broadband Internet access, the digital divide among countries is wide:

Figure 2. Average diffusion of internet use, by income inequalities. Note: Each line measures, respectively, average internet users (per 100 people) of low developing countries, developed countries and the whole world from 1997-2007.
Source: International Telecommunication Union

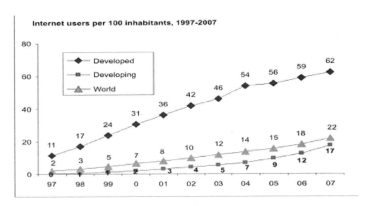

High-income countries account for nearly three-quarters (74.0%) of total broadband subscribers worldwide; Whereas e-commerce is commonplace in the developed world, it has not taken off in developing economies partly due to the lack of financial facilities (such as credit cards and insurance services) that can support online sales and purchase. Additionally, prices for broadband Internet in developing countries are higher than in developed countries, thus putting broadband services beyond the reach of ordinary consumers. (International, 2007)

The new communication technology is said to provide access to global knowledge resources, since it allows users to share their knowledge, resources and experiences of different people.

Despite rapid increase in information communication technologies in developed countries, there exists a digital divide between rich, poor, urban and rural/remote areas in developing countries. The challenge of expanding the telecommunications network in developing countries to reach the whole population needs to overcome two

separate" gap" …These gaps are: The market efficiency gap and the access gap. (Navas-Sabater, D.A., and Juntunen, n.d.)

Kofi Anan, UN secretary general also in his message for the World Telecommunication day –May 17th 2004 – emphasized on digital divide between countries:

Digital divide can be for a number of reasons: access to education or training, lack of money to buy the required equipment, or lack of access because of the problems obtaining the required communications links or services to get online. Some states have produced good research than others. Although accessing to Internet is not only criteria and other factors such as the quality of connection and auxiliary services, processing speed and other capabilities of computer used must be considered. It is clear that developed nations with the resources to invest in and develop ICT infrastructure are reaping enormous benefits from the information age.

Table 1. (1)Internet usage and world population statistics are for June 30, 2008.(2) Demographic (population) numbers are based on data from the US Census Bureau. (3) Internet usage information comes from data published by Nielsen//Net Ratings, by the International Telecommunications Union, by local NIC, and other reliable sources. (4) For definitions, disclaimers, and navigation help, please refer to the site surfing guide, now in ten languages.

World Regions	Population (2008 Est.)	Internet Users Dec/31, 2000	Internet Usage Latest Data	% Population (Penetration)	Usage % of World	Usage Growth 2000-2008
Africa	955,206,348	4,514,400	51,065,630	5.3%	3.5%	1,031.2 %
Asia	3,776,181,949	114,304,000	573,538,257	15.2%	39.3%	401.8 %
Europe	800,401,065	105,096,093	384,633,765	48.1%	26.4%	266.0 %
Middle East	197,090,443	3,284,800	41,939,200	21.3%	2.9%	1,176.8 %
North America	337,167,248	108,096,800	248,241,969	73.6%	17.0%	129.6 %
Latin America/ Caribbean	576,091,673	18,068,919	139,009,209	24.1%	9.5%	669.3 %
Oceania/ Australia	33,981,562	7,620,480	20,204,331	59.5%	1.4%	165.1 %
WORLD TOTAL	6,676,120,288	360,985,492	1,458,632,361	21.8 %	100.0 %	304.1 %

Source: www.internetworldstats.com.

As we observed, developing countries are suffering from the dearth of Information Communication Technologies infrastructure and consequently the benefits of them in education systems. But how can developing countries bridge the digital divide? In the first stage authorities in developing countries must identify the barriers, then attempt to eliminate them, in that case they can bridge the digital divide that exists between them and developed countries."

If we want to identify barriers of internet use, optimistically as Kofi Anan did there are three barriers: *price of Internet access, language, and a shortage of infrastructure.*

Society today is characterized and dominated by applications of modern information and communication technology (ICT) virtually in all aspects of human endeavors for information access, processing and dissemination. Consequently, the impact of ICT utilization has cut across economics, politics, education, medicine, and other fields of human development. Through the use of ICT, modern society has been described as an information age and the knowledge economy. Thus access to ICT, the internet technology in particular, has provided people with a foundation for building up and applying knowledge globally and particularly in developing nations. According to the reports, ICT is the key for economic development and growth; it offers opportunities for global integration while retaining the identify of traditional societies.

According to the reports there are different factors that influence internet use such as: Lack of access to the internet, Lack of/ inadequate skills to browse the internet/ check e-mail, Lack of financial capacity to pay the bill by internet users, Poor internet services (e.g. low response time, network fluctuation, etc.), Poor maintenance culture of the available facilities, e.g. computers at the internet cyber café.

The fact shows that the digital divide is far from being solved. The ICT pushes the society forward into a knowledge age but at the same time brings us a new challenge. Because of the differences of the information infrastructure, educational level and information literacy, gaps of information, knowledge, opportunity and income between the developed and the developing countries and between the well educated, high income groups and not well educated, low income groups, are increasing.

So, the digital divide is still real. Because the majority of the world population live on the other side of the digital divide and they need IT for basic living. That is why the World Telecommunications Day (May 17th) chose "ICT for all: empowering people to cross the digital divide "as the theme for 2002. (Jianzhong, 2002, pp.18-24).

While the information is in principle available to all, in practice it tends to be accessed more by the wealthy and higher educated. The very poor rarely exercise their rights fully. They may be able to take advantage of information that is disclosed automatically, in the media for example, but they are less likely to request information themselves-hindered perhaps by unfamiliarity with the processes, illiteracy, cost, the time needed, the difficulty of making a request or simply because they fear, or do not trust public officials. The very poor are therefore most likely to benefit via the activities of NGOs or other institutions of civil society. (Asia-Pacific Human Development Report, 2008)

Although we can name other some barriers such as: *Social and Legal Constraints*, including censorship and denial of access: There are a number of countries who attempt to strictly control access to the Internet and to Internet resources. The systems used to enforce such constraints, most notably proxy servers, inevitably affect the performance and currency of available data, and inevitably limit the breadth of available information, the range of resources accessed, and the number of people who have access to even that data which has not been proscribed. Many authoritarian regimes translate a long and successful history of control over other information and communication technologies into strong control of internet development within their borders. Potential challenges to the state may arise from Internet use in several areas: the mass public, civil society, the economy, and the international community. Authoritarian states will likely respond to these challenges with a variety of reactive measures: restricting Internet access, filtering content, monitoring on-line behavior, or even prohibiting Internet use entirely. The restrictions on access to the technology raise the question of whether the development of the information society and its impact on the private, working and public lives of people requires democracy to be underpinned with' communication rights'. (Saheb, 2005)

A clear finding from the work of all these initiatives is the strong push given to the English language as a result of IT, with French and Spanish struggling to keep us. As Irna Orellana of RDS in Honduras puts it, "Most of the search engines are in English, and they are the most popular ones." The Internet is definitely driving the use of English – its one of the reasons to learn English. (Hijab, 2001)

The Role of ICT and the Digital Divide

In the global economy, information and communication technologies (ICTs) play a vital role: International trade is highly dependent on the accumulation and dissemination of information and knowledge; In many countries, the business environment can be vastly improved as business licensing and other bureaucratic procedures are streamlined thanks to e-governance; Information infrastructure thus weighs heavily in the decision of international companies as to where to set up new business and investment; ICT enables developing countries to become active participants in international trade and integrate into the global knowledge-based economy; In particular, mobile technology has enabled farmers and fishermen from rural communities to gain price information

and new customers without the need to go through the middleman; ICT also allows many developing countries to make a leap towards higher value-added production and services. For example, India and China have become strong players in the ICT industry in terms of both software development and manufacturing of ICT goods such as mobile phones and computers.

In terms of ICT skills, the literature increasingly promotes the need to go beyond teaching IT skills, and emphasizes e-literacy or media skills. (Cushman, and Kleen, 2006) These promote developing peoples' ability to analyze, evaluate and create information. A shift towards a more learner-focused approach and teaching a wide range of e-literacy skills is also encapsulated in two recent documents – the ICT Skill for Life standard and the ICT Skill for Life Core Curriculum. However, it appears that the link between funding and accredited courses results in the necessity to follow specific curricula, with little time for learner-led activities or discussions. (QCA, 2007)

Society today is characterized and dominated by applications of modern information and communication technology (ICT) virtually in all aspects of human endeavors for information access, processing and dissemination. Consequently, the impact of ICT utilization has cut across economics, politics, education, medicine, and other fields of human development. Through the use of ICT, modern society has been described as an information age and the knowledge economy. Thus access to ICT, the internet technology in particular, has provided people with a foundation for building up and applying knowledge globally and particularly in developing nations. The World Bank(2002) in its report contended that, in the rapidly evolving electronic environment, developing countries face opportunity costs if they delay greater access to and use of information infrastructure and information technology (IT), which together make up ICT. According to the report, ICT is the key for economic development and growth; it offers opportunities for global integration while retaining the identity of traditional societies. ICT can also increase the economic and social being of poor people, empower individuals and communities; and enhance the effectiveness and efficiency of the public sector. (Bank, 2002)

This refers to the availability as well as affordability of computers with multimedia performance capabilities and with broadband connectivity to the internet. In a time where so much content and contact is on the internet, anything less than broadband access to multimedia can be considered a competitive disadvantage. (Sharma, and Azura, 2005)

Reaffirm the strong correlation (although they concede this does not necessarily mean causation) between the ability to communicate over distances and time using technology and economic growth. The digital divide, while pass in its prognosis, remains a demarcation between "haves" and "have lesses" (UNESCO, 2005).

Among others, caution against the fallacies of present policy measures that tend to favor the economic or intellectual elite in the mistaken belief that this would be more impactful. Therefore the concept of ICT accessibility has to be broadened to ensure that there is greater deliberative democracy, which is essentially what is required in a knowledge society. In this sense, universal suffrage for ICTs means that the availability and cost of access to broadband internet allows a knowledge society to presume that participation is open to all who need them. (Ergazakis, Metaxiotis, and Psarras, 2006).

The importance of information and communication technologies (ICTs) as powerful tools for socio-economic development is now widely acknowledged not only among large corporations but small business enterprises as well. However, for ICT to be effectively deployed as engines of economic development existing IT skills gap both in developed and developing countries must be addressed. Additionally, pervasive use of ICT in the economy depends on well-trained human resources for developing relevant applications,

supporting and maintaining systems. Moreover, investment in human capital, research and development is becoming increasingly recognized as a critical factor in preparing citizens to participate in the digital age.

The digital divide is information inequality which can be reduced through information accessibility, information use and information sharing as well as dissemination. Given that ICT infrastructure is partly prepared, information society citizens can rely on librarians' roles in the increased utilization of information. Furthermore, librarians can help people interact intimately as well as efficiently with new information technologies to locate, use, process, organize, create, communicate and manipulate information and information resources and somehow find an appropriate identity and status in the electronic virtual world.

Information Infrastructures

Many countries in the developing world still lack the most basic forms of information and communications infrastructure. There are enormous gaps between the technologically advanced, industrialized societies of the world and the developing nations in the availability of information and communication services. Of all the gaps that exist between the South and the North, none is growing faster than the information gap. (Ahsanullah, 2002)

Infrastructure is one of the key foundations for building an information society and bringing the benefits of ICTs to all. Especially, public intervention in facilitating the establishment of the basic network infrastructure is vital. Such public infrastructure would reduce cost of entry for new companies into the market and substantially reduce the risk of business. Both of these would also reduce cost of information for the general public. (Information have`s and have not`s, 2007)

Basic infrastructure includes buildings and power resources; many countries lack power generation and distribution facilities adequate to running computers or Network Infrastructures except in large cities, and access can be limited and/or sporadic even there. Solutions involving the use of small scale local power generation (solar power and fuel cells) are becoming increasingly workable, but a high bandwidth Network Infrastructure often depend on the backbone provided by a power infrastructure.

The Internet is built on a complex layering of data networks, with a variety of top level Network Service Providers (NSPs) interconnecting a wide variety of localized networks, including schools, business, governments, and local Internet Service Providers (ISPs). Individual local ISPs will provide end users and smaller businesses with one or more of a variety of connectivity options, including dial-up modem access, broadband cable network access, radio frequency network access, and others. End users and small businesses will, in many cases, use this connectivity to connect multiple machines to the Internet via a local area network (LAN). (Saheb, 2005)

Although, in future scenario for internet usage, developed countries will continue to offer a solid consumer base for ICT products and services, the future expansion of the ICT industry will be driven by growth momentum in developing countries. Thanks to their younger age structure, larger populations and lower labour costs, manufacturers of ICT goods (e.g. mobile phones and computers) will be increasingly attracted to developing countries to invest and set up production .An increasing number of developing countries will improve their business environments through e-government and e-business. This will help to facilitate national and international business transactions and boost economic growth in these counties. (International, 2007)

THE ROLE OF GOVERNMENT AND E-GOVERNANCE IN DIMINISHING THE DIGITAL DIVIDE

E-government is a common term used for the concepts like e-services, e-democracy and above all, e-administration. It is the use of information and communication technology to increase the access to, and delivery of the government services to benefit citizens, business partners, public and private sectors. E-Government engages the automation or computerization of existing paper-based procedures that will rapid new methods of management. It is a connection between the government authorities, the private sector and the citizens. Above all, it aims to advance the government's resources in the direction of an effective control to increase the country's social, political and economic resources for development. (E-Government, 2007)

E-governance projects, can bridge the digital divide and spread the benefits of ICT especially to rural citizens, enable them access to digital services and help address and hopefully eliminate the rural/urban digital divide. (E-Government projects will bridge digital divide, spread ICT benefits)

Connecting people by making investments in the technology is comparatively an easier job than bringing and keeping them online. The key to encourage citizens in developing countries to use the Internet would be to provide them with compelling content and services that meet their primary needs. E-government perse is an unlikely key for bridging the digital divide. The notion that technologies can prescribe their own course of action is mythical. The responsibility for technological outcomes lies in the social order between individuals, groups and institutions through which lives are organized. There is, however, synergy to be created between technology and social context. This is not deterministic synergy it will vary by context and will therefore entail adaptation of the technology and social context. If there is no prior experience of using computers, then there is probably no relevant social context. In some aspects, this may make it easier to introduce new technology, as there will be no old values or context to change; however, a context has to be created. If the existing context for information is informal or non-paper driven, automation may be difficult. In both situations, new rules will have to be learnt and accepted. When leapfrogging, one must be careful to identify both technical and social considerations, ensuring that the technology is not embedded to the detriment of the social order. Further, one should not assume that there is only one way to leapfrog all social contexts will have one or more different leapfrogging solutions. By most measures, developing countries continue to struggle with the implementation of viable e-governance strategies. (Basu, 2006)

Information can be used in various ways some being more productive than others. Hence the demand for information (the willingness of individual to pay a price for it) also depends on the ability of the individual consumer to utilize information. It also depends on the consumer's awareness level of the availability and source of information.

It can be argued that government has a role in enhancing awareness and capability of the people to use information properly and thereby increase demand. Such enhanced demand would create a business case for the market to exist.(Information Have's and Have not's, 2007)

In addition, E-Government is about a process of reform in the way governments work, share information and deliver services to external and internal clients for the benefit of both government and the citizens and businesses that they serve.

E-Government harnesses information technologies, such as Wide Area Networks (WAN), Internet, World Wide Web, and mobile computing by government agencies to reach out to citizens, business, and other aims of the government to:

- Improve delivery of services to citizens
- Improve interface with business and industry

- Empower citizens through access to knowledge and information, and
- Make the working of the government more efficient and effective.

The resulting benefits could be more transparency, greater convenience, less corruption, revenue growth, and cost reduction. So in order to bridging the digital divide, NGOs and grass root organizations that catalyze and manage the community building process needs to be improved. Applications that draw a large cliental that pays for the information services, ensure economic viability that empowers rural citizens and enables formation of communities Technology that makes rural access inexpensive and robust. (Bhatnagar, 2004)

Many different institutions, some related to incipient state organizations and others to private associations, emerged to provide the public goods required for the proper functioning of markets and for reducing transaction costs. (The knowledge explosion and the knowledge divide)

It is a fair generalization that thus far the generation of technology has been confined to a few countries and is becoming increasingly capital-intensive, making it more difficult for developing countries to catch up. Also more and more R&D is increasingly originating in the private sector. The private companies that produce new goods and services that improve human outcomes are motivated. These companies expend huge amounts on R&D and capture the returns to such expenditures by staying ahead of the competition. These private institutes ease the communication between government and people and help people getting information faster and easier and getting more information. The qualification of IT and ICTs in this process, help diminishing digital divide and the role of it is inevitable. Increasingly, global attitudes toward technology are being shaped by important non-governmental organizations (NGOs), especially as non-state actors start to play a greater role in global governance.

As yet, there is relatively little research on the social impact of privatizing social services. Most investigations have focused on economic efficiency rather than impact on redistribution and the poor. If policy is weak before privatization, it will also be weak after privatization. Privatization is clearly no substitute for a responsible policy of redistribution. (Asia-Pacific Human Development Report, 2008)

As a result, we can conclude that in market economies, both the public and private sector can promote digital opportunity. Government has an important role to play in establishing an enabling environment for investment and market competition, as well as intervening to achieve socio-economic goals in areas to create balanced growth in reality. The roles of governments and the private sector overlap and include additional elements: first positive incentives stimulating market dynamics and second, measures are preventing uneven development (for example by use of regulatory criteria or restrictions). (World Information Society Report, 2007)

THE RELATIONSHIP BETWEEN HUMAN DEVELOPMENT AND DIGITAL DIVIDE

Human Resource Development

The importance of information and communication technologies (ICTs) as powerful tools for socio-economic development is now widely acknowledged not only among large corporations but small business enterprises as well. However, for ICT to be effectively deployed as engines of economic development existing IT skills gap both in developed and developing countries must be addressed. The Digital Opportunity Task Force emphasizes human resources development through systematic training and education as critical if countries have to reap digital divides. Additionally, pervasive use of ICT in the economy depends on well- trained human resources for developing relevant applications, supporting and maintaining systems. Moreover, investment in human capital, research and development is becoming increasingly recognized as a critical factor in preparing citizens to participate in the digital age. Enhancing the information literacy in developing countries is one of the most important strategies in order to decreasing the digital divide. (ICT skills readiness for the emerging global digital economy among small business in developing countries, 2007)

The Impact of the Digital Divide on Skills Development

There has been a great deal of discussion about the impact of digital information resources, particularly around what has been termed the digital divide, or the split between those that have access to digital information resources and those who do not. In general, the digital divide applies internationally. However, (Norris 2001) discusses three types of digital divide:

Social (within countries), global (between countries) and democratic (those unable to use ICTs to take part in public life). The (social) digital divide has an impact upon information professionals in developed environments, with many libraries lacking resources and technical support, and staff needing continuously to acquire appropriate training in order to deliver up-to-date services and troubleshoot equipment. (Bill and Melinda Gates Foundation, 2004)

Regarding the *global* digital divide, Lim, (1999) suggests that too much emphasis has been placed upon the development of ICT infrastructure in developing countries, and not enough consideration has been given to human resource development.(Lim, 1999).

However, in order to understand how ICTs impact upon skills development in developing countries, it is necessary to recognize the situation that currently exists regarding the ICT infrastructure. For example, in Africa, one in a hundred people have access to a PC; the few Internet Service Providers are comparatively expensive; power supplies may be unreliable (even non-existent) and telecommunications are sparse, with the 90% of the population living in rural areas having only 50% of the telephone lines .(Jensen, 2002)

Suggests that many ICT users are self-taught, and are capable of developing an understanding of ICTs through the experience of utilizing them. If this is the case, then countries unable to provide extensive access to ICTs are inevitably marginalized as they are less likely to produce capable self-taught persons. However, Steinmueller's suggestion does indicate a more optimistic scenario for those developing environments progressively providing access to ICTs, as it suggests that staff may be able to gain at least some degree of expertise through self-learning. (Steinmueller, 2001)

The Information Literacy Needs Attention

Education system in information age has slight alteration and just some sort of education systems has become popular solely in developed countries. Developing countries are still suffering from digital gap. They can't keep up with the changes in socio-economic system during the twentieth century. So an up-to-date education system should be consistent with current socio-economic system that has named information society, which means it should be based on concepts from information and consumer services.

The need for adequate scientific and technical literacy in a nation's workforce, an important element in the development of science and technology capabilities, has been recognized as nations strive to raise their living standards. This is now perceived as an everybody working knowledge of science, is as necessary as reading and writing for a satisfactory way of life in the modern world. In an era where economic growth based on the production of primary goods is proving to be increasingly uncertain and difficult to sustain,

the call for improved human resources that can competitively turn out ever more sophisticated goods and services rings true in rich and poor nations alike. So, science and technology capabilities of most developing countries are far too limited to deal adequately with the challenges of economic advance, social progress and environmental sustainability. Thus, they should work hard on their human development programs and invest on their education and literacy. (The knowledge explosion and the knowledge divide, 2001)

Judging by these experiences, the most problematic issue is lack of support to training and maintenance. This was emphasized even more frequently than cost or lack of infrastructure, by groups throughout the world. "Training, training, training", says Mike Jensen, one of the first activists in the Association for Progressive Communications. Health Link encourages a "mentor/supportive" approach to training, doing as much on site as possible, and following up with repeat visits. (Hijab, 2001)

Information has its existence, since the existence of human being. With the advent of ICTs and computers, the delivery of information has become easy, inexpensive and every ones cup of tea. As information is increasingly codified in digital forms, new skills are needed to operate the technology to search for, organize, manage information and use it to solve problems and create new knowledge and cultural products. The greatest challenge for society in 21st century is to keep pace with the knowledge and technological expertise necessary for finding and evaluation information. Information literacy is a survival skill in the information age. Instead of drowing in the abundance of information that floods their lives, information literate people know how to find, evaluate, and use information effectively to solve a particular problem or make a decision. Libraries, which provide a significant public access point to such information and usually at no cost, must play a key role in preparing people for the demands of today's information society.

(Presidential Committee on Information Literacy: Final Report, n.d.)

Technological literacy, a broad understanding of the human-designed world and our place in it, is an essential quality for all people who live in the increasingly technology-driven 21st century. (The New Digital Divide: Media Literacy, broadening participation? Inclusive education? Digital equity, 2007)

What are the features of information Society that education systems must be commensurate with ?

The information society is a new kind of society. Specific to this kind of society is the central position information technology has for production and economy. Information society is seen as successor to industrial society. Closely related concepts are post-industrial society (Daniel Bell), post-Fordism, post-modern society, knowledge society, information revolution, and information society. Applications of information and communication technologies (ICTs) are making dramatic changes in economic and social development that these tectonic economic and social changes have been characterized by terms such as "knowledge economy" and "learning society", conveying the notion that knowledge and learning are now at the core of economic productivity and social development. Nowadays information communication technologies are the nervous system of contemporary society, transmitting and distributing sensory and control information, and interconnecting myriad interdependent units. These technologies consist Electronic Mass Media such as Cable Television, pay Television Services, Interactive Television, Wireless Cable Systems, Streaming Media, Radio broadcasting, Direct Broadcast Satellite, Computers and Consumer Electronic such as Multimedia computers Video Games, The Internet and the World Wide Web, Office Technologies, Internet Commerce, Virtual and Augmented Reality, Home video and Digital Audio and Technology and Satellite technologies such as Local and Long Distance Telephony,

Broadband Networks, Residential Gateways and Home Networks, Satellite Communication, Distance Learning, Wireless Telephony, Video conferencing. (Saheb, 2005)

Education is essential in these parts of the world. Training and improving already existing skills is the first step in establishing any form of economy. Utilizing labor and skills will allow for countries to evaluate and determine what their strongest assets are in the trade world. Once this is established, and a monetary system is developed, a democracy is also needed. With a democratic leadership the people can make decisions for themselves, and provide for their futures. After such communities are established, then technology can start to integrate into the picture. However, substantial amounts of education are needed to train workers on how such technologies work, and how they can benefit the culture. Many of these small countries must rely on trade to be viable. They must learn to utilize their assets and resources adequately. "Improved training, particularly at secondary and vocational levels, will be necessary for the effective functioning of the economies," With a strong educational foundation, many of these countries will continue to flourish, while others will begin a new venture with economic growth and stability. Building an economic base, education and training can lead to more substantial technology integration. Producing energy and dispersing this energy is the next step. After power supplies are in tact, communities can begin to slowly integrate technology.

Education is the key to this integration, and without proper training and understanding, resistance of the Western influence is likely. When societies learn to utilize their own strengths and resources, the feeling of ownership leads to determination. This determination along with assistance, allows for integration to begin.

As we continue to bring technology into Third World, developing countries and less developed countries, let us keep in mind the main reason for this integration. It is not to control their markets and trade; it is to bring them to a higher level economically and socially. When we begin to integrate strictly for our own gain, the global network will fail. Many countries do not encourage the technology and free market/free trade ideal. They are opposed or skeptical of the Western influence that might also invade their culture. With a tyrannical government, this idea of integration will never work. People in these situations are not valued, and they are not able to acquire rights that allow them to even consider integration and its possibilities. Poverty is such a huge problem in many of these countries. Unless a political structure is in place, economic development is nearly impossible, and without the economic backing, the poverty will never diminish. Programs implemented in the past by the US and other countries have not always succeeded. Again, this is a case where we must learn from the trials and mistakes of past integration in order to continue in the process today. Not only will the less developed countries benefit, the developed countries will see a boost in political, economic, and educational aspects of all cultures. (Sipe-Haesemeyer,2005) on the other hand, The Internet has become such vital part of our society and cultures that is often difficult to imagine how we ever functioned without it. The idea that "knowledge is power" has become possibly one of the most quoted (and east understood) truisms of the Information Society. There are many ways of looking at knowledge or information, especially when we consider the *volume* of information that becomes readily available through computer networks and databases. Anthony Smith, In his book "*The Geopolitics of Information*" addresses the context in which we think of this continuous stream of information: "It is possible to view information as a social resource of a special kind rather than as a produced commodity, a resource which enables other resources to function productively since it is the existence of salient information which determines the value and existence of other resources."

He adds: "The problems of privacy, access, commercial privilege, public interest, are problems of allocation and priority and value of the kind that every society has had to debate incessantly in history and now has to do so again in this new guise."

Smith's suggestion that there is "geopolitics" to information itself is an interesting one. It is premise worth examining in some detail. Originally the subject of geopolitics focused upon the analysis of geographical influences on power relationships in international politics"

.However, technological developments in the later half of this century have allowed many states (and other social organisms) to overcome limitations placed upon them by geographical location. In the modern context, geopolitics is less and less geography bound and today might be better defined as a study of relationships between space and power as these apply to social organisms. (Harris, 1996)

In order for developing countries to accept the Internet and use it effectively, these countries must agree upon some type of policy to ensure success. "Developing countries must create a framework of political, legal and economic conditions that guarantee equality of opportunities and create incentives for trade and investment,". Most of these countries still have political systems that are imperfect to those in more developed countries. "In the rankings of economic freedom, most developing countries obtain poor scores in critical areas such as legal stability, size of government, regulation and sound monetary policy," These impediments often keep these countries in poverty. With the Internet and world support, it would be possible for these developing countries to break out of this lifestyle. Some of these countries have not yet accepted globalization and they have not embraced economic liberalization. Perhaps with better campaigning and education of the importance of such ideals, the countries would more graciously accept these concepts and help improve their countries. Most of these countries have political institutions that spend too much money and borrow too much to even consider individual rights for its people . With our attempts at open trade and cultural integration, it is hoped that technology can help break individuals in these countries free from the oppression they face with such rule. (Sipe-Haesemeyer, 2005)

Lack of capital, inadequate markets, and weak institutions are demonstrably inadequate. The crucial element that has been largely ignored is the cultural: that is to say, values and attitudes that stand in the way of progress. Some cultures, above all those of the West and East Asia, have proven themselves more prone to progress than others. The conclusion that culture matters goes down hard. The implication is that all cultures are equally worthy, and those who argue to the contrary are often labeled ethnocentric, intolerant or even racist. A similar problem is encountered with those economists who believe that culture is irrelevant that people will respond to economic signals in the same way regardless of their culture.

But a growing number of academics, journalists and politicians are writing and talking about culture as a crucial factor in societal development, and a new paradigm of human progress is emerging but the vast majority of countries still lags far behind. Of the six billion people who inhabit the world today, fewer than one billion are to be found in the advanced democracies. More than four billion live in what the World Bank classifies as "low-income" or "lower middle income" countries. (Harrison, n.d.)

As a conclusion, with the *proper education, reliable information, and having right to have information,* these communities can develop a democratic society where people are allowed to view and process information and make logical conclusions on their own.

THE ROLE OF LIBRARIES, LIBRARIANS AND DIGITAL DIVIDE

Nowadays, terms such as "knowledge-based society", "sustainable development" and so forth are frequently heard. In the world today, information is "a resource for development", and "the absence of reliable information is an epitome of underdevelopment"(Huang, and Russell, 2006)

Special librarians, who have access to information, have an important role in developing countries, in order to delivering proper and reliable information to people. So they can affect on promoting learning and information literacy programs.

Libraries will be called upon to provide authentic and reliable information, evolve strategic alliances, participate in network activities and contribute to the bridging of the digital divide. They will emerge as technology experts, guides, researchers, analysts, knowledge engineering, editors, navigators, gatekeepers, brokers and asset managers. Conclusively, librarians will need to acquire new skills to access net resources, and develop new strategies and services to meet the challenges of the knowledge age. (Omekwu, 2006)

These days, Libraries have more important role than before in developed and also in developing countries. They are emerging as one of the most important vehicles for bridging the digital divide as they increase the availability of technology to patrons and elevate the technical expertise of staff. Providing libraries with computers and librarians with training on how to use the new information technology is one of the most important solutions in order to bridging the digital divide all around the world. Libraries, with their long history of providing free access to information, are a natural vehicle for leading this effort to expand public access to technology. A key component of assuring the sustainability of these efforts is an intern program, which works to faster relationships between various kinds of libraries, specially library schools and public libraries by hiring library science students to help with computer installation and training. These activities help ensure that every library is prepared to maintain and sustain a high level of technological access for all patrons.

There is strong evidence that this and other similar efforts are making a dent in the digital divide. The U.S. National Commission on Libraries and Information Science (NCLIS) recently issued the results of its 2000 Internet Connectivity Study, which measured the level of connectivity, public access, training support and technology funding, current and anticipated, for staff and the public. The NCLIS found that in the last two years, Internet connectivity in public libraries has increased from 83 percent of libraries being connected to over 95 percent and in the same time period, libraries have nearly doubled the number of public access workstations (Bascom, and Melinda, 2001).

Libraries must train and teach their patrons to handle new electronic information formats as never before. They teach computer skills, internet surfing, information searching and providing various electronic services for the local citizens.

In the electronic service context, Librarian's roles will become more prominent as educators, information managers, information management consultants, custodians of information, information providers and publishers, change agents and custodians of library facilities:

- As educators, librarians can increase awareness among their clients of information networks, their contents and potential use.
- As information managers, librarians need access to information resources of many types, in many disciplines. They have the skills to build navigation tools for networked resources in the same way that develop navigation tools for published information in library catalogues and national bibliographies.

- As information management consultants, librarians can help network users build and maintain personal information systems, which provide access to the subset of networked information sources relevant to each user's work.
- As custodians of information, librarians are facing apparent challenge to their role, as physical resources migrate into electronic form and on- demand electronic delivery becomes more common.
- As information providers, librarians can make available much more widely collections which now can be sued only within a single physical library location.
- As change agents, library staff can lobby managers and governments as appropriate, for network access for themselves and their users.
- As custodians of library facilities, library can provide workstations, network gateways, printers and software that may not be otherwise available to the public. (Omekwu, 2006)

Librarians should confirm themselves even stronger than before thought their knowledge and skills and they should change their attitude towards the new environment, if they want to have an important role in order to diminish the digital divide. In this respect "librarians must redesign their service menu for their customers through thinking functionally. Under the present conditions where the Internet has become very popular, they should concentrate on the professional information services which can be provided only by libraries and librarians. For that purpose, we need to review the various IT devices and information services."

While the digital divide is expanding, the role and responsibility of librarians and libraries are increasing. So policy makers should consider the vital role that librarians can play in the realization of a knowledge-based society and sustainable development.

So it is emphasized that proper access to the information, is the key to alleviate the obstacles to information access, and so diminish the educational and information divide and totally digital divide within each country. Yet we must not overlook that there are basic, essential requirements – economic, social, political, and cultural – that must be taken into consideration to overcome the digital divide and thus gain equally access to information. (Aqili, 2008)

In this situation, Librarians and librarians have worked to bridge the divide between the information "haves" and "have- not's" for more than 100 years. (Digital divide, (2002))

Developing countries try hard in order to diminish digital divide. Libraries throughout North America have used resources provided by the Foundation to support their own individual efforts to increase public access to information. In the Yukon Territory, librarians established a mobile computer lab that travels to remote areas not served by a local library. In St. Louis, technology centers were installed in libraries serving inner-city neighborhoods. Students from the surrounding neighborhood use the technology centers to do homework after school. In Michigan, local libraries installed the first public workstations with Internet access. (Bascom, and Melinda, 2001)

As one of the library's missions, user education has been developed to help build up the learning skills for users regardless of age, race, language, religion, sex and physical ability. The term "information literacy" is evolved from the library education, for instance, the skill of catalogue search.

The Role of Digital Libraries in Diminishing the Digital Divide

While the information and communication technologies (ICTs) in general, and the Internet and the world wide web in particular, have made life easier by facilitating easy communication with virtually everyone, and easy access to information located virtually anywhere in the world, they have also widened the gap between the rich and the poor.

Digital libraries make use of ICT and the web to provide access to the local and remote digital information sources and services. Therefore, accessibility to the basic ICT and the Internet is a pre-requisite to the development and use of digital libraries. There are many other factors too. The two most important issues are the cost of building and maintaining sustainable digital library systems and services, and achieving the required information literacy standards so as to exploit the full benefits of digital libraries. Digital libraries can play a significant role in bridging the gap.

Developing countries, especially the least developed countries, that struggle to meet the basic human needs, cannot afford to spend such huge amount of money required for research and development of digital libraries. In addition, there are many other problems that stand in the way of digital library development in the developing countries. Consequently, libraries have long been suffering from financial and other crises such as lack of the appropriate technology, trained manpower, etc. Libraries have also been affected by a number of social problems, the primary ones being the poor literacy rates. While governments are struggling to improve the levels of basic literacy, proper use of library and information services call for another level of literacy – the information literacy that is absolutely necessary for people to become good information users. Due to the lack of suitable technologies and trained manpower, and above all due to the lack of financial resources, most libraries in the developing countries do not even have fully developed and up-to-date OPACs, let alone full-fledged automated library management systems, and digital libraries. Hence compared with the developed world scenario, libraries in the developing countries are already left behind by at least one generation. Digital divide and lack of resources for digital library research and development may increase the gap far more significantly between library and information services in developed and developing countries.

Five specific areas where digital libraries can promote developments in the developing countries:

1. In the dissemination of humanitarian information
2. In facilitating disaster relief by providing the appropriate information
3. In the preservation and propagation of indigenous culture
4. In building collections of locally-produced information, and
5. In creating new opportunities to enter the global marketplace.

To this we can add another important point that can be applicable to any digital library: digital libraries can facilitate lifelong learning which is the key to success in this fast changing world.

The following is a short list of problems or issues that stand in the way of digital library research and development in the developing countries:

- Shrinking library budget that forces the library management to struggle to maintain a minimum standard of services leaving no room for new ventures and developments
- Lack of financial support specifically for digital library research and development
- Absence of fully developed and up-to-date OPACs, and little access to online information resources – on-line data bases, e-journals, etc.
- Poor ICTs – computers and networks
- Poor facilities for access to ICT, especially the Internet
- Stringent government and institutional policies on Internet access
- Lack of trained manpower
- Poor information literacy rate that causes lack of appreciation of modern information services and their use.

The list may go on and on. Any experienced library manager from a developing country can surely add quite a few more points to the above list. In short, existing libraries in the developing countries are struggling for their mere existence. Of course there are many reasons for the lack of resources for library development. In countries where citizens still struggle for reliable sources of food, water, medical care and educational opportunities, bridging the digital divide may seem like a lofty goal, and that is why digital library development is way down the list of priorities of governments and institutions. (Chowdhury, 200?)

As digital libraries become part of the traditional library infrastructure, it will be vital to deal with a number of issues. A major risk to digital objects is technological obsolescence of the devices to read them. Likewise, a major worry is the funding for the regular refreshing. Digital preservation will be an ongoing operation, requiring a regular future expense. Experts have projected that over the next 20 years, with all the potential new ways to create, receive and transmit information, we will receive 50 times as much as we have had in the past. So digitizing our libraries should be one of the proper solutions in order to bridging the digital divide all over the world. (Mutual, 2007)

CONCLUSION AND RECOMMENDATIONS

Closely linked to a nation or society's scientific and technological capabilities and to the issue of scientific literacy, is its people's ability to access and effectively utilize the rapidly growing flow of information. Despite the ongoing knowledge explosion, however, entire nations and millions of individuals, particularly in the developing world, are ill-equipped to be part of an emerging global "information society" due to factors such as inadequate education, social and political exclusion, and sheer lack of financial resources. (The knowledge explosion and the knowledge divide, 2001)

The digital divide is shrinking in terms of Internet usage around the world and it has reduced sharply over recent years. The prevalence of the digital divide in developing countries is a serious threat to effective utilization of information for socio-economic development and nation building. Governments and relevant international/non-governmental organizations should introduce appropriate programs that will entice people to consider careers in science and technology. In addition they should provide internet access and technology education for people irrespective of their career in order to bridge the observed digital divide.

One serious form of digital divide in developing economies as shown by the survey is that of educational/ literacy level of the citizenry. In developed nations, the vast majority of the populace are educated and/literate. In developing countries, however, where there is a high incidence of illiteracy, a lot of people are cut off from having access to vital information especially through computers and the internet, unlike in telephony. This is explicit since an illiterate person can only make use of Internet through intermediation. Most of these illiterate people in developing countries are not even aware of the existence or usefulness of ICT. Hence, governments, relevant international organizations and non-government organizations (NGOs), etc., should embark on enlightenment and/awareness programs regarding ICT, particularly the Internet and its applications in different fields of human endeavor. This will encourage the illiterate/uneducated section of our population to begin to make use of available Internet cyber cafes at least through intermediation for relevant and specialized information on business, farming, fishing etc. Then a long-term measure will be for governments to embark on policies that will improve literacy level in developing countries as obtained in the developed countries. In addition,

general computer literacy programs should be organized by public institutions/ministries in the country to reduce the level of the digital divide due to lack of skills in modern computer technology among their staff. Respective governments/agencies should therefore make the internet facilities available in our public institutions: schools, tertiary institutions, ministries, etc. for ease of access (e.g. free access or subsidized financial cost) Relevant governments and their agencies should also embark on the provision free or subsidized public internet cyber café in developing countries, as well as rural communities, to bring Internet access to the low income earners.

It also recommends the following five strategies to help make progress toward digital equity:

1. Legitimize the significant role culture plays in students' educational experience.
2. Continue to challenge perceptions about the role of technology in education.
3. Encourage others to recognize the critical link between technology, professional development and classroom practice.
4. Create opportunities for students to access technology outside the classroom.
5. Continue to seek funding for technology in spite of challenges.(TheNew Digital Divide: Media Literacy, broadening participation? Inclusive education? Digital equity,2007)

So the Internet and related technologies, generally information communication technologies, can provide information and tools that extend the fastest and newest ways of learning and can establish new kinds of education systems that will foster learning in an interactive, digitalized and hypertext atmosphere and this will be vital task of all the countries over the world to prepare these infrastructures that are useful for both students and teachers.

As we know, one of the underlying causes of the digital divide is unequal access to technology and uneven ability and knowledge to implement and use that technology. ICTs are a major force for development in the modern economy, but many people still remain unconnected. Creation of "technological parks" by the central and regional, and municipal governments, creation of "technological business incubators" by the universities and other academic institutions to entrepreneurs interested in exploring new business venues. These incubators would provide technical, business and technological management assistance. Promotion of clusters and networks of medium and small enterprises in specific sectors and localities, specializing in specific aspects of productive services, which exchange products and services and share a series of supporting services to achieve greater collective and individual efficiency. Promotion of linkage between national firms and transnational firms that would purchase local products to make them available in global markets, promotion of strategic alliances between national enterprises in key sectors for the transformation of national resource, creation and promotion of capacity-building and professional training specialized for the productive social priority sectors and etc are some of the strategic and policies to bridge the knowledge divide specially in developing countries. (The knowledge explosion and knowledge divide, 2001)

In addition, there are some solutions but community computer and Internet kiosks have emerged as the preferred medium for bringing the benefits of the information and communication technologies (ICTs) to rural communities in developing countries. These kiosks are being used to deliver a host of services such as education, health care, agriculture, e-government, and communication (email, voice mail ...). The National e-governance Action plan of the government of India has placed great emphasis on these kiosks as the main vehicle for developing e-government services in rural areas.

One obvious implication of this is to make more and more e-government services available through the kiosks, which would save time and costs, in terms of a reduced number of visits to the government offices and less corruption, to the users. As kiosks become more and more ubiquitous in our countryside, it is important that we pay serious attention to ensure that no one is left out from their benefits. (Bridging the rural digital divide, n.d.)

In order to integrate technology, it will take more than simply installing a few phone cables. Telecommunication infrastructures need to be in place for the Internet to be successful in these countries. Costs of computers and other equipment often hinder these countries from logging onto the web. The dial-up fee is also outrageous for only a short amount of Internet hours. English is the dominant language of the Internet, posing a problem for many countries. Since global communication is made up largely of Internet usage, those who do not speak English might have little desire to become part of the World Wide Web. Perhaps developing more web material in local languages, lower costs of equipment, and providing easier access will help to integrate technology into these less developed countries. The price of computers remains a major obstacle to wider household penetration, especially in developing countries.

Countries need to have access to lower cost computers and they need to have easy and affordable access to the phone lines and Internet. As a more developed country, we need to learn from the successful and unsuccessful attempts at integrating technology. Not only will these less developed countries benefit from the integration, developed countries will benefit politically, economically, and educationally. (Sipe-Haesemeyer, 2005)

The digital divide can never be contained in isolation but the effort has to be multi-dimensional and multi-pronged. ICTs are one of the enabling tools to bridge digital divide. Creation of ICT infrastructure and content are core methodologies and a thrust to technology growth in a planned manner will certainly lessen the gap. While digital divide is an issue of recent concern, technology divide has been as issue for much longer. There are two approaches to enable a wider population to benefit from technology and information revolutions; one is to enhance level of literacy (basic, functional technology and computer education amongst masses) and another is to design appropriate IT tools around the capabilities of users (such as Simputer that employs audio/visual input/output, without need to be literate; low cost telephony and data communication—VOIP and wireless communication.

REFERENCES

Ahsanullah, A. (2002). *Information Technology Services for Rural Communities of Developing Countries toward poverty Alleviation*. Dhaka: Faruque & Aulad Hassain.

Alextbox, J. (2006). *Digital divide: The three stages*. Retrieved May 4, 2008, from http://www.useit.com/alertbox

Aqili, V. I. (2008). Bridging the digital divide: The role of librarians and information professional in the third millennium. *The Electronic Library, 26*(2), 226–237. Retrieved from http://www.emeraldinsight.com/0264-0437.htm. doi:10.1108/02640470810864118

Asia-Pacific Human Development Report. (2008). Retrieved from http://hdr.undp.org/en/reports/regional reports /featured regional report 2008/RHDR_full.pdf

Bank, W. (2002). *Information and communication technologies: a world bank group strategy*. Washington, DC: The World Bank Group.

Bascom, B. B., & Melinda, G. F. (2001, March 5). *Libraries are connection millions to the internet*. Retrieved from http://www.digitaldivide.net/articles/view.php?ArticleID

Basu, S. (2006). *E-Government and developing countries: role of technology and law*. Retrieved from http://www.digital divide.net/articles/view.php?article ID=601

Bhatnagar, S. (2004). *Universal e-Government and digital divide*. Retrieved from http://www.apdip.net/projects/2004/public-services/presentations/bhatnagar.ppt

Bill and Melinda Gates Foundation. (2004). *Toward equality of access: the role of public libraries in addressing the digital divide*. Retrieved from http://www.gatesfoundation.org/nr/Downloads/libraries/uslibraries/reports/TowardEqualityof

Bridging the rural digital divide. (n.d.). Retrieved from http://www.hindu.com/op/2005/04/12/stories/2005041200161500.htm

Chowdhury, G. G. (200?). *Digital divide: How can digital libraries bridge the gap?* Retrieved from http://www.cis.strath.ac.uk/research/publications/papers/strath_cis_publication_334.pdf

Cushman, M., & Klecun, E. (2006). *How (can) nonusers engage with technology: bridging in the digitally excluded. Social inclusion: Social and Organizational implication for information systems*. New York, NY: Springer.

Digital divide. (2002). Retrieved from http://www.ala.org/oitp/digital divide

E-Government. (2007). Retrieved from http://electronic-government.blogspot.com

E-Government projects will bridge digital divide, spread ICT benefits. (n.d.). Retrieved from http://www.indianexpress.com

Ergazakis, K., Metaxiotis, K., & Psarras, J. (2006). A coherent framework for building successful KCs in the context of the knowledge-based economy. *Knowledge Management Research & Practice, 4*(1), 56–59.

Euromonitor International. (2007). *The global digital divide*. Retrieved from http://www.euromonitor.com/The_global_digital_divide Key points

Foulger, D. (2001). *The cliff and continuum: defining the digital divide*. Retrieved April 28, 2008, from http://pages.prodigy.net/davis_foulger/articles/cliffandcontinum.htm

Foundation, B. (2002). *Digital divide basics fact sheet*. Retrieved from http://www.ctcnet.org/ctc/benton/DigitalDivideBasics.doc

Grace, J. K., Kenny, C., & Qiang (2004). *Information and communication technologies and broad-based development: a partial review of the evidence*. Washington, DC: The World Bank.

Harris, B. (1996, December 14). *Geopolitics of Cyberspace*. Retrieved from http://Blakeharris.com/site/the-geopolitics-of-cyberspace/

Harrison, L. E. (n.d.). *Cultural matters*. Retrieved from http://www.arakpmg.com.ph/pttaf/content/culture2%matters.pdf

Hijab, N. (2001). *People's initiatives to use IT for development*. Retrieved from http://hdr.undp.org/en/reports/global/hdr2001/papers/hijab-1.pdf

Huang, J., & Russell, S. (2006). The digital divide and academic achievement. *The Electronic Library*, 24(2), 160–173. doi:10.1108/02640470610660350

ICT skills readiness for the emerging global digital economy among small business in developing countries. (2007). *Library Hi Tech, 25*(2), 231-245.

Information haves and have nots. (2007). *Public Policy Alternatives Weekly E-Governance & Development Insights, 1*(1).

International Telecommunication Union. (n.d.). Retrieved from http://www.itu.int/ITU-D/ict/statistics.

Internet World State. (n.d.). Retrieved from http://www.internetworldstats.com.

Jensen, M. (2002). *African Internet Status: a report*. Retrieved from http://www.sn.apc.org/africa/afstat.htm

Jianzhong, W. (2002). `s role in bridging the digital divide: the case of community libraries in shanghai. In 68th IFLA council and general conference* (pp. 18–24). Library.

Klecun, E. (2008). Bridging lost sheep in to the fold: questioning the discourse of the digital divide. *Information Technology & People, 21*(3), 267–272. Retrieved from http://www.emeraldinsight.com/0959-3845.htm. doi:10.1108/09593840810896028

Lim, E. (1999). Human resource development for the information society. *Asian Libraries, 8*(5), 82–100. doi:10.1108/10176749910275975

Mutula, S. M. (2007). Paradigms shifts in information environment: prospects and challenges African libraries. *Library Hi Tech, 25*(3), 396–408. Retrieved from http://www.emeraldinsight.com/0737-8831.htm. doi:10.1108/07378830710820970

Navas-Sabater, D. A. & Juntunen, N. (n.d.). *Telecommunication and information services for the poor: toward a strategy for universal access*. Washington, DC: The World Bank.

Noh, Y. H., & Yoo, K. (2008). Internet, inequality and growth. *Journal of Policy Modeling, 30*, 1005–1016. Retrieved from http://www.Sciencedirect.com. doi:10.1016/j.jpolmod.2007.06.016

Norris, P. (2000). *The world wide digital divide: information poverty, the internet and development*. Retrieved from http://ksghome.harvard.edu/~pnorris/Acrobat/psa2000dig.pdf

Norris, P. (2001). *Digital divide: civic engagement, information poverty and the internet worldwide*. Cambridge, UK: Cambridge University Press.

Omekwu, C. O. (2006). Managing information and technology: critical roles for librarians in developing countries. *The Electronic Library, 24*(6), 847–863. doi:10.1108/02640470610714260

Presidential Committee on Information Literacy. *Final Report.* (n.d.). Retrieved May 25, 2007, from http://www.ala.org/ala/acrl/acrlpubs/whitepapers/presidential.htm

QCA. (2007). *Skill for life ICT curriculum,* Retrieved from http://www.qca.org.uk/libraryAssets/media/skill_for_life_ict_curriculum_jan07.pdf

Saheb, T. (2005). ICT education and digital divide in developing countries. *Global Media Journal, 4*(7). Retrieved from http://lass.calumet.purdue.edu/cca/gmj/fa05/gmj-fa05-saheb.htm

Scrutiny of Acts and Regulations Committee. (2005). Retrieved April 28, 2007, from http://www.parliament.vic.gov.au/sarc/E-Democracy/Final_Report/Glossary.htm

Sharma, R., & Azura, I. M. (2005). Bridging the digital divide in Asia- challenges and solutions. *International Journal of Technology. Knowledge and Society, 1*(3), 15–30.

Steinmueller, W. (2001). ICTs and the possibilities for leapfrogging by developing countries. *International Labour Review, 140*(2), 193–210. doi:10.1111/j.1564-913X.2001.tb00220.x

The digital divide. (n.d.). Retrieved February 19, 2009, from http://dl.filmaust.com.au/module/113/

The knowledge explosion and the knowledge divide. (2001). Retrieved from http://hdr.undp.org/en/reports/global/hdr2001/papers/sagasti-1-1.pdf

The new digital divide, media literacy, broadening participation? Inclusive education? Digital equity. (2007). Retrieved from http://thornburgcenter.blogspot.com/2007/06/new-digital-divide-media-literacy.html

UNESCO. (2005). *From the information society to knowledge society.* Paris: UNESCO Publishing.

World Information Society Report. (2007). Retrieved February 19, 2009, from http://ITU.int/osg/spu/publications/world information society/2007/WISR07-chapter4.pdf

Chapter 17
Digital Divide and Economic Wealth:
Evidence from Asia–Pacific Countries

Shampa Paul
Institute of Economic Growth, New Delhi, India

ABSTRACT

This chapter aims at identifying and analyzing the factors that have resulted in a digital divide in Asia-Pacific countries. There are several factors that can be used as proxy of the digital divide. In this study, Internet density has been used as a proxy of the digital divide along with other variables such as gross domestic product, computer density, telephone density, & information and communication technology expenditure. Using data from 1995 to 2007 for 10 countries, the study finds evidence of the pivotal role played by communication infrastructure in the diffusion of ICTs, and there is also a high correlation between Internet usage and telephone density. It appears that GDP has been a major factor influencing varying degrees of the diffusion of ICTs and the consequent digital divide.

INTRODUCTION

The traditional societies are realising the relevance of knowledge in everyday life, and due to which are getting converted into knowledge driven societies. Therefore, knowledge–driven societies are giving rise to knowledge–driven economies. This is a global phenomenon, hence nations that have less access to knowledge are less privileged whereas nations with better access to knowledge become privileged and advanced. It is now the aim of all the nations whether rich or poor, to minimise or bridge the digital divide by introducing information and communication technologies (ICTs) in different activities. Libraries and public institutions are playing a major role in this initiative.

The importance of ICTs as powerful tool for socio-economic development is being widely acknowledged not only by large countries but also

DOI: 10.4018/978-1-61520-767-1.ch017

by small ones as well. However, existing gaps in ICT skills both in developed and developing countries are to be addressed so that ICT is effectively used as engine of economic development. Globally, the Internet has wide spread use as ICT tool. It provides a powerful means of accessing information. According to Grace et al., 2004, in developing countries the Internet offers a cheap and versatile mechanism of connecting users with a global repository of information. The social significance of Internet in broadening and enhancing access to information worldwide has been recognized. It offers promise in delivery of basic services like education and health information to far reaching regions.

The diffusion of Internet though rapid has been highly asymmetrical among different countries. The advanced societies in the world have witnessed the fastest penetration of ICTs. The term 'Digital Divide' is used to describe the divide or gap of digital information between individuals, institutions and countries owing to different socio-economic levels in terms of opportunities available to access ICTs and the Internet. The diffusion and production of ICTs that has led to the digital divide are unevenly distributed among the nations (Mansell and When, 1998).

Although Chowdhury, 2004 argues that improved access to ICT and Internet are not the only factors for reducing the digital divide. But one should not forget that the availability of proper ICT tools is necessary to overcome the gap. It is necessary to look at some of the following factors which separately or in combination help to minimize this divide.

1. Economics: much of the information is only available from the Internet and so it is the libraries, archives and other public institutions to come forward to increase accessibility.
2. Information: with good technology and adequate authorized access, it is easy to find the required information for a particular task.

3. Technology: the information we are talking about is computer maintained and computer accessed, in particular it is accessed across the Internet and through the World Wide Web. If a person or organization does not have a computer, network access, reliable access, high speed access, then finding and using this information ranges from impossible to difficult.
4. Tools: proper access tools like protocols, formats, standards are necessary so as to make the operation of bridging the gap becomes easy.

Thus, phrase 'digital divide' refers to the unequal and disproportionate pace of development in societies in having access to digital infrastructure and services. The revolutionary changes in computer and telecommunication networks along with the global explosion in knowledge have created unprecedented changes in the flow of trade, finance, information, knowledge and its management in and among nations, which has undoubtedly affected the information science area. Key variables such as grant, skilled manpower, infrastructure, quality software etc, are important, as they are likely to have a differential impact on the consequences of accessing information and knowledge (Paul, 2002).

As is well known, per capita income between the rich and poor countries is widely divergent. Although there is little clear-cut association of ICTs and income levels, studies in United States show that ICT adoption leads to equality among social classes and races (DiMaggio et. al., 2001). Asian countries have generally experienced a lower rate of ICT adoption in comparison to non-Asian countries. The ICT diffusion in these countries is low relative to their level of potential as predicted on the basis of their current level of GDP per capita (Lal & Paul, 2004).

Bridges.org (2002) provides the statistics for regional distribution of Internet users, showing the penetration of Internet in Asia-Pacific countries at only 28.9% (167.86 million) as compared to the World total of 100% (580.78 million). The Asia-Pacific countries have been following different paths of economic development for the last two decades, due to which the diffusion of computer usage is uneven. As can be seen in Fig. 1, the density of Internet users (per 100 people) is showing an increasing trend across the countries.

The statistics indicates the digital gap, far from narrowing, seems to be widening. This gives a cause for concern given that the developing countries are starting from a lower level and might therefore be expected to grow at a faster rate but the picture seems to be different.

Their study intends to analyse the factors that have influenced the digital divide in the Asia-Pacific countries, using Internet usage as a proxy of digital divide. Internet users are considered in this study due to the fact that inequality of Internet access, knowledge of search strategies, and the extent of Internet use to evaluate the quality of information have increased. Needless to add, computers are required for Internet access and for a wide range of tasks from commonplace tasks like word processing, data entry and electronic mail to high-end usage.

The organisation of the remainder of the paper is as follows: Data sources and methodology are presented in Section 2. Hypotheses are formulated in Section 3 and Section 4 discusses the results.

The findings of the study are summarised in Section 5.

DATA SOURCES AND METHODOLOGY

This study uses data of 10 countries from 1995 to 2007. The variables that have been used in the analysis are: GDP per capita, Internet users, computer density, ICT expenditure, and telephone density. The ICT expenditure data availability is only for period 2000 to 2006. The annual data for all the variables have been taken from the World Development Indicators (2008). We are presenting data for 2003 in Table 1 because data for PC density for Japan are missing from 2004 onward. In order to make proper comparison we are presenting data for 2003 for all the countries in Table 1.

It can be seen from Table 1 that high-income countries show greater diffusion of Internet. Although with the exception of Korea which, though a high income country, does not show high ICT expenditure, there seems to being a high correlation between national income (GDP) of a country and penetration of Internet.

Figure 1. Internet density in Asia-Pacific countries

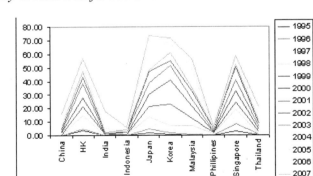

Table 1. Sample data used in the study

Country	GDP(USD)	Per capita ICT expenditure (USD)	Internet users (per 100)	Computer density (per100)	Telephone density (per 100)
China	1209.00	94.10	6.17	3.91	20.39
Hong Kong	26361.58	1227.19	47.50	55.69	56.28
India	511.54	21.42	1.74	0.88	3.95
Indonesia	872.36	33.59	3.76	1.29	3.75
Japan	37227.27	2175.78	48.26	40.72	47.15
Korea	12245.18	984.72	61.07	50.68	52.51
Malaysia	4033.07	314.93	34.95	16.98	18.49
Philippines	1042.96	54.55	4.93	3.51	4.11
Singapore	23619.25	1766.71	51.89	61.73	45.92
Thailand	2277.30	127.33	9.71	4.87	10.68

Data source: World Development Indicators (2008); data pertains to year 2003

HYPOTHESES

It is expected that the driving force behind the diffusion of the Internet is the quality of telecommunication infrastructure available in a country. In addition to this, PC density, ICT infrastructure, and the economic wealth of a country also play an important role. In this study the Internet users are taken in terms of per 100 persons. Although the Internet revolution has gripped the whole world, the accessibility of Internet depends on the infrastructure available. In developing economies, Internet access from homes is not a common phenomenon. Users have to access the Internet from common service providers such as kiosks, cyber cafes etc. The penetration of Internet users along with compound annual growth rate (CAGR) of Asia-Pacific countries is presented in Table 2.

As seen from Table 2, the Internet penetration has not been even throughout the region. The increase is more prominent in China @94% whereas Singapore and Hong Kong have grown only @25% during the sample period. India has shown a growth rate of 70% in this period. The remainder of this section presents the hypotheses regarding the variables used in the analysis.

Gross Domestic Product (GDP)

GDP per capita represents the economic wealth of a country in this study. This has been a major factor in the production and diffusion of new technologies. ICTs in general and the Internet in particular are very different from earlier technological innovations. The most distinctive character of the new technologies is that they are knowledge rather than capital intensive (Oyeyinka and Lal 2005). GDP is a prerequisite for the penetration of Internet. Individual income and institutional financial capital are expected to influence the growth of Internet. It is hypothesized that countries with more economic wealth are expected to experience a higher rate of Internet diffusion. It has been found that the growth in Internet hosts per capita is influenced by income per capita and Internet access cost of that country (Kiiski and Pohjola 2002).

Telephone Density (TELE)

The variable has been defined as the number of telephone mainlines per 100 inhabitants. In the 1980s, the use of computers was limited to in-house data processing. As a result, communication

Table 2. Internet users in Asia-Pacific countries

Year	China	Hong Kong	India	Indonesia	Japan	Korea	Malaysia	Philippines	Singapore	Thailand
1995	0.00	3.25	0.03	0.03	1.59	0.81	0.15	0.03	2.84	0.10
1996	0.01	4.66	0.05	0.06	4.37	1.61	0.85	0.06	8.17	0.23
1997	0.03	10.40	0.07	0.19	9.16	3.56	2.31	0.14	13.17	0.64
1998	0.17	14.47	0.14	0.25	13.40	6.70	6.75	1.13	19.10	0.84
1999	0.71	21.19	0.28	0.44	21.37	23.30	12.31	1.46	24.00	2.16
2000	1.78	27.83	0.54	0.92	29.95	40.50	21.38	2.02	32.27	3.79
2001	2.65	38.74	0.68	2.01	38.46	51.49	26.69	2.57	41.08	5.78
2002	4.62	43.31	1.58	2.12	46.47	55.17	32.33	4.40	50.29	7.78
2003	6.17	47.50	1.74	3.76	48.26	61.07	34.95	4.93	51.89	9.71
2004	7.25	51.26	3.24	2.59	62.21	65.68	42.22	5.31	58.12	11.14
2005	8.51	51.76	5.48	3.58	66.75	68.35	48.87	5.46	58.61	11.56
2006	10.44	54.99	10.81	4.74	68.52	70.47	53.57	5.80	59.07	13.34
2007	15.91	57.20	17.80	5.76	73.57	71.75	56.50	6.03	58.84	21.02
CAGR	**94.02**	**25.83**	**70.89**	**53.79**	**32.61**	**44.27**	**52.40**	**53.18**	**24.15**	**51.56**

Data source: World Development Indicators (2008).

technology had no impact on the use of computers. However, in the 1990s, the idea of distributed computing and electronic networks came into existence, leading to the integration of computer and communication technologies. Applications of ICTs can now be seen in almost every domain of activity from manufacturing to education and services. Hence, the use of computers has become dependent on the availability of a national and global communication infrastructure. Telephone density is part of the telecommunications network since it provides the last mile connectivity to the end users. It is expected that higher telephone density can result in more Internet usage.

Computer Density (COMP)

Computer density is measured as the number of computer users per 100 persons. Since the word 'computer' is almost synonymous to 'personal computer' (PC) in today's world, the terms PC density and computer density have been used interchangeably. Access to Internet in households

is usually through personal computers (PCs), whereas at the institutional level, the Internet is accessible through both the local area networks and PCs. The local area networks consist of PCs and dumb terminals. Although households and kiosks dominate Internet access, the availability of a PC is not a necessary condition for Internet access. Therefore, PC density is expected to emerge as a significant determinant of Internet diffusion.

Information and Communication Technology Expenditure

Information and communication expenditure has been measured in USD as per capita expenditure on ICTs. These new technologies are a fundamental feature of knowledge based economies and are considered to be an important driver of current and future productivity improvements. ICT expenditure is crucial as it diffuses new technologies in the form of IT (information technology) equipment, services, and software. Since this factor plays an important role in estimating the overall

Figure 2. Internet usage and GDP per capita in USD

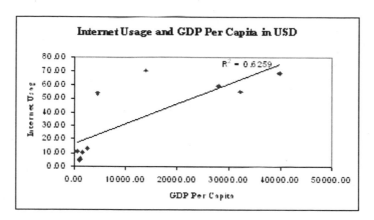

telecommunication infrastructure of a country, it has been considered in this study despite many gaps in the data.

RESULTS

The data on the relationship between Internet users and the other variables have been analysed graphically showing trend lines. The trends are presented in Fig. 2-5. Figure 2 shows the relationship between the density of Internet users and the economic wealth of the countries. The extent to which the income of a country influences Internet use can be explained by R^2 of the trend line between Internet users and GDP, which is 0.62. This indicates that the diffusion of Internet in a

country depends upon its economic wealth. Also from the correlation matrix of China and Japan it is evident that the income of a country strongly influences the telecommunication infrastructure. In developing regions like India and Thailand, the picture is the same.

Likewise, Fig. 3 presents the relationship between Internet use and telephone density. The value of R^2 of the trend line between these variables is 0.69. This proves the high dependence of Internet users on the telephone mainlines in a country. It also indicates that the telephone density is more important than GDP in explaining the Internet diffusion in the sample countries.

The Fig 4 shows the relationship between Internet usage and PC density. The value of R^2 at 0.89 is quite high. This confirms the hypothesis

Figure 3. Internet users and telephone density

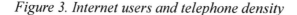
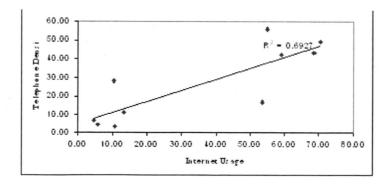

Figure 4. Internet users and PC density (2003)

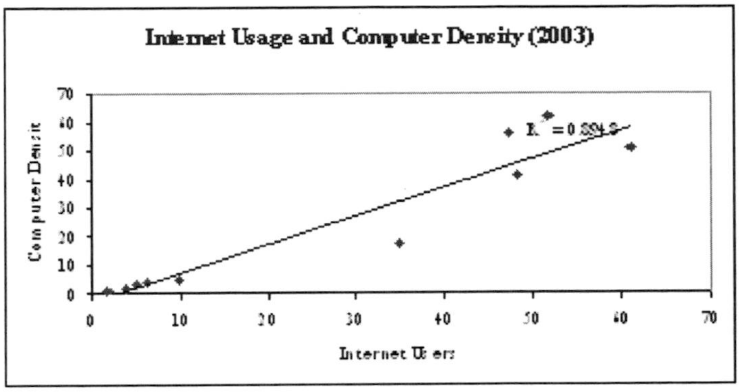

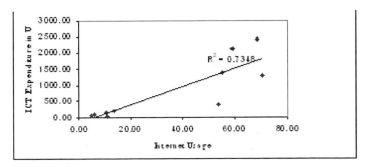

that Internet usage depends upon the computer density of a country. Due to non availability of PC Density data for Japan after 2003, data for all the countries pertaining to 2003 are considered for the analysis presented in Fig. 4.

From Fig. 5 it is clear that Internet usage depends on the respective countries, ICT expenditure. With increase in ICT expenditure, the number of Internet users will increase.

In order to obtain a more robust relationship the correlation matrices of all the countries have been calculated. These are presented in the Appendices I to X.

The correlation matrix of China, India, Indonesia and Korea shows more than 90% dependence of Internet usage on telephone density, whereas in Japan and Malaysia Internet diffusion depends more on PC density. The emergence of telephone density as a highly significant variable supports the hypothesis that the telecommunication infrastructure plays a crucial role in the digital divide.

SUMMARY AND CONCLUSION

The study aims at identifying and analysing the factors that have resulted in the digital divide in the Asia-Pacific countries. The country-specific variables that have been used in the analysis are: Computer density, GDP per capita, telephone density, and per capita information and communication expenditure. The data have been collected from the World Development Indicators (2008). The period taken for data analysis is 1995 to 2000,

Figure 5. The relationship between Internet users and ICT expenditure in USD has been shown in Fig. 5.

due to the non-availability of information for all the countries for subsequent years. The findings of the study suggest that the density of Internet users and PCs influences the Internet diffusion. The findings are in accordance with expectations.

The implications that have emerged from the study are two-fold: First, there is a need to reorient national telecommunication and economic policies to promote ICTs, which in turn will boost the economic growth. Second, the governments of the developing countries need to encourage the use of PCs. Greater use of computers in academic institutions, government organizations and small business enterprises will encourage their diffusion through the society. This will further reduce the digital divide.

ACKNOWLEDGMENT

My special thanks are due to Dr. K. Lal, UNU, Maastricht, Netherlands whose constant help and comments have improved the quality of the paper to a considerable extent.

REFERENCES

Balasubramanian, S., Valarmathi, C., & Narmatha, T. (2002). Digital Divide: Problems and Solutions. In Kaul, H. K., & Baby, M. D. (Eds.), *Library and Information Networking NACLIN 2002* (pp. 369–374). New Delhi: DELNET.

Bridges.org. (2002). *Spanning the digital divide*. Retrieved May 24, 2006, from http://www.bridges.org

Chowdhury, G. G. (2004). Access to Information in Digital Libraries: Users and Digital Divide. In *International Conference on Digital Libraries: Knowledge Creation, Preservation, Access and Management, Conference Proceedings* (pp. 56-64). New Delhi: TERI.

DiMaggio, P., Hargittai, E., Neuman, W. R., & Robinson, J. P. (2001). Social implications of the Internet. *Annual Review of Sociology, 27*, 307–336. doi:10.1146/annurev.soc.27.1.307

Grace, J., Kenny, C., & Zhen-Wei Qiang, C. (2004). Information and Communication Technologies and Broad-Based Development: A partial Review of the Evidence. *World Bank Working Paper, No. 12.*

Kaul, S. (2002). Digital Divide: Are we experiencing the era of technological 'haves' and 'have nots? In Kaul, H. K., & Rama Reddy, E. (Eds.), *Library and Information Networking NACLIN 2001* (pp. 345–358). New Delhi: DELNET.

Kiiski, S., & Pohjola, M. (2002). Cross-country Diffusion of the Internet. *Information Economics and Policy, 14*(2), 297–310. doi:10.1016/S0167-6245(01)00071-3

Lal, K., & Paul, S. (2004). Digital divide and international orientation: Evidence from Asia Pacific countries. *The ICFAI journal of Applied Economics, 3*(2), 31-41.

Mansell, R., & Uta, W. (Eds.). (1998). *Knowledge Societies: Information Technology for Sustainable Development.*Oxford, UK: Oxford University Press.

Oyelaran-Oyeyinka, B., & Lal, K. (2005). Internet diffusion in sub-Saharan Africa: A cross-country analysis. *Telecommunications Policy, 29*, 507–527. doi:10.1016/j.telpol.2005.05.002

Paul, J. (2002). Narrowing the digital divide: initiatives undertaken by the Association of South-East Asian Nations (ASEAN). *Electronic Library and Information Systems, 36*(1), 13–22. doi:10.1108/00330330210426085

(2008). *World Development Indicators*. Washington, DC: World Bank.

APPENDIX

Appendix: Table 3. Correlation matrix (China)

	COMP	GDP	ICT	INTERNET	TELE
COMP	1.00				
GDP	0.98	1.00			
ICT	0.98	0.98	1.00		
INTERNET	0.99	0.99	0.97	1.00	
TELE	0.98	0.97	0.98	0.98	1.00

Appendix: Table 4. Correlation matrix (Hong Kong)

	COMP	GDP	ICT	INTERNET	TELE
COMP	1.00				
GDP	0.86	1.00			
ICT	-0.80	-0.61	1.00		
INTERNET	0.92	0.79	-0.75	1.00	
TELE	-0.93	-0.71	0.79	-0.95	1.00

Appendix: Table 5. Correlation matrix (India)

	COMP	GDP	ICT	INTERNET	TELE
COMP	1.00				
GDP	0.95	1.00			
ICT	0.93	0.98	1.00		
INTERNET	0.99	0.95	0.93	1.00	
TELE	0.22	0.46	0.49	0.20	1.00

Appendix: Table 6. Correlation matrix (Indonesia)

	COMP	GDP	ICT	INTERNET	TELE
COMP	1.00				
GDP	0.94	1.00			
ICT	0.96	0.99	1.00		
INTERNET	0.87	0.89	0.87	1.00	
TELE	0.92	0.96	0.95	0.79	1.00

Appendix: Table 7. Correlation matrix (Japan) continued.

	COMP	GDP	ICT	INTERNET	TELE
COMP	1.00				
GDP	0.69	1.00			
ICT	-0.98	-0.58	1.00		
INTERNET	0.98	0.59	-0.98	1.00	
TELE	-0.99	-0.75	0.95	-0.97	1.00

Appendix: Table 8. Correlation matrix (Korea)

	COMP	GDP	ICT	INTERNET	TELE
COMP	1.00				
GDP	0.88	1.00			
ICT	0.75	0.95	1.00		
INTERNET	0.97	0.95	0.88	1.00	
TELE	-0.80	-0.91	-0.92	-0.91	1.00

Appendix: Table 9. Correlation matrix (Malaysia)

	COMP	GDP	ICT	INTERNET	TELE
COMP	1.00				
GDP	0.93	1.00			
ICT	0.87	0.98	1.00		
INTERNET	0.99	0.95	0.90	1.00	
TELE	-0.98	-0.97	-0.95	-0.98	1.00

Appendix: Table 10. Correlation matrix (Philippines)

	COMP	GDP	ICT	INTERNET	TELE
COMP	1.00				
GDP	0.98	1.00			
ICT	0.99	0.97	1.00		
INTERNET	0.84	0.86	0.85	1.00	
TELE	0.03	-0.08	0.06	-0.01	1.00

Appendix: Table 11. Correlation matrix (Singapore)

	COMP	GDP	ICT	INTERNET	TELE
COMP	1.00				
GDP	0.91	1.00			
ICT	-0.18	0.16	1.00		
INTERNET	0.94	0.75	-0.35	1.00	
TELE	-0.97	-0.92	0.06	-0.91	1.00

Appendix: Table 12. Correlation matrix (Thailand)

	COMP	GDP	ICT	INTERNET	TELE
COMP	1.00				
GDP	0.99	1.00			
ICT	0.96	0.97	1.00		
INTERNET	0.95	0.96	0.91	1.00	
TELE	0.89	0.88	0.79	0.96	1.00

Compilation of References

(2003). Western States Digital Standards Group. Accessed March 2005 at http://www.cdpheritage.org/digital/scanning/documents/WSDIBP_v1.pdf.

(2008). World Development Indicators. Washington, DC: World Bank.

Alliance for Permanent Access. (n.d.). Retrieved from http://www.alliancepermanentaccess.org/

Abdul Kalam, A. P. J. (2004). Inaugural Speech, "Digital Library and its Multidimensions." In *International Conference on Digital Libraries (ICDL-2004),* 24-27 February 2004, New Delhi.

Abdul Kalam, A.P.J. (2005). *Address to the Nation by the President of India.* Delivered on the eve of 56th India's Republic Day – 2005.

Abels, E. (1996).The email reference interview: electronic mail library queries. *RQ, 35*(3), 345-58.

Abram, S. (2005). Web 2.0 — huh?! library 2.0, librarian 2.0. *Information Outlook, 9*(12), 44–46.

Acharya, S. S. (2004). Sustainable Agriculture and Rural Livelihoods. In Sundaram, K. V., Moni, M., & Jha, M. M. (Eds.), *Natural Resources management and Livelihood security: Survival Strategies and Sustainable Policies.* Delhi: Concept Publishing Company.

Adobe Systems Inc. (1992). *TIFF Revision 6.0.* Retrieved March 2005, from

Adobe Systems Inc. (2005). *Adobe PDF.* Retrieved March 2005, from and Information Resources. Retrieved March 2005, from Archives. Retrieved March 2005, from at http://www.tasi.ac.uk/advice/creating/quality.html

Agarwal, P. K. (1999). India's national internet backbone. *Communications of the ACM, 42*(6), 53–58. doi:10.1145/303849.303862

Agnew, G. (2008). *Digital Rights Management: A Librarian's Guide to Technology and Practice.* Oxford: Chandos.

Ahmad, R. (2002, December). Forging a Sustainable Development Model: The Malaysian way. *Development, 45*(4), 74–79. doi:10.1057/palgrave.development.1110409

Ahsanullah, A. (2002). *Information Technology Services for Rural Communities of Developing Countries toward poverty Alleviation.* Dhaka: Faruque & Aulad Hassain.

Ahuja, A. (1996). Chaining the Unchained Books: Copyright as an Infringement on the Philosophy of Library Science. *DESIDOC Bulletin of Information Technology, 16*(6), 5–10.

Alemneh, D. (n.d.). *Metadata Quality Assessment: A Phased Approach to Ensuring Long-term Access to Digital Resources.* Retrieved from http://www.asist.org/Conferences/AM09/posters/80.pdf

Alexander, B. (2006, March/April). Web 2.0: A new wave of innovation for teaching and learning. *EDUCAUSE Review, 41*(2), 32–44.

Alextbox, J. (2006). *Digital divide: The three stages.* Retrieved May 4, 2008, from http://www.useit.com/alertbox

Alikhan, S., & Mashelkar, R. (2004). *Intellectual Property Rights and Competetive Strategies in the 21ˢᵗ Strategies.* The Hague: Kluwer Law International.

Al-Khalifa, H. S., & Davis, H. C. (2006). Harnessing the wisdom of crowds: how to semantically annotate Web resource using folksonomies. In *Proceedings of IADIS Web Applications and Research 2006 (WAR2006).* Retrieved from http://eprints.ecs.soton.ac.uk/13158/

Ambati, V., Balakrishnan, N., Reddy, R., Pratha, L., & Jawahar, C. V. (2006). The Digital Library of India project: process, policies and architecture. In *Proceedings of the International Conference on Digital Libraries*, New Delhi, December 5 - 8, 2006.

American Library Association. (1989). *Final Report, Presidential Committee on Information Literacy.* Retrieved from http://www.ala.org/acrl/nili/ilit1st.html

Amsen, E. (2006). Who Benefits from Science Blogging? *Hypothesis Journal, 4*(2).

Ananda, T. B., & Reddy, R. B. (1996). Copyright in the Information Age: Librarian's Viewpoint. *DESIDOC Bulletin of Information Technology, 16*(6), 17–19.

Anderson, C. (2006). *The Long Tail: How endless choice is creating unlimited demand.* London: Random House Business Books.

Anderson, J. (2002). The New-Look PADI: The National Library of Australia's Subject Gateway. *Gateways.* Retrieved from http://www.nla.gov.au/pub/gateways/archive/60/p20a01.html

Aqili, V. I. (2008). Bridging the digital divide: The role of librarians and information professional in the third millennium. *The Electronic Library, 26*(2), 226–237. Retrieved from http://www.emeraldinsight.com/0264-0437.htm. doi:10.1108/02640470810864118

Arms, W. (2000). *Digital Libraries.* Cambridge, MA: MIT Press.

Arms, W. Y. (1995 July). Key concepts in the architecture of the digital library. *D-lib Magazine.*

Arms, W. Y. (2000). Automated digital libraries: how effectively can computers be used for the skilled tasks of professional librarianship? *D-Lib Magazine, 6*(7/8). Retrieved from http://www.dlib.org/dlib/july00/arms/07arms.html. doi:10.1045/july2000-arms

Arms, W. Y. (2001). *Digital libraries.* Cambridge, MA: MIT Press.

Arms, W. Y., Blanchi, C., & Overly, E. A. (1997). An Architecture for information in Digital libraries. *D-Lib Magazine, 3*(2). Retrieved April 28, 2009, from http://www.dlib.org/dlib/february97/cnri/02arms1.html

Art Museum Image Consortium. (n.d.). Retrieved from http://www.amico.org/

Arunachalam, S. (2002). *ICT-enabled knowledge centers for the rural poor – a success story from India.* Retrieved February 4, 2009, from http://www.utsc.utoronto.ca/~chan/istb01/readings/ICTenabledknowledge.pdf

Ashlin, A., & Ladle, R. (2006). Environmental Science Adrift in the Blogosphere. *Science, 312*(5771), 201. doi:10.1126/science.1124197

Asian Development Bank Institute. (2004). *Proceedings of the Regional Workshop on Building e-Community Centres for Rural Development*, Bali/Indonesia.

Asia-Pacific Human Development Report. (2008). Retrieved from http://hdr.undp.org/en/reports/regional reports /featured regional report 2008/RHDR_full.pdf

Association of Research Libraries. (n.d.). *Definition and purpose of digital libraries.* Retrieved June 5, 2009, from http://sunsiteberkeley.edu/ARL/definition.html

Atkinson, R. J. (1997). Towards a more secure internet. *IEEE Computers, 30*(1), 57–61.

Baker, D., & Evans, W. (2008). *Digital Library Economics: Digital library economics: An academic perspective.* Oxford, UK: Chandos Publishing.

Balakrishnan, N. (2005). Universal Digital Library – Future Research Directions. *Journal of Zhejiang University. Science, 6A*(11), 1204–1205. doi:10.1631/jzus.2005.A1204

Balakrishnan, N., Reddy, R., Ganapathiraju, M., & Ambati, V. (2006). Digital Library of India: a testbed for Indian language research. *TCDL Bulletin, 3*(1).

Balasubramanian, S., Valarmathi, C., & Narmatha, T. (2002). Digital Divide: Problems and Solutions. In Kaul, H. K., & Baby, M. D. (Eds.), *Library and Information Networking NACLIN 2002* (pp. 369–374). New Delhi: DELNET.

Bank, W. (2002). *Information and communication technologies: a world bank group strategy*. Washington, DC: The World Bank Group.

Bar-Ilan, J. (2007). The use of Weblogs (blogs) by librarians and libraries to disseminate information. *Information Research, 12*, Paper 323. Retrieved October 17, 2008, from http://InformationR.net/ir/12-4/paper323.html

Bascom, B. B., & Melinda, G. F. (2001, March 5). *Libraries are connection millions to the internet*. Retrieved from http://www.digitaldivide.net/articles/view.php?ArticleID

Basu, S. (2006). *E-Government and developing countries: role of technology and law*. Retrieved from http://www.digital divide.net/articles/view.php?article ID=601

Bawden, D. (2001). Information and digital literacies: a review of concepts. *The Journal of Documentation, 57*(2), 218–259. Retrieved from http://gti1.edu.um.es:8080/jgomez/hei/intranet/bawden.pdf. doi:10.1108/EUM0000000007083

Bawden, D., & Robinson, L. (2001). Training for information literacy: diverse approaches. In Graham, C. (Ed.), *Online Information 2001: Proceedings* (pp. 87–90). Oxford: Learned Information.

Bearman, D. (n.d.). *Issues facing the Art Museum Image Consortium*. Retrieved from http://www.mcn.edu/conference/MCN98/sessions_thursday.html

Beer, D., & Roger, B. (2007). Sociology and of and in Web 2.0: Some Initial Considerations. *Sociological Research Online, 12*(5). Retrieved from http://www.socresonline.org.uk/12/5/17.html.

Bell, S. (2005). Where the Readers Are. *Library Journal*, 8-12. Retrieved February 17, 2009, from http://nrs.harvard.edu/urn-3:hul.eresource:abiinfor

Beresford, P. (2007). Web Curator Tool. *Ariadne*, 50.

Berners-Lee, T. (1998). Realizing the potential of the Web. In Lloyd, P., & Boyle, P. (Eds.), *Web-Weaving*. London: Butterworth-Heinemann.

Berners-Lee, T., Hall, W., Hendler, J., Shadbolt, N., & Weitzner, D. (2006). Creating a science of the Web. *Science, 313*(5788), 769–771. doi:10.1126/science.1126902

Berube, L. (2007). *On the Road Again: The next e-innovations for public libraries?* Retrieved from http://www.bl.uk/about/cooperation/pdf/einnovations.pdf

Besser, H. (1995d). From Internet to Information Super-Highway. In Brook, J., & Boal, I. A. (Eds.), *Resisting the Virtual Life: The Culture and Politics of Information* (pp. 59–70). San Francisco: City Lights.

Bhatnagar, S. (2004). *Universal e-Government and digital divide*. Retrieved from http://www.apdip.net/projects/2004/public-services/presentations/bhatnagar.ppt

Bhatnagar, S., et al. (2009). *M. S. Swaminathan Research Foundation's Information Village Research Project (IVRP), Union Territory of Pondicherry*. Retrieved February 4, 2009, from http://siteresources.worldbank.org/INTEMPOWERMENT/Resources/14654_MSSRF-web.pdf

Bhattacharjee, R. (2002). *Public Libraries Section, Country Report: India*. International Federation of Library Associations and Institutions. Retrieved September 30, 2008, from http://www.ifla.org/VII/s8/annual/cr02-in.htm

Bhattacharya, P. (2004). Advances in digital library initiatives: a developing country perspective. *The International Information & Library Review, 36*(3), 165–175. doi:10.1016/j.iilr.2003.10.008

Bhoovigyan Vikas Foundation. (2002). *International Conference on Sustainable Agriculture, Water Resources Development and Earth Care Policies*. New Delhi (India).

Bill and Melinda Gates Foundation. (2004). *Toward equality of access: the role of public libraries in addressing the digital divide.* Retrieved from http://www.gatesfoundation.org/nr/Downloads/libraries/uslibraries/reports/TowardEqualityof

Boon, S., & Webber, S. (2009). *Information Literacy Blog.* Retrieved February 18, 2008, from http://information-literacy.blogspot.com/

Borgman, C. (2000). *From Gutenberg to the Global Information Infrastructure: Access to information in the networked world.* Cambridge, MA: MIT Press.

Borgman, C. (2003). Personal digital libraries: creating individual spaces for innovation. In *NSF/JISC Post Digital Library Futures Workshop,* June 15-17, Cape Cod, Massachusetts. Retrieved from http://www.sis.pitt.edu/~dlwkshop/paper_borgman.html

Borgman, C. L. (1996). *Social aspects of digital libraries.* Retrieved November 2, 2006, from http://is.gseis.ucla.edu/research/dl/UCLA_DL_Report.html

Borgman, C. L. (1999). What are digital Libraries? Competing Versions. *Information Processing & Management, 35*(3), 227–243.

Boutin, P. (2008). Twitter, Flickr, Facebook Make Blogs Look So 2004. *Wired Magazine.* Retrieved December 3, 2008, from http://www.wired.com/entertainment/theweb/magazine/16-11/st_essay

Brakker, N., & Kujbyshev, L. (1994). Information resources on cultural heritage: some problems of integration. *INSPEL, 33*(4), 199–208.

Breeding, M. (2006). Web 2.0? let's get to web 1.0 first. *Computers in Libraries, 26*(5), 30–33.

Bridges.org. (2002). *Spanning the digital divide.* Retrieved May 24, 2006, from http://www.bridges.org

Bridging the rural digital divide. (n.d.). Retrieved from http://www.hindu.com/op/2005/04/12/stories/2005041200161500.htm

Brookover, S. (2007). Why We Blog. *Library Journal, 132,* 28-31. Retrieved 2/18/2009, from http://nrs.harvard.edu/urn-3:HUL.ejournals:sfx954921392997

Brown, A. (2003). *Digital Preservation Guidance Note 1: Selecting File Formats for Long-*

Bryant, T. (2006). Social Software and academia. *EDUCAUSE Quarterly, 2,* 61–64.

Bundy, A. (2004). One essential direction: information literacy, information technology fluency. *Journal of eLiteracy, 1*(1). Retrieved December 22, 2004 from www.jelit.org/archive/00000006/

Butler, D. (2005, December 1). Science in the web age: Joint efforts. *Nature, 438,* 548–549. doi:10.1038/438548a

Butler, D. (2006, March 14). *The scientific Web as Tim originally envisaged.* Tutorial session on Web 2.0 in Science, Bio-IT world Conference.

Caldwell, T. (2005). Pen a Blog Buster. *Information World Review,* 16-17. Retrieved 2/17/2009, from http://nrs.harvard.edu/urn-3:hul.eresource:abiinfor

Campbell, D. (2000). Australian subject gateways: political and strategic issues. *Online Information Review, 24*(1), 73–77. doi:10.1108/14684520010320266

Campbell, J. D. (1992). Shaking the conceptual foundations of reference: a perspective. *RSR. Reference Services Review, 20*(4), 29–35. doi:10.1108/eb049164

Campbell, J. D. (2000). Clinging to traditional reference services. *Reference and User Services Quarterly, 39*(3), 223–227.

Canadian Heritage Information Network. (2002). *Creating and Managing Digital Content.*

Caplan, P. (2004). Building a digital preservation archive: tales from the front. *The Journal of Information and Knowledge Management Systems, 34*(1), 38–42.

Caplan, P. (2008). *The Preservation Of Digital Materials; Expert Guides To Library Systems And Services.* Chicago, IL: American Library Association.

Carbo, T. (1997). *Mediacy: knowledge and skills to navigate the information highway. Paper present at the Infoethics conference.* Monte Carlo.

Casey, M. (2006a, January 3). Born in the biblioblogosphere. *LibraryCrunch.*, 2006.

Casey, M. (2006b). *LibraryCrunch: bringing you a library 2.0 perspective.*

Casey, M. E., & Savastinuk, L. C. (2006). Library 2.0: Service for the next-generation library. *Library Journal.* Retrieved 2/18/2009, from http://www.libraryjournal.com/article/CA6365200.html

Casey, M. E., & Savastinuk, L. C. (2007). *Library 2.0: A Guide to Participatory Library Service.* Newark, NJ: Information Today, Inc.

Casey, M., & Savastinuk, L. C. (2006). Library 2.0. *Library Journal, 131*(14).

Caslon Analytics. (2007 February). *Moral Rights. Caslon Analytics Intellectual Property.* Braddon, ACT, Australia: Caslon Analytics. Retrieved from http://www.caslon.com.au/ipguide18.htm

CASPAR D1201. *Conceptual Model – Phase 1.* (2007). Retrieved from http://www.casparpreserves.eu/Members/cclrc/Deliverables/caspar-guidelines/at_download/file

Cervone, H. (2001). Making decisions: methods for digital library project teams. *OCLC Systems & Services, 21*(1), 30–35. doi:10.1108/10650750510578127

Chad, K., & Miller, P. (2005). *Do Libraries matter?* Retrieved at March 15, 2009, from http://www.talis.com/downloads/white_paper/DoLibrariesMatter.pdf

Chad, K., & Miller, P. (2005). *Do Libraries Matter? The Rise of Library 2.0.* Retrieved February 19, 2008, from http://www.talis.com/applications/resources/white_papers.shtml

Chapman, S. (2000). Considerations for project management. In Sitts, M. K. (Ed.), *Handbook for digital projects: a management tool for preservation and access* (pp. 31–42). Andover, MA: Northeast Document Conservation Center.

Chen, H. (2000). Introduction to the special topic issue: part 2. *Journal of the American Society for Information Science American Society for Information Science, 51*(4), 213–215. doi:10.1002/(SICI)1097-4571(2000)51:3<213::AID-ASI1>3.0.CO;2-R

Chowdhary, G., & Margariti, S. (2004). Digital reference services: a snapshot of the current practices in Scottish libraries. *Library Review, 53*(1), 50–60. doi:10.1108/00242530410514793

Chowdhary, G., Poulter, A., & McMenemy, D. (2006). Public Library 2.0. *Online Information Review, 30*(4), 454–460.

Chowdhury, G. (2002). Digital libraries and reference services: present and future. *The Journal of Documentation, 58*(3), 258–283. doi:10.1108/00220410210425809

Chowdhury, G. G. (200?). *Digital divide: How can digital libraries bridge the gap?* Retrieved from http://www.cis.strath.ac.uk/research/publications/papers/strath_cis_publication_334.pdf

Chowdhury, G. G. (2004). Access to Information in Digital Libraries: Users and Digital Divide. In *International Conference on Digital Libraries: Knowledge Creation, Preservation, Access and Management, Conference Proceedings* (pp. 56-64). New Delhi: TERI.

Chowdhury, G. G., & Chowdhury, S. (2001a). *Searching CD-ROM and Online Information Sources.* London: Library Association Publishing.

Chowdhury, G. G., & Chowdhury, S. (2001b). *Information Sources and Searching on the World Wide Web.* London: Library Association Publishing.

Chowdhury, G. G., & Chowdhury, S. (2003). *Introduction to Digital Libraries.* London: Facet Publishing.

Chu, H., and Krichel, T. (2003). NEP: current awareness service of the RePEc Digital Library. *D-Lib Magazine, 9*(12). Retrieved

Cleveland, G. (1998). *Digital Libraries: Definitions, Issues and challenges.* Retrieved April 20, 2001, from www.ifla.org/VI/5/op/udtop8/ udtop8.html

Clyde, L. A. (2004). *Weblogs and Libraries.* Oxford, UK: Chandos Publishers, Ltd.

Cohen, S. (2000). My Library: personalized electronic services in the Cornell University Library. *DLibMagazine, 6*(4). Retrieved April 05, 2009, from www.dlib.org/dlib/april00/mistlebauer/04 mistlebauer.html

Coleman, A. (2002). The road ahead for education in digital libraries. *D-Lib Magazine, 8* (7/8). Retrieved June 18, 2009, from http://www.dlib.org/dlib/july02/coleman/07coleman.html

Controller General of Patents. Designs and Trademarks. (n.d.). *Frequently Asked Questions.* Department of Industrial Policy and Promotions, Ministry of Commerce and Industry. Retrieved from http://www.patentoffice.nic.in/

Controller General of Patents. Designs and Trademarks. (n.d.). *Frequently Asked Questions.* Office of the Registrar of Trademarks. Retrieved from http://ipindia.nic.in/tmr_new/default.htm

Cornell University Library. (n.d.). Retrieved from http://www.library.cornell.edu/

Cornish, G. P. (2005). Electronic Information Management and Intellectual Property Rights. *Information Services & Use, 25,* 59–68.

Coulter, P., & Draper, L. (2006). Blogging It into Them: Weblogs in Information Literacy Instruction. *Journal of Library Administration, 45*(1/2), 101–115. doi:10.1300/J111v45n01_06

Council on Library and Information Resource. (2005). *CLIR Publication No. 129.*

Crawford, W. (2006). Library 2.0 and 'Library 2.0.' *Cites and Insights, 6.* Retrieved from http://cites.boisestate.edu/civ6i2.pdf

Cronin, B. (2005). *Dean's Notes: BLOG: see also Bathetically Ludicrous Online Gibberish.* Retrieved February 19, 2008, from http://www.slis.indiana.edu/news/story.php?story_id=958

Crow, B., & Longford, G. (2000). Digital Restructuring: gender, class and citizenship in the information society in Canada. *Citizenship Studies, 4*(2), 207–230. doi:10.1080/13621020050078096

Cruz, J. M. B., Kritchel, T., & Trinidad, J. C. (2003, September). *Organizing current awareness in a large digital library.* Paper presented at the Conference on Users in the Electronic Information Environments, Espoo.

Cunningham A. Metadata Standards in Australia – An Overview. 2005. Presentation at Queensland State Archives March 2005. National Archives of Australia. Creating and Managing Digital Content. 2002. Canadian Heritage Information Network. Accessed March 2005 at http://www.chin.gc.ca/English/Digital_Content

Cushman, M., & Klecun, E. (2006). *How (can) nonusers engage with technology: bridging in the digitally excluded. Social inclusion: Social and Organizational implication for information systems.* New York, NY: Springer.

Cyberspace Law and Policy Centre, University of New South Wales. Retrieved March

Dalsgaard, C. (2006). Social Software: E-learning beyond learning management systems. *European Journal of Open, Distance and E-learning.* Retrieved February 18, 2008, from http://www.eurodl.org/materials/contrib/2006/Christian_Dalsgaard.htm

Das, A. K. (2008). *Open Access to Knowledge and Information: Scholarly Literature and Digital Library Initiatives – the South Asian Scenario.* New Delhi: UNESCO. Retrieved February 1, 2009, from http://dlist.sir.arizona.edu/2281/01/Open%5FAccess%5FBook.pdf

Das, A. K., Dutta, C., & Sen, B. K. (2007). Information Retrieval Features in Indian Digital Libraries: A Critical Appraisal. *OCLC Systems & Services: International Digital Library Perspectives, 23*(1), 92–104. doi:10.1108/10650750710720793

Das, A. K., Sen, B. K., & Dutta, C. (2005). *Digitization of scholarly materials in India for distance and open learners.* Paper presented ICDE International Conference, New Delhi. Retrieved June 15, 2009, from http://openmed.nic.in/1217/01/Anup_Kumar_Das_ICDE_Conference_05.pdf

Das, J. (2003). Copyright in Library. In *Knowledge Management in Special Libraries, XXIV All India Conference of IASLIC,* Dehradun (pp. 255-260).

Data Dictionary—Technical Metadata for Digital Still Images. (2003). National

Day, M. (2003). *Collecting and Preserving the World Wide Web, Version 1.0.* JISC: Bristol, UK. Retrieved from http://www.jisc.ac.uk/uploaded_documents/archiving_feasibility.pdf

De Sàez, E. E. (1993). *Marketing concepts for Libraries and Information services.* London: Library Association Publishing.

Deegan, M., & Tanner, S. (2004). Conversion of primary sources. In S. Schreibman, R. Siemans, & and J. Usworth (Ed.), A companion to digital humanities. Oxford: Blackwell Publishing.

Deegan, M., & Tanner, S. (Eds.), *Digital Preservation.* London: Facet Publishing.

DELOS. (2007). *The DELOS Digital Library Reference Model: Foundations for Digital Libraries, version 0.96.* Retrieved from http://www.delos.info/files/pdf/ReferenceModel/DELOS_DLReferenceModel_096.pdf

Dempsey, L. (2006, April). Libraries and the Long Tail: Some Thoughts about Libraries in a Network Age. *D-Lib Magazine, 12*(4). Retrieved from http://www.dlib.org/dlib/april06/dempsey/04dempsey.html. doi:10.1045/april2006-dempsey

Dempsey, L., et al. (1996). *eLIB Standards Guidelines version 1.0, Feb. 1996.* Retrieved from: http://www.ukoln.ac.uk/services/elib

Department of Information Technology. (n.d.). Retrieved September 30, 2008, from http://mit.gov.in

Devi, P., & Surachand Singh, K. L. (2008). Information needs of the rural people. In Dhawan, S. M. (Eds.), *Shaping the future of special libraries* (pp. 115–124). Delhi: Ane Books.

Digital Curation Centre (DCC). (n.d.). Retrieved from http://www.dcc.ac.uk

Digital divide. (2002). Retrieved from http://www.ala.org/oitp/digital divide

Digital Imaging for Archival Preservation and Online Presentation: Best Practices. (2001). Michigan State University. Retrieved March 2004 at

Digital Library Federation (DLF). (n.d.). Retrieved from www.clir.org/diglib/

Digital Library of India. (n.d.). Retrieved July 1, 2009, from http://dli.iiit.ac.in/

Digital library. (n.d.). LIS Wiki. Retrieved June 05, 2009, from http://liswiki.org/wiki/Digital_library#Definition

Digital Library. (n.d.). Wikipedia: the free encyclopedia. Retrieved June 5, 2009, from http://en.wikipedia.org/wiki/Digital_library

Digital Preservation and Storage. (2004). Technical Advisory Service for Images.

Digital Preservation Europe. (n.d.). Retrieved from http://www.digitalpreservationeurope.eu/

digitisation on demand. National Archives of Australia. Retrieved March 2005, from

Digitization Disposal Policy. *Policy on the authorization of the early disposal of original paper records after digitization.* (2006). Queensland State Archives. Retrieved April 2006, from http://www.archives.qld.gov.au/government/ddp.asp

Dikshit, S. (2000, December 10). Growth in Internet connections lopsided. *The Hindu.* Retrieved from http://www.hindu.com/2000/12/10/stories/0210000t.htm

DiMaggio, P., Hargittai, E., Neuman, W. R., & Robinson, J. P. (2001). Social implications of the Internet. *Annual Review of Sociology, 27,* 307–336. doi:10.1146/annurev.soc.27.1.307

Directory of Open Access Repositories - OpenDOAR. (n.d.). Retrieved June 30, 2009, from http://www.opendoar.org/

DISNIC. (n.d.). Retrieved September, 30, 2008 from http://disnic.nic.in

Dr. S. R. Ranganathan. (n.d.). Retrieved September, 30, 2008 from http://drtc.isibang.ac.in/DRTC/srr/index.html

Drabenstott, K. M. (1994). *Analytical Review of the Library of the Future.* Washington, DC: Council on Library Resources.

DRAMBORA. (n.d.). Retrieved from http://www.repositoryaudit.eu/

drtc.isibang.ac.in/bitstream/1849/232/1/paperY_Malik.pdf (n.d.).

DSpace. (n.d.). Retrieved May 18, 2009, from http://www.dspace.org

Dublin Core: (n.d.). Retrieved September, 30, 2008 from http://dublincore.org/

Ebersole, J. L. (1994). *A Review of Protecting Intellectual Property Rights on the Information Superhighway.* Washington, DC: Information Industry Association.

Eden, B. (2001). Managing and directing a digital project. *Online Information Review, 25*(6), 396–400. doi:10.1108/14684520110412948

Efimova, L. (2004). *Discovering the iceberg of knowledge work: A weblog case.* Paper presented at the OKLC 2004. Retrieved January 25, 2008, from https://doc.telin.nl/dscgi/ds.py/Get/File-34786

E-Government projects will bridge digital divide, spread ICT benefits. (n.d.). Retrieved from http://www.indianexpress.com

E-Government. (2007). Retrieved from http://electronic-government.blogspot.com

Electronic Records Management Guidelines. (2004). Minnesota State Archives. Accessed

Ellis, F. (2000). *Rural Livelihood Diversity in Developing Countries: Analysis, Policy, Methods. School of Development Studies/University of East Anglia.* Oxford, UK: Oxford University Press.

Engineering, Monash University. Retrieved March 2005, from

EPrints. (n.d.). Retrieved May 18, 2009, from http://www.eprints.org

Ergazakis, K., Metaxiotis, K., & Psarras, J. (2006). A coherent framework for building successful KCs in the context of the knowledge-based economy. *Knowledge Management Research & Practice, 4*(1), 56–59.

Euromonitor International. (2007). *The global digital divide.* Retrieved from http://www.euromonitor.com/The_global_digital_divide Key points

European Commission. (1991). *Information Technology Security Evaluation Criteria (ITSEC): Provisional Harmonised Criteria, Version 1.2 Document COM (90) 314.* Brussels: European Commission. Retrieved from http://www.ssi.gouv.fr/site_documents/ITSEC/ITSEC-uk.pdf

Express Computer. (2003, October 6). *Swaminathan using IT for rural development.* Retrieved February 4, 2009, from http://www.expresscomputeronline.com/20031006/indiacomputes01.shtml

FaceBook. (n.d.). Retrieved from http://www.facebook.com/

February 15, 2009, from www.dlib.org/dlib/december03/chu/12chu.html

Ferguson, C. (2000). Shaking the conceptual foundations, too: integrating research and technology support for the next generation of information service. *College & Research Libraries, 61*(4), 300–311.

Ferguson, C., & Bunge, C. (1997). The shape of services to come: values-based reference service for the largely digital library. *College & Research Libraries, 58*(3), 260.

Fernandez-Molina, J. C. (2003). Laws Against the Circumvention of Copyright Technological Protection. *The Journal of Documentation, 59*(1), 41–68. doi:10.1108/00220410310458000

Fialkoff, F. (2005). The Power of Blogs. *Library Journal, 130*(6), 8–8.

Ficther, D. (2003). Why and How to Use Blogs to Promote Your Library's Services. *Information Today, 17.* Retrieved October 17, 2008, from http://www.infotoday.com/mls/nov03/fichter.shtml

File Formats and Compression. 2004. Technical Advisory Service for Images. Accessed March 2005 at http://www.tasi.ac.uk/advice/creating/fformat.html#ff2

Fisher, W. (2003). The electronic resources librarian position: a public services phenomenon. *Library Collections, Acquisitions & Technical Services, 2*(1), 3–17. doi:10.1016/S1464-9055(02)00303-2

Flicker, D. (2000). *Harvard's Library Digital Initiative: Building a First Generation Digital Library Infrastructure.* Retrieved from http://www.dlib.org/dlib/november00/flecker/11flecker.html

Flickr. (n.d.). Retrieved from http://www.flickr.com/

Formats. 2002. *Digital Preservation Coalition.* Retrieved March 2005, from

Foulger, D. (2001). *The cliff and continum: defining the digital divide.* Retrieved April 28, 2008, from http://pages.prodigy.net/davis_foulger/articles/cliffandcontinum.htm

Foundation, B. (2002). *Digital divide basics fact sheet.* Retrieved from http://www.ctcnet.org/ctc/benton/DigitalDivideBasics.doc

Fountain, R. (2005). *Wiki Pedagogy.* Dossiers Pratiques, Profetic. Retrieved from http://www.profetic.org:16080/dossiers/dossier_imprimer.php3?id_rubrique=110

Fox, E., & Urs, S. (2002). Digital libraries. *Annual Review of Information Science & Technology, 36,* 503–589. doi:10.1002/aris.1440360113

Frappr. (2006). Retrieved from http://www.frappr.com/

Frey, F. (2000). *Guides to Quality in Visual Resource Imaging.* Council on Library and.

Frey, J. G. (2006). *Free The Data.* WWW 2006 Panel Discussion, Edinburgh, UK, March 25, 2006. Retrieved from http://eprints.soton.ac.uk/38009/

Ganapathiraju, M., Balakrishnan, M., Balakrishnan, N., & Reddy, R. (2005). Om: One tool for many (Indian) languages. *Journal of Zhejiang University. Science, 6A*(11), 1348–1353. doi:10.1631/jzus.2005.A1348

Garrett, J., & Waters, D. (Eds.). (1996). *Preserving Digital Information, Report of the Task Force on Archiving of Digital Information commissioned.* The Commission on Preservation and Access and The Research Libraries Group. Retrieved from http://www.ifla.org/documents/libraries/net/tfadi-fr.pdf

Gartner. (n.d.). Retrieved September, 30, 2008 from http://www.gartner.com/

Gawrylewski, A. (2008). *Library 2.0: Secrets from science librarians that can save you hours of work.* Retrieved from http://www.the-scientist.com/2008/11/1/82/1/

General Guidelines for Scanning. (1999). *Colorado Digitization Project.* Retrieved March.

Gertz, J. (2000). Selection for preservation in the digital age. *Library Resources & Technical Services, 44*(?), 97–104.

Ghosh, A. (1997). Internet bandwidth: India needs a backbone. Retrieved May 22, 2009, from http://www.ieo.org/backbone.html

Giaretta, D. (2009). Significant Properties, Authenticity, Provenance, Representation Information and OAIS. Paper in iPRES, San Francisco, 5&6 October 2009.

Giaretta, D. (June 2007). The CASPAR Approach to Digital Preservation. *IJDC 2*(1), 2007. Retrieved July 25, 2008, from http://www.ijdc.net/ijdc/article/view/29/32

Gillespie, J., Fair, P., Lawrence, A., & Vaile, D. (2004). Coping when Everything is Digital? *Digital Documents and Issues in Document Retention – White Paper.* Baker & McKenzie 2005 from http://www.bakercyberlawcentre.org/ddr/

Glister, P. (1997). *Digital Literacy.* Hoboken, NJ: John Wiley And Sons Inc.

Glogoff, S. (2005). Instructional Blogging: Promoting Interactivity, Student-Centred Learning, and Peer Input.

Innovate: Journal of Online Education, 1. Retrieved February 19, 2008, from http://innovateonline.info/

Glogoff, S. (2006). The LTC wiki: experiences with integrating a wiki in instruction. In Mader, S. L. (Ed.), *Using Wiki in Education.*

Glossary of Archival and Recordkeeping Terms. 2004. Queensland State Archives. Accessed March 2005 at http://www.archives.qld.gov.au/downloads/GlossaryOfArchivalRKTerms.pdf

Goldsmith, R. E. (1999). The personalized marketplace: beyond the 4Ps. *Marketing Intelligence & Planning, 17*(4), 178–185. doi:10.1108/02634509910275917

Gordon, R. S. (2005). Revenge of the NextGen People. *Library Journal, 130*(9), 78–78.

Gorman, M. (2003). *Enduring Library.* Chicago, IL: American Library Association.

Gorman, M. (2005). Revenge of the Blog People! *Library Journal, 130*(3), 44–44.

Gorman, M. (2007). The wrong path and the right path: the role libraries in access to, and preservation of, cultural heritage. *New Library World, 108*(11-12), 479–489. Retrieved from http://www.emeraldinsight.com/0307-4803.htm. doi:10.1108/03074800710838236

Governments. 2003. Ohio Electronic Records Committee. Retrieved March 2004 at

Grace, J. K., Kenny, C., & Qiang (2004). *Information and communication technologies and broad-based development:a partial review of the evidence.* Washington,DC: The World Bank.

Grace, J., Kenny, C., & Zhen-Wei Qiang, C. (2004). Information and Communication Technologies and Broad-Based Development: A partial Review of the Evidence. *World Bank Working Paper, No. 12.*

Graham, P. S. (1995). Requirements for the Digital Research Library. *College and University Research Libraries, 56*(4), 331–339.

Greenstein, D. (2000). Digital Libraries and Their Challenges. *Library Trends, 49*(Fall), 290–303.

Greenstein, D. (2002, March 15). Digital Library Orchestrating Digital Worlds. *Library Journal.*

Griffiths, J. R., & Brophy, P. (2005). Students searching behavior and the web: use of academic resources and Google. *Library Trends, 53*(4), 539–554.

Gronroos, C. (1994). Relationship marketing: strategic and tactical implications. *Management Decision, 34*(3), 5–14. doi:10.1108/00251749610113613

Grout, C., Purdy, P., & Rymer, J. (2000). *Creating digital resources for the visual arts: standards and good practice.* Oxford: Oxbow Books.

Gudiva, V., Raghavan, V., Grosky, V., & Kasanagottu, R. (1997). Information Retrieval on the World Wide Web. *IEEE Internet Computing, 1*(5), 58–68. doi:10.1109/4236.623969

Guidelines for management, appraisal and preservation of electronic records. (1999).

Guthrie, K., Griffiths, R., & Maron, N. (2008). Sustainability and revenue models for online academic resources. *Ithaka Online.* Retrieved from http://www.ithaka.org/.../sustainability-and-revenue-models-for-online-academic-resources

Guy, M. (2006). Wiki or Won't He? A Tale of Public Sector Wikis. *Ariadne, 49.* Retrieved from http://www.ariadne.ac.uk/issue49/guy/.

Habib, M. (2006). Conceptual model for academic library 2.0. *Michael Habib's weblog on library and information science.* Retrieved from http://mchabib.blogspot.com/2006/06/conceptual-model-for-academic-library.html

Habib, M. (2006). *Toward Academic Library 2.0: Development and Application of a Library 2.0 Methodology.* Unpublished Master's Dissertation, University of North Carolina, Chapel Hill.

Haigh, S. (1996). Optical Character Recognition (OCR) as a Digitization Technology. *Network Notes, 37.*

Hall, H., & Davison, B. (2007). Social software as support in hybrid learning environments: The value of the blog as a tool for reflective learning and peer support.

Library & Information Science Research, 29(2), 163–187. doi:10.1016/j.lisr.2007.04.007

Hancock, A. (2002). Notes on information literacy. In *WSIS Focus - World Summit on the Information Society*. Retrieved from http://www.ideography.co.uk/wsis-focus/positions/hancock_01.html

Harris, B. (1996, December 14). *Geopolitics of Cyberspace*. Retrieved from http://Blakeharris.com/site/the-geopolitics-of-cyberspace/

Harrison, L. E. (n.d.). *Cultural matters*. Retrieved from http://www.arakpmg.com.ph/pttaf/content/culture2%matters.pdf

Harter, S. (1996, September). *What is a digital library? Definitions, content and issues*. Paper presented at KOLISS DL '96: International Conference on Digital Libraries and Information Services for the 21st Century, Seoul.

Hedstrom, M. (2004). Digital preservation: A time bomb for digital libraries. *Computers and the Humanities, 31*(3), 189–202. doi:10.1023/A:1000676723815

Herry, R., & Powell, A. (2006). Digital Repositories Roadmap: looking forward. *UKOLN*. http://www.ukoln.ac.uk/repositories/publications/roadmap-200604/rep-roadmap-v15.pdf

Hijab, N. (2001). *People's initiatives to use IT for development*. Retrieved from http://hdr.undp.org/en/reports/global/hdr2001/papers/hijab-1.pdf

Hilton, D., & Warr, P. (2004). *Unlocking Queensland's Picture Heritage – Picture Queensland Digital Imaging Workshop Course Notes*. State Library of Queensland.

Hofman, J. (2009). *Introducing Copyright: A Plain Language Guide to Copyright in the 21st Century*. Vancouver, Canada: Commonwealth of Learning.

Holley, R. (2004). Developing a digitization framework for your organization. *The Electronic Library, 22*(6), 518–522. doi:10.1108/02640470410570820

Horton, S. (2004). *Web Style Guide 2nd Edition: PNG Graphics*. Retrieved March 2004 at http://www.webstyleguide.com/graphics/pngs.html

How To Fix Bad Scans. (2004). Dixie State College of Utah. Retrieved March 2005, from http://cit.dixie.edu/vt/vt2600/bad_scans.asp

http://chnm.gmu.edu/digitalhistory/links/cached/chapter3/link3.45.CD

http://cit.dixie.edu/vt/vt2600/bad_scans.asp

http://partners.adobe.com/asn/developer/pdfs/tn/TIFF6.pdf

http://www.adobe.com/products/acrobat/adobepdf.html

http://www.ala.org/ala/mgrps/divs/alcts/resources/preserv/01alaprespolicy.cfm

http://www.archives.gov/research_room/arc/arc_info/techguide_raster_june2004.pdf

http://www.archives.qld.gov.au/publications/PublicRecordsAlert/PRA105.pdf

http://www.archives.qld.gov.au/publications/PublicRecordsAlert/PRA205.pdf

http://www.cdpheritage.org/digital/scanning/documents/WSDIBP_v1.pdf

http://www.clir.org/PUBS/archives/ensuring.pdf

http://www.ctie.monash.edu.au/EMERGE/multimedia/JPEG/COMM03.HTM

http://www.dpconline.org/graphics/medfor/media.html

http://www.historicalvoices.org/papers/image_digitization2.pdf

http://www.jasc.com/tutorials/scantip.asp

http://www.library.cornell.edu/preservation/tutorial/quality/quality-01.html

http://www.library.cornell.edu/preservation/tutorial/quality/quality-02.html

http://www.naa.gov.au/Publications/corporate_publications/digitising_TLing.pdf

http://www.naa.gov.au/recordkeeping/dirks/dirksman/dirks.html

http://www.nationalarchives.gov.uk/electronicrecords/advice/pdf/procedures2.pdf

http://www.niso.org/standards/resources/Z39_87_trial_use.pdf

http://www.ohiojunction.net/erc/imagingrevision/revisedimaging2003.html

http://www.pcworld.idg.com.au/index.php/id;11700291 96;fp;2;fpid;1585691688

http://www.prepressure.com/formats/tiff/fileformat.htm

http://www.prov.vic.gov.au/vers/standard/standard

http://www.rlg.org (n.d.).

http://www.slq.qld.gov.au/__data/assets/file/5449/sd1_meta_v1.2.doc

http://www.slq.qld.gov.au/__data/assets/file/6289/How_of_Metadata.doc

http://www.slq.qld.gov.au/__data/assets/word_doc/32645/sd2_current.doc

Huang, J., & Russell, S. (2006). The digital divide and academic achievement. *The Electronic Library, 24*(2), 160–173. doi:10.1108/02640470610660350

Hughes, L. M. (2004). *Digitizing Collections. Strategic Issues for The Information Manager.* London: Facet Publishing.

Hull, R., & Dreher, S. (2001). Into the middle of the thing (with apologies to Horace), developing a system to manage a grant-funded digital collection project. *Collection Management, 26*(3), 29–38. doi:10.1300/J105v26n03_04

Humes, B. (1999). *Understanding Information Literacy.* Retrieved from http://www.ed.gov/pubs/UnderLit/

ICDL. *2004.* (2004). Retrieved September, 30, 2008 from http://www.teriin.org/events/icdl/icdl2004rprt.htm

IConnect Online. (2002). Retrieved February 4, 2009, from http://www.iconnect-online.org/Stories/Story.import4612

ICT skills readiness for the emerging global digital economy among small business in developing countries. (2007). *Library Hi Tech, 25*(2), 231-245.

ILA Preservation policy. (n.d.). Retrieved from 2005 Queensland State Archives.

Image Quality Working Group of ArchivesCom. (1997). *Technical Recommendations for Digital Imaging Projects.* Retrieved March 2005, from http://www.columbia.edu/acis/dl/imagespec.html

Imaging Best Practices. (2003). University of California, Berkley. Retrieved March 2005, from http://www.lib.berkeley.edu/digicoll/bestpractices/image_bp.html

IMLS. *A Framework of Guidance for Building Good Digital Collections.* (n.d.). Retrieved from http://www.imls.gov/pubs/forumframework.htm

Indian Council of Scientific and Industrial Research. (2009). *About TKDL.* Retrieved February 1, 2009, from www.tkdl.res.in/tkdl/langdefault/common/AboutTKDL.asp

Indian Ministry of Communication and Information Technology. (2004). *Digitization of Culture - Background Note for Asia IT Ministers' 2nd Summit, Hyderabad.* Retrieved February 1, 2009, from http://www.asiaitsummit.nic.in/Digitisation.pdf

Indian Ministry of Communication and Information Technology. (2009). *National Digital Libraries Cell: List of Projects and Current Status including Achievements.* Retrieved February 1, 2009, from http://www.mit.gov.in/default.aspx?id=325

Indiana Digital Library. (2004). *Suggested Technical Metadata Elements.* Retrieved March. 2005 from http://www.statelib.lib.in.us/www/isl/diglibin/techmeta.pdf

Indira Gandhi National Centre for Arts. (2002). *National Mission for Manuscripts.* Retrieved September 30, 2008 from http://ignca.nic.in/nl002203.htm

Information haves and have nots. (2007). *Public Policy Alternatives Weekly E-Governance & Development Insights, 1*(1).

Information Resources. Retrieved March 2005, from http://lyra2.rlg.org/visguides/

Information Standards Organization and AIIM International. Retrieved March 2005, from

International Development Research Centre. (n.d.). Retrieved April 2, 2009, from http://www.idrc.ca/en/ev-1-201-1-DO_TOPIC.html

International Telecommunication Union. (n.d.).Retrieved from http://www.itu.int/ITU-D/ict/statistics.

Internet World State. (n.d.). Retrieved from http://www.internetworldstats.com.

Jain, P. K., Jindal, S. K., & Babbar, P. (2006). Digital libraries in India. *The International Information & Library Review, 38*(3), 161–169. doi:10.1016/j.iilr.2006.06.003

Janes, J. (2003). *Introduction to Reference Work in the Digital Age.* New York: Neal-Schuman.

Jantz, R. (2001). Technological discontinuities in the library: Digital projects that illustrate new opportunities for the librarian and the library. *IFLA Journal, 27,* 74–77. doi:10.1177/034003520102700207

Jasc Software Inc. (1999). *Scanning Tips and Techniques.* Retrieved October 2004, from http://www.jasc.com/tutorials/scantip.asp

Jayawardana, C., Hewagamage, K. P., & Hirakawa, M. (2001 a). Personalization tool for active learning in digital libraries. *Journal of Academic Media Librarianship, 8*(1). Retrieved March 28, 2009, from wings.buffalo.edu/publications/mcjrnl/v8nl/active.html

Jayawardana, C., Hewagamage, K. P., & Hirakawa, M. (2001 b). A personalized information environment for digital libraries. *Information Technology and Libraries, 20*(4), 185–197.

Jeevan, V. K. J. (2004). Digital library development: identifying sources of content for developing countries with special reference to India. *The International Information & Library Review, 36,* 185–197. doi:10.1016/j.iilr.2003.10.005

Jensen, M. (2002). *African Internet Status: a report.* Retrieved from http://www.sn.apc.org/africa/afstat.htm

Jeon-Slaughter, H., Herkovic, A. C., & Keller, M. A. (2005). Economics of scientific and biomedical journals: where do scholars stand in the debate of online journal pricing and site license ownership between libraries and publishers? *First Monday.* Retrieved June 28, 2006, from http://www.firstmonday.org/issues/issue10_3/jeon/index.html

Jianzhong, W. (2002). `s role in bridging the digital divide: the case of community libraries in shanghai. In *68th IFLA council and general conference* (pp. 18–24). Library.

JISC Technology and Standards Watch. (2007). *Web 2.0.* Retrieved from http://www.blyberg.net/2006/08/18/go-go-google-gadget/

JISC. (n.d.). Supporting. *Education and Research.* Retrieved from http://www.jisc.ac.uk.

Joint Conference on Digital Libraries. (n.d.). Retrieved September, 30, 2008 from http://www.jcdl.org.

Jose, S. (2007). Adoption of open source digital library software packages: a survey. In M. K. Kumar (Ed.), *Proceedings of CALIBER 2007: 5th International Convention on Automation of Libraries and Research Institutions,* Punjab University, Chandigarh. Retrieved June 6, 2009, from http://eprints.rclis.org/8750/1/Sanjojose.pdf

JPEG Image Coding Standard. (1998). Centre for Telecommunications and Information

JSTOR. (n.d.). Retrieved from http://www.jstor.org

Kalasampada Product Brochure. (n.d.). Retrieved July 2, 2009, from http://ignca.nic.in/kalasampada.pdf

Kalra, H. P. S. (2004). Efforts towards digitization of libraries in India: problems and prospectus. *The International Information & Library Review, 33*(2/3), 197–204.

Kansa, E., & Schultz, J. (2004 1st August). *Perspectives on cultural heritage and intellectual property.* Alexandria Archive Institute.

Kasowitz, A., Bennett, B., & Lankes, R. D. (2000). Quality standards for digital reference consortia. *Reference and User Services Quarterly, 39*(4), 355–364.

Kaul, H. K. (1998). *Library resource sharing and networks*. New Delhi: Virgo.

Kaul, S. (2002). Digital Divide: Are we experiencing the era of technological 'haves'and 'have nots? In Kaul, H. K., & Rama Reddy, E. (Eds.), *Library and Information Networking NACLIN 2001* (pp. 345–358). New Delhi: DELNET.

Kelly, B. (2002). Archiving the UK domain and UK websites. In Proceedings of Web-archiving: managing and archiving online documents and records, London, March 25, 2002.

Kenney, A. R., & Chapman, S. (1996). *Digital imaging for libraries and archives*. Ithaca, NY: Dept. of Preservation and Conservation, Cornell University Library.

Kessler, J. (1996). *Internet digital libraries: The International Dimension*. Boston: Artech House Publishers.

Kiiski, S., & Pohjola, M. (2002). Cross-country Diffusion of the Internet. *Information Economics and Policy, 14*(2), 297–310. doi:10.1016/S0167-6245(01)00071-3

Klang, M. (2008). Open access barriers: an action research. In Avgerou, C., Smith, M. L., & van den Besselaar, P. (Eds.), *Social Dimensions of Information and Communication Technology Policy* (pp. 335–348). doi:10.1007/978-0-387-84822-8_23

Klecun, E. (2008). Bridging lost sheep in to the fold: questioning the discourse of the digital divide. *Information Technology & People, 21*(3), 267–272. Retrieved from http://www.emeraldinsight.com/0959-3845.htm. doi:10.1108/09593840810896028

Koelman, K. J., & Helberger, N. (2000). Protection of Technological Matters. In *Copyright and Electronic Commerce: Legal Aspects of Electronic Copyright Management* (pp. 165–227). The Hague: Kluwer Law International.

Koskinen-Olsson, T. (2001). *Secure IPR Content on the Internet*. Paper presented in the Second International Conference on Electronic Commerce and Intellectual Property, Geneva, 19-21 September. Retrieved from http://www.ecommerce.wipo.int/meetings/2001/conference/presentations/pdf/Koskinen.pdf

Kukulska-Hulme, A. (2006). Learning activities on the move. In *Handheld learning conference*, 12th Oct 2006, London. Podcast retrieved from http://www.handheld-learning.co.uk.

Lagoze, C., Krafft, D., & Payette, S. (2005). What is a digital library anyway? Beyond search and access in the nsdl [Electronic Version]. *D-Lib Magazine*. Retrieved from doi:10.1045/november2005-lagoze

Lakshmana Moorthy, A. (2006). Copyright Issues in Digitization Era. In Moorthy, A. L., & Laxman Rao, N. (Eds.), *Technology Managemnt in Libraries: Festchrift Volume in Honour of Dr. E Rama Reddy*. New Delhi: Allied.

Lakshmana Moorthy, A., & Karisiddappa, C. R. (2000). Copyright in networked environment. In R. Vengan, H.R. Mohan & K.S. Raghavan (Ed.), *CALIBER-2000: Seventh National Convention on Information Services in a Networked Environment* (pp. 4.18--4.30). Ahmedabad, India: INFLIBNET Centre.

Lakshmana Moorthy, A., & Karisiddappa, C. R. (2005). *Copyright Issues in Digital Environment*. Paper presented in the Seminar on Perspectives in Intellectual Property Rights, 13-14th August, 2005, Dharwar (pp. 32-52). Retrieved from http://drtc.isibang.ac.in:8080/xmlui/bitstream/handle/1849/362/Copyright-Hubli.pdf?sequence=1

Lakshmana Moorthy, A., Prahalada Rao, M., & Karisiddappa, C. R. (2001). Intellectual property rights of electronic information in the age of digital convergence. In *NACLIN 2001: Networking of Digital Resources for National Development: Papers of the Fourth National Annual Convention on Library and Information Networking* (pp.583-589). New Delhi, India: DELNET.

Lal, K., & Paul, S. (2004). Digital divide and international orientation: Evidence from Asia Pacific countries. *The ICFAI journal of Applied Economics, 3*(2), 31-41.

Lancaster, F. W. (1978). *Toward Paperless Information Systems*. New York: Academic Press.

Laningham, S. (Ed.). (2006). *Tim Berners-Lee*. Podcast retrieved from http://www-128.ibm.com/developer-works/podcast/

Lankes, D. R. (Eds.). (2000). *Digital Reference Services in the New Millennium; Planning Management and Evaluation*. New York: Neal Schuman Publishers Inc.

Lankes, D., Collins, J. W., & Kasowitz, A. S. (2000). *Digital Reference Service in the New Millennium: Planning, Management, and Evaluation*. New York: Neal-Schuman.

Lankes, R. D. (2004). The digital reference research agenda. *Journal of the American Society for Information Science and Technology, 55*(4), 301–311. doi:10.1002/asi.10374

Leonard, G. D. (1993). *Multiculturalism and library services*. New York: Haworth Press.

Lesk, M. (1997). *Practical Digital Libraries: Books, Bytes, and Bucks*. San Francisco: Morgan Kaufman.

Leurs, L. (2001). *The TIFF file format*. Retrieved March 2005, from

Levy, D. M., & Marshall, C. C. (1995). Going Digital: A Look at Assumptions Underlying Digital Libraries. *Communications of the ACM, 58*(4), 77–84. doi:10.1145/205323.205346

Levy, S., & Stone, B. (2006). The New Wisdom of the Web. *Newsweek*. Retrieved from http://www.msnbc.msn.com/id/12015774/site/newsweek/page/5/

Library 2.0 Theory: Web 2.0 and Its Implications for Libraries. (n.d.). Retrieved from http://www.webology.ir/2006/v3n2/a25.html

Library 2.0. (2009, February 6). Wikipedia, The Free Encyclopedia. Retrieved February 19, 2009, from http://en.wikipedia.org/w/index.php?title=Library_2.0&oldid=268990356

Library of Congress. (1998). *Manuscript Digitization Demonstration Project*.

Library/Research Department. Retrieved March 2005, from

Library/Research Department. Retrieved March 2005, from

LibraryThing. (2006). Retrieved from http://www.librarything.com/

Licklder, J. C. R. (1965). *Libraries of the future*. Cambridge: MIT Press.

Lim, E. (1999). Human resource development for the information society. *Asian Libraries, 8*(5), 82–100. doi:10.1108/10176749910275975

Ling, T. (2002). *Taking it to the streets: why the National Archives of Australia embraced digitisation on demand*. National Archives of Australia. Accessed March 2005 at http://www.naa.gov.au/Publications/corporate_publications/digitising_TLing.pdf

Liu, Y. Q. (2004a). Is the education in digital libraries adequate? *New Library World, 105*(1196/1197), 60–68. doi:10.1108/03074800410515273

Liu, Y. Q. (2004b). Best practices, standards and techniques for digitizing library materials: a snapshot of library digitization practices in the USA. *Online Information Review, 28*(5), 338–345. doi:10.1108/14684520410564262

Liu, Y., Myers, J., Minsker, B., & Futrelle, J. (2007). *Leveraging Web 2.0 technologies in a Cyberenvironmnt for observatory-centric environmental research*. Presented at The 19th Open Grid Forum (OGF19), Jan 29th – Feb 2nd 2007, North Carolina, USA. Retrieved from http://www.semanticgrid.org/OGF/ogf19/Liu.pdf

Loptin, L. (2006). Library digitization projects, issues and guidelines: a survey of literature. *Library Hi Tech, 24*(2), 273–289. doi:10.1108/07378830610669637

Lynch, C. (1994). The Integrity of Digital Information: Mechanics and Definitional Issues. *Journal of the American Society for Information Science American Society for Information Science, 45*(10), 737–744. doi:10.1002/(SICI)1097-4571(199412)45:10<737::AID-ASI4>3.0.CO;2-8

Lynch, C. (2001). The battle to define the future of the book in the digital world. *First Monday, 6*(6). Retrieved March 10, 2009, from http://www.firstmonday.orh/issues/issues6_6/lynch/index.html

Lynch, C. A. (1994). Rethinking the integrity of the scholarly record in the networked information age. *Educom Review, 29*(2). Retrieved April 28, 2009, from http://www.educause.edu/pub/er/review/reviewArticles/29238.html

Lynch, C. A. (2005, July/August). Where Do We Go From Here? The Next Decade for Digital Libraries. *D-Lib Magazine, 11*(7/8).

Lynch, C. A. (2007, June 19). *Networked Information Applications and Future Internet Developments*. Presented at the event "Internet Innovation: Applications and Architectures, An Industry Perspective on Internet Research," in Santa Clara, CA.

LZW Patent Information. 2005. Unisys Corporation. Accessed March 2005 at http://www.unisys.com/about__unisys/lzw/

Making of America. (n.d.). Retrieved from http://quod.lib.umich.edu/m/moagrp/

Malik, M., & Jain, A. K. (2006). Digital Library: Link to E-learning. In *ICT Conference on Digital Learning Environment*, Bangalore, 11–13 January. Retrieved from http://72.14.235.132/search?q=cache:MYRR4Ten8dYJ:https://drtc.isibang.ac.in/bitstream/handle/1849/232/paperY_Malik.pdf%3Fsequence%3D1+This+modular+approach+is+fundamentally+liberating+since+it+permits+libraries+to+think+creatively+about&cd=1&hl=en&ct=clnk

Maness, J. M. (2006). Library 2.0 theory: Web 2.0 and its implications for libraries. *Webology, 3*(2), 25. Retrieved March 10, 2009, from www.webology.ir/2006/v3n2/a25.html

Mansell, R., & Uta, W. (Eds.). (1998). *Knowledge Societies: Information Technology for Sustainable Development*. Oxford, UK: Oxford University Press.

March 2005, from http://tasi.ac.uk/advice/delivering/metadata.html

March 2005, from http://www.mnhs.org/preserve/records/electronicrecords/erguidelinestoc.html

March 2005, from http://www.tasi.ac.uk/advice/creating/fformat.html#ff2

March 2005, from http://www.w3.org/Graphics/PNG/

Marchionini, G., & Fox, E. A. (1999). Progress toward digital libraries: augmentation through integration. *Information Processing & Management, 35*(3), 219–225.

Marchionini, G., & Komlodi, A. (1998). Design of interfaces for information seeking. *Annual Review of Information Science & Technology, 33*, 89–12.

Martin, A. (2004). *What is eLiteracy?* IT Education Unit, University of Glasgow, Glasgow. Retrieved from http://www.iteu.gla.ac.uk/eliteracy/whatiseliteracy.html

Masanes, J. (2006). *Web Archiving*. Berlin: Springer-Verlag. doi:10.1007/978-3-540-46332-0

Maxwell, S., & Franken Berger, T. R. (1992). *Household Food Security: Concepts, Indicators and Measurement*. New York: UNICEF.

Mcclure, C. R. (2002). *Statistics, Measures And Quality Standards For Assessing Digital Reference Library Services: Guidelines And Procedures*. Syracuse, NY and Tallahassee, FL: Syracuse University and Florida State University.

McCray, A. T., & Gallagher, M. E. (2001). Principles for digital library development. *Communications of the ACM, 44*(5), 49–54. doi:10.1145/374308.374339

McDaniel, L. M. (2000, August 18). *Barriers and recommendations to the implementation and use of advanced technology in native American communities*.

Mchombu, K. (1996). *Impact of information technology on rural development: background, methodology and progress*. Retrieved February 4, 2009, from http://archive.idrc.ca/books/focus/783/mchombu.html

Mchombu, K. (1999). *Information provision for rural development 2: measuring the impact of information on rural development*. Retrieved February 4, 2009, from http://idrinfo.idrc.ca/archive/corpdocs/115513/finalrep.99.pdf

Mchombu, K., & Cadbury, N. (2006). *Libraries, literacy and poverty reduction: a key to African development.* Retrieved February 4, 2009, from http://www.bookaid.org/resources/downloads/Libraries_Literacy_Poverty_Reduction.pdf

McKiernan, G. (2001). *LiveRef(Sm), a registry of real-time digital reference services.* Retrieved March 15, 2009, from http://www.public.iastate.edu/~CYBERSTACKS/Liveref.htm

Mehra, B., & Srinivasan, R. (2007). The Library-Community Convergence Framework for Community Action: Libraries as Catalysts of Social Change. *Libri, 57,* 123–139. doi:10.1515/LIBR.2007.123

Mendham, S. (2005). JPEG 2000. *IDG Communications.* Retrieved March 2005, from

Menon, M. (1996). Copyright Problems in Library Services. Guest Editorial. *DESIDOC Bulletin of Information Technology, 16*(6), 3.

Metadata and Digital Images. 2004. Technical Advisory Service for Images. Accessed March 2005 at http://tasi.ac.uk/advice/delivering/metadata.html

Miller, P. (2005). Web 2.0: building the new library. *Ariadane, 45.*

Miller, P. (2005). Web 2.0: Building the new library. *Ariadne, 45.* Retrieved February 19, 2008, from http://www.ariadne.ac.uk/issue45/miller/intro.html

Miller, P. (2005a). *Do libraries matter?: The rise of library 2.0* [White Paper]. Talis. Retrieved from http://www.talis.com/downloads/white_papers/DoLibrariesMatter.pdf

Miller, P. (2005b, October). Web 2.0: building the new library. *Ariadne, 45.* Retrieved from http://www.ariadne.ac.uk/issue45/miller/.

Miller, P. (2006). *Library 2.0 - the challenge of disruptive innovation.* Retrieved February 19, 2008, from http://www.talis.com/applications/resources/white_papers.shtml

Miller, P. (2006, January 31). *Introducing the Library 2.0 gang.* Recorded telephone conference as part of the Talking with Talis podcast series. Retrieved from http://talk.talis.com/archives/2006/02/introducing_the.html

Miller, P. (2006a). Coming together around library 2.0: a focus for discussion and a call to arms. *D-Lib Magazine, 12*(4). Retrieved from http://www.dlib.org/dlib/april06/miller/04miller.html. doi:10.1045/april2006-miller

Miller, P. (2006b). *Library 2.0 - the challenge of distruptive innovation* [White Paper]. Talis. Retrieved from http://www.talis.com/resources/documents/447_Library_2_prf1.pdf

Minerva Europe. (2004). *Cultural Website Quality Principles: Celebrating European cultural diversity by providing access to digital cultural content.* Retrieved from http://www.minervaeurope.org/publications/tenqualityprinciples.htm

Mitchell, E., & Gilbertson, K. (2008). Using Open Source Social Software as Digital Library Interface. *D-Lib Magazine, 14*(3/4). doi:10.1045/march2008-mitchell

Mittal, R., & Mahesh, G. (2008). Digital libraries and repositories in India: an evaluative study. *Program: Electronic Library and Information Systems, 42*(3), 286–302. doi:10.1108/00330330810892695

Moni, M. (2002). *Digital Libraries in Rural India: A digital opportunity for sustainable development.* Invited talk on the National Technology Day, May 11, 2002.

Moni, M. (2002). *Digital Opportunities for Responsive Administration in India: Electronic Administration of Services to Citizens.* Internal Note sent to e-Governance Division of Department of Information Technology, 2002.

Moni, M., & Vijayaditya, N. (1990). *DISNIC – A NICNET Based District Government Informatics Programme in India.* Hyderabad, India: Indian Computing Congress.

Moving Theory into Practice. (2003). *Digital Imaging Tutorial.* Cornell University.

MS Swaminathan Research Foundation. (n.d.). Retrieved April 3, 2009, from http://www.mssrf.org

Muddiman, D. (2001). Open to all? The Public Library and Social exclusion: Executive Summary. *New Library World, 102*(1163/1164), 154–157. doi:10.1108/03074800110390626

Mutula, S. M. (2007). Paradigms shifts in information environment: prospects and challenges African libraries. *Library Hi Tech, 25*(3), 396–408. Retrieved from http://www.emeraldinsight.com/0737-8831.htm. doi:10.1108/07378830710820970

MySpace. (n.d.). Retrieved from http://www.myspace.com/

National Archives and Records Administration (US). (2004). *Technical Guidelines for Digitizing Archival Materials for Electronic Access.* Retrieved March 2005, from

National Archives of Australia. Retrieved December 2005, from

National Informatics Centre. (1998 June). *Project Proposal For Wired Village Project at Warana Nagar, Maharashtra.* Retrieved September, 30, 2008 from http://www.mah.nic.in/warana/

National Science Foundation Cyberinfrastructure Council (NSF). (2007). *Cyberinfrastructure Vision for 21st Century Discovery.* Retrieved from http://www.nsf.gov/pubs/2007/nsf0728/nsf0728.pdf

National Science Foundation. (n.d.). Retrieved from http://www.nsf.gov

Navas-Sabater, D. A. & Juntunen, N. (n.d.).*Telecommunication and information services for the poor: toward a strategy for universal access.* Washington,DC: The World Bank.

Nestor Working Group Trusted Repositories – Certification. (2006). *Catalogue of Criteria for Trusted Digital Repositories.* Retrieved from http://edoc.hu-berlin.de/series/nestor-materialien/8en/PDF/8en.pdf

Nichani, M., & Rajamanickam, V. (2001). Grassroots KM through Blogging. *Elearningpost.com.* Retrieved January 4, 2009, from http://www.elearningpost.com/features/archives/001009.asp

Noerr, P. (2000). *Digital library tool kit.* Sun Microsystems. Retrieved from http://www.sun.com/products-n-solutions/edu/libraries/digitaltoolkit.html

Noerr, P. (2003). *The Digital Library Toolkit* (3rd Ed.). Sun Microsystems, Inc. Retrieved January 16, 2009, from www.sun.com/products-n-solutions/edu/whitepapers/digitaltoolkit.html

Noh, Y. H., & Yoo, K. (2008). Internet, inequality and growth. *Journal of Policy Modeling, 30,* 1005–1016. Retrieved from http://www.Sciencedirect.com. doi:10.1016/j.jpolmod.2007.06.016

Norris, P. (2000). *The world wide digital divide: information poverty, the internet and development.* Retrieved from http://ksghome.harvard.edu/~pnorris/Acrobat/psa2000dig.pdf

Norris, P. (2001). *Digital divide: civic engagement, information poverty and the internet worldwide.* Cambridge, UK: Cambridge University Press.

Northeast Document Conservation Center. (n.d.). *NEDCC Handbook for digital projects: A management tool for preservation and access.*

Notess, G. R. (2006). The terrible twos: web 2.0, library 2.0, and more. *Online, 30*(3), 40–42.

O' Reilly, T. (2005). *What is Web 2.0? Design patterns and business models for the next generation of software.* Retrieved February 13, 2009, from http://www.oreillynet.com/pub/a/oreilly/tim/news/2005/09/30/what-is-web-20.html

O'REILLY. T. (2003, April 6). The Architecture of Participation. *ONLamp.com.* Retrieved from http://www.oreillynet.com/pub/wlg/3017

OAIS. (2002). *Reference Model for an Open Archival Information System.* Retrieved July 25, 2008, from http://public.ccsds.org/publications/archive/650x0b1.pdf

Oman, R. (1998). From Scourge to Savior: How Digital Technology will Save Authorship in the Age of the Internet. In WIPO Internet Forum on the Exercise and Management of Copyright and Neighbouring Rights in the Face of the Challenges of Digital Technologies, Sevilla, 14-16 May (pp. 207-26). Geneva: WIPO.

Omekwu, C. O. (2006). Managing information and technology: critical roles for librarians in developing countries. *The Electronic Library, 24*(6), 847–863. doi:10.1108/02640470610714260

Ostrow, S. (1998 February). *Digitizing historical pictorial collections for the Internet.* CLIR. Retrieved from http://www.clir.org/pubs/reports/ostrow/pub71.html

Owen, M., Grant, L., Sayers, S., & Facer, K. (2006). *Social Software and Learning.* Bristol, UK: FutureLab. Retrieved from http://www.futurelab.org.uk/research/opening_education/social_software_01.htm

Oxfam Canada. (n.d.). Retrieved April 2, 2009, from http://www.oxfam.ca/

Oyelaran-Oyeyinka, B., & Lal, K. (2005). Internet diffusion in sub-Saharan Africa: A cross-country analysis. *Telecommunications Policy, 29*, 507–527. doi:10.1016/j.telpol.2005.05.002

Pace, A. K. (2003). *The Ultimate Digital Library; Where the New Information Players Meet.* Chicago, IL: American Library Association.

Pannone, J. (2007-2009). Robbins Library Notes. Retrieved November 6, 2008, from http://blogs.law.harvard.edu/pannone/

Parliament of India Library. (n.d.). Retrieved September 30, 2008, from http://parliamentofindia.gov.in Planning Commission, Government of India: *Five Year Plans. 10th Plan (2002-2007).* Volume 2, Chapter 3.2. Retrieved September, 30, 2008 from http://planningcommission.nic.in/plans/planrel/fiveyr/10th/volume2/v2_ch3_2.pdf.

PARSE. *Insight project.* (n.d.). Retrieved from http://www.parse-insight.eu

Pasquinelli, A. (2002). Digital Library Technology Trends. Retrieved from http://www.lib.buu.ac.th/webnew/libtech/digital_library_trends.pdf

Paul, J. (2002). Narrowing the digital divide: initiatives undertaken by the Association of South-East Asian Nations (ASEAN). *Electronic Library and Information Systems, 36*(1), 13–22. doi:10.1108/00330330210426085

Placing, K., Ward, M., Peat, M., & Teixeira, P. (2005). *Blogging Science and science education.*

PNG (Portable Network Graphics). (2004). *World Wide Web Consortium.* Retrieved.

Pomerantz, J., & Stutzman, F. (2004). *Lyceum: A Blogsphere for Library Reference.* Retrieved February 17, 2009, from http://www.ibiblio.org/fred/pubs/Lyceum.pdf

Prahallad, K., & Black, A. (2005). A text to speech interface for Universal Digital Library. *Journal of Zhejiang University. Science, 6A*(11), 1229–1234. doi:10.1631/jzus.2005.A1229

Prahallad, L., Prahallad, K., & Ganapathiraju, M. (2005). A simple approach for building transliteration editors for Indian languages. *Journal of Zhejiang University. Science, 6A*(11), 1354–1361. doi:10.1631/jzus.2005.A1354

Prakash, K. (2008-2009). *Distance Library Services.* Retrieved November 6, 2008, from http://kshema-distancelibraryservices.blogspot.com/

Presidential Committee on Information Literacy. *Final Report.* (n.d.). Retrieved May 25, 2007, from http://www.ala.org/ala/acrl/acrlpubs/whitepapers/presidential.htm

Pscanningguidelines.html.

Public Record Office Victoria. (2004). *Management of Electronic Records PROS 99/007* (Version 2). Retrieved March 2005, from

Public Record Office, The National Archives (UK). Retrieved March 2005, from *Public Records Alert No 1/05: Day batching of records.* (2005). Queensland State

Public Records Alert No 2/05: Understanding and applying recordkeeping metadata.

QCA. (2007). *Skill for life ICT curriculum,* Retrieved from http://www.qca.org.uk/libraryAssets/media/skill_for_life_ict_curriculum_jan07.pdf

Quality Assurance. (2004). *Technical Advisory Service for Images.* Retrieved March 2005

Queensland State Archives March 2005. National Archives of Australia.

ReadNepal. (n.d.). Retrieved April 3, 2009, from http://www.readglobal.org/nepal.asp

Recordkeeping in Brief No. 11: Digital Imaging and Recordkeeping. 2003. State Records New South Wales. Accessed March 2005 at www.records.nsw.gov.au/publicsector/rk/rib/rib11.htm

Regional Poverty Profile, S. A. A. R. C. *(RPP).* (2003). Retrieved April 3, 2009, from http://www.saarc-sec.org/data/pubs/rpp2005/pages/frameset-2.htm

Reichardt, R., & Harder, G. (2005). Weblogs: Their use and application in science and technology libraries. *Science & Technology Libraries, 25,* 105-116. Retrieved February 18, 2009, from http://nrs.harvard.edu/urn-3:HUL.ejournals:sfx958480310487

Renda, M. E., & Straccia, U. (2005). A personalized collaborative digital library environment: A model and an application. *Information Processing & Management, 41*(1), 5. doi:10.1016/j.ipm.2004.04.007

Revised Digital Imaging Guidelines for State of Ohio Executive Agencies and Local

RLG-OCLC. (2002). *Report on Trusted Digital Repositories: Attributes and Responsibilities.* Retrieved from http://www.oclc.org/programs/ourwork/past/trustedrep/repositories.pdf

Roelofs, G. (2005). *Multiple-image Network Graphics.* Retrieved March 2005, from http://www.libpng.org/pub/mng

Roes, H. (2001). Digital libraries and education: trends and opportunities. *D-Lib Magazine, 77*(8). Retrieved March 20, 2009, from http://dlib.org/dlib/july01/07roes.html

Rogers, A. (2006, September). Get Wiki with it. *Wired, 14*(9), 30–32.

Röll, M. (2004). *Distributed KM – Improving knowledge workers' productivity and organizational knowledge sharing with weblog-based personal publishing.* Paper presented at the Blog Talk 2.0, "The European Conference on Weblogs.

Roosendal, H., Huibers, T., Guerts, P., & van der Vet, P. (2003). Changes in the value chain of scientific information: economic consequences for academic institution. *Online Information Review, 27*(2), 120–128. doi:10.1108/14684520310471734

Roper, T. (2009). *Tom Roper's Weblog.* Retrieved February 18, 2009, from http://tomroper.typepad.com/

Rose, J. B. (2005). Community Telecentres: Assessing their impact and viability. In *The National Symposium on «Information and Communication Strategies for Grassroots development,* 4-5 March, University of Madras, Chennai, India.

Rosenfeld, L., & Morville, P. (1998). *Information architecture.* Cambridge, MA: O'Reilly.

Rothenberg, J. (1999). *Ensuring the Longevity of Digital Information.* Council on Library.

RSS. *(file format).* Wikipedia. Retrieved from http://en.wikipedia.org/wiki/RSS_(protocol)

Rudner, L. (2000). Who is going to mine digital library resources? And how? *D-Lib Magazine, 6*(5). Retrieved from http://www.dlib.org/dlib/may00/runder/05runder.html. doi:10.1045/may2000-rudner

Rutherford, L. L. (2008). Building participative library services: the impact of social software use in public libraries. *Library Hi Tech, 26*(3), 411–423. doi:10.1108/07378830810903337

Saha, N. C. (2006). Copyright Implications in Open Access Environment. In *XXII National Seminar of IASLIC* (pp. 193–200). Kolkota.

Saheb, T. (2005). ICT education and digital divide in developing countries. *Global Media Journal, 4*(7). Retrieved from http://lass.calumet.purdue.edu/cca/gmj/fa05/gmj-fa05-saheb.htm

Saracevic, T., & Dalbello, M. A. (2001). A survey of digital library education. In. *Proceedings of American Society for Information Science, 38,* 209–223.

Sauers, M. P. (2006). *Blogging and RSS: A Librarian's Guide.* Newark, NJ: Information Today.

Schatz, B. R., & Chen, H. (1999). Digital Libraries: Technological Advances and Social Impacts (Guest Editors' Introduction). *IEEE Computer, 32*(2), 45–50. doi:. doi:10.1109/2.745719

Schlachter, E. (1997). The Intellectual Property Renaissance in Cyberspace: Why Copyright Law Could be Unimportant on the Internet. *Berkley Technology Journal, 12*(1). Retrieved from http://www.law.berkeley.edu/journals/btlj/articles/vol12/Schlachter/html/reader.html

Schonfield, R. C., King, D. A., Okerson, A., & Fenton, G. (2004). Library periodicals expenses: comparison of non-subscription costs of print and electronic formats on life cycle basis. *D-Lib Magazine, 10*(1). Retrieved February 28, 2009, from http://www.dlib.org/dlib/january04/schonfeld/01 schonfeld.html

Schrecker, D. L. (2008). Using Blogs in Academic Libraries: Versatile Information Platforms. *New Library World, 109*(3/4), 117–129. doi:10.1108/03074800810857586

Scrutiny of Acts and Regulations Committee. (2005). Retrieved April 28, 2007, from http://www.parliament.vic.gov.au/sarc/E-Democracy/Final_Report/Glossary.htm

Secker, J. (2008). *Case Study 4: blogging and libraries.* Retrieved February 17, 2009, from http://clt.lse.ac.uk/Projects/Case_study_four_report.pdf

Secker, J., & Price, G. (2007). Libraries, social software and distance learners: blog it, tag it, share it! *New Review of Information Networking, 13*(1), 39–52. doi:10.1080/13614570701754536

Seethalakshmi, R. (2005). Optical character recognition for printed Tamil text using Unicode. *Journal of Zhejiang University. Science, 6A*(11), 1297–1305. doi:10.1631/jzus.2005.A1297

Senthilkumaran, S., et al. (2003). *Using ICTs in development: Information village research project, Pondicherry.* Paper presented at World Congress – Engineering and Digital Divide, at Tunis, 12-19 October 2003.

Shanhi, R. (2006). Web 2.0: data, metadata, and interface. Retrieved from http://www.rashmisinha.com/archives/05_08/web2-data-metadata-interface.html

Sharari, S. A. (2006). Intellectual Property Rights Legislation and Computer Software Piracy in Jordan. *Journal of the Social Sciences, 2*(1), 7–13. doi:10.3844/jssp.2006.7.13

Sharma, A. (2001). *Digital Noise, Film Grain. Digital Photo Techniques.* Retrieved March. 2005 from http://www.phototechmag.com/sample/sharma.pdf

Sharma, R. K., & Vishwanathan, K. R. (2001). Digital libraries: developments and challenges. *Library Review, 50*(1), 10–15. doi:10.1108/00242530110363190

Sharma, R., & Azura, I. M. (2005). Bridging the digital divide in Asia- challenges and solutions. *International Journal of Technology. Knowledge and Society, 1*(3), 15–30.

Sherman, C. (2000). Reference resources on the Web. *Online, 24*(1), 52–56.

Shidhulai Swanirvar Sangstha. (2008). Retrieved April 3, 2009, from http://www.shidhulai.org/

Shukla, S., & Gautam, J. N. (2008). Role of ICTs in rural development. In Dhawan, S. M. (Eds.), *Shaping the future of special libraries* (pp. 125–132). Delhi: Ane Books.

Shukla, V. N., Arora, K. K., & Gugnani, V. (2004). *Digital library: language centered research, test beds and applications.* Retrieved May 15, 2008, from www.cdacnoida.in/technicalpapers/PaperICDL1.pdf

Skipper, M. (2006). Would Mendel have been a blogger? *Nature Reviews. Genetics, 7*, 664. doi:10.1038/nrg1957

Sloan, B. G. (1998). Service perspectives for the digital library remote reference services. *Library Trends, 47*(1), 117–143.

Smith, A. (2001). *Developing Sustainable Digital Library Collections: Strategies for Digitization.* Digital Library Federation Council on Library and Information Resources. Retrieved from http://www.clir.org/pubs/reports/pub101/contents.htm

Smith, M. (2003). D-Space: an open source dynamic digital repository. *D-Lib, 9*(1). Retrieved April 8, 2004, from http://www.dlib.org/dlib/january03/smith/01smith.html

SPRI Museum & Archives: access policy and plan (2006-2009). (2008). Retrieved from http://www.spri.cam.ac.uk/museum/policy/access.html

Standard, D. (2003). *1 – Cataloguing and Metadata for Digital Images.* State Library of.

Standard, D. (2003). *2 – Digital capture, format & preservation.* State Library of.

Stanley, T. (2006). *Web 2.0: Supporting Library Users.* QA Focus, UKOLN. Retrieved from http://www.ukoln.ac.uk/qa-focus/documents/briefings/briefing-102/briefing-102-A5.doc

Star, S. L., & Griesemer, J. R. (1989). Institutional Ecology, 'Translations' and Boundary Objects: Amateurs and Professionals in Berkeley's Museum of Vertebrate Zoology. *Social Studies of Science, 19*, 387–420. doi:10.1177/030631289019003001

Steinmueller, W. (2001). ICTs and the possibilities for leapfrogging by developing countries. *International Labour Review, 140*(2), 193–210. doi:10.1111/j.1564-913X.2001.tb00220.x

Stephens, M. (2006). Exploring Web 2.0 and libraries. *Library Technology Reports, 42*(4), 8–14.

Stephens, M., & Casey, M. E. (2005). *Where Do We Begin? A Library 2.0 Conversation with Michael Casey.* ALA Techsource Blog. Posted to http://www.alatechsource.org/blog/2005/12/where-do-we-begin-a-library-20-conversation-with-michael-casey.html

Straw, J.E (2000). A virtual understanding: the reference interview and question negotiation in the digital age. Reference & User Services Quarterly, 39(4), 376-9.

Sun Microsystems. (n.d.a). Retrieved from http://www.sun.com

Sun Microsystems. (n.d.b). White Paper. Retrieved from http://www.sun.com/software/whitepapers/wp.../wp-dhbrown99.pdf

Swan, A. (2006). Overview of scholarly communication. In Jacobs, N. (Ed.), *Open Access: Key Strategic, Technical and Economic Aspects.* Oxford, UK: Chandos Publishing.

Tanner, S. *From Vision to Implementation – strategic and management issues for digital collections. 2000. The Electronic Library – strategic, policy and management issues seminar. Accessed March 2005 at http://heds.herts.ac.uk/resources/papers/Lboro2000.pdf*

Tanner, S. (2006). Handbook on cost reductions in digitisation. *Minerva online.* Retrieved from http://www.minervaeurope.org/.../CostReductioninDigitisation_v1_0610.pdf

Tanner, S. (2009). The economic future for digital libraries: a 2020 vision. In Baker, D., & Evans, W. (Eds.), *Digital Library Economics: An academic perspective.* Oxford, UK: Chandos Publishing.

Techsource Blog, A. L. A. Library Technology Reports. (n.d.a). *Review of Web 2.0 and Libraries: Best Practices for Social Software.* Retrieved 2/20/2009, from http://www.alatechsource.org/ltr/web-20-and-libraries-best-practices-for-social-software

Techsource Blog, A. L. A. Library Technology Reports. (n.d.b). *Review of Web 2.0 & Libraries, Part 2: Trends and Technologies.* Retrieved February 20, 2009, from http://www.alatechsource.org/ltr/web-20-libraries-part-2-trends-and-technologies

Tenopir, C. (2001). Virtual reference services in a real world. *Library Journal, 126*(12), 38–40.

Tenopir, C., & Ennis, L. A. (2001). Reference services in the new millennium. *Online, 2*(4), 40–45.

Term Preservation. National Archives (UK). Retrieved March 2005, from http://www.nationalarchives.gov.uk/preservation/advice/pdf/selecting_file_formats.pdf

TerraServer-USA. (n.d.). Retrieved from terraserver-usa.com/default.aspx

The Ashden Awards for Sustainable Energy. (2007). *Case Study: Shidhulai Swanirvar Sangstha, Bangladesh.* Retrieved from http://www.ashdenawards.org/winners/shidhulai

The digital divide. (n.d.). Retrieved February 19, 2009, from http://dl.filmaust.com.au/module/113/

The DIRKS Manual: A Strategic Approach to Managing Business Information. (2003).

The knowledge explosion and the knowledge divide. (2001). Retrieved from http://hdr.undp.org/en/reports/global/hdr2001/papers/sagasti-1-1.pdf

The new digital divide, media literacy, broadening participation? Inclusive education? Digital equity. (2007). Retrieved from http://thornburgcenter.blogspot.com/2007/06/new-digital-divide-media-literacy.html

The Preservation Management of Digital Material Handbook, Chapter 5: Media and

Theodore, R. (2005 January). Rural development. *Yojana.*

Thornely J. The How of Metadata: Metadata Creation and Standards. 1999. 13th National Cataloguing Conference, October 1999, Accessed March 2005 at http://www.slq.qld.gov.au/__data/assets/file/6289/How_of_Metadata.doc

Tibbo, H. R. (1995). Interviewing techniques for remote reference: electronic versus traditional environments. *The American Archivist, 58*(3), 294–310.

Townsend, S., et al. (n.d.). *Digitising history.* Retrieved from http://hds.essex.ac.uk/g2gp/digitising_history/index.html

TRAC. (2007). *Trustworthy Repositories Audit & Certification: Criteria and Checklist.* Retrieved from http://www.crl.edu/PDF/trac.pdf

Traditional Knowledge Digital Library (n.d.). Wikipedia: the free encyclopedia. Retrieved July 1, 2009, from http://en.wikipedia.org/wiki/Traditional_Knowledge_Digital_Library

Traditional Knowledge Digital Library. (n.d.). Retrieved from http://www.tkdl.res.in/tkdl/langdefault/common/Home.asp?GL=Eng

Tuck, J. (2005a, November 24). *Collection Development and Web Publications at the British Library.* PowerPoint presentation at Digital Memory, Tallin. Retrieved from http://www.nlib.ee/html/yritus/digital_mem/24-2-tuck.ppt

Tuck, J. (2005b.) *Creating Web Archiving Services in the British Library.* DLF Fall Forum, Nov 9, 2005. Retrieved from http://www.diglib.org/forums/fall2005/presentations/tuck-2005-11.pdf.

Tuck, J. (2007). Author's notes. In *Memories for Life: the future of our pasts*, British Library, London, Dec 12th 2006. Retrieved from http://www.memoriesforlife.org/events.php

Tudhope, D., Koch, T., & Heery, R. (2006). *Terminology Services and Technology: JISC state of the art review.* UKOLN/JISC: Bristol, UK. Retrieved from http://www.ukoln.ac.uk/terminology/JISC-review2006.html

Turender, H. (2002). Digital reference: trends, techniques and changes. *Library Hi Tech News, 19*. Retrieved from http://masetto.emeraldinsight.com/v1=9380369/cl=29/nw=1/rpsv/cw/mcb/07419058/v19.

Twidale, M. B., Nicholas, D. M., & Paice, C. D. (1997). Browsing is a collaborative process on online systems, example of ARIADANE. *Information Processing & Management, 33*(6), 761 783. doi:10.1016/S0306-4573(97)00040-X

Tyson, J. (2003 December). *How Scanners Work.* How StuffWorks. Retrieved from http://www.howstuffworks.com

UNESCO. (2001). *Universal Declaration on Cultural Diversity.* Retrieved February 1, 2009, from http://www.un-documents.net/udcd.htm

UNESCO. (2002). *Memory of the World: general guidelines to safeguard documentary heritage. CII-95/WS-11rev February 2002. Heritage Collections Committee of the Cultural Ministers Council. (1995). National conservation and preservation policy for movable cultural heritage.* Canberra, Australia: Department of Communications and the Arts.

UNESCO. (2005). *From the information society to knowledge society.* Paris: UNESCO Publishing.

United Nations. (2005). *Millennium Development Goals.* Retrieved February 4, 2009, from http://www.un.org/millenniumgoals (Accessed on 2.4.2009)

United States Patent and Trademark Office. (n.d.). *Trademark, Copyright or Patent*. Washington, DC: USPTO. Retrieved from http://www.uspto.gov/web/offices/tac/doc/basic/trade_defin.htm

Universal's encyclopedia of important central acts and rules (Vol. 6). (2004). New Delhi: Universal Law Publishing.

University Library Blogs. (2009). Retrieved February 18, 2009, from http://homer.gsu.edu/blogs/library/

University of California. *Berkeley*. (n.d.). Retrieved from http://berkeley.edu/

Upadhyay P. K., Moni M., & Vijayaditya N. (2004). Digital Library Initiatives in India. *Libraries, Information & Knowledge, 21(1)*.

UThink Blogs. (2009). Retrieved February 18, 2009, from http://blog.lib.umn.edu/uthink/start.phtml

Van der Wal, T. (2005). *Folksonomy definition and Wikipedia*. Retrieved from http://www.vanderwal.net.

Varmazis, C. 2006. *Web 2.0: Scientists Need to Mash It Up*. BIO-IT World.com. http://www.bio-itworld.com/newsitems/2006/april/04-06-06-news-web2

Varnum, K. (2006). *RSS4Lib: Innovative ways libraries use RSS*. Retrieved from http://blogs.fletcher.tufts.edu/rss4lib/

Venkatasubramaian, K. (2002). *Presidential Address.* Delivered at the Seminar on Electronic Libraries in Rural India, 11 May 2002.

Venkatasubramanian, K. (2001, December 4). Education & Poverty. *The Hindu*. Retrieved June 30, 2006 from http://www.hinduonnet.com/thehindu/op/2001/12/04/stories/2001120400060100.htm

Vinje, T. (1999). Copyright Imperiled. *European Intellectual Property Review, 21*(4), 197–207. Retrieved from http://www.eblida.org/ecup/publica/vinje.rtf.

Virtual Reference Desk. (2000). *Facets of quality for digital reference services* (Version 4). Retrieved January 12, 2009, from www.vrd.org/facets-10-00.shtml

Voice Counts, Y. (2008). Retrieved February 18, 2009, from http://blog.fairfield.edu/summerreading2008/

Wasik, J. M. (1999). Building and maintaining digital reference services. *ERIC Digest*. Retrieved March 15, 2009, from http://www.ed.gov/databases/ERIC_Digests/ed427794.html

Watson, E. F. (2003). *Developing Library and Information Services for Distance Education*. Retrieved February 18, 2009, from http://www.col.org/resources/publications/trainingresources/knowledge/Pages/library.aspx

Webber, S., & Johnston, B. (2000a). Conceptions of information literacy: new perspectives and implications. *Journal of Information Science, 26*(6), 381–397. doi:10.1177/016555150002600602

Webber, S., & Johnston, B. (2000b). *The information literacy class at Strathclyde University*. Paper presented at the SCONUL Conference 2000. Retrieved from http://dis.shef.ac.uk/literacy/sconuljuly.pdf

WikiBios. (n.d.). Retrieved from http://www.wikibios.com/

Wikipedia. (n.d.). Retrieved from http://www.wikipedia.com

Wikipedia. (n.d.). *Steganography*. Retrieved from http://en.wikipedia.org/wiki/Steganography

Wilder, S. J. (2002). New hires in research libraries demographic trends and hiring priories. *ARI, 221*(5).

Williams, J. B., & Jacobs, J. (2004). Exploring the use of blogs as learning spaces in the higher education sector. *Australasian Journal of Educational Technology, 20*(2), 232–247.

Wilson, D. T., & Yowell, S. S. (2008). Resourceful Blogging: Using a blog for information sharing. *Medical Reference Services Quarterly, 27*(2), 183–210. doi:10.1080/02763860802114660

Wilson, W. (2003). Building and managing a digital collection in a small library. *North Carolina Library, 61*(3), 88–97.

Wiseman, N., Rusbridge, C., & Griffin, S. M. (1999). The Joint NSF/JISC International Digital Libraries Initiative. *D-Lib Magazine, 5*(6). Retrieved from http://www.dlib.org/dlib/june99/06wiseman.html

World Bank. (1999). *World development report 1998/99: Knowledge for development. Oxford, UK: World Bank.* Oxford: University Press.

World Bank. (2003). Multi-Stakeholder Regional Consultation for International Assessment on Role of Agricultural Science and Technology in reducing hunger, improving rural livelihoods and stimulating environmentally sustainable economic growth. Organized by The World Bank, 12-13 May 2003, New Delhi.

World Bank. (2009). *South Asia: Data, Projects and Research.* Retrieved April 3, 2009, from http://web.worldbank.org/WBSITE/EXTERNAL/COUNTRIES/SOUTHASIAEXT/0.pagePK:158889~piPK:146815~theSitePK:223547.00.html

World Book Encyclopedia. (n.d.). Community. In World Book Encyclopedia (Vol. 4., pp. 245). Chicago: World Book.

World Information Society Report. (2007). Retrieved February 19, 2009, from http://ITU.int/osg/spu/publications/worldinformationsociety/2007/WISR07-chapter4.pdf

Yongqing, M., Clegg, W., & O'Brien, A. (2006). Digital library education: the current status. In *JCDL '06. Proceedings of the 6th ACM/IEEE-CS Joint Conference on Digital Libraries, 2006* (pp. 165–74). Retrieved June 15, 2009, from http://ieeexplore.ieee.org/stamp/stamp.jsp?arnumber=04119115

Z39. *50.* (n.d.). Retrieved from www.loc.gov/z3950/agency/

Zhuo, F. (2006). Blogs in American Academic Libraries: An Overview of Their Present Status and Possible Future Use. In L. Feng et al. (Eds.), Proceedings of Web Information Systems – WISE 2006 Workshops WISE 2006 International Workshops, Wuhan, China, October 23-26, 2006 (Vol. 4256, pp. 145-152). Heidelberg: Springer.

Zorich, D. M. (2003). *A Survey of Digital Cultural Heritage Initiatives and Their Sustainability Concerns.* Council on Library and Information Resources, Washington, DC. Retrieved April 8, 2004, from http://www.clir.org/pubs/abstract/pub118abst.html

About the Contributors

Dr.Tariq Ashraf is M.A. in Political Science from Hindu College, University of Delhi and holds PG and Doctoral degrees in Library & Information Science from Department of Library & Information Science, University of Delhi. Currently with University of Delhi, he has earlier worked at institutins like Indian Institute of Management, Lucknow, and Centre For Policy Research, New Delhi. A regular contributor to LIS literature and research ,Dr. Ashraf is twice winner of international paper contest held by American Society for Information Science and Technology (ASIST). He is a council member, Gerson Lehrman Group, USA for a wide ranging LIS consulting assignments.

Dr. Jaideep Sharma is a gold medalist from University of Delhi and is currently Associate Professor at Indira Gandhi National Open University. He is an expert in the areas of Information Literacy and Competencies Programmes and recognized as a key resource person in these areas. As a keen researcher, he has widely contributed to several scholarly journals of repute. Dr.Sharma is associated with prestigious online course of IGNOU and regularly anchors programmes for the distant and e- learners.

Puja Anand Gulati, an M.Phil. in Library & Information Science is currently with Shaheed Bhagat Singh College of University of Delhi and has been associated previously with UNICEF and British Council, New Delhi. Ms. Gulati is an extensively ICT trained person and is credited with successful implementation of several library modernization projects .She regularly contributes to LIS literature and is an active library professionals associated with several prestigious associations and organisations.

* * *

Leila Nemati Anaraki is a PhD student of Library and Information Science with the Department of Library and Information Studies in Islamic Azad University, Science and Research Branch, Tehran, Iran.

Jagdish Arora is the Director of UGC-INFLIBNET, Ministry of Human Resource Development, Government of India, New Delhi.

M. Ishwara Bhat is a Librarian at the Birla Institute of Technology and Science, Pilani, Rajasthan. Dr. Bhat previously worked as Regional Manager for Northern India for British Council Libraries, Delhi.Dr. Bhat has delivered lectures in various universities including Karnatak, Bangalore, AP Open University, IGNOU, Lucknow, Delhi and Kurukshetra universities. Research interests include marketing of libraries and information centres, Customer service, Human Resource management in libraries, Children libraries, Reading habit development, and Village knowledge centres.

Arun Kumar Chakraborty holds a Ph.D. from Vidyasagar University, West Bengal, India and As-sociateship in Documentation and Information Science i.e. equivalent to MLISc. from Indian Statistical Institute (ISI), Documentation Research and Training Centre (DRTC), Bangalore, India. He serves as the chief of Bose Institute (BI) Library designated "Librarian". He is a life member of a number of Library Associations in India and abroad such as Indian Association of Special Libraries and Information Centre (IASLIC); Indian Library Association, Delhi; Bengal Library Association (BLA), Kolkata, India and Society for Information Science (SIS). He is Standing Committee member of International Federation of Library Associations (IFLA), Netherland, of Genealogy and Local History Section (2009-2013). He is also the General Secretary of Indian Association of Special Libraries and Information Centre (IASLIC) www.iaslic1955.0rg since 2007 up to 2010.

Pravin Kumar Choudhary qualification includes M.Sc., AIS, LLB, DM & PGDPM. He has over thirteen years of Professional Experience in the Documentation, Information management using ICT & modern Library administration and management. He has a keen interest to study different issues concerning LIS professionals in I.T dominated era. He is regularly contributing to national and inter-national books, journals, conferences & seminars. He has already presented sixteen papers at different forums. He is currently working as Sr. Manager (Documentation) in DLF Limited, New Delhi (India). His current major assignment includes establishment of State of the Art Documentation and Information Centre, DMS implementation for DLF Group of Companies. He has got keen interest towards Intellectual Property Right Issues and Marketing of Information Products and Services in digital era.

Anup Kumar Das is an advance researcher in the Centre for Studies in Science Policy at Jawaharlal Nehru University (JNU), India and a UNESCO Expert in the areas of Communication and Information. He was awarded doctoral degree from the Jadavpur University, India in 2008. He has published a number of papers in different journals and presented papers in different international/ national conferences. His recent work includes 'Open Access to Knowledge and Information: Scholarly Literature and Digital Library Initiatives – the South Asian Scenario', UNESCO, New Delhi, 2008. A list of his publications and presentations is available at http://anupkumardas.blogspot.com

Chaitali Dutta is Associate Professor in the Department of Library and Information Science, Jadavpur University, Kolkata, India. Other than her professional contributions in journals and conferences, she is also a creative writer and poet and publishes widely in Bengali little magazines. She was a principal investigator in a UNESCO-sponsored research study titled "Information Literacy Competency and Readership Study of Five Specific Localities in Urban, Industrial and Semi-Urban Areas of Kolkata Metropolitan City' in 2008. She completed her doctoral study from the University of Calcutta, India.

Shantanu Ganguly has done B.Sc (Botany), M.Sc (Ecology and Environment), Masters in Library and Information Science, Post Graduate Diploma in Management (specialization in Marketing), Post Graduate Diploma in Computer Application. Currently, he is pursuing PhD in Library and Information Science in the area of Information Service Marketing. He is working as Fellow, Library and Informa-tion Center, TERI, New Delhi.He has served several reputed organizations in and around Delhi such as Delhi University (DU), Voluntary Health Association of India (VHAI), and National Productivity Council (NPC), Tata Energy Research Institute (TERI), Institute for Integrated Learning in Management (IILM), and Indian Institute of Management (IIM), Lucknow etc. While working in IIM, Lucknow he was heading both Lucknow and NOIDA Campus. He has almost 18 years of experience in the field of library and information services. He is consultant to several organizations in setting up their library and information centers. He also served as Academic Counsellors to several institutions such as IG-NOU, VMOU to develop their course modules. During his stay at IILM, he developed the passion of teaching and started taking sessions in UG and PGP levels on Business Communications. In IILM, he was promoted to Associate Professor (Business Communication) and Head, Library and Information Centers in IILM. He has been served as Associate Editors for several reputed national journals and newsletters. He has published several papers in national and international refereed journals. He has been invited by several reputed Universities and institutions to take special sessions on "Information Service Marketing" etc.

Ramesh C. Gaur is Librarian & Head, Kalanidhi Division (Professor Grade) at Indira Gandhi National Centre for the arts (IGNCA), New Delhi. A Fulbright Scholar, Dr. Gaur is a Science graduate with Ph.D in Library and Information Science, with exposure to several-advanced training programme on the applications of IT to Library Management. After rich exposure in corporate environment, he joined IMT Ghaziabad where his first major achievement of automating the Library and transforming it into a state-of-the-art establishment, hailed by all concerned. This feat he replicated at the famed Tata Institute of Fundamental Research, Mumbai and also at Management Development Institute (MDI), Gurgaon. Digitization and Digital Archiving of Indian Cultural Heritage is the main focus of his work at Indira Gandhi National Centre for Arts.

David Giaretta is Deputy Chair at Data Archive Ingestion Working Group of CCSDS, Oxford, United Kingdom.

Azadeh Heidari is a PhD student of Library and Information Science with the Department of Library and Information Studies in Islamic Azad University, Science and Research Branch, Tehran, Iran.

S. C. Jindal is currently head of Central Science Library, University of Delhi and an eminent library professional known for his expertise in the areas of Information literacy, e-resources and digital content creation. He is author of a three volume pioneering study on Digital Libraries and contributes regularly to LIS literature.

Bharat Kumar is the Assistant Librarian for the Management Development Institute in Gurgaon, India.

Madaswamy Moni is a senior technocrat of National Informatics Centre (Department of Information Technology, Government of India), currently working as its Deputy Director General. With more than 24 years of professional experience, he has held several prestigious assignments. He pioneered to establish the District Information System of National Informatics Centre (DISNIC) in 27 Sectors of importance, which included Agriculture, Education, Industries, Rural Development, Microlevel Planning, Animal Husbandry, Fisheries, Water Resources etc, for implementation in about 520 districts of

India, with the establishment of NICNET in districts, during 1987-96. His forte is ICT Diffusion and Infusion for achieving sustainable agricultural and rural development in India. He was instrumental in organising the national conference on "Informatics for Sustainable Agricultural Development (ISDA-95)" in May 1995, which gave the "road map" for ICT diffusion in the agricultural sector.

Shweta Pandey is currently working as Assistant Librarian at Knowledge Resource Center, Indus World Business School: (A Career Launcher Education Foundation Initiative) Greater Noida (UP). She is graduated in Psychology from Isabella Thobourn College, Lucknow. Shweta holds her Masters in Library & Information Science from Babasaheb Bhimrao Ambedkar University, Lucknow and posses intensive hands on training from IIM, Lucknow. She has published papers in proceedings and presented in conferences. Her research interest includes: Users need analysis, Information Seeking Behavior, E-learning and Library Management, Cognitive & Behavioral psychology application in Library and Information Science.

Jason A. Pannone is the Librarian for Robbins Library, Department of Philosophy, Harvard University, in Cambridge, Massachusetts.

Shampa Paul holds M. Phil (LIS) degree. In addition she earned M.A. (Economics) degree from Himachal University. Currently she is Ph.D scholar in Library and Information Science, University of Delhi. She has published several research papers in refereed journals. She was a first place winner in the international paper competition organized by American Society for Information Science and Technology (ASIS&T) 2007, USA. She has been working at the Institute of Economic Growth (IEG) since November 1998. She regularly teaches to Indian Economic Service Probationers, Indian Statistical Services Officers, and participants of other training programmes organized by IEG.

Kshema Prakash is presently overseeing the electronic resource facilities including e-journals, internet based services, Arts & Social Sciences collection, and library website development in Central Library of Dayalbagh Educational Institute (Deemed University). She is an active member of DEI Libraries Computerization Committee and has put in 11 years of administrative experience. She is also serving as Coordinator for Distance Library Services of DEI to its various study centres across the country and overseas. Dr. Kshema has been the recipient of Vice -Chancellor's Gold Medal in B.Lib.I.Sc. and MLIS for securing highest marks. She has authored 3 invited book chapters, 14 research papers and articles. She is also involved in developing self learning material for distance learning pro](rammes and translation work. Her research interests are Change Management, Systems Approach to Change Management in Library & Information Centres, Distance/Off-campus Library Services, and Information Literacy & Bibliographic Instruction. She is a life member of Systems Society of India (SSI), and Indian Association of Special Libraries & Information Centres (IASLIC).

Manisha Saksena worked as Librarian with Entrepreneur Development Institute Ahmadabad, India. She is currently living in the USA to pursue her research interests.

Bimal Kanti Sen graduated in Science with Distinction and obtained his Diploma in Library Science from the University of Calcutta. He obtained his Master's degree in Library in Information Science from the University of Delhi obtaining First Class and standing First and earned his PhD from Jadavpur

University working on the history of Indian scientific periodicals. Dr Sen served INSDOC for more than 30 years working on various capacities and heading among others Russian Science Information Centre; National Centre on Bibliometrics; Education and Training Division and National Science Library. He served the University of Malaya as a Visiting Professor from 1995 to 1999. During his career as an academic spanning well nigh four decades he has taught a number of subjects including Cataloguing, Classification, Information sources, Collection development, Information and Society, Bibliometrics and Technical writing. During his career he has classified more than a hundred thousand documents. Dr Sen has guided more than 50 students for their dissertations and contributed more than 200 papers, authored/edited one dozen books, wrote about 25 course materials for Indira Gandhi National Open University, and edited half a dozen journals. His books among others include On Bengali Scientific Terminology (Bengali); Glossary of Library and Information Science Terms (English-Bengali); In Search of Knowledge; Directory of Scientific Research Institutions in India, 2nd ed.; Growth of Scientific Periodicals in India (1788-1900); Growth of Scientific Periodicals in India (1901-1947); and DDC Readymade. For his academic contributions, Dr, Sen has received a number of awards including Prof S. Dasgupta Memorial Gold Medal (University of Delhi); Dr. T. M. Das Foundation Award for popular science writing in Bengali; Tincori Dutt award for Best Writing in Library and Information Science published in Granthagar; and Distinguished Leadership Award by American Biographical Institute. His biodata figures in about a dozen biographical sources. In academic pursuit he has traveled far and wide including USA, USSR, Malaysia, Bangladesh, Pakistan, and Nepal.

K. Santi Swarup has wide teaching experience in the areas of Principles of Management, Statistics, Corporate Finance, Financial Services, Security Analysis and Portfolio Management. He holds keen research interest in Small Business Management, Investment Management, and Financial Services. He has 26 publications in Indian journals and in 10 books to his credit.

Pradip Kumar Upadhyay is presently working as Technical Director and Officer Incharge, Library, National Informatics Center(NIC), Department of Information Technology, Ministry of Communication and Information Technology, Government of India, Block-A, CGO Complex, Lodhi Road, New Delhi- 110003. His research area includes library technology projects and activities at NIC, creation of rural electronic libraries and community information centers in India, digital libraries in government organizations, National Digital Library, networking of Government Libraries, modernization and networking of public libraries and community information centers in India. He has an M. Sc in Physics from University of Delhi and also a Masters Degree in Library and Information Science from University of Delhi. He was Member Convener of MCIT Library Consortium from 2004-2008 and now continuing as member of this consortium committee. He is Fulbright Scholar (2002-2003) from Graduate School of Library and Information Science, University of Illinois, USA. He has visited a number of Community Information Networks initiatives and Digital library Projects in USA and Canada. He has published a number of research papers in the area of Information and Communications Technology applications in Library Science. He is winner of SIG III International Paper Contest 2006 for the paper 'e-Granthalaya: Moving Towards Rural Digital Library for Sustainable Rural Livelihoods'.

Index

Symbols

16MEuros 146
(non) ownership model 25
("Perpetual") access 24

A

absence of action plans 201
academic librarian 90, 96, 97, 98, 99, 102, 103, 104
academic librarian bloggers 102, 103, 104
academic libraries 90, 91, 93, 94, 98, 103, 104, 133
academic library blogs 90, 94, 95, 99, 103
Academic publishing 108
Accessibility testing 161
accessing information and knowledge 312
Acrobat Capture 2.0 45
ADF (Automatic Document Feeder) 68
Age of Information 128
aggregated 119
Agricultural Information 256
Alliance for Permanent Access 150, 154
alternative models of e-learning 98
Amazon.com 31, 32
America II project 24
American Library Association (ALA) 3, 98
analog data 136
Analogue collection 133
analogue information 40
analogue objects 189
AntBase 127
AntWeb 127
Archival Storage 42
Art Museum Image Consortium (AMICO) 26, 27

Arts and Letters Daily (A&LD) 29
ASCII (American Standard Code for Information Interchange 51
ASCII files 44, 48
Asia Foundation 258
Asia-pacific countries 311
Asia-Pacific countries 311, 312, 313, 314, 315
Asiatic Society 237, 246
Association for Computing Machinery (ACM) 3
Association Littéraire et Artistique Internationale (ALAI) 227
Association of College and Research Libraries (ACRL) 98
Authenticity 136
average life span of webpages 119
Ayurveda, Yoga & Naturopathy, Unani, Siddha and Homoeopathy-(AYUSH) 198

B

backing up data 82
Barriers to Access 235
Berne Convention 227, 228
best-seller phenomenon 112
biblioblogosphere 91
bibliographic information 20
bibliographic instruction 90, 98, 99, 101, 103
bibliographic records 110
bilateral treaties 227
binary digits 41
Biodiversity 259
bit 65, 68, 69, 70, 71, 72, 73, 74, 75, 77, 82, 85

Bit depth 69, 71
bit level 138
bit-mapped page image 43, 65, 72
Bitonal or binary scanning 47
bitonal scanning 71, 73
Bit range 77
Bit-stream Copying 82
Blogging 90, 93, 96, 97, 98, 99, 105,
    106, 107
boat libraries 258, 259
Book Delivery Act 250
Book Eye Scanners 78
Books Delivery Act 239, 251
book superstore 31
Boolean 44
Business Software Alliance 223

C

Cable Television 300
California Digital Library 9
Canonicalization 83
CASPAR-based archival system 157
CASPAR Conceptual Model 155
CASPAR project 146, 155
CD-R piracy 226
certification Management 145
Changing technologies 10
Changing Trends in LICs 108
Charging for access 15
Chemical impregnation 223
CiteULike 127
Citizen IT Interface 269
civil society 252, 261, 262, 263
Clearly Significant Properties 147
Client/Server Library Information Architecture
    171
Coalition for Networked Information (CNI) 3
Coalition for Networked Resources 4
Collaboration 15
Collaborative Digital Library 206
collecting and preserving web 108
collection development 133, 137
collection development policy 118
collection management 6
Colour images 70
colour management 48

colour scanning 47, 48, 49, 53
CombeChem work 126
commodities 110
commodity distribution divisions 111
Commonwealth of Learning (COL) 98
Communication Networks 266, 269, 282
Community Information 265, 266, 269,
    273, 274, 275, 276, 279, 282, 283
Community Information and Com-
    munication Centres (CICC)
    265, 266, 269, 276, 282, 283
Community Information projects 262
community library system 261
Community Multimedia Centre (CMC) 273
compound annual growth rate (CAGR) 314
Compression 48, 49, 69, 71, 81, 82
compression algorithms 71
computer and communication technologies 161
Computer density 314, 315, 317
computerized library 19
Computer literacy 163, 164
Computer Museum 82
computer museum approach 138
content management system 27
continuum of choice 288
Converting information 41
Cooperating 34
Cooperative Development 272
cooperative purchasing 33
cooperative resource sharing environment 24
Copyright 225, 226, 227, 228, 229, 232,
    233, 234
Copyright Act 238, 239, 242, 243, 244, 250
Copyright-cultural heritage 235
copyright laws 24, 227, 228
copyright protected 228
Cost/benefit analyses 154
Council of Scientific and Industrial Research
    (CSIR) 197, 232
Counterfieting 226
crawler technology 121
creation of metadata 4
cryptography 224, 230
Cryptography 230
Cultural Archives 243, 250
cultural assets 6

cultural digitization 109
cultural diversity 207, 220
cultural heritage material
236, 240, 241, 244, 249, 250
Cultural Informatics Laboratory (CIL) 235
cultural institutions 240, 250
cultural memory 118
cultural products 299
Curation Persistent Identifiers - CPID) 157
current storage equipment 5
Customer relationship 160
Customer Relationship Management (CRM)
176

D

daily posting 101, 102
data abstraction 84
Data Bank of the arts 242
data encoding 85
data integrity 85
data recovery companies 85
DCC [Digital Curation Centre] 155
Delhi Public Library 239
delivery of services 162
DELOS 125, 129
DELOS conceptual model 125
Department of Information Technology (DIT)
272
Designated Community 145, 146, 147, 148,
149, 150, 155, 156
Designs Act 2000 225
developing countries 252, 253, 286, 291,
299, 301, 304
developing digital libraries 200
developmental issues 103
development information activities 260, 263
Dialog Alerts 171
diffusion of Internet 312, 313, 316
Digital access 16
digital archiving 5
Digital cameras 53, 78
digital collection
108, 126, 127, 184, 185, 192
digital content 134, 144
Digital Content Management System 277
digital conversion 6, 11

Digital conversion 85
digital curation 145
Digital Curation Centre (DCC) 151, 158
digital current awareness service 95
Digital divide 286, 287, 292, 304, 308, 309
digital document system 66
digital environment 160, 162, 166, 168,
173, 177, 178
digital formats 1, 5, 10, 11, 31
Digital imaging 51, 61, 65, 140
digital imaging technology 5, 7
digital infrastructure OAIS 145
digital kiosks 202
digital libraries , 1, 2, 3, 4, 5, 7, 8, 9, 10,
11, 12, 13, 15, 16, 17, 18, 19, 20,
21, 22, 23, 24, 26, 27, 28, 29, 35,
36, 37, 38, 40, 59, 61, 90, 108, 109,
110, 114, 125, 126, 127, 129, 130,
31, 134, 135, 141, 160, 161, 165,
180, 182, 265, 276, 277, 278, 279,
280, 281, 283, 284, 285, 286, 289,
304, 305, 308
digital library development 304, 305
Digital library education 185, 205
Digital Library Federation (DLF) 3, 17, 134
digital library initiatives 20, 39, 184, 185,
187, 192, 196, 203
Digital Library of India 184, 187, 197, 198,
203, 204, 206, 207, 208, 209, 210,
211, 212, 213, 216, 220, 221
Digital Library Problems 90
digital library research 184
digital library services 19, 161, 167, 176
digital library systems 208
digital library technologies 221
Digital library use 20
Digital literacy 163
digitally preserved information 35
digital management 229
Digital Management of Copyright Act (DMCA)
227
Digital materials 140
digital object 81, 82, 83, 84, 85, 166, 169
Digital Object 146, 147
digital object creation 166
digital objects 5, 6, 7, 8, 10, 11, 145, 146,
147, 149, 150, 153, 157, 189

digital preservation 9, 10, 11, 12, 19, 145, 146, 150, 154, 155, 156, 239, 250, 251

Digital Preservation Europe [DPE] 151

Digital Preservation-legal issues 235

Digital preservation requirements 9

digital preservation strategy 85, 138

Digital raw materials 137

digital reference services (DRS) 160, 164, 165, 166, 167, 173, 182

digital replacements 6

Digital Repositories 151, 152, 159

digital repository 189, 192

digital repository applications 123

digital resources 24, 26, 27, 34, 36

Digital Rights Management (DRM) 223, 229

digital storage strategies 133

digital technologies 19, 36, 136, 184, 185

digital text 40, 169

Digital watermarking 231

Digitisation 40, 41, 42, 54, 55, 58, 59, 61, 231

digitisation project 41

digitization 65, 81, 86, 88, 135, 137, 140, 141, 143, 144

digitization activities 6

digitization of documents 67, 85

digitization process 189

digitization programs 12

digitization projects 190, 202, 204

digitization recommendations 66

Digitized documents 206

digitized material 240, 241, 249, 250

digitized resources 25

Digitizing 34

digitizing documents 7

digitizing learning objects 188

DigiTool 186

DISNIC 269, 273, 284, 285

DISNIC-PLAN Project 269

dissemination methods 254

Distance Education 90, 97, 98, 101, 104, 107

Distance Library Services 100, 101, 102, 103, 106

Distance Library Services blog 101

distributed computing and electronic networks 315

DMS packages 43

document image processing (DIP) 43, 68

Document Management Systems (DMS) 43, 68, 79, 80

document object model (DOM) 171

dot-com bust 113

dot per inch (dpi) 47

DRAMBORA (Digital Repository Audit Method Based on Risk Assessment) 151

Drum scanners 53, 77

DSpace 186, 191, 192, 193, 195, 202, 204

dynamic database 121

dynamic information 253

E

e-activities 162

E-bank project 127

e-books 169, 178

e-book standards 31

e-commerce 4, 31, 292

e-Community centre 269, 270, 273

economic activity 289

economic advance 299

economic development 286, 287, 288, 293, 294, 295, 298, 301, 306

Economic wealth 311

Economies-of-scale 111

e-databases 172

Educational Information 256

educational structures 134

e-Governance 269, 272, 273, 281, 282, 283, 285, 286, 289, 294, 296, 297, 307, 308

E-Government projects 296, 308

e-government services 307

e-Granthalaya 266, 279, 280, 281, 283

e-journals 30, 31, 169, 170

e-learning 165, 170

Electrical and Electronics Engineers (IEEE) 3

Electric Library 171

electronic book prize 32

electronic books 178

Electronic Business XML (ebXML) 23

Electronic Commerce 36

Electronic connectivity 268
electronic content 25
electronic contracting 226
electronic conversion 64
electronic data interchange (EDI) 35
Electronic Document Management Goals 64
electronic documents 65, 66
electronic documents/records 65
Electronic Filing System (EFS) 43, 68, 80
electronic information 66
electronic information servers 31
electronic library 1
Electronic Management System (EMS) 229
Electronic Mass Media 300
Electronic publications 190
Electronic record 239
Electronic Records Management 64, 86
electronic reference book 178
electronic reference services 27
electronic sources 133
electronic storage 38
electronic systems 30
Elsevier's Contents Direct Service 171
emerging digital libraries 254
emerging technologies 171
emulation 83, 85, 133, 138, 139, 239
emulator programs 83
Encapsulation 26
Encoded Archival Description (EAD) 27
ENCompass 27
Encryption 230
EPrints 195, 204
E- publishing 160
ERNET India 211
exchanging information 95
Extensible Hypertext Markup Language
    (XHTML) 171
Extensible Markup Language (XML) 22, 171
Extensible Stylesheet Language (XSL) 171

F

faculty perspective 165
Farmer's Dairy 256
Feature Extraction 50
Federation of Indian Chambers of Commerce
    of India (FICCI) 232

File format 69, 75
File size 75
Fixity 135, 136
FLAG (Fibre optic Loop Around the Globe)
    202
Flatbed scanner 53, 77
folksonomies 109, 112, 126, 128
formal ontologies 126
format migration 133, 138, 139
Format Normalization 138, 139
free access to information 302
Free Software Foundation 231
full-text search 41, 44
Functionality testing 161
future of libraries 186

G

geographical information systems (GIS) 77
Get It at Gutman 94
Gigabit networks 200
Girl Children's Right Association 259
Glasgow University Library (GUL) 177
global digital divide 286, 290, 298, 309
global governance 297
global knowledge resources 289, 292
global marketplace 305
global phenomenon 311
Go Go Google Gadget 116
Google Docs 83
government-level organisation 154
Government of India Library Association
    (GILA) 275
Graphics Interchange Format (GIF) 73
graphic user interfaces 110
Grassroots level access to Information (Net-
    working) 265, 268, 282
Grassroots level Information access (Contents)
    265, 268, 282
Gray scale scanning 47
grey scale images 70
growth in agricultural production (GAP) 267

H

Hand-held scanners 52, 53
Hardware loading 226
harvesting of metadata 185

heritage collections 208, 221
hi definition televisions (HDTVs) 171
Higher Education (HE) libraries 262
human-designed world 300
humanitarian information 305
human progress 302
human resources and skills 35
Human Rights 259
hybrid library 175

I

ICT applications 271, 282
ICT infrastructure 200, 201, 298, 314
ICT policies 16
ICT utilization 293, 294
IGNCA collections 242
Ignorance of the copyright laws 227
illegal copying 223, 231
Illubabor community 261
Illustrated 249
Image editing applications 54
Image enhancement 46, 48, 72
image quality 47, 48, 49, 53
IM applications 123
independent information providers 111
indexing information 4
indexing services 30
Indian Association of Teachers of Library and
        Information Science (IATLIS) 275
Indian copyright act 1957 237
Indian Copyright Act and IT Act 239
Indian cultural heritage v, xi, 196, 197,
        235, 236, 239, 240, 241, 250, 251
Indian culture 236
Indian digital library initiatives 206, 207, 221
Indian Institute of Information Technology and
        Management (IIITM) 187
Indian Institute of Science Bangalore (IISc)
        210, 215
Indian Institute of Science (IISc) 195
Indian IT Act 2000 239
Indian Library Association (ILA) 275
Indian System of Medicine and Homoeopathy
        (ISM&H) 198
Indigenous Digital Library 206

Indira Gandhi National Centre for the Arts
        (IGNCA) 196, 235, 241, 242
INFORD 2 260
information and communication technologies
        (ICT) 165, 184, 199, 207, 255, 268,
        286, 287, 289, 291, 293, 294, 295,
        298, 300, 304, 307, 311
Information economy 311
information literacy 162, 163, 164, 173,
        178, 179, 181, 183, 286, 299
information literacy instruction 93, 95
information management consultants 303
Information Provision for Rural Development -
        INFORD1 260
information service 31
Information Society (IS)
        268, 287, 298, 301, 310
information storage and retrieval 133, 134
Information Technology Act 250
information technology (IT) 270, 294
Information Technology Security Council
        (ITSEC) 230
'Information Village' 255
instant messaging (IM) 112, 123
institutional repositories 184, 185, 195, 203
INTACH (Charles Wallace bequest) 248
intangible cultural heritage 236, 237, 244
Intangible Cultural Heritage 236, 237, 250
intangible cultural heritage (ICH) 236
Integrated Library Software (ILS) 92
intellectual custodians 280
intellectual property 2, 4, 11
Intellectual Property Rights (IPR) 224
Intelligent Character Recognition 50
interactive video games 37
interface customization 109
International Convention for the Protection of
        Artistic and Literary Works 227
International Copyright Order 1958 228
International Development Research Centre
        260, 263
International Federation for Information Pro-
        cessing (IFIP) 195
International Federation of Library Associa-
        tions and Institutions (IFLA) 3, 279

International Internet Preservation Consortium (IIPC) 120
International Telecommunication Union (ITU Group 4) 49
Internet adoption 288
Internet connectivity 200
Internet diffusion 311, 314, 315, 316, 317, 318
Internet piracy 226
Internet Public Library 171
Internet Service Providers (ISPs) 255
intertwingled 115
'invisible' Web 120
IT applications 21
IT infrastructure 190
IT manpower 240, 250

J

Japan Patent Office (JPO) 219
Jeff Bezos 31
Joint Conference on Digital Libraries (JCDL) 278
Joint Photographic Experts Group (JPEG) 72
JPEG2000 84
JPEG (Joint Photographic Expert Group) 49
JSTOR 14, 15, 28, 29, 38

K

Kalasampada 187, 196, 197, 198
key ideas behind Web 2.0 112
Khuda Bakhsh Oriental Public Library 237, 246
knowledge age 293, 302
Knowledge Base 148, 149, 150, 156, 157
knowledge-based society 279, 302, 303
Knowledge connectivity 268
knowledge–driven societies 311
Knowledge Economy (KE) 268
knowledge enterprise 4, 21
knowledge institutions 274
"knowledge-intensive" techniques 265, 268, 282
Knowledge Management 277, 278, 283
knowledge management environments 126
knowledge requirements of the poor 252
knowledge sharing 257, 262, 263

knowledge society 266, 268, 269, 275, 276, 277, 282
knowledge work 96, 105

L

lack of access 287, 292
LASSIE Project 97
Learning Management System (LMS) 96
learning objects 188, 189
learning objects repository 188, 189
librarianship 133, 142, 185
Library 2.0 91, 92, 93, 97, 98, 105, 106, 108, 112, 116, 117, 123, 124, 125, 129, 130, 131, 160, 174, 179, 180, 181
library automation 110, 111, 241
library collections 177
library collection services 133
library-community convergence framework (LCCF) 275
library community culture 94
Library Digital Initiative 28, 38
library functions 127
library literacy 163, 164
library management systems (LMS) 187
library networking 108
library portal 91
library resources 20, 35
library services 91, 92, 94, 95, 97, 98
library systems 135
Library Technology 90, 92, 107
Libray Crunch blog 116
LIS professionals 175, 176
Literacy Mission and Poverty Alleviation 275, 276
LOCKSS (Lots of Copies Keeps Stuff Safe) 82
Logical Data View 139
Longerty 81
Long Tail 92
long term preservation 11, 15, 148
long-term preservation strategy 82
long-term storage 11
Lossless Compression 71
Lossy Compression 71
LZW compression 49

M

Madrid System for the International Registration of Marks 225
major problems faced by the users 249
Malawi National Library Services 260, 261
managing a digitization project 191
Manuscript Conservation Centres (MCC-s) 245
Manuscript Resource Centres (MRC-s) 245
Manuscripts Library 246, 247, 248
MARC (machine readable catalog) 8, 19, 23
Market connectivity 268
market reach 290
mass-distributed information 111
materials for digitisation 41
Matrix / Template Matching 50
Mediaeater Reference Desk 171
Media literacy 163, 164
MediaWiki 109
memex 19
Memorandum of Understanding (MoU) 100
Metadata 19, 23, 24
Metadata elements 189
Metadata Encoding and Transmission Standards (METS) 24
metadata standards 8, 23
Micro Enterprise Groups 259
Microfilm Scanner 78
migration 82, 83, 85, 239
"migration on request" approach 83
Millennium Development Goals 253, 264
Ministry of Culture 237, 241, 250, 251
moral rights 224, 225, 227, 228, 231
Mosaic 113
mounted digital cameras 191
MOUS 249
Multimedia programs 259
multimedia servers 34
multimedia technologies 241
Multiple Livelihood Opportunities (MLO) 267
Multiple Referencing 42
"Multipurpose Community Telecentre" (MCT) 273

N

Nammavur Seithi 256
National Commission on Libraries and Information Science (NCLIS) 303
National Council of Educational Research and Training (NCERT) 280
National Digital Preservation Programme (NDPP) 251
National e-Governance Programme (NeGP) 281
national income (GDP) 313
National Informatics Centre (NIC) 269
National Information 242
National Knowledge Commission (NKC) 275
National Library of Australia 26, 38
National Library of Kolkata 239
National Mission for Manuscripts (NMM) 190, 235
National Mission on Libraries 251
National Policy on Library and Information system (NAPLIS) 275
National Science Foundation (NSF) 20, 21, 38
Nature Protocols 126
Nepal National Library 258
Networked Digital Library 206
networked environment 162, 165
networked information space 24
Networked knowledge societies 207
Networked Library 266
Networking of Information 268
Networking of People 268
Network literacy 163
network pipelines 31, 32
Neural Networking 50
new communication technology 289, 292
new digital technologies 286
new economy 288
NewJour 30
new technologies 21, 30, 32, 36
new technology revolution 161
non-governmental organizations (NGOs) 297
non-Indian languages 207
non-print material 250

O

OAIS Reference Model 145, 146, 151, 156
OAIS-type archives 156
OA journals 231
OA models 231
OA publishing 231
objections to blogging 91, 102, 104
Object Relational Database Management Systems (ORDBMS) 171
OCRed 41, 43, 44, 45, 46, 50, 57, 62
OCR (Optical Character Recognition) 45, 50, 60
OEM privacy/ Unbundling 226
older versions 26
OmniPage 65
online copyright laws 227
Online Cultures 108
online environment 162
open access movement 231
open access (OA) 15, 236, 249, 250, 251
open access repositories 203
open and distance learning (ODL) 188
Open Archival Information System OAIS 146
Open Archives 254
Open source movement 16
open source software (OSS) 160, 174, 184, 1 86, 192, 195, 199
Open systems architecture 22
Open Text Mining Interface (OTMI) 115
optical character recognition (OCR) 46, 63, 67
option assessment matrix 191
owner of copyright 238
Oxfam Canada 261, 264

P

PARSE.Insight project 145, 150, 155, 158
Participative citizenship 162
"passive" preservation 138
Patent protection 224
patron questions 177
PDF normal 46
penetration of Internet 312, 313, 314
personal collections 235, 243
personal computers (PCs) 315
personal digital assistants (PDAs) 171

personal information system (PIS) 143
personalized information environment (PIE) 167
photo-documentation 249
photo editing software 4
Photo-Multiplier (Vacuum) Tubes (PMTs) 53
photo-negatives 248
physical information 15
physical media 40, 41, 58
physical objects 24
planners and policymakers 266
platform-one window 165
Portable Document Format (PDF) 73
Portable Network Graphics (PNG) 73
potential customer 176
Poverty Alleviation 266, 275, 276, 283
PovertyNet 267
preservation community 11
preservation infrastructure 151, 153, 154, 156, 158
Preservation of digital materials 9
preservation policies 26
preservation policy 25
preservation problem 142
Preservation programmers 84
preservation programs 6
preservation treatment 136
"Preserving Access to Digital Information" (PADI) 26
preserving digital content 8
preserving the bits 119
Prime space 133
Printed books/documents 66
printed resource 168
print magazines 30
procedural barriers 254
proper policy guidelines 236
ProQuest 14
proximity operators 44
"public face" of library 104
public libraries 26, 29, 32
Public Libraries Act 251
public policy debate 33
Pub Med Central 30
Pub SCIENCE 30

Q

Quality check 75, 76
quality of images 187

R

Rampur Raza Library 237, 246
rare books 235, 236, 242
R&D activities 15
READ Foundation Nepal 258
ReadNepal 257, 264
really simple syndication (RSS) 173
re-coding 84
re-compiling 84
Reference librarians 160, 179
Reference Library of IGNCA 248, 250
reference questions 177
Reference Services 90, 107, 160, 166, 168,
     172, 179
regional development 265, 266, 269, 282
Regional Mega Scanning Centres (RMSCs)
     210
Regional Poverty Profile (RPP) 253
Re-keying the Data 44
relationship marketing (RM) 176
Relevant governments 306
reliability, availability, and serviceability (RAS)
     8
renderability of digital information 135
repository 24, 27, 28, 29, 38
Repository Audit and Certification (RAC) 151
Representation Information 146, 147, 148,
     149, 150, 152, 153, 154, 155, 156,
     157, 158
reproduce a work 229
reproduction cost 247
Reprography Unit of IGNCA 248
Rescue content 85
Research libraries 19, 37
Research Libraries Group (RLG) 26, 33
research literature 195
Resolution 46, 47, 63, 69, 70, 72
Resource node 126
resource sharing 91, 101
restricted access 249
retrieval of information 65

Return on Investment (ROI) 283
Robot crawlers 120
Robots Exclusion Protocol 120
RSS feeds 113, 124
Rural Connectivity 265
rural digital libraries 266, 283
Rural Education and Development Foundation
     of Nepal (READ Foundation) 257
rural poor 252, 253, 263
Rural Population 280
Rural Public Libraries 266, 275, 282

S

SAFE (South Africa Far East) 202
Scanning Software 76
Scholarly Research 108, 115
Science and Technology (S&T) 267
SEA-ME-WE (III) (South East Asia, Middle
     East and Western Europe) 202
Security Measure 42
security mechanisms 201
Self Help Groups (SHGs) 257
SEMANTIC Technologies 283
sharpening 72, 75
Sheet-Feed Scanners 77
Shidhulai 258, 259, 260, 264
Significant Property 147, 148
Simple Object Access Protocol (SOAP) 22
skill-based literacies 164
Slide scanners 53, 78
slowly integrate technology 300
social action 290
social bookmarking 91, 97, 101
social inclusion 162, 266, 269, 276, 282
social interaction 108, 117, 123
social media 112, 116
Social Networking 108
social networking issues 206
social progress 299
social significance of Internet 312
social software 90, 91, 92, 93, 96, 97, 98,
     105, 106, 107, 108, 109, 114, 115,
     117, 127
social software technologies 115
social trends 185

socio-economic development 286, 295, 298, 306, 311
Sociology of Digitization 108
sociology of Web 2.0 109
sociotechnical artifacts 109
sociotechnical systems 110
Soft lifting 226
Software reengineering 84
source code 84
Standard General Markup Language (SGML) 22
steganography 230, 234
storage and retrieval systems 2
Storage capacity 8
Storage Facility 153, 154
storage space 65
Sufficient internet bandwidth 202
sustainable consumption 265, 268, 282
sustainable development 1, 265, 267, 268, 269, 270, 282, 285, 302, 303
sustainable digitization program 1, 12
sustainable national development 266

T

Tagged Image File Format (TIFF) 73
Tagging 124, 126
tangible cultural heritage 236, 237
technical services 19, 34
technological developments 110
Technology emulation 26
Technology Information Forecasting Cell (TIFAC) 232
technology preservation 82, 138
technology sector market crash 112
Technology Trends 108
TechWatch report 117
telecommunication infrastructure 314, 316, 317
Telecottage 273
telephone density 311, 313, 315, 316, 317
Teraserver project 29
Term of copyright 238
TextBridge 65, 67
textual artifacts 32
textual images 65
The IT Action Plan 277

threshold 46, 48, 63, 69, 71
TKDL 206, 207, 208, 217, 218, 219, 220, 221, 222
Trade and Merchandise Marks Act 225
Trademark 224, 225, 234
Trade Related Aspects of Intellectual Property Rights (TRIPS) 228
Traditional Knowledge Digital Library 206, 207, 208, 217, 220
Traditional Knowledge Digital Library (TKDL) 197, 198
Traditional Knowledge Systems 251
Traditional libraries 32, 186, 187
traditional library infrastructure 305
traditional library services 254
Transform library services 108
Trustworthy Repositories Audit and Certification: Criteria and Checklist (TRAC) 145

U

ubiquitous electronic access 30
UDL portal 209, 210
UK Web Archiving Consortium (UKWAC) 118
UML diagram 146
Uncompressed images 49, 71
Understandability 136
UNESCO Universal Declaration on Cultural Diversity 206, 207, 258
United Nations Development Programs (UNDP) 291
United States Patent and Trademark Office (USPTO) 219
Universal Description, Discovery and Integration (UDDI) 22
Universal Digital Library project 208, 212
Universal Digital Library (UDL) 208
universal virtual computer 85, 138, 139
Universal Virtual Machine 138, 139
University Grants Commission 190
Unrestricted Client Access 226
Usability testing 161
user-centred change 112, 116
user expectations 116
user-friendly interfaces 187
user-generated content 108, 126
users opinions 175
UThink Blogs 95, 107

V

vector scanners 77
Version Migration 82
VHF duplex radio devices 255
Viability of a digital file 136
Video Frame Grabber 78
village knowledge centers 254
Village Knowledge Centers (VKCs) 268
violating copyright 227, 229
ViolaWWW 113
virtual learning environment (VLE)
   1, 4, 21, 118
virtual libraries 1, 142, 168
virtual machine 133, 139
Virtual Reference Desk (VRD) 173
virtual superstore 31
Virtual Village Hall 273
VKC Research Project 254

W

WARANA Experiment 270
WARC storage format 118
Water User Association 259
Web 1.0 113, 123
Web 2.0 application 124
Web 2.0, consumers 128
Web 2.0 functionality 108
Web 2.0 ideas and services 121
Web 2.0-style applications and services 116
Web 2.0-type social annotations 114
Web-based archiving tools 121
web-based federated search application 165
Web-based publications 122

Web-based reference 161, 171
Web-enabled device 2
Web-enabled services 160
Web harvesting management system (Web
   Curator Tool) 118
Web Services Description Language (WSDL)
   23
Wide Area Networks (WAN) 297
Wide Area Usage 42
wiki-based glossary of technical terms 114
WikiBios 124, 132
wikis 109, 113, 114, 115, 117, 121, 122,
   123, 124
Wimax 291
window-one platform 165
WIPO Copyright Treaty (WCT) 228
Women's Rights 259
WordPress blogging software 109
workflows 145, 156, 157
world brain 19
World Development Indicators
   313, 314, 315, 317
World Intellectual Property Organisation
   (WIPO) 218, 219, 227
world's largest bookstore 31
World Telecommunication day 292
World Trade Organization (WTO) 228
WorldWide Web 122
World Wide Web libraries 134
World Wide Web (WWW) 72

Y

Your Voice Counts! 95